STUDIES IN INDIAN COINS

D.C. Sircar

MOTILAL BANARSIDASS
INTERNATIONAL
DELHI

Reprint Edition : Delhi, 2023
First Edition : Delhi, 1968

ISBN : 978-81-962137-4-9

Also available at

MOTILAL BANARSIDASS INTERNATIONAL

H. O. : 41 U.A. Bungalow Road, (Back Lane) Jawahar Nagar, Delhi - 110 007
4261 (basement) Lane #3, Ansari Road, Darya Ganj, New Delhi - 110 002
203 Royapettah High Road, Mylapore, Chennai - 600 004
12/1A, 2nd Floor, Bankim Chatterjee Street, Kolkata - 700 073
Stockist : Motilal Books, Ashok Rajpath, Near Kali Mandir, Patna - 800 004

Printed in India
MOTILAL BANARSIDASS INTERNATIONAL

Dedicated to

the Memory of my Teacher
D.R. Bhandarkar
to whom I owe my Interest in
the Study of Ancient Indian Numismatics

And

of the Great Numismatists
E.J. Rapson *and* **S.H. Hodivala**
whose Writings have been my
Greatest Source of Inspiration.

CONTENTS

CONTENTS

PREFACE

Sometime ago, at the request of my friends, I published a volume incorporating many of my papers on Indian historical geography, which had earlier appeared mostly in various Indian periodicals. It is a matter of satisfaction to me that, in spite of its defects, the publication was received favourably by the students of the subject. Some European scholars suggested that my studies in the other aspects of Indian history and culture should better be likewise made available in similar volumes, especially to the students in Europe where copies of many Indian periodicals are not obtainable. This sympathetic and appreciative suggestion encouraged me to collect my papers on Indian numismatics in the volume now placed before the public.

As in my *Studies in the Geography of Ancient and Medieval India*, so also in the present volume, sometimes more papers than one have been clubbed together and discussions on several problems have been brought under one Chapter for the sake of the facility of presentation. Thus nearly 35 papers and notes, published at different dates during the past 25 years, have been presented in this volume in eighteen Chapters and three Appendices. The size of the Chapters varies, a few of them being lengthy and others smaller. Some of the papers have been suitably modified in the course of revision.

Many of the papers incorporated in the volume appeared originally in the *Journal* of the Numismatic Society of India, to which I have to express my thanks for honouring me by electing me its President for the years 1955 and 1956.

The authorities of the periodicals, in which my papers were published previously, have placed me under a debt of gratitude by their kindness in allowing me to include the articles in the present work.

The sources of the different Chapters and Appendices are indicated below.

I. Adapted from a Bengali article contributed to the

Bhāratakoṣa appearing under the auspices of the Vaṅgīya Sāhitya Pariṣat, Calcutta.

II. *Journal of the Numismatic Society of India*, Varanasi (Banaras, Benares), Vol. XVIII, 1956, pp. 1 ff.

III. *Ibid.*, Vol. XV, 1953, pp. 136 ff.; Vol. XVI, 1954, pp. 40 ff.

IV. *Ibid.*, Vol. XIV, 1952, pp. 128 ff.; Vol. XIII, 1951, pp. 183 ff.; Vol. XXIII, 1961, pp. 297 ff.

V. *Epigraphia Indica*, Delhi, Vol. XXXV, 1963-1964, pp. 247 ff.

VI. *Ibid.*, pp. 69 ff.

VII. *Journal of the Numismatic Society of India*, Vol. IV, 1942, pp. 149 ff.; Vol. XXII, 1960, pp. 168 ff.

VIII. *Indian Historical Quarterly*, Calcutta, Vol. XXXIII, December 1957, pp. 269 ff.

IX. *Annual Report on Indian Epigraphy*, Delhi, 1956-57, pp. 21 ff., 126 ff.

X. *Journal of the Numismatic Society of India*, Vol. XXIV, 1962, pp. 1 ff.; *Our Heritage*, Calcutta, Vol. VIII, 1962, pp. 69 ff.

XI. *Journal of the Numismatic Society of India*, XXVIII, 1966, pp. 211ff.; *Indian Numismatic Chronicle*, Patna, Vol. II, 1961, pp. 206 ff.; *Epigraphia Indica*, Vol. XXXIII, 1959-1960, pp. 95 ff.; *Journal of Indian History*, Vol. XL, Trivandrum, 1962, pp. 533 ff.

XII. *Journal of the Numismatic Society of India*, Vol. XV, 1953, pp. 229 ff.

XIII. *Ibid.*, Vol. XXI, 1959, pp 137 ff.; *Annual Report on Indian Epigraphy*, 1959-60, pp. 31-32, 170.

XIV. *Suparṇa* (J. Ph. Vogel Commemoration Volume in the press); *Journal of the Numismatic Society of India*, Vol. XIV, 1952, pp. 80 ff.; Vol. XXVIII, 1966, pp. 90 ff.

XV. *Journal of the Numismatic Society of India*, Vol. XX, 1958, pp. 192 ff.; *Epigraphia Indica*, Vol. XXXII, 1957-1958, pp. 329 ff.

XVI. *Journal of the Numismatic Society of India*, Vol. VII, 1945, pp. 78 ff.

XVII. *Ibid.*, pp. 82 ff.; Vol. XVI, 1954, pp. 264 ff.

XVIII. *Ibid.*, Vol. VII, 1945, pp. 87 ff.; XXVI, 1964, pp. 127 ff.

Appendix I. *Ibid.*, Vol. XVIII, 1956, pp. 10 ff., 226 ff.

" II. *Indian Historical Quarterly*, Vol. XXIV, September 1948, pp. 242 ff.

" III. *Numismatic Chronicle*, London, 1963, pp. 213 ff.

I have always found it risky to form an opinion on the reading of coin-legends on the basis of the unsatisfactory illustrations in Indian periodicals, without examining the original coins or their casts. But, in India, it is not easy to get coins on loan or their satisfactory casts for study. I am therefore specially thankful to Dr. A. N. Lahiri, an old pupil of mine, who rendered me great help in this respect as one of my Assistants when I was Government Epigraphist for India at Ootacamund. It is, in most cases, the plaster-casts of coins, which Dr. Lahiri prepared in the course of his official tours and placed at my disposal on his return to headquarters, that enabled me to detect errors in the published readings of the legends of a number of coins discussed in several of my papers included in this volume. Likewise Sri G. Bhattacharya assisted me in examining the Peṭlūri-pālem hoard of Śaka coins (Chapter IX). I am also grateful to my former pupil, Sri Dilip Kumar Ganguly, who kindly translated into English one of my articles, originally written in Bengali, for Chapter I. The index is the work of Sri Samares Bandyopadhyay, another pupil of mine, who has also helped me in various other ways.

In order to enhance its usefulness to the students of Indian numismatics, a large number of interesting coins have been illustrated in the Plates appended to the work. Dr. Lahiri has been of considerable help to me in this matter.

It is quite possible that many errors have crept into the pages and that I have failed to make the book as useful to the students of Indian numismatics as was my earnest desire. Nevertheless, it will be a great satisfaction to me if the volume succeeds in creating genuine interest in the study of coins in the minds of educated Indians and also in improving the standard of numismatic research in our country even in the smallest degree. For the errors I may have committed, I crave the indulgence of the readers and request them to be so good as to draw my attention to them, so that they may be rectified in the future.

The size and weight of coins have not been uniformly indicated in inches or centimetres and in grains or grams respectively. But their conversion is easy if one remembers that 1 centimetre=.39 inch and 1 inch=2.54 centimetres, while 1 grain=·065 gram and 1 gram=15·38 grains.

University of Calcutta,
Jan. 26, 1968.

D. C. Sircar

CHAPTER I

SURVEY OF INDIAN NUMISMATICS

The English word *numismatics,* which owes its origin to Latin *numisma* (i. e. currency), signifies 'the study of coins.' The Indians of antiquity would sometimes designate the subject as *Paurāṇa-śāstra,* i.e. the science that dealt with the old silver currency known as the Purāṇa. Proficiency in this branch of learning is stated to have required a study of the *Rūpasūtra* and the scrutiny of numerous coins, old and new. The student was then in a position to ascertain the significance of the symbols on the coins and to recognise the place of their origin and the artisan who was responsible for minting them.

The word *numismatics* is often translated into the Neo-Indo-Aryan languages by such expressions as *mudrā-vidyā, mudrā-tattva, mudrā-vijñāna,* etc., and therefore numismatics, as a source for the reconstruction of ancient Indian history, may be called *pratna-mudrā-vidyā,* etc., in these languages. But, since the word *mudrā* conveys different meanings in Sanskrit, *pratna-mudrā-vidyā,* etc., may also signify the study of old seals and similar other objects. Words like *rūpa, rūpya,* etc., which are used in Sanskrit in the sense of currency, have likewise different meanings and cannot be regarded as more suitable than *mudrā* in this respect.

The importance of coins as a source of history is less felt in those countries where regular historical chronicles of the early period are available. But they are of outstanding importance for the reconstruction of ancient Indian history, because this subcontinent did not produce in early times a Herodotus or Thucydides, a Livy or Tacitus. The coins often offer the names of persons or institutions that were responsible for their issue. Of them, only some are known from epigraphic and literary records.

At the infancy of human civilisation, the people had to produce or procure their necessities by dint of their own labour. In course of time, the practice of barter came into vogue and a cultivator could get from a weaver a piece of cloth in exchange for a quantity of his produce. But a drawback in the barter system is that it requires the coincidence of the respective needs of the parties concerned, viz. the buyer and the seller. Therefore, with the progress of civilisation, the need for a permanent and satisfactory medium of transaction was gradually felt. In the early period, often the cow seems to have been regarded as a unit of wealth, and a commodity could be purchased in exchange for a cow, the quantity of the article being determined by the number and value of the animals. But it was then difficult to buy a small article which would cost much less than a cow. To alleviate this difficulty, articles like cowrie-shells, etc., used as ornaments in early human society, were also prevalent as the media of exchange. Gradually these were supplanted by metallic pieces and the use of this medium of exchange ultimately led to the introduction of coins. After all, a coin is merely a piece of metal having definite shape and weight and bearing recognised symbols on its face, impressed upon it by a responsible authority. A gold piece of the value of a cow served as a sort of currency in some countries of antiquity.

The introduction of coins is a landmark in the history of civilisation and is a great achievement of the human race. The development of trade and commerce is impossible without money, while the happiness and prosperity of human society depend largely on the ease with which one's necessities can be procured. The introduction of coins in the economic life of man solved such problems to a great extent.

The class of coins which finds frequent mention in ancient Indian epigraphic and literary sources is the Kārṣāpaṇa. The name *Kārṣāpaṇa* is derived from *karṣa*, the weight of the coins being one *karṣa* which was regarded as equal to 80 Ratis or 146.4 grains. Literary records speak of Kārṣāpaṇas of gold, silver and copper. The gold Kārṣāpaṇa was also known as Suvarṇa and Niṣka, whereas the silver one was called Purāṇa or Dharaṇa and likewise the copper Kārṣāpaṇa bore the popular designation of Paṇa. Two facts, however, deserve mention in this connection. In the first place, although reference to the gold-Kārṣāpaṇa, Suvarṇa or Niṣka is frequent in early literature, curiously enough, very few coins of this class have so far been discovered in India. This would imply that it was circulated to a very limited extent and that its use as a piece of metal or ornament was more popular In the second place, since silver was a costly metal in ancient India, the weight of the silver-Kārṣāpaṇa (Purāṇa or Dharaṇa), though it was still called Kārṣāpaṇa (i. e. the coin weighing one Karṣa), was reduced from 80 Ratis to 32 Ratis or 58.56 grains. Another interesting fact is that coins of the same metal, but showing variation in weight, etc., were often known by the same designation. As for instance, the gold currency of the Kuṣāṇas (about 124 grains), the silver money of the Śakas of Western India (about 36 grains), the Varāha or Suvarṇa-gadyāṇa (48 Ratis) of South India, and the Māḍa, Māḍā or Māḍai (probably 40 Ratis) of the same region were often called Suvarṇa, Kārṣāpaṇa, Suvarṇa (or Niṣka) and Kārṣāpaṇa respectively.

The silver-Kārṣāpaṇa, otherwise called Purāṇa or Dharaṇa, was in circulation throughout India. The weight of the coins was indicated by Indian authorities by that of the Raktikā or Kṛṣṇala (Rati), i.e. the red-and-black seeds of the Guñjā berry (about 1.83 grains). Thus 5 Ratis = 1 Māṣaka; 80 Ratis or 16 Māṣakas = 1 Kārṣāpaṇa. In the case of silver, the table was quoted as follows : 2 Ratis = 1 Māṣaka; 32 Ratis or 16 Māṣakas = 1 Kārṣāpaṇa. The Rati is still the recognised standard of measurement in wide areas of North India, though in the South, especially in the Tamil-speaking region, the Mañjāḍi seed serves as the radical unit of measurement. In South India, 10 Mañjāḍis were regarded as equivalent to one Kaḷañju seed and a gold or silver coin weighing a Kaḷañju also bore the name of Kaḷañju. Since the measurement of the silver-Kaḷañju was practically the same as that of the silver-Kārṣāpaṇa, Purāṇa or Dharaṇa, the silver-Kaḷañju was the silver-Kārṣāpaṇa of the south. South Indian writers of the medieval period, however, speak of 1 Mañjāḍi = 2 Ratis and 20 Mañjāḍis or 40 Ratis = 1 silver-Kaḷañju or Dharaṇa. But these silver coins were no other than the above-mentioned Māḍa, Māḍā or Māḍai, which was in circulation in the south in the period in question. The equation of a Mañjāḍi with 1 silver-Māṣaka or 2 Ratis (i.e. 3.6 grains), in an attempt to interconnect the northern and southern systems of weighing, is interesting to note, even though it was not strictly accurate.

Although the use of the Mañjāḍi, in place of Rati, as the unit of measurement came to be confined to the southern areas of the country in later days, there is some evidence to believe that this weight standard was prevalent in North India at an early period. References to the gold-Śatamāna are noticed in Vedic literature. The weight of a silver-Śatamāna, also called Pala or Niṣka, is given by Manu as 320 Ratis. It is apparent from the very name Śatamāna, 'weighing one hundred units of measurement', that the unit measure of a gold or silver Śatamāna of 320 Ratis was an object which weighs 3⅕ Ratis and a hundred of which would conform to one Śatamāna in weight. It seems that this unit measure, weighing a little more than 3 Ratis, is no other than the Mañjāḍi.

It has to be noticed that it is extremely difficult, if not impossible, to find any two seeds of Raktikā or Mañjāḍi, the weight of which would be identical. Some foreign scholars have tried in their own way to find out the actual weight of a seed, generally depending on the average weight of a seed from the weight of a hundred chosen specimens; but they are not unanimous in their conclusion. The weights of the Rati and Mañjāḍi, as recorded by Vincent A. Smith, are 1.825 and roughly 5 grains respectively, whereas Alexander Cunningham estimated them as 1.83 and 5.736 grains respectively and Walter Elliot calculated the weight of the Mañjāḍi as 4.8 grains. However, as has already been pointed out, the silver-Kaḷañju was called Kārṣāpaṇa in South India, and, therefore, we may say that approximately 10 Mañjāḍis=1 silver-Kaḷañju or Kārṣāpaṇa =32 Ratis; and 10 silver-Kaḷañjus or Kārṣāpaṇas = 1 Śatamāna=320 Ratis.

As stated earlier, although the standard weight of silver-Kārṣāpaṇas was 32 Ratis, several coins of approximate weights were also called Kārṣāpaṇa. Mention may be made, in this connection, of the silver currency of the Śaka rulers. The weight of a Greek drachm was 67.5 grains and the silver coins of the Śakas of Western India, the weight of which was not more than 36 grains, may be hemidrachms or half-drachms. On the contrary, the weight of the silver-Kārṣāpaṇa, Purāṇa or Dharaṇa, was a little more than 58 grains. Even then, the people regarded the Śaka currency as three-fourths of the ancient silver Kārṣāpaṇa, i.e. as a coin weighing 24 Ratis or 42 grains. This, however, may be a rough calculation and not an exact estimate. The purchasing capacity of the Kārṣāpaṇa of two different weights would naturally vary, and the public were not ignorant of this, though they were unable to detect minute differences. There may also have been the question of metallic purity.

Silver-Kārṣāpaṇas have been discovered extensively from all regions of India and the number of Paṇas or copper-Kārṣāpaṇas, that have so for been discovered, also is not negligible. The latter is thicker than the former. This class of copper and silver money is described in English as 'punch-marked' coins. This is because, for the manufacture of these coins, strips were first cut out of a metal sheet and small rectangular pieces cut from these strips would pass as coins after certain symbols were hammered on one or both of their faces by means of separate punches. The marks on each coin are sometimes many, but occasionally few. An adjustment of the weight was made by cutting small bits off one or more corners of the heavier pieces and this would lead to a deviation of their rectangular shape. Some punch-marked coins are also found to be circular in shape. Later on, similar coins, especially of copper, were cast from moulds.

It is clear from the attempt to adjust the weight by snipping small bits from the edges of the coins that the people responsible for minting them were conscious about the exactitude of their weight. A large number of old coins discovered in various parts of India, however, betray divergences in weight, and this may be accounted for by such factors as the defect of the system of measuring with the help of seeds, the dishonesty on the part of those who used the coins, the circulation of coins of several denominations, etc. Smaller coins like $\frac{1}{8}$, $\frac{1}{4}$, $\frac{1}{2}$ and $\frac{3}{4}$ of the standard money were in circulation, while issues of higher denominations like $1\frac{1}{4}$, $1\frac{1}{2}$, 2, $2\frac{1}{2}$, etc., of the original were also not rare. Coins would become lighter in consequence of everyday use. Moreover, the weight of coins might vary in accordance with the change in the relative market value of the metal. Further, many unscrupulous and dishonest people tried to chip off metal bits from the coin-pieces. In view of these circumstances, it is extremely difficult to ascertain the original weight of the ancient coins discovered in various parts of the country from time to time.

Among the coins of the 'punch-marked' class, the rectangular silver bars are generally believed to be the oldest. Some of these bars are bent in shape. The punch-marked silver bars were not manufactured by cutting the pieces out of silver sheets as is the case with the ordinary punch-marked coins of silver, which are thinner. Although legends are conspicuous by their absence on the face of the punch-marked coins, they bear numerous symbols, e.g., bird, animal, human figure, tree, hill, river, sun, crescent, wheel, etc. The exact significance of many of the symbols still remains uncertain.

There is some evidence to suggest that punch-marked coins were current in India even before the birth of Lord Buddha in the sixth century B. C., and that their circulation in South India continued as late as the fifth century A. D. But long before this later date, the alien invaders of North-West India had introduced in this country coins with legends and, in the course of time, the Indians followed them in issuing coins with inscriptions. At the same time, the cast and die-struck coins also came into circulation.

Cast coins of copper, a large number of which do not bear any legend, were generally made by pouring molten metal into earthenware moulds. Anvils and punches with a wide face were needed for striking coins from dies. A shallow depression, slightly wider than the coin-flan, was cut out on the surface of the anvil and figures, etc., were engraved on it negatively. Similar symbols were often also incised on the face of the punches. The die-struck coins were manufactured by placing the face of a punch upon a metal-flan put inside the depression on the heated anvil and striking at the back of the punch only once with a hammer. A large number of coins belonging to this class bear symbols only on the obverse. As regards the mode of manufacture, this was the method employed in India even as late as the age of the Peshwās. The difference between the punch-marked and the die-struck coins is that, while in the case of the former, different symbols were impressed by separate punches, in that of the latter, all the symbols on its obverse were impressed by a single punch.

There is considerable divergence of opinion among numismatists as regards the problem as to who issued the punch-marked coins. Formerly it was held that this coinage was issued by merchant-guilds and corporate bodies and not by the royal authority. Now, however, it is generally believed that these were state issues. But there is some evidence to show that all the punch-marked coins were not state issues and that some of them at least were struck by private agencies, with or without the permission of the Government. Buddhaghoṣa, the celebrated Buddhist scholar of the fifth century A.D., narrates in his *Visuddhimagga* how a moneyer-goldsmith, after carefully scrutinizing a number of Kārṣāpaṇa coins, could determine the village, town, mountain-slope or river-side where a coin was minted and also the *Ācārya* (i.e. the master-goldsmith) who was responsible for its manufacture. What is important to note here is that Buddhaghoṣa does not say that the moneyer could detect as to which royal authority issued a particular coin.

Although some of the Indian rulers of the ancient and medieval periods had their own mints, coining of money was generally entrusted to leading goldsmiths who were, however, not allowed to deviate from the traditional system prevalent in the state. Sometimes, the privilege of issuing and circulating coins was enjoyed by the royal favourites or State officials. That the coins on which the names of particular towns are written were introduced by the corporate bodies of the towns in question admits of no doubt. From the ancient city of Takṣaśilā (Taxila) in the Rawalpindi District, West Pakistan, a number of coins have been unearthed, which bear the names of certain *Naigamas* or the merchants' corporation or city-guild of particular localities. The use of ordinary metal pieces as coined money was also not rare.

The Muhammadan rulers, who gradually established themselves in various parts of India in the early medieval period, exercised almost absolute authority in the matter of issuing coins, though that does not seem to have been the case with most ruling families in ancient India. It has, however, to be admitted that, even during the Muhammadan rule, the use of early coins, foreign money and cowries was continued. The cowries, imported to the Indian markets from the Maldive Islands, were used by the people as coined money. Needless to say that it was not possible for any state to imprint the mark of royal authority upon cowries.

Besides the Kārṣāpaṇas, references to Māṣakas of iron, wood and lac are met with in Pali literature. According to the commentators, the Kārṣāpaṇa was of three different varieties, viz., gold, silver and copper. As regards the Māṣaka of iron, it is said that they were made of copper, iron or some other metal. The wooden Māṣaka has been interpreted as a coin made of hard wood or pieces of bamboo, palm-leaf, etc., whereas the Māṣaka of lac was manufactured by impressing symbols upon small balls of lac, gum, etc. These coins had only practical, but no real, value and cannot be regarded as State issues.

The ancient kingdom of Bactria in Northern Afghanistan formed a part of the Greek empire of the Seleucid dynasty of Western Asia. About the middle of the third century B. C., the local Greek governors of Bactria asserted their independence by throwing off the allegiance of their Seleucid overlords. During the first half of the subsequent century they succeeded in establishing their hegemony over a considerable portion of Northern India. A large number of beautifully executed circular coins of these Greek kings of Bactria and India have been discovered. The Indo-Bactrian coins are generally made of silver according to the Hellenic or a modified weight standard. They usually bear the names as well as the busts of the rulers who issued them. The appearance of legends on indigenous Indian money may be traced to this Greek influence, although the Indians took a long time to issue coins of similar beauty and execution. The Greeks were followed in North-Western India by the Scythians, Parthians and Kuṣāṇas in succession. The Kuṣāṇas introduced a gold currency which served as the prototype of the gold coinage of the Imperial Gupta rulers who established themselves in Bihar and Eastern U. P. in the first quarter of the fourth century A. D. and soon extended their power and influence over wide areas of India.

Most of the Indo-Greek coins show on their obverse the name of the issuer in Greek, and on their reverse, the Prakrit rendering of the Greek legend usually in Kharoṣṭhī but rarely in Brāhmī. It is well known that Kharoṣṭhī was prevalent in the north-western regions while Brāhmī was popular in the rest of the country. The system of issuing bilingual and biscriptal coins was followed by the Scythian and Parthian rulers. It is interesting to note that the Kuṣāṇa emperors of the house of Kaniṣka used only Greek in their coin legends, although they ruled over a more extensive region of North India than their predecessors. The silver currency of the Śaka rulers of Western

India, who flourished between the second and fourth centuries, have their legend in an admixture of Prakrit and Sanskrit written in the Brāhmī script, though traces of Greek legend are noticed in some of their earlier issues.

At first the Greek rulers of Bactria issued coins of the Attic (i.e. Greek) standard of weight (1 Drachm=67.5 grains); but, when they annexed the north-western part of India, they started issuing silver coins regarded by some as of the Persian standard (1 Siglos=86.45 grains). A large number of Drachms, Hemidrachms, Didrachms and various small denominations like the obol have been discovered in Bactria. The weight of a Didrachm and a Hemidrachm, according to the modified standard, was about 160 and 40 grains respectively.

The Bactrian issues of the Hellenic rulers show the Greek legend only; but their Indian coins, as indicated above, bear on the reverse the Prakrit translation of the Greek legend. This Prakrit legend was written in the Kharoṣṭhī alphabet with the exception of certain square issues of Pantaleon and Agathocles, on which it is written in Brāhmī. The celebrated Indo-Greek king Eucratides I (c. 175-155 B. C.) imitated the old Persian emperors in assuming the title 'Great King' (cf. *Basileos Megalou*) on his coins. In his later issues, this was translated as *Mahārāja* which became a popular regal title among later Indian rulers. Generally, the obverse of the Indo-Greek coins shows the bust of the king, whereas the reverse depicts the figures of Greek divinities. Although the great majority of these coins are made of silver, a few are found to be of gold, copper and nickel. An interesting feature of these coins is the use of monograms or symbolical conjuncts of Greek letters on them. The occurrence of Kharoṣṭhī monograms on Indo-Greek coinage is also met with.

The issue of Indo-Greek coins of the modified standard is explained by the fact that North-Western India was once included within the dominions of the Achaemenids of Persia. Some scholars believe that the Persian rulers had circulated their silver money called Siglos (86.45 grains) and their gold coin called Daric (about 133 grains) in the Indian part of their empire. Alexander the Great of Macedon, while staying in India from 327 B. C. to 324 B. C., is believed to have circulated some copper coins. It appears that silver coins with the figure of the Athenian owl were minted in India during the same period. Some Indologists are of the opinion that king Saubhūti (Sophytes), an Indian contemporary of Alexander, struck coins with Greek legends.

The Euthydemians and the Eucratidians, the two rival Greek houses that were involved in a long-drawn struggle for supremacy, issued an interesting series of coins, which numismatists describe as 'pedigree coins'. Generally these coins bear the name of the person commemorated upon the obverse and, on the reverse, the name of the issuer. Similar medals associated with the name of Eucratides I display on their obverse the busts and names of his father Heliocles and mother Laodice. It is worth observing that, while Heliocles is represented as bareheaded, his wife Laodice bears a diadem, demonstrating thereby that she had royal blood in her veins. This would suggest that the claim of Eucratides I to the throne was derived from his mother who was in all probability a Seleucid princess.

On certain coins, the name of queen Agathocleia appears on the obverse, while Strato I is mentioned on the reverse. On others, we find the name of Strato I alone and some of these coins represent him in the portrait as a man of advanced years. From this, it has been conjectured that, at the time of his accession to the throne, Strato I was a minor, and his mother Agathocleia was governing the principality on behalf of her son. Agathocleia's name seems to suggest that she was either a daughter or a sister of king Agathocles, and the striking similarity of her coinage with Menander's may indicate that she was the queen of the latter. It has however been recently suggested that Strato and Agathocleia were husband and wife.

The coins of the Scytho-Parthian kings resemble those of the Indo-Greek rulers to a large extent. The reverse of these coins represents numerous divinities, which are generally Hellenic, but occasionally Indian. The joint issues, like the Agathocleia-Strato I coins referred to above, occupy a subordinate position in Indo-Greek coinage. Such, however, is not the case with the Scytho-Parthian coins, a number of which are joint issues. The Scythian coins bear the name of the reigning king in Greek on the obverse, while their reverse shows in Prakrit the name and title of the heir-apparent. Thus the name of Azilises occurs on the reverse of the coins of Azes I just as

Azes II is mentioned on the reverse of the issues of Azilises. The *Mahākṣatrapas* and *Kṣatrapas* belonging to the Śaka family of Western India issued coins in their respective names at the same time. Sometimes the reverse of the Scytho-Parthian coins bears the name of a viceroy.

Formerly, the circulation of gold coins in India was extremely limited; but, with the foundation of the Kuṣāṇa dynasty in the first century A.D., gold coinage became popular. It may be said that no genuine silver issues of the Kuṣāṇas have been discovered. The coins of the Kaniṣka group of kings show only Greek legend. The striking characteristic of the money of Kaniṣka I and Huviṣka is that they bear upon their reverse the figures and names of numerous gods and goddesses which were worshipped in the vast Kuṣāṇa empire embracing wide area of Northern India and Central Asia. Of the Indian deities appearing on Kaniṣka's coins, mention may be made of Śākyamuni Buddha and the god Śiva represented anthropomorphically, whereas the issues of Huviṣka display the figures as well as the names of such Indian divinities as Umā, Skanda-Kumāra, Viśākha, Mahāsena, etc. The occurrence of the Indian deities on their coins may be associated with the fact that the Kuṣāṇa kings adopted Indian religious faiths. The gold currency of the Kuṣāṇa rulers after Vāsudeva, which betrays poor workmanship and depreciation in the purity of gold, exhibit writing in Brāhmī characters.

With the decline of the Kuṣāṇa empire, the north-western region of India came under the sway of the Sasanid dynasty of Persia. The coins of the later rulers of Western India bear clear traces of Sasanian influence. The so-called Gadhiyā or Gadhaiyā coins current in that region were regional imitations of Sasanian prototypes. Copper coins imitated from the Kuṣāṇa originals were in circulation in Orissa for several centuries after the decline of the Kuṣāṇas.

The coins of the Śaka rulers of Western India, who flourished between the beginning of the second century A. D. and the close of the fourth century, are made of silver and are small in size. From the last quarter of the second century, these coins show the date of their issue in the Śaka era behind the royal head on the obverse. When the celebrated Gupta emperor Candragupta II conquered Western India from the Śakas about the beginning of the fifth century A. D., he issued silver coins for that region in imitation of the Śaka currency, though the Śaka date was replaced by years of the Gupta era. This fact demonstrates the influence of the local types upon the coinage of ancient India. Like the Imperial Guptas, some Śātavāhana rulers of about the second half of the second century A.D., e. g. Vāsiṣṭhīputra Śātakarṇi and Gautamīputra Yajña-Śātakarṇi, issued silver coins in imitation of the silver money of the Śakas for circulation in the district that had previously formed part of the Śaka kingdom.

In connection with the influx of foreign coins in ancient India, we should not fail to take notice of a large number of Roman coins discovered in various parts of India, especially in the coastal regions of the south. The Kuṣāṇa monarchs melted the Roman gold coins that entered in the North Indian markets and minted their gold issues weighing 124 grains in accordance with the Roman weight standard. In South India, besides original Roman coins, we have also their local imitations and both were in circulation in the market for a long time.

While the foreign rulers like the Greeks, Scythians and Parthians were exercising their supremacy over North-Western India, there arose in Northern India a large number of smaller states, both monarchial and republican. The existence of these is known only from their coins. During the period of Kuṣāṇa paramountcy, they were relegated to the status of vassal states; but, with the decline of Kuṣāṇa power towards the beginning of the third century A. D., many of them re-asserted their independence. Coins of several such kingdoms and republics have been unearthed at various sites like Kauśāmbī (modern Kosam near Allahabad), Mathurā, Ahicchatrā (mod. Rāmnagar in the Bareilly District), Ayodhyā (near Fyzabad), Nagarī (near Chitodgadh), Nagar (in the Tonk District), etc. These states, however, lost their importance in the fourth century A. D., with the rise of the Guptas. As mentioned earlier, the Śaka kingdom of Western India was also annexed to the Gupta empire about the beginning of the next century.

The Śātavāhana rulers of Andhra nationality ruled over a considerable portion of the Deccan from the latter half of the first century B.C. down to the first quarter of the third century

A. D. Coins of these kings, which were generally made of lead, copper, billon and potin, have been discovered in large numbers.

The coins of the Śātavāhana rulers bear upon their obverse various symbols such as the hill, tree, animals and several other objects, while their reverse is often occupied by the so-called Ujjain symbol. It is worth noting that the Śātavāhana issues discovered in Madhya Pradesh generally show an elephant on their obverse.

Gautamīputra Śātakarṇi (c. 106-30 A. D.), the most illustrious king of the Śātavāhana dynasty, is known to have restruck the silver coins of the contemporary Śaka ruler of Western India, viz., Nahapāṇa of the Kṣaharāta family, after having killed the latter and annexing the Śaka territories. Some of Gautamīputra's successors, e.g., Vasiṣṭhīputra Śātakarṇi and Gautamīputra Yajña-Śātakarṇi, issued some coins in silver and, as mentioned earlier, these coins were imitated from the Śaka coinage.

A few Śātavāhana coins, showing a double-mast ship, and thus testifying to the prevalence of maritime trade and commerce, have been found on the eastern coast of the Far South. The name of the king, as given on these pieces, is illegible; but it is very probable that they were issued by either Vāsiṣṭhīputra Puḷumāyi or Gautamīputra Yajña-Śātakarṇi.

The gold coinage of the Imperial Guptas, which displays superb artistic merit, beautiful execution and a great variety of types and motifs, occupies a place of outstanding importance in Indian numismatics. One of the greatest kings of this family, Samudragupta (c. 335-76 A. D.), issued a large number of coins of the Standard type, in which we have on the obverse the standing figure of the king with a standard in one of his hands and, on the reverse, the goddess Lakṣmī seated on throne. There is hardly any doubt that this type of Samudragupta's coins is a close imitation of the Ardokhsho type of Kuṣāṇa coins circulating in the East Punjab region under the later Kuṣāṇas of the third century A. D. Although Samudragupta's coins show variation in respect of their devices, many of them betray Kuṣāṇa inspiration. It is interesting to note that Samudragupta bore the name of Kāca in his first series of coins just as Jahāngīr and Shāh Jahān are referred to by their original names, viz. Salim and Khurram, in some of their early issues.

The weight of early Gupta coinage, which was evidently based upon the Kuṣāṇa standard, was about 124 grains though afterwards it was changed to the traditional Indian Suvarṇa standard of 146 grains. The gold coins of the Imperial Guptas were usually known as Dīnāra (Roman *Denarius*). One of the characteristic features of Gupta gold coins is that their legends, written in Sanskrit, are mostly metrical, the usual metres being the Upagīti and Indravajrā-Upendravajrā. These coins furnish us with numerous otherwise unknown epithets of the Gupta suzerains.

Samudragupta is known to have issued a number of coin-types, of which mention may be made of the Lyrist and Aśvamedha types, the first depicting the king as playing on the lyre and the second bearing the figure of the sacrificial horse. On certain types of his coins, the king is shown holding a bow and arrow, or a battle-axe, or as slaying a tiger. In this connection, attention may be drawn to an interesting series of coins which give the name of his parents Candragupta I and Kumāradevī on the obverse, and that of his mother's clan, *i. e.* the Licchavis, on the reverse. These coins were in all probability, commemorative medals, struck by Samudragupta in memory of his parents, in order to point expecially to the Licchavi blood in his veins, the king's birth from a girl of the Licchavis being prominently mentioned in the official records of the Guptas. Although Candragupta I was the founder of the Imperial Gupta family, it was his illustrious son and successor Samudragupta who established the greatness of the family and was apparently the first king of the dynasty to start numismatic activity. The commemorative medallions of Samudragupta may well be compared with those of Eueratides I showing the names and busts of the parents of the Indo-Greek king. No genuine silver and copper issues, which can be attributed to Samudragupta, have so far been discovered.

Of the gold coinage issued by Candragupta II Vikramāditya (c. 376-414 A. D.), reference may be made to the Archer, Lion-slayer, Horseman, *Chatra* and Couch types. A number of silver coins and a few copper pieces of Candragupta II have also been found. In a unique gold coin, the king is represented as standing before the god Viṣṇu and is described as *Cakra-*

vikrama. As pointed out earlier, Candragupta II issued silver coins in imitation of the Kṣatrapa silver issues and they were inteded for circulation in the Śaka territory in Western India, which he had annexed to his empire. Although the circulation of the Gupta silver coinage, known as Rūpaka, was originally restricted to the western provinces, in the course of time it came to be used in the Gangetic plains also.

Continuing the numismatic activity of his predecessors with remarkable zest and vigour, Kumāragupta I (c. 414-55 A. D.) issued gold coins of various types, *e. g.*, the Aśvamedha, Kārttikeya, Lyrist, Swordsman, Archer, Elephant-rider, Lion-slayer, Tiger-slayer, *Chatra* and Rhinoceros-slayer. On a certain type of coins, the king is known to be described as *Apratigha* (unconquerable). The marginal legend on this coin-type cannot be satisfactorily deciphered and that is why there has been considerable divergence of opinion among numismatists as regards the real significance of the scene represented on the obverse. In this scene, the king seems to be depicted as a depressed young boy being encouraged by a male and a female divinity standing on either side. Kumāragupta I also minted an extensive silver coinage, one class of which shows a peacock and a metrical legend. On certain coins, the king is shown in the company of his queen, whereas, on some other issues, he is shown slaying a lion while riding on an elephant.

It was during the reign of Skandagupta (455-67 A. D.) that the weight of the gold coinage was increased to conform to the traditional Suvarṇa standard. The degradation of the Gupta currency, from the point of view of grace and purity of metal, is noticeable from the close of the fifth century A. D.

Among the early coins discovered in Bengal, we have silver punch-marked issues and a number of coins of both the Kuṣāṇas and the Guptas. The copper plates found in this region bear witness to the fact that the Gupta gold and silver coins were respectively known as Dīnāra and Rūpaka and that 16 Rūpakas were equivalent to 1 Dīnāra. The Kalighat hoard contained a few coins of the later Gupta rulers. Among the rulers of Eastern India who flourished after the Gupta age and imitated the coinage of the Guptas, Śaśāṅka (c. 600-25 A. D.), the lord of Gauḍa, was the most prominent.

It is a matter of regret that no coins of either the Pālas or the Senas of East India have as yet come to light. We have to note that the simultaneous use of cowries and old coins along with the current money would have sometimes prompted the ruling authorities to abstain from striking fresh coins of their own. The copper plate inscriptions of the Sena rulers show that the amount of land-revenue was assessed in Kapardaka-Purāṇas. The *Kapardaka* is a cowrie whereas the *Purāṇa*, as we have seen, is the same as the silver-Kārṣāpaṇa. *Kapardaka-Purāṇa* would therefore signify 'a Purāṇa calculated in cowries'. 80 cowries were considered to be equal to one Paṇa or copper-Kārṣāpaṇa, and 16 Paṇas or 1280 cowries were regarded as equivalent to one Purāṇa or silver-Kārṣāpaṇa, otherwise called Cūrṇi, etc. Of course, this rate was liable to variation from age to age and country to country.

Several royal houses like the Kalacuri, Gāhaḍavāla, Cāhamāna, etc., which were holding sway in North India during the early medieval period, are known to have struck coins. Among the Kalacuri rulers of Ḍāhala, Gāṅgeyadeva Vikramāditya (c. 1015-41 A. D.) issued gold coins with the old Gupta device of seated Lakshmī. This coin-type was imitated by the Candella rulers who flourished at a slightly later date. The silver coinage of the Cāhamānas showing a bull and a horseman was a close copy of the Śāhī currency that was long prevalent in North-Western India. The Turkish Muhammadan invaders of North India also at first adopted this device for their coinage.

We have a number of copper coins of the medieval rulers of Kashmir. The gold and silver currency of king Harṣa (1089-1111 A. D.) exhibits the head of an elephant. This coin type, as we learn from the testimony of the *Rājataraṅgiṇī*, was of Karṇāṭa origin.

Of the coins of South India, mention may be made of certain thick gold pieces bearing the boar symbol, which are believed to have been issued by the early Cālukya rulers. Some of them are cup-shaped and are known as Padma-ṭaṅka. It may be noted in this connection that the gold coins current in South India during the medieval period were generally known as Varāha (probably so called for the boar symbol), their alternative name being gold-Gadyāṇa (48 Ratis). It is often referred to as Pon or Hon (Sans. *Suvarṇa*) in Kannaḍa, Niṣka in

Sanskrit inscriptions and Kaḷañju or Māḍai in Tamil literature. This Māḍai (Sans. *Māṣa*) is written in the Telugu-Oriya records as Māḍa, Māḍā, Māḍha or Māḍhā and its weight is said to have been about 40 Ratis. There were also Gadyāṇas and Māḍais made of silver. The Varāha was called Pagodi, Pagode or Pagoda by the Europeans, the name being derived from the Sanskrit *Bhagavatī* (i. e. the Mother-goddess) as is suggested by the appearance of the figures of gods, goddesses or temples on these coins. A class of small gold coins, known as Paṇam (English *Fanam*) and weighing about 5 or 6 grains were in circulation in the Tamil-speaking areas and it is almost certain that the Accu and Gulikā coins mentioned in the Tamil texts were no other than these Paṇams. The Eastern Gaṅga rulers of Orissa appear to have issued this type of coins. Mention has already been made of the gold and silver Kaḷañju current in South India. The small copper coins of this region were generally known as Kāśu, spelt *Cash* by the Europeans.

The coins of the Imperial Coḷas are characterised by three symbols, viz., fish, bow and tiger. Some scholars believe that the tiger, fish and bow were the national emblems of the Coḷas, Pāṇḍyas and Keralas respectively and that the coins bearing the aforesaid symbols testify to the Coḷa occupation of the Pāṇḍya and Kerala kingdoms. On certain silver issues of the celebrated Coḷa emperor Rājarāja I (985-1016 A. D.), we find the deformed bust of the king and the royal name inscribed in the Nāgarī script. Rājarāja introduced his coins in Ceylon after the annexation of Northern Ceylon to the Coḷa kingdom. The Coḷa coinage served as the prototype for the currency of the indigenous rulers of Ceylon, who flourished at a later period.

Several gold coins of the Fish-type, belonging to the Pāṇḍya rulers, have been discovered. In this connection, mention may be made of some silver pieces of a king called Vīra-kerala, which bear legend in the early medieval Nāgarī characters. The Eastern Cālukya kings are known to have struck the boar-type coins. Certain light pieces of gold bearing the names of some of the well-known kings of this dynasty, viz., Cālukyacandra or Śaktivarman I (999-1011 A.D.) and Rājarāja I (1019-61 A.D.) have been found in the Cheduwa island on the Arakan coast.

Some of the rulers of the Later Western Cālukya dynasty issued coins bearing the lion and temple symbols. King Permāḍi Vikramāditya VI (1076-1127 A.D.) was a contemporary of the celebrated Kashmirian monarch Harṣa. The evidence of the *Rājataraṅgiṇī* referred to above would suggest that Vikramāditya VI struck elephant-type coins which were imitated by Harṣa of Kashmir. Unfortunately, however, no coin of this type bearing the Cālukya king's name has as yet come to light. The anonymous gold coins bearing the representation of the forepart of an elephant are known among numismatists as the 'Gajapati Pagoda', though it would appear from the testimony of the *Rājataraṅgiṇī* that such coins were struck or allowed to be struck by the later Cālukya rulers of Karṇāṭa.

Recently a few copper pieces of king Pratāparudra I (1163-95 A. D.) of the Kākaṭīya dynasty of Warangal have been discovered. They have Nandināgarī legend and no symbols. At a later period the rulers of Vijayanagara struck coins in gold, silver and copper, in accordance with the prevalent style in South India. We find several symbols on these coins such as the bull, elephant, a number of divinities and the imaginary double-faced eagle called Gaṇḍabheruṇḍa.

By the first half of the eighth century A. D., the Arab Muhammadans effected the conquest of Sind; but it was after many years that they started issuing coins. In the early years of the eleventh century, Sulṭān Maḥmūd of Ghaznī succeeded in establishing Ghaznavid supremacy over the Punjab region. By the close of the twelfth and the commencement of the thirteenth century A. D., Turkish Muslims extended their authority upon the plains of Northern India and, in the fourteenth century, practically the whole of South India was subjugated by them.

The Muslim rulers regarded the issue of coins to be a special prerogative of an independent monarch. Coins issued by the Muhammadan kings of India were generally an imitation of the coinage of the Muslim countries in Western Asia. They usually bear legends on both sides, but no symbols. Generally, on the obverse of this coinage, we have the *Kalima* or the Creed of Islam in Arabic (i. e. *lā Ilāhī il Allāh Muḥammad Rasūl Allāh,* "Allāh is the one and only God and Muḥammad is His Prophet,") and, on the reverse, the name and titles of the king and the place as well as the date of minting. But there are some coins which are square in shape and bear legends in Nāgarī characters and also some symbols. These coins exhibit considerable Indian influence which, however, was not a permanent feature of the Indo-Muslim coinage.

Sulṭān Maḥmūd issued the silver Dirham or Taṅka from the city of Maḥmūdpur (i. e. Lahore) in A. H. 418 and 419. It shows on the obverse the *Kalima* in Arabic and, on the other side, its Sanskrit rendering in Nāgarī characters (*Avyaktam=ekaṁ Muhamadaḥ avatāraḥ nṛpatiḥ Mahamūdaḥ Avyaktīya-nāmni ayaṁ Taṅkaḥ Mahamūdapure ghaṭitaḥ Tājikīyena saṁvatā* 418 or 419). After him, no other Muhammadan ruler struck coins of this type.

Towards the close of the twelfth century A. D., Muḥammad of Ghūr adopted the Gāhaḍavāla device of seated Lakṣmī for his own gold currency. The Sulṭāns belonging to the so-called Slave dynasty issued coins called Dehlīwāl which bear, on one side, the well-known device of the Cauhān horseman and, on the other, the bull of Śiva as well as the royal name in Nāgarī characters. The weight of their coins, generally made of billon (mixture of silver and copper), was about 56 grains. Their gold issues were similar to those in billon. Sulṭān Iltutmish (1211-36 A. D.) issued coins of a type in which the Sulṭān is represented on horseback. In 1228 A. D., Al Mustansir, the then Khalifa of Bagdād, granted him a charter confirming his sovereignty in India. It was in commemoration of this cordial relation with the Khalifa that, towards the end of his rule, the Sulṭān struck coins with the former's name on the obverse and his own on the reverse. Although the said Khalifa died in 1242 A. D., his name continued to appear on the currency of the Delhi Sulṭāns as late as the reign of Ghiyāsuddīn Balban (1266-87 A. D.). The theoretical weight of the silver coins of Iltutmish was about 175 grains and coins of this type in gold and silver were issued by the Delhi Sulṭāns till the days of Muḥammad bin Tughluq Shāh. The silver coin of this weight was the predecessor of the later Rūpiya. This coin often called Taṅka, was $\frac{1}{10}$ of the gold coin of the same weight in value.

Sulṭān Alāuddīn Muḥammad Shāh (1294-1316 A. D.) of the Khaljī dynasty was the first Indo-Muslim ruler to quote dates in the Hijrī reckoning in his billon currency, though his copper issues do not bear any date. On his Taṅkas, the Sulṭān describes himself as 'the Second Alexander', 'the Right-hand of the Khilāfat,' etc., while his son and successor Quṭbuddīn Mubārak (1316-29 A. D.) calls himself 'the Khalifa of the Lord of Heaven and Earth'.

The reign of Muḥammad bin Tughluq (1325-51 A.D.) constitutes an important epoch in the coinage of the Delhi Sultanate. During the early years of his reign, Muḥammad followed his predecessors and issued gold and silver coins weighing about 175 grains; but shortly afterwards, these were supplanted by the gold Dīnār and the silver Adalī weighing about 202 and 144 grains respectively. It seems that this change was due to an attempt to adjust the relative values of gold and silver. The early series of Muḥammad's coins bears the names of the first four Khalifas along with the *Kalima*. In 1340 A.D., he dispatched an emissary to Egypt to the Abbasid Khalifa Al Mustakfī in order to secure confirmation of his sovereignty and accordingly issued coins with the Khalifa's name. But it was found later on that Al Mustakfī had already passed away and therefore the name of the next Khalifa Hākim Abu'l Abbās Aḥmad was inserted in the later series of his coins.

The silver Taṅkas of Muḥammad bin Tughluq were equivalent to 48 and 50 Jitals in Northern and Southern India respectively. The billon pieces like Do-Gānī, Sas-Gānī, Āṭh-Gānī, Bārah-Gānī and Solah-Gānī, (i. e. 2, 6, 8, 12 and 16 Jītal pieces), were in circulation in the North respectively as $\frac{1}{24}$, $\frac{1}{8}$, $\frac{1}{6}$, $\frac{1}{4}$, and $\frac{1}{3}$ of a Taṅka, whereas in the South, 25 Gānī (25 Jitals $= \frac{1}{2}$ Taṅka) and 10 Gānī (10 Jital $= \frac{1}{5}$ Taṅka) coins were put into use.

Muḥammad made serious efforts to popularise the use of certain copper and brass tokens as silver and billon coins, as is indicated by the legend appearing on them. This class of coins bear the inscription, 'Obedience to the Sulṭān is obedience to God.' Although he was an orthodox Muhammadan, he nevertheless used Nāgarī characters on some of his issues. But the attempt of the Sulṭān proved abortive, because the public were generally unwilling to accept the copper or brass coins as silver ones and, moreover, the market was flooded with a large number of forged coins of this type.

The coinage of Fīrūz Shāh (1351-88 A. D.) shows the name of Khalifa Abu'l Abbās. His billon coins, like the similar issues of Muḥammad, weigh 144 grains. The issue of this coin-type was continued during the reign of the later Sulṭāns whose silver coins are rare. Buhlūl Lodī (1451-89 A. D.) introduced the silver Bahlolīs and a copper currency, the weights of which were 145 and 140 grains respectively.

At a later period, when the power of the Turkī Sultanate of Delhi was fast declining, almost all the provinces of the kingdom, with the exclusion of Delhi and its neighbourhood, threw off their allegiance to the central government and asserted independence. Bengal did not accept the suzeraignty of Delhi for a long period. The Sulṭāns of Bengal struck silver coins of about 166 grains, which display a striking similarity to those of the Delhi Sulṭāns. Shamsuddīn Iliyās Ṣhāh (1343-57 A. D.), following the celebrated Khaljī emperor, assumed the proud title of 'the Second Alexander' on his coins. Another independent Sulṭan of Bengal, Alāuddīn Husen Shāh (1493-1518 A. D.), described himself as the conqueror of Kāmrū (i. e., Kāmarūpa) and Kamta and of Urīsa (Orissa) and Jājanagar on his issues.

Sulṭān Bāyazid Shāh was succeeded by his son Fīrūz Shāh on the throne of Bengal in A. H. 817 (*i. e.* 1414-15 A. D.). During this period, Rājā Gaṇeśa, originally a Hindu Zamindar, grew powerful enough to seize the throne of Bengal. But, guided by political motives, he did not ascend the throne himself, but gave it to his son Yadu after converting him to Islām under the name of Jalāluddīn. Certain coins of Jalāluddīn, bearing the dates A. H. 818 (1415-16 A. D.) and 819 (1417-18 A. D.) have come to light. But in the year 1339 of the Śaka era (1417-18 A. D.), Rājā Gaṇeśa reconverted his son to Hinduism and himself ascended the throne. He struck silver coins from the mints at Pāṇḍunagara (Pandua), Suvarṇagrāma (Sonargaon) and Chāṭigrāma (Chittagong) under his newly assumed name Danujamardana. After Gaṇeśa *alias* Danujamardana, his son Yadu or Jalāluddīn, continued to issue coins from Chāṭigrāma and Pāṇḍunagara under the name of Mahendradeva. But, shortly afterwards, he embraced Islām once again and started issuing coins under the name Jalāluddīn from A. H. 821, *i.e.* 1418-19 A. D., onwards.

Although Kashmir lay beyond the jurisdiction of the Delhi Sultanate, the influence of the coinage of Quṭbuddīn Mubārak

Khaljī can be clearly traced on the silver issues circulated by the independent Sulṭāns of Kashmir. Along with the silver coins, a few brass and lead issues of the Sulṭāns of Kashmir have been discovered.

Muḥammad bin Tughluq appointed a governor in Madurā after his conquest of the Tamil-speaking regions of South India. But, in 1334 A. D., Jalāluddin Ahsan Shāh, the governor of Madurā, assumed independence. This Sulṭān as well as his successors struck money in copper and billon. A few gold pieces of this dynasty have also been found.

Alāuddīn Hasan Bahman Shāh laid the foundation of the famous Bahmanī kingdom (1347-1518 A. D.) in the Deccan towards the middle of the fourteenth century. The legend on Bahmanī coins mentions the metropolitan city of Gulbarga as Ahsanābād. During the reign of Alāuddīn II Aḥmad Shāh (1435-57 A. D.), Bīdar was made the capital of the kingdom and, from this time, the name of the new capital began to appear on the coins. The gold and silver issues of the Bahmanī dynasty betray the influence of the coins of Sulṭān Alāuddīn Khaljī of Delhi. Certain early silver issues of the Bahmanī Sulṭāns weigh between 15 and 26 grains. But, during the latter half of his reign, Aḥmad Shāh II struck coins in copper, the weight of which varied from 27 to 255 grains.

Towards the close of the fifteenth century, five separate principalities were rising into prominence on the ruins of the Bahmanī kingdom. These were the kingdoms of the Imād Shāhīs of Berar, the Nizām Shāhīs of Ahmadnagar, the Quṭb Shāhīs of Golconda, the Adil Shāhīs of Bijāpur, and the Barīd Shāhīs of Bīdar. Of the coins issued by the Sulṭāns of these different kingdoms, the silver Lārin of Sulṭān Ali II (1656-72 A. D.) of Bījāpur, resembling fishing hooks, deserves special mention. It is worth noting that even as late as the twentieth century, the Bijāpur prototypes were copied by the Sulṭāns of the Maldive Islands.

The Sharqī Sulṭāns of Jaunpur struck a large number of coins, mostly in billon and copper, which betray the influence of the Delhi Sulṭāns. Sulṭān Husen Shāh of Jaunpur had to retire from Jaunpur in 1476 A.D. as a result of the reverses he suffered at the hands of Sulṭān Buhlūl Lodī of Delhi; but the circulation of his billon issues was continued for the next three decades. At the same time, the copper coins of Buhlūl's brother Barbak Shāh were circulated from the city of Jaunpur. It may be noted that the coinage of some of the Jaunpur Sulṭāns, like that of Jalāluddīn Muḥammad Shāh (*i. e.* Yadu, son of Rājā Gaṇeśa) of Bengal, bears the legend in the Tughra style of writing.

Of the Sulṭāns of Malwa, Hūshang Shāh (1405-32 A. D.) was the earliest to strike coins and it was his son and successor Muḥammad Shāh I (1436-68 A. D.) who started coining money in billon. The chief characteristic of the Malwa coins of this period is that the great majority of them are square in shape. They served as the prototype for the coinage of a large number of rulers including the illustrious Rāṇā Sāṅgā of Citoḍ.

Among the Sulṭāns of Gujarāt in Western India, Aḥmad Shāh I (1411-43 A. D.), who is credited with the foundation of the city of Aḥmadnagar, is believed to be the first issuer of coins. It appears that a Rati was considered by the Gujarāt Sulṭāns as equivalent to 1.85 grains in weight in accordance with the standard of metrology prevailing in Gujarāt. In A. H. 850 (1446-47 A. D.), Maḥmūd II issued coins with a versified legend in the Persian language. This is for the first time that we notice the occurrence of a Persian verse on Indian coinage. Certain coins of the Gujarat Sulṭāns are valuable from the historical point of view since they give us the genealogy of the royal family beginning with its founder Zafar Shāh down to the reigning monarch. Sulṭān Muzaffar Shāh III (1562-72 A. D.) is said to have authorised the ruler of Navānagar in Kathiawar to strike copper-Korī. The chieftains of Junagadh and Porbandar continued to issue this type of coin, bearing corrupt Gujarātī legend, for a long time.

Bābur (1526-30 A. D.), who laid the foundation of the Mughul dominion in India, as well as his son Humāyun (1530-40 and 1555-56 A. D.) adopted the Central Asian standard for their coinage. There silver issues were known as Shāhrūkhī or Dirham. On certain coins of Bābur, the name of the imperial mint is given as Urdū (*i. e.* the Camp). Some specimens of the gold coins of Humāyun have come to light. It is interesting to note that the copper issues of these two Mughul emperors do not bear the names of their issuers. During the early years of his reign, Akbar circulated gold and silver coins in conformity with the currency of his immediate predecessors.

Sher Shāh (1539-45 A. D.), the great Afghān ruler of the Sūr dynasty, exhibited great originality and wisdom in the regulation of currency. He may be regarded as the predecessor of Akbar who adopted several of his monetary measures. Sher Shāh issued silver and copper coins, weighing about 178 and 330 grains respectively, half, one-fourth, one-eighth and one-sixteenth pieces of the currency being also in circulation during his reign. In later times, these silver and copper coins came to be known as Rūpiya and Dām (*i. e.* ancient *Dramma*) respectively. The coins of the Sūr dynasty, struck from various places in the empire, bear the names of the emperors in Nāgarī as well as Arabic characters. Their gold coins are rare.

Although the foundation of the Mughul empire in India was laid long before his accession, the brilliant numismatic activity of the Mughuls really started with the reign of Akbar. The Mughul coinage occupies an important place in the history of the numismatics of the world. Certain Mughul issues are said to have weighed 2000 Tolas; but they were apparently meant for donation and were not intended for circulation. Of the heavy coins, a unique silver piece of Aurangzeb, weighing 225 Tolas, and a 200-Muhar gold piece of Shāh Jahān have been found. Generally, a Muhar weighed between 170 and 175 grains, and during the reign of Akbar, it was equivalent to ten silver Rūpiyas, the average weight of which was about 178 grains. We have the 5-Muhar pieces of Akbar and Jahāngīr and some Double-Rūpiyas of the later Mughal emperors. Besides these, one 10-Rūpiya piece of Ṣhāh Ālam II has come to light. We also meet with certain Mughul coins which are slightly heavier in weight than the Rūpiyas and Muhars. The earliest mention of the Rūpiya to indicate the silver coinage of the Mughul emperors occurs on certain issues of Akbar, struck in the 47th year of his reign.

The Mughul emperors issued a special series of coins, in both gold and silver, which were meant for distribution among the audience on festal occasions. These were known as Nisār, Nūr Afshān or Khair Kabūl. Aurangzeb introduced the Dirham Shar-ī for convenience in the realisation of the Jizya tax which had been imposed upon the Hindus.

The Mughul Dāms, which were based on the copper

currency of Sher Shāh, weighed between 320 and 330 grains. These were generally called Fulūs (copper) or Sikka Fulūs (copper coins). The $\frac{1}{2}$-Dām, $\frac{1}{4}$-Dām and $\frac{1}{8}$-Dām pieces were called Nishfi, Dāmrā and Dāmrī respectively. But, during the reign of Aurangzeb, when the value of copper rose high, the imperial mint-masters were issuing Dāms or Fulūs weighing about 220 grains.

Akbar struck copper Ṭaṅkās of 644 grains, 10 Ṭaṅkīs being equivalent to 1 Ṭaṅkā. Smaller coins like $\frac{1}{2}$, $\frac{1}{4}$, $\frac{1}{8}$ and $\frac{1}{16}$ Ṭaṅkā pieces were also in circulation. Likewise, 2-Ṭaṅkī and 4-Ṭaṅkī pieces were also issued.

As was the case with the currency of early Muhammadan rulers, the early series of Akbar's coins, which are square or circular in shape, bears the *Kalima* on the obverse and the name of the king on the reverse. But, from 1579 A. D. which witnessed the promulgation of his new religious system known as Dīn-i-Ilāhī, the legend *Allāhu Akbar* (Allāh is Akbar or great) began to appear on the obverse of his coins. The Ilāhī coinage of Akbar, issued from the thirtysecond year of his reign, bears the inscription *Allāhu Akbar Jalla jalālahu* which means "Allāh is Akbar or great; His majesty is well-renowned." Instead of the date in the Hijrī era, these coins show his regnal year, i. e. the date in the Ilāhī era, as well as the name of the Persian solar month. This practice continued till the early part of Shāh Jahān's reign.

The Ilāhī coins were either square or circular. Some of Akbar's coins, struck in the fiftieth year of his reign, are very beautiful. They bear the figures of ducks, eagles, etc. In this connection, mention may be made of certain $\frac{1}{2}$-Muhars of Akbar, depicting the figures of Rāma and Sītā.

The gold and silver issues of Jahāngīr are valuable from the artistic point of view. He struck different types of coins with novel Persian stanzas in the legend. The name of his queen Nūr Jahān is found associated with his own name in the verse occurring on certain coins of Jahāngīr. In his thirteenth regnal year, Jahāngīr started to issue coins with the zodiacal signs, *e.g.*, Aries, Taurus, etc. Certain coins of Jahāngīr, regarded by some scholars as minted for making gifts to the courtiers, depict the emperor as holding a wine-cup. Some coins of this emperor bear the creed of the Ilāhī faith, viz.,

Allāhu Akbar, on the obverse and the solar symbol on the reverse.

The matchless elegance which characterises the issues of Jahāngīr is conspicuous by its absence on the coins of his son and successor Shāh Jahān. This emperor imitated his celebrated ancestor Tīmūr who assumed the proud epithet of Sāhib Kirān (the Lord of the Favourite Planet) and called himself 'the Second Sāhib Kirān'. Murād and Shujā, two of the four princes involved in a fratricidal struggle for Shāh Jahān's throne, struck coins with the title 'the Second Sikandar' towards the closing years of the reign of Shāh Jahān.

The copper coins of Akbar, with the exception of the Taṅkā and Ṭaṅkī, generally do not bear the name of the king. But the copper issues of the later Mughul emperors show the name of the ruler and the date in the Hijrī era as well as in the regnal reckoning.

The Mughul emperors issued their coins from different mints, scattered throughout their dominions. The appearance of various marks on Mughul money goes back to the days of Humāyun. They seem to be the symbols of the different mints. It is not unlikely that the change of the mint-masters was indicated by modification of the symbols.

Towards the close of Mughul rule, several ruling chiefs enjoyed the privilege of coining money. These local coins, circulated in the name of the Mughul emperors continued to be issued from different parts of the country for many years. The Indian issues of Nādir Shāh, who invaded India in 1739 A. D., and Aḥmad Shāh Abdālī, who invaded the country later, were more or less direct imitations of the Mughul coinage.

In the thirteenth century A. D., the Ahoms, belonging to the Shān tribe of Burma, established their political hegemony over the ancient kingdom of Prāgjyotiṣa or Kāmarūpa, which consequently came to be known as Asama or Assam. The coins of the early Ahom rulers bear the figures of various tribal divinities of their own, like Leṅgdun, Phatu, Cheṅg, etc., together with the name of the ruler in the Ahom language. When they became Hinduised, the Ahom kings started using Sanskrit in the legend of their monetary issues. The practice of quoting dates in the Śaka era also came into vogue from this time. Śukhen Muṅg (1509-59 A. D.) was the first Ahom king to strike coins, whereas the coins bearing Sanskrit legend in

Bengali-Assamese characters were issued for the first time during the reign of Sūryanārāyaṇa (1611-49 A. D.). Some of the coins of the Ahom rulers are octagonal in shape. Certain Ahom kings of the eighteenth century A. D. used the Persian language in their coin-legend in imitation of the Mughul coinage. The weight of early Ahom coins is 176 grains. Coins of their smaller denominations like $\frac{1}{2}$, $\frac{1}{4}$, $\frac{1}{8}$, etc., were also in circulation.

The coinage of the rulers of Jayantapura or Jaintiyā resemble the currency of the later Ahom monarchs. But king Govindacandra of Kachar struck coins which show the date in the Śaka era in a verse in the *Anuṣṭubh* metre. The coins of the rulers of Tripurā, bearing the Śaka date in numerical figures, are similar to those of the Ahom kings.

In the seventeenth century, the Malla king Mahendramalla of Nepāl secured the permission to issue coins from the Mughul emperor. King Pratāpamalla (1639-89 A. D.) issued silver coins which are more or less direct imitations of the coinage of the emperor Jahāngīr. By 1768 A. D., Nepāl fell into the hands of the Gorkhās who struck coins in gold, copper and silver, the last class corresponding to the Malla coinage. The coins of king Jaggajjayamalla (1702-32 A. D.) of Nepāl served as the prototype of the Tibetan silver Ṭaṅkās.

Śivājī, the celebrated founder of the Marāṭhā empire, issued coins in his own name. Numerous monetary issues of his successors as well as the Peshwās who followed them have been discovered. The gold coins and Rūpiyas (Pagoda, Fanam, Rupee, etc.) current in South India were struck by the Peshwās at Poona and various other places. Likewise, other Marāṭhā rulers like the Bhonsles of Berar, the Gāekwāḍs of Baroḍā, the Sindhiās of Gwalior and the Holkars of Indore had their mints at different places. The Marāṭhās, after they had established their supremacy over Ahmadābād in 1752 A. D., introduced coins of the Mughul style, with the addition of a hook symbol. The Rājput states like Jaipur, Jodhpur, Bīkāner, etc., had their own mints.

The Nizāms of Hyderābād struck coins in the name of the Mughul emperors as late as 1857 A. D., employing only the first letter of their own names; but, in their later issues, the name of the Mughul emperors was replaced by theirs.

The Rohilas had their mints at various places of Rohilkhand. The Nawābs of Oudh struck coins in the name of the the Mughul emperors. They bore the representation of the fish and were known generally as the Maslīdār. Ghāziuddīn Haidar issued coins in his own name in 1818 A.D. when he assumed the title of king. There are two interesting varieties of the silver coins of Oudh, the first of them being issued by Shujauddīn in 1774 A. D. after the defeat of the Rohilas at the battle of Miran Kātrā and the second by Ghāzīuddīn on Muḥarram 1 of A. H. 1235 on the occasion of his coronation. These coins bear a graceful bust of the king . A few coins of the Maslīdār type, bearing the date A. H. 1229 and *Subah Avadh* in the legend have been regarded by scholars as the issues of the Sepoy leaders of Lucknow, struck at the time of the Mutiny.

Haidar Alī of Mysore generally issued the Varāha or Hon (Pagoda) and Paṇam (Fanam) coins of South India; but his illustrious son Tīpū not only continued his father's coin-types, but also introduced Muhars, Rūpiyas, etc. Coins of smaller denominations like $\frac{1}{2}$, $\frac{1}{4}$, $\frac{1}{8}$ and $\frac{1}{16}$ Rūpiya pieces were also put in circulation during his reign, while the copper coins of the value of 20, 10, 5 and 2½ Kāśu were issued.

The coins of Tīpū were known by various designations, viz., Fāruqī (*i.e.*, Varāha of the value of ½ Muhar), Haidarī (2-Rūpiya), Ahmadī (Rūpiya), Johrā (*i.e.*, copper coin of the value of 20 Kāśu), etc. The copper money of Tīpū bear the elephant device on the obverse. There is some peculiarity in the dating of Tīpū's currency. His early issues bear the dates in the Hijrī era; but his later coins show them in the Mawlūdī era counted from 571 A. D., when Prophet Muḥammad was believed to have been born. It may be noted that Tipū gave different names to the different years of his reign. In the enumeration of numerals, he gave up the well-known Abjad reckoning and introduced the new 'Abtas' system. The coins of Tīpū are of singular beauty. After his overthrow by the British, Kṛṣnarāja Oḍeyar (1799-1868 A. D.) struck coins first with the representation of the bust of an elephant and then with that of a lion. His coins bear the legend in Kannaḍa instead of Persian.

The Sikh Khālsās forming a bulwark against the aggression of Aḥmad Shāh Abdālī grew very powerful in the Punjab region and introduced the Govind Shāhī coins from the city of Lahore in 1764. They bore the name of Guru Govind Singh in a Persian verse. The Nānak Shāhī coins were issued from Amritsar in 1777. One of the chief characteristics of the Sikh coinage is that it bore the date in the Vikrama era.

Ranjit Singh, the celebrated Sikh king of the Punjab, is known to have struck two types of coins, the first showing the legend in Persian and the second bearing Gurmukhī legend. But his Kashmir issues display the simultaneous use of the Persian and Gurmukhī legends. The coins of Ranjit Singh have the legend *Akālsahāī Gur Nānakjī* and bear a symbol in place of the king's name. Originally he adopted the leaf symbol which was later on substituted by the sign first of the peacock's feather and then of the mirror. His coins issued from Lahore in Vikrama Saṁvat 1885 bear the representation of Guru Nānak and his Muhammadan disciple Mardāna. Some of the copper coins of Ranjit Singh weighed about 600 grains.

The silver issues of Ranjit with a Persian verse served as the prototype for the silver coinage of the rulers of Paṭiālā, Nāvā, Jhind, Kaithal, etc., as well as of the Dogra chiefs of Kashmir. The initials *I. H. S.* in English occur on certain coins of Kashmir.

The rulers of the medieval period generally did not bother with the number of coins to be introduced or withdrawn from the market. It was the merchants and bankers who decided whether the number of the coins in the market should be augmented or reduced. According to their necessity, they purchased metal and got coins struck through the mints. The duty of the State was to verify the purity of the metal and the uniformity of the coins in regard to their weight and shape. It is likely that a similar system was also in vogue in ancient India.

But the Mughul emperors regarded their mints as a source of income. In order to keep the mints running, the people were compelled to get new silver coins struck every year. The value of coins diminished by 3 percent a year after the date of their issue and by 5 per cent after 2 years. In order to avoid loss, the people would therefore like to get their coins reminted at the end of the year. Of course, they had to pay rebate at the rate of 2 per cent. Under this system, the mints used to get sufficient work and thereby added to the income of the imperial treasury. The Government had also the opportunity to effect slight changes in the metal content and weight of the currency if they considered that necessary. During the Mughul regime, the silver Rupee was the standard coin while gold and copper issues bore metal value only.

As stated above, towards the close of the Mughul rule, petty feudatory chiefs sometimes enjoyed the privilege of striking coins, whereas foreign currency also was not obsolete in the market. Thus a large number of silver coins of different shape and weight and of various grades of metallic purity flooded the market. This explains the existence of nearly one thousand different coins of gold and silver in the Indian market during the latter half of the eighteenth century. When a number of coins were brought to a shrof or moneyer, he had to determine their value in the current Mughul silver coin after carefully examining the weight and metallic purity of each specimen.

Coins naturally lost some weight in consequence of everyday use and of several other factors. While paying their taxes in these old coins, people had therefore to pay a heavy discount. The peasants were ignorant of the actual value of the coins which they received by selling their crops. Under these circumstances, the suffering of the people knew no bounds. Such was also the condition prevailing during the early period of the British rule; but the Anglo-Indian Government's attempts to alleviate the people's misery ultimately became successful.

In 1685 A. D. the English East India Company obtained permission to issue coins in India. They circulated the gold Varāha (Pagoda) coins of South India and silver and copper coins of the European type. In the beginning, they struck coins in the name of the Mughul emperors. Certain coins, issued by the Company in Mumbai or Bombay, bear the name of Farrukhsiyar (1713-19 A. D.). In 1742 A. D., the Company procured a Farmān from the Mughul emperor Muḥammad Shāh granting the privilege of striking coins of the type of those of the Nawābs of Arcot. After 1765 A.D., when the Company received the Diwānī of Bengal, Bihār and Orissa, it was trying to establish gradually a monopoly in the matter of issuing coins.

We have already mentioned how, during the early period of British rule in India, the Rupee lost 3 per cent of its value after one year and 5 per cent after two years. In order to remedy the grievance of the people, Warren Hastings provided that, from 1773 onwards, only one date of the reign of the Mughul emperor Shāh Ālam II should be mentioned on the coins, that is to say, the date would remain unaltered on the coins for a considerable period of time. In 1789, Lord Cornwallis declared that a good coin, in spite of its mutiliated condition, should not be rejected, but that its value should be determined in accordance with its weight. At the same time, the system of re-issuing good coins which were mutiliated was introduced. Moreover, the Government continued to circulate coins in large numbers. From 1794, Indo-British coins were recognised as the only legal tender and the silver Rupee was the standard coin. 64 Pice or 16 Annas would make a Rupee, fractions of which were also in circulation. Copper coins of the value of $\frac{1}{2}$, $\frac{1}{4}$ and $\frac{1}{12}$ of a copper Pice were issued at the same time.

In the twentieth century, when the price of silver rose high, the practice of striking the Rupee first in an alloy of silver instead of pure silver and finally in the cheap metal called nickel was adopted. Currency notes were also introduced.

During the British period, Hyderabad, Travancore, Gwalior, Alwar, Baroda and some other Native States exercised the right of issuing coins. Their coinage was generally influenced by the Indo-British standard. The weight of the small silver Chakram of Travancore was based on that of the ancient gold Paṇam.

The year 1947 marked the termination of British rule in India and shortly afterwards India (excluding Pakistan but absorbing the former Native States) was declared a republic. The new Government of the Indian Republic introduced the decimal system of currency, according to which 100 Pice would be equal in value to one Rupee. Coins of the value of 2, 3, 5, 10, 25 and 50 Pice were issued in large numbers, the tendency being to avoid s lver and copper and the round strape in the smaller denominations. The new Pice, called Nayā Paisā for some time, is smaller than the old Pice in size, weight and value.

BIBLIOGRAPHY

Works on Indian numismatics can be divided into three classes; *viz.* (i) books on coins including the Catalogues of various collections and their Supplements; (ii) periodicals specially meant for publishing articles on Indian numismatics, and (iii) periodicals and other works dealing with Indian coins along with various subjects. Some monographs on Indian numismatics originally appeard in periodicals.

i

S. Ahmed, *Supplementary Catalogue of the Coins in the Indian Museum, Calcutta, Vol. II*, 1939.

J. Allan, *Catalogue of the Coins of Ancient India [in the British Museum]*, London, 1936.

„ *Catalogue of the Coins of the Gupta Dynasties and of Śaśāṅka king of Gauḍa [in the British Museum]*, London, 1914.

„ *Catalogue of the Coins in the Indian Museum*, Vol. IV (Native States), Oxford, 1928.

A. S. Altekar, *Catalogue of the Gupta Gold Coins in the Bayana Hoard*, Bombay, 1954.

„ *The Coinage of the Gupta Empire*, N. S. I., 1957.

D. R. Bhandarkar, *Lectures on Ancient Indian Numismatics*, Calcutta, 1921.

R. D. Banerji, *Prācīn Mudrā* (Bengali), Calcutta, B. S. 1322 (1915 A. D.).

P. N. Bhattacharya, *A Hoard of Silver Punch-marked Coins from Purnea*, Mem. A. S. I., No. 62, Delhi.

N. K. Bhattasali, *Catalogue of the Coins in the Dacca Museum*, 1936.

„ *Coins and Chronology of the Early Independent Sulṯāns of Bengal*, 1922.

B. B. Bidyabinod, *Supplementary Catalogue of the Coins in the Indian Museum, Calcutta, Vol. I (Non-Muhammadan Series)*, Calcutta, 1923.

G. B. Bleazly, *List of Coins and Medals belonging to Pratap Singh Museum, Srinagar, Kashmir*, 1908.

A. W. Botham, *Catalogue of the Provincial Coin Cabinet in Assam*, 1930.

C. J. Brown, *Catalogue of the Coins in the Provincial Museum, Lucknow*, Vols. I and II (Mughal Emperors), Oxford, 1920.

„ *Catalogue of the Coins of the Guptas, Maukharis, etc.*,

in the Provincial Museum, Lucknow, Allahabad, 1920.
,, *The Coins of India*, Culcutta, 1922.

S. K. Chakrabortty, *A Study of Ancient Indian Numismatics*, Mymensingh, 1931.

H. W. Codrington, *Ceylon Coins and Currency*, Colombo 1924.

O. Codrington, *A Manual of Musalman Numismatics*, London, 1904.

A. Cunningham, *Coins of Alexander's Successors in the East*, London, 1873 (originally published in the *Numismatic Chronicle*, 1868-73).
,, *Coins of Ancient India from the earliest times down to the 7th century A. D.*, London, 1891.
,, *Coins of the Indo-Scythians*, London, 1892 (originally published in the *Numismatic Chronicle*, 1888-92).
,, *Coins of the Later Indo-Scythians*, 1894 (cf. *Numismatic Chronicle*, 1893).
,, *Coins of Medieval India from the 7th Century down to the Muhammadan Conquests*, London, 1894.

P. Dayal, *Catalogue of Coins of the Sulṭāns of Delhi* [*in the Provincial Museum, Lucknow*], Allahabad, 1925.

T. Desikachari, *South Indian Coins*, 1933.
,, *South Indian Epigraphy and Numismatics*, 1916.

E. Drouin, *Monnaies des Grands Kouchans*, 1896.
,, *Chronologie et Numismatique des Rois Indo-Scythes*, 1888.

Chas. Duroiselle, *Catalogue of Coins in the Phayre Museum, Rangoon*, Rangoon, 1924.

W. Elliot, *Coins of Southern India*, 1886.

P. Gardner, *Catalogue of the Coins of the Greek and Scythic Kings of Bactria and India* [*in the British Museum*], London, 1886.

P. L. Gupta, *Punch-marked Coins in the Andhra Pradesh Government Museum*, Hyderabad, 1961.

E. Herzfeld, *Kushano-Sasanian Coins*, Mem. A. S. I, No. 38, Delhi, 1930.

S. H. Hodīvālā, *Historical Studies in Mughal Numismatics*, Calcutta, 1923.

G. H. Khare *Catalogue of Coins in the Bhārat Itihās Saṁśodhak Maṇḍal, Poona*, 1933.

A. N. Lahiri, *Corpus of Indo-Greek Coins*, Calcutta, 1965.

S. Lanepoole, *Catalogue of the Coins of the Mughal Emperors* [*in the British Museum*], London, 1892.

„ *Catalogue of the Coins of the Muhammadan States of India* [*in the British Museum*], London, 1885.

„ *Catalogue of Coins of the Sulṭāns of Delhi* [in *the British Museum*], London, 1884.

E. Loventhal, *The Coins of Tinnevelly*, Madras, 1888.

J. J. Michael, *List of Coins in the MacMohan Museum, Quetta*, Quetta, 1912.

D. Prasad, *Observations on the Silver Punch-marked Coins of Ancient India and their Age*, Benares, 1931.

M. Rama Rao, *Sātavāhana Coins in the Andhra Pradesh Government Museum*, Hyderabad, 1961.

„ *Select Sātavāhana Coins in the Madras Government Museum*, Madras, 1959.

T. M. Rangachari and T. Desikachari, *Dravidian Coins—The Pāṇḍyas and Coḷas and their Coinage.*

E. J. Rapson, *Catalogue of the Coins of the Andhra Dynasty, the Western Kṣatrapas, the Traikūṭaka Dynasty and the Bodhi Dynasty* [*in the British Museum*], London, 1908.

„ *Indian Coins*, Strassburg, 1898.

B. N. Reu, *Coins of Marwar*, Jodhpur, 1946.

T. W. Rhys-Davids, *Ancient Coins and Measures of Ceylon*, 1877.

C. J. Rodgers, *Catalogue of Coins in the Indian Museum, Calcutta*, Parts III (1895) and IV (1896).

„ *Coin Collecting in North India*, Allahabad, 1894.

S. C. Roy, *The Stratigraphic Evidence of Coins in Indian Excavations and Some Allied Issues*, N. S. I.

B. Sahni, *Technique of Casting Coins in Ancient India*, N. S. I., 1945.

A. von Sallet, *Nachfolger Alexanders des Grossen in Bactrien und Indien*, Berlin, 1883 (originally published in *Zeitschrift für Numismatik*, 1879-83).

C. R. Singhal, *Bibliography of Indian Coins*, Vol. I (Non-Muhammadan Series, Bombay, 1950) and Vol. II (Muhammadan and Later Series), N. S. I.

„ *Catalogue of the Coins of the Gujarat Sulṭāns* [*in the Prince of Wales Museum, Bombay*].

„ *Mint-towns of the Mughal Emperors*, N. S. I.

V. A. Smith, *Catalogue of the Coins in the Indian Museum, Calcutta*, Vol. I (Part I—The Early Foreign Dynasties and the Guptas; Part II—Ancient Coins of Indian Types; Part III—Persian, Medieval, South Indian and Miscellaneous Coins), Oxford, 1906.

E. Thomas, *Ancient Indian Weights*, 1865.

" *Chronicles of the Pathan Kings of Delhi*, London, 1871.

E. Thurston, *History of the Coinage of the Territories of the East India Company in the Indian Peninsula and Catalogue of the Coins in the Madras Museum*, Madras, 1890.

H. V. Trivedi, *Catalogue of the Coins of the Nāga Kings of Padmāvatī*, Gwalior, 1957.

R. H. C. Tufnell, *Hints to Coin Collectors in Southern India*, Madras, 1889.

W. H. Valentine, *The Copper Coins of India*, London, 1914.

E. J. Walsh, *The Punch-marked Coins from Taxila*, Mem. A. S. I., No. 59, Delhi, 1939.

R. B. Whitehead, *Catalogue of the Coins in the Punjab Museum, Lahore*, Vol. I (Indo-Greek Coins), Oxford, 1914; Vol. II (Coins of the Sulṭāns of Delhi and their Contemporaries); Vol. III (Coins of the Mughal Emperors).

" *The Pre-Muhammadan Coins of North-Western India*, New York, 1922.

H. N. Wright, *Catalogue of the Coins of the Indian Museum, Calcutta*, Vol. II (Part I—The Sulṭāns of Delhi; Part II—Contemporary Dynasties in India), Oxford, 1907; Vol. III (Mughal Emperors of India), Oxford, 1908.

" *The Coinage and Metrology of the Sulṭāns of Delhi*, Delhi, 1936.

ii

Even several years before the foundation of the Numismatic Society of India in 1910, arrangements had been made for the publication of a 'Numismatic Supplement' as part of the *Journal* of the Asiatic Society, Calcutta. No. I of these Supplements appeared in the Volume of the Journal for the year 1904 and No. XLVII, which is the latest, in that for the year 1937. The arrangement was discontinued when the Numismatic Society of India resolved to publish its own *Journal*, of which

Vol. I appeared as pertaining to the year 1939 and Vol. XXIII (Golden Jubilee Volume) relating to 1961 was published some years ago. The Society has also published several issues of a series entitled 'Numismatic Notes and Monographs'. Another periodical entitled *The Indian Numismatic Chronicle* is being published by the Bihar Research Society, Patna, since 1960.

iii

There are numerous periodicals and books that fall in this class. Amongst periodicals, mention may be made of the *Asiatic Researches*, *Journal of the Asiatic Society* (Calcutta), *Numismatic Chronicle* (London), *Journal of the Royal Asiatic Society* (London), *Journal of the Bihar and Orissa Research Society*, etc., etc. The Annual Reports of the Archaeological Survey of India and of some of the Museums also fall into this class.

Amongst books, we may include *Cambridge History of India*, Vol. I, 1922; *A Comprehensive History of India*, Vol. II, 1957; W.W. Tarn's *The Greeks in Bactria and India*, 1951; A.K. Narain's *The Indo-Greeks*, 1957; J.N. Banerjea's *Development of Hindu Iconography*, 1956 (Chapter IV, pp. 108-57), D.C. Sircar's *Select Inscriptions*, *Indian Epigraphy* (pp. 428-34) and *Indian Epigraphical Glossary* (pp. 428-42), etc., etc. Publications like the *Corolla Numismatica* (Numismatic essays in honour of Barclay V. Head), Oxford, 1906, would also fall into this class. Cf. also *Encyclopaedia Britannica* (s. v. *Rupee*), *Hobson-Jobson* (s. v. *Rupee*, *Fanam*, *Pagoda*, etc.), Wilson's *Glossary of Judicial and Revenue Terms* (s.v. *Rūpiya*, etc.), etc., etc.

CHAPTER II

NUMISMATIC STUDIES IN INDIA

The number of serious students of numismatics was few among Indians for a long time after they had begun to participate with European scholars in the work of the reconstruction of India's lost history of the early period, when she made most of her significant contributions to the civilization of the world. Of late, the position has somewhat changed. The number of Indians taking interest in the ancient and medieval coins of India has increased and Indian membership of the Numismatic Society of India has swelled appreciably. The Central and State Governments are exhibiting greater appreciation of the Society's work. The issues of the Society's journal are coming out regularly every year, while its annual session, held about the end of the year, has become a regular feature. In order to encourage studies in Indian coins, the Society is awarding medals to energetic students of numismatics. An upflow of Indian enthusiasm in numismatic studies is evidenced by certain recent publications, notably A. S. Altekar's *Catalogue of the Gupta Gold Coins in the Bayana Hoard*, 1954. The Society has also undertaken the publication of several interesting monographs. Recently the Epigraphical Branch of the Archaeological Survey has seriously undertaken the study of coins, and arrangements have been made for the publication of notices of coins examined by the Branch in the *Annual Report on Indian Epigraphy* and of articles on coins, especially the inscribed ones, in the pages of the *Epigraphia Indica*. A few Indian Universities have now provided for the study of coins in their M.A. courses in Ancient Indian History and Islamic History.

These are no doubt good signs; but unfortunately there is a dark side of the picture too. Our numismatic studies still suffer from various drawbacks. We shall have to improve the position and strive hard to reach the goal.

Numismatic studies and research in India have not yet been as popular as they should be. Most of our Universities have not yet provided for the study of Indian coins of any period.

Even the few that have made provision for the study of regional history (e. g. ancient history of Assam in the Gauhati University and history of Orissa in the Utkal University) or ancient Indian history or Islamic history have in most cases failed to introduce the study of coins in the courses in question. There is no special post of a teacher (Lecturer, Reader or Professor) of numismatics in any of the Indian Universities. As yet coins do not play any part in the teaching of history and geography in the schools and colleges of India.

Another point, which deserves attention, is the narrowness of our approach. We are not interested in the study of the ancient, medieval and modern coinage of other countries. A large number of Roman coins have been discovered in India; but there is hardly anybody amongst us, who may be regarded as capable of doing full justice to them. We deal with the coins of the Bactrian and Indo-Greek rulers without sufficient knowledge of ancient Greek coinage. This shows that we are far less inquisitive than scholars in other countries, who extend their investigation and research to all parts of the world. Even in regard to India, a study of the late medieval and modern coins, especially the medieval issues of South India, the Indo-British coins and medals and the coinage of the recently dissolved Native States, has so far drawn little attention. As a matter of fact, there should be a sort division of labour and collaboration among Indian scholars for a planned progress in the field of numismatic studies.

Our Museums show scant enthusiam in collecting coins issued in different ages in various parts of India herself, not to speak of the other countries of the world, or in completing their sets even when they have already some specimens of a particular class. Not only is the study of the medieval coinage of South India a neglected subject, very few North Indian Museums have representative collections of South Indian coins in their cabinets. Many of the types and varieties of Indo-Greek coins recently discovered in Afghanistan very quickly reached the cabinet of the British Museum in London; but nobody in India is known to have made an attempt to collect any of them. The authorities of institutions like the British Museum and the American Numismatic Society collect coins of all ages and all parts of the world and are always after the wanted types or varieties of coins to complete particular sets. This is why even for studying coins of some period of Indian history we have often to refer to the rich collections of the British Museum. It is high time that our institutions discard their narrow outlook. The activities of the Numismatic Society of India should also not be confined to the study of Indian coins alone.

An unfortunate feature of most of our Museums is that they have got no qualified numismatist on their staff. As repositories of coins, our Museums have a great responsibility, although they do not appear to be quite conscious of it. The recording of treasure-trove coins received by them from time to time in the registers and putting them securely in iron safes are not the only things they are expected to do. An examination of those coins, publication of periodical reports on them and preparation of their descriptive and illustrated catalogues are absolutely necessary. Some Museums devote a small space on their numismatic acquisitions in their annual reports without satisfactory description and illustration of the important specimens. Such scrappy treatment of coins is of little use to the students of numismatics. In case they cannot be suitably treated in the museum reports, arrangements should better be made for their publication in research journals like the one published by the Numismatic Society of India. Important numismatic acquisitions of a Museum may also be illustrated in picture post-cards. Typical specimens of coins or at least their metal or plaster casts, suitably coloured and endowed with descriptive labels, should be properly exhibited in the Museums. There should be arrangements for the preparation of casts of coins and they should be supplied to persons and institutions that are interested in numismatic research and may require them for study either free of cost or at nominal price. Museums should also afford facilities to students of numismatics to examine the coins in their cabinets.

Our National Museum may be made the richest storehouse of Indian coins of all periods and the greatest centre of numismatic studies in the country. A band of qualified numismatists may be employed on its staff for the preparation of an exhaustive and comprehensive series of catalogues of Indian coins with a view to collecting the required specimens according to that list. A board of Numismatic Advisers may also be constituted for the guidance of such workers. As most of the coin collections in the Museums and private hands in India remain as yet unexamined, the said employees of the National Museum may be engaged in the proper examination of these collections in which hundreds of important types and varieties of old coins are known to be lying uncared for and unpublished. This process would make a large number of duplicate coins available for the cabinet of the National Museum either by purchase or by exchange and transfer. Metal casts of unique specimens in these collections should also be secured for the National Museum. The Archaeological Survey, the Universities that have arranged for the study of numismatics in the Post-Graduate classes and the Numismatic Society of India may also be invited to help in the examination of such collections and in the preparation of their catalogues. The numismatists of the National Museum and other students of the subject may be deputed from time to time to the Museums in foreign countries like Pakistan, Afghanistan, Iran and Russia, which contain very large number of coins in which students of Indian history would be interested, with a view to securing casts of unique Indian coins and purchasing rare and important specimens. In this way alone we may develop in India a supreme collection of coins for the study of our history. But, side by side with Indian coins, the National Museum should acquire representative collections of coins of all ages and all countries of the world.

In the Western countries, archaeological missions to other lands and exploration and excavation of important sites therein are often sponsored by private organizations and financed by rich individuals. The people in our country are accustomed to look to the Government for such works. There are some persons in this country, who have the hobby of collecting coins among other curios and antiquities. But, since they are not numismatists themselves, their collections may be contaminated with forged specimens. Attempts should be made for acquiring genuine coins from such private collections for one or the other of the museums in India and, while selling them to the museums, their owners should be guided not merely by the instinct of getting as high a price as possible for their possessions but by the nobler sentiment of serving a national cause. In the Western countries rich people often purchase rare coins at great costs only for the purpose of presenting them to a museum. This noble practice may be emulated by our rich men.

At present the Mints of India have no connection with numismatic studies in the country nor with the Numismatic Society of India. Lively co-operation between the Society and the Masters of the Mints is, however, likely to be beneficial to both the parties. It is really unfortunate that none of the Indian Mints is known to have any numismatist on its staff. The Mint authorities have, moreover, little idea about the value of the preservation of their old records and of the pattern-coins struck in the Mints in the past. This is why a student of Indo-British coins often gets from them vague, evasive or meaningless answers to his queries. On being asked about the respective mint-marks on Indo-British coins of different reigns, a Master of one of our mints is known to have replied, "This information is of a confidential nature and is not given to outsiders." This evasive reply seems to be due to the fact that the officer had no time to read the old records of the Mint or such records were either lost or insufficiently or unmethodically preserved so that they were not easily available to him. It is extremely desirable that our Mints publish periodical pamphlets regarding their activities. By publishing illustrated booklets on coins struck in the Mints as well as those issued by counterfeiters they may render a distinct service to the country. Such publications will educate the people as to how to detect counterfeit coins and thereby check the flourishing business in unauthorised coins that is causing serious loss to our national exchequer year after year.

The main difficulty in the progress of numismatic studies in India is the fact that, while, for doing full justice to the task facing us, we require a good number of trained numismatists, there are only a few serious and succesful students of the subject amongst us. It is a pity that, neither in epigraphy nor in numismatics, the right types of trainees are available in numbers. The paucity of genuine epigraphists and numismatists in India is no doubt due to the difficult nature of the subjects in question. The correct reading of a word in a damaged passage in an inscription may baffle the decipherer for fifty times and occur to him in his fiftyfirst attempt or not at all. Sometimes a damaged passage cannot be deciphered without the help of a similar passage elsewhere. Satisfactory decipherment and interpretation of a record also require very sound knowledge of the language in which it is written as well as of a large number of similar records. The legends on coins are usually worn out and incomplete. The most important thing to decipher in them is again the name of the issuer, and it is common experience that a name, if damaged or incomplete, is considerably more difficult to restore than an ordinary expression. Moreover while, on the one hand, the satisfactory and successful study of an epigraph or a coin does require the knowledge of a large number of other inscriptions and coins, on the other, very few Indian students of coins have sound knowledge of epigraphy and palaeography. Proficiency in epigraphy and numismatics involves a good deal of patient and laborious work. Unfortunately many of our students are not distinguished by their perseverence and diligence, but exhibit, on the other hand, the unscholarly tendency to theorising apparently due to an eagerness to ascend to fame without delay. As a result of this, we see sometimes very poor specimens of work on Indian epigraphy and numismatics in the journals published from different parts of the country. Often the published epigraphic texts are found to be full of misreading and without any sense at all and very clearly show that the authors made no attempt to understand them.

Another weakness of our students is that often they show scant regard for truth and are inclined to stick to their suggestions, based on insufficient study or data, even after they are shown to be totally wrong. We have therefore to develop among our younger research workers a strong critical acumen and a genuine love of truth. But a danger in the way is that, because the standard of scholarship is as yet not very high in our country, whatever a research worker publishes is likely to bring him some reputation as a scholar. Publication of any stuff is also not difficult as there are numerous journals which would publish even an article that is worthy only of the wastepaper basket. Unfortunately this creates a false sense of self-confidence and pride in the author, which leads to further deterioration in the standard of his work.

In this connection, attention may be drawn to another class of people in the field, who stand in the way of the progress of epigraphic and numismatic research. They are the followers of what may be described as the dog-in-the-manger policy. If an inscription or a hoard of coins happens to fall in their hands, they immediately declare the intention to publish the results of their study of the material in due course. Really, however, they are incapable of doing proper justice to the work and are therefore shy to publish anything on the subject. But they are very particular that better students of the subjects do not get an opportunity of examining and publishing the material.

From one point of view, the study of numismatics is at a greater disadvantage than that of epigraphy. Inscriptions are generally illustrated from inked impressions, on the basis of which the published transcript of an epigraph can be more easily checked than the legend, etc., of coins which are illustrated from photographs. Since the coins are often rubbed out and their unsatisfactory illustrations do not in many cases help us much in checking their descriptions, irresponsible writings on coins are more likely to go unchallenged than those on inscriptions. We may note in this connection how a few years ago some ordinary Gaṅga Fanams were attributed to a ruler of Bolangir-Patna in Orissa on the basis of an imaginary reading of their legend.[1]

The *Journal of the Numismatic Society of India* may well make a serious attempt to raise the standard of numismatic research in India and there is no doubt that its efforts will be ultimately crowned with success. It is better for it to publish a few well-written articles rather than a good deal of unsatisfactory stuff and to see that quality is not sacrificed to quantity. The journal should be printed in a better press and the illustrations of coins should be as satisfactory as possible.

The raising of the standard of the journal, and through it that of numismatic studies in the country, is primarily the responsibility of elderly scholars in the field of research. It is they who are to set up a high standard to be followed by the younger scholars. It is, however, deplorable that even the works of some of our front-rank numismatists cannot be regarded as a model in this respect as they are often full of speculations and errors.

A very elderly and distinguished student of Indian epigraphy and numismatics once read the letters *sagamānamaha* on certain coins found in Hyderabad, associated the legend with

1. *JNSI*, Vol. V, pp. 61-64; also see below.

śakyamānā of the Purāṇas and found in both of these expressions the name of the Śaka king Māna of the Mahiṣa dynasty. In a decade, a good deal was written on this early Śaka ruling family of Hyderabad and a number of coins were attributed to the same king and other members of his family.[1] But the existence of the Śaka dynasty of Hyderabad is entirely based on speculation. Firstly, we know that the names of the Śaka rulers of ancient India did not usually begin with the tribal designation *Śaka* while there are names like *Śakasena* and *Śakaśāta* or *Śakaśātakarṇi* among people who were not Śakas. Under the circumstances, even if the reading of the letters *sagamānamaha* is accepted and is taken to yield *śakamānamahiṣa* (we do not agree with the rendering), it is impossible to be confident without further evidence that a Śaka king is actually referred to. Secondly, it is equally impossible to be definite that the Puranic *śakyamānā* (which has other variants) really refers to a Śaka named Māna in view of the fact that the tribal name *Śaka,* quite well known to the Puranic chroniclers, would not in that case have possibly been modified in the context. Thirdly, on some coins attributed to the same ruler, the legend was originally supposed to read *mahāsenāpatisa radajiputasa sagamānacuṭukulasa,* in which *radajiputasa* was later corrected to *bharadajaputasa,* although the intended reading of the expression is no doubt *bharadajiputasa,* i. e. *bhāradvājī-putrasya.* It may be pointed out that the metronymic *Bhāradvājīputra,* 'born of a lady belonging to the Bhāradvāja-gotra,' does not appear to suit a Śaka king very well. Fourthly, the author's interpretation of *cuṭukulasa* (found to be *cuṭukasa* on some specimens) or *sagamānacuṭukulasa* as 'of Śaka Māna who is of the Cuṭu family' is obviously unwarranted. It is also difficult to believe that one and the same person described himself on some of his coins as a scion of the Mahiṣa dynasty and on others as that of the Cuṭu family. Fifthly, although the existence of a Cuṭu family of Śātakarṇis ruling from Banavāsi in the North Kaṇara District was accepted by scholars, it was not a Śaka dynasty. To avoid this difficulty, the utterly unconvincing suggestion that the Cuṭus of Banavāsi may have borrowed the

1. Cf. *JNSI,* Vol. XI, pp. 1 ff.; Vol. XII, pp. 90 ff.; Vol. XV, pp. 115 ff.; 120; Vol. XVI, pp. 74-75; *IHQ,* Vol. XXII, pp. 34 ff.; Vol. XXVI, pp. 216-22; Vol. XXVII, pp. 341-46. See also below.

epithet *cuṭukula* from the inscriptions and coins of the Śaka king Māna has been offered as if Māna's imaginary inscriptions are already well known.

Another ancient Indian ruling family that has been recently created in the same fashion is that of the Sebakas or Sevakas.[1] In one case, the letters *sapusa* only are stated to be clear on a coin; but they were conjectured to have formed a part of *sirikasapusiva* which was then supposed to yield the name of king Kaśipuśiva Sebaka.[2] Not only, however, is the name Kaśipuśiva absolutely imaginary, but his attribution to the Sebaka dynasty is a great flight of fancy. Similarly, on a few coins of different types, the following groups of letters are said to be clear on different specimens: *tasa* on one, *raño* on another, *kosiki* on the third and *kosikiputasa* on the fourth, although in some cases the reading of the letters is uncertain; but all the coins were supposed to have been issued by a Śātavāhana king named Kauśikīputra Śātakarṇi who was further supposed to have enjoyed 'a fairly long reign'.[3] The speculative nature of the suggestion ascribing the issuer of the said coins to the Śātavāhana family is, strangely enough, clearly demonstrated by the author himself elsewhere[4] as the ruler is there assigned to the imaginary Mahiṣa dynasty, even though he forgets to explain how the typical Śātavāhana name *Śātakarṇi* should have been adopted by the Mahiṣas of Śaka origin. There is, however, really no valid reason to believe that all the coins referred to were issued by a particular king styled Kāuśikīputra. The suggestion that his name was Śātakarṇi is only imaginary and therefore extremely doubtful, not to speak of his ascription to the Śātavāhana or Mahiṣa family and the long reign assigned to him.

As an illustration of careless mistakes creeping in the writings of front-rank numismatists, we may refer to a small note from the pen of one of the learned Editors of the *JNSI*.[5] The note in 39 lines bristles with errors of both fact and language, the most glaring of which may be noticed here. It is said,

1. Cf. *JNSI*, Vol. VII, pp. 94 ff., Vol. VIII, pp. 107; Vol. XIII, pp. 137 ff.
2. *Ibid.*, Vol. XIII, p. 137.
3. *Ibid.*, Vol. XIII, pp. 119, 134; cf. Vol. VIII, pp. 116 ff.
4. *Ibid.*, Vol. XIII, p. 135.
5. *Ibid.* Vol. XVI, pp. 120-29.

"Agathocles and Pantaleon issued some copper coins, purely Indian in shape, metrology, motifs and legends. They are squarish in size and have legends in Brāhmī or Kharoṣṭhī only, Greek script being altogether omitted." But it is well known that such coins struck by Pantaleon bear legends both in Greek and Brāhmī and that on none of his coins of this type is Kharoṣṭhī used and Greek discarded. There are two types of similar coins issued by Agathocles, of which one bears legends in both Greek and Brāhmī and the other in Kharoṣṭhī only. It is again extremely difficult to believe that the said coins were struck according to the Indian weight standard. Their recorded weights are known to range between 159.2 and 192 grains. These have no appreciable relation with the Indian *Paṇa* standard of 80 *Ratis* or 146.4 grains. On the other hand, we have copper coins of the Bactrian Greek kings Diodotus and Euthydemus weighing 169 and 160 grains and of king Demetrius and Eucratides weighing between 88 and 95 grains. It will be seen that the above coins of Diodotus and Euthydemus correspond in weight to the lighter amongst the coins of Pantaleon and Agathocles whose heavier issues have double the weight of the coins of Demetrius and Eucratides. It is said that the Greek (Attic) copper unit was the Chalkaus weighing 67.2, grains. The heavier coins therefore may be 3-Chalkaus (201.6 grains) and the lighter issues 2-Chalkaus (167 grains) pieces unless it is believed that the lighter weight of the latter is due to corrosion. It is further said, "The Guptas continued the type of their predecessors the Śāka (sic) rulers, and appear on their coins as offering oblations in fire while dressed in Scythian dress." Here is a clear confusion between Śaka and Kuṣāṇa. Of course, the Guptas are known to have imitated the silver coinage of the Śakas of Western India; but they appear in Turkish dress not on their silver issues but on their gold coins imitated from the coinage of the Kuṣāṇas. It is also said, "Kaniṣka, Huviṣka and Vāsudeva introduced a large number of Indian deities like Vāta, Skanda, Kārtikeya (sic), Mahāsena, the Sun, etc., besides continuing Śiva and the Buddha." There are several errors in the statement. In the first place, Vāsudeva did not introduce any Indian deity on his coin types, but merely continued the representation of Śiva introduced by one of his predecessors. Secondly, Vāta (Oado) and the Sun-god (Miiro, Miuro or Mioro) on the Kuṣāṇa coins were Iranian (and not Indian) deities. Thirdly, there is no mention of Kārttikeya in the legend of Kuṣāṇa coins so far discovered. They are known to mention only Mahāsena, or Skanda-kumāra and Mahāsena, or Skanda-kumāra, Viśākha and Mahāsena. Then again it is said, "Some of the Achaemenian *Darics* are counter-marked with Indian symbols." The fact, however, is that some of the Persian silver coins called *Siglos* (not the Persian gold coin called *Daric*) bear marks resembling Brāhmī or Kharoṣṭhī letters or symbols on the Indian punch-marked coinage.

A popular practice among Indian numismatists is to discover fanciful names from coin-legends which are not satisfactorily decipherable. The doubtful reading *mahagāmakasamaha* supposed to yield the name of king Sumahāgrāmaka[1] and the equally conjectural reading [*Mahara*]*ja-ra*[*ja*]*dhasa Dhamadamadhara*[*sa*] believed to yield the name of *Mahārāja Rājādhirāja* Dharmadamadhara[2] are cases in point. Such attempts to create historical figures out of speculative readings is most deplorable especially because they set a rather unwholesome example to youngesters in the field of research. They also put those students of history who have no opportunity to examine the original coins at a great disadvantage because the illustrations of the coins are usually unsatisfactory.

What has been said above is merely to illustrate the low standard of our numismatic research and is not meant to discredit anybody in particular. We should coolly and dispassionately think over the position and devise ways and means to raise the standard of our research.

1. *JNSI*, Vol. XII, pp. 92 f.; *Hyd. Mus. Num. Ser.*, No. 7. See also below.

1. *JNSI*, Vol. XII, pp. 1 ff.; *Anc. Ind.*, No. 5, pp. 97, 100.

CHAPTER III

ŚATAMĀNA AND ŚĀṆA

I

The address, delivered by the President of the Numismatic Society of India at Nagpur in December 1950 and printed in the Society's Journal, Vol. XII, Part ii, pp. 188 ff., contains an interesting reference to the silver coin called Śatamāna, weighing 100 Ratīs or 180 grains, and its subdivisions.[1] It was suggested that the Śatamāna had several subdivisions such as Ardha-Śatamāna or half Śatamāna (50 Ratīs or 90 grains), Pāda-Śatamāna or one-fourth Śatamāna (25 Ratīs or 45 grains), and Pādārdha-Śatamāna (also called Śāṇa) or one-eighth Śatamāna ($12\frac{1}{2}$ Ratīs or $22\frac{1}{2}$ grains). In this connection reference has also been made to the coins called Triṁśatka and Viṁśatika supposed to be weighing respectively 60 Ratīs or 108 grains and 40 Ratīs or 72 grains and being $\frac{3}{5}$ and $\frac{2}{5}$ of the Śatamāna in weight and value. Thus the existence of an elaborate system of coinage has been traced on the basis of the Śatamāna. The name Śatamāna literally means 'measuring a hundred' and the basis of the measurement has been supposed to be the Raktikā or Ratī, usually regarded as weighing 1.83 grains. On a later occasion the same scholar says, "We know from other sources that the Śatamāna coin was one hundred *rattīs* (Ratīs) in weight"[2] although the evidence regarding the actual weight of the Śatamāna, referred to here, has unfortunately not been discussed. Here also weights of the coins of the Śatamāna series have been quoted. In this list, Ardha-Śāṇa (i.e. one-sixteenth Śatamāna) has been mentioned as weighing $6\frac{1}{4}$ Ratīs. It seems that the existence in ancient India of a silver coin called Śatamāna weighing 100 Ratīs and its many subdivisions has already been accepted by the students of Indian numismatics.[3] It has been said that 'a coin called Ardha-Śatamāna of 50 *rattīs* or 90 grains is well-known from grammatical literature',

1. *Op. cit.*, pp. 194-95.
2. *Ibid.*, Vol. XIV, p. 25.
3. Cf. *ibid.*, pp. 42 ff.

although the name of the work mentioning the weight of the half-Śatamāna has not unfortunately been disclosed.

In his *Lectures on Ancient Indian Numismatics*, pp. 55 ff., D. R. Bhandarkar drew the attention of scholars to the mention of the coin called Śatamāna in Kātyāyana's *Śrautasūtra*,[1] Pāṇini's *Aṣṭādhyāyī*,[2] Kātyāyana's *Vārttika*,[3] *Śatapatha Brāhmaṇa*,[4] *Taittirīya Brāhmaṇa*[5] and *Vājasaneyi-saṁhitā*.[6] He also pointed out that Sāyaṇa in his commentary on the *Śatapatha* passages explains Śatamāna as a round plate weighing one hundred *mānas* and takes *māna* to indicate a Ratī. It will be seen that Sāyaṇa's interpretation of Śatamāna involves two suggestions, viz. (1) that it was a plate and (2) that it weighed 100 Ratīs. Bhandarkar ridicules Sāyaṇa's ignorance in failing to recognize the Śatamāna as a coin and observes, "The case is not unlike that of Nāgojībhaṭṭa who, while commenting on the celebrated passage from the *Mahābhāṣya*.........interprets Mauryas as idol-makers. But just as no scholar will now understand Mauryas to mean idol-manufacturers, but take them to denote the Maurya princes only, no one can similarly explain the term Śatamāna in the way in which Sāyaṇa has done, but he must interpret it to denote the Śatamāna coin alone." Disposing thus of one of the two suggestions of Sāyaṇa, Bhandarkar takes up the other one and concedes, "Śatamāna may, however, have been one hundred *mānas* or *guñjā* berries (Ratīs) in weight as explained by Sāyaṇa". It may be noticed that the above statement of Sāyaṇa forming a part of his fantastic interpretation of Śatamāna is the 'evidence' in favour of the coin or metallic courrency called Śatamāna being 100 Ratīs in weight. A. B. Kieth[7] also speaks of the mention 'in the *Brāhmaṇas* of the Śatamāna, a piece of gold in weight equivalent to a hundred Kṛṣṇalas,' but does not give any reference.[8]

Bhandarkar understood Śatamāna in the sense of a gold

1. XV. 181-83.
2. V. 1. 27.
3. On Pāṇini, V. 1. 29.
4. V. 4. 3. 24 and 26; V. 5. 5. 16; XII, 7. 2. 13; XIII, 2. 3. 2; in one case described as *vṛtta* or round.
5. I. 7. 6. 2; I. 2. 7. 3.
6. III. 2. 6. 3; II. 3. 11. 5.
7. *Cambridge History of India*, Vol. I, p. 137.
8. Cf., however, *Ved. Ind.*, s. v. *māna* and *kṛṣṇala*.

coin and not a silver one. He quoted the following two passages of the *Śatapatha Brāhmaṇa* : (1) *suvarṇaṁ hiraṇyaṁ bhavati rūpasy=ev=āvaruddhai Śatamānaṁ bhavati śat-āyur=vai puruṣaḥ*; (2) *hiraṇyaṁ dakṣiṇā suvarṇaṁ Śatamānaṁ tasy=oktam*, and observed, "it will be seen that here Suvarṇa is associated with Śatamāna, and both are called *hiraṇya* or gold." We are however not sure whether the word *hiraṇya* in this context should be interpreted only as 'gold'. The original meaning of this word was gold or any other precious metal; but it latter developed the sense of coined gold or money.[1] Sometimes *hiraṇya* is taken to mean besides gold, also silver, any precious metal and wealth or property.[2] Although therefore the Śatamāna may have been a gold coin (or currency) as suggested by Bhandarkar, the possibility of its being a silver currency cannot be ruled out, especially in view of the fact that later evidence associates it usually with silver.

It may be pointed out that certain earlier writers on the subject took Śatamāna mentioned by Kātyāyana to be a silver coin or weight, although the same name was believed by them to have been given in the *Śatapatha Brāhmaṇa* to a gold coin or weight ; but Bhandarkar does not refer to them. Thus E. Thomas, in his *Ancient Indian Weights*,[3] observed, "Prof. Weber has collected from the Sūtras and later Vedic writings a number of references to money weights,[4] the most interesting of which are the notice of the silver Śatamāna by Kātyāyana,[5] the immediate successor of Pāṇini, and the mention of a 'yellow-gold Śatamāna' (*hiraṇyaṁ suvaraṇaṁ Śatamānam*) in the *Śatapatha Brāhmaṇa*."[6] But, as we have indicated above, it is not absolutely certain that the word *hiraṇya* has always been used in the *Śatapatha Brāhmaṇa* in the sense only of gold and not of 'any bright metal (especially silver)'.

Elsewhere in his work,[7] Bhandarkar makes the following observation on the Śatamāna : "We do not find any trace of this coin in literature or in inscriptions after the beginning

1. Cf. Monier-Williams, *Sans.-Eng. Dictionary*, s. v.
2. Apte, *Practical Sans.-Eng. Dictionary*, s. v.
3. *The International Numismata Orientalia*, Vol. I, Part i, p. 35.
4. *Zeitschrift*, Vol. XV, 1861, pp. 138-39.
5. XX. 26.
6. XII. 7. 2, etc.
7. See p. 182.

of the Christian era. No doubt that word occurs in the *Amarakoṣa*......But there is no such evidence to show that by Śatamāna the *Amarakoṣa* is referring to some coin of its period. The mere occurrence of the word Śatamāna in this lexicon is, therefore, of no consequence, for lexicons have to take cognizance of all words whether there are any objects corresponding to them or not." This observation is due to misunderstanding as Bhandarkar believed Śatamāna to be only a gold coin weighing 100 Ratīs. It appears that the learned scholar did not care to consult Kṣīrasvāmin's well-known commentary on the *Amarakoṣa*, which explains *śatamāna* as *rūpya-pala* (i.e. one Pala of silver) on the authority of the *Yājñavalkyasmṛti*, although elsewhere in his work (p. 180) Bhandarkar recognises the silver Śatamāna mentioned by Manu and Yājñavalkya.

The *Yājñavalkyasmṛti* (I. 364-65) says :

dve Kṛṣṇale rūpya-Māṣo Dharaṇaṁ ṣoḍaś=aiva te ।
Śatamānaṁ tu daśabhir=Dharaṇaiḥ Palam=eva tu ॥

According to this authority, therefore, the Śatamāna, otherwise called Pala, is a money weight of silver equal to 10 Dharaṇas or 160 silver Māṣas or 320 Kṛiṣṇalas (Ratīs). The same view is expressed by the *Manusmṛti*,[1] which says :

dve Kṛṣṇale samadhṛte vijñeyo raupya-Māṣakaḥ ।
te ṣoḍaśa syād=Dharaṇaṁ Purāṇañ=c=aiva rājatam ॥
...Dharaṇāni daśa jñeyaḥ Śatamānas=tu rājataḥ ॥

The only difference between the two authorities is that the *Manusmṛti* does not apply the name Pala to the Śatamāna, although it applies that name to the gold measure or currency weighing 320 Ratīs in the same context:[2]

pañca-Kṛṣṇalako Māṣas=te Suvarṇas=tu ṣoḍaśa ।
Palaṁ Suvarṇāś=catvāraḥ Palāni Dharaṇaṁ daśa ॥

It may be pointed out in this connection that the passage *pūrv-oktāś=catvāraḥ Suvarṇā eko rājato Niṣko bhavati*, occurring in Vijñāneśvara's *Mitākṣarā* commentary on the *Yājñavalkya-smṛti*,[3] seems to apply the name 'silver Niṣka' to the silver Śatamāna or Pala weighing 320 Ratīs. It will therefore be seen that Bhandarkar would have found little difficulty in trac-

1. VIII. 135-37.
2. VIII. 134-35.
3. I. 365.

ing the mention of the metallic currency called Śatamāna in works of a date later than the beginning of the Christian era, if he would not have taken (wrongly, in our opinion) it to signify only a gold coin weighing 100 Ratīs. The *Manusmṛti* may be assigned to a date about the third century A.D., while the *Yājñavalkyasmṛti* is possibly later by a century or so.

That the silver Śatamāna or Pala or Niṣka weighing 320 Ratīs was regarded as the standard currency in some parts of India even at a much later date seems to be suggested by certain early inscriptions discovered in Orissa. In an article entitled 'Some Karasāsanas of Ancient Orissa,' published in *J.R.A.S.*, 1952, pp. 4-10, we have shown how, in specifying the fixed rent for an area of land payable annually, early Orissan documents usually quote the amount in *Rūpya-Pala*, often contracted into *Rū-Pla*. The Asiatic Society's plate of Gayāḍatuṅga[1] records the grant of Torogrāma at the fixed annual rent of 9 silver Palas. The Talcher plate[2] of the same ruler records the grant of another area, of which the cess called *tṛṇodaka* was fixed at 4 Palas of silver. The Talcher plate[3] of Kulastambha similarly speaks of the grant of a village called Siṅgagrāma with its *tṛṇodaka* fixed at 2 Rūpya-Palas. We also noticed that the Puri Plate (B) of Kulastambha[4] actually contains the passage *Kara-śāsana Rū-Pla* 10, i.e. *Kara-śāsana Rūpya-Pala* 10. The Jurada grant[5] of Neṭṭabhañja quotes the royal dues for a village as 4 Rūpya-Palas while the amount of another 4 Rūpya-Palas is stated to have been payable as Khaṇḍapāla-muṇḍamola (tax to be paid for the maintenance of the officer in charge of a Khaṇḍa or sub-division or of the Khaṇḍāits). The Ganjam insciption[6] of Pṛthvīvarman records the grant of a village with the annual rent fixed at 4 Rūpya-Palas. Two records of the Somavaṁśī king Mahābhavagupta I Janamejaya[7] mention the grants of villages with the amounts of rent fixed respectively at 5 and 8 Rūpya-

1. *J.A.S.B.*, 1909, pp. 348 ff.
2. *Ibid.*, 1916, pp. 293-94.
3. *Ep. Ind.*, Vol. XII, pp. 156-59.
4. Cf. *J.A.S.B.*, Vol. LXIV, Part i, pp. 123 ff.
5. *Ep. Ind.*, Vol. XXIV, pp. 15-20.
6. *Ibid.*, Vol. IV, pp. 198-201.
7. *Ibid.*, Vol. III, pp. 340-44; *J.P. A.S.B.*, 1905, pp. 12-13.

Palas. The expressions used in these records are : *prativarṣe c=ātra karaṁ pañca-Rūpya-Palāni niṣṭaṅkya* and *prativarṣa-dātavya-rūpyak-āṣṭa-Pala-kara-dānaṁ viviścitya.* The expression *rūpyak-āṣṭa-Pala* suggests that, although Rūpya-Pala was regarded as the standard, eight of which were the fixed annual rent in this case, there was in actual use no silver coin weighing 320 Ratīs. This suggestion is strengthened by the Madras Museum plates[1] which quote the rent of a village as *Rūpyaka-Pla* 10 *A-Mā* (*Ādya-Māṣa*) 2 *Gu* (*Guñjā*) 4, because in this case the fraction of the Rūpya-Pala or Ādya-Māṣa given in Guñjā could not probably have been a coin. Moreover, the fact that no silver coin weighing 320 Ratīs has ever been discovered practically settles the issue. The Angul plate[2] represents queen Dharmamahādevī as granting a village with the rent fixed at 3 Pala-Rūkas. *Rūka* in this case is either a mistake for *Rūpyaka* or the same as Telugu *rūka* derived from Sanskrit *rūpyaka* and meaning 'money'. In any case, the above instances make it abundantly clear that the silver Pala or Śatamāna weighing 320 Ratīs was regarded as the standard of calculation in monetary transactions in early medieval Orissa. Thus the old Śatamāna was not entirely out of use as late even as the medieval period.

It may be mentioned in this connection that medieval Orissan inscriptions often speak of a coin called Māḍha which was both of gold and silver. Oriya lexicons recognise the word *Māḍha* in the sense of the weight of half a Tolā or Karṣa (i.e. 40 Ratīs). The gold or silver Māḍha of medieval Orissa was therefore the one-eighth Śatamāna (otherwise called Śāṇa) and points to the continuity of the use of the old Śatamāna standard down to quite recent times.[3] As the *Śatapatha Brāhmaṇa* also speaks of the gold Śatamāna, it can be linked with the Orissan Māḍhas of gold. The same word occurs in Telugu as *Māḍa,* which not only means any coin or money but also an old gold coin weighing roughly about 25 grains.

Thomas observed,[4] "The exotic designation Śatamāna, 'one hundred measures', equally points to Aryan influences.

1. *Ep. Ind.*, Vol. XXVIII, pp. 44 ff.
2. Misra, *Orissa under the Bhauma Kings*, pp. 50 ff.
3. Cf. *Ep. Ind.*, Vol. XXVIII, p. 306. Cf. Tamil *Māḍai*, a coin name probably derived from Sanskrit *Māṣa*.
4. *Op. cit.*, p. 12.

We can appreciate the motives which induced the northern races to devise the *Śata-raktika*, or 'one-hundred Rati piece', out of existing units of value; but it is difficult to devise the object or meaning of 'one hundred measures' which do not fit in with either of the national metrical schemes. The special total of 320 Ratis is equal to 960 barley corns. Accepting the latter seed as the natural Aryan unit, the $\frac{1}{100}$ part of this sum would be 3.2 Ratis or 9.6 barley corns—a broken subdivision, which can only be accounted for by a theoretical rather than a practical assertion of the decimal system." But the learned writer seems to have been groping in the dark.

The belief that the weight of the Śatamāna was 100 Ratīs is no doubt based on the name which literally means 'measuring 100', i.e. 'made up of 100 units of measurement', and on the conjecture that this unit of measurement is no other than the well-known Ratī. But, as we have seen, the evidence of the *Manusmṛti* and *Yājñavalkyasmṛti* leaves hardly any doubt that the suggestion is absolutely unwarranted. These authorities make it quite clear that the unit of measurement, one hundred of which made up the Śatamāna weighing 320 Ratīs, was not one Ratī but actually $3\frac{1}{5}$ Ratī or 5.8 grains. It is very interesting to note that this is roughly the weight of the Mañjāḍi. Smith says, "The metric system of Southern India appears to be based upon the weight of two kinds of seeds, the Mañjāḍi (*Adenanthera pavonina*) averaging about five grains Troy, and the Kaḻañju, Molucca bean or Bonduc nut (*Caesalpinia bonduc, Guilandina bonducella*), which was considered as equivalent to ten Mañjāḍis......in practice the Kaḻañju weight did not differ widely from the northern standard of 32 Ratis, to which the punch-marked silver coins were struck. These punch-marked coins which occur all over India north and south......The southern specimens may be regarded as roughly equivalent to a Kaḻañju."[1] Walter Elliot in his *Coins of Southern India*, p. 48, note 2, gives the weights of the Mañjāḍi and Kaḻañju according to himself respectively as 4.8 and 48 grains but according to Alexander Cunningham respectively as 5.736 and 57.36 grains; and he also says,[2] "It may there-

1. *Cat. C. Ind. Mus.*, Vol. I, p. 310.
2. *Op. cit.*, p. 49.

fore be reasonably inferred that the Eldling or Purāṇa is simply a silver Kaḷañju." Elsewhere in the same work,[1] Elliot observes, "By whatever name the Elding was known in other parts of India, it probably in the South may have taken the designation of the weight Kaḷañju." It will be seen that scholars regard 10 Mañjāḍis or 1 Kaḷañju as roughly equal to 1 silver Dharaṇa=Purāṇa=Kārṣāpaṇa of 32 Ratīs. According to this rough estimate, 100 Mañjāḍis or 10 Kaḷañjus would make 10 Dharaṇas or Purāṇas or Kārṣāpaṇas or 320 Ratīs. This leaves little doubt regarding Mañjāḍi being the unit of measurement, one hundred of which made up the Śatamāna. The suggestion was already offered by S. K. Chakrabortty.[2] But it seems that it has been altogether ignored by later writers on the subject. Chakrabortty also pointed out that the Śatamāna was a metallic currency, but not actually a coin in the real sense of the term. The prevalence of the silver Śatamāna or Pala standard as the basis of calculation in monetary transactions as well as of the Māḍha coins weighing half a Tolā in the Kaliṅga area of Southern India as late as the medieval period seems also to be significant in this connection.

The adoption of the Śatamāna based on a Nonaryan weight system in the economic life of the Aryans at a fairly early date need not surprise us. Scholars have now traced various Nonaryan elements in the culture of the Aryans settled in India and intermixed with the Nonaryan peoples.[3] In the field of monetary calculation, 16 Māṣas making 1 Purāṇa-Dharaṇa-Kārṣāpaṇa, 16 Paṇas making 1 Kāhaṇa and 16 Annas making 1 Rupee may be traced to the 'use of the multiple 16' by the pre-historic people of the Indus valley, who were Nonaryans.[4]

The above discussion will show that, if an elaborate system of silver currency based on the weight standard of the Śatamāna was really prevalent in any part of Ancient India, the weights of those pieces were as follows : (1) Śatamāna=320 Ratīs (585.6 grains), (2) ½ Śatamāna=160 Ratīs (292.8 grains), (3) ¼ Śatamāna=80 Ratīs (146.4 grains), (4) ⅛ Śatamāna (known to be called Śāṇa also)=40 Ratīs (73.2 grains), and

1. See pp. 50-51.
2. *A Study of Ancient Indian Numismatics*, 1931, pp. 27, 437 ff.
3. Cf. *The Vedic Age*, ed. Majumdar, pp. 14 ff.
4. Cf. Piggot, *Pre-Historic ndia*, p. 181.

(5) $\frac{1}{16}$ Śatamāna (said to be called $\frac{1}{2}$ Śāṇa also)=20 Ratīs (36.6 grains). It will be seen that $\frac{1}{4}$ Śatamāna weighed 80 Ratīs or one Karṣa (146.4 grains). Attention in this connection may be drawn to what we have said as to the evidence supplied by the *Kauṭilīya Arthaśāstra*, *Amarakoṣa* and its commentary regarding the weight of the silver Kārṣāpaṇa:[1] "It is clear that the silver Kārṣāpaṇa weighing 146.4 grains (or slightly less as indicated by the *Arthaśāstra*) was known in some parts of the country at least theoretically, although we have no silver punch-marked coins of this weight. The very name Kārṣāpaṇa (i.e. a coin weighing one Karṣa), applied to the silver coin, also suggests that its original weight, even if theoretical, was 80 Ratīs." Thus the Śatamāna would not appear to have been entirely unrelated to the Kārṣāpaṇa as it was originally 4 times a Kārṣāpaṇa, while the later silver Purāṇa was $\frac{1}{10}$ of it in weight. The silver Māḍhas (40 Ratīs) of medieval Orissa prove the genuineness of the tradition regarding the silver Kārṣāpaṇa weighing 80 Ratīs.

It may be further pointed out in this connection that the designation of a unit of one hundred Ratīs was not entirely unknown in ancient India. But it was not styled Śatamāna. On another occasion,[2] we referred to the various weights of the Karṣa (the same as that of the Paṇa or Kārṣāpaṇa) recognised in ancient Indian literature and noticed that Karṣa was sometimes regarded as weighing 100 Ratīs. We also know how Buddhaghoṣa's *Samantapāsādikā* says :

tadā Rajagahe vīsati-Māsako Kahāpaṇo hoti, tasmā pañca-Māsako Pādo, and how according to Nārada : *Māṣo viṁśatimo bhāgaḥ Paṇasya parikīrtitaḥ*. The *Mitākṣarā* (on the *Yājñavalkya-smṛti*, I. 365) makes the point absolutely clear : *pañca-Suvarṇa-Pala-pakṣe viṁśati-Māṣaḥ Paṇo bhavati......catuḥ-Suvarṇa-Pala-pakṣe tu ṣoḍaśa-Māṣaḥ Paṇo bhavati.*

II

A. S. Altekar's article entitled 'Origin and Early History of Coinage in Ancient (sic) India' published in *JNSI*, Vol. XV,

1. *JNSI*, Vol. XIV, p. 131. See also below, p. 77.
2. *JNSI*, Vol. XIII, pp. 187 ff.; Vol. XIV, p. 129. See below, pp. 74-75.

Part i, pp. 1ff., dwells on the weight of the Śatamāna in a number of places : "......silver Śatamānas which weighing 100 *rattis* would give a weight of about 175 grains" (p. 7); "Most probably it (i.e. the Śatamāna) weighed a hundred *Kṛṣṇalas* or *rattis*, i.e. 175 grains" (p. 16); "Śatamāna undoubtedly weighed 100 *rattis* or 175 grains" (p. 18); "Most probably its (i.e. of the Śatamāna) weight was a hundred *raktikās* (175 grains) as its name obviously indicates......silver Śatamāna being 100 *rattīs*..." (p. 20); "a silver Śatamāna had come into vogue weighing hundred Rattis or 175 grains" (p. 21); etc. In spite of the discrepancy between 'most probably' on the one hand and 'undoubtedly' and 'obviously' on the other, there can be no doubt about the firmness of the belief of the author who further refers to the 'silver Śatamāna of 100 Ratti standard' in one of his many editorial notes (cf. p. 60). Some of the contributors of other papers in the said issue of the journal have also shown their inclination in favour of the general belief that the Śatamāna was a coin weighing one hundred Ratīs (see pp. 30, 63, etc.).

Altekar speaks of the gold currency prevalent 'during the age of the Later Saṁhitās, Brāhmaṇas and Upaniṣads' and of its three denominations, viz., Niṣka, Suvarṇa and Śatamāna. In regard to the weight of these three denominations, he says, "Śatamāna undoubtedly weighed 100 *rattis* or 175 grains. In later times, Suvarṇa and Niṣka followed the weight standard of 80 and 320 *rattis* respectively. The same may have been the case in this period also" (p. 18). Thus his approach to the weight problem of the Śatamāna on the one hand and that of the Niṣka and Suvarṇa on the other is different. He thinks that the Śatamāna was a coin of gold and not of silver during the age in question and says, "Śatamāna is mentioned by Kātyāyana also (c. 4th century B.C.); but, as gold coin, it seems to have gone out of vogue in later times. It will be soon shown that a silver Śatamāna being 100 *rattis* [in weight] came into vogue by c. 500 B.C." (p. 20). The ascription of Kātyāyana to the fourth century B.C. and of the beginning of the silver Śatamāna currency to circa 500 B.C. as well as the statement that 'there is no reference to any silver currency in the Vedic literature' (p. 21), however, does not appear to be quite consistent with what has been further said at p. 21 : "The *Kātyāyana Śrautasūtra*, while describing the Aśvamedha sacrifice in Chapter XVI, refers to a *dakṣiṇā* of [a] hundred gold Śatamānas.........But later it again refers to a *dakṣiṇā* in Śatamāna, but adds that the Śatamāna was to be of silver in one case......There is thus some literary evidence to show that at about 600 B.C., which is generally (sic) taken to be the time of the Śrautasūtras, a silver Śatamāna had come into vogue, weighing [a] hundred Rattis or 175 grains." It is difficult to understand why Kātyāyana has been attributed to the fourth century B.C. but his *Śrautasūtra* to about 600 B.C. and why the beginning of the silver Śatamāna currency has been assigned to circa 500 B.C. in one place, but to circa 600 B.C. in another. It is equally unintelligible to us why the *Kātyāyana Śrautasūtra* (a Vedāṅga work of the Kalpa class) has not been recognised as a treatise pertaining to the 'Vedic' literature. But we are not much concerned with such discrepancies for the present. Let us see what evidence has been offered to prove the often-repeated statement that the Śatamāna was a coin weighing one hundred Ratīs and also the suggestion that it was a coin of gold and not of silver in the age of the Brāhmaṇas.

In regard to the first point, Altekar quotes the following passage. from Karka's commentary on the *Kātyāyana Śrautasūtra* : *vṛtt-ākārau raktikā-śata-mānau* (literally 'two round objects weighing one hundred Ratīs'), and says, "In later times Śatamāna was taken by Manu and Yājñavalkya as a silver coin weighing 160 *māṣakas* or 10 *dharaṇas*......It is extremely doubtful whether the Śatamāna of the Brāhmaṇa period was [a] silver coin in view of its being expressly described as *hiraṇya*."[1]

It will be seen that Karka's interpretation of the expression *śatamāna* is similar to that of Sāyaṇa, referred to and commented on by Bhandarkar,[2] and does not prove that this late commentator understood the word to indicate a coin or currency. Altekar therefore seems to deduce too much from Karka's interpretation of *śatamāna* as an object weighing one hundred Ratīs. Moreover, accepting for argument's sake that Karka speaks of the Śatamāna coin weighing one hundred Ratīs, it is unintelli-

1. Cf. p. 16, note 2.
2. *Ancient Indian Numismatics*, p. 57; above, p. 49.

gible why his opinion has been regarded as earlier and more authoritative than that of the ancient works of Manu and Yājñavalkya, in which the word *māna* in the designation *Śatamāna* has been used in a different sense. It appears to us that late authors like Sāyaṇa and Karka were as ignorant of the nature and weight of the Śatamāna as the twentieth century writers on ancient Indian numismatics and that their opinion has little value when it is opposed to that of much earlier authorities like Manu and Yājñavalkya.

As regards the meaning of the word *hiraṇya* in Vedic literature, we have already suggested that sometimes it was used to indicate 'silver'. This fact has been recognised by the learned compilers of the *Vedic Index*, when they say, "Gold is described sometimes as *harita*, 'yellowish',[1] sometimes as *rajata*, 'whitish'[2] when probably 'silver' is alluded to."[3] Elsewhere in the same work,[4] it is further said, "*Rajata* as an adjective with *hiraṇya*[5] designates 'silver', and ornaments (*rukma*),[6] dishes (*pātra*)[7] and coins (*niṣka*)[8] 'made of silver,' are mentioned."[9] Under the circumatances, we find it difficult to accept Altekar's suggestion that the word *hiraṇya* always means 'gold' in Vedic literature. Moreover, the mention of silver Niṣkas in the *Pañcaviṁśa Brāhmaṇa* (side by side with the reference to the silver Śatamāna in the *Kātyāyana Śrautasūtra*, referred to above) seems to render Altekar's statement that 'there is no reference to any silver currency in the Vedic literature'[9] unwarranted.[10] The *Vedic*

1. Cf. *Kāṭhaka Saṁhitā*, X. 4; *Śatapatha Brāhmaṇa*, XII. 4. 4. 6; *Ṣaḍviṁśa Brāhmaṇa*, II. 9.

2. Cf. *Taittirīya Saṁhitā*, 1. 5. 1. 2; *Śatapatha Brāhmaṇa*, XII. 4. 4. 7; XIII. 4. 2. 10, etc.

3. *Op. cit.*, Vol. II, p. 505.

4. See p. 197.

5. Cf. *Taittirīya Saṁhitā*, 1. 5. 1. 2; *Kāṭhaka Saṁhitā*, X. 4; *Śatapatha Brāhmaṇa*, XII. 4. 4. 7; XIII. 4. 2. 10; XIV. 1. 3. 4, etc.

6. Cf. *Śatapatha Brāhmaṇa*, XII. 8. 3. 11.

7. Cf. *Taittirīya Brāhmaṇa*, II. 2. 9. 7; III. 9. 6. 5.

8. Cf. *Pañcaviṁśa Brāhmaṇa*, XVII. 1. 14.

9. *Op. cit.*, p. 21.

10. Altekar himself refers to the mention of silver Niṣka in the *Pañcaviṁśa Brāhmaṇa* 'in connection with the Vrātyas', but explains it away by saying, "the Vrātyas...used to wear it as an ornament. [The] Vrātyas were an outlandish people. We can therefore very well assume that there exist-

Index[1] rightly points out that 'as early as the *Ṛgveda*[2] traces are seen of the use of Niṣkas as a sort of currency,' although Indian students of numismatics have often confused *currency* with *coin*.[3] Apparently Niṣka and Śatamāna were different names of both the gold and silver currencies weighing 320 Ratīs.

V. S. Agrawala says, "In the *Śatapatha Brāhmaṇa* (XII. 2. 2. 2) it is stated : 'Gold and silver will be the fee for the sake of variety to correspond to the manifold form of the deity, and that *dakṣiṇā* will be Śatamāna, since a human being lives for one hundred years' (*rajataṁ hiraṇyaṁ nānā-rūpatayā Śatamānaṁ bhavati śatāyur=vai puruṣaḥ*; *S. B.*, VIII. 4. 2. 10). Here is a definite reference to a silver Śatamāna of 100 parts, i.e. 100 *ratti* weight. Manu mentions the silver Śatamāna as equal to 10 *dharaṇas* or 120 *rattis* in weight (VIII. 137); but no actual specimen of a silver punch-marked coin conforms to the extraordinary weight of 560 grains."[4]

As regards Agrawala's support to the view respecting Śatamāna as a coin weighing one hundred Ratīs, it seems to us, as already indicated above, to be a mere speculation unsupported by any evidence worth the name. Of course he refers to the non-availability of ancient coins of the real Śatamāna weight standard of 320 Ratīs, but does not notice that, as noted above, Śatamāna was essentially a metal weight and not a coin in the real sense of the term. Moreover, the argument is irrelevant as the Śatamāna of 320 Ratīs, mentioned in the works of Manu and Yājñavalkya, cannot be regarded as a figment of imagination. The absence of actual coins weighing 320 Ratīs therefore does not prove that the Śatamāna was a coin weighing one hundred Ratīs. Similarly, the existence of coins weighing one hundred Ratīs in ancient India does not prove that such coins were called Śatamāna. As indicated above, there is evidence to show that the designation of ancient Indian coins which were one hundred Ratīs in weight was Kārṣāpaṇa. A class of Kārṣāpaṇas weighing one hundred Ratīs is

ed no silver currency among the Aryans of the Vedic period" (*op. cit.*, p. 10). But the Vrātyas were certainly Indians and it is impossible to *prove* that they were Nonaryans although anything can be *assumed*.

1 Vol. I, pp. 454-55.

2. Cf. I. 126. 2.

3. Cf. Bhandarkar, *op. cit.*, pp. 65 ff.

4. *JNSI*, Vol. XV, p. 30.

mentioned in old works which appear to us more authoritative than a twentieth century guess based on late and doubtful traditions that are opposed to older authorities and are hardly of any value at all. The supporters of the view that the word *māna* in the designation *Śatamāna,* known from the *Śatapatha Brāhmaṇa* and the *Kātyāyana Śrautasūtra,* means a Ratī have to explain why the same word has been used in the same designation in an altogether different sense in the *Manusmṛti* and *Yājñavalkyasmṛti.* Such an explanation has not as yet been offered and is not likely to be forthcoming so far as we can see. Considering the dearth of silver in ancient India, it is impossible to believe that the currency weighing only 100 Ratīs in earlier times was made as heavy as 320 Ratīs in the age of the works of Manu and Yājñavalkya. We know how the old silver Kārṣāpaṇa of 80 Ratīs was later made of 32 Ratīs only.

III

We have tried to show that the ancient Indian gold and silver currency called Śatamāna (also called Pala and Niṣka) was 320 Ratīs in weight (not 100 Ratīs as has been supposed by some modern writers) and that the Śāṇa (which was one-eighth of the Śatamāna according to the *Mahābhārata,* III. 134. 15) weighed 40 Ratīs or one-half of a Tolā of 80 Ratīs. It is also contended that the unit, one hundred of which made a Śatamāna, was not the Ratī, as has been erroneously supposed by some modern writers, but the Mañjāḍi weighing 3⅕ Ratīs. It may of course be argued that the Kṛṣṇala or Raktikā (i.e. Ratī) and not the Mañjāḍi should be regarded as the unit of measurement in connection with ancient Indian coins and currencies since the former is 'frequently referred to in the Saṁhitās and Brāhmaṇas' while the latter 'is not mentioned in them at all.'[1] One has to admit that the word Kṛṣṇala is found in the *Taittirīya, Maitrāyaṇī* and *Kāṭhaka Saṁhitās* and in other Vedic works such as the *Taittirīya Brāhmaṇa,*[2] although the name Raktikā is later. We cannot however ignore the fact that many words used in the Vedic literature, including a few indicating particular weights, have not yet been properly understood. Take, for example, the

1. *Ibid.*, p. 148.
2. Cf. *Vedic Index,* Vol. I, p. 185.

word *mṛḍa*, *pṛḍa* or *pruḍ*.[1] Passages like *aṣṭāmṛḍaṁ hiraṇyam* and *aṣṭā-pruḍ-ḍhiraṇyam* no doubt show that this was a small metallic weight or currency. Who can say that *mṛḍa*, *pṛḍa* or *pruḍ* was not the ancient name of the modern Mañjāḍi ?

That the Śatamāna, otherwise called Pala and Niṣka, was 320 Ratīs in weight is definitely proved by ancient Indian authorities including the *Manusmṛti*. This has already been made clear in our arguments set forth above. There is equally undisputable proof in favour of our suggestion that the weight of the Śāṇa was originally 40 Ratīs.

The *Śabdakalpadruma* explains the word *tolaka* (i.e. modern Tolā) as follows : *Śāṇa-dvaya-parimāṇam=iti Śabdamālā*; *aśīti-Rakti-parimāṇam*, etc. Thus, according to the Sanskrit lexicon entitled *Śabdamālā*, the weight of the Śāṇa was half of that of a Tolā, i.e. 40 Ratīs. This view is very clearly supported by the *Vaidyakaparibhāṣā* quoted in the *Śabdakalpadruma*, s. v. *Māṣa* and by Gaṅgādhara's commentary on the *Carakasaṁhitā*.[2] The *Vaidyakaparibhāṣā* says : *Guñjābhir=daśabhir=Māṣaḥ Śāṇo Māṣa-catuṣṭayam*, i.e. 10 Guñjās (Ratīs) make 1 Māṣa and 4 Māṣas (40 Ratīs) make one Śāṇa. Gaṅgādhara gives the weight of the Śāṇa in the following words : *daśa-Guñj-ātmaka-Māṣaka-catuṣṭayena tulya iti* ; *etac=c=ānyatr=oktaṁ "Guñjābhir=daśabhiḥ prokto Māṣako Brahmaṇā purā* । *catvāro Māṣakāḥ Śāṇas=tad-dvayaṁ Kola-saṁjñitam* ॥" *dvau Śāṇau Draṅkṣaṇaṁ Kolaṁ Badaraṁ Tolakañ=ca paryāyeṇa vidyāt*. According to this authority therefore a Śāṇa was equal to 4 Māṣakas each of which weighed 10 Guñjās (Ratīs). Thus according to Gaṅgādhara, a Śāṇa was 40 Ratīs in weight and 2 Śāṇas made 1 Tolaka (i.e. Tolā of 80 Ratīs). This weight of the Śāṇa has been supported by Gaṅgādhara by a quotation from an older authority saying that, according to an ancient view attributed to the god of creation, 10 Guñjās (Ratīs) make 1 Māṣaka, 4 Māṣakas make one Śāṇa, and 2 Śāṇas make 1 Kola. Gaṅgādhara further points out that the said Kola was otherwise known as Draṅkṣaṇa, Badara and Tolaka (i.e. Tolā). Thus Śāṇa is stated to have been 40 Ratīs or ½ Tolā in weight.

1. Cf. *Kāṭhaka Saṁhitā*. XI. I; XIII. 10; *Taittirīya Saṁhitā*, III. 4. 1. 4, etc.; Pāṇini's *Aṣṭādhyāyī*, III. 1. 123.

2. Kalpasthāna, Chapter 12. Cf. *JNSI*, Vol. XV, p. 151.

The above traditions giving the weight of the Śāṇa as 40 Ratīs no doubt support in very clear terms the combined testimoney of the *Mahābhārata* and the early Dharmaśāstra works that the Śatamāna (otherwise called Pala and Niṣka) weighed 320 Ratīs and that the Śāṇa was one-eighth of the Śatamāna.

There are certain other traditions apparently later than the above, which quote a lighter weight for the Śāṇa and sometimes also of the Śatamāna and other denominations. Thus the *Bhāvaprakāśa*,[1] gives the system of measurement prevalent in the Kaliṅga country in the following stanzas :

Māṣo Guñjābhir=aṣṭābhiḥ saptabhir=vā bhavet kvacit ।
caturbhir=Māṣakaiḥ Śāṇaḥ sa Niṣkaṣ=Ṭaṅka eva ca ॥
Gadyāṇo Māṣakaiḥ ṣaḍbhiḥ Karṣaḥ syād=daśa-Māṣakaiḥ ।
catuṣ-Karṣaiḥ Palaṁ proktaṁ daśa-Śāṇa-mitaṁ budhaiḥ ॥

According to this authority, 8 Guñjās (Ratīs) make 1 Māṣa (although, he says, sometimes 7 Guñjās were also taken to be equal to 1 Māṣa),[2] 4 Māṣakas (i.e. 32 Ratīs) make 1 Śāṇa otherwise called Niṣka and Ṭaṅka, 6 Māṣakas (i.e. 48 Ratīs) make 1 Gadyāṇa, 10 Māṣakas (i.e. 80 Ratīs) make 1 Karṣa, and 4 Karṣas make 1 Pala which was equal to 10 Śāṇas. It will be seen that, instead of the original 2 Śāṇas=1 Karṣa (80 Ratīs), here we find 2½ Śāṇas=1 Karṣa (Tolā), although the weight of the Pala (i.e. Śatamāna) remain 320 Ratīs as of old so that not 8 but 10 Śāṇas were now regarded as equal to a Pala. We have to note that 32 Ratīs, given here as the weight of the Śāṇa, were the weight of the well-known silver coin called Purāṇa and Dharaṇa and the popularity of these coins may have been at the root of the modification of the Śāṇa weight in this case. It is interesting to note that the Śāṇa (here also called Ṭaṅka and Niṣka) has elsewhere been actually called Dharaṇa. We may also note here that Bhāskarācārya's

1. *Ibid.*, p. 152.

2. That this modified weight of the Māṣaka, *viz.* 7 Ratīs=1 Māṣaka, was mentioned only as a side issue is suggested by the well-known weights of the Karṣa (viz. 80 Ratīs) and Pala (viz. 320 Ratīs). There is no authority in favour of the attribution of the weights 70 Ratīs and 280 Ratīs respectively to the Karṣa (Tolā) and Pala. We know that there was a tendency to attribute a higher weight to the Karṣa. Sometimes the Karṣa or Tolā was regarded as 96 Ratīs or 100 Ratīs or 120 Ratīs in weight and rarely 1 Karṣa was taken to be equal to 2 Tolakas (Tolās). Cf. below, pp. 74-75.

Līlāvatī mentions the Gadyāṇa weighing 48 Ratīs. It has further to be noticed that this Gadyāṇa was equal to 1½ Dharaṇas of the 32 Ratī standard and was ½ of the later and heavier Tolā of 96 Ratīs.

The identification of the Śāṇa with the Ṭaṅka and Niṣka with reference to the Kaliṅga country is interesting. The medieval coins of that area in both gold and silver were called Māḍha or Māḍa which was 40 Rātīs in weight, although it is believed to have been modified in later times to 24 Ratīs being ¼ of the later Tolā of 96 Ratīs.[1] Different kinds of Māḍas are mentioned in inscriptions; e.g. Malla-māḍa,[2] Malla-nandi-māḍa,[3] Surabhi-māḍa,[4] Gaṇḍa-māda,[5] Kulottuṅga-māḍa[6] Gandhavāraṇa-māḍa,[7] Cāmara-māḍa,[8] Gandhahasti-māḍa[9] and Uttama-gaṇḍa-māḍa.[10] Often the Padmanidhi-gaṇḍa-māḍa and Padmanidhi-malla-māḍa[12] are added to the list and it is believed that the coin is sometimes called Padmanidhi only.[13] The name of the coins would then remind us of the Padma-ṭaṅkas.[14] It is however to be noted that in these and many other cases the word *padmanidhi* has been used in the inscriptions in the sense of a sacred deposit made in a temple treasury.[15] Gandhavāraṇa-maḍa and Gandha-hasti-māḍa are apparently the same coin. It is interesting to note that the Gaṇḍa-māḍa is sometimes called Kārṣāpaṇa,[16] Niṣka[17] and Gaṇḍa-niṣka.[18] The name Kulottuṅga-māḍa, ap-

1. Cf. *J. K. H. R. S.*, Vol. I, pp. 152-53.
2. *S. I. I.*, Vol. VI, Nos. 932, 1179, etc.
3. *Ibid.*, No. 1180, dated Śaka 1138.
4. *Ibid.*, Vol. V, No. 1270, dated Śaka 1096.
5. *Ibid.*, Nos. 1154, 1172, 1244; Vol. VI, Nos. 712, 860, 904, 932, 957, etc.
6. *Ibid.*, Vol. IV, No. 1052.
7. No. 232 of 1897, dated Śaka 1089.
8. No. 227 of 1887, dated Śaka 1060.
9. No. 234 of 1897.
10. Nos. 208 and 236 of 1897, dated Śaka 1034.
11. *S. I. I.*, Vol. VI, Nos. 1031, 1037.
12. *Ibid.*, No. 752.
13. Cf. *J. K. H. R. S.*, *op. cit.*, p. 155.
14. Smith, *Catalogue of Coins*, pp. 311, 317.
15. Cf. *S. I. I.*, Vol. V, Nos. 907, 1244, 1248.
16. *J. K. H. R. S.*, *op. cit.*, p. 152.
17. *Ep. Ind.*, Vol. V, p. 32; *S. I. I.*, Vol. VI, No. 960, dated Śaka 1283. In *Ep. Ind.*, the coin has been taken to be a half Pagoda. The Varāha or Pagoda is often regarded as a double Hon of 32 Ratis (Thomas, *Ancient Indian Weights*, p. 42, note 4).
18. *S.I.I.*, Vol. VI, Nos. 932 and 1137, dated Śaka 1212.

parently Māḍas issued by the Coḷa-Cālukya king Rājendra-Kulottuṅga I (1070-1120 A.D.), suggests that the issue of some of the Māḍa coins similarly named have to be attributed to particular kings. Some scholars believe that 'Māḍa was a piece of gold of the weight of 40 Ratīs and not a stamped coin.'[1] But there appear to have been Māḍas of silver. This is clearly indicated by the fact that sometimes Māḍas are specifically mentioned as of gold.[2] M. M. Chakravarti pointed out that, in medieval Orissa, 5 silver Māḍas were considered to be equal to 1 Māḍa of gold[3] although this seems to suggest a higher weight for the silver Māḍa than that of the gold one. In this connection the epithet 'small', applied to the Gaṇḍa-māḍa in some records,[4] is also interesting to note. Moreover the varieties of the Māḍas mentioned in inscriptions clearly suggest that the different types could be distinguished by the people easily so that they could not have been merely undistinguishable pieces of the same weight.[5]

Wilson's Glossary explains Ṭaṅka as 'a weight of silver equal to four Māṣas...a coin, a stamped coin in general...a coin formerly current (in the Telugu country), but now used only in account; equal to four silver Fanams; there was also a gold Tanka and a copper coin similarly named, both obsolete." According to an inscription of the Kaliṅga area,[6] thirtythree *Veṇḍi* or silver Ṭaṅkas were given as the current price of a piece

1. *J. K. H. R. S.*, *op. cit.*, p. 153.
2. *Ibid.*, p. 157.
3. *Ibid.*, p. 156.
4. Cf. *S.I.I.*, Vol. VI, No. 932.
5. Considering the meanings of the words in the names of the coins such as *malla* (a wrestler), *nandin* (Śiva's bull), *surabhi* (a fabulous cow), *gaṇḍa* (a rhinoceros), *gandhavāraṇa*. or *gandhahastin* (an elephant in rut), and *cāmara* (a chowrie), it is tempting to suggest that these referred to particular representations on the coins in question. *Uttama* may be the well-known *biruda* of the Coḷa king Madhurāntaka (c. 969-85 A.D.). There are references in inscriptions to several other Choḷa coins called Rājarāja-māḍa, Rājendracoḷa-māḍa, etc. (cf. *J.K.H.R.S.*, *op. cit.*, p. 132). A class of old coins weighing four Ratīs is known in Orissa as Cāmara (*ibid.*, p. 154). The same was the weight of the Oriya Cinā, ten of which were equal to a Māḍa (*ibid.*, p. 153).
6. *S.I.I.*, Vol. V, No. 1250.

of land. The passage *deulabhaṇḍāraku padmanidhi śāśukāni koḍie ṭaṅka dei*[1] seems to use the word *ṭaṅka* in the sense of money which is stated to have been given as *padmanidhi* (deposit) in Śāśukānis and cowries. The Śāśukāni is often mentioned in inscriptions as the Śāśukāni-ṭaṅka,[2] although the name Ṭaṅka without any specification is also met with.[3] The earliest mention of the Śāśukāni-ṭaṅka has been traced in an inscription of Śaka 1323 corresponding to 1401 A.D.[4] There cannot be any doubt that this Śāśukāni is the same as the billon coin called Ṣaṣghānī which was issued by the Sulṭāns of the Tughluk dynasty and was widely popular during the reigns of Muḥammad bin Tughluk (1325-51 A.D.) and Fīrūz Shāh (1351-88 A.D.). The Ṣaṣghānī was six Jitals in value. As 48 Jitals were regarded as equal to one silver coin (Ṭaṅka) of the Sulṭāns, the Ṣaṣghānī was ⅛ of a Sulṭānī Ṭaṅka.[5] The standard weight of the silver Ṭaṅka of the Delhi Sulṭāns since the days of Iltutmish (1211-36 A.D.) was 100 or 96 Ratīs while Nāṣīruddīn Mahmūd (1245-65 A.D.) is supposed to have introduced the gold Ṭaṅka of the same weight. Thus the value of the Ṣaṣghānī was equal to that of 12½ or 12 Ratīs of silver, though its weight was higher.

In quoting the system of measurement prevalent in the Magadha country, the same *Bhāvaprakāśa* (*loc. cit.*) says :

ṣaḍbhis=tu Raktikābhiḥ syān=Māṣako Hema-Dhānakau ।
Māṣaiś =caturbhiḥ Śāṇaḥ syād=Dharaṇaḥ sa nigadyate ॥
Ṭaṅkaḥ sa eva kathitas=tad-dvayaṁ Kola uchayate ।
Kṣudrako Vaṭakaś=c=aiva Draṅkṣaṇaḥ sa nigadyate ॥

The *Śārṅgadharasaṁhitā*[6] says the same thing in the same words. According to this view, 6 Raktikās (Ratīs) make 1 Māṣaka (otherwise called Hema or Dhānaka), 4 Māṣas make 1 Śāṇa (otherwise called Dharaṇa and Ṭaṅka) and 2 Śāṇas make 1 Kola (otherwise called Kṣudraka, Vaṭaka and Draṅkṣaṇa). In this scheme, the Śāṇa, also called Dharaṇa and Ṭaṅka, weighed 24 Ratīs (i.e. ¼ of the later and heavier Tolā of 96 Ratīs). It is interesting to note that the same Dharaṇa (Śāṇa) of 24 Ratīs is mentioned in Bhāskarācārya's *Līlāvatī*. This

1. *J.K.H.R.S.*, *op. cit.*, p. 153, note 20.
2. *S.I.I.*, Vol. VI, Nos. 707, 919 and 1160.
3. *Ibid.*, Nos. 697 and 748.
4. *S.I.I.*, Vol. VI, No. 919.
5. Wright, *Coinage and Metrology of the Sulṭāns of Delhi*, p. 398.
6. *JNSI*, Vol. XV, p. 151.

modification of the Dharaṇa or Śāṇa seems to have been due to the popularity of the silver coins of foreigners like the Śaka Satraps of Western India. We have seen how these Śaka silver coins were regarded as three-fourths of the standard silver Kārṣāpaṇa (Dharaṇa or Purāṇa) of 32 Ratīs.[1] The theoretical weight standard of these coins was therefore 24 Ratīs although they essentially followed the weight of the hemi-drachm of a modified standard issued by the Indo-Greek kings, viz. 43.2 grains theoretically, but about 37 or 38 grains actually.[2]

There are some other traditions which indicate a further modification of the weight not only of the Śāṇa, but sometimes even of the Śatamāna.

Keśava's *Kalpadrukośa*[3] has the following on the weight of the Śāṇa :

dvābhyāṁ Yavābhyāṁ Guñjā syāt pañca tā Māṣa-Māṣakau ।
sa eva Hemadhānyo nā taiś=caturbhis=tu Śāṇakaḥ ॥
Ṭaṅko='strī Dharaṇaṁ Śāṇa-dvayaṁ Kolas=tu Daṅkṣamaḥ ।
Kṣudramo Vaṭakaḥ Kolau Karṣaṁ puṁsi napuṁsake ॥

He also says that 4 Karṣas make 1 Pala (Śatamāna) and 10 Dharaṇas make 1 Śatamāna, apparently imitating the early Dharmaśāstra writers. In any case, here we find that 5 Guñjās (Ratīs) make 1 Māṣa, Māṣaka or Hemadhānya, 4 Māṣas make 1 Śāṇaka (Śāṇa) also called Ṭaṅka and Dharaṇa, 2 Śāṇas make 1 Kola or Daṅkṣama or Kṣudrama or Vaṭaka, and 2 Kolas make 1 Karṣa. Thus, according to this scheme, the Śāṇa is one-fourth of a Karṣa of 80 Ratīs. The weight of the Śāṇa is also clearly given as 20 Ratīs. It will be seen that this authority quotes the weight of the Śāṇa, which is one-half of its original weight of 40 Ratīs. This has resulted in the equation of 4 Śāṇas to 1 Karṣa instead of the original 2 Śāṇas = 1 Karṣa.

This new weight of the Śāṇa is also found in several other works including Yādavaprakāśa's *Vaijayantī*. This authority speaks of the old Śatamāna when he says :

te='ṣṭau Yavaḥ ṣoḍaśa tu Yavā Māṣo='thavā tribhiḥ ।
Yavair= Guñjā pañca Guñjā Māṣaḥ kupye tu sapta tāḥ ॥
Rūpya-Māṣo dvi-Guñjo vā Dharaṇaṁ ṣoḍaś=aiva te ।

1. Cf. Rapson, *Indian Coins*, p. 21; *Catalogue*, clxxxiv.
2. G. O. S. ed., pp. 189 f.
3. Oppert's ed., p. 189.

Śatamānaṁ tu daśabhir=Dharaṇaiḥ Palam=eva ca ||[1]

It is stated that 16 Yavas or 5 Guñjās (Ratīs of 3 Yavas each) make 1 Māṣa of gold and silver and 7 Ratīs make 1 Māṣa of the base metals, although the silver Māṣa of 2 Ratīs, Dharaṇa of 16 such Māṣas (32 Ratīs) and Śatamāna or Pala of 10 Dharaṇas (320 Ratīs) are quoted from the early Dharmaśāstras. Moreover, at the same time, Yādavaprakāsa also says :

Yaḥ pañca-Kṛṣṇalo Māṣaḥ kupye vā sapta-Kṛṣṇalaḥ |
tau dvau Māṣāv=Arṇikā syāl=Lohitikaṁ tri-Māṣakam ||
Śāṇo Maṇḍaḥ Picūlaṁ ca Māṣaḥ syuś=catur-ādayaḥ |
Maṅkṣuṇaṁ sapta-Māṣaṁ syād=Aṇḍikā syāc=catur-Yavā |
Drakṣaṇaṁ Drakṣuṇaṁ Kolaṁ Vaṭakaṁ c=āṣṭa-Māṣake ||
tṛtīye Dhvānakā Śāṇa-bhāge Māṣās=tu ṣoḍaśa |
Suvarṇo='kṣaḥ Picuḥ Pāṇiḥ Karṣo='strī Kroḍa-Binduke ||
Viḍālapādakaṁ Haṁsapadaṁ Grāsagrahaṁ Ta(To)laṁ |
Śatamānaṁ tu Karṣe dve Śuktir=Aṣṭamikā Nalā ||

It is stated that, counting on the basis of 5 Ratīs=1 Māṣa of gold and silver and 7 Ratīs=1Māṣa of base metals, 2 Māṣas=1 Arṇikā, 3 Māṣas=1 Lohitīka, 4 Māṣas=1 Śāṇa, 5 Māṣas=1 Maṇḍa (Māḍa ?), 6 Māṣas=1 Picūla, 7 Māṣas=1 Maṅkṣuṇa, 8 Māṣas=1 Drakṣaṇa, Drakṣuṇa, Kola or Vaṭaka, 16 Māṣas=1 Suvarṇa, Akṣa, Picu, Pāṇi, Karṣa, Kroḍa, Binduka, Viḍālapādaka, Haṁsapada, Grāsagraha or Tola, and 2 Karṣas=1 Śatamāna, Śukti, Aṣṭamikā or Nalā. As regards gold and silver therefore 20 Ratīs make 1 Śāṇa, 80 Ratīs make 1 Suvarṇa, Karṣa or Tola, and 160 Ratīs make 1 Śatamāna. It will be seen that not only the Śāṇa but even the Śatamāṇa has been quoted here as having one-half of its original weight. This modification of the Śatamāna weight is no doubt due to the influence of its relation with the Śāṇa, viz. 8 Śāṇas=1 Śatamāna. It seems to us that the modification of the Śāṇa weight to 20 Ratīs was due to the popularity of a type of coins of this weight (¼ Tolā) prevalent in certain parts of India.

It may be noted in this connection that there is evidence to prove the existence of a class of popular coins in the Deccan, which were apparently issued according to the 20

1. *JNSI*, Vol. XIII, pp. 188 ff.

Ratī (36.6 grains) standard. These are silver coins belonging to the sixth century Kalacuri king Kṛṣṇarāja. Their great popularity and fairly wide distribution are indicated not only by their discovery in hoards found at Karad in the Satara District, at Devalana in the Nasik District, at Malgaon in Salsette and in Bombay, but also by their mention as Kṛṣṇarāja-rūpaka in an inscription of the eighth century found in the Nasik District.[1] Their recorded weight is about 33 grains.[2] There are several other types of early Indian coins of the same weight which were all imitated from the silver currency of the Śaka Satraps.

In the above discussion we have made an attempt to classify the different traditions regarding the weight of the Śāṇa and to put the modifications of the Śāṇa weight in a sort of chronological order. We have thus seen : (1) that, according to the combined strength of the evidence of the *Mahābhārata* and the early Dharmaśāstra writers, the Śatamāna was 320 Ratīs in weight while the Śāṇa was one-eighth of it and therefore weighed 40 Ratīs and that this weight of the Śāṇa is clearly supported by the *Śabdamālā* and the *Vaidyakaparibhāṣā* as well as a tradition quoted by Gaṅgādhara in his commentary on the *Carakasaṁhitā*; (2) that, according to the Kaliṅga system of measurement as quoted in the *Bhāvaprakāśa*, the Śāṇa weighed 32 Ratīs and was one-tenth of a Pala (otherwise called Śatamāna according to the early Dharmaśāstra writers); (3) that, according to the *Śārṅgadharasaṁhitā* as well as the Magadha system of measurement quoted in the *Bhāvaprakāśa*, the weight of the Śāṇa was 24 Ratīs; and (4) that, according to works like Keśava's *Kalpadrukośa* and Yādavaprakāśa's *Vaijayantī*, the modified Śāṇa weighed only 20 Ratīs while, according to the *Vaijaiyantī*, the weight of the modified Śatamāna was 160 Ratīs only. Although the works containing these four traditions regarding the weight of the Śāṇa can hardly be classified into a strictly chronological order, it is not improbable that the decrease in the weight of the Śāṇa from the original 40 Ratīs to 32 Ratīs, 24 Ratīs and 20 Ratīs resulted from the modification in the weight of the standard silver or gold coin in various parts of the country. Particular weights may have been popular in particular localties.

1. Cf. *The Classical Age*, ed. Majumdar, p. 149.
2. Elliot, *Coins of South India*, p. 149.

The expression *Śāṇa-pāda*, 'one-fourth of the Śāṇa', is taken in the Dictionaries to mean the Māṣa whatever be the latter's weight in Ratīs. The authorities discussed above clearly state that 4 Māṣas make 1 Śāṇa. The late *Śabdaratnasamanvaya-koṣa* of king Shāhjī (accession 1683 A.D.) of Tanjavur also says : *Śāṇo Māṣa-catuṣṭaye.*[1] Of all the authorties examined by us, only the *Carakasaṁhitā*[2] equates 1 Śāṇa with 3 Māṣakas :

ṣaḍ-Dhvaṁśyas=tu Marīciḥ syāt ṣaṇ-Marīcyas=tu Sarṣapaḥ ।
aṣṭau te Sarṣapā raktās=Taṇḍulaś=c=āpi tad-dvayam ॥
Dhānyamāṣo bhaved=eko Dhānyamāṣa-dvayaṁ Yavaḥ ।
Aṇḍikā te tu catvāras=tāś=catasras=tu Māṣakaḥ ॥
Hemaś=ca Dhānakaś=c=okto bhavec=Chāṇas=tu te trayaḥ ।
Śāṇau dvau Draṅkṣaṇaṁ vidyāt Kolaṁ Badaram=eva ca ॥
vidyād=dvau Draṅkṣaṇau Karṣaṁ Suvarṇaṁ c=Ākṣam=eva ca ।
Biḍālapadakaṁ c=aiva Picuṁ Pāṇitalaṁ tathā ॥
Tindukaṁ ca vijānīyāt Kavalagraham=eva ca ।
dve Suvarṇe Palārdhaṁ syāc=Chuktir=Āṣṭamika tathā ॥
dve Palārdhe Palaṁ Muṣṭiḥ Prakuñco='tha caturthikā ।

According to this scheme, 6 Dhvaṁśīs=1 Marīcī, 6 Marīcīs=1 Sarṣapa, 8 Red Sarṣapas=1 Taṇḍula, 2 Taṇḍulas=1 Dhānyamāṣa, 2 Dhānyamāṣas=1 Yava, 4 Yavas=1 Aṇḍikā, 4 Aṇḍikās=1 Māṣaka, etc., 3 Māṣakas=1 Śāṇa, 2 Śāṇas=1 Draṅkṣaṇa or Kola or Badara, 2 Draṅkṣaṇas=1 Karṣa or Suvarṇa or Akṣa, etc., 2 Suvarṇas=1 Palārdha, etc., and 2 Palārdhas=1 Pala, etc. As the Karṣa or Suvarṇa weighed 80 Ratīs and the Pala 320 Ratīs, the intended weight of the Śāṇa, which is stated to be one-fourth of the former and one-sixteenth of the latter, seems to be 20 Ratīs as in the last of the four views on the Śāṇa weight discussed above. It has however to be pointed out that the students of Indian medicine understood the *Carakasaṁhitā* Śāṇa to be weighing no less than 40 Ratīs (cf. Gaṅgādhara's commentary on the *Carakasaṁhitā* quoted above). Their Karṣa and Pala were therefore of heavier weights. Another curious fact is that often the Māṣa of exactly the same weight as assigned to it by the *Carakasaṁhitā* was regarded by the students of medicine as one-

1. G. O. S. ed., p. 107.
2. N.S.P. ed., p. 675.

fourth of the Śāṇa, one-sixteenth of the Karṣa and one-sixty-fourth of the Pala quite in conformity with the other schemes of calculation. In this connection attention of scholars may be drawn to the *Aṣṭāṅgahṛidaya*[1] of Vāgbhaṭa II, which says :

ṣaḍ-Vaṁśyas=tu Marīcī syāt ṣaṇ-Marīcyas=tu Sarṣapaḥ ।
Taṇḍulaḥ Sarṣapās=tv=aṣṭau Dhānyamāṣas=tu tau Yavaḥ ॥
tāv=Aṇḍikā caturbhis=tair=Māṣakaḥ Śāṇakas=tathā ।
dvau Śāṇau Vaṭakaḥ Kolaṁ Badaraṁ Draṅkṣaṇaś=ca tau ॥
Akṣaṁ Picuḥ Pāṇitalaṁ Suvarṇaṁ Kavalagrahaḥ ।
Karṣo Biḍālapadakaṁ Tindukaḥ Pāṇimāṇikā ॥ etc.

According to this scheme, 6 Vaṁśīs=1 Marīcī, 6 Marīcīs=1 Sarṣapa, 8 Sarṣapas=1 Taṇḍula, 2 Taṇḍulas=1 Dhānyamāṣa, 2 Dhānyamāṣas=1 Yava, 4 Yavas=1 Aṇḍikā, 4 Aṇḍikās=1 Māṣaka, 4 Māṣakas=1 Śāṇaka, 2 Śāṇas=1 Vaṭaka, Kola, Badara or Draṅkṣaṇa, and 2 Vaṭakas=1 Akṣa, Suvarṇa or Karṣa, etc. It will be seen that the *Bhāvaprakāśa* scheme, barring small variations of reading here and there, is exactly the same as that of the *Carakasaṁhitā* with the only noteworthy difference that the former gives 4 and the latter 3 as the number of Māṣas in the Śāṇa. Considering the weight of the Śāṇa as given by other authorities and the points of similarity between the *Bhāvaprakāśa* and *Carakasaṁhitā* schemes, it seems that the *Carakasaṁhitā* Māṣa, although it looks to have exactly the same weight as the Māṣa of the *Bhāvaprakāśa*, is really heavier than the latter. The commentators on the *Carakasaṁhitā* have tried to explain this away. We have seen how Gaṅgādhara offers the suggestion rather arbitrarily that the Śāṇa of the *Carakasaṁhitā* was equal to 4 Māṣas of 10 Ratīs each, i.e. to 40 Ratīs. The commentator Cakrapāṇidatta says the same thing in a different way : "3 Māṣakas make 1 Śāṇa. In this scheme of measurement, 48 Māṣakas make 1 Pala which is equal to a Pala containing 64 Māṣakas of 10 Ratīs each. Therefore 24 Dhānyamāṣas are equal to 10 Ratīs. Thus 64 Māṣakas of 10 Ratīs each are counted as of 24 Dhānyamāṣas each and as equal to 1536 Dhānyamāṣas. In this way, a Pala weighing 64 Māṣakas of 10 Ratīs each becomes equal to the Pala weighing 48 Māṣakas of 32 Dhānyamaṣas each. It is also observed in the *Suśrutasaṁhitā* that 12 Dhānyamāṣas make 1

1. Dravyakalpa, Chapter VI; N. S. P. ed., p. 775.

Suvarṇamāṣa, 64 of which make 1 Pala. Then 64 Māṣakas of 32 Dhānyamāṣakas each weigh 768 Dhānyamāṣas. Thus Suśruta's measurements of Pala, etc., are respectively one-half of those of Dṛḍhabala (as quoted in the *Carakasaṁhitā*). Thus in the *Suśrutasaṁhitā* the Māṣa weighs 5 Ratīs, because it is said that Dṛḍhabala's measurements are according to the system of Magadha and Suśruta's measurements belong to the Kaliṅga system although Jatūkarṇa gives the weight of the Māṣa as 6 Ratīs."

The following passage occurring in the *Aṣṭāṅgasaṅgraha* (Kalpasthāna, Chapter 8) and quoted by Aruṇadatta in his commentary on the *Aṣṭāṅgahṛdaya*[1] gives the same weight of the Śāṇa : *ṣaḍ-Vaṁśyo Marīcī; tāḥ ṣaṭ Marīcyaḥ Sarṣapa ucyate; aṣṭau Sarṣapās=Taṇḍulaḥ; tau dvau Taṇḍulāv=eko Dhānyamāṣaḥ; tau dvau Dhānyamāṣau Yavaḥ; ataḥ paraṁ caturguṇa-vṛddhyā Aṇḍikā-Māṣaka-Śāṇa-Karṣa-Pala-Kuḍava-Prasth-Āḍhaka-Droṇa-Vahāḥ kalpyante; evaṁ caturbhir=Māṣakaiḥ Śāṇasya parimāṇaṁ paricchidyate; Dharaṇam tu Palasya daśamo bhāgaḥ.* It may be pointed out that the *Carakasaṁhitā* in its present form is assigned by scholars to the eighth or ninth century A. D. while the *Aṣṭāṅgahṛdaya* of Vāgbhaṭa II and the *Aṣṭāṅgasaṅgraha* of Vāgbhaṭa I are ascribed respectively to the eighth and the seventh century A.D.[2] There is no doubt that the Śāṇa of the *Carakasaṁhitā*, which was of the same weight as the Śāṇa of the *Aṣṭāṅgahṛdaya* and *Aṣṭāṅgasaṅgraha*, was understood by the students of Indian medicine to weigh 40 Ratīs.

In view of the facts noted above, to say that 'the silver Śāṇa coin was much lighter; it was $\frac{1}{8}$ of a Śatamāna or 12.5 Rattīs in weight'[3] seems to be merely what may be called begging the question. The supporters of the view that the Śatamāna and Śāṇa were respectively 100 and 12½ Ratīs in weight should better not depend entirely on their imagination, but try to trace at least a single passage from the vast literature of ancient India going clearly in favour of their contention.

1. *Op. cit.*, p. 776.
2. Cf. Kieth, *History of Sanskrit Literature*, pp. 506 ff.
3. *J.N.S.I.*, Vol. XV, p. 152.

CHAPTER IV

KAUṬILYA AND BUDDHAGHOṢA ON COINS

I

It is well known to numismatists that *Dharaṇa* was the name usually applied to a particular measure used in weighing silver and also to a silver coin of that weight, while *Paṇa* was similarly the name often applied to a weight as well as a coin of copper. But it is difficult to reconcile the evidence of the *Kauṭilīya Arthaśāstra* in regard to Paṇa and Dharaṇa with what is known about them from other sources.

The Smṛtis of Manu,[1] Yājñavalkya[2] and Viṣṇu[3] agree remarkably in offering the following table for the weights of gold, silver and copper.

Gold

18 Gaura-sarṣapas (white mustard seeds)	= 1 Kṛṣṇala (Guñjā berry, also called Raktikā, i.e. modern Ratī)			
90 ,,	= 5 ,,	= 1 Māṣa		
1440 ,,	= 80 ,,	= 16 ,,	=1 Suvarṇa	

Silver

36 ,,	= 2 ,,	= 1 Rūpya-māṣa (i.e. Māṣa of silver)		
576 ,,	= 32 ,,	16 ,,	= 1 Dharaṇa or Purāṇa (also called silver-Kārṣāpaṇa by Manu according to one interpretation)	

1. VIII. 133 ff.
2. I. 363 ff.
3. IV. 4 ff.

Copper

1 Karṣa = 1 Paṇa or Kārṣāpaṇa

None of these authorities gives the weight of the Karṣa, from which the name Kārṣāpaṇa was apparently derived ; but the *Amarakoṣa* (Vaiśyavarga, 85-86) says that 5 Guñjās (Ratīs) = 1 Ādya-māṣa and 16 Ādya-māṣas = 1 Karṣa which is therefore equivalent to a modern standard Tolā. This view is supported by other authorities including, as will be seen below, Kauṭilya's *Arthaśāstra*. Thus the weight of the gold Suvarṇa and copper Paṇa or Kārṣāpaṇa is 16 Māṣas =80 Ratīs=1440 Gaura-sarṣapas, while the silver Dharaṇa, Purāṇa or Karṣāpaṇa weighs 16 Rūpya-māṣas=32 Ratīs =576 Gaura-sarṣapas. The weight of a Guñjā berry or Ratī is now usually regarded as 1.83 grains. The gold Suvarṇa and copper Paṇa or Kārṣāpaṇa therefore weigh 146.4 grains and the silver Dharaṇa, Purāṇa or Kārṣapaṇa only 58.56 grains.

In connection with the table quoted above, it may be noted that the names Paṇa and Kārṣāpaṇa were sometimes exclusively applied to the copper coin weighing one Karṣa or 80 Ratīs. Thus the *Mitākṣarā*[1] refers to Manu and says : *Karṣa-sammitas=tāmra-vikārah Paṇa-saṁjño bhavati Kārṣāpaṇaś=ca.*[2] But there is no dearth of references in ancient Indian literature to the name Kārṣāpaṇa being applied to the coins of all the three metals, viz., gold, silver and copper,[3] while, as we shall see below, the name was often applied exclusively to the silver coin. The name Paṇa was likewise generally used to indicate the copper coin; but, as will be shown below, we have authorities speaking of the gold or the silver Paṇa. There is also divergence of opinion in regard to the weight of the copper Paṇa which is 1 Karṣa or 80 Ratīs according to most of the authorities. Nārada[4] and some other authors[5] speak of the Paṇa as weighing 20 Māṣas : *Māṣo viṁśatimo bhāgaḥ Paṇasya parikīrtitaḥ.*[6] This

1. On Yājñavalkya, I. 365.
2. The same opinion is expressed by the *Smṛticandrikā* quoted by Kane in his *History of Dharmaśāstra*, Vol. III, p. 120, note.
3. Cf. *JNSI*, Vol. XIII, pp. 184 ff. ; below, pp. 93, etc.
4. Pariśiṣṭa, verse 58.
5. Cf. *Mitākṣarā* on Yājñavalkya, I. 365.
6. Cf. *JNSI*, Vol. XIII, pp. 187 ff.

would make a Paṇa=100 Ratīs. A Paṇa weighing 120 Ratīs is suggested by the *Agni Purāṇa*[1] : *Kṛṣṇalāṇāṁ tathā ṣaṣṭyā Karṣārdhaṁ Rāma kīrtitam.* But these Paṇas of 100 and 120 Ratīs may have been really $1\frac{1}{4}$ and $1\frac{1}{2}$ Paṇas of the standard weight, which were prevalent in certain areas.[2] Similarly, Bhāskarācārya's *Līlāvatī*[3] makes 24 Ratīs=1 Dharaṇa, and 48 Ratīs =2 Dharaṇas=1 Gadyāṇaka. This Dharaṇa was only $\frac{3}{4}$ of the Dharaṇa weighing 32 Ratīs, which is known from authorities like Manu.

In chapter 40 of the *Kauṭilīya Arthaśāstra*,[4] we have the following information regarding the weights of the Suvarṇa or Karṣa and Dharaṇa.

Gold

5 Guñjās (Ratīs)	=	1	Suvarṇa-māṣa (i.e. Māṣa of gold)	
80 ,,	=	16	,,	= 1 Suvarṇa or Karṣa

Silver

88 Gaura-sarṣapas	=	1	Rūpya-māṣa (i.e. Māṣa of silver)	
1408 ,,	=	16	,,	= 1 Dharaṇa

It will be seen that Kauṭilya's view in regard to the weights of gold tally with those of Manu, Yājñavalkya and Viṣṇu cited above; but what he says about the weights of silver is quite different. Kauṭilya's silver Māṣa weighs 88 Gaura-sarṣapas, while the silver Maṣa of the other authorities is only 36 Gaura-sarṣapas in weight. Thus the Rūpya-māṣa of the *Arthaśāstra* is in weight more than double the Rūpya-māṣa known from other sources. Kauṭilya's Dharaṇa is consequently much heavier than the silver Dharaṇa, Purāṇa or Kārṣāpaṇa weighing 32 Ratīs (58.56 grains) and seems to weigh about 145.14 grains. It can hardly be ignored that Kauṭilya's silver

1. Chapter 227, verse 2.
2. According to the *Śabdakalpadruma* (s. v. *tolaka*), the apothecaries' Karṣa is equal to two Tolakas and is therefore 160 or 192 Ratīs in weight.
3. I. 3.
4. Shamasastry's translation, p. 113.

Dharaṇa is just a few grains lighter than the Karṣa (146.4 grains), which is the weight of the gold Suvarṇa of all authorities including Kauṭilya himself as well as of the copper Paṇa or Kārṣāpaṇa of Manu, Yājñavalkya and Viṣṇu. The only difference between Kauṭilya's silver Māṣa and the Māṣa of gold and copper of other authorities is that, while the former weighs 88 Gaura-sarṣapas, the weight of the latter is 90 Gaura-sarṣapas. There is thus a small difference of only two white mustard seeds.

D. R. Bhandarkar notices the above peculiarity of Kauṭilya's Dharaṇa and observes,[1] "Those who have read Cunningham's book entitled *Coins of Ancient India* must be familiar with his remark that India produced little or no silver. Kauṭilya on the other hand speaks of varieties of silver and in no place gives us the impression that it was scarce in his time. Is it possible that shortly after Kauṭilya the sources of producing silver in India began to fail and that consequently, as silver became scarce and increased in value, the Purāṇa had to be diminished in weight?" Strangely however the learned author offers an altogether contradictory suggestion elsewhere in the same work.[2] Here he says, "Kauṭilya's *Arthaśāstra* allowed as much as 31.25 per cent of alloy in silver coins, whereas the silver Kārṣāpaṇas assayed by Cunningham contained only 20 per cent of it. This means that, during the period when Kauṭilya lived, silver had become so expensive that economic exigencies necessitated a higher percentage of alloy being mixed with it in order that the original standard of value might be maintained."

That Bhandarkar's first suggestion is wrong is demonstrated clearly by the fact that authorities, later not only than the author of the *Arthaśāstra* but also than the works of Manu and others, sometimes speak of a silver Kārṣāpaṇa one Karṣa or 80 Ratis in weight. We have seen how the *Amarakoṣa* (c. sixth century A.D.) defines Karṣa as of the above weight. Now the same work[3] further says :

Kārṣāpaṇaḥ kārṣikaḥ syāt kārṣike tāmrike Paṇaḥ.

Kṣīrasvāmin, the celebrated commentator on the *Amarakoṣa*, who possibly flourished about the eleventh century A.D.,

1. *Carmichael Lectures : Ancient Indian Numismatics*, p. 94.
2. See p. 162.
3. *Loc. cit.*, verse 88.

gives the following explanation of the passage quoted above :

Karṣa-sambandhinā paṇyate vyavahriyate='nena rūpya-rūpakeṇa Kārṣāpaṇaḥ; Karṣaḥ pramāṇam=asya kārṣikaḥ; tāmramayaṁ Karṣa-pramāṇaṁ tu rūpyaṁ Paṇaḥ.

Thus the *Amarakoṣa* seems to take one Karṣa weight of gold and silver as Kārṣāpaṇa and of copper as Paṇa, while the commentator clearly says that Kārṣāpaṇa is a silver coin weighing one Karṣa (80 Ratīs) and that Paṇa is a copper coin of the same weight. Kṣīrasvāmin applies the name Kārṣāpaṇa exclusively to the silver coin and the name Paṇa exclusively to the copper coin and this is supported by the tradition[1] equating 16 Paṇas [of cowries] with one Kāhaṇa (Prakrit *Kahāvaṇa*, Sanskrit *Kārṣāpāṇa*). In any case, it is clear that the silver Kārṣāpaṇa weighing 146.4 grains (or slightly less, as indicated by the *Arthaśāstra*) was known in some parts of the country at least theoretically, although we have no silver punch-marked coins of this weight. The very name Kārṣāpaṇa (i.e. a coin weighing one Karṣa), applied to the silver coin, also suggests that its original weight, even if theoretical, was 80 Ratīs.

In Chapter 78 of the *Arthaśāstra* (cf. *op. cit.*, p. 229), Kauṭilya says :

Suvarṇān=Māṣakam=apaharato dvi-śato daṇḍaḥ; rūpya-Dharaṇān=Māṣakam=apaharato dvādaśa-Paṇaḥ.

It is said that, if a goldsmith steals, in the process of making coins, one Māṣa from the gold coin called Suvarṇa, he will be fined 200 [Paṇas] while his fine will be 12 Paṇas if he steals one Māṣa from a silver Dharaṇa. This passage is interesting for several reasons. In the first place, not only are the words *Suvarṇa* and *Dharaṇa* appear to be used here in the specific sense of coins of gold and silver respectively, but the standard coin is mentioned as Paṇa although it is conspicuous by its absence in Kauṭilya's discussion on the weights of the metals. Secondly, a very rough estimate of the relative value of gold and silver is possible on the basis of the amounts of fines for stealing one Māṣa of gold or silver from the coins inspite of the amount of

1. *JNSI*, Vol. VII, p. 83; Vol. XIII, p. 185.

alloy in them. The ratio between gold and silver thus comes roughly to 1 to 16.6. Reference in this connection may be made to the late medieval work *Śukranītisāra*[1] according to which gold was sixteen times the value of the same weight of silver which again was eighty times the price of the same weight of copper. As Kauṭilya's Suvarṇa and Dharaṇa are practically of the same weight standard, it may be inferred that 16 silver Dharaṇas made one gold Suvarṇa. We know that the equation of 16 silver coins with one gold coin is indicated not only by Bhāskarācārya's *Līlāvatī* (I. 2) according to which 16 Paṇas or 4 Kākinīs or 80 cowrie-shells are equated to a silver Dramma and 16 Drammas to 1 gold Niṣka, but also by the Baigram plate of 448 A.D.[2] in which we have 16 silver Rūpakas equated to one gold Dīnāra although the weight of the gold and silver coins was not in all cases the same and the relative value of the two metals would differ.

But the most important question that arises now is in regard to the value of Kauṭilya's Paṇa. An interesting passage in Chapter 33 of the *Arthaśāstra*[3] says : "The Superintendent of Mint (*Lakṣaṇādhyakṣa*) shall carry on the manufacture of silver coins (*rūpya-rūpa*) made up of four parts (i.e. one-fourth) of copper and one-sixteenth (Māṣa) of any one of the metals *tīkṣṇa*, *trapu*, *sīsa* and *añjana*. There shall be a Paṇa, a half Paṇa, a quarter and an one-eighth. Copper coins (*tāmara-rūpa*), made up of four parts of alloy (*pādājīva*) shall be a Māṣaka, half Māṣaka, a Kākanī and half a Kākanī." As indicated by a commentator, who is supported by Nārada,[4] Kākanī is one-fourth of a Māṣa. Kauṭilya thus speaks of the minting of the silver coins entitled Paṇa, Ardha-Paṇa, Pāda-Paṇa and Aṣṭa-bhāga-Paṇa as well as of copper coins called Māṣa, Ardha-Māṣa, Pāda-Māṣa (Kākanī) and Aṣṭa-bhāga-Māṣa (Ardha-Kākanī).

It is very interesting to note that Kauṭilya does not speak of the minting of gold coins at all, although reference is made elsewhere in the *Arthāśāstra* to the making of the Suvarṇa by the goldsmith. Thus the gold coinage appears to have been outside ordinary use, as is also indicated by the evidence of other

1. IV. 2. 92-93.
2. *Select Inscriptions*, p. 343.
3. *Op. cit.*, pp. 86-87.
4. Pariśiṣṭa, verse 58 (Kākinī = $\frac{1}{4}$ of Māṣa and of Paṇa).

sources available on the subject.[1] A similar position of the gold coins prevailed in India also in the period of the great Mughuls. About the gold coins of Akbar, Moreland observes,[2] "The coins in regular use were silver and copper. Gold coins were also struck; but most of the twentysix denominations may be described as 'fancy' and the three which were struck regularly were rarely found in circulation being too large for retail transactions and being sought mainly in order to be hoarded." It is also interesting to note that Akbar's revenue was registered in the copper coins called Dām weighing a little over 1 Tolā and 8 Māṣas[3] while cowrie-shells were widely used as money by the poorer classes of the subjects of the Mughul emperor.[4]

Another interesting feature of the above passage of the *Arthaśāstra* is that the word *rūpa* (in *rūpya-rūpa* and *tāmra-rūpa*) has been used in the sense of 'a coin'. We have seen that the name Rūpaka is applied to the silver coin in Kṣīrasvāmin's commentary on the *Amarakoṣa* and in the Baigram plate. This name of the silver coin can also be traced in works like the *Bṛhatsaṁhitā* (81.12-13). But the word *rūpa* in the general sense of a coin is peculiar, as it essentially means a mark or figure. A coin was thus usually called a *rūpya* owing to a *rūpa* being imprinted on it by the stroke of a hammer.[5] The *Kāśikā* says : *nighātikā-tāḍanādinā Dīnārādiṣu rūpaṁ yad=utpadyate tad=āhatam=ity=ucyate; āhataṁ rūpam=asya rūpyo Dīnāraḥ; rūpyaṁ Kārṣāpaṇam.*[6] *Rūpya* is the later silver *Rūpiya* of the Muslims.

But the most important indication of the passage in question is that Paṇa and Māṣaka are regarded as the standard coins respectively of silver and copper while the silver coin elsewhere mentioned in the *Arthaśāstra* itself as Dharaṇa is passed over in silence. As we have suggested elsewhere,[7] this copper Māṣaka may be no other than the copper Paṇa of 80 Ratīs, so called because it was one-sixteenth of the standard silver coin in value. But it is really strange that the name Paṇa, given to the copper coin of 80 Ratīs by most authorities, should have

1. Cf. *JNSI*, Vol. XIII, pp. 184 ff. See also below, pp. 92 ff.
2. *India at the Death of Akbar*, p. 55.
3. *Hobson-Jobson*, s. v.
4. Cf. *JNSI*, Vol. VII, pp. 85 ff.
5. Cf. *ibid.*, p. 80.
6. Kane, *op. cit.*, p. 126, note.
7. *JNSI*, Vol. XIII, pp. 184 ff. ; below, pp. 92 ff.

been used by Kauṭilya to indicate exclusively the standard silver coin. A commentator explains Kauṭilya's silver Paṇa as Kārṣāpaṇa possibly implying thereby that it is the same as Kauṭilya's silver Dhraṇa of a little less than 80 Ratīs. It should be remembered that the standard Dharaṇa of 32 Ratīs is not recognised by the *Arthaśāstra*.

There is a controversy amongst scholars about the nature and value of Kauṭilya's Paṇa which is the standard coin very often mentioned or implied in the *Arthaśāstra* in the specification of salaries and fines. In Chapter 93 of the work,[1] Kauṭilya prescribes the various grades of salaries to be paid to the king's officials and dependants as 48000, 24000, 12000, 8000, 4000, 2000, 1000, 500, 250, 120 and 60 of the standard coin, no doubt Paṇa. The chief conductor of sacrifices, the teacher [of the princes], the chief minister, the chief priest, the commander-in-chief of the army, the crown-prince, the queen-mother and the chief queen were each to receive 48000, while the artisans and craftsmen (carpenters, etc.) were alloted 120 and servants doing miscellaneous work 60 only. Scholars are not agreed as to the value of the coin (Paṇa) intended and the period for which the salary was to be paid. K. P. Jayaswal[2] holds that the salaries were yearly and that the Paṇas were coins of silver. V. R. R. Dikshitar[3] thinks that the salaries were to be paid monthly, while K. V. Rangaswami Aiyangar[4] believes that the salaries were paid monthly in gold Paṇas. P. V. Kane holds that the salaries were meant by Kauṭilya to be paid monthly in copper Paṇas.[5]

As to the question whether the salaries mentioned in the *Arthaśāstra* were intended to be monthly or annual, attention of scholars may be drawn to the following passage occurring in Chapter 28 of the work :

triśataṁ catuḥpañcāśac=c=āhorātrāṇāṁ karma-saṁvatsaraḥ; tam=Āṣāḍhī-paryavasānam=ūnaṁ pūrṇaṁ vā dadyāt.

Shamasastry translates it as follows : "Three hundred and fiftyfour days and nights is a working year. Such a work (actually, such a year, i.e. such annual work) shall be paid

1. *Op. cit.*, pp. 276-77.
2. *Hindu Polity*, II, p. 136.
3. *Mauryan Polity*, p. 151.
4. *Ancient Indian Polity*, pp. 44-45.
5. *Op. cit.*, pp. 120 ff.

for more or less in proportion of its quantity at the end of the month of Āṣāḍha." This may suggest that the salaries of the royal officials, as mentioned in the *Arthaśāstra*, were paid on an annual basis. Such a custom was partially followed in the Zamindarī estates of Eastern India till recent times The Zamindar's officials in the rural areas often took amounts of money or quantities of corn, etc., out of their salary as occasions demanded; but the accounts of the amounts payable to them for the year were cleared only during the principal season for collection of revenue from the tenants or at the end of the financial year. Wilson's *Glossary of Judicial and Revenue Terms* recognises the word *Sāliāna* in the sense of such annual salaries. Thus the suggestion that the salaries of the royal officials as mentioned in the *Arthaśāstra* are annual is not improbable.

But Kane[1] draws our attention to Manu, VII. 125-26, saying that the wages for the lower class of menial servants of the king (such as those who sweep the house and bring water, according to Kullūka) was one Paṇa a day while that of a superior menial servant were 6 Paṇas a day and that the former (according to Kullūka who prescribes a graded increase in the case of the latter class) was to get in addition one pair of garments or cloth every six months and every month a Droṇa (i.e. 1024 Muṣṭis or handfuls according to Kallūka, nearly $1\frac{1}{4}$ or $1\frac{1}{2}$ or 2 Maunds) of paddy. Kane observes, "Artisans and craftsmen were, according to Kauṭilya, to get 120 Paṇas. If this were yearly, they would get only 10 Paṇas a month, while, according to Manu quoted above, even the lowest menial was to get a Paṇa a day. Therefore, 120 Paṇas of copper were the monthly salary of an artisan [according to Kauṭilya]."

It will however be seen that Kauṭilya specifically describes Paṇa as a silver coin while he may have spoken of annual and not monthly salaries. If calculated on this basis, an artisan, according to the *Arthaśāstra*, received 10 silver coins a month. We have seen how 16 copper coins were usually regarded as equivalent to one silver coin. Wilson's *Glossary* points out that, from this fixed relation between the Kāhaṇa (Kārṣāpaṇa) and Paṇa, the word *paṇa* is often used in Orissa to indicate the sixteenth of any given unit. In that case, an artisan's daily

1. *Op. cit.*, pp. 123 ff.

salary comes roughly to 5⅛ copper coins which may be compared with the salary of 6 Paṇas prescribed by Manu for a superior servant of the king.

The above rates of wages, prescribed by Kauṭilya and Manu, may also be fruitfully compared with those prevalent in the days of the Mughul emperor Akbar (1556-1605 A.D.). From a careful study of the *'Ain-i-Akbarī*, Moreland[1] shows that Akbar sanctioned the following daily rates of wages : ordinary labourers 2 Dāms, superior labourers 3 to 4 Dāms, carpenters 3 to 7 Dāms and builders 5 to 7 Dāms. The Dām was a copper coin a little over 1 Tolā and 8 Māṣas in weight and $\frac{1}{40}$ of the silver Rūpiya in value. In this connection Moreland has also pointed out that the purchasing power of an Akbarī Rūpiya was nearly 6 Indian Rupees in 1912 (i.e. before the First World War) and that the Dām was approximately 2¼ Annas in value. He concludes, "In several instances the lowest of servants were entitled to less than two Rupees monthly (65 Dāms for a sweeper, 60 for a camel-driver, 70 for a wrestler, and so on), while the bulk of the menials and of the ordinary foot-soldiers began at less than three Rupees. The mininum for subsistence at the Court is probably marked by the lowest grade of slaves who were allowed one Dām daily, equivalent to three-quarters of a Rupee monthly in the currency of the time."

The salaries of the higher royal officers as given in the *Arthaśāstra* may be similarly compared with those of Akbar's officers styled Mansabdārs, as known from the *'Ain-i-Akbarī.*[2] But such a comparison is not likely to be fruitful for various reasons. More profitable will be a comparison of the *Arthaśāstra* figures with the salaries of royal officers as known from the *Rājataraṅgiṇī*[3]. Bhaṭṭa Udbhaṭa, court-poet of the eighth century Kashmirian king Jayāpīḍa, received a daily salary of 100000 cowries probably paid in 500 Khārīs of grain. According to Stein's calculation, which is based on the equation of 100 cowries (Kashmiri *hat*, Sanskrit *śata*) with an Akbarī Dām as suggested by Abul Fazl, Udbhaṭa's salary comes to about 25 Akbarī Rupees a day. Similarly the storekeeper (*Gañjavara*) Lavaṭa received a daily salary of 2000 cowrie-shells (½

1. *Op. cit.*, pp. 56, 190-92.
2. Blochman's trans., Vol. I, 1939, pp. 247-59.
3. Cf. Stein's trans., Vol. II, p. 327.

Akbarī Rupee) from king Śaṅkaravarman (883-902 A.D.), and king Ananta (1028-63 A.D.) allowed his favourite officials Rudrapāla and Diddāpāla respectively 150000 cowries (37½ Akbarī Rupees) and 80000 cowries (20 Akbarī Rupees) a day. It will be seen that the court-Pandit received the equivalent of about 9000 silver coins a year, the officers 13500 and 7200 and the store-keeper 180. Kauṭilya prescribes the followihg rates in addition to those noticed above: 24000 for the officer in charge of the palace-gate, the superintendent of the harem, the chief judge, the collector-general and the chamberlain; 12000 for a prince, the nurse of a prince, the chief of the constables, the officer in charge of a town, the superintendents of law or commerce and of manufactories, the members of the council of ministers, and the governors of districts and of boundaries; 8000 for the chiefs of military corporations, elephant force, cavalry, chariots and infantry and for commissioners; 4000 for the superintendents of infantry, cavalry, chariots and elephants, and the guards of timber and elephant forests; 2000 for the chariot-driver, the physician of the army, the trainer of horses, the chief carpenter and the chief animal-rearer ; 1000 for the foreteller, the reader of omens, the astrologer, the reader of the Purāṇas, the story-teller, the bard, the retinue of the priest and all superintendents of Departments; 500 for trained soldiers, the staff of accountants and writers and the trumpet-blowers; 250 for musicians.

Sometime ago,[1] we ourselves expressed doubts whether Kauṭilya's Paṇa was really a silver coin of that name. Our argument was then based on the following fact. It is well-known that ancient Indian works on law speak often of the three fixed fines or amercements called Sāhasa, viz. *prathama-sāhasa* (first amercement), *madhyama-sāhasa* (middlemost amercement) and *uttama-sāhasa* (highest amercement). According to Śaṅkhalikhita quoted by Kane,[2] the first amercement amounts to 24 to 91 Paṇas, the middling to 200 to 500 Paṇas and the highest to 600 to 1000 Paṇas in proportion to the value of the matter in dispute or the nature of the injury caused. Manu[3] and Viṣṇu[4] state that the first, middling and highest amercements are respectively 250,

1. See *JNSI*, Vol. VII, p. 83, note 3.
2. *Op. cit.*, p. 393.
3. VIII. 138.
4. IV. 10.

540 and 1080 Paṇas, while Nārada[1] says that the lowest limits of the three amercements are respectively 100, 500 and 1000 Paṇas and that the highest amercement may include death penalty, forfeiture of all property, banishment, branding and cutting off of a limb. There is absolutely no doubt that Manu and others mean by Paṇa the copper coin of 80 Ratis. Now in Chapter 74 of the *Arthaśāstra*, Kauṭilya gives the following specification of the three fixed fines : (1) first amercement—between 48 and 96 Paṇas, (2) middlemost amercement—between 200 and 500 Paṇas, and (3) highest amercement—between 500 and 1000 Paṇas. It will be seen that, broadly speaking, there is not a very great disagreement amongst the authorities on the amounts of the amercements and it is really difficult to believe that in the above specification of the amounts of the fixed fines, while most authorities speak of Paṇa as a copper coin, Kauṭilya alone regards it as a silver coin which again, if it is the same as his Dharaṇa, weighs nearly 80 Ratīs. It was therefore suggested that by Paṇa in these cases Kauṭilya probably means really the well-known copper coin of 80 Ratīs and not the silver Paṇa mentioned elsewhere in the *Arthaśāstra*.

In pursuing the above line of argument, it may be further pointed out that often the same amounts of Paṇas for particular offences are prescribed by Kauṭilya and, say, Yājñavalkya who undoubtedly uses the name Paṇa for the copper coin. We may quote here a few instances to illustrate the point although they may be easily multiplied. In Chapters 89-90 of the *Arthaśāstra*, Kauṭilya prescribes the following punishments : (1) when one falsely accuses another of theft, while in reality the latter is guilty of adultery, the complainant shall be fined 500 Paṇas ; he who lets off an adulterer by receiving money shall pay a fine of eight times that amount ; (2) adultery with a nun shall be punished by a fine of 24 Paṇas ; (3) A man forcing his connection with a harlot shall be fined 12 Paṇas, while many persons committing rape on a single such woman shall each of them pay a fine of 24 Paṇas. The above three regulations may be compared with Yājñavalkya, II. 301, 293 and 291 respectively. It will be seen that the numbers of Paṇas prescribed by Yājñavalkya for the offences in question are exactly the same as in the *Arthaśāstra* with only a slight modification

1. Sāhasa, verses 7-8.

in the case of a man forcing his connection with a Dāsī being made punishable by a fine of 10 Paṇas (instead of 12 Paṇas as prescribed by Kauṭilya). We must not be understood to suggest that there is no great difference between Kauṭilya and Yājñavalkya in the specification of fines. As a matter of fact there is often considerable divergence of opinion between the two authorities. As for instance, according to Kauṭilya, a man having sexual connection with a woman against the order of nature or with another man shall pay the first amercement (between 48 and 96 Paṇas according to the *Arthaśāstra*); but the same offences are punishable by a fine of 24 Paṇas only by Yājñavalkya.[1] The point to which we are inclined to invite attention is that the same amounts of Paṇas for particular offences have often been prescribed by both Kauṭilya and Yājñavalkya and that this fact creates a difficulty in regarding Kauṭilya's Paṇa as a silver coin when Yājñavalkya's Paṇa was certainly a copper coin. It will also be noticed that there are cases where the fine for a particular offence prescribed by Yājñavalkya is only 24 Paṇas but by Kauṭilya between 48 and 96 Paṇas, i.e. between double and four times of Yājñavalkya's amount. This may no doubt suggest that Kauṭilya's Paṇa was really a copper coin (Māṣa, $\frac{1}{16}$ of the standard silver coin in value), which was described in the *Arthaśāstra* as of silver through confusion. But there are other considerations which render such a theory not entirely beyond the range of doubt.

It seems that just as the name Kārṣāpaṇa was applied to the coins and weights of gold, silver and copper although it was often exclusively used to indicate the silver coin, the name Paṇa, even if it was often regarded as the exclusive appelation of the copper coin, was similarly sometimes applied to coins of gold and silver as well. The application of the name Paṇa to coins of metals other than copper is not restricted to the *Arthaśāstra* which speaks of the silver Paṇa. The *Rājanītiprakāśa* (part of Mitramiśra's *Vīramitrodaya* of the 17th century)[2] refers to the gold Paṇa which is also mentioned by Bhāruci referred to by Kane.[3] That Paṇas of gold and silver were both known in ancient India is further supported by the use of the word in

1. II. 293.
2. Chowkhamba series, p. 294.
3. *Op. cit.*, p. 393, note.

South India. Wilson's *Glossary* says under *Paṇa* : "The same word becoming *Paṇam* is Tamil and Malayalam signifies 'money', also a small coin, both of silver and gold, transformed by European pronunciation to *Fanam* : the gold Paṇam was properly the sixteenth of a Hūn."[1]

Another fact that cannot be ignored in this connection is the great divergence of views about the metal in which the fines were to be paid. Kane (*op. cit.*, p. 393, note) observes, "According to Vijñāneśvara, the figures of fines in such verses as Manu, VIII. 378, where no metal is specified, the Paṇas are those of copper, while according to Bhāruci, quoted in the *Sarasvatīvilāsa*, p. 150, they are of gold. The *Sarasvatīvilāsa* remarks that local usage is to be followed. The *Vyavahāramayūkha*[2] states that, in all texts about fines, the mention of a number without specifying the object to which it refers is to be deemed to refer to Paṇas, that Paṇa is a copper piece one Karṣa in weight and that Karṣa is one-fourth of a Pala (320 Ratīs). Bṛhaspati, quoted by the *Smṛticandrikā*,[3] states that the table in Manu[4] beginning with dust particle in a beam and ending with Kārṣāpaṇa is to be followed in ordeals and fines." According to Kātyāyana,[5] whatever fine is prescribed in the Smṛti texts is to be paid in Paṇas of copper or their equivalent; but, where the fine is given as $\frac{1}{4}$ or $\frac{1}{2}$ of a Māṣa, the gold Māṣa is meant and, when it is specified in full Māṣas, they are meant to be of silver.

That the fines were often realised in terms of silver coins is also demonstrated by epigraphic evidence. A Gujarat inscription of the sixth century A.D.,[6] among various cases, prescribes for abusing and assault $6\frac{1}{4}$ Rūpakas and for infliction of wounds 48 Rūpakas, while Viṣṇu[7] prescribes for the same offences respectively 36 and 64 Paṇas of copper. A Kannaḍa inscription of the eleventh century[8] speaks of the fines of 2 Paṇas for abusing, 12 Paṇas for asault, 3 Gadyāṇas for drawing out the

1. For the gold and silver Paṇams prevalent in South India during the medieval period, see *Hobson-Jobson*, s.v. *Fanam*.
2. See p. 255.
3. Vol. II, p. 991.
4. VIII. 132-36.
5. Cf. *op. cit.*, p. 394.
6. *J.R.A.S.B.*, Letters, Vol. XVI, p. 118; *Ep. Ind.*, Vol. XXX, p. 175.
7. V. 66-67.
8. *Ep. Ind.*, Vol. XX, p. 66.

dagger, 12 Gadyāṇas for stabbing and 3 Gadyāṇas for adultery committed by a bachelor. Gadyāṇa or Gadyāṇaka was a silver coin 48 Ratīs in weight and was equal to 1½ standard Dharaṇa-Purāṇa-Kārṣāpaṇas of silver, although a gold coin called Gadyāṇaka is also known, e.g., from another inscription of the same area.[1] The Paṇa of the Kannaḍa inscription may be a silver Fanam. The *Arthaśāstra*[2] generally prescribes 12 Paṇas for abusing, and for assault with or without the infliction of wounds 48 and 24 Paṇas respectively.[3] It will be seen that 48 Rūpakas are also prescribed for inflicting wounds in the sixth century inscription referred to above. The authorities apparently differed often in regard to the amount of fine for a particular offence. But a comparison of the views of the *Arthaśāstra* with those of others does not show beyond doubt that Kauṭilya's Paṇa was not a silver coin as stated in the *Arthaśāstra*.

The above discussion will show that the fines, sometimes given specifically in Paṇas and often mentioned without such specification, were usually regarded as payable in copper Paṇas, but that there was no absolute unanimity amongst the authorities on the subject. Thus, while it is not altogether impossible that Kauṭilya's Paṇa is represented as a silver coin in the *Arthaśāstra* owing to a confusion and is really the copper coin of that name weighing 80 Ratīs, the possibility of the *Arthaśāstra* representing a genuine tradition regarding the silver Paṇa recognised in some areas of the country in a certain age is not precluded. But it is difficult to be definite on this point in the present state of our knowledge, and we now hesitate to characterise Kauṭilya's description of the silver Paṇa as a mistake due to confusion. The commentator's interpretation of Kauṭilya's Paṇa apparently as a silver Kārṣāpaṇa can hardly be ignored in this connection. Moreover, why should we be suspicious about the quite clear description of the Paṇa and its subdivisions in the *Arthaśāstra* when no other case of similar confusion has been detected in any other part of the work ?

Before concluding this section we consider it necessary to take into account Kane's arguments in favour of taking

1. *Ep. Ind.*, Vol. III. pp. 6-7.
2. Chapter 75.
3. Chapter 76.

Kauṭilya's Paṇa as a copper coin. He says,[1] "Kauṭilya (in V. 3) says that......60 Paṇas were to be the equivalent of one Āḍhaka of corn (*ṣaṣṭi-vetanasy=āḍhakaṁ kṛtvā hiraṇy-ānurūpaṁ bhaktaṁ kuryāt*). An Āḍhaka came to only 256 Muṣṭis (handfuls) of corn and even in famine times one Āḍhaka could not have cost 60 silver Paṇas, much less golden ones. In V. 3, Kauṭilya declares that an ordinary Dūta should get ten Paṇas for a journey of one Yojana and twice the wages for each Yojana upto one hundred. A Yojana, according to Kauṭilya himself[2] is equal to 8000 Dhanus (according to another reading, 4000 Dhanus), a Dhanus being equal to four Aratnis (each Aratni being 24 Aṅgulas). So, taking the highest figure, a Yojana was at the most about 9 or 10 miles (or only 4½ or five miles according to the other reading). To hold that 10 silver Paṇas were allowed to an ordinary Dūta for going even ten miles (which he could cover in half a day or less) would be too much." A careful examination of the two points raised would however show that both of them are wrong.

In the first place, the passage *ṣaṣṭi-vetanasy=āḍhakaṁ kṛtvā hiraṇy-ānurūpaṁ bhaktaṁ kurtyāt* has been misunderstood by both Kane and Shamasastry, but has been correctly interpreted by U. N. Ghoshal[3] and R.G. Basak.[4] What Kauṭilya means to say is that a royal servant getting 60 Paṇas will get in addition to his *vetana* one *Āḍhaka* of corn as *bhakta* (additional allowance)[5] in corn according to the corresponding rate. The provision of *bhakta* is similar to that mentioned in Manu, VII. 126. The payment of *bhakta* in addition and in proportion to *vetana* to royal servants is well known from various other sources.

Kane moreover seems to have confused Kauṭilya's Āḍhaka with a different measurement of the same name. This will be clear from the following analysis. According to Manu,[6] 4 Suvarṇas (i.e. Karṣas of gold) make one Pala (or Niṣka) and 10 Palas one gold Dharaṇa, while 10 silver Dharaṇas make one silver Śatamāna. Manu therefore speaks of one kind of Pala (gold) which is 4 Karṣas (i.e. Tolās) or 320 Ratīs in weight and two kinds of Dharaṇa, the silver Dharaṇa

1. *Op. cit.*, pp. 123-25.
2. II. 20.
3. *Hindu Revenue System*, p. 156.
4. Bengali translation of the *Arthaśāstra*, Vol. II, pp. 51-52.
5. Cf. Wilson's *Glossary*, s. v. *bhāta*.
6. VIII. 134-37.

weighing 32 Ratīs and the gold Dharaṇa 40 Tolās or 3200 Ratīs. Yājñavalkya (I. 363-65) however speaks of two kinds of Pala, the gold Pala weighing either 4 or 5 Suvaraṇas (i. e. 4 Tolās=320 Ratīs, or 5 Tolās=400 Ratīs the former variety being also called Niṣka) and gives the second name 'silver Pala' to the silver Śatamāna weighing 320 Ratīs. Kauṭilya[1] on the other hand speaks of the Pala of gold weighing 4 Karṣas (Tolās) and of the Dharaṇa of silver weighing 88 Gaura-sarṣapas (nearly one Tolā) in connection with the weights of metals as well as of a Pala weighing 10 Dharaṇas used in measuring grains, etc. The heavier Pala of Kauṭilya thus seems to be about 10 Tolās in weight, although a commentator says that this Pala, called Dharaṇa-pala, is heavier by one Karṣa than the usual Pala (of 4 Karṣas or of 10 Dharaṇas ?). The Arthaśāstra further says that the royal Droṇa weighs 200 Palas, the public Droṇa 187½ Palas, the servants' Droṇa 175 Palas and the harem Droṇa 162½ Palas, and that Droṇa, which is equal to 4 Āḍhakas or 16 Prasthas or 64 Kuḍavas, is $\frac{1}{16}$ of a Khārī, $\frac{1}{20}$ of a Kumbha and $\frac{1}{200}$ of a Vaha. The servants' Droṇa of the *Arthaśāstra* is thus about 1750 Tolās in weight and a servants' Āḍhaka about 437½ Tolās (nearly 5½ Seers). This small quantity of paddy was possibly the daily or monthly allowance of a royal servant earning 60 Paṇas a year ; but it is difficult to be definite on this point. It may be noticed in this connection that the Droṇa and Āḍhaka recognised in different parts of the country were not always of the same weight. Kauṭilya's Droṇa is about ½ Maund and Khārī about 9 Maunds. These weights may be compared with those of the systems referred to by Kṣīrasvāmin[2] and by Kullūka.[3] According to the first view, 4 Palas (16 Tolās according to Manu, 16 or 20 Tolās according to Yājñavalkya) or Muṣṭis (handfuls) = 1 Kuḍava, 4 Kuḍavas=1 Prastha, 4 Prasthas=1 Āḍhaka, 8 Āḍhakas=1 Droṇa, 2 Droṇas=1 Sūrpa; 1½ Sūrpas=1 Khārī, 2 Sūrpas=1 Goṇī or Bhāra, 4 Bhāras=1 Vaha. According to the other scheme, 8 Muṣṭis (handfuls)=1 Kuñci, 8 Kuñcis = 1 Puṣkala, 4 Puṣkalas=1 Āḍhaka, 4 Āḍhakas= 1 Droṇa, 16 Droṇas=1 Khārī, 20 Droṇas=1 Kumbha, 10 Kumbhas

1. *Arthaśāstra*, Chapter 40.
2. On Amara, Vaiśyavarga, verse 88.
3. On Manu, VII. 126.

= 1 Vāha. It will be seen that the Āḍhaka of the former system is equal to 64 Muṣṭis (handfuls) or Palas (i.e. $3\frac{1}{8}$ or 4 Seers according to Manu and Yājñavalkya) and is $\frac{1}{8}$ of the Droṇa ($25\frac{3}{8}$ or 32 Seers), while it is 256 Muṣṭis and is $\frac{1}{4}$ of the Droṇa according to the latter system. Thus the Droṇa of the first system is only a half of the same denomination in the second system and neither of the two tallies exactly with Kauṭilya's Droṇa.

It should also be noted that, from what we know of the prices of paddy and rice in different parts of ancient India, even 60 copper Paṇas would be far too much for '256 Muṣṭis' (at the most about 20 Seers or half a Maund according to some) of paddy. Stein has shown[1] how in ancient Kashmir during the rule of the Hindu kings the price of a Kashmir Khārī (177 pounds, nearly $2\frac{1}{4}$ Maunds) of paddy was 200 cowrie-shells (only 36 cowries in a year of exceptional abundance) which rose in the fifteenth century to 300 cowries, how in Akbar's time the price of the same quantity of paddy was fixed at about $13\frac{1}{8}$ Dāms of copper, and how in Bengal in the 14th century 25 Delhi Rothls (about 9 or $7\frac{3}{4}$ Maunds) of rice or 80 Delhi Rothls (about $28\frac{3}{4}$ or $24\frac{7}{10}$ Maunds) of paddy were sold at a silver Dīnār. Even at the end of the 17th century, 580 pounds ($7\frac{1}{4}$ Maunds) of rice were sold at Chittagong in East Bengal for a Rupee. According to a tradition, 8 Maunds of rice were sold at a Rupee at Dacca during the viceroyalty of Shāista Khān about the same time.[2] In an interesting article entitled 'Prices of Foodstaff in Tirhoot since the last Decade of the Eighteenth Century',[3] the author records the following prices of rice and paddy at Muzaffarpur in 1796 : Vasumatī rice first and second sorts at 22 Seers and 1 Maund $7\frac{1}{2}$ Seers a Rupee; Uṣṇa rice first and second sorts at 1 Maund $11\frac{3}{4}$ Seers and 1 Maund 12 Seers a Rupee ; paddy first and second sorts at 2 Maunds 5 Seers and 2 Maunds 10 Seers a Rupee. We have also to note that 60 copper Paṇas were equivalent to $3\frac{3}{4}$ silver coins in ancient Indian currency and that the purchasing power of the copper Paṇa and silver Kārṣāpaṇa was very considerably higher than even

1. *Rājataraṅgiṇī*, trans., II, pp. 308-28.
2. Cf. *JNSI*, Vol. VII, p. 82, note 3.
3. *Journal of the Bihar Research Society*, Vol. XXXVII, Parts 3-4, pp. 145 ff.

the Dām and Rūpiya of the Mughal period. Thus 60 Paṇas for half a Maund of paddy would be an utter absurdity in any period of Indian history before the twentieth century.

The Dūta of the *Arthaśāstra*[1] was not an ordinary servant as understood by Kane. The passage in question has been translated by Shamasastry as follows : "A messenger of middle quality shall receive 10 Paṇas for each Yojana he travels and twice as much when he travels from 10 to 100 Yojanas." It will be seen that the *madhyama* type of Dūta mentioned here was not a regular employee of the king. The epithet *madhyama* again shows that he was not of the type of a menial servant. His was thus a temporary appointment without salary but on the basis of a travelling allowance. Considering the facts that his food and other necessaries (conveyances, etc.) were not provided for, his travelling allowance at the rate of 10 silver coins per ten (or even five) miles cannot be regarded as high. Moreover, Kauṭilya seems to refer to the Yojana as the distance to be covered by the Dūta both while going and coming back. An illustration of the journey of a Dūta of the *madhyama* type is possibly furnished by the *Rājataraṅgiṇī*[2] in the story of the poet Mātṛgupta who had to travel to Kashmir as a messenger of king Vikramāditya with practically no help from the latter.

II

The celebrated Buddhist author Buddhaghoṣa, who flourished in the fifth century A.D., is said to have been born of a Brāhmaṇa family residing in the village of Ghoṣagrāma near Bodhgayā, near Gayā in the Gayā District of Bihar.[3] Students of ancient Indian numistmatics have often drawn upon his famous commentaries on the Buddhist canonical works in Pāli for information regarding ancient Indian coinage.[4]

1. Cf. Chapters 16 and 127.
2. III. 129 ff.
3. *J.U.P.H.S.*, Vol. VI, p. 156, note; Law, *The Life and Works of Buddhaghosha*, pp. 1-24. Some scholars regard him as a Teliṅga of South India (*The Classical Age*, ed. Majumdar, p. 395). It seems that, even if he was originally a North Indian, he lived in the South for many years.
4. See, e. g., D. R. Bhandarkar, *Carmichael Lectures*: *Ancient Indian*

In the *Pātimokkha*,[1] there is the following regulation for the Buddhist monks: *yo pana bhikkhu jātarūpa-rajataṁ uggaṇheyya vā uggaṇhāpeyya vā upanikkhittaṁ vā sādiyeyya nissaggiyaṁ pācittiyaṁ.* It says that the monks should not accept or cause any one to accept *jātarūpa* or gold and *rajata* or silver. The expression *jātarūpa-rajata* ocurring in the above passage has been explained in the *Suttavibhaṅga* section of the *Vinaya Piṭaka* as well as in Buddhaghoṣa's *Kaṅkhāvitaraṇī* (commentary on the *Pātimokkha*) and *Samantapāsādikā* (commentary on the *Vinaya Piṭaka*) in the following words:[2]

(1) *Jātarūpaṁ nāma satthuvaṇṇo vuchchati. Rajataṁ nāma Kahāpaṇo Loha-māsako Dārumāsako Jatu-māsako ye vohāraṁ gacchanti* (*Suttavibhaṅga*;)

(2) *Jātarūpa-rajatan=ti suvaṇṇañ=c=eva rūpiyañ=ca. Api ca Kahāpaṇa-Lohamāsaka-Dārumāsaka-Jatumāsak-ādayo pi ye vohāram gacchanti sabbe te idha rajatan=t=eva vuttā* (*Kaṅkhāvitaraṇī*);

(3) *Jātarūpa-rajatan=ti. Jātarūpaṁ nāma suvaṇṇassa nāmaṁ......Kahāpaṇo ti sovaṇṇamayo vā rūpiyamayo vā pākatiko vā. Loha-māsako ti tamba-loh-ādihi kata-māsako. Dāru-māsako ti sāra-dāruṇā vā veḷupesikāya vā antamaso tāḷa-paṇṇena pi rūpaṁ chinditvā kata-māsako. Jatu-māsako ti lākhāya vā niyyāsena vā rūpaṁ samuṭṭhāpetvā kata-māsako* (*Samantapāsādikā*).

In the first of the three extracts quoted above, 'gold' has been taken merely in the sense of the metal, while 'silver' has been taken to mean coins such as the Kārṣāpaṇa (apparently of silver) and the Māṣaka of *lauha* (generally meaning 'iron'), wood and lac. The second extract explains both 'gold' and 'silver' as metals, but, at the same-time, points out that the latter here includes whatever is used as money, e.g., the Kārṣāpaṇa of silver, the Māṣaka of *lauha*, wood and lac and similar other coins. These two passages would thus suggest (1) that there were no coins of gold, (2) that the Kārṣāpaṇa was made of silver only, (3) that the Māṣaka was made of *lauha*, wood, lac, etc., but not of silver, and (4) that the Māṣakas were so called probably not because they were one *māṣaka*

Numismatics, 1921, pp. 81, 98, 126, 128, 140 ff., 159 f,; Rhys Davids, *Ancient Coins and Measures of Ceylon* (*International Numismata Orientalia*), etc.

1. See V. Bhattacharya's ed., Calcutta, p. 21.

2. *Op. cit.*, p. 162.

in weight, but because they were one-sixteenth in value of the standard silver coin called Kārṣāpaṇa.[1] We know from the *Amarakoṣa*[2] that the weight of a Kārṣāpaṇa was one Karṣa which was the weight of sixteen Māṣakas (called *Ādya-Māṣaka* showing thereby that there was at least another *Māṣaka* of a different weight) or eighty Guñjās or Ratīs, i.e. 146.4 grains, while a Karṣa weight of gold was called Suvarṇa and the same weight of copper was known as Paṇa. Manu[3] gives the same information in regard to the gold Suvarṇa and the copper Paṇa; but, as regards silver, he says that two Ratīs of silver (instead of five Ratīs as in the case of gold and copper) made one silver Māṣa, sixteen of which made one Purāṇa or Dharaṇa (58.56 grains), otherwise called Kārṣāpaṇa.[4] It will be seen that the implications of the two extracts analysed above do not tally with the information supplied by the *Amarakoṣa* and the *Manusmṛti*. The details of the third extract quoted above, strangely enough, also differ from that of the other two in one important respect.

Although the third extract quoted from Buddhaghoṣa's *Samantapāsādikā* explains 'gold' as a metal, it speaks of three different kinds of Kārṣāpaṇas, viz. (1) gold Kārṣāpaṇa (apparently the same as Suvarṇa) (2) silver Kārṣāpaṇa, and (3) ordinary Kārṣāpaṇa (probably the same as Paṇa). This shows that Kārṣāpaṇa of both gold and copper were also known. The gold Kārṣāpaṇa may have been ignored by Buddhaghoṣa in his *Kaṅkhāvitaraṇī* list because it was rare and was not in common use. This is perfectly borne out by the absence of punch-marked coins in gold against the abundance of silver and copper punch-marked coins.[5] The absence of the quite common and very widely used copper Paṇa (called 'ordinary' elsewhere by Buddhaghoṣa himself) however seems to be explained by the details of the Lauha-Māṣaka furnished by the *Samantapāsadikā*. The expression *lauha-māṣaka* has been explained as the Māṣaka made of *tāmra* (copper), *lauha* and others (i.e. other

1. Cf. *J.U.P.H.S.*, Vol. VI, p. 171.
2. Vaiśya-varga, verses 85-88.
3. VIII. 34-36.
4. Manu, VIII. 136 may be understood as follows: (1) *te ṣoḍaśa syād=Dharaṇaṁ Purāṇaś=c=aiva rājataḥ Kārṣāpaṇas=tu*; (2) *vijñeyas=tāmrikaḥ kārṣikaḥ Paṇaḥ*.
5. See Allan, *Catalogue of Indian Coins : Ancient India*, p. clx.

metals). The word *loha* or *lauha* means 'iron, copper, brass, any metal' and the expression '*lauha* and others' has apparently been used in the sense of any cheap metal other than copper which is separately mentioned. It appears, as already indicated above, that a copper Māṣaka was not so called because it was only one *Māṣaka* (five Ratīs or 9.15 grains) in weight, but because it was regarded as one-sixteenth of the silver Kārṣāpaṇa in value.[1] As sixteen Paṇas [of cowries] were considered equal in value to a Kāhaṇa (i.e. Kahāvaṇa, Kahāpaṇa, Kārṣāpaṇa) down to quite recent times,[2] the suggestion suits well if the copper Māṣaka of Buddhaghoṣa is regarded as a copper Paṇa or Kārṣāpaṇa of eighty Ratīs (146.4 grains). It further explains the omission of the quite common copper Paṇa or Kārṣāpaṇa from the *Kaṅkhāvitaraṇī* list of coins. Thus the copper Māṣaka mentioned in the list of Māṣakas and the copper Kārṣāpaṇa put in that of the Kārṣāpaṇas in the *Samantapāsādikā* would appear to have been the same coin, or at least similar coins, put under different heads. If it is believed that the weight of the Māṣakas of cheap metals like copper, iron, brass, lead, etc., was determined by their intrinsic value (depending on the current market prices of the metals) as one-sixteenth of the standard silver coin, it will also explain the impossibility of classifying the punch-marked coins discovered in different parts of India according to definite weight standards.[3] This of course does not explain the great variety of the weight standard noticed also in the silver punch-marked coins. An important factor in the great diversity in the weight standard of the ancient Indian coins seems also to be the fact that the basic Māṣaka weight was not the same in different localities and periods even in regard to the same metal. We have already noticed that Manu's silver Māṣaka was much smaller than his gold or copper Māṣaka. The *Śabdakalpadruma*, s. v. *Māṣaka*, quotes some authorities speaking of Māṣaka of five, six, seven and eight Ratīs. In Wilson's *Glossary of Judicial and Revenue Terms*, 1885, s. v. *Māṣa*, there is the following note on the same weight: "An

1. The relative value of silver and copper would in that case stand as 32 Ratīs to 1280 Ratīs, i.e., as 1 to 40. Cf. Nārada on Māṣa = Paṇa (above, p. 78).

2. Cf. Allan, *op. cit.*, p. clix.

3. Rapson, *Catalogue of Indian Coins : Andhras*, etc., pp. clxxx ff.; Allan, *loc. cit.*

elementary weight in the system of goldsmiths' and jewellers' weights throughout India, and the basis of the weight of the current silver coin; it is variously reckoned at 5, 8, or 10 Ratis...; the average weight of the Māṣa, according to Mr. Colebrooke, was 17$\frac{3}{8}$ grains (troy): the actual weight of several examined in England, sent from different parts of India, varied from 14$\frac{7}{10}$ grains to 18$\frac{1}{2}$ grains; the Benares Māṣa weighed 17$\frac{1}{40}$ grains. Mr. Prinsep, from the weight of several Akbarshāhī rupees the standard weight of which was 11$\frac{1}{4}$ Māṣas, valued the latter at 15$\frac{1}{2}$ grains; as now fixed by law as one-twelfth of the Tolā of 180 grains, the Māṣa weighs 15 grains."

Buddhaghoṣa's *Samantapāsādikā* explains the wooden Māṣaka as those made of strong wood and of bits of bamboo and includes in this category even the Māṣaka that was made by cutting in a figure on a piece of palmyra leaf. Apparently the palmyra-leaf Māṣaka could not have been one Māṣaka in weight. As the intrinsic value of the Māṣaka made of wood, bamboo or palm leaf could hardly have been one-sixteenth of either the silver or even the copper Kārṣāpaṇa, they appear to have been of the nature of the modern currency notes. The same appears to have been the case with the lac Māṣaka explained as those made by producing a figure on a quantity of lac or gum. It is tempting to suggest that the metallic Māṣakas were regarded as one sixteenth of the standard silver coin, while the non-metallic Māṣakas stood in the same relation to the standard coins of cheap metals like copper. Although there is evidence to show that metallic coins weighing one-sixteenth of the standard money of silver and other metals were also not unknown,[1] they were probably not common everywhere.

The passages, quoted from Buddhaghoṣa's *Kaṅkhāvitaraṇī* and *Samanatapāsādikā* and analysed above, give very valuable information about ancient Indian currency. Another interesting passage was quoted by D. R. Bhandarkar from Buddhaghoṣa's *Visuddhimagga*.[2] The passage runs as follows :

1. Cf. Allan, *op. cit.*, pp. clxii-iii.

2. *A.S.I.*, *A.R.*, 1913-14, p. 226; cf. *Carmichael Lectures*, *op. cit.*, pp. 99-100. See also *Visuddhimaggo*, P.T.S. ed., pp. 437, 515; below, pp. 202-03.

yathā hi heraññika-phalake ṭhapitam Kahāpaṇa-rāsiṁ eko a-jāta-buddhi-dārako eko gāmika-puriso eko heraññiko ti tīsu janesu passamānesu a-jāta-buddhi-dārako Kahāpaṇānaṁ citta-vicitta-dīgha-caturassa-parimaṇḍala-bhāva-mattam=eva jānāti idam manussānaṁ upabhoga-paribhogaṁ ratana-sammataṁ ti na jānāti; gāmika-puriso citta-vicittādi-bhāvaṁ jānāti idaṁ manussānaṁ upabhoga-paribhogaṁ ratana-sammataṁ ti ca, ayaṁ cheko ayaṁ kūṭo ayaṁ addha-sāro ti idaṁ pana vibhāgaṁ na jānāti; heraññiko sabbe pi te pakāre jānāti jānanto ca Kahāpaṇaṁ āloketvā pi jānāti ākoṭita-saddaṁ sutvā pi gaṁdhaṁ ghāyitvā pi rasaṁ sāyitvā pi hatthe dhārayitvā pi amukasmiṁ nāma gāme vā nagare vā pabbate vā nadī-tīre vā kato ti pi amuk-ācariyeṇa kato ti pi jānāti.

Bhandarkar explains the passage in the following words : "It describes how a lot of coins lying on a wooden slab would strike an inexperienced boy, a man from the village and a shroff or money-changer. The boy would notice simply that some coins are oblong, some round and some elongated in shape. The rustic would know all this and also that coins were like gems, worthy objects of enjoyment to mankind. The shroff, on the other hand, not only would be conversant with all this but also would be in a position to decide after handling the coins in a variety of ways (such as looking at them, hearing the sound they produce by being struck at, smelling them, licking them and touching them) as to which of them were struck at which village, mufassil town, capital city, mountain and river bank and also by what mint-master."

The learned scholar points out, on the strength of this passage, that every place which issued coinage in ancient India had its own distinguishing mark or marks stamped on it, by observing which the shroff of that age could at once tell from which place any particular coin came. Elsewhere[1] Bhandarkar says how, according to Buddhaghoṣa's commentary on the *Mahāvagga*, a man who had to learn the *Rūpasūtra* (*i.e.* a set of rules concerning figures on the coins, or concerning coins) used to turn many Kārṣāpaṇas over and over and look at them. He further refers to Buddhaghoṣa's statement that there were other kinds of money which were current in different parts of the country, although they were not mentioned by him, and that

1. *Carmichael Lectures, op. cit.*, pp. 126, 128.

they were of bone or skin or the fruits or seeds of trees and might be with or without any *rūpa* or figure raised on them.[1]

There is one passage in Buddhaghoṣa's *Samantapāsādikā* which seems to have been imperfectly utilised by earlier writers.[2] C. D. Chatterjee quoted and interpreted the passage fully in his paper entitled 'Some New Numismatic Terms in Pali Texts,' published in the *Journal of the U. P. Historical Society*, Vol. VI, 1933, pp. 156-73.[3] The passage runs as follows :

Tadā Rājagahe vīsati-Māsako Kahāpaṇo hoti, tasmā pañca-Māsako Pādo. Etena lakkhaṇena sabba-janapadesu Kahāpaṇassa catuttha-bhāgo Pādo ti veditabbo. So ca kho porāṇassa Nīla-Kahāpaṇassa vasena, na itaresaṁ Rudradāmak-ādīnaṁ.

Chatterjee also quotes in this conection the following two passages from the *Sāratthadīpanī* (commentary on Buddhaghoṣa's *Samantapāsādikā* by Sāriputra) and the *Vinayatthamañjūsā* (commentary on Buddhaghoṣa's *Kaṅkhāvitaraṇī* by Buddhanāga who flourished in the twelfth century A.D.) :

(1) *Iminā va sabba-janapadesu Kahāpaṇassa vīsatimo bhāgo Māsako ti, idaṁ=ca vuttam=eva hot=īti daṭṭhabbaṁ. Porāṇa-satth-ānurūpa-lakkhaṇa-sampannā uppāditā Nīla-Kahāpaṇā ti veditabbā. Rudradāmena uppādito Rudradāmako. So kira Nīla-Kahāpaṇassa ti-bhāgaṁ agghati* (*Sāratthadīpanī*);

(2) *Porāṇakassa ti porāṇa-satth-ānurūpam=uppāditassa lak-khaṇa-sampannassa Nīla-Kahāpaṇa-sadisassa Kahāpaṇassa; etena Rudradāmak-ādīni parikkhipati...Māsako nāma Porāṇakassa vīsatimo bhāgo yā loke Mañjeṭṭhī ti pi vuccati* (*Vinayatthamañjusā*).

Chatterjee points out that the passage from the *Samanta-pāsādikā* together with those from the commentaries of Sāriputra and Buddhanāga yields the names of the following coins: (1) Rudradāmaka, (2) Rudradāmakādi, (3) Nīla-Kārṣāpāṇa, (4) Pāda of the Nīla-Kārṣāpaṇa, and (5) Māṣaka of the Nīla-Kārṣāpaṇa. His translation of the *Samantapāsādikā* passage runs as follows : "At that time at Rājagaha (Rājagṛha), one Kahāpaṇa was equal to twenty Māsakas; wherefore one Pāda was equal to five Māsakas. By this standard it is to be under-

1. *bid.*, pp. 140-41.
2. P.T.S. ed., Vol. II p. 297; cf. Bhandarkar, *Carmichael Lectures*, *op. cit.*, p. 111.
3. See also Chatterjee's paper entitled 'Some Numismatic Data in Pali Literature' published in the *Buddhistic Studies*, ed. B.C. Law, Calcutta, 1931, Chapter XV, pp. 283-452.

stood that, in all the provinces, the quarter of a Kahāpaṇa is a Pāda. But this is in respect of the ancient Nīla-Kahāpaṇa and not of these latter-day Rudradāmaka coins and those which have been modelled after it."

It is no doubt unfortunate that the expression *Rudradāmakādi*, which merely means 'the Rudradāmaka and others (i.e. other silver coins or Kārṣāpaṇas)' has been understood by the learned writer to indicate two classes of coins, viz. (1) Rudradāmaka and (2) Rudradāmakādi. As regards the latter, Chatterjee takes it to denote the monetary issues which had been modelled after the standard money of Rudradāman I, composed of silver. According to him, "The term *Rudradāmakādi* thus indicates the silver issues of the successors of Rudradāman I." The suggestion is, however, altogether untenable in view of the facts that the silver coins of the Śakas of Western India are of a single type following the weight standard of the Graeco-Indian hemi-drachms and weighing between 34 and 36 grains (the standard weight was, however, a little higher) instead of 58.56 grains (the weight of Manu's Purāṇa or Dharaṇa, otherwise called the silver-Kārṣapaṇa), although they are mentioned as Kārṣāpaṇa in epigraphic records,[1] and that it was hardly possible for the ordinary people of the fifth century to distinguish the silver issues of Rudradāman from those of the other Śaka rulers of Western India. There is absolutely no doubt that Buddhaghoṣa and his commentators speak of the whole class of the Śaka silver coins as *Rudradāmaka* after the greatest and most famous of the Śaka rulers of Western India, viz. Rudradāman I (c. 130-55 A.D.), and that Chatterjee's suggestion about a different class of similar coins, called Rudradāmakādi, is entirely imaginary. The class seems also to include non-Śaka silver coins of about the same weight standard such as those of the Śātavāhanas[2] and the Guptas.[3]

The statement of the *Sāratthadīpanī* that Rudradāmaka was the name of the coins issued by Rudradāman discloses the interesting fact that the great Śaka ruler was remembered long after the end of his rule in the second century A.D. and the

1. Rapson, *op. cit.*, p. clxxxiv.
2. *Ibid.*, p. lxxxix. See also below, pp. 107 ff.
3. Allan, *Catalogue of Indian Coins : Gupta Dynasties*, p. lxxxvi.

extirpation of the Śakas of Western India by the Imperial Guptas about the close of the fourth century. The Śaka coins must have been in circulation at least as late as the fifth century when Buddhaghoṣa flourished, if not much later still.

The *Sāratthadīpanī* says, in explaining the reason why the Pāda should indicate the fourth of the old Kārṣāpaṇa and not of the new Rudradāmaka Kārṣāpaṇa, that the value of a Rudradāmaka was only three-fourths of a Nīla-Kārṣāpaṇa. Buddhaghoṣa applies the epithet *purāṇa* (i.e. old or old-fashioned) to the Nīla-Kārṣāpaṇa, while his commentators say that this coin was what was manufactured with special marks according to the specifications of ancient treatises (such as the *Rūpasūtra* mentioned in Buddhaghoṣa's commentary on the *Mahāvagga*). The Nīla-Kārṣāpaṇa was no doubt the silver Kārṣāpaṇa called Purāṇa (a term actually used in the description of the coin by Buddhaghoṣa) or Dharaṇa and weighing 58.56 grains. If, as seems probable, the theoretical weight of the Rudradāmaka or Śaka style Kārṣāpaṇa was about 40 grains or slightly more,[1] it was actually three-fourths of the Purāṇa or old silver-Kārṣāpaṇa in weight and value. The passages make it clear that both old-fashioned and new style Kārṣāpaṇas were in use side by side and that the manufacture of the old-fashioned Kārṣāpaṇas was going on. The *Vinayatthamañjusā* actually speaks of the manufacture of Kārṣāpaṇas *resembling* the Nīla-Kārṣāpaṇa.

As to the epithet *nīla* (*i.e.* blue) applied to the old silver Kārṣāpaṇa, Chatterjee says, "That silver punch-marked coins tend to develop a bluish tint by a long process of time and usage is not an unfamiliar fact with the numismatists. The acquisition of this colour is the effect of the alloy (of about 20 per cent of copper) that inevitably went into the composition of the silver pieces." He points out that the silver punch-marked coin is called only Kārṣāpaṇa in the *Piṭakas*, while the epithet *nīla* came to be applied, at a later period, 'when the Kārṣāpaṇa pieces then available had become sufficiently coated with verdigris deposit through oxidation in the long course of time.' The suggestion may be true in spite of the fact that the

1. Chatterjee thinks that these coins had the theoretical weight-standard of 42 grains.

name was not only applied to old issues, but also often to the contemporary issues of the old-fashioned coin probably on analogy. It may be argued that the epithet *nīla* or 'blue' points to the potin (an admixture of copper, tin, lead, etc., having a bluish appearance) coins issued by the Śātavāhana kings and some of the Śaka rulers of Western India. This, however, seems to be improbable, as the potin coins could hardly have been regarded as having considerably more value than the Rudradāmaka or silver coins of the Śakas of Western India as well as of the Śātavāhanas, Guptas and others.

In connection with the Nīla-Kārṣāpaṇa (i.e. Blue Kārṣāpaṇa), Chatterjee draws our attention to the Kāla-Kārṣāpaṇa (*i.e.* Black Kārṣāpaṇa) mentioned by Buddhaghoṣa.[1] He says, "As in Pāli the two words, *nīla* and *kāla* are not identical in sense, we cannot possibly take Kāla-Kahāpaṇa to be synonymous with Nīla-Kahāpaṇa ...As regards the Kāla-Kahāpaṇa, the black colour is of course derived from the metal of these coins, viz. copper." As copper coins, when even slightly old, look blackish, Chatterjee's suggestion may be right.

The Pāda, which was one-fourth of a silver Kārṣāpaṇa (of the older variety and of the new-fangled Rudradāmaka and other varieties) seems to have been usually a coin of a cheaper metal or material, one-fourth of the latter in value and of various weights and only rarely a silver coin which was one-fourth of the standard silver coin in weight. The Māṣaka, which was one-twentieth of the silver Kārṣāpaṇa, was rarely a silver coin[2] one-twentieth of the latter in weight, but was sometimes a small coin of a cheap metal and often of other cheaper material, regarded as one-twentieth of the silver Kārṣāpaṇa in value.

Chatterjee is no doubt right in identifying the Mañjeṭṭhī, a synonym of the Māṣaka according to the *Vinayatthamañjusā*,

1. The reference is to the *Dhammapadaṭṭhakathā*, III, 254. See P.T.S. *Pali-Eng. Dict.*, s. v. *Kahāpaṇa*.

2. Silver Māṣakas are not unknown. In his Memoir on the Punch-marked coins from Takṣaśilā, Walsh has described 79 minute silver coins found in one of the boards, weighing between 2.3 and 2.86 grains, which may be regarded as silver Māṣakas, whose theoretical weight would be 3·5 grains. See also V.S. Agrawala's article entitled 'A Note on Some Minute Punch-marked Coins' (*JNSI*, Vol. XIII, pp. 164 ff.) which describes some specimens of silver-Māṣakas found in the former N.W.F.P.

with the South Indian Mañjāḍi. He quotes Bālambhaṭṭa to show that this weight (called Majjāṭikā by Bālambhaṭṭa) was equal to two Ratīs[1] and that 20 Mañjeṭṭhīs were equal to one Kaḻañju or Dharaṇa. This would appear to refer to the standard silver coin being 40 Ratīs (73 grains) in weight instead of 32 Ratīs as prescribed by Manu. This was probably the Māḍa.

III

It is admitted that the different symbols on the punch-marked silver coins, known in ancient India as Purāṇa, Dharaṇa or Raupya-Kārṣāpaṇa and weighing 32 Ratīs (a little over 58 grains) theoretically, were stamped by means of separate punches and not by a single die. But there is difference of opinion among scholars as to whether the symbols were punched all at the same time by the issuing authority or by different people at different dates.

V. A. Smith thought that 'the numerous obverse punches seem to have been impressed by the different moneyers through whose hands the pieces passed, and the reverse marks may be regarded as the signs of approval by the controlling authority.'[2] But the same grouping of the symbols noticed on a large number of coins from a single hoard, as pointed out by other writers, proves that generally they were stamped on the coins at the same time by the issuing authority.[3] This problem has thus been solved satisfactorily.

Another difference of opinion relates to the question as to who issued the punch-marked coins. Smith observed that 'the punch-marked coinage was a private coinage issued by guilds and silver smiths with the permission of the ruling authority.'[4] But, after systematic studies of the coin-hoards of definitely known provenance, D. B. Spooner, D. R. Bhandarkar and E. J. Walsh suggested that the punch-marked coins were issued by a central authority, i.e. the State.[5] Among later

1. According to Wilson's *Glossary*, the weight of the Mañjāḍi is four grains avoirdupois. See also above, pp. 54-55.
2. *Catalogue of Coins in the Indian Museum*, Vol. I, p. 133.
3. Cf. Allan, *op. cit.*, *Anc. Ind.*, p. xix; etc.
4. *Loc. cit.*
5. See Spooner in *ASI, AR*, 1905-06, p. 153; Bhandarkar in *Carm.*

writers commenting on Smith's views, J. N. Banerjea says, "There is little doubt that the marks were those of a central authority that guaranteed the genuineness of the metal and the correctness of the weight."[1] S. K. Cakrabortty says that practically all or the majority of the coins examined by Smith are surely State issues ; but, at the same time, he also maintains that originally the punch-marked coins were being issued by private bankers whose symbols have not yet been recognised by scholars owing to insufficient study and to the fact that the private issues were mostly called back and given new impress when the State entered into the field.[2]

In our opinion, there is some evidence to show that all punch-marked coins were not issued by the State, that some of them were certainly 'issued by guilds and silversmiths' as Smith suggested and that such coins were in circulation side by side with those issued by the States. The evidence is primarily supplied by a passage in Buddhaghoṣa's *Visuddhimagga* composed in the 5th century A.D. and it has been known to the students of Indian numismatics for about half a century now.[3] The belief regarding 'the absence of information from literary sources' on the punch-marked coins, as expressed in Allans' *Catalogue* (published in 1936 and referred to above) does not appear to be fully justified.[4]

The well-known *Visuddhimagga* passage has been quoted above, and we have seen that it clearly describes how a hoard of Kārṣāpaṇas lying on a goldsmith's or money-changer's tray would strike a child, a rustic and another goldsmith or money-changer differently. The child would know only that the coins have many symbols on them (*citra-vicitra*) and are oblong, square or round, but not that they could be used like gems for our enjoyment. The rustic would know all what the child knows and also that the coins could be used by us for enjoyment like gems; but he would not know the difference among them, e. g., which is

Lect., 1921, pp. 98-99; Walsh in *MASI*, No. 19; *JRAS*, Suppl., October 1924, p. 175; etc.

1. *Comp. Hist. Ind.*, Vol. II, ed. Sastri, p. 777.
2. *Stud. Anc. Ind. Num.*, pp. 129-30.
3. Cf. D.R. Bhandarkar in *ASI, AR*, 1913-14, p. 226; *Carm. Lect.*, 1921, pp. 99-100; see also *JNSI*, Vol. XIII, pp. 183 ff. and above, pp. 96-97.
4. *Op. cit.*, p. xix. Allan himself refers to the literary evidence elsewhere in his work (cf. lxxiii-lxxiv).

genuine, which is a forgery and which is now half its original value. But the goldsmith or money-changer would not only know all that is known to the child and the rustic, but much more than that. After looking at the coins, and examining them in various ways such as hearing the sound they make when struck, smelling and licking them and taking them in his hand, he would understand which *Ācārya* made them and at which village, town, hill or river-bank they were made. The word *ācārya* has been used here in the sense of 'a master goldsmith.'[1]

The passage makes it abundantly clear that the symbols on the Kārṣāpaṇas or punch-marked coins only indicated the place wherein a particular piece was made and the goldsmith who made it. Apparently, none of the symbols indicated the State in which it was made or by which it was issued. If there was any such symbol, that would have naturally been regarded as far more important than the others and Buddhaghoṣa could have hardly failed to mention it. Thus the manufacture of the Kārṣāpaṇas, referred to in the *Visuddhimagga* passage, was not directly associated with the State. Of course whether the goldsmith manufactured them with the State's permission is not known from it. The minting of coins from villages is also an interesting information supplied by the passage.

There is another passage in Buddhaghoṣa's *Samantapāsādikā*, which also has been quoted and explained above.[2] It means to say that the weight of the Kārṣāpaṇa was 20 Māṣakas at Rājagṛha so that its quarter weighed 5 Māṣakas and that, likewise, the quarter of a Kārṣāpaṇa was known as Pāda in other territories also, though this was true only with reference to the old-type Blue Kārṣāpaṇa and not to other new Kārṣāpaṇas like the Rudradāmaka, *i.e.* the silver coins of about 36 grains issued by Rudradāman I (c. 130-55 A.D.) and other Śaka kings of Western India. Apparently no coin equivalent to ¼ of the Rudradāmaka-Kārṣāpaṇa is recognised here.

The above *Samantapāsādikā* passage shows that the punch-marked coins, here called 'the old-type Blue Kārṣāpaṇa', were

1. Cf. *P. T. S. Pali-Eng. Dict.*, s. v. *ācariya*. Buddhaghoṣa being a South Indian (see above, p. 91, note 3), it is interesting to note that the word is used in the sense of 'an artisan' (a goldsmith, mason, carpenter, etc.) in the South Indian languages.

2. See p. 96; *JNSI*, Vol. VIII, p. 188.

in circulation as late as the 5th century when Buddhaghoṣa flourished and also that they were current side by side with State issues like the silver coins of the Śakas of Western India. It is also clear that the Śaka coins remained in circulation centuries after their issue.

As we have seen, the later commentators[1] bring out the difference between the old-type Blue Kārṣāpaṇa and the new Kārṣāpaṇa called Rudradāmaka and state that the latter was $\frac{3}{4}$ of the former in value. According to one commentator, the old-type Blue Kārṣāpaṇa was made by stamping symbols on them in accordance with the *Paurāṇa-śāstra*, i.e. a book dealing with the Purāṇa coin such as the *Rūpasūtra*[2] (*porāṇa-satth-ānurūpa-lakkhaṇa-sampannā uppāditā*). Another commentator says that the old-type Kārṣāpaṇas were made in accordance with the *Paurāṇa-śāstra* by impressing symbols on them and that they resembled the Blue Kārṣāpaṇa (*porāṇa-satth-ānurūpam=uppāditassa lakkhaṇa-sampannassa Nīla-Kahāpaṇa-sadisassa Kahāpaṇassa*). These passages, as we have already seen, show that the punch-marked coins were manufactured as late as the 5th century, if not also later, long after the other types of coins, sometimes bearing names of kings who issued them, appeared in the field. There is little doubt that the old-type Kārṣāpaṇas are the same coins as mentioned in the *Visuddhimagga* apparently as private issues.

The question now is whether a king would like to issue punch-marked coins anonymously in the 5th century or later when coins bearing the kings' names began to be used in various parts of the country from before the beginning of the Christian era. It is difficult to answer the question. But we consider it unlikely that the Śātavāhana kings issued coins of their usual types only in cheap metals like copper, lead and potin, but, at the same time, also the punch-marked coins in silver. If, therefore, the punch-marked coins were in circulation during the Śātavāhana age, as they apparently were since that age was earlier than the days of Buddhaghoṣa, they were probably private issues.

We have also seen that the *Suttavibhaṅga* section of the

1. Above, pp. 97 ff.; cf. *JNSI*, XIII, pp. 188-90.
2. Cf. Bhandarkar, *Carm. Lect.*, 1921, p. 126. According to Buddhaghoṣa, while learning the *Rūpasūtra*, one had to turn over and over many Kārṣāpaṇas and look at them. See above, pp. 96-97.

Vinayapiṭaka mentions Kārṣāpaṇa along with the Lauha-Māṣaka, Jatu-māṣaka and Dāru-māṣaka coins and Buddhaghoṣa's *Samantapāsādikā* explains the second and third respectively as

(1) those made of bits of wood and bamboo and pieces of palmyra leaves on which figures were cut in (*sāra-dāruṇā vā veḷu-pesikāya vā antamaso tāla-paṇṇena pi rūpaṁ chinditvā kata-māsako*), and

(2) those made of a quantity of lac or gum with the impression of figures (*lākhāya vā niyyāsena vā rūpaṁ samuṭṭhāpetvā kata-māsako*).[1] It is doubtful whether the State issued coins of such flimsy material. They can only be local issues.

We have some copper coins bearing the names of certain localities like Tripurī, Ujjayinī, Kauśāmbī and Vārāṇasī[2] and it is hardly possible to prove that they were not issued by local bodies pertaining to the places in question. The same is the case with similar coins bearing the word *negamā* (Sanskrit *naigamāḥ*) meaning 'traders' or 'members of an administrative board pertaining to a town'.[3] Lumps of copper, known as the *Ḍhabuā*, coin were not State issues.[4]

But the question is not of the private minting of coins of cheap material. Generally speaking, minting of coins in ancient India does not appear to have been different from that in the dominions of the Peshwas. We are told that in the times of the Peshwas, coinage was not a monopoly, either private or governmental. "Not a few people were apparently licensed to mint coins which naturally varied in their weight, purity and types from place to place. No wonder then that there were a plethora of coins of various sorts. Even in a single town, various kinds of coins were in circulation. Obviously these were exchanged at a rate which varied according to the metal used in the coins."[5]

It is well known that, in the late medieval period, coins of various ages and countries passed as currency in the Indian market.[6] That the same position held good in the early period

1. See above, pp. 92 ff.; *JNSI*, XII, p. 183.
2. Allan, *op. cit.*, pp. 239, 262; *JNSI*, XI, pp. 9-10; XII, pp. 134-35; etc.
3. Cf. Allan, *op. cit.*, p. cxxvi; *Ep. Ind.*, Vol. XXXV, p. 5.
4. Cf. *JNSI*, Vol. VI, pp. 55 ff.
5. *Ibid.*, Vol. IX., p. 50; cf. VII, pp. 78 ff. See also below.
6. *Ibid.*, Vol. VII, pp. 87 ff. See below.

also is proved by available evidence. The currency of the old Rudradāmaka coins in Buddhaghoṣa's age, as referred to above, of the silver coins of Kalacuri Kṛṣṇa of the 6th century even in the 8th century[1] and of early Roman coins in the markets especially of South India has to be remembered in this connection.[2] Under the circumstances, it is difficult to believe that coins minted by anybody anywhere could have been effectively prevented from being circulated in the ancient Indian market.

When punch-marked coins manufactured centuries ago were in circulation, it seems to us practically impossible to check additions to the old stock by guilds and silversmiths from time to time especially in view of the fact that the said coins were used all over India while the whole country was never under a single suzerain and that often there was no effective administration in many areas.

1. Cf. *Ep. Ind.*, XXV, pp. 225 ff.; Bhandarkar's *List of Inscriptions*, No. 1206; etc.
2. Cf. Brown, *The Coins of India*, p. 58.

Chapter V

SILVER COINS OF VĀSIṢṬHĪ-PUTRA ŚĀTAKARNI

I

Two silver coins of the Śātavāhana king Vāsiṣṭhī-putra Śātakarṇi[1] (second century A.D.), bearing his bust on the obverse, have so far been known. Like silmilar coins of Gautamīputra Yajña-Śātakarṇi, they were imitated from the silver issues of the Śakas of Western India and were apparently meant for circulation in the northernmost areas of the Śātavāhana dominions, which had been recently reconqured from the Śakas. The first of the two coins of Vāsiṣṭhī-putra Śātakarṇi was published by A. S. Altekar[2] and the second by Dinkar Rao.[3]

The legends on the obverse and reverse of the first coin (size—round, ·6″; weight—28 grains) was read by Altekar respectively as *raño Vasiṭhī-putasa* [*Sātakaṇisa*][4] and *Ara*[*kaṣa Vāsiṭhi-putaṣa hi*] *ru-Hatakaṇiṣa*, though the reading is admittedly tentative and the illstrations of the coin do not enable us to check his reading of most of the letters. But, although Altekar thought otherwise, the legends and symbols, etc., on both the silver coins of Vāsiṣṭhī-putra Śātakarṇi appear to be identical.

The published illustration of the second coin, now in the possession of D. Rao of Hyderabad, is quite unsatisfactory. But we had an opportunity of examining some plaster casts of the coin, a study of which helped us in tracing some errors in the published readings and interpretations of the legends. Its reverse legend, which was not formerly correctly read and interpreted, is of great importance as it not only helps us in restoring a damaged word in the legend on the reverse of the similar coins of Yajña-Śātakarṇi,[5] but also throws new light on

1. This name is spelt as both *Śātakarṇi* and *Sātakarṇi* while the name of the family, to which the kings bearing this name belonged, is spelt both as *Śātavāhana* and as *Sātavāhana*.

2. *JNSI*, Vol. XI, pp. 59 ff., Plate II, Nos. 5-6.

3. *Ibid.*, Vol. XXI, pp. 9-12, Plate I, No. 4, with Altekar's comments at pp. 13-17.

4. Probably *siri* has been omitted before the name by Altekar through oversight.

5. The legends on the obverse and reverse of Yajña-Śātakarṇi's coins were read by Rapson as *raño Gotamaputasa siri-Yaña-Satakaṇisa* and......*ṇaṣa Gotama-putaṣa hiru-Yaña-Hātakaṇiṣa* respectively (*Catalogue*, p. 45).

the Dravidian language and alphabet of about the second century A.D. Two eye-copies of this legend, one prepared by Rao and another by Altekar, have been published.[1] Neither of them is true to the original though Rao's copy is closer to the original than Altekar's.

The obverse of the coin exhibits the bust of the king to right and circular legend in normal Brāhmī characters of about the second century A.D., above the back of the head and to the front of the bust. This legend was read by Rao as *siri-Sātakaṇisa raño Vāsiṭhī-putasa*. Although the arrangement of the words in the legend looks like the above, we are inclined to read the right half beginning from XII (*raño Vāsiṭhī-putasa*) before the left half ending at XII (*siri-Sātakaṇisa*) since this is the case with the reverse legend. We therefore read *raño Vāsiṭhī-putasa siri-Sātakaṇisa* (Sanskrit *rājñaḥ Vāsiṣṭhī-putrasya śrī-Śātakarṇeḥ*), '[This is the coin] of the illustrious Śātakarṇi, the son of Vāsiṣṭhī (i.e., a lady belonging to a family of the Vāsiṣṭha *gotra*)].' This is also what Rapson has done in respect of the obverse and reverse legends of the silver coins of Yajña-Śātakarṇi.[2]

The reverse of the coin exhibits a number of symbols and a circular legend in Southern Brāhmī characters along the border. This legend has been read by Rao as *Arihaṇaṣa vāla-daṇḍa-dhā-Kaṇaṣa tiru-Hātakaṇiṣa*. He explains *arihaṇa* as 'the killer of enemies', *vāla-daṇḍa-dhā* as 'one who holds swords and sceptre' and *Kaṇa* as standing for *Kṛṣṇa* which, in his opinion, may have been a secondary name of the king in question or indicate 'one who is like Kṛṣṇa'. The difficulty in accepting Rao's interpretation of *vāla-daṇḍa-dhā* has been pointed out by Altekar. But the said reading of the passage is also impossible and Rao's reading and interpretation of *arihaṇa* and his explanation of *Kaṇa* are equally unsatisfactory.

Altekar reads the legend on the reverse of the coin as *Tiru-Hātakaṇiṣa arahaṇaṣa Vāhiṭha-Sathakaṇaṣa* explained as '[Coin of] the worshipful Vāhiṭha (or Vāhiṭhī, i.e., Vāsiṣṭhī-putra) Śātakarṇi of the respectable Śātakarṇi [dynasty].' But this is as unsatisfactory as Rao's reading and interpretation.

In the first place, it is impossible to believe that the same

1. *JNSI*, Vol. XXI, p. 13.
2. *Catalogue*, p. 45.

name has been written here once as *Hātakaṇi* and for a second time as *Sāthakaṇi.*

Secondly, it is not explained why, in *Sathakaṇaṣa*, *ṣ* at the beginning has a shape altogether different from that of the same letter at the end.

Thirdly, the name of the family, to which the issuer of the coin belonged, was Śātavāhana and not Śātakarṇi.

Fourthly, Altekar says, 'The legend also shows the Tamilian practice of changing *ta* into *tha* in the word *Sāthakaṇiṣa.*' But his reference to a Tamil practice in support of the change of *t* to *th* is due entirely to misunderstanding. The Tamil alphabet has only *t* for the four letters *t*, *th*, *d* and *dh* of the Sanskritic alphabet and likewise *ṭ* for *ṭ*, *ṭh*, *ḍ* and *ḍh*, though intervocal *t* and *ṭ* are pronounced as *d* and *ḍ* respectively. The Tamil practice, which Altekar has misunderstood, is really that, when Tamil words or names are written in Roman characters, the sounds of *t* and *d* are reproduced respectively by *th* and *dh* only to distinguish them from those of *ṭ* and *ḍ* which are written in English by *t* and *d* respectively.[1]

Fifthly, in Altekar's opinion, *Vāhiṭha* or *Vāhiṭhī* is an abridged form of *Vāsiṣṭhī-putra*. Since, however, the words *Vāsiṣṭha* or *Vāsiṣṭhī* (a man or woman belonging to the Vāsiṣṭha *gotra*) and *Vāsiṣṭhī-putra* (a man born of a lady belonging to a family of the Vāsiṣṭha *gotra*) have significantly different meanings, we have doubts whether a sensible and responsible mint-master could have used the former in the sense of the latter.

Sixthly, Altekar's interpretation of *arahaṇa* as *arhaṇa*, 'the worshipful one', does not appear to be happy, because *arhaṇa* really means 'worship' and not 'worshipful.'

In our opinion, Rapson was perfectly right in thinking that the legends on the obverse and reverse of the similar coins of Yajña-Śātakarṇi differ only in script and phonology but are identical in contents,[2] while Altekar is certainly wrong in think-

1. Altekar thinks that the mint officer hailed form the Tamil country and that after having spelt *Sātakaṇisa* as *Ṣāthakaniṣa*, 'he then perhaps realised that that was not the pronunciation in his master's dominions and so he spelt the word the second time as Hātakaṇiṣa' (*op. cit.*, p. 15). Apart from the quite unconvincing nature of the conjecture, it may be pointed out that, in the legend as read by Altekar and quoted above, the word *Hātakaṇiṣa* appears first and *Ṣāthakaṇiṣa* later.

2. Cf. *Catalogue*, pp. xc-xci.

ing that the legends of the present coin offer a phenomenon quite different from those of the coins of Yajña-Śātakarṇi and that the obverse legend on it is considerably different in contents from the legend on the reverse.[1]

The passage, which both Rao and Altekar have read wrongly, is quite clearly *Vahaṭṭi-mākaṇaṣa* and is certainly not *vāladaṇḍadhā-Kaṇaṣa* or *Vāhiṭha-Sathakaṇaṣa* which are both meaningless.

As we have seen, the obverse legend of the coin under study reads *raño Vāsiṭhī-putasa siri-Sātakaṇisa* (Sanskrit *rājñaḥ Vāsiṣṭhī-putrasya śrī-Śātakarṇeḥ*), '[This is the coin] of the illustrious king Śātakarṇi, son of Vāsiṣṭhī.' There is no doubt that this legend in Sanskritic Prakrit was translated into Dravidian Prakrit in the reverse which in our opinion clearly reads : *arahaṇaṣa Vahiṭṭi-mākaṇaṣa tiru-Hātakaṇiṣa*. In this, *ṣa* is used for *sa* to indicate the sixth case-ending while *arahaṇa* and *mākaṇa* are derived from Dravidian words meaning 'king' and 'son' respectively. Rapson rightly conjectured that the word in five or six syllables on the reverse of Yajña-Śātakarṇi's coins, which Bhagwanlal Indraji wrongly read as *Caturapaṇaṣa* though he was himself sure only of its last two *akṣaras* (viz. *ṇaṣa*), was probably equivalent to *raño*.[2]

The first of the two words is equivalent to Tamil and Malayāḷam *aracaṉ* or *araśaṉ*; Kannaḍa *arasa, arasu*; Tulu *arasu*. In this word, viz. *arahaṇa*, *ha* represents the change of *s* or *ś* to *h* as in *Sātakarṇi* or *Śātakarṇi* modified to *Hātakaṇi*; cf. also the change of Sanskrit *śrī*=Prakrit *siri* to *hiru* on the coins of Yajña-Śātakarṇi. The second word stands for Tamil and Malayāḷam *makaṉ* (*magaṉ*), *maka* (*maga*) ; Kannaḍa *magan maga, magam* ; Tulu *mage*. It will be seen that the Dravidian words ending in a final consonant have been made to end in *a* as in cases like Tamil *nīr* and *mīṉ* adopted in Sanskrit as *nīra* and *mīna*, the latter probably coming back to Tamil as *mīṇam*. In *māgaṇa*, whether *mā* and *ṇa* are intentional cannot be determined. It may, however, be pointed out that the word *arahaṇa* is spelt with *ṇ* also on the coins of Yajña-Śātakarṇi. But, even if *ṇ* is regarded as due to a Prakrit convention, the length of the

1. *JNSI*, Vol. XXI, p. 15.
2. *Catalogue*, p. xci.

vowel in *mā* may be assigned to the original pronunciation of the word.[1]

Vahiṭṭi is of course the same as Sanskrit *Vāsiṣṭhī*=Prakrit *Vāhiṭṭi* with the absence of aspiration while *tiru* is the modification of Sanskrit *śrī*=Prakrit *siri* as used in modern Tamil. The word *tiru*, as we have seen, is written as *hiru* in the reverse legend of Yajña-Śātakarṇi's coins. As regards *śrī*=*siri*=*hiru*, Rapson drew attention to *Śāta*=*Sāta*=*Hāla* and *Śakti*=*Haku* as known from literary and epigraphic records relating to the Śātavāhana family.

It is interesting to note that the originals of neither of the two words of Dravidian origin used in the legend, viz. *araśaṉ*=*arahaṇa* and *makaṉ*=*mākaṇa*, are now traceable in Telugu[2] which appears to have been the mother-tongue of the Śātavāhana kings called Andhra in the Purāṇas. That the phonology and vocabulary of Telugu were much nearer Tamil in the second century A.D. seems also to be clear from the occurrence of the two words in the Prakrit legend on the coin under study. It is further clear, as already known, that Tamil has retained some of the characteristics of the original Dravidian language till the present time while greater impact of Sanskrit has caused their disappearance from Telugu.

The palaeography of the reverse legend exhibits close resemblance of the characters with those of the reverse legend on the similar coins of Yajña-Śātakarṇi. The letters that are written in forms different from those of normal Brāhmī are *m*, *ṣ* and *h*. The letter *m* as reproduced by Rapson from Yajña-Śātakarṇi's coins has a shorter and more angular form than the same letter on the present coin; but this longish form with the roundish lower limb is remarkably similar to the form of *m* as found in the Aritapatti and Arikamedu inscriptions.[3] It

1. A Dravidian palaeographical characteristic, indicated by the Bhattiprolu inscriptions (*Ep. Ind.*, Vol. II, p. 324), is the representation of a consonant with the inherent *a* by an *ā-mātrā*-like sign except when it was endowed with an *anusvāra*. We do not think that this has any bearing on the length of *mā* which is noticed in the word in a few early Tamil inscriptions.

2. Cf., however, *maganru* used in the sense of 'son' in Telugu inscriptions (*SII*, Vol. X, Nos. 602, 632, etc.). As regards *araśan*, A. N. Narasiṁha (*A Grammar of the Oldest Kanarese Inscriptions*, p. 277) gives *arasu* as a Telugu word without quoting any reference.

3. See *Ancient India*, No. 2, p. 110, on the shorter form of the letter with roundish bottom in the inscriptions from Madurai, Sittannavasal and various places in the Tirunelveli District other than Arittapatti.

is difficult to say whether the modified forms of the letters, at least of *h* and *ṣ* which did not exist in the Dravidian language, were used to indicate a modification in the sounds. We have seen that *s* in Prakrit *siri* has been represented by *h* and *t* while, in Prakrit *Sātakaṇisa*, the first *s* is represented by *h* and the second by *ṣ* although the sound of neither existed in Dravidian. It is not impossible that the letter *h* represented a half aspirate and *ṣ* the Dravidian *c*=*ś* (a sound like *ts*).

But the more important palaeographical feature of the legend under study is the dot placed to the right of *ṭ* in *Vahaṭṭi* to indicate final *ṭ*. This dot, called *puḷḷi* in Tamil and now universally used only in Tamil amongst the alphabets of the Dravidian group of languages, is indicated by a dot above the consonant. It is found in Tamil inscriptions only rarely from about the 7th century A.D.[1] That the fashion of indicating the final consonant by a *puḷḷi* was known in Tamil writing in still earlier times is indicated by the *Tolkāppiyam* which does not appear to belong to a date later than the 5th century A.D.[2] But the present coin not only shows that the fashion was known in the second century A.D. but also that it was originally used in writing other languages of the Dravidian group such as early Telugu. Although the *puḷḷi* is now put above a letter in Tamil writing, the dot is placed to the right of the consonant in the legend of our coin probably to distinguish this sign of a final consonant from the usual *anusvāra* mark. Thus the *puḷḷi* may have been put to the right of the consonant in the early centuries of the Christian era.

King Vāsiṣṭhī-putra Śātakarṇi who issued the coin under study is known from the Kanheri inscription[3] of his queen who was a daughter of the Śaka *Mahākṣatrapa* Rudradāman I (c. 130-55 A. D.). As we have suggested elsewhere,[4] he was apparently a co-uterine brother of Vāsiṣṭhī-putra Puḷumāvi, son of Gautamī-putra Śātakarṇi ((c. 106-30 A.D.), and was not identical with Puḷumāvi as supposed by Rapson. Because he is not quite clearly mentioned in the Purāṇas, we formerly supposed that he may have been a viceroy of his

1. See T. N. Subramaniam, *SITI*, Vol. III, Part ii, pp. 1540-41.
2. See Sūtra 15 stating that 'a pure consonant will have a dot added to it'; cf. T. N. Subramaniam, *op. cit.*, p. 1508.
3. See Rapson, *op. cit.*, p. li, No. 17.
4. *The Age of Imperial Unity*, p. 205.

father-in-law Rudradāman I in Aparānta ((Northern Konkan) or, if he ruled as a king, the said tract may have been conquered by him after Rudradāman's death.[1] But the issue of the coins would suggest that he ruled as a king for some time. Since Puḷumāvi appears to have been the immediate successor of Gautamī-putra Śātakarṇi, Vāsiṣṭhī-putra Śātakarṇi must have been a successor of Puḷumāvi.[2] Before the discovery of Vāsiṣhṭhī-putra Śātakarṇi's silver coins, the Śātavāhana conquest of Aparānta from the successors of Rudradāman I was ascribed to Yajña-Śātakarṇi[3] who ruled about the close of the second century A.D. But, as will be seen below, there is some reason to believe that Gautamī-putra and his successors succeeded in retaining their hold not only over the Nasik-Poona region, but also over the Thana District (Aparānta).

The use of the Dravidian script and the Dravidian Prakrit (resembling Tamil more than Telugu) in the legend of this and a few other Śātavāhana silver issues belonging to Puḷumāvi and Yajña is very interesting. As we have seen, the Śātavāhana kings were Andhras while wide areas of the present-day Telugu-speaking tract, inhabited by the people called Āndhra, formed parts of their dominions. They may or may not have ruled over any part of the land where the Tamil language is now spoken. Apparently Telugu, which was in olden times closer to Tamil than it is now, was the mother tongue of the Śātavāhanas and they wanted to exhibit their Dravidian character by using an admixture of that language and Sanskritic Prakrit in the reverse legend on their coins meant for circulation in the northernmost provinces conquered from the Śakas. The real reason for their eagerness to exhibit their Dravidian origin in the said area, where the coins of the Śakas were in popular use, cannot be determined.

On the inadequate evidence of Yajña-Śātakarṇi's silver coins, Rapson suggested that the occurrence of the 'local Prakrit, perhaps containing Dravidian elements, peculiar to the Kistna District', 'like that of the alphabet associated with it, on the

1. *Loc. cit.*

2. The name of Puḷumāvi has been read on a silver coin of the same type as Vāsiṣṭhī-putra Śātākarṇi's, which was published in *JNSI*, Vol. XIV, pp. 1-3, Plate I. b, Nos. 1-2.

3. *The Age of Imperial Unity*, p. 206.

coins of Śrī-Yajña struck in Western India must, no doubt, be regarded as a reminiscence of the old home of the race in the Telugu country and may be compared to the use of Kharoṣṭhī on the coins of Bhūmaka, Nahapāna and Caṣṭana.'[1] There are, however, some difficulties in accepting this view. Firstly, it does not explain why this dialect and alphabet are found only in a few issues of the Later Śātavāhanas, which were specially meant for circulation in a limited area in the northern part of their dominions. Secondly, there is little evidence that the original home of the Śātavāhana dynasty was in the Krishna District while there is some evidence to show that the Andhra people moved southwards to the present-day Telugu-speaking area from the Vindhyan region.[2] The use of the Dravidian Prakrit and alphabet may have been more widely spread in the age in question.

Description

(Silver ; round—·7" diameter ; 28 grains)

Obverse: Bust of the king to right; his frizzled hair tied with a ribbon; crest-jewel, offering a side view and looking like a flower to front, above the forehead;[3] legend in two parts above the back of the head and to the front of the bust; the right part beginning from XII reads : *raño Vasiṭhīpu*[*tasa*], and the left part beginning at VIII and ending at XII reads : *siri-Sātakaṇisa.*

Reverse : Ujjayinī symbol surmounted by a crescent to the left and six-peaked hill surmounted by a crescent to

1. *Op. cit.*, p. xic.
2. *The Age of Imperial Unity*, p. 194.
3. Rao thinks that the king's frizzled hair is 'tied in a knot by a decorative ribbon at the centre of his forehead in a peculiar style, so as to form a round ball resembling a flower bouquet.' See also S.V. Sohoni in *JNSI*, Vol. XVII, pp. 100 ff. But Altekar points out that the said 'object can also be a crest jewel'. He also doubts whether 'frizzled hair can be tied in a knot', though Rao probably means a knot of the ribbon and not of the hair. The object is, however, clearly a flower design and the flat position in which it is depicted shows that it offers only the side view of the decorative jewel above the king's forehead. The same object is also found above the forehead of the king on the similar coins of Yajña-Śātakarṇi.

the right; wavy line below and rayed sun between the two crescents above; continuous circular legend around starting from and ending at XII : *arahaṇaṣa Vahaṭṭi-mākaṇaṣa tiru-Hātakaṇiṣa.*

II

The Periplus of the Erythraean Sea, composed about the eighth decade of the first century A.D.[1] says, "Beyond the Gulf of Baraka (Dvārakā in Kathiawar) is that of Barygaza (Bharu-kaccha, Bharoch or Broach on the mouth of the Naramdā in Southern Gujarat) and the coast of the country of Ariaka which is the beginning of the kingdom of Mambarus (apparently a Śaka Satrap) and of all India. That part of it (the kingdom of Mambarus) lying inland and adjoining Skythia (Śakasthāna in the lower valley of the Indus) is called Abiria (Ābhīra), but the coast is called Syrastrene (Surāṣṭra or Kathiawar)."[2]

There is difference of opinion among scholars on the identification of the land called Ariaka. Lassen took it to be a mistake for *Larika* standing for Lāṭa (the Nausari-Broach region of South Gujarat), while Bhagwanlal Indraji considered it to be the same as Aparāntikā (Aparānta or the Northern Konkan about the Thana District).[3] The separate mention of both Ariake and Larike in the Geography of Ptolemy (composed about the middle of the second century A.D. on the basis of material collected a little earlier), however, makes it clear that *Ariaka* does not stand for *Larika*. The author of the *Periplus*, it appears, included Larika or Lāṭa in Ariaka which has to be identified with Aparānta, since Śuppara (Sūrpāraka, the capital of Aparānta) was located in Ariaka as we shall see below.

1. For the date of the *Periplus*, see below, pp. 119 ff.

2. Schoff's trans., p. 39. The *Periplus* also says, "In these places there remain even in the present time signs of the expedition of Alexander, such as ancient shrines, walls of forts and great wells." These antiquities, probably seen by the author himself, may be associated with Alexander's stay in the land of the lower Indus for some months waiting for the Etesian winds for the dispatch of a part of his forces under Nearkhus by the sea before his own departure from India with the remainder of the army by land in the year 324 B.C. Cf. Smith, *EHI*, 1924, pp. 108-09.

3. Schoff, *op. cit.*, pp. 174-75.

Ptolemy first gives the places in Syrastrene (Kathiawar), next those in Larike (Southern Gujarat) and then those of Ariake which he calls 'Ariake of the Sadenoi'.[1] In the land of Larike, he locates the mouth of the river Mophis (Mahī) and on the Gulf of Barygaza in the same country (as we shall see later) the mouth of the Namades (Narmadā) and a locality called Nausaripa (Navasārikā, modern Nausari in the Surat District). Larike is therefore undoubtedly the same as Lāṭa. On the other hand, the geographer locates in the coast of Ariake the places called Souppara (Sūrpāraka, modern Sopara in the Thana District) and Semyla (modern Chaul in the same District, 23 miles to the south of Bombay).[2] This Ariake is no doubt identical with Aparānta or the Thana region (Northern Konkan).

The *Periplus* seems to include Ariaka, comprising Prolemy's Larike or Lāṭa, in the territory of Mambarus who had his capital at Minnagara near Barygaza. Thus, about 80 A. D., both Lāṭa and Aparānta appear to have formed parts of the Śaka kingdom of Western India. The same state continued till the time of the Kṣaharāta-Śaka Satrap Nahapāna (119-24 A.D.) who ruled over wide areas of Western India as far as the Nasik-Poona region of Maharashtra in the south. There is an early Jain tradition that Nahapāna had his capital at Bharukaccha which was repeatedly attacked by the Śātavāhana king of Pratiṣṭhāna (i.e. Gautamī-putra Śātakarṇi, c. 106-30 A.D.), who ultimately conquered it.[3] The partial destruction of Bharukaccha as a result of this struggle may have led the next Śaka Satrap Caṣṭana (Tiastenes) to make Ujjayinī (Ozene) his headquarters, as we learn from Ptolemy's Geography.

It will be seen that, while the *Periplus* includes Ariaka in the kingdom of Mambarus, Ptolemy mentions Ariake as the land of the Sadenoi and apparently includes Larike in the kingdom of Caṣṭana. A second section in Ptolemy's Geography

1. *La Géographie de Ptolémée : L' Inde (VII,* 1-4), ed. Renou, pp. 3-4 (Section 6).

2. Hippokoura (116° 15'—16° 30') in Ariake may be different from Hippokoura (119° 45'—19° 30') described elsewhere (*op. cit.*, p. 36, Section 83) as the capital of Baleokouros, usually identified with Viḷivāyakura of the Kolhapur coins.

3. Cf. *JBROS*, Vol. XVI, p. 288.

says that, in the country of Larike, the market town of Barygaza lay to the west of the river Namades (Narmadā) while, among the towns lying to the east of that river, there was Ozene (Ujjayinī), the capital of Tiastenes (Caṣṭana).[1]

Who were the Sadenoi occupying Ariake when the Kārdamaka-Śaka ruler Caṣṭana was holding Larike in the forties of the second century A.D.? That they were no other than the Śātavāhanas appears to be clear from a third section of Ptolemy's Geography wherein Baithana (Pratiṣṭhāna on the Godāvarī in the Aurangabad District of Maharashtra), capital of Siroptolemaios (Śrī-Puḷumāvi who was the son of Gautamī-putra Śātakarṇi and ruled in c. 130-59 A.D.), and the town of Tagara (modern Ter in the Osmanabad District of Maharashtra) are located in the same country to the west of the river Bendas.[2]

The Śātavāhana occupation of Aparānta before the Śaka conquest of Western India is referred to in the *Periplus* which says, "The market-towns of this region are, in order, after Barygaza; Suppara (Sūrpāraka, Sopara) and the city of Kalliena (Kalyāṇa in the Thana District, 33 miles north-east of Bombay) which in the time of the elder Saraganus (an early Śātavāhana king named Śātakarṇi) became a lawful market-town; but since it came into the possession of Sandanes (identifiable with a Kuṣāṇa emperor; see below), the port is much obstructed, and Greek ships landing there may chance to be taken to Barygaza under guard."[3]

About 124 A.D., the later Śātavāhana king Gautamī-putra Śātakarṇi (c. 106-30 A.D.) overthrew the Kṣaharāta-Śaka ruler Nahapāna and not only occupied the Nasik-Poona region and Northern Konkan (Aparānta), but even succeeded in annexing Malwa (Ākara and Avanti) and Kathiawar (Surāṣṭra).[4] But Gautamī-putra is known to have lost much of the conquered territory to the Kārdamaka-Śakas before his

1. Renou, *op. cit.*, pp. 28-29 (Section 63). Larike thus seems to have comprised the Ujjayinī region. Nasika is given here as a town in Larike. But modern Nasik in Maharashtra was in the possession of the Śātavāhanas. The Kārdamaka-Śakas could not recover the Nasik-Poona region from the Śātavāhanas.

2. *Ibid.*, p. 35 (Section 82).

3. Schoff, *op. cit.*, p. 43. Kalyāṇa is located in Aparānta in a Kanheri inscription (Lüders' *List of Brāhmī Inscriptions*, No. 113).

4. See *The Age of Imperial Unity*, ed. Majumdar, p. 201.

death about 130 A.D. In that year, the dominions of Kārdamaka Caṣṭana and his grandson Rudradāman (who ruled jointly with his grandfather as a sub-king) included Kutch, while the Junagadh inscription (150 A.D.) states that Rudradāman twice defeated Śātakarṇi (Gautamī-putra Śātakarṇi), the lord of Dakṣiṇāpatha, though the latter was not extirpated because of the closeness of relations between the two rulers. The inscription further says that Aparānta and the other districts in the northern part of Gautamī-putra's empire were then in the possession of the Kārdamaka-Śakas. As regards the closeness of relations between Gautamī-putra Śātakarṇi and Rudradāman, we know that the former's younger son Vāsiṣṭhī-putra Śātakarṇi married the latter's daughter.[1]

The reference to two wars between Rudradāman (who was originally a sub-king under his grandfather Caṣṭana) and Gautamī-putra may suggest that there were two stages in the reconquest of the northern districts of Gautamī-putra's kingdom by the Kārdamaka-Śakas. Probably the Malwa-Kathiawar area was conquered before the conquest of Aparānta and the neighbouring regions. The absence of any mention of Lāṭa in the list of territories in the possession either of Gautamī-putra or of Rudradāman appears to suggest that it was included in the administrative unit of Aparānta as indicated by the statement of the *Periplus* referred to above.

The question now is whether the whole of Aparānta was reconquered by the Kārdamaka-Śakas as suggested by the Junagadh inscription or parts of it still remained in the hands of Gautamī-putra and his successors as is indicated by Ptolemy's Geography. It has to be noted that, while Ptolemy locates the Śātavāhana capital in Ariake, epigraphic records of the Kārdamakas are conspicuous by their absence in the Nasik-Poona region as well as in the Northern Konkan, though a number of inscriptions of the successors of Gautamī-putra Śātakarṇi have been discovered in the said areas. Thus we have the Nasik and Karle (Poona District) inscriptions of Vāsiṣṭhī-putra Puḷumāvi (c. 130-59 A.D.), the Kanheri (Thana District) inscription of Vāsiṣṭhī-putra Śātakarṇi (c. 159-66 A.D.), the Nasik

1. *Ibid.*, p. 183; also Rapson's analysis of the epigraphic and numismatic data (*Catalogue*, pp. xxvi ff., cviii ff.).

and Kanheri inscriptions of Gautamī-putra Yajña-Śātakarṇi (c. 178-202 A.D.), etc., etc.[1] Formerly we had Śaka type silver coins of Yajña-Śātakarṇi, which were apparently issued for circulation in areas previously under the Śakas and one of them was found at the base of the ruined Buddhist establishment at Sopara. This led to the belief that Yajña conquered Aparānta from the Kārdamaka-Śakas.[2] But coins of the same type issued by Vāsiṣṭhī-putra Puḷumāvi and Vāsiṣṭhī-putra Śātakarṇi have also been recently discovered.[3] Thus the Nasik, Poona and Thana Districts appear to have remained in the possession of Gautamī-putra and his successors. Ptolemy's representation of Ariake as the land of the Sadenoi (Śātavāhanas) is therefore justifiable, while his inclusion of Larike (comprised in Ariaka according to the author of the *Periplus* who, as we have seen, seems to be supported by the Śātavāhana and Śaka inscriptions) apparently in the territory of Tiastenes of Ozene shows that the northern part of the Ariaka of the *Periplus* (i.e. Larike or Lāṭa) was reoccupied by the Śakas.

According to some scholars, Ptolemy distinguishes Ariake of the Sadenoi from Ariake of the Pirates, comprising the coast country towards the south stretching as far down as the country of Lymirike (Damirika of the *Periplus*, i.e. Tamiḻaka or Draviḍa) which seems to have included the land of the Kerala-putra (the king of Kerala).[4] This extension of Aparānta in the south seems to be supported by Kālidāsa's *Raghuvaṁśa* (IV. 54-58) wherein the river Muralā is probably mentioned as the boundary between Kerala and Aparānta.[5]

III

The anonymous Greek work entitled *Periplus maris Erythrae* was translated into English by McCrindle in the *Indian Anti-*

1. See Rapson's *Catalogue of Indian Coins*, pp. l-liii; *Ep. Ind.*, Vol. XXXV, p. 250. For the dates of the kings, cf. Sircar, *Suc. Sāt.*, p. 390.
2. Rapson, *op. cit.*, p. cxxi.
3. *Ep. Ind.*, Vol. XXXV, pp. 247 ff.; see also above, pp. 107 ff.
4. S. N. Majumdar Sastri, *McCrindle's Ancient India as described by Ptolemy*, p. 45. Cf. the *Periplus* locating Tyndis, one of the first markets of Damirika, in the kingdom of the Kerobothra (Schoff, *op. cit.*, p. 44).
5. Mallinātha, the South Indian commentator on the *Raghuvaṁśa*, regards the Muralā as a river in the Kerala country, while the South Indian product entitled *Avantīsundarīkathā* speaks of the sports of the Aparānta elephants in the waters of the Muralā (cf. Sircar, *Select Inscriptions*, p. 453, note 1).

quary, Vol. VIII, 1879, pp. 108 ff.,[1] while W.H. Schoff's annotated English translation of the work appeared in 1912. McCrindle dates the *Periplus* between 80 and 89 A.D. and Schoff suggests 60 A.D. as the date of its composition, though he later expressed his preference for 80 A.D.[2] The date 246 or 247 A.D. proposed by Reinaud was considered impossible by V. A. Smith who regarded Kennedy's date 70 or 71 A.D. to be the best authenticated.[3] For many years, the composition of the *Periplus* is being referred to by scholars to the eighth decade of the first century A.D., i.e. a few decades after Hippalus' discovery of the sea-route to India described in the work and fixed by Vincent at about 47 A.D.[4]

On the basis of a recent study of the evidence of South Arabian archaeology, it has been suggested that the *Periplus* was composed during Nahapāna's time about the beginning of the 3rd century A.D. Jacqueline Pirrenne says, "Les derniers rois de Qatabān ont frappé monnae, disions-nous, entre 100 et 200; Charibaél devrait se situer immediatement aprés eux, á une époque où le *Periple* nomme Charibaél et ignore Qatabān."[5] Unfortunately the conclusion seems to ignore totally not only Rapson's admirable analysis of the numismatic evidence regarding Nahapāna's contemporaneity with Caṣṭana, but also the valuable light thrown on the problem by statements contained in the work itself :

1. "Beyond this region.........there follows the coast district of Skythia (Śakasthāna).........from which flows down the river Sinthus (Indus).........This river has seven mouths...... they are not navigable except the one at the middle, at which, by the shore, is the market town, Barbarikum. Before it, there lies a small island, and inland behind it is the metropolis of Skythia, Minnagara; it is subject to Parthian princes who are constantly driving each other out.........

1. McCrinddle's work was also separately published in the same year.
2. See Schoff, *The Periplus of the Erythraean Sea*, p. 15; V. A. Smith, *Early History of India*, 1924, p. 245, note.
3. Smith, *loc. cit.*; Kennedy in *JRAS*, 1918, p. 112.
4. Schoff, *op. cit.*, p. 8.
5. *Le Royaume Sud Arab de Qatabān et sa datation d'aprés l'archéologie et les sources classiques jusqu'au Periple de la mer Erythrée*, Louvain, 1961, p. 200; cf. H. de Contenson, 'Les premiers rois d' Axoum d'aprés déccuvertes recentes' in *Journal Asiatique*, 1960, No. 1, pp. 75 ff.

2. "Beyond the gulf of Baraka (Dvārakā) is that of Barygaza (Bharukaccha, Broach) and the coast country of Ariaka (Lāṭ-Āparānta) which is the beginning of the kingdom of Mambarus and of all India. That part of it lying inland and adjoining Skythia is called Abiria (Ābhīra); but the coast is called Syrastrene (Surāṣṭra).........The metropolis of this country is Minnagara from which much cotton cloth is brought down to Barygaza......

3. "The country inland from Barygaza is inhabited by numerous tribes.........Above these is the very warlike nation of the Baktrians who are under their own king......

4. "Inland from this place and to the east is the city called Ozene (Ujjayinī), formerly a royal capital.........

5. "The market-towns of this region are, in order, after Baryagaza: Suppara (Sūpāraka, Sopara), and the city of Kalliena (Kalyāṇa) which, in the time of the elder Saraganus, became a lawful market-town; but, since it came into the possession of Sandanes, the port is much obstructed, and Greek ships landing there may chance to be taken to Barygaza under guard."[1]

If these five extracts are studied in the light of certain known facts of Indian history, they would suggest that the *Periplus* was composed considerably before 200 A.D. Their implications are summarily discussed below.

1. The Periplus mentions Minnagara, the capital of the land of the Śakas in the lower valley of the Indus, as subject to the Parthian princes who were constantly driving each other out. The Junagadh inscription[2] of [Śaka] 72 (150 A. D.) states that the countries of Sindhu and Sauvīra, together covering the lower Indus valley, formed parts of the dominions of the Śaka *Mahākṣatrapa* Rudradāman of Western India, who was then very probably a semi-independent subordinate of the Kuṣāṇas. The discovery of the inscriptions[1] of Kaniṣka and Vāsiṣka near Bahawalpur and Bhopal points to the inclusion of

1. See Schoff, *op. cit.*, p. 37 (para. 38), p. 39 (para. 41), p. 41 (para. 47), p. 42 (para. 48), p. 43 (para. 53).

2. Cf. *Select Inscriptions*, p. 172, text line 12. Some of these territories, besides Sindhu and Sauvira, were East and West Malwa (Ākar-Āvanti), North and South Kathiawar (Ānarta-Surāṣṭra), the Sābarmatī valley (Śvabhra), the Marwar region (Maru), Kutch (Kaccha), the Northern Konkan (Lāṭ-Āparānta), etc.

the lower Indus valley and Malwa in the Kuṣāṇa empire. Under these circumstances, it is extremely difficult to place Parthian rulers at the capital of the said territory after Kaniṣka I and Rudradāman. On the other hand, the lower valley of the Indus seems to have formed a part of the kingdom of the Parthian king Gondopherenes (c. 21-46 A.D.) and 'the Parthian princes driving each other out' may easily be regarded as having ruled at the capital of Skythia during the period of Parthian decadence in India some time after the death of Gondophernes about the middle of the first century A.D.

2. The country of Ariaka (Lāṭ-Āparanta) on the Gulf of Barygaza as well as Syrastrene (Surāṣṭra) on the coast and Abiria (Ābhīra country) adjoining the lower Indus valley are mentioned as parts of the dominions of Mambarus who had his capital at Minnagara (different from Minnagara, the capital of Skythia) not very far from Barygaza or Broach. This Mambarus was apparently a Śaka Satrap; but his identification with the Kṣaharāta-Śaka Satrap Nahapāna is unsatisfactory since Nahāpāna is known to have had his capital at Broach itself. As will be seen below, Mambarus should be referred to a period earlier than Nahapāna's time.

Jinadāsagaṇin (seventh century A.D.), commenting on Bhadrabāhu's *Āvaśyakasūtraniryukti*, speaks of Nahavāhana (Nahavāṇa of the original *gāthā*), i.e. Śaka Nahapāna, as having his capital at Bharukaccha (Broach) and as an enemy of the Sātavāhana (i. e., the Śātavāhana king) who ruled at Paiṭhāna (Pratiṣṭhāna, modern Paithan in the Aurangabad District) and led frequent attacks on Nahavāhana's capital.[2] Thus Nahapāna had his capital at Broach, and Minnagara in the same neighbourhood appears to have been the capital of the Śakas of Western India at an earlier date since the successors of Nahapāna (i. e. the Kārdamaka-Śakas) are known to have made their headquarters at the city of Ujjayinī as we shall presently see. Mambarus therefore flourished earlier than Nahapāna.

The Śātavāhana king Gautamī-putra is represented in one of the records of his son Puḷumāvi as the destroyer of the Śakas

1. See *ibid.*, pp. 135-36.
2. Cf. *A Comprehensive History of India*, Vol. II, ed. K. A. Nilakanta Sastri, p. 279.

and other barbarians, as the extirpator of the Kṣaharāta clan to which the Śaka Satrap Nahapāna belonged and as the lord of such territories as Surāṣṭra, Aparānta, Ākara and Avanti which were apparently acquired as a result of his victory over the Śaka ruler.[1] Gautamī-putra's own inscriptions[2] show not only that he was present in the vicinity of Nasik in connection with a military expedition apparently against the Śakas, but also that he granted lands in the Nasik-Poona region, which had been previously in the possession of or had been granted by Śaka Ṛṣabhadatta, Nahapāna's son-in-law and viceroy of the said area. There is also a hoard of Nahapāna's coins restruck by Gautamī-putra Śātakarṇi, which was discovered at Jogalthembi in the Nasik District.[3] All these point to Gautamī-putra's success against Nahapāna. But the territories the Śātavāhana king conquered from the Śaka ruler were mostly recovered soon by the Kārdamaka-Śakas under Caṣṭana and Rudradāman apparently under orders of the Kuṣāṇa overlords.

The contemporaneity of king Siroptolemaios of Baithana (i.e. Gautamī-putra Śātakarṇi's son and successor Vāsiṣṭhī-putra Śrī-Puḷumāvi of Pratiṣṭhāna) and Tiastenes of Ozene (i. e. the Kārdamaka-Śaka Satrap Caṣṭana of Ujjayinī) is proved by the *Geography* of Ptolemy (middle of the second century A. D.).[4] According to the Andhau inscriptions,[5] Caṣṭana was ruling jointly with his grandson Rudradāman in the [Śaka] year 52=130 A. D. Rudradāman's Junagadh inscription[6] of 150 A. D. states that he twice defeated Śātakarṇi, lord of Dakṣiṇāpatha, whom he did not extirpate owing to the closeness of relations existing between the two rulers. This Śātakarṇi has to be identified with Gautamī-putra, and the closeness of relationship is explained by the Kanheri inscription[7] referring to Vāsiṣṭhī-putra Śātakarṇi (no doubt a younger brother of Vāsiṣṭhī-putra Puḷumāvi and son of Gautamī-putra) as the husband of a daughter of *Mahākṣatrapa* Rudra[dāman]. Caṣṭana

1. See *Select Inscriptions*, pp. 196-97, text lines 2, 5 and 6.
2. *Ibid.*, pp. 191-92; also p. 165, and Lüders' *List of Inscriptions*, Nos. 1099 and 1105.
3. Rapson's *Catalogue of Coins*, pp. lxxxviii ff.
4. VII. i. 63 and 82.
5. *Select Inscriptions*, pp. 167 ff.
6. *Ibid.*, pp. 169 ff., text line 12.
7. Lüders' *List*, No. 994.

and Rudradāman succeeded in recovering from Gautamī-putra Śātakarṇi the territories the latter had conquered from Nahapāna with the exception of the southernmost areas.

The above discussion will show that the Śātavāhana king Gautamī-putra Śātakarṇi was a contemporary of the Śaka rulers Nahapāna, Caṣṭana and Rudradāman and that the dates in Nahapāna's records, years 41-46,[1] should be referred to the Śaka era so as to yield 119-24 A. D. The Śātavāhana king ousted Nahapāna from the Malwa and Gujarat regions in or shortly after 124 A.D., but was himself driven back by Caṣṭana and Rudradāman by 130 A.D.

It will therefore be seen that Nahapāna (119-24 A. D.) had his capital at Broach, and Caṣṭana (130 A. D.) and apparently his successors had their headquarters at Ujjayinī,[2] and that these Śakas were ruling over the area under the occupation of Mambarus of Minnagara according to the *Periplus*. The work therefore appears to have been composed before 119 A. D. It is significant that, about the middle of the second century A.D., Ptolemy mentions the same Śaka city as Minagara, but not as the capital of any ruler.[3] If Minnagara was no capital city in the middle of the second century A. D., it could have been the capital of Mambarus at an earlier date and not at a later date, because the Śaka capital from Ptolemy's time was at Ujjayinī. The territory over which Mambarus is stated to have ruled was moreover a part of the dominions of the Kṣaharāta and Kārdamaka-Śakas, and Mambarus could have ruled over that area only at an earlier period.

3. If the *Periplus* was composed at about 80 A. D., the warlike Baktrians ruled by their own king may be indentified with the Kuṣāṇas since during the reigns of Kadphises I and II, the Kuṣāṇa headquarters were in Northern Afghanistan. But if the composition of the work is ascribed to 200 A. D., who could have been the Baktrians ruled by their own king ? Baktria then was an integral part of the mighty empire of the Kuṣāṇas, with its capital at Puruṣapura (Peshawar), and the Baktrians

1. *Select Inscriptions*, pp. 157 ff.
2. Note the tradition regarding the Extirpator of the Śakas (Śakāri Vikramāditya) having made Ujjayinī his capital and the mention of a West Indian Śaka ruler of the third century A.D. in a Nagarjunikonda inscription as the *Mahārāja* of Ujjayinī (*Select Inscriptions*, p. 221).
3. VII. i. 63.

were then certainly not an independent people under their own king. It is interesting in this connection to note that, according to Chinese evidence, the people of Ta-hia (Baktria), who were easily subdued by the Yueh-chi were unskilled in war and devoted to commerce and were wanting in cohesion.[1]

4. Ozene or Ujjayinī is mentioned as a city which had been formerly the capital of a ruler, but was no royal city just when the *Periplus* was composed. This apparently refers to a period earlier than the second quarter of the second century A.D. when theKārdamaka-Śakas made Ujjayinī their capital. About the time of the composition of the *Periplus*, it seems to have been an ordinary city of the dominions of Mambarus, although it had been previously not only the capital of the ancient Avanti-janapada but also the headquarters of the local rulers who issued the punch-marked coins with the so-called Ujjayinī symbol.[2]

5. Kalliena or Kalyāṇa in the Thana District (ancient Aparānta) formed part of the dominions of the Elder Saraganus (Śātakarṇi) during whose rule it was a peaceful market town sometime before the date of the composition of the *Periplus*. But, when the work was composed, Kalyāṇa was under Sandanes and there was not only much obstruction to trade, even Greek ships landing there were liable to be seized and taken to Barygaza under guard. This passage refers to the Early Śātavāhana rule in Aparānta and its occupation later by the Śaka-Kusāṇas. We have seen that, about 124 A.D., the Śātavāhana king Gautamī-putra Śātakarṇi conquered Aparānta from Śaka Nahapāna, but soon lost its northern part to the Kārdamaka-Śakas who, however, never succeeded in re-occupying Aparānta proper (i.e. the Thana District of Maharashtra). There is no name like Mambarus in the Kārdamaka family. There seems also to be no place for Sandanes about 200 A.D. when the port appears to have been a part of the dominions of the Śātavāhana king Gautamī-putra Yājña-Śātakarṇi (c. 174-203 A. D.) or one of his immediate successors.[3]

1. *The Age of Imperial Unity*, ed. Majumdar, p. 137.
2. Cf. Allan's *Catalogue of Indian Coins* (Ancient India), pp. cxli ff.
3. Cf. *The Age of Imperial Unity*, pp. 205 ff. For the identification of Sandanes with a Kuṣāṇa overlord of the Śakas of Western India, cf. Lévi, *Journ. As.*, Tome CCXXVII, pp. 61 ff.; Bailey, *Khotanese Texts*, Vol. II, pp. 201 ff.; *BSOS*, Vol. XII, pp. 926 ff.

Chapter VI

ALLEGED COINS OF THE MAHIṢA KINGS

I

It is well known to the students of Indian numismatics that V. V. Mirashi has been trying for the past many years to prove the existence of a Mahiṣa dynasty of Śaka nationality founded by a king named Māna and of certain other rulers of that family as also to show that these Mahiṣa kings ruled over the southern part of the former Hyderabad State. The theories are based on his reading and interpretation of the legends on certain coins mostly discovered in the said area. It may also be known to our numismatists that we have often expressed the opinion that Mirashi's readings of the coin legends are doubtful and that his interpretations of the legends are still more dubious. But it has sometimes been complained that we have only characterised the published readings of the coin legends and their interpretations as unsatisfactory without offering any reading and interpretation ourselves.[1]

Our difficulty was that we were not prepared to commit without examining the coins and satisfying ourselves with the reading of the legends and their interpretation. Recently we had an opportunity of examining plaster-casts of some of the coins in the Hyderabad Museum including what Mirashi has published as those issued by the kings of the so-called Mahiṣa dynasty, and are now fortunately in a better position to express our opinion on them.

Mirashi has recently discussed, in the *Journal of the Numismatic Society of India*, Vol. XVIII, pp. 116-21, the history of his study of the coins of a ruler whom he calls the Śaka king Māna of the Mahiṣa dynasty. This story indicates the following stages

1. Cf. *JNSI*, Vol.XVIII, 1956, pp. 6 ff., 116 ff., 124 ff. Mirashi's articles on the coins in question are referred to below. Our comments on some of his theories based on these coins were offered earlier in *op. cit.*, Vol. XII, pp. 50 ff.; *IHQ*, Vol. XXVII, pp. 174 ff.; Vol. XXIX, pp. 294 ff.

in the development of his interesting theory about the kings of the Mahiṣa dynasty.

(1) In 1946, Mirashi received inked impressions of two coins in the possession of Hurmuz Kaus of Hyderabad and published them in the *Indian Historical Quarterly*, Vol. XXII, pp. 34 ff. and Plate. The legend on the coins was read and translated by him as follows : *Raṁño Saga-Māna-Mahasa*[*sa**] (Sanskrit *Rājñaḥ Śaka-Māna-Mahiṣasya*), '[This coin is] of the Śaka king Māna of the Mahiṣa dynasty'. From the illustration, however, it is quite clear that not only *sa*, put in brackets with an asterisk after *mahasa*, is untraceable on the coins and is admittedly an imaginary addition, but there is also no trace of the word *raṁño* on them.[1] His interpretation of the legend was influenced by the Puranic passage *Śakyamānābhavad=rājā Mahiṣīṇāṁ* (v. l. *Mahiṣyāṇāṁ*) *mahīpatiḥ*. It seems that he corrected *Śakyamānābhavad°* to *Śaka-Māno='bhavad°* and *Mahiṣīṇāṁ* or *Mahiṣyāṇāṁ* to *Mahiṣāṇāṁ*. The territory over which the Śaka king 'Māna the Mahiṣa' ruled was located by him in the region around Māhiṣmatī, i. e. modern Māndhātā or Maheshwar on the Narmadā. As, however, will be seen below, the letters *mahasa* constitute the first part of the word *Mahāsenāpatisa* found on other coins of the same ruler and therefore the existence of the Mahiṣa dynasty has no foundation at all.

(2) In 1949, Mirashi received photographs of two coins discovered in the course of excavations, the first at Kondapur and the second at Maski, from Khwaja Muhammad Ahmed, then Director of Archaeology, Hyderabad, and published them in the *Journal of the Numismatic Society of India*, Vol. XI, pp. 1 ff. and Plate.[2] He also published a note on the responsibility of the Śaka kings of the Mahiṣa dynasty for the spread of the Śaka era in South India in the *Proceedings of the Indian History Congress*, Cuttack Session, 1949, pp. 45 ff., as well as in the *Indian Historical Quarterly*, Vol. XXVI, 1950, pp. 216 ff. The fragmentary legend on the said two coins from Kondapur and Maski,

1. What has been read as *raṁño* with the remarks, 'These two *akṣaras* appear very thin and crampled for want of space', is really a small symbol of six arches (i.e. a six-peaked hill), which is partly rubbed off.

2. The article was reprinted in *Numismatic Series*, No. 3—'Some Coins of the Mahiṣa Dynasty', Hyderabad Museum, 1950, with illustration of the Kondapur and Maski coins as well as the two coins published in the *Indian Historical Quarterly*, Vol. XXII.

as he read it, ends with the letters *mahasa* which were taken to stand for Sanskrit *Mahiṣa* and he ascribed the Kondapur coin to the same Śaka king Māna of the Mahiṣa dynasty. The legend on the Maski coin was read by Mirashi as *yasasa Mahasa-[sa*]* which suggested to him a Mahiṣa king with his name ending in the word *yaśas*, supposed to have been a later member of the family founded by the Mahiṣa-Śaka king Māna, though elsewhere he applies the name Yaśa to this king.[1] On the basis of the discovery of these coins at Kondapur in the Medak District and Maski in the Raichur District, he now suggested that the territory ruled by the kings of the Mahiṣa-Śaka dynasty comprised the southern part of the former Hyderabad State, which in his opinion was called Māhiṣaka in ancient times.[2] It was also suggested that the said Mahiṣa-Śaka house of Southern Hyderabad was an offshoot of the Kṣaharāta-Śaka family of Western India. But, as has already been indicated above, *Mahasa......* actually stands for *Mahāsenāpatisa*. The dynastic and personal names of the issuer of the coins, which have been misunderstood even though they are quite clear, are being discussed below and it will be seen that they have nothing to do either with the Śakas or with any Mahiṣa dynasty.

(3) Two notes were published by Mirashi in the *Journal of the Numismatic Society of India*, Vol. XII, 1950, pp. 87-89 and pp. 90-91 with Plates.[3] The subject of the first of the two notes is a coin in the possession of Hurmuz Kaus, which bears the legend *Saga-Māna-Cuṭukasa*, '[This coin is] of the Śaka Māna Cuṭuka,' as read and interpreted by Mirashi. It was now suggested that this Śaka king named Māna-Cuṭuka belonged to the family founded by the Śaka ruler Māna who himself as well as some of his successors (like......*yaśas* or *Yaśa* referred to above) assumed the dynastic name *Mahasa*=Sanskrit *Mahiṣa*.

1. *Numismatic Series*—'Coins of King Sumahāgrāmaka from Kondapur Excavations', No. 7, Hyderabad Museum, 1950, p. 2. In our opinion, the reading of what has been read as *yasa* is uncertain.

2. For our comments on the location of the Mahiṣa country in the southern part of the former Hyderabad State, cf. *JNSI*, Vol. XII, pp. 50 ff.; *IHQ*, Vol. XXVII, pp. 174 ff.

3. The coins dealt with in the second note were also published in the *Numismatic Series*, No. 8.—'Some More Mahiṣa Coins from Kondapur Excavations', Hyderabad Museum, 1950.

As will be seen below, Mirashi later regarded *Cuṭuka* as a shortened form of *Cuṭu-kula* which is, according to him, an epithet of Śaka-Māna and means 'belonging to the Cuṭu family'. But we have pointed out elsewhere[1] that 'Śaka Māna' could have scarcely been described on some of the coins as 'Māna the Mahiṣa' and on others as 'Māna the Cuṭuka (i. e. Cuṭu)'.

The subject of the second note of Mirashi is a number of coins on which the complete legend was read by him as *Mahā-senāpatisa Radaji-putasa Saga-Māna-Cuṭukulasa*, with the remarks that sometimes *Senāpati-puta* and *Cuṭuka* occur in the legend instead of *Mahāsenāpati* and *Cuṭukula* respectively. As a matter of fact, however, the seventh and eighth letters of what actually reads *Mahasenapatisa Bharadaji-putasa* (i. e. the letters *sa bha*) were wrongly read as *puta*. But the word *Cuṭuka* has been rightly regarded by Mirashi as a shortened form of *Cuṭukula*, although his interpretation of the expression, as will be seen below, is wrong.

(4) In an article in the same journal, Vol. XV, 1953, pp. 115 ff. and Plate, Mirashi published another coin of the so-called *Mahāsenāpati* Śaka Māna from Kondapur, which helped him to correct the reading *Radaji-puta* of the legend on similar coins, published by him previously and referred to above, to *Bharadaja-puta* (Sanskrit *Bharadvāja-putra*). The legend is now read as *Mahāsenāpatisa Bharadaja-putasa Saga-Māna-Chuṭu-kulasa* (Sanskrit *Mahāsenāpateḥ Bharadvāja-putrasya Śaka-Māna-Cuṭu-kulasya*) and translated as '[This coin is] of the *Mahāsenāpati* Śaka Māna, the son of Bharadvāja, who is of the Çuṭu family.' It is also suggested that Śaka Māna had issued these coins earlier when he was a *Mahāsenāpati* while his coins bearing the epithet *raṁño* were issued at a later date after his assumption of royal title. Mirashi further observes, "In two other respects, these Kondapur coins differ from those found elsewhere. They mention his (i. e. Śaka Māna's) family as *Cuṭu-kula* which is shortened to *Cuṭuka* in one case (see above, Vol. XII, p. VIII, Coin 8). On the other coins, he mentions instead the epithet *Mahasa* (Sanskrit *Mahiṣa*) derived from the country under his rule. He seems to have been well known as the king

1. *JNSI*, Vol. XVIII, p. 8.

of the Mahiṣas."[1] But, as we have pointed out above, the word *raṁño* does not actually occur on the coins in question. Elsewhere,[2] we commented on the interpretation of *Saga-Māna-Cuṭu-kulasa* (Sanskrit *Śaka-Māna-Cuṭu-kulasya*) as 'of the Śaka Māna belonging to the Cuṭu family' as quite unsatisfactory. If that was the meaning intended, the passage would have been worded as *Cuṭu-kulasa Saga-Mānasa* (Sanskrit *Cuṭu-kulasya Śaka-Mānasya*) or at least *Cuṭu-kula-Saga-Mānasa* (Sanskrit *Cuṭu-kula-Śaka-Mānasya*). There is no instance of the mention of a person and his dynasty in an extremely awkward compound expression like *Saga-Māna-Cuṭu-kula*, as Mirashi's interpretation would involve.

II

There is another interesting fact to which attention of scholars should be drawn in this connection. The occurrence of the epithet *Mahāsenāpatisa* on these coins suggests quite clearly that the letters *mahasa* read on the same ruler's other issues published by Mirashi earlier, does not stand for *Mahisa*[*sa**] (Sanskrit *Mahiṣasya*), 'of the Mahiṣa', but for *Mahāse*[*nāpatisa**] (Sanskrit *Mahāsenāpateḥ*), 'of the *Mahāsenāpati* (i. e. great *Senāpati* or commander of forces)'. Considering, however, the arrangements of the words in the passage *Sagamāna Mahāse*-[*nāpatisa**] on this group of coins as well as the size of both the coins of this group and of the letters in the legend, it appears to us that the full legend here may have been *Sagamāna Mahāsenāpatisa Cuṭukasa* (or *Cuṭukulasa*) and that the epithet *Bharadaji-putasa* (Sanskrit *Bhāradvājī-putrasya*, 'of one who is the son of a lady born in a family belonging to the Bhāradvāja *gotra*') may have been omitted for the sake of space. In any case, it is clear that the flans of these coins were considerably smaller than the die. As will be seen below, what Mirashi takes to be *Saga-Māna* (i.e. *Śaka-Māna*) we are inclined to take as *Sagamāna* (i. e. *Sagamānaṁ*), 'of the Sagamas (i. e. belonging to the Sagama family)'.

In our opinion, Coin No. 1, the inked rubbing of which has been published in the *Numismatic Series*, No. 8, Plate I, reads

1. *Op. cit.*, p. 117.
2. *JNSI*, Vol. XVIII, p. 8.

Bharadaji and not *Bharadaja* and the legend fully preserved on Coin No. 5 on the same Plate[1] and incompletely on some others read *Mahasenapatisa Bharadaj* [*i*]-*putasa Sagamāna Cuṭukulasa.* The natural inclination of any student of Sanskrit and Prakrit would be to take the passage to stand for Sanskrit *Mahāsenāpateḥ Bhāradvājī-putrasya Sagamānāṁ Cuṭukulasya* and to translate it as '[This coin is] of *Mahāsenāpati* Bhāradvājī-putra Cuṭukula of the Sagamas (i. e. belonging to the Sagama dynasty)'. *Sagamāna Cuṭukula* may be compared to numerous such passages occurring in early South Indian inscriptions, e. g., *Pallavāṇa Sivakkhaṁdavamo* (Sanskrit *Pallavānāṁ Śivaskandavarmā*), 'Śivaskandavarman of the Pallava family', occurring in the Hirhadagalli plates.[2] Whether *Sagama* is a Dravidian name or stands for Sanskrit *Saṅgama* or *Saṅgrāma* cannot be determined, although these are familiar personal names,[3] easily applicable to families, and the medieval Saṅgama dynasty (1336-1485 A.D.) of Vijayanagara is well known to us.

The language of the passage also shows beyond doubt that *Cuṭukula* here has to be taken as a personal name. There is certainly no other satisfactory explanation of the passage. To some of our readers, however, *Cuṭukula* as a personal name would appear rather awkward, since the word *kula* forming its second part means 'a family' in Sanskrit. Of course, Monier-Williams' *Sanskrit-English Dictionary* recognises Rājakula-bhaṭṭa occurring in the *Kathāsaritsāgara* as the personal name of a poet. But there is reason to believe that, just as *Mihirakula* was Sanskritised from Persian *Mihrgul*, *Cuṭukula* is likewise the Sanskritised form of a Dravidian personal name.

We have certain coins found in the Karwar region, some of which bear the legend *Raño Cuṭukaḍānaṁdasa*, '[This coin is] of king Cuṭukaḍānanda', and others with the legend *Raño Muḍānaṁdasa*, '[This coin is] of king Muḍānanda', both the groups being exactly similar in type.[4] There is no doubt that these coins were issued by two rulers (apparently

1. This is the same as Coin No. 6 in Plate VIII of *JNSI*, Vol. XII.
2. *Select Inscriptions*, p. 437.
3. Bhandarkar's List, Nos. 123, 1557, 1560, etc.
4. Rapson, *Catalogue of the Coins of the Andhra Dynasty*, etc., pp. lxxxii-lxxxiv, 59-60, Plate VIII, Nos. G. P. 2, 235, G. P. 3, and Nos. G. P. 4.

related to each other) whose personal names were Cuṭukaḍānanda and Muḍānanda. There also cannot be any doubt that the personal name *Cuṭukaḍānanda* occurs in its Sanskrit garb as *Cuṭukulānanda* in the name of Hāritīputra Viṇhukaḍa-Cuṭukulānaṁda Śātakarṇi of an inscription[1] from Banavasi and of Hāritīputra Viṇhukaḍḍa-Cuṭukulānanda-Śātakarṇi of another inscription[2] from Malavalli. We have seen above that coins, wrongly attributed by Mirashi to king Māna of the Mahiṣa dynasty, represent the personal name of the issuer in some cases as *Cuṭukula* and in others in a shortened form as *Cuṭuka* which is the same as *Cuṭu* with the *svārthika* suffix *ka* added to it.[3] This fact would suggest that *Cuṭukula,* the Sanskritised form of Dravidian *Cuṭukaḍa,* was another slightly shortened form of the personal name *Cuṭukaḍānanda-Cuṭukulānanda.* It is of course difficult to say whether *ānanda,* the third element in the name, is also the Sanskritised form of a Dravidian word. But that personal names with this element were popular in certain areas of the Deccan seems to be suggested by names like Muḍānanda found on the Karwar coins referred to above and Viṣṇurudraśivalānanda-Śātakarṇi of Vanavāsa (modern Banavāsi in the North Kanara District, Mysore) mentioned in the Nagarjunikonda inscription[4] of the time of the Ābhīra king Vasuṣeṇa.

The above discussions will make it clear that whatever has been said during the past many years about the existence of kings of the Mahiṣa-Śaka dynasty and their rule over the southern part of the old Hyderabad State, on the basis of the erroneous reading and interpretation of the coin legends dealt with above, is without any foundation.

Cuṭukula, who issued the coins discussed above and enjoyed the official designation *Mahāsenāpati*, seems to have been the military governer of a district or its subdivision within the dominions of some king who cannot be identified in the present state of our knowledge. It appears that he flourished as a semi-inde-

1. *Ibid.*, p. liii, No. 25; Lüders' List, No. 1186; above, Vol. XXXIV, pp. 239 ff.
2. Rapson, *op. cit.*, p. liv; Lüders' List, No. 1195.
3. The addition of this suffix is quite common in early epigraphic records.
4. *Indian Archaeology*, 1958-59, p. 8; *Ep. Ind.*, Vol. XXXIV, p. 197.

pendent ruler when the Śātavāhana power was fast declining. The issue of coins by such subordinate rulers is illustrated by certain coins bearing the legend *Sadakana Kaḷalāya-mahāraṭhisa* (Sanskrit *Śātakānāṁ Kaḷalāya-mahārāṣṭriṇaḥ*), '[This coin is] of the *Mahārāṣṭrin* Kaḷalāya of the Śātaka family'.[1] The official designation *Mahārāṣṭrin* means 'the great *Rāṣṭrin* or ruler of a *rāṣṭra*', i.e. 'a chief of the *Rāṣṭrins*', and *rāṣṭra* means a group of villages or the subdivision of a district. The word *rāṣṭrin* reminds us of the designation *Rāṣṭrakūṭa*, 'head of a *rāṣṭra*', coined on the analogy of *Grāmakūṭa*, 'head of a *grāma* or village'.[2] Another similar designation is *Rāṣṭramahattara* mentioned along with *Grāmamahattara.*[3]

In this connection reference may be made to certain other coins published by Mirashi in the *Journal of the Numismatic Society of India.* In a small note in Vol. XV, p. 120 and Plate, he published a coin in the possession of Hurmuz Kaus of Hyderabad. In the fragmentary legend on the coin, Mirashi could not read anything besides the letters *sivalasa maha* which induced him to attribute the issue to a Mahiṣa king named Śivala. We, however, consider the suggestion quite unwarranted. In the first place, he admits the existence of a letter like *ka* before *si.* Thus the name may have been one ending in *śivala* as in the case of Vishṇurudraśivalānanda-Śātakarṇi of a Nagarjunikonda inscription referred to above. Secondly, the two letters *maha* may suggest anything like *Mahārāja*, *Mahāsenāpati*, *Mahārāṣṭrin*, *Mahāgrāmika*,[4] *Mahātalavara*,[5] etc., and there is no reason to confine ourselves to *Mahiṣa* even if such an epithet was known from epigraphic and numismatic records. But, as we have shown above, *Mahiṣa* does not occur in the legend of any Indian coin so far discovered.

1. Rapson, *op. cit.*, pp. 58-59. The name Śātaka applied to the family or clan of Kaḷalāya reminds us of the Sātiya-putra, Satiya-putra or Satika-putra mentioned in Rock Edict II of Aśoka to indicate 'the king of the Sātiya, Satiya or Satika people' and of the Śāntikas mentioned by Varāhamihira along with the Aparānta and Haihaya peoples, and by Parāśara (*Bṛhatsaṁhitā*, XIV. 20 and Utpala's commentary).

2. For *Rāṣṭrakūṭa*, see *Ep. Ind.*, Vol. XXV, pp. 25 ff., and for *Rāṣṭrin* the same as *Rāṣṭrika*=Prakrit *Raṭhika*, see *ibid.*, Vol. I, pp. 1 ff.

3. Cf. *Rāṣṭra-grāma-mahattara* (*Ind. Ant.*, Vol. V, pp. 114 ff.).

4. For the coin of a *Mahāgrāmika*, see *JNSI*, Vol. XXII, pp. 168 ff., and below, pp. 140 ff.

5. For coins issued by a *Mahātalavara* or *Talavara* whose name ended in *saha* (*i.e. sīha*=Sanskrit *siṁha*), see *JNSI*, Vol. XV, pp. 117 ff.

APPENDIX

I

COINS OF CUṬUKULA OF THE SAGAMA DYNASTY

Type I.—Elephant : : Ujjayinī Symbol;[1] *Copper*

Obverse :—Elephant with uplifted trunk to right ; *Svastika* above the back of the elephant ; legend around in thick characters : *Sagamāna Mahās[enāpatisa]...*

Reverse :—Ujjayinī symbol with orbs having each a pellet in double circle; *Svastika* between each pair of orbs.

1. [Hurmuz Kaus, Hyderabad : *IHQ*, Vol. XXII, p. 34, Plate at p. 35, figure A; *Numismatic Series*, No. 3, Plate II, figure b-2.]

Size—squarish, 1″×·9″; Weight—130 grains ; Legend—*...gamana Maha[se]...*

2. [Hurmuz Kaus, Hyderabad: *IHQ*, Vol. XXII, p. 34, Plate at p. 35, figure B; *Numismatic Series*, No. 3, Plate II, figure b-1.]

Size—rectangular, .95″ × ·75″ (thick); Weight—180 grains; Legend—*Sagamāna [Ma]*... There is a six-peaked hill symbol near the end of the elephant's tail.[2]

Type II.—Svastika[3] : : *Thunderbolt and Arrow ; Lead and Copper*

Obverse :—*Svastika* and legend around : *Mahāsenāpatisa Bharadaji-putasa Sagamāna Cuṭukasa* (or *Cuṭukulasa*).

Reverse :—In pellet border, thunderbolt with arrow pointed downwards on right or left.

Variety A-1 : Lead, Squarish

Class I : Issuer's name—*Cuṭu...*

1. [Hyderabad Museum (from the Kondapur excavations) : *JNSI*, Vol. XII, p. 90, Plate VIII, No. 2 ; *Numismatic Series*, No. 8, p. 1, Plates I-II, No. 1.]

Size—.9″×·8″; Weight—115 grains; Legend—*... [ha]-sanapatisa Bharadaji-putasa Sagamāna Cu[ṭu]...*; arrow to the left of the thunderbolt.

2. [Hyderabad Museum (from the Kondapur excava-

1. The Ujjayinī symbol connects this type with Type III below.
2. The symbol has been wrongly regarded by Mirashi as the word *raṁño*.
3. The *Svastika* connects this type with Type III below

tions) : *JNSI*, *loc. cit.*, No. 4; *Numismatic Series*, *loc. cit.*, No. 3.]

Size—.8″×.75″; Weight—128 grains ; Legend—...... *Bharadaja-patasa Sagamana*...; arrow probably to the left of the thunderbolt.

3. [Hyderabad Museum (from the Kondapur excavations) : *JNSI*, *loc. cit.*, No. 5; *Numismatic Series*, *loc. cit.*, No. 4.]

Size—.75″×.75″; Weight—112 grains ; Legend—...*tasa Bharadaja-putasa Sagamāna*...; arrow to the right of the thunderbolt.

Class II : Issuer's name—*Cuṭuka*.

4. [Hyderabad Museum (from the Kondapur excavations) : *JNSI*, *loc. cit.*, No. 3; *Numismatic Series*, *loc. cit.*, No. 2.]

Size—.9″×.65″;[1] Weight—77 grains; Legend—...[*ta*]*sa* [*Bha*]*radaja-putasa Sagamāna Cuṭu*[*kasa*] ; arrow to the right of the thunderbolt.

5. [Hyderabad Museum (from the Kondapur excavations) : *JNSI*, *loc. cit.*, No. 8; *Numismatic Series*, *loc. cit.*, No. 7.]

Size—.7″×.7″; Weight—80 grains; Legend—*Mahāsena*-[*patisa*]...[*puta*]*sa Sagamana Caṭakasa* ; arrow to the left of the thunderbolt.

Variety B-1 : Lead, Round—big; Issuer's name—*Cuṭukula*.

1. [Hyderabad Museum (from the Kondapur excavations) : *JNSI*, *loc. cit.*, No. 6; *Numismatic Series*, *loc. cit.*, No. 5.]

Size—1.8″ in diameter ; Weight—458 grains; Legend—*Mahāsenāpatasa* [*Bharada*]*ja-pata*[*sa*] *Sagamana Cūṭakūlasa*; the arrow is obliterated.

2. [Hyderabad Museum (from the Kondapur excavations) : *JNSI*, Vol. XV, p. 115, Plate VI, Nos. 1-2.]

Size—1.7″ in diameter; Weight—666 grains; Legend—*Mahāsenāpatisa Bharadaja-putasa Sagamāna Cuṭukulasa*.

Variety B-2 : Copper, Round—small; Issuer's name—lost.

1. [Hyderabad Museum (from the Kondapur excavations): *JNSI*, Vol. XII, p. 90, Plate VIII, No. 9; *Numismatic Series*, No. 8, p. 1, Plates I-II, No. 8.]

Size—.8″ in diameter; Weight—80 grains; Legend—...[*Bha*] *radaja-putasa Sa* [*ga*]...; arrow to the left of the thunderbolt.

1. The size is quoted by Mirashi differently as .95″×.85″ in *JNSI*, Vol. XII, p. 90. It is difficult to say which of the two quotations is correct.

Type III.—Svastika : : Ujjayinī Symbol;[1] *Lead, Round*

Obverse :—*Svastika* and partially preserved legend around : ... [*sa*] *Bharadaja-putasa* [*Sagamā*]*na*...

Reverse :—Ujjayinī symbol as on Type 1, but with crescent above.

1. [Hyderabad Museum (from the Kondapur excavations) : *JNSI, loc. cit.*, No. 7; *Numismatic Series, loc. cit.*, No. 6.]

Size—.75″ in diameter; Weight—115 grains.

Type IV.—Lion : : Ten-peaked Hill;[2] *Lead, Round*

Obverse :—Lion[3] to right with tail hanging down; *Svastika* above the back of the lion ; symbol looking like tree-in-railing to the left of the *Svastika*; Legend—*Ma*[*hasa*]...

Reverse :—In double-lined square, ten-peaked hill with a dot in each of the curves surmounted by a crescent which is flanked by what looks like ploughs.

1. [Hyderabad Museum (from the Maski excavations): *JNSI*, Vol. XI, p. 2, Plate II, No. 10; *Numismatic Series*, No. 3; p. 3, Plate II, figure a-2.]

Size—1.05″ in diameter; Weight—210 grains ; Legend —*Maha*[*sa*]...[4]

II

COINS NOT ASSIGNABLE TO CHUṬUKA-CHUṬUKULA

Type V.—Lion : : Ujjayinī Symbol;[5] *Lead, Roundish*

1. The *Svastika* connects this type with Type II and the Ujjayinī symbol with Type I above.

2. The lion connects this type with Type V while the ten-peaked hill reminds us of the six-peaked hill on the reverse of Type VI, although the issuers of Types V-VI cannot be regarded as members of the Sagama dynasty without further evidence.

3. Mirashi regards the animal as a horse.

4. Mirashi reads : *s*[*i*]*r*[*i*]...*yasasa Mahasasa* and assigns the coin to a person named ...yaśaḥ or Yaśa of the so-called Mahiṣa dynasty.

5. The lion connects this type with Type V while the ten-peaked hill reminds us of the six-peaked hill on the reverse of Type VI, although the issuers of Types V-VI cannot be regarded as members of the Sagama dynasty without further evidence as already indicated in note 2 above.

Obverse :—Lion with upraised tail to left; legend above—*Maharaṭhisa* (?)...

Reverse :—Ujjayinī symbol with a pellet in each orb.

1. [Hyderabad Museum (from the Kondapur excavations) : *JNSI*, Vol. XI, Plate II, p. 1; No. 9; *Numismatic Series*, No. 3, p. 1, Plate II, figure a-1.]

Size—.75″ in diameter; Weight—72.5 grains.

Type VI.—Crescent : : Six-peaked Hill ; Lead, Roundish

Obverse :—Crescent. Legend (to be read from the outer side) around—...*sivalasa*[2] *maha*...[3]

Reverse :—Similar to the reverse device of Type IV ; but the hill is six-peaked.

1. [Hurmuz Kaus, Hyderabad : *JNSI*, Vol. XV, p. 120, Plate VI, Nos. 6-7.]

Size—85″ in diameter; Weight—54 grains.

III

COINS OF MAHĀRĀṢṬRIN CUṬUKULA

Among the coins in the Hyderabad Museum, of which plaster-casts were examined by me, there is one bearing the standing lion on the obverse and the tree-in-railing and Ujjayinī symbols on the reverse as well as the legend *Mahāraṭhisa Cuṭukulasa* (Sanskrit *Mahārāṣṭriṇaḥ Cuṭukulasya*),' [This coin is] of *Mahārāṣṭrin* Cuṭukula'. From the specimen examined, it is not possible to say whether an expression like *Sagamāna* has been cut off before *Mahāraṭhisa.* Therefore, in the present state of our knowledge, it is difficult to determine whether *Mahārāṣṭrin* Cuṭukula of this coin is identical with *Mahāsenāpati* Bhāradvājī-putra Cuṭuka or Cuṭukula of the Sagama dynasty, whose coins have been discussed above. The identification is, however, not totally precluded by the difference in the official designations *Mahārāṣṭrin* and *Mahāsenāpati* since the same person often enjoyed more than one such designation and, as we have seen above,

1. Mirashi reads the legend as ...*na Mahasasa* [*sa*] and assigns the coin to the so-called Māna Mahiṣa.

2. The name of the issuer of this is probably not *Śivala* but ends in that expression

3. It is difficult to say whether this stands for *Mahāsenāpati*, *Mahāraṭhi* or any other similar official designation beginning with *mahā*.

a subordinate of Ābhīra Vasuṣeṇa is known from a Nāgārjunikoṇḍa inscription to have enjoyed three official designations at a time, viz. *Mahāgrāmika*, *Mahātalavara* and *Mahādaṇḍanāyaka*. There are innumerable cases of this kind in later inscriptions.

Another coin of a similar type in the same collection bears the imperfect legend *Mahāraṭhisa* ... and may have been issued by *Mahārāṣṭrin* Cuṭukula referred to above. A third coin in the same collection bears the figure of a humped bull on the obverse and the representation of a six-peaked hill, a *Svastika* and the Ujjayinī symbol on the reverse. Only three *akṣaras* of the legend on this coin are clear and they read ...*kalasa*, probably the latter part of the expression *Cuṭukulasa*. It is, however, not possible to say from the specimen at our disposal whether the legend mentioned Cuṭukula as *Mahāsenāpati* or as *Mahārāṣṭrin*.

Type I.—Lion to left : Ujjayinī Symbol, etc.; Lead

Obverse :—In incused area, lion with upraised tail standing to left ; circular legend—*Mahāraṭhisa Cuṭukulasa*.

Reverse :—In a square enclosure, symbols, of which only three are seen on the flan, viz. a zig-zag line, above which on the left is an Ujjayinī symbol with a dot in each orb and, on the right, a tree-in-railing.

1. [Hyderabad Museum]

Size—round, .8 inch in diameter; Weight—not recorded; Legend—[*Mahāra*]*ṭhisa C*[*u*] *ṭukulasa*.

2. [Hyderabad Museum]

Size—round, .9 inch in diameter; Weight—74 grains; Legend—*Maharaṭhi*[*sa*] ...... The reverse is blurred.

Type II.—Bull to left : Ujjayinī Symbol, etc.; Lead

Obverse—In an incuse area, humped bull to left; Legend—...*Cuṭukulasa*.

Reverse :—In a square enclosure, six-peaked hill, to the left of which is a *Svastika* and, to the right, portion of an Ujjayinī symbol; above the *Svastika* is a partially preserved udefinable symbol.

1. [Hyderabad Museum]

Size—round, .95 inch in diameter; Weight—127.9 grains; Legend (to the right)—...*kalasa*.

CHAPTER VII

COINS OF SEMI-INDEPENDENT RULERS

I

K. N. Puri published his report on the excavations at Rairh in the old Jaipur State, conducted by him during 1938-39. The following note occurs at p. 50 of Puri's work entitled *Excavations at Rairh* : "*Senāpati Coins.*—(Pl. XXVI, 6-8). A group of six coins (5 rectangular and one round) bears the epigraph 'Senāpati Vachāghosa' in early Brāhmī characters of about the 3rd-2nd century B. C. which may be rendered 'of the Commander-in-chief Vachāghosa." The correct reading is however not *Senāpati* but *Senāpatisa*. This is not only the reading of the Plate, but also that of the legend printed at p. 66 of the same work.. The actual reading is therefore *Senāpatisa Vachāghosa,* according to Puri. The author does not suggest the existence of the traces of another *akṣara* after the above, nor would the representations of these coins permit space for any. There is thus a grammatical difficulty in accepting Puri's interpretation of the legend. 'Of the commander-in-chief Vachāghosa' would require *Senāpatisa Vachāghosasa*. *Senāpatisa Vachāghosa* has to be translated 'Of the *Senāpati* Vachāgho,' although Vachāghosa (=Sans. *Vatsaghoṣa*) would have been a beautiful name. Puri appears to be quite confident about the sign for *o*; but the facsimiles of the coins published in his work are not quite helpful for the verification of the reading. The originals may be examined to see if the actual reading of the name is *Vachāgha* (Sanskrit *Vatsārghya*) or *Vachāya* (Sanskrit *Vatsārya*).

As regards, the date of the *Senāpati* coins from Rairh, we do not consider them much earlier than the first century B. C. Again, the said *Senāpati* was probably not merely a commander-in-chief. Superior royal officers like a general were often made governors of a province. Cf., *e.g.*, the case of *Mahāsenāpati* Skandanāga, governor of the Śātavāhanīyāhāra under the Śātavāhana king Puḷumāvi.[1] The appointment of military

1. Cf. Sircar, *The Successors of the Sātavāhanas*, p. 19.

officers as governors of a frontier district or a troubled area, threatened by enemies or rebels, is a recognised practice in all ages. Later feudatory titles like *Mahārāja-Mahāsenāpati*[1] refer to the same custom. It seems that the Rairh coins were issued by a *Senāpati* who was the semi-independent provincial governor of some unknown king. We shall refer below to coins issued by chiefs bearing official designations such as *Mahāsenāpati*, *Mahāgrāmika*, *Talavara* or *Mahātalavara*, *Mahārāṣṭrin*, etc., who seem to have been semi-independent governors of various parts of the Śātavāhana empire, on the decline of the Śātavahanas.

In this connection, Puri has pointed to the same title used with the name of Puṣyamitra Śuṅga. The *Mālavikāgnimitra* calls him a *Senāpati* when he was celebrating an Aśvamedha and even when his son Agnimitra was a *Rājan* at Vidiśā. This shows that Kālidāsa in the 4th-5th century A. D. knew Puṣyamitra only as a *Senāpati* and not as a *Rājan*. The suggestion is most eloquently supported by the Ayodhyā inscription,[1] palaeographically assignable to the close of the first century B. C., as therein a person closely related to Puṣyamitra calls him *Senāpati* and *dvir-aśvamedha-yājin*, but not a *Rājan*. Again the *Harivaṁśa* probably refers to Puṣyamitra as a *Senānī*[2] which is the same as *Senāpati*. These facts appear to show that, whatever be the reason, Puṣyamitra never assumed any royal title.[3] He possibly posed to have been merely the *Senāpati* of a Maurya king even after he became the supreme ruler of the empire of the Later Mauryas, although the suggestion does not totally agree with all the traditions that have come down to us about the founder of the Śuṅga royal family.

II

In a small note appearing in the *Journal of the Numismatic Society of India*,[4] V. V. Mirashi published four lead coins which he attributed to a king named Sumahāgrāmaka. The coins are stated to have been discovered in the course of excavations at Kondapur, a village in the Kalabgur Taluk of the Medak District of the old Hyderabad State and Mirashi received them

1. Sircar, *Select Inscriptions*, p. 96.
2. Sircar, *Suc. Sāt.*, p. 349.
3. Cf. *JNSI*, Vol. IV, p. 16, note 1.
4. Vol. XII. 1950, pp. 92-93 and Plate V.

from Khwaja Muhammad Ahmed, then Director of Archaeology, Hyderabad. A similar note on the coins was also published by Mirashi in the *Numismatic Series*, No. 7, 'Coins of King Sumahāgrāmaka from Kondapur Excavations', Hyderabad Museum, 1950, pp. 1-2 and Plate.

The coins are roundish in shape (1" or 1.05" in diameter). The weight of the four coins is recorded as—162, 214, 168 and 142 grains. They have a *Svastika* on the obverse with a *ha*-like symbol above and the legend running round it. Of the symbols on the reverse which is more or less rubbed off on all the specimens, only traces of the Ujjayinī symbol are noticed in some cases. The legend is only partially preserved because the flans of the coins were smaller than the die.

The preserved portions of the incomplete legend were read on the four specimens as follows :

(1) *Samahagāma[kasa]*,
(2) *Mahagāmakasa ma[ha]*,
(3) *[Sa]mahagāma*, and
(4) *Samaha..*

The characters of the legend were assigned to the third century A. D. in the note published in the journal and to the second or third century A. D. in the *Numismatic Series*, No. 7.

The legend *Samahagāmakasa maha*, as made out by Mirashi, was taken by him to stand for Sanskrit *Sumahāgrāmakasya maha*... and translated as '[This coin is] of Sumahāgrāmaka Maha...' He discussed the question whether the concluding letters of the legend can be read as *Mahasa* (Sanskrit *Mahiṣa*) and whether the issuer could have belonged to the Mahiṣa dynasty, the existence of which was inferred from the legend on certain other coins read and interpreted by him as *Saga-Māna-Mahasa[sa*]* (Sanskrit *Śaka-Māna-Mahiṣasya*), '[This coin is] of Śaka Māna of the Mahiṣa dynasty'. But he expressed his doubt that the letter after *maha* at the end of the legend on the second of the four Kondapur coins, referred to above, may not be *sa*.

While expressing our doubts about the ascription of the coins to a king named Sumahāgrāmaka, we had occasion to suggest the reading *Maṭhari-putasa* (Sanskrit *Māṭharī-putrasya*) for what has been read by Mirashi as *maha*... at the end of the legend on the Kondapur coin in question.[1] Mirashi, however,

1. *JNSI*, Vol. XVIII, p. 10.

complained that we merely expressed our doubt about the existence of king Sumahāgrāmaka, but did not offer any constructive suggestion. Thus he says, "Dr. Sircar does not explain how he would explain *Samahagāmaka*. Is it a territorial designation ? Have we come across a similar one anywhere else ? In the absence of any clue to the correct interpretation of this legend, why not take it tentatively as a coin of Sumahāgrāmaka, though the name may appear rather queer ?"[1]

Our difficulty was that we were not prepared to go far without examining the coins to our satisfaction. Recently we had an opportunity of examining some plaster-casts of the coins in the Hyderabad Museum, a study of which enables us to offer our suggestion regarding the reading and interpretation of the legend on the Kondapur coins.

On a careful examination of the illustrations and casts of the Kondapur coins in question, we find that the legend reads: *Mahagāmakasa Maṭhari-putasa ...sa* (Sanskrit *Mahāgrāmikasya Māṭharī-putrasya ...sya*), '[This coin is] of *Mahāgrāmika* Māṭharī-putra ...'. Unfortunately the personal name of the issuer of the coins, who enjoyed the official title *Mahāgrāmika* and the metronymic *Māṭharī-putra* (i. e. the son of a lady born in a family belonging to the Māṭhara *gotra*), is not preserved in any of the specimens.

The official designation *Mahāgrāmika* (literally, 'the great *Grāmika* or head of a village', i. e. 'a chief of the *Grāmikas*') occurs in early South Indian records. Thus the Nāgārjunikoṇḍa inscription of the time of Ābhīra Vasuṣeṇa mentions Kauśikī-putra Śivaśepa of the Peribiḍeha family as enjoying the designations *Mahāgrāmika*, *Mahātalavara* and *Mahādaṇḍanāyaka*,[2] while *Grāmika* meaning 'the head of a village' is well known from numerous instances of its occurrence in epigraphic and literary sources. The expression *Mahāgrāmika* means an officer having jurisdiction over a territorial unit called a *mahāgrāma* or a group of villages each under a *Grāmika*. We know of the use of the word *mahāgrāma* or *grāmāhāra* in early South Indian inscriptions. Thus an inscription of Kadamba Bhogivarman (sixth century A. D.) mentions Tagare-mahāgrāma

1. *Ibid.*, p. 123.
2. *Indian Archaeology*, 1958-59, p. 8; *Ep. Ind.*, Vol. XXXIV, p. 197.

which consisted of twenty-four *pallīs* and was situated in the Tagare *viṣaya* (district),[1] while the *grāmāhāra* of Sahalāṭavī consisting of twelve villages is mentioned in an earlier inscription.[2] *Mahāgrāma* was thus the subdivision of a district, another name for which was *rāṣṭra* as known from South Indian records. We have the *Rāṣtrakūṭa*, 'head of a *rāṣṭra*', an expression coined on the analogy of *Grāmakūṭa*, 'head of a village', in numerous inscriptions.[3] Some other official designations of a similar import are *Rāṣṭramahattara*, *Rāṣṭrin* and *Rāṣṭrika*.[4]

The issue of coins by a subordinate ruler who was the governor of the subdivision of a district is well known from other instances offered by early South Indian numismatics. As we have already seen, there are coins[5] bearing the legend *Sadakana Kaḻalāya-mahāraṭhisa* (Sanskrit *Śātakānāṁ Kaḻalāya-mahārāṣṭriṇaḥ*), '[This coin is] of the *Mahārāṣṭrin* Kaḻalāya of the Śātaka clan or family'. The designation *Mahārāṣṭrin* (literally, 'the great *Rāṣṭrin*', i. e. 'a chief of the *Rāṣṭrins*') is derived from *Rāṣṭrin*, i. e. the ruler of a *rāṣṭra* which, as indicated above, was the subdivision of a district or a territorial unit consisting of a group of villages, similar to a *mahāgrāma*. It appears that the *Mahāgrāmika* who issued the coins under study and the other issuers of coins bearing subordinate titles were ruling semi-independently when the Śātavāhana power was fast declining.[6]

In this connection, we may also refer to the coins issued by persons enjoying the official designation *Mahāsenāpati* (literally, 'the great *Senāpati* or commander of forces,' *i. e.* 'a chief of the *Senāpatis*') who was probably the military governor of a district or a subdivision. Mirashi published some coins on which the legend has been read and interpreted by him as *Mahāsenāpatisa Bharadaja-putasa Saga-Māna-Cuṭu-kulasa* (Sans-

1. *The Successors of the Sātavāhanas*, p. 305.
2. *Ibid.*, pp. 249-50.
3. See, *e. g.*, the Ellora plates of Dantidurga (*Ep. Ind.*, Vol. XXV, pp. 25 ff.).
4. *Rāṣṭrika* occurs as *Raṭhika* in Prakrit epigraphs, *e. g.*, the Hirahadagalli plates (*Ep. Ind.*, Vol. I, pp. 1 ff.). For *Rāṣṭramahattara*, cf. the passage *Rāṣṭra-grāma-mahattara* in the Kavi plates (*Ind. Ant.*, Vol. V, pp. 114 ff.). For *Rāṣṭrin*, see below.
5. Rapson, *Catalogue of the Coins of the Andhra Dynasty*, etc., pp. 57-58.
6. For coins issued by a *Talavara* or *Mahātalavara*, see *JNSI*, Vol. XV, pp. 117-19.

krit *Mahāsenāpateḥ Bharadvāja-putrasya Śaka-Māna-Cūṭu-kulasya*). '[This coin is] of *Mahāsenāpati* Bharadvāja-putra Māna, the Śaka, who belongs to the Chuṭu family.'[1] As we have already suggested, the correct reading of what had been read as *Bhara-daja* is *Bharadaji* (Sanskrit *Bhāradvājī*)[2] while the interpretation of *Saga-Māna-Cuṭukula* as 'Śaka Māna of the Cuṭu family' is unconvincing.[3] We have also shown that the legend may stand for Sanskrit *Mahāsenāpateḥ Bhāradvājī-putrasya Saṅgamānāṁ* (or *Saṅgrāmāṇāṁ*) *Cuṭukulasya*, '[This coin is] of *Mahāsenāpati* Bhāradvājī-putra Cuṭukula (the Sanskritised form of a Dravidian personal name) belonging to the Saṅgama or Saṅgrāma dynasty'. In the same connection, we have also tried to prove that what Mirashi has read on some coins of the same person as *Saga-Māna-Mahasa*[*sa**] and interpreted as *Śaka-Māna-Mahiṣasya*, '[This coin is] of the Śaka [king] Māna of the Mahiṣa dynasty', really stands for *Sagamāna Mahā-senāpatisa*, Sanskrit *Saṅgamānāṁ* (or *Saṅgrāmaṇāṁ*) *Mahā-senāpateḥ* ..., '[This coin is] of *Mahāsenapati* ... belonging to the Saṅgama or Saṅgrāma dynasty'.[4]

In any case, it is clear that there is no basis for the existence of a king named Sumahāgrāmaka just as the theory regarding the rule of a Śaka-Mahiṣa dynasty over the southern parts of the old Hyderabad State is based on the erroneous reading and interpretation of certain coin-legends.

1. *JNSI*, Vol. XV, pp. 115 ff.
2. *Ibid.*, Vol. XVIII, p. 7.
3. *Ibid.*, p. 8.
4. See *Ep. Ind.*, Vol. XXXV, pp. 69 ff.; above, pp. 126 ff.

Chapter VIII

DATE OF ĪŚVARADATTA'S COINS

Mahākṣatrapa Īśvaradatta issued silver coins of the same type as those of the Śaka *Kṣatrapas* and *Mahākṣatrapas* of Western India with dates in his regnal reckoning instead of the Śaka era. His coins issued in his first and second regnal years are known and he apparently ruled for a short time (nearly two years or a little above one year) over the Śaka dominions as a usurper. There is difference of opinion among scholars as to the period to which Īśvaradatta's rule should be assigned.

Bhagawanlal Indraji believed that Īśvaradatta began to rule in 249 A. D. and founded the Traikūṭaka-Kalacuri-Cedi era starting from that year.[1] The suggestion was based on the fact that, when he wrote, no coin of the Śaka *Mahākṣatrapas*, from Śaka 171 (249 A. D.) to 176 (254 A. D.), was known.

Rapson later pointed out that there was no such break in the continuity of the coins issued by the Śaka *Mahākṣatrapas* between Śaka 171 and 176.[2] On the other hand, he observed that the treatment of the eye in Īśvaradatta's portrait on his coins prevailed during the period *c.* Śaka 127-70 (205-48 A. D.), that the resemblance of the portrait is strongest to those of Vīradāman, Yaśodāman I and Vijayasena who flourished between Śaka 156 (234 A.D.) and 172 (250 A. D.) and that the form of the letter *kṣa* in Īśvaradatta's coin legend is later than Śaka 130 (208 A. D.) while the rounded shape of *pa* is earlier than about Śaka 160 (238 A. D.). Rapson was therefore inclined to place Īśvaradatta's rule in the gap between Śaka 158 (236 A. D.), the last recorded date of *Mahākṣatrapa* Dāmasena, and Śaka 161 (239 A. D.), the earliest date of *Mahākṣatrapa* Yaśodāman I as known to him.

D. R. Bhandarkar, while discussing the Sarvania hoard of Śaka coins supplying the date Śaka 160 (238 A. D.) for *Mahākṣatrapa* Yaśodāman I, commented on Rapson's arguments regarding the palaeography of Īśvaradatta's coin legend, his

1. *JRAS*, 1890, p. 657.
2. *Catalogue*, pp. cxxxv f., 136-39.

portrait on the coins and the treatment of the eye in it.[1] He was inclined to place Īśvaradatta's rule between Śaka 110 (188 A. D.) and 113 (191 A. D.) since, according to Rapson, *Mahākṣatrapa* Rudrasiṁha I issued during the said period coins with the humbler title *Kṣatrapa* in Śaka 110 and 112. The humiliation of Rudrasiṁha I in the period in question was suppossed by Rapson to be due to the usurpation of power by Jīvadāman,[2] but by Bhandarkar to that by Īśvaradatta.[3] It has, however, to be admitted that Īśvaradatta, who issued coins in his first and second regnal years, may have ruled for a little over one year only and that this period may well be accommodated between Śaka 158 and 160 (236-38 A. D.).

P. L. Gupta has recently drawn our attention to a coin issued by Rudrasiṁha I as *Mahākṣatrapa* in Śaka 112 (190 A. D.)[4] and he considers the reading *Kṣatrapa* on the coins of that year by Rapson as doubtful.[5] He further suggests that the title *Kṣatrapa* found on a few coins of Rudrasiṁha I issued in Śaka 110 (188 A. D.) may have been due to the engraver's error and not to any reduction in the status of the ruler. It has, however, to be pointed out that, even accepting the date as read by Gupta, it is possible to accommodate Īśvaradatta's rule of a little over one year about Śaka 111 (189 A. D.) as suggested by Bhandarkar.

Gupta's own solution of the problem is simple. He refers to the Uparkot, Sarvania and Sonepur hoards, in which Īśvaradatta's coins were found, and to the Vasoj, Junagadh, Sanchi, Gondarmau and Karad hoards which do not contain any coin of that ruler, and concludes : "Now, his (Īśvaradatta's) coins are found in three hoards all of which include the coins of Svāmi-Rudrasena III. The two hoards, which include his coins for the first year only, have the latest coins of Svāmi-Rudrasena III, dated 273, and the hoard that includes the coin of the second year has the coins of Svāmi-Rudrasena III for the years from 284 to 301 also. Sanchi and Gondarmau hoards also have the coins of Svāmi-Rudrasena III; but in them his latest known

1. *ASIAR*, 1913-14, p. 229.
2. *Op. cit.*, p. cxxiv.
3. *Op. cit.*, p. 230.
4. *JNSI*, Vol. XVII, p. 94.
5. *JBBRAS*, Vol. XXX, 1955, p. 52.

dates are 272 and 270 respectively. The absence of Īśvaradatta's coins from these hoards suggests that his coins had not come in existence at least till 272. They came in existence in 273 or a little later. These facts, if viewed properly, unmistakably suggest that Īśvaradatta ousted Svāmi-Rudrasena III in 273 or a little later and usurped his entire dominion. This menace caused panic among the people and they buried their treasures during the beginning of Īśvaradatta's reign. This is well supported by the fact that we do not possess any coin of Svāmi-Rudrasena III after 273 till the year 284."[1]

Unfortunately Gupta, who is inclined to place Īśvaradatta more than a century later than the period suggested by Indraji, Rapson and Bhandarkar, has totally ignored Rapson's arguments not only about the portraiture on Īśvaradatta's coins but also about the palaeography of their legends. The consideration of palaeography seems to us to be especially important in this case, since the letters in Īśvaradatta's coin legend are certainly of a date much earlier than those in the legends on the coins of Svāmi-Rudrasena III. Gupta also ignores the fact that the first and second regnal years of Īśvaradatta scarcely fill up the gap between Śaka 273 and 284 (351-62 A. D.) in the reign of Svāmi-Rudrasena III. But the most curious thing is that Gupta has nothing to say about the discovery of hoards in which the coins of Īśvaradatta have been found along with only those of the predecessors Svāmi-Rudrasena III and without a single issue of that ruler.

In a short note entitled 'A List of the Hoards of Silver Coins of the Western Kṣatrapas' published in the *Journal of the Numismatic Society of India*, Vol. XVIII, 1956, pp. 220-21, Gupta himself has referred to one such hoard. Of the three hoards mentioned in this note in addition to the eight referred to in his paper on *Mahākṣatrapa* Īśvaradatta referred to above, the one from Shirwal near Junīr was noticed in the *Journal of the Bombay Branch of the Royal Asiatic Society*. Vol. II, 1844-47 (July 1847), pp. 377-80, by John Stevenson. This hoard contains some coins of Īśvaradatta, but none of Svāmi-Rudrasena III. The latest Śaka coins in it are those issued by *Kṣatrapa* Rudrasiṁha II who was the son of Svāmi-Jīvadāman and whose coins bear

1. *Op. cit.*, p. 55.

dates ranging between Śaka 227 (305 A. D.) and 238 (316 A.D.), although coins attributed by Stevenson to *Kṣatrapa* Agadāman, son of *Kṣatrapa* Rudrasaha, may really belong to *Kṣatrapa* Yaśodāman II (Śaka 238-54=316-32 A.D), son of Rudrasiṁha II.[1] The earliest coins of the hoard appear to belong to *Mahākṣatrapa* Vijayasena (Śaka 162-72=240-50 A. D.), son of *Mahākṣatrapa* Dāmasena. Similar is the case with the recently discovered Peṭlūripālem hoard.[2]

This hoard was discovered by a peasant while digging the earth at the village of Peṭlūripālem in the Narasaraopet Taluk in the Guntur District of Andhra Pradesh. The hoard consists of 238 silver coins of the Śakas of Western India from *Kṣatrapa* Vīradāman (Śaka 156-60= 234-38 A.D.) to Yaśodāman II (Śaka 238-54=316-32 A.D.) with only one of Īśvaradatta and a few badly preserved and unattributable pieces. It will be seen that the latest Śaka coins of the hoard are those belonging to *Kṣatrapa* Yaśodāman II who flourished in Śaka 238-54 (316-32 A. D.).

It has to be noticed that the Shirwal hoard offers Īśvaradatta's coins along with Śaka coins of the period between the rule of *Mahākṣatrapa* Vijayasena (Śaka 162-72=240-50 A.D.) and of Rudrasiṁha II (Śaka 227-38=305-16 A.D.) or Yaśodāman II (Śaka 238-54=316-32 A.D.) while in the Peṭlūripālem hoard his coin is found along with the issues of Śaka rulers from Vīradāman (Śaka 156-60=234-38 A. D.) down to Yaśodāman II (Śaka 238-58=316-32 A. D.). Hence, if it be believed that Īśvaradatta ruled for a short time about the period represented by the coins found in these two hoards, Rapson's suggestion assigning him to about Śaka 159=237 A. D. would appear to be more reasonable than Bhandarkar's theory placing him about Śaka 111=189 A. D. and Gupta's view assigning his rule to about Śaka 274=352 A. D. Gupta's theory also appears to be wrong, as indicated above, in view of the palaeography of Īśvaradatta's coin-legends, which points to a date much earlier than that of the coins of Svāmi-Rudrasena III.

The real cause of the absence of the coins of Svāmi-Rudra-

1. Cf. Rapson, *op. cit.*, p. 107, note 1.

2. *Annual Report on Indian Epigraphy for the Year* 1956-57, pp.21 ff.; below, pp. 150 ff.

sena III between Śaka 273 and 284 (351-62 A. D.) appears to have been his defeat in the hands of the Gupta emperor Samudragupta (c. 335-76 A. D.) whose Allahabad pillar inscription speaks of his victory over one of the rulers of Āryāvarta named Rudradeva who was very probably the Śaka ruler Svāmi-Rudrasena III of Western India.[1] As we have suggested elsewhere, the Śakas of Western India appears to have been subdued by Samudragupta, but that they threw off the Gupta yoke after about a decade and were finally extirpated by Candragupta II Vikramāditya, son of Samudragupta, about the close of the fourth century.

There is a general belief among the Indian students of numismatics that hoards of coins were interred in ancient India only when there was a political unrest in the country and Gupta seems to be a subscriber to this view; but the practice of interring accumulated wealth in cash was common in all parts of ancient and medieval India. It was a popular practice in the villages in many parts of the country as late as the closing years of the last century. The reason is that, on the one hand, there were no Savings Banks in ancient and medieval India as we have now and, on the other, often the lives of the people were insecure and their wealth lay at the mercy of thieves and robbers. Of course the unsocial elements were occasionally kept under check by vigourous and capable rulers.

As regards the hoards of Śaka coins discussed here, one of them was found outside the dominions of the Śakas whose political fortunes might not have much to do with the interment of the coins.

1. *Proc. IHC*, Madras, 1944, pp. 78 ff. Cf. the Yādava king Rāmacandra's name sometimes quoted as Rāma, Rāmadeva and Rāmarāja (Rāmrāy). See *Ep. Ind.*, Vol. XXV, pp. 221, 223; Vol. XXXV, p. 51; etc.

Chapter IX

PEṬLŪRIPĀLEM HOARD

The hoard, consisting of a large number of silver coins belonging to the Western Kṣatrapa dynasties, came from the village of Peṭlūripālem in the Narasaraopet Taluk of the Guntur District, Andhra Pradesh. The coins were originally discovered in a copper urn by a superstitious peasant who abandoned them when the vessel containing them disintegrated in an attempt to raise it from the ground. They were later picked up by cowherds from whom, on receipt of information relating to the find, the police recovered, under the Treasure Trove Act, 238 coins in three lots of 52, 16 and 170 pieces. At my request, J. P. L. Gwynn, then Collector of Guntur, kindly placed the entire lot of 238 coins at my disposal for examination in 1957.

It is interesting to note that all the coins of the Peṭlūripālem hoard belong to the *Kṣatrapas* and *Mahākṣatrapas* of Western India, though the hoard has been discovered far away from their dominions. As will be seen below, the coins of the hoard were issued by rulers who flourished between 234 and 332 A.D. and this is the period when the Ikṣvākus were ruling over the Guntur region from their capital at Vijayapurī in the Nāgārjunikoṇḍa valley. We know that the Ikṣvākus were matrimonially related to the Śakas of Western India. One of the queens of Ikṣvāku Vīrapuruṣadatta (second half of the third century A. D.) was Rudradharabhaṭṭārikā, daughter of the *Mahārāja* of Ujjayinī, while king Ehuvala Śāntamūla (close of the third and the first half of the fourth century A. D.), son of Vīrapuruṣadatta, married Varmabhaṭā, daughter of a *Mahākṣatrapa* belonging to the Bṛhatphala *gotra*.[1] It is also known that the Ikṣvāku kingdom was occupied by the Ābhīra king Vasuṣeṇa of Western India for a short time in the latter half of the third century A.D.[2] But these facts do not clearly explain the discovery of a hoard of exclusively West Indian coins in the Ikṣvāku domi-

1. See *The Successors* of the *Sātavāhanas*, pp. 22-23; *Ep. Ind.*, Vol. XXXIV, p. 21.
2. *Ep. Ind.*, Vol. XXXIV, pp. 196 ff.

nions. It seems that an inhabitant of Peṭlūripalem lived for some time in the Śaka dominions for trade or for service and returned home with his earnings, though he died before he had an opportunity to utilise the amount. It is also possible that a West Indian trader went to Peṭlūripālem in connection with his business, but died there before finishing his work.[1] The interment of the hoard may be explained by some local trouble like the Pallava threat or, more probably, the almost chronic insecurity of movable property from the menace of burglars and dacoits in the age when there was no bank of the modern type as already indicated above.

Three of the coins are so badly damaged that they cannot be identified. Another three (Nos. 233-35) are interesting in that they bear, on both the obverse and the reverse, the bust of the king instead of the usual bust and legend respectively. This was obviously the result of defective minting. Rapson does not appear to have come across any such coin. It seems that, at the time of striking, the coin just struck previously was not removed from the anvil (representing the reverse die), but a coin-blank was placed on it and hammered with the upper obverse die. The second blank would, thus, get on the obverse the normal impression of the obverse die, but, on the reverse, the negative impression of the obverse of the previously struck coin.

The entire hoard consists of only silver coins and the earliest of them belongs to *Kṣatrapa* Vīradāman, son of Dāmasena. This fact corroborates the statement of Rapson that potin coinage was discontinued by the dynasty some time after Śaka 158 (236 A. D.), *i. e.* after the reign of Dāmasena. The weight of the coins varies from 25 to 37½ grains, though a few weigh even 23 grains. These coins were known in ancient India as Rudradāmaka-kārṣāpaṇa. The weight-standard of the coins, based on that of the Graeco-Indian hemi-drachm, was regarded as three-fourths of the Indian silver Kārṣāpaṇa or Purāṇa of 32 *Ratis* or 58.56 grains, *i.e.* 24 *Ratis* or 43.92 grains.[2]

For about two hundred and seventy years, the Western Kṣatrapa rulers faithfully followed the coin-pattern set by Nahapāna who, in his turn, imitated for his coins the hybrid Indian

1. The presence of the Śakas at the Ikṣvāku capital is indicated by the epigraphical and sculptural records discovered at Nāgārjunikoṇḍa (cf. *Ep. Ind.*, Vol. XX, p. 37; *Mem. ASI*, No. 53, Plate X c).

2. *JNSI*, Vol. XIII, pp. 188 ff.; above, pp. 98ff.

drachm of the Graeco-Indian kings in size, weight and fabric. The Western Kṣatrapa coins bear dates from the reign of Jīvadāman, son of Dāmajadaśrī I, the date being recorded in Brāhmī symbols on the obverse behind the king's head. The reverse has the three-peaked hill surmounted by crescent and the star besides the usual legend. This hill device was most probably imitated from the Śātavāhanas and maintained by the members of Caṣṭana's house on their silver issues, the humped bull or the elephant appearing only on their potin issues. Generally, on all the coins, the crescent and the star are placed to the left and right respectively of the three-peaked hill on the reverse. But on a few coins this arrangement is reversed, *i.e.* the crescent is put to the right and the star to the left of the three-peaked hill. This change has been considered as something striking by Rapson, although he has noted that; on some of the coins (Variety B) of *Mahākṣatrapa* Dāmasena and *Kṣatrapa* Dāmajadaśrī II, this irregularity has crept in. In the present collection, this feature is noticed on a coin of *Mahākṣatrapa* Bhartṛdāman, dated in the year 214 (No. 146). It appears that the irregularity was due to a defect in the die. In almost all cases, the legend is written around the reverse design in such a way that the ruling monarch's name ends over the star. But, on the coins bearing the star and crescent in reversed positions, the arangement of the legend is different. A brief account of the coins belonging to different rulers is given below. The irregular features of some of the coins may indicat eancient forgery.

1. Vīradāman (Śaka 156-60=234-38 A. D.).—The earliest coin found in the hoard belongs to Vīradāman who is known to have ruled merely as a *Kṣatrapa*, as all the coins discovered so far attribute to him only this title. On the coins of his son Rudrasena II also, he is styled as *Kṣatrapa*. Only three coins of the present hoard belong to him (Nos. 1-3) and they bear the dates Śaka 150 + and 157.

2. Īśvaradatta.—Only one coin (No. 4), issued in his first regnal year, belongs to Īśvaradatta often supposed to have belonged to the Ābhīra race. From his assumption of the full royal title *Mahākṣatrapa*, he has to be regarded as having temporarily superseded Śaka rule. Rapson was inclined to place Īśvaradatta's rule sometime about Śaka 159, while D. R. Bhandarkar

assigns it to about Śaka 111 as we have seen above.[1] The date behind the bust of the king on the obverse of the coin is missing.

3. Vijayasena (Śaka 160-72=238-50 A. D.)—Altogether thirteen coins (Nos. 5-17) belong to Vijayasena, son of *Mahākṣatrapa* Dāmasena and they range in date between Śaka 162 and 172. Vijayasena's coins may be singled out for their beautiful execution and careful representation of the characters in the legend. All the thirteen coins were issued by the ruler as *Mahākṣatrapa*, the earliest of them probably bearing the date Śaka 162 (No. 5). No. 15 seems to be dated in Śaka 172, in which year his reign is believed to have terminated.

4. Dāmajadaśrī III (Śaka 172 or 173 to 176=250 or 251 to 254 A. D.).—To *Mahākṣatrapa* Dāmajadaśrī III, son of *Mahākṣatrapa* Dāmasena and brother of *Mahākṣatrapa* Vijayasena, belong altogether 11 coins (Nos. 18-28). On all these specimens, Dāmajadaśrī, like Vijayasena, is described as *Mahākṣatrapa*.

On two coins (Nos. 29-30), probably belonging to Dāmajadaśrī III, the name of the ruler who issued them is not traceable. The ruler himself was a *Mahākṣatrapa* and the son of *Mahākṣatrapa* Dāmasena. The date portion of one coin is damaged. On the other, two symbols out of the three may tentatively be read as 100+50+x= or 100+70+x. We know that *Kṣatrapa* Vīradāman, son of *Mahākṣatrapa* Dāmasena, ruled between Śaka 156 and 160. If the reading of the date is 100+50+x, then it cannot belong to any son of *Mahākṣatrapa* Dāmasena other than Vīradaman. But Vīradāman is not known to have ruled as *Mahākṣatrapa* and, even on the coins of his son Rudrasena II, he is simply styled as *Kṣatrapa*.

5. Rudrasena II (Śaka 176?-196=256?-274 A. D.).—A good number of coins, fiftythree (Nos. 31-83) in all, belong to *Mahākṣatrapa* Rudrasena II, son of *Kṣatrapa* Vīradāman. Rudrasena II succeeded his uncle Dāmajadaśrī III sometime between Śaka 176 and 179. He also ruled as a *Mahākṣatrapa*. Though a large number of coins were issued by him, in most of the issues, the date cannot be read satisfactorily. The earliest date recorded on his coins in the hoard under study may be

1. For discussions on the problems of Īśvaradatta's date, see *JBBRAS*, Vol. XXX, 1955, pp. 52 ff.; *IHQ*, Vol. XXXIII, pp. 269-74; above, pp. 145 ff.

176 (No. 34) and the latest 196 (No. 76). On his coins Nos. 35-37, the numerical symbol for 70 appears without a loop below. Nos. 84-85, though no name can be traced on them, may be assigned to Rudrasena II in view of the dates.

6. Viśvasiṁha (Śaka 199-200+x=277-278+x A. D.).—Viśvasiṁha succeeded his father Rudrasena II. He is always represented on the coins as Vi (or Vī) śvasīha. The names of thetwo rulers Viśvasiṁha and Viśvasena are writen in such a way that only the mention of their father helps us to identify the ruler correctly. The dates on Viśvasiṁha's coins issued as *Mahākṣatrapa* are all damaged. According to Rapson, he might have ruled as *Mahākṣatrapa* from Śaka 201 with his brother Bhartṛdāman ruling as *Kṣatrapa* till Śaka 211 when the latter assumed the office as *Mahākṣatrapa*. In the present hoard, one coin (No. 140) of *Mahākṣatrapa* Bhartṛdāman gives the date clearly as Śaka 210 while, on some other issues of the ruler, the dates, though cut off, bear traces of two symbols which appear to suggest years varying between Śaka 204 and 209. In all, twentysix coins (Nos. 86-111) of the hoard belong to Viśvasiṁha.

7. Bhartṛdāman (Śaka 201-17=279-95 A. D.).—The number of coins of Bhartṛdāman in the present hoard are considerable like those of Rudrasena II. Altogether eighty coins (Nos. 112-91) belong to him. But, in most cases, the dates are cut off. No. 140 was issued by *Mahākṣatrapa* Bhartṛdāman in Śaka 210 and Nos. 133-37 probably in 204. The date on No. 126 issued as *Mahākṣatrapa* looks like 180 although year 180+x actually falls in the reign of his father *Mahākṣatrapa* Rudrasena II. On many of Bhartṛdāman's coins, *ha* in the expression *Mahākṣatrapasa* looks like *na* and once *pa* in *Kṣatrapasa* (No. 158) similarly resembles *na*. On No. 189, *Mahākṣatrapa* Rudrasena, father of Bhartṛdāman, is called *Kṣatrapa*, a fact which is not corroborated by any other evidence. This may have been due to the carelessness of the die-maker. The symbols of the crescent and star are reversed in No. 146 as in variety B of his coins illustrated by Rapson. It should be noted, however, that this coin was issued by Bhartṛdāman as *Mahākṣatrapa*.

On 12 coins (Nos. 192-204), the name of the issuing ruler is missing. From the dates, 210 and 212, tentatively readable on two of the coins (Nos.196, 198), it is possible to suggest that both belong to *Mahākṣatrapa* Bhartṛdāman.

8. Viśvasena (Śaka 214?-226=294-304 A. D.).—In all, twenty coins (Nos. 205-24) belong to Viśvasena who was the son and successor of Bhartṛdāman and ruled as a *Kṣatrapa*. The earliest date recorded on the coins is 216, although the last numerical sign in some cases (Nos. 208-10) may be read as 4 instead of 6. On No. 212 the date 216 is clear. Besides the representation of *ha* in *Mahākṣatrapa* looking like *na*, *kṣa* resembles *kcha* at least in three cases (Nos. 219, 221, 223). On No. 223, *da* in *Bhartṛdāman* looks like *na*.

Three coins (Nos. 225-27) belong to the son of *Mahākṣatrapa* Bhartṛdāman, the name of the ruler being cut off. But one of them possibly bears the date 214 or 216. The coins may therefore be ascribed to Viśvasena.

The name of Bhartṛdāman looks like *Bharatṛapana* on No. 225 and the usual order of the letters in the legend is also changed. No. 228 cannot be ascribed to any particular ruler.

10. Rudrasiṁha II (Śaka 225?-235+x=303-313+x A.D.).—Viśvasena was followed by *Kṣatrapa* Rudrasiṁha II, son of Svāmi-Jīvadāman belonging to a different branch of the Western Kṣatrapa family. Svāmi-Jivadāman bears no royal title. It is not improbable that he was a brother of Bhartṛdāman. Only two coins (Nos. 229-30) may be attributed to Rudrasiṁha II. But the legends on them are worn out and it is difficult to determine whether the reading is *Rudrasahasa* or *Rudrasanasa*. *Va* and *ha* are written like *na* and the arrangement of the letters of the legend on the two coins is changed. Rudrasiṁha II is supposed to have ruled from Śaka 226 or 227. But No. 229 bears a damaged date of which the last digit may be read as 5 (i. e. 225) thus indicating a slightly earlier date for the king.

11. Yaśodāman II (Śaka 238-54=317-32 A. D.).—Yaśodāman, son and successor of Rudrasiṁha II, is represented in the hoard by only two coins (No. 231-32), the date on which may possibly be read as 240. He was a *Kṣatrapa* like his father Rudrasiṁha II. Though the name of Yaśodāman is damaged on No. 232, it may be assigned to him on the basis of the date and the name of the issuer's father. But, as on the coins of Rudrasiṁha II, his father's name looks like *Rudrasana*.

I. *Kṣatrapa* Vīradāman (Śaka 156-60)

1	Śaka [100+50]+x	Silver, round. Size—.6″ (diameter). Weight—32 grains. *Obverse*—Ornamental border of corrupt Greek legend; bust of king to right in the usual close-fitting cap. Date behind head. *Reverse*—Pellet border; hill of 3 peaks surmounted by crescent; beneath—wavy line, left—crescent, right—star of 7 dots. Legend—(II) *rajño Mahakṣatrapasa [D]āmas[e]na-putrasa ra[jñaḥ Kṣatrapasa] V[ī]radāmnaḥ.* Cf. Rapson, *Catalogue*, p. 118, Plate XIII, No. 433.
2	Do.	Do. Weight—32½ grains. *Obverse* and *Reverse*—As on No. 1. Legend : (II) *rajño [Mahā]kṣatrapasa Dāmasanasa putrasa rajñaḥ Kṣatrapa[sa Vī]ra[dām*]na[ḥ*].* Cf. *loc. cit.*
3	Śaka [100+50+7]	Do. Weight—35 grains. *Obverse* and *Reverse*—As on No. 1. Legend : (II) *rajño [Maha]kṣatrapasa Dāmasanasa putrasa rajñaḥ Kṣatrapasa Vīradāmnaḥ.* *A.R.Ep.*, 1956-57, Plate VI, No. 1

II. *Mahākṣatrapa* Īśvaradatta (c. Śaka 159)

4	Regnal Year 1	Do. Weight—30 grains. *Obverse*—As on No. 1; but without date. *Reverse*—As on No. 1; but with star of 6 dots. Legend : (II) *r[ā]jño Mahakṣatrapasa Īśva[ra*]datta[sa] va[r*]ṣe [pra]...* Cf. Rapson, *op. cit.*, p. 124, Plate XIII, No. 473.

III. *Mahākṣatrapa* Vijayasena (Śaka 160-72)

5	Śaka [100+60+2]	Do. Weight—35 grains. *Obverse*—As on No. 1. *Reverse*—Pellet border; symbols blurred ; only star clear. Legend : (II) *rajño Mahakṣatrapasa Damasana-putrasa ra[jño] Maha-[kṣatrapasa] Vijayasenasa.* Cf. *ibid.*, p. 130,Plate XIV,No. 495.
6	Śaka 100+60+4	Do. Weight—30 grains. *Obverse* and *Reverse*—As on No. 1. Legend : (II) *rajño Mahakṣatrapasa Damasena-putrasa rajño Mahakṣatra-pasa Vijayasenasa.* *A. R. Ep.*, 1956-57, Plate VI, No. 2; cf. *Rapson,* p. 132, Plate XIV, No. 508.
7	Śaka 100+60+9	Do. Weight—25 grains. *Obverse*—As on No. 1. *Reverse*—As on No. 5. Legend : (II).........*[sa]na-putrasa rajño Mahakṣatrapasa Vijaya.........* Cf. Rapson, *op. cit.*, p. 134, Plate XIV, No. 534.
8	Do.	Do. Weight—32½ grains. *Obverse* and *Reverse*—As on No. 1. Legend : (II) *rajño Mahakṣatrapasa Damasana-[putrasa] [rā*][jño] Mahakṣatrapasa V[i]ja[yasanasa].* Cf. *loc. cit.*
9	Śaka [100+60+9]	Do. Weight—32½ grains. *Obverse* and *Reverse*—As on No. 1. Legend : (II) *rajño Mahakṣatrapasa Dāmasena-putrasa rajño [Maha]kṣa-tra[pasa ......sanasa].* Cf. *loc. cit.*
10	Do.	Do. Weight—30 grains. *Obverse* and *Reverse*—As on No. 1.

		Legend : (II) *rajño Mahakṣatrapasa Dāmasena-putrasa rajño [Maha]kṣa-trapasa [Vijayasanasa].* Cf. *loc. cit.*
11	Do.	Do. Weight—30 grains. *Obverse* and *Reverse*—As on No. 1. Legend : (II) *rajño Mahakṣatrapasa Damasena-putrasa rajño Mahakṣatra-pasa Vijayasenasa.* *A. R. Ep.*, 1956-57, Plate VI, No. 3.
12	Śaka [100+70+-]+x	Do. Weight—32½ grains. *Obverse* and *Reverse*—As on No. 1. Legend : (II) *rajño Mahakṣatrapasa Damasana-putrasa rajño Mahakṣatra-pasa V[i]jayasanasa.* *A.R.Ep.*, 1956-57, Plate VI, No. 4.
13	Do.	Do. Weight—30 grains. *Obverse*—As on No. 1. *Reverse*—Pellet border; symbols blur-red. Legend : (II) *[ra]jño Mahakṣatra-pasa Damasana-putrasa rajño Maha-kṣatrapasa V[ija]yasanasa.*
14	Śaka [100+70+1]	Do. Weight—35 grains. *Obverse*—As on No. 1. *Reverse*—As on No. 1; but with star of 8 dots. Legend : (II) *rañjo Mahakṣatra......* *......[putrasa] rajño Mahakṣatrapasa Vijayasanasa.* Cf. Rapson, *op. cit.*, p. 136, Plate XIV, No. 551.
15	Śaka [100+70+2]	Do. Weight—32½ grains. *Obverse* and *Reverse*—As on No. 1. Legend : (II) *rajño Mahakṣatrapasa*

		Damasana-putra[sa] ra[jño Mahakṣatrapasa Vijayasana]sa. Cf. *ibid.*, p. 136, Plate XIV, No.554.
16	Damaged	Do. Weight—30 grains. *Obverse.*—As on No. 1. *Reverse*—As on No. 1; but star of 5 dots. Legend : (II) *rajño Mahakṣatrapasa Damasana-putrasa rajño Mahakṣatrapasa V[ijayasana]sa.*
17	Do.	Do. Weight—35 grains. *Obverse*—As on No. 1. *Reverse*—As on No. 1; but with star of 6 dots. Legend : (II) *rajño Maha[kṣatrapasa] Damasana-putrasa rajño Mahakṣatrapasa V[i]jayasenasa.*

IV. *Mahākṣatrapa* Dāmajadaśrī III (Śaka 172 or 173 to 176)

18	Śaka [100]+x+x	Do. Weight—37½ grains. *Obverse* and *Reverse*—As on No. 1. Legend : (II) *rajñ[o Mahak[kṣatra]-pasa Damasena-putrasa rajño Mahakṣatrapasa Damama[ja]daśr[riya]..*
19	Śaka [100+70]+x	Do. Weight—27 grains. *Obverse*—As on No. 1. *Reverse*—As on No. 1; but with star of 5 dots. Legend : (II) *rajño [Maha]kṣatrapa-[sa Da]ma[senaputrsa] rajño [Mahakṣatrapasa Damajadaśr]iya..* Cf. Rapson, *op. cit.*, p. 139, No. 568.
20	Śaka [100+70+2]	Do. Weight—37½ grains. *Obverse* and *Reverse*—As on No. 19. Legend : (II) *rajño Mahakṣatra[pasa ......putra...rajño Maha]kṣatrapasa Damajadaśr[i]ya..* The numerical sign for 70 is without loop.

		Cf. *ibid.*, p. 137, Plate XIV, No. 556.
21	Śaka [100+70+4]	Do. Weight—30 grains. *Obverse* and *Reverse*—As on No. 1. Legend : (II) *rajño Mahakṣatra......* *rajño [Maha]kṣatrapasa Damajadaśriyaḥ.* Cf. *ibid.*, p. 138, Plate XIV. No. 559.
22	Do.	Do. Weight—30 grains. *Obverse* and *Reverse*—As on No. 1. Legend : (II) *rajño [Maha]kṣatra... [putrasa] rajño Mahakṣatrapasa Damajadaśri[ya]..* Cf. *loc. cit.*
23	Do.	Do. Weight—27 grains. *Obverse* and *Reverse*—As on No. 1. Legend : (II) *rajño [Maha]kṣatra-[pasa Damasana]-pu[trasa Maha]-kṣatra[pasa] Dama[ja]da[śriyaḥ].* Cf. *loc. cit.*
24	Śaka [100+70+5]	Do. Weight—32½ grains. *Obverse* and *Reverse*—As on No. 1. Legend : (II) *rajño Mahakṣatra[pasa Da]masana-putra[sa] rajño [Maha]-kṣatra[pasa Da]maja[da]śr[i]ya..* cf. *ibid.*, p. 138, Plate XIV, No. 561.
25	Do.	Do. Weight—30 grains. *Obverse*—As on No. 1. *Reverse*—As on No. 1; but with star of 8 dots. Legend : (II) *rajño Mahakṣatrapasa Damasana-putrasa rajño Mahakṣatra-pasa Damajadaśriya..* *A. R. Ep.*, 1956-57, Plate VI, No. 5.
26	Śaka [100+70+6]	Do. Weight—32½ grains.

		Obverse—As on No. 1. *Reverse*—As on No. 1; but with star of 5 dots. Legend : (II) *rajño Mahakṣatrapasa [Dāmasana]-putrasa rajño Mahakṣatrapasa Da[ma]jada[ś]r[i]ya..* *A.R.Ep.*,1956-57, Plate VI, No. 6.
27	Damaged	Do. Weight—32½ grains. *Obverse*—As on No. 1. *Reverse*—Pellet border; symbols blurred. Legend : (II) *rajño Mahakṣatrapasa Damasana-putrasa rajño ......ya. .*
28	Do.	Do. Weight—32½ grains. *Obverse* and *Reverse*—As on No. 1. Legend : (II) *rajño Mahakṣatrapasa Damas[e]na-putrasa rajño Mahakṣatra......[darśiya]. .*
29	Śaka [100+70+x	Do. Weight—30 grains. *Obverse* and *Reverse*—As on No. 1. Legend : (II).........*kṣatra[pasa] Damasana-putrasa rajño Mahakṣatra...* The second numerical symbol is irregular in shape.
30	Damaged	Do. Weight—32½ grains. *Obverse* and *Reverse*—As on No. 1. Legend : (II) *rajño Mahakṣatra-[pasa] Dama[sena]-putrasa rajño [Mahakṣatra]*.........

V. *Mahākṣatrapa* Rudrasena II (Śaka 178?-196)

31	Śaka [100]+x+x	Do. Weight—30 grains. *Obverse*—As on No. 1. *Reverse*—Pellet border; symbols blurred. Legend : (II) *rajñaḥ Kṣatrapa...... putrasa rajño Mahakṣatrapasa Rudra-[senasa].* Cf. Rapson, *op. cit.*, p. 145, Plate XV, No. 614.

32 Do. Do. Weight—30 grains.
Obverse—As on No. 1.
Reverse—As on No. 1; but with the star blurred.
Legend : (II) *rajña ...pasa Vīra-dāma-putrasa rajño Mahakṣatra......*
Ru[*dra*]......
Cf. *loc. cit.*

33 Śaka [100+70]+x Do. Weight—27 grains.
Obverse—As on No. 1.
Reverse—As on No. 1; but with star of 4 dots.
Legend : (II) *rajña*[*ḥ*] *Kṣatrapasa Vīradama-putrasa rajño Mahakṣa-trapasa Rudra*[*senasa*].
Cf. *ibid.*, p. 141, Plate XV, No. 581.

34 Śaka [100+70+6] Do. Weight—32 grains.
Obverse and *Reverse*—As on No. 1.
Legend : (II) *rajñaḥ Kṣa*[*trapasa*] *V*[*ī*]*radama-putrasa rajño Mahakṣa-trapasa Rudrasenasa.*

35 Śaka [100+70+9] Do. Weight—32 grains.
Obverse and *Reverse*—As on No. 1.
Legend : (II) [*rajña*]*ḥ Kṣatrapasa* [*Vī*]*radama-putrasa rajño Mahakṣtra-pasa Rudra*[*sa*]......
The sign for 70 is irregularly shape.

36 Śaka 100+[70]+9 Do. Weight—35 grains.
Obverse—As on No. 1.
Reverse—As on No. 1; but with star of 4 dots.
Legend : (II) *rajñaḥ......Vīradama-putrasa rajño Mahakṣatra*[*pasa*] *Rudra*[*senasa*].
Do.

37 Do. Do. Weight—32½ grains.

		Obverse—As on No. 1; but with star of 6 dots. Legend : (II) *rajñaḥ Kṣatra......ra... putra[sa] rajño Mahakṣa......[Rudra]-sanasa.* The numerical signs in the date are of irregular shape.
38	Śaka 100+80	Do. Weight—30 grains. *Obverse* and *Reverse*—As on No. 1. Legend : (II) *rajña[ḥ] Kṣatra... [Vi]radama-putrasa rajño Mahakṣa-trapasa Rudra[senasa].* Cf. Rapson, *loc. cit.*, p. 142, No. 583.
39	Śaka 100+[80]	Do. Weight—37½ grains. *Obverse*—As on No. 1. *Reverse*—As on No. 1; but with faint traces of the star. Legend : (II) *rajña.........[da]-ma-putrasa rajño Mahakṣatrapasa Rudrasenasa.* Cf. *loc. cit.*
40	Śaka [100+80]	Do. Weight—30 grains. *Obverse* and *Reverse*—As on No. 1. Legend : (II) *rajñaḥ Kṣatrapasa Vīradama-putrasa rajño Mahakṣatra-pasa Rudrasenasa.* Cf. *loc. cit.*
41	Do.	Do. Weight—30 grains. *Obverse*—As on No. 1. *Reverse*—As on No. 1; but with star of 4 dots. Legend : (II) *rajñaḥ Kṣatrapasa V[ī]ra[dama]-putrasa rajño Maha-kṣatrapasa Rudra.........* Cf. *loc. cit.*
42	Do	Do. Weight—32½ grains.

Obverse and *Reverse*—As on No. 1.
Legend : (II) *rajñaḥ Kṣatrapasa Vīradama-putrasa rajño Mahakṣatra...* [*Rudra*]......
Cf. *loc. cit.*

43 Do. Do. Weight—27 grains.
Obverse—As on No. 1.
Reverse—As on No. 1; but without pellet border.
Legend : (II) *rajñaḥ Kṣatrapasa Vīrada*[*ma*]*-putrasa rajño Mahakṣatrapasa Rudras*[*e*]*nasa.*
Cf. *loc. cit.*

44 Do. Do. Weight—35 grains.
Obverse—As on No. 1.
Reverse—As on No. 1; but with star of 4 dots.
Legend : (II) *rajña*[*ḥ*] *Kṣatrapasa Vīradama-putrasa rajño Mahakṣatrapasa Rudrasanasa.*
Cf. *loc. cit.*

45 Do. Do. Weight—30 grains.
Obverse—As on No. 1.
Reverse—As on No. 1; but with star of 5 dots.
Legend : (II) *rajña*[*ḥ*] *Kṣatrapasa Vīradāma-putrasa rajño Mahakṣatra-*[*pa*]*sā Rudra.* [*nasa*].
Cf. *loc. cit.*

46 Śaka [100+80 or 90] Do. Weight—32 grains.
Obverse—As on No. 1.
Reverse—As on No. 1; but with star of 4 dots.
Legend : (II) *rajñaḥ Kṣatrapasa V*[*ī*]*radama-putrasa rajño Mahakṣatrapasa Rudrasenasa.*
A.R. Ep., 1956-57, Plate VII, No. 7.

47 Do. Do. Weight—32 grains.
Obverse—As on No. 46.
Reverse—Pellet border; symbols blurred; traces of the hill symbol and the wavy line.
Legend : (II).........*sa V[ī]radama-putrasa rajño Mahakṣatrapasa Ru[dra]*........

48 Śaka 100+80+x Do. Weight—32½ grains.
Obverse and *Reverse*—As on No. 47.
Legend : (II) *rajñaḥ Kṣatrapasa V[ī]radama-putrasa rajño Mahakṣatrapasa Rudrasenasa.*
Cf. Rapson, *loc. cit.*, p. 144, No. 601.

49 Śaka 100+80+6 Do. Weight—32½ grains.
Obverse—As on No. 1.
Reverse—As on No. 1; but star of 5 dots.
Legend : (II) *rajña[ḥ] Kṣatrapasa Vīradāma-putrasa rajño Mahakṣatrapasa Rudrasanasa.*
The letter *sa* in *Mahakṣatrapasa* is not properly formed.
Cf. *ibid.*, p. 143, Plate XV, No. 590; see *A. R. Ep.*, Plate VII, No. 8.

50 Śaka 100+80+[6] Do. Weight—27 grains.
Obverse—As on No. 49.
Reverse—Pellet border; symbols blurred.
Legend : (II) *rajñaḥ Kṣatrapasa Viradama-[pu]...........[Rudra]senasa.*
Cf. Rapson, *loc. cit.*

51 Do. Do. Weight—32½ grains.
Obverse and *Reverse*—As on No. 49.
Legend : (II) *rajñaḥ Kṣatrapasa V[ī]ra[dama]-putrasa rajño Maha-*

		kṣatrapasa [*Rudra*]......... Cf. *loc. cit.*
52	Śaka [100+80+9]	Do. Weight—30 grains. *Obverse*—As on No. 1. *Reverse*—As on No. 1; but with star of 4 dots. Legend : (II) *rajñaḥ Kṣatrapasa V*[*ī*]*radama-putrasa rajño Mahakṣatrapasa Rudrasenasa.* Cf. *ibid.*, p. 144, Plate XV, No. 600.
53	Do.	Do. Weight—37½ grains. *Obverse*—As on No. 1. *Reverse*—As on No. 49. Legend : (II) *rajña*[*ḥ Kṣa*]...... [*putra*]. *rajño Mahakṣatrapasa Rudrasenasa.* Cf. *loc. cit.*
54	Do.	Do. Weight—27 grains. *Obverse*—As on No. 1. *Reverse*—As on on No. 1; but with star of 5 dots. Legend : (II) [*rajñaḥ Kṣatrapa*]*sa Vīradama-p*[*utrasa*] *rajño Mahakṣatrapasa Rudra*......... Cf. *loc. cit.*
55	Do.	Do. Weight—30 grains. *Obverse* and *Reverse*—As on No. 1. Legend : (II) *rajñaḥ Kṣatrapasa* [*V*]*ī*]*ra*]*dama-pu*[*t*]*ra*......[*Rud*]*rasenasa.* Cf. *loc. cit.*
56	Do.	Do. Weight—30 grains. *Obverse*—As on No. 1. *Reverse*—As on No. 1; but with star of 6 dots.

		Legend : (II) *rajñaḥ Kṣatrapasa V[i]rad[ā]ma-putrasa [ra]jño Mahakṣatrapasa Rudrasenasa.* Cf. *loc. cit.*
57	Do.	Do. Weight—32½ grains. *Obverse* and *Reverse*—As on No. 1. Legend : (II) *rajñaḥ Kṣatra...... [pu]trasa rajño Mahakṣatra[pa]sa Rudras[e]nasa.* Cf. *loc. cit.*
58	Do.	Do. Weight—35 grains. *Obverse*—As on No. 1. *Reverse*—As on No. 1; but with the star damaged. Legend : (II) *ra[jñaḥ Kṣatra]pasa [Vīradama-putrasa] rajñ[o] Ma-[hakṣatra]......Rudra......* Cf. *loc. cit.*
59	Do.	Do. Weight—27 grains. *Obverse*—As on No. 1. *Reverse*—Pellet border; symbols damaged. Legend : (II) *[rajñaḥ Kṣa]...... ra[da]ma-putrasa rajño Mahakṣa... [Rudra]......* Cf. *loc. cit.*
60	Do.	Do. Weight—32½ grains. *Obverse*—As on No. 1. *Reverse*—As on No. 1; but with star of 6 dots. Legend : (II) *rajña[ḥ] Kṣatrapasa Vīradama-putra[sa] rajño Mahakṣatra[pasa] Rudras[e]nasa.* Cf. *loc. cit.*
61	Do.	Do. Weight—23 grains. *Obverse*—As on No. 1.

Reverse—As on No. 1; but with star of 4 dots.
Legend : (II) *rajñaḥ Kṣatrapasa V[īra]d[ā]ma-putrasa rajño Mahakṣatra[pasa] Rudras[e]nasa.*
Cf. *loc. cit.*

62 Do. Do. Weight—30 grains.
Obverse and *Reverse*—As on No. 1.
Legend : (II) *rajña[ḥ Kṣat]ra-[pa]sa V[ī]radama-putrasa rajñ[o] Mahakṣatrapasa Rudra.........*
Cf. *loc. cit.*

63 Do. Do.
Obverse—As on No. 1.
Reverse—As on No. 1; but with the star damaged.
Legend : (II) *rajñaḥ Kṣatra[pa]sa Vīradama-putrasa rajñ[o] Ma[hakṣa-trapasa] Rudas[e]nasa.*
Cf. *loc. cit.*

64 Do. Do.
Obverse and *Reverse*—As on No. 1.
Legend : (II) *rajñaḥ Kṣatra[pasa Vī]ra[da]ma-put[r]asa rajño Mahakṣatrapasa Rudrasenasa.*
Cf. *loc. cit.*

65 Do. Do. Weight—35 grains.
Obverse—As on No. 1.
Reverse—As on No. 1; but with star of 4 dots.
Legend : (II) *rajñaḥ Kṣatrapasa Vīradama-putrasa rajñ[o Mahakṣa-tra. sa] Rudra[se]nasa.*
Cf. *loc. cit.*

66 Do. Do. Weight—30 grains.

		Obverse—As on No. 1. *Reverse*—Pellet border; symbols damaged. Legend : (II) *rajña[ḥ Kṣatra]... Vara[dama]-putrasa rajño Mahakṣatrapasa Rudrasenasa.* Cf. *loc. cit.*
67	Do.	Do. *Obverse*—As on No. 1. *Reverse*—As on No. 1; but with star of 4 dots. Legend : (II) *rajñaḥ Kṣatrapasa Vīradama-putrasa rajño Mahakṣatra-[pasa] Rudra[senasa].* Cf. *loc. cit.*
68	Śaka [100]+ 80+[9]	Do. Weight—$32\frac{1}{8}$ grains. *Obverse*—As on No. 1. *Reverse*—As on No. 1; but with star of 5 dots. Legend : (II) *rajña[ḥ Kṣatrapasa] V[ī]radāma-putrasa [ra......Rudra]...* Cf. *loc. cit.*
69	Do.	Do. Weight—30 grains. *Obverse*—As on No. 1. *Reverse*—As on No.1; but with star of 6 dots. Legend : (II) *rajñaḥ Kṣatrapasa V[ī]radāma-putra[sa rajño ......tra]-pasa Rudrasanasa.* Cf. *loc. cit.*
70	Do.	Do. Weight—$32\frac{1}{8}$ grains. *Obverse*—As on No. 1. *Reverse*—As on No. 1; but with star of 5 dots. Legend : (II) *[rajña]......V[ī]ra-dama-putrasa rajño Mahakṣatrapasa Rudra......* Cf. *loc. cit.*

71	Śaka 100+80+[9]	Do. Weight—27 grains. *Obverse*—As on No. 1. *Reverse*—Pellet border; symbols damaged. Legend : (II) *rajñaḥ Kṣatrapasa V[ī]radāma-putra......[kṣatrapasa] Rudrasanasa.* Cf. *loc. cit.*
72	Do.	Do. Weight—32½ grains. *Obverse*—As on No. 1. *Reverse*—As on No. 1; but with star of 5 dots. Legend: (II) *[ra]jñaḥ [Kṣatra]-pasa Vīradāmà-putrasa rajñ[o] Mahakṣatra[pasa] Rudrasanasa.* *A. R. Ep.*, 1956-57, Plate VII, No. 9.
73	Śaka 100+80+9	Do. Weight—27 grains. *Obverse*—As on No. 1. *Reverse*—Pellet border; symbols blurred; star of 6 dots Legend: (II) *rajñaḥ Kṣatrapasa Vīradama-putrasa rajño Mahakṣatrapa-[sa Rudra]senasa.*
74	Do.	Do. Weight—27 grains. *Obverse* and *Reverse*—As on No. 1. Legend : (II) *rajña[ḥ] Kṣa...... rad[ā]ma-putrasa... Mahakṣatrapasa Rudrasenasa.* Gf. Rapson, *loc.cit.*; see *A. R. Ep.*, 1956-57, Plate VII, No. 10.
75	Śaka [100+90]	Do. Weight—30 grains. *Obverse*—As on No. 1. *Reverse*—As on No. 1; but with star of 6 dots. Legend : (II)...*V[ī]ra...[putra]sa rajño Mahakṣatrapa[sa] Rudra......*

76 Śaka 100+90+[6] Do.
Obverse—As on No. 1.
Reverse—As on No. 1; but with star of 5 dots.
Legend : (II) *rajñaḥ Kṣatrapasa Vīradama-p... Kṣatra[pasa] Rudra[e]-nasa.*
Cf. Rapson, *loc. cit.*, p. 145, Plate XV, No. 612.

77 Cut off Do. Weight—35 grains.
Obverse—As on No. 1.
Reverse—Pellet border; symbols damaged.
Legend : (II) *rajñaḥ Kṣatrapasa Vīradama-putra[sa rajño] ...kṣatra... Rudra[e]nasa.*

78 Do. Do. Weight—30 grains.
Obverse—As on No. 1.
Reverse—As on No. 1; but with the star damaged.
Legend : (II) *rajñaḥ Kṣatrapasa Vīradama-pu[t]ra...[rajño...... Kṣatra sa] Rudrasenasa.*

79 Do. Do. Weight—32½ grains.
Obverse—As on No. 1.
Reverse—As on No. 1; but with star of 5 dots.
Legend : (II) *rajñaḥ Kṣatrapasa V[ī]ra[dā]ma-[p]u[t]ra[sa] ra[jño Maha]kṣatrapasa Rudrasenasa.*

80 Do. Do. Weight—27 grains.
Obverse and *Reverse*—As on No. 79.
Legend : (II) *rajñaḥ Kṣatrapasa V[ī]radama-putrasa rajño Maha-kṣatra[pasa] Rudras[e]nasa.*

81	Damaged	Do. Weight—30 grains. *Obverse*—As on No. 1. *Reverse*—As on No. 1; but with star of 4 dots. Legend : (II) [*rajñaḥ Kṣatrapa*]*sa Vīradama-putrasa rajño Mahakṣatra*... *Ru*[*d*]*ra*......
82	Do.	Do. Weight—32½ grains. *Obverse*—As on No. 1. *Reverse*—Pellet border; symbols damaged. Legend : (II) [*rajñaḥ Kṣatra*...... *putrasa*] *rajño Mahakṣatrapasa Rudrasenana.* Damaged.
83		Do. *Obverse*—As on No. 1. *Reverse*—As on No. 1; but with no trace of the crescent. Legend : (II) *rajñaḥ Kṣatrapasa V*[*ī*]*radama-putrasa rajñ*[*o*] *Maha-kṣatra*[*pasa Ru . se*]*nasa.*
84	Śaka 100+80+[2]	Do. *Obverse*—As on No. 1. *Reverse*—Pellet border; symbols blurred. Legend : (II) ...*Kṣatrapasa Vīra-dama-putrasa rajño Mahakṣa*[*tra*]...
85	Śaka [100+80+9]	Do. *Obverse*—As on Nol 1. *Reverse*—Pellet border; hill; star of 5 dots; no crescent. Legend : (II) *rajñaḥ Kṣatrapasa Viradāma-putra*[*sa*] *rajñ*[*o*].........

VI. *Kṣatrapa* Viśvasiṁha (Śaka 199-200+x)

86	Śaka [100+x+x]	Do. Weight—27 grains.

		Obverse—As on No. 1. *Reverse*—Pellet border; symbols blurred. Legend: (II) *ra[jño Mahakṣatra]-pasa Rudrasana-putra[sa] rajñaḥ Kṣatrapasa Viśvasīhasa.*
87	Do.	Do. *Obverse* and *Reverse*—As on No. 1. Legend : (II) *rajñ[o] Mahakṣa-trapasa Rudrasana-p[utrasa] rajñaḥ Kṣatra[pasa] V[iś]va......*
88	Śaka [100+90] +x	Do. Weight—32½ grains. *Obverse* and *Reverse*—As on No. 1. Legend : (II) *rajño Mahakṣatra-pasa Rudra[se]na-putra . [rajñaḥ Ksatrapasa] ...s[ī]hasa* Cf. Rapson, *loc. cit.*, p. 148, Plate XV, No. 629.
89	Śaka [100+90+9]	Do. Weight—27 grains. . *Obverse* and *Reverse*—As on No. 1. Legend : (II) *rajñ[o Mahakṣatra-pasa] Rudra[sena]-putrasa rajñaḥ Kṣatrapasa V[ī]śvas[īhasa].*
90	Do.	Do. *Obverse*—As on No. 1. *Reverse*—Pellet border; symbols blurred. Legend : (II) *rajño Mahakṣa[trapa]. [Rudra]...p[ut[ra[sa] rajñaḥ Kṣatra-pasa Viśvasīhasa.* Cf. Rapson, *loc. cit.*, No. 88.
91	Do.	Do. Weight—32½ grains. *Obverse*—As on No. 1. *Reverse*—As on No. 1; but with the star damaged. Legend : (II)......*[pasa] Rudra-sana-putrasa rajñaḥ Kṣatrapa[sa...... ś[va...].*

92	Śaka [x+x+9]	Do. *Obverse*—As on No. 1. *Reverse*—As on No. 1; but with star of 4 dots. Legend : (II) *rajño Mahakṣatrapasa Rudra [sena-putrasa] rajñaḥ Kṣatra [pasa Viś] vas [i] ha [sa].*
93	Śaka 200	Do. *Obverse* and *Reverse*—As on No. 1. Legend : (II) *rajño [Mahakṣatra]... Ru...... [putrasa] rajñaḥ Kṣatrapasa V[i] śvas.[i] hasa.* Cf. Rapson, *loc. cit.*, p. 148, Plate XV, No. 634.
94	Do.	Do. Weight—25 grains. *Obverse* and *Reverse*—As on No. 1. Legend : (II) *rajño Maha[kṣa]... ...na-putra [sa rajñaḥ Kṣatrapasa] V[i]śvas[i]hasa.* Cf. *loc. cit.*
95	Do.	Do. *Obverse*—As on No. 1. *Reverse*—As on No. 1; but with the star damaged. Legend : (II) *rajño Mahakṣatrapasa Rudras[ena-pu[t]ra . [rajñaḥ Kṣatra]......va[sī]hasa.*
96	Cut off	Do. Weight—27 grains. *Obverse*—As on No. 1. *Reverse*—Pellet border; symbols blurred. Legend : (II) *rajño Maha[kṣatra... Rudra...putra . rajñaḥ Kṣa]trapasa V[ī]śvasīhasa.*
97	Do.	Do. *Obverse*—As on No. 1.

		Reverse—As on No. 1; but with star of 5 dots. Legend : (II) *rajño Mahakṣatrapasa Rudrasena-putra............ [Viś] va [sīhasa].*
98	Do.	Do. Weight —30 grains. *Obverse*—As on No. 1. *Reverse*—As on No. 1; but with star damaged. Legend : (II) *rajño Mahakṣatrapasa Rudras [e] na-putrasa rajña [ḥ] Kṣa [tra]......... [sīhasa].*
99	Do.	Do. Weight—32½ grains. *Obverse*—As on No. 1. *Reverse*—Pellet border; symbols blurred. Legend : (II) *rajño Mahakṣatrapasa Rudras [ena] . trasa .... V [i] śvasīhasa.* *A.R.Ep.*, 1956-57, Plate VII, No.11.
100	Do.	Do. *Obverse* and *Reverse*—As on No. 1. Legend : (II) *rajño Mahakṣatrapasa [Rudrase...... rajñaḥ Kṣatrapasa] V [i] śvasī [ha] sa.* Damaged.
101	Do.	Do. Weight—30 grains. *Obverse* and *Reverse*—As on No. 1. Legend : (II) *rajño ...kṣa... [pa] sa Rudrasana-putrasa rajñaḥ Kṣatra- [pasa Viś] va......* Cf. Rapson, *loc. cit.*
102	Do.	Do. Weight—30 grains. *Obverse*—As on No. 1. *Reverse*—As on No. 1; but with star of 4 dots.

		Legend : (II) *rajño Mahakṣatrapasa Rudrasena-pu[t]ra[sa] rajñaḥ Kṣatra[pasa] V[iś]vas[īha]sa.*
103	Do.	Do. Weight—32½ grains *Obverse*—As on No. 1. *Reverse*—As on No. 1; but with star of 6 dots. Legend : (II) *rajño ......kṣatra ...Rudra...[p]u[t]rasa rajñaḥ Kṣatrapasa Viśvasīha[sa].* Damaged.
104	Do.	Do. Weight—27 grains. *Obverse* and *Reverse*—As on No. 1. Legend : (II) *rajñ[o] Mahakṣatrapasa Rudras[e]na-putrasa rajña[ḥ] Kṣatra...... V[iś]vas[ī]hasa.*
105	Do.	Do. Weight—30 grains. *Obverse*—As on No. 1. *Reverse*—Pellet border; symbols damaged. Legend : (II) *rajñ[o Mahakṣa]tra[pasa] Rudra.........[putrasa] rajño Kṣatrapasa Viśvas[īha]sa.*
106	Damaged	Do. Weight—32½ grains. *Obverse*—As on No. 1. *Reverse*—Pellet border; symbols blurred; star of 6 dots. Legend : (II) *rajño Mahakṣatra[pasa] Rudrasena-putrasa [rajñaḥ] Kṣatra......Vi[ś]vas[īhasa].* Damaged.

VII. *Mahākṣatrapa* Viśvasiṁha (Śaka 201-204 ?)

107	Cut off	Do. Weight—23 grains. *Obverse* and *Reverse*—As on No. 1. Legend : (II) *[rajño Ma]...........*

		Rudra.........p[ut][rasa] rajñ[o] Mahakṣatrapasa Viśva[sīhasa]. Damaged.
108	Do.	Do. Weight—27 grains. *Obverse* and *Reverse*—As on No. 1. Legend : (II) *rajñ[o] Mahakṣatra ... Rudrasena-pu[tra]sa rajño Mahakṣatrapasa Viśvasīhasa.*
109	Do.	Do. *Obverse*—As on No. 1. *Reverse*—Pellet border; symbols damaged; star of 4 dots. Legend : (II) *ra[jñ]o Mahakṣatra-[pasa] Rudra...[p]u[t]ra]. [rajño]...kṣa[t]ra[pasa] V[i]śva-s[ī]ha[sa].*
110	Do.	Do. Weight—32½ grains. *Obverse*—As on No. 1. *Reverse*—As on No. 1; but with star of 4 dots. Legend : (II) *rajño Mahakṣatra... Rudra...put]ra[sa] rajñ[o] Mahakṣatrapasa Viśvas[īhasa].*
111	Do.	Do. *Obverse*—As on No. 1. *Reverse*—Pellet border; symbols damaged; traces of the star. Legend : (II)[*rajño Maha*]*kṣatrapasa Rudrasena-putrasa rajñ [o Mahakṣat] ...V[iś]va[sīhasa].* Damaged.

VIII. *Kṣatrapa* Bhartṛdāman(Śaka 201-204 ?)

112	Śaka [200+x]	Do. Weight—30 grains. *Obverse*—As on No. 1. *Reverse*—As on No. 1; but with star

		of 5 dots. Legend : (II) [*rajño Maha*]*kṣa-trapasa Rudrasana-putrasa rajña*[*ḥ*] *Kṣatra......tṛi......* Cf. Rapson, *loc. cit.*, p. 154, Plate XV, No. 668.
113	Śaka [200+1]	Do. Weight—32½ grains. *Obverse* and *Reverse*—As on No. 1. Legend : (II) [*rajña......tra . rajñaḥ Kṣa*]*trapasa Bhartṛdamnaḥ.* Cf. *ibid.*, p. 153, No. 667.
114	Śaka [200+4]	Do. Weight—32½ grains. *Obverse* and *Reverse*—As on No. 1. Legend : (II) *rajño Mahakṣatra...* [*Rudra*] *...putra . rajñaḥ Kṣatrapasa Bhartṛdamnaḥ.* Cf. *ibid.*, p. 154, No. 671.
115	Do.	Do. *Obverse*—As on No. 1. *Reverse*—As on No. 1; but with star of 6 dots. Legend : (II) *rajñ*[*o Mahakṣa*]-*trapasa Rudrasana-putrasa rajñaḥ* [*Kṣatrapasa ...mna.*].
116	Do.	Do. Weight—35 grains. *Obverse*—As on No. 1. *Reverse*—As on No. 1; but with star of 4 dots. Legend : (II) *rajño Ma*[*hakṣatra... Rudra...putra*] . *rajñaḥ Kṣatrapasa Bha*[*r*]*tṛdamnaḥ.* The numerical sign for 4 looks like having a loop below. Cf. Rapson, *loc. cit.*
117	Do.	Do. Weight—32½ grains.

		Obverse—As on No. 1. *Reverse*—As on No. 1; but with the star damaged. Legend : (II) [*rajño Mahakṣatra*]... ...*rajñaḥ Kṣatrapasa Bhartṛdamnaḥ*. Damaged. Cf. *loc. cit.*
118	Cut off	Do. Weight—30 grains. *Obverse*—As on No. 1. *Reverse*—As on No. 1; but with star of 4 dots. Legend : (II) *rajño Mahakṣatrapasa Rudrasana-putrasa rajña*[*ḥ Kṣatra*]......*mnā*..
119	Do.	Do. Weight—35 grains. *Obverse* and *Reverse*—As on No. 1. Legend : (II) [*raño...kṣatra... R*]*u*[*d*]*ra*[*sena-putrasa*] *rajñaḥ Kṣatrapasa Bha*[*r*]*tṛ*......[*mnaḥ*].
120	Do.	Do. *Obverse* and *Reverse*—As on No. 1. Legend : (II) [*rajño...Kṣatra*]... *Ru*[*d*]*ra*[*sena*]-*putrasa rajñaḥ Kṣatrapasa Bha*[*r*]*tṛdamna*.. Damaged.
121	Do.	Do. *Obverse*—As on No. 1. *Reverse*—As on No. 1; with star of 6 dots. Legend : (II) *ra*[*jño Mahakṣatrasa*] *Rudrasana-putrasa rajñaḥ Kṣatrapasa Bha*[*r*]*tṛdamnaḥ*.
122	Do.	Do. *Obverse* and *Reverse*—As on No. 121. Legend : (II) *rajño Mahakṣatra-*

		pasa Rudrasana-putrasa rajña[ḥ] Kṣatrapasa Bhartṛdamna[ḥ].
123	Do.	Do. *Obverse*—As on No. 1. *Reverse*—As on No. 1; but with the star of 7 dots to the left of the hill and the crescent to its right. Legend : (II) [*rajño Mahakṣa*]-*trapasa Rurdasana-putrasa rajñaḥ* [*Kṣatrapa...tṛ*]. *mna...* Variety B of Rapson, *loc. cit.*
124	Do.	Do. Weight--27 grains. *Obverse*—As on No. 1. *Reverse*—As on No. 1; but with the star cut off. Legend : (II) [*rajño ...kṣatrapa*]*sa Rudrasena-putrasa rajñaḥ* [*Kṣatra... ...tṛ*]...
125	Do.	Do. *Obverse*—As on No. 1. *Reverse*—As on No. 1; but with the star blurred. Legend : [II] *rajño Mahakṣatra-pasa R*[*u*]*dra......*[*putrasa rajñaḥ Kṣatrapasa Bhar*]*tṛdāmnaḥ.*

IX. *Mahākṣatrapa* Bhartṛdāman (Śaka 204 ?-217)

126	Śaka [100+80?]+x	Do. *Obverse* and *Reverse*—As on No. 1. Legend : (II).........*rajño Maha-kaṣtrapasa Bhartṛ*[*da*]... The date is irregular and doubtful. Bhartṛdāman reigned from the Śaka year 201 as a *Kṣatrapa.*
127	Śaka [200+?]	Do. Weight—32½ grains. *Obverse* and *Reverse*—As on No. 1.

		Legend : (II) *rajño Mahakṣatra-pasa Ru[dra...putra. rajño Ma. kṣa]trapasa Bhartṛdamna..* Do.
128	Do.	Do. Weight—30 grains. *Obverse*—As on No. 1. *Reverse*—Pellet border; hill of two peaks; crescents; dots of the star mixed up with the letters of the legend. Legend : (II) *rajñ[o] Mahakṣa-trapasa Rudrasena-putrasa rajño Maha-kṣatra[pa...tṛdamna.].* Do.
129	Śaka [200+?]	Do. *Obverse* and *Reverse*—As on No. 1. Legend : (II) *rajño Mahakṣatra-[pasa Ru[drasana-putrasa ra[iño Mahakṣa]tra. [sa] Bhartṛdamna..* Do.
130	Śaka [200+?]; cut off	Do. *Obverse* and *Reverse*—As on No. 1. Legend : (II) *rajño Ma[hakṣatra... Rudra...putrasa] rajño Mahakṣa-trapasa Bhartṛdamna..* Do.
131	Do	Do. *Obverse* and *Reverse*—As on No. 1. Legend : (II) *rajño Mahakṣatra-pasa Rudra[sena]-putrasa rajño [Mahakṣa]tra[pasa Bhart]ṛ[damna.].* Do.
132	Do.	Do. *Obverse* and *Reverse*—As on No. 1. Legend : [II] *rajño Mahakṣatra-[pa]sa Rudra[sena-putrasa] rajño Mahakṣatrapasa Bhartṛdamna..* The *ha* in *Mahakṣatrapasa* looks

		like *na*. Do.
133	Śaka [200+4]; cut off	Do. Weight—35 grains. *Obverse*—As on No. 1. *Reverse*—Pellet border; symbols blurred. Legend : (II).........*rajño Mahakṣatrapasa Bhartṛ*.... Do. Damaged.
134	Do	Do. Weight—32½ grains. *Obverse*—As on No 1. *Reverse*—As on No. 1; but with the symbols damaged. Legend : (II) *rajño Mahakṣatra-[pasa] Rudra...[putra. rajño ...kṣatrapa]sa Bha[rtṛdamna]*.. Do.
135	Śaka [200+4]	Do. Weight—32 grains. *Obverse*—As on No. 1. *Reverse*—As on No. 1; but with star of 3 dots. Legend : (II) *rajño...kṣatrapa. Rudra...[putra]sa rajño Mahakṣatrapasa Bha[r]tṛdām]na*..
136	Do.	Do. Weight—30 grains. *Obverse*—As on No. 1. *Reverse*—Pellet border; symbols blurred. Legend : (II) ....[*kṣatrapasa*] *Rudrasana-*[*putra*. *rajño* ... *kṣatra*......*tṛ*...... Do.
137	Śaka 200+[4]	Do. *Obverse*—As on No. 1.

		Reverse—As on No. 1; but with star cut off. Legend : (II) ....[*Rudrasena*]-*putrasa rajño* [*Mahakṣatra*]......*Bha*-[*rt*]*ṛi*...... Damaged; doubly struck.
138	Śaka [200+9]; cut off	Do. *Obverse* and *Reverse*—As on No. 1. Legend : (II) *rajño Mahakṣatra*-[*pasa*] *Rudra*...[*p*]*u*[*t*]*ra*[*sa*] *rajñ*[*o*] *Mahakṣatrapasa Bhartṛdāmna*.. *Ha* in *Mahakṣatrapasa* looks like *na*. Damaged.
139	Śaka 200+10	Do. Weight—32½ grains. *Obverse*—As on No. 1. *Reverse*—No pellet border; hill; crescent; star of 5 dots. Legend : (II) ......[*pu*]*trasa rajño Mahakṣatrapasa Bha*...... Doubly struck. The letter *bha* is written below the letter *sa* of *Mahakṣatrapasa*. Do.
140	Do.	Do. *Obverse*—As on No. 1. *Reverse*—As on No. 1; but with star of 5 dots. Legend: (II) [*rajño* ...*ksatra*]... *Rudra* ...*putrasa rajño Mahakṣatrapasa* [*Bhartṛ. mna.*]. Do.
141	Śaka [200]+10+[1]	Do. Weight—30 grains. *Obverse*—As on No. 1. *Reverse*—Pellet border; symbols

		blurred; star damaged. Legend : (II) [*rajño ...kṣatra*]...... ......*putrasa rajño Mahakṣatrapasa Bhartṛdamna.*]. Cf. Rapson, *loc. cit.*, p. 156, Plate XVI, No. 678.
142	Śaka [200+x+2]; cut off	Do. Weight—32½ grains. *Obverse*—As on No. 1. *Reverse*—No pellet border; symbols blurred. Legend : (II) [*rajño...hakṣatrapasa*] *Rudra*[*sena*]*-putrasa rajño Mahakṣatra*[*pasa Bhart*]*ṛ.*[*m*]*na...*
143	Śaka [200+x+2]	Do. Weight—35 grains. *Obverse* and *Reverse*—As on No. 1. Legend : (II) [*rajño*] *Mahakṣatrapasa Rudrasa*[*na-putrasa rajño ... kṣatrapasa......mna.*].
144	Śaka [200+10+4]	Do. Weight—30 grains. *Obverse* and *Reverse*—As on No. 1. Legend : (II) *rajño* [*Mahakṣa*]-*trapasa Rudrasana-putrasa ra*[*jño Ma*]*hakṣatrapasa Bhartṛdamna..* *Ha* in *Mahakṣatrapasa* looks like *na*. Cf. Rapson, *op. cit.*, p. 158, Plate XVI, No. 690; see *A. R. Ep.*, 1956-57, Plate VII, No. 13.
145	Śaka 200+10+4	Do. Weight—27 grains. *Obverse*—As on No. 1. *Reverse*—As on No. 1; but with star damaged. Legend : (II) ...[*Mahakṣatrapasa Rudra...putrasa rajño Mahakṣa*]*trapasa Bhartṛ...* Cf. Rapson, *loc. cit.*
146	Śaka 200+[10+4]	Do. *Obverse*—As on No. 1.

Reverse—As on No. 1 ;but, on the left, star of dots; right—crescent (?). Legend : (II) *rajño Mahakṣatrapaa-[sa] Ru[dra......p]u[t]ra[s rajño Mahakṣatrapaṣa Bhartṛdamna[ḥ]*. Variety B of Rapson, *loc. cit.*; see *A. R.Ep*:, 1956-57, Plate VII, No. 14.

147 Śaka 200+ [x+4] — Do.
Obverse—As on No. 1.
Reverse—Pellet border; symbols damaged.
Legend : (II) *rajño [Mahakṣatra-pasa] Rudrasana-putrasa rajño Mahakṣatrapasa Bhartṛda[mna.]*.
Ha in the first *Mahakṣatrapasa* looks like *la* and *pa* in the second *Maha-kṣatrapasa* like a vertical line.

148 Śaka [200+x+4]; cut off — Do.
Obverse—As on No. 1.
Reverse—No pellet border; rest as on No. 144.
Legend : (II) *rajñ[o] Mahakṣa-trapasa Rudrasana-putrasa rajño Ma[hakṣatra.........mna.]*.

149 Śaka 200+[10+4]; cut off — Do. Weight—30 grains.
Obverse—As on No. 1.
Reverse—Pellet border; symbols damaged.
Legend : (II) ....*[putrasa] rajño Mahakṣatrapasa Bha t[ṛ]da-[mna]*..
Cf. Rapson, *loc.cit.*,as No. 145 above.

150 — Do. Weight—32½ grains.
Obverse—As on No. 1.
Reverse—As on No. 1; but with the star cut off.
Legend : (II)..............*[Rudrase]*-

na-putrasa rajño Mahakṣatrapasa......
[*tṛ*]....

151 Cut off

Do. Weight—35 grains.
Obverse—As on No. 1.
Reverse—As on No. 1; but with star of 5 dots.
Legend : (II) *rajñ*[*o Maha*]*kṣatrapasa Rudrasana-putrasa rajño Ma*[*kakṣatra......tṛdamna.*].

152 Do.

Do. Weight—27 grains.
Obverse and *Reverse*—As on No. 1.
Legend : (II) *rajño......*[*kṣatra... Rudra*]*...putrasa rajño Mahakṣatrapasa Bhartṛdamna..*
Ha in *Mahakṣatrapasa* looks like *na.*

153 Do.

Do.
Obverse—As on No. 1.
Reverse—As on No. 1; but with star damaged.
Legend : (II) *rajño* [*Mahakṣatrapasa Ru*]*......trasa rajño Mahakṣatrapasa* [*Bhartṛ. mna.*].
Do.

154 Do.

Do.
Obverse and *Reverse*—As on No. 1.
Legend : (II) [*rajño*] *Mahakṣatrapasa Rudrasana-putrasa rajñ*[*o*] *......kṣatra......tṛ. mna.*].

155 Do.

Do. Weight—32 grains.
Obverse—As on No. 1.
Reverse—As on No. 1; but with the star cut off.
Legend : (II).........*Rudrasana-putrasa rajño Mahakṣatra*[*pa...tṛ*]...
Ha in *Mahakṣatrapasa* looks like *na.*

No.	Condition	Description
156	Damaged	Do. Weight—27 grains. *Obverse*—As on No. 1. *Reverse*—Pellet border; faint traces of the symbols. Legend : (II) ....[*putrasa rajño*] *Ma*[*hakṣatrapasa Bhartṛ*]...
157	Damaged and cut off	Do. Weight—32½ grains. *Obverse* and *Reverse*—As on No. 1. Legend : (II) *rajño* [*Mahakṣatra*] ......*Ru*[*drasena-putrasa*] *rajño* [*Mahakṣatrapasa*] *Bhartṛdāmna*.. *Ha* in *Mahakṣatrapasa* looks like *na*.
158	Do.	Do. Weight—35 grains. *Obverse* and *Reverse*—As on No. 1. Legend : (II) *rajño Maha*[*kṣatra*... ......*rajño*...*kṣa*]*trapasa Bhartṛdāmnaḥ*. *Pa* in ...*kṣatrapasa* looks like *na*.
159	Do.	Do. Weight—30 grains. *Obverse*—As on No. 1. *Reverse*—As on No. 1; but with star of 4 dots. Legend : (II) *rajño*......[*kṣatra*...... *Rudra*......*putra*] . *rajño Mahakṣatrapasa* [*Bhartṛdamna*.]. Damaged.
160	Do.	Do. Weight—35 grains. *Obverse* and *Reverse*—As on No. 1. Legend : (II) [*rajño Maha*]......... ...*putrasa rajño Mahakṣatrapasa Bhartṛ. mna*.].
161	Do.	Do. Weight—30 grains. *Obverse*—As on No. 1. *Reverse*—As on No. 1; but with dots of the star mixed up with the

		letters of the legend. Legend : (II) *ra[jño......trapasa] Rudra[sena-putrasa rajño Mahakṣatra ...Bhart]ṛ[dam]na..*
162	Damaged and cut off	Do. Weight—32½ grains. *Obverse*—As on No. 1. *Reverse*—As on No. 1; but with the star damaged. Legend : (II) *[rajño Mahakṣatrapasa] Rudrasana-putrasa ra[jño Mahakṣatra......tṛ...mna.].*
163	Cut off	Do. Weight—30 grains. *Obverse*—As on No. 1. *Reverse*—Pellet border; symbols damaged. Legend : (II) ....*[sa] rajño Mahakṣatrapasa Bha[r]tṛ......* Damaged.
164	Do	Do. Weight—32½ grains. *Obverse* and *Reverse*—As on No. 1. Legend : (II) *rajño Mahakṣatra-[pasa] Rudra[sena-putrasa rajño Mahakṣatrapasa] Bhartṛdamna..* Do.
165	Do.	Do. *Obverse*—As on No. 1. *Reverse*—As on No. 1; but with dots of the star mixed up with letters of the legend. Legend: (II) *rajño Mahakṣatra-[pa]sa Rudras[e]na-putrasa rajño Mahakṣa]tra[pasa Bhartṛdamna.].*
166	Faint traces	Do. *Obverse*—As on No. 1. *Reverse*—Pellet border; symbols blurred.

Legend : (II) *raj[ño Mahakṣa]tra-[pasa] Ru[d]ra...[putrasa] rajño [Mahakṣatrapasa Bhartṛ[damna.].* Damaged.

167	Rubbed off	Do. *Obverse*—As on No. 1. *Reverse*—As on No. 1; but with symbols damaged. Legend : (II).........*[trasa] rajño Mahakṣatrapasa Bha......* Do.
168	Cut off	Do. Weight—30 grains. *Obverse*—As on No. 1. *Reverse*—As on No. 1; but with star of 6 dots and one dot possibly mixed up with the hill symbol. Legend : (II) *rajñ[o......kṣatrȧ...... Rudra...pu]trasa rajño Mahakṣatrapasa Bha[r]tṛdamna[ḥ].*
169	Damaged.	Do. *Obverse*—As on No. 1. *Reverse*—As on No. 167. Legend: (II) ....*[putrasa] rajño Mahakṣatrapasa Bhatṛ[da]...*
170	Do.	Do. Weight—23 grains. *Obverse* and *Reverse*—As on No. 1. Legend : (II) *[rajño ...kṣatrapasa Rudra] ......rajño Mahakṣatrapasa Bhatṛ.[mna.].* Damaged.
171	Cut off	Do. Weight—27 grains. *Obverse*—As on No. 1. *Reverse*—Pellet border; symbols blurred; no trace of star. Legend ; (II) *ra[jño Mahakṣatrapasa Rudra...trasa] rajñ[o]*

		Mahakṣatra [*pasa Bhar*] *tṛi* [*damnaḥ*]. Damaged
172	Do.	Do. Weight—30 grains. *Obverse*—As on No. 1. *Reverse*—As on No. 1; but with star of 4 dots. Legend : (II) .... *rajño Mahakṣatrapasa Bha* [*r*] *tṛ*-[*damna.*].
173		Do. *Obverse*—As on No. 1. *Reverse*—As on No. 1; but with star cut off. Legend : (II)......... [*tra*......] *Rudra...putra*] *sa rajño Mahakṣatra*-[*pasa ...tṛ*]...
174	Damaged; traces of 200	Do. Weight—32½ grains. *Obverse*—As on No. 1. *Reverse*—As on No. 1; but with dots of the star mixed up with the letters of the legend. Legend : (II) *raj* [*ño Maha*] *kṣa-trapasa Rudra* [*sena-putra*]. *rajña... kṣatra......tṛ.mna..* Damaged.
175	Very faint	Do. Weight—35 grains. *Obverse*—As on No. 1. *Reverse*—As on No. 1; but with star of 5 dots. Legend : (II) *rajño Mahakṣatra-pasa Rudrasena*-[*putra. rajña... kṣatra...tṛ...mna.*].
176	Damaged	Do. *Obverse*—As on No. 1. *Reverse*—No pellet border; symbols damaged.

		Legend : (II) *ra[jño]...trapasa R[u]d[ra]s[e]na-putrasa rajño Ma[ha.........mna.].* Damaged.

X. *Kṣatrapa* or *Mahākṣatrapa* Bhartṛdāman

177	Śaka [200+2?]; cut off and indistinct.	Do. Weight—30 grains. *Obverse*—As on No. 1. *Reverse*—Pellet border; symbols damaged. Legend : (II) [*rajño Maha......... ....trapa]sa Bha[rtṛdamna.].* Damaged. Cf. Rapson, *loc. cit.*, p. 154, Plate XV, No. 668.
178	Śaka 200+[4]	Do. Weight—35 grains. *Obverse*—As on No. 1. *Reverse*—As on No. 1; but with the star of 6 dots. Legend : (II) *rajño Mahakṣatra-[pasa Rudra ....tṛda]mnaḥ.* Cf. *loc.cit.*, as No. 177 above.
179	Śaka [200+10+1]	Do. *Obverse*—As on No. 1. *Reverse*—As on No. 1; but with star blurred. Legend : (II) *rajño Mahakṣatrapa-[sa Rudra...putra......kṣatra......tṛ-damna.].* *Ha* in *Mahakṣatrapasa* looks like *na.* Damaged. Cf. *loc.cit.*, as No. 141 above.
180	Śaka [200+x+1]	Do. Weight—25 grains. *Obverse*—As on No. 1. *Reverse*—As on No. 1; but with dots of the star mixed up with the letters of the legend. Legend : (II) *rajño Mahakṣatra-[pasa Rudra]...... Bhartṛdamnaḥ.*

181 Damaged. Do. Weight—27 grains.
Obverse—As on No. 1.
Reverse—As on No. 1; but with star of 4 dots.
Legend : (II) *rajño Mahakṣatra-pasa Rudra......[tṛda]mnȧ...*
Damaged.

182 Do. Do. Weight—35 grains.
Obverse—As on No. 1.
Reverse—Pellet border; symbols damaged.
Legend : (II) ......[*kṣa*]*trapasa Bhartṛda*[*mna*].
Do.

183 Do. Do. Weight—30 grains.
Obverse—As on No. 1.
Reverse—As on No. 1; but with dots of the star mixed up with the letters of the legend.
Legend : (II) *rajño Mahā*[*kṣatra ....Bhartṛda*]*mnaḥ.*
Do.

184 Cut off Do.
Obverse—As on No. 1.
Reverse—Pellet border; hill of 3 peaks; no crescent; star of 6 dots.
Legend : (II) *rajño Mahakṣatrapasa Ru*[*dra...........tṛ*]. *mna..*

185 Damaged Do.
Obverse—As on No. 1.
Reverse—Pellet border; symbols blurred.
Legend : (II) *rajño Mahakṣatrapasa Ru*[*dra...........tṛ*]*damnaḥ.*
Damaged.

186 Cut off Do.
Obverse and *Reverse*—As on No. 183.

Legend : (II) *rajño Mahakṣatra-[pasa Rudra............kṣatrapasa Bhar]tṛdamna[ḥ].*

187 Do. Do. Weight—35 grains.
Obverse—As on No. 183.
Reverse—Pellet border; symbols damaged.
Legend : (II) *rajño Mahakṣa[tra......tṛ]damnaḥ.*
Damaged.

188 Slight traces Do. Weight—32½ grains.
Obverse—As on No. 1.
Reverse—As on No. 1; but with star of 5 dots.
Legend : (II) *rajña Ma[hakṣatra ......Rudra]...........trapasa Bhartṛ-[da]mna..*
Do.

189 Do. Do. Weight—30 grains.
Obverse—As on No. 1.
Reverse—As on No. 1; but with the star and the crescent above the hill cut off.
Legend : (II) *rajña. Kṣatrapasa Rudra[sa......putra.........da]mnaḥ.*
On this coin Rudrasena II, father of Bhartṛdāman is described as *Kṣatrapa* instead of *Mahākṣatrapa*. This is due to the carelessness of the die-cutter.
Damaged.

190 Do. Do. Weight—32 grains.
Obverse—As on No. 1.
Reverse—Pellet border; symbols damaged.

Legend: (II) *rajñ[o].........kṣatrapasa Bhartṛdam[na]ḥ.*
Do.

191 Do. — Do. Weight—30 grains.
Obverse—As on No. 1.
Reverse—As on No. 1; but with the star blurred.
Legend : (II) *rajño Mahakṣatrapasa Ru[dra...........Bhar]tṛdamna..*
Rudrasena seems to be spelt as *Rūdrasena.*
Do.

XI. *Kṣatrapa,* son of Rudrasena II

192 Śaka [200+4] — Do. Weight—25 grains.
Obverse and *Reverse*—As on No. 1.
Legend : (II) *[rajño] Mahakṣatrapasa Rudrasana-putra[sa rajñaḥ Kṣatra]......*

193 Śaka [200+x+2]; rubbed off; slight traces — Do. Weight—30 grains.
Obverse—As on No. 1.
Reverse—Pellet border; hill of two peaks; traces of the star and crescents.
Legend : (II)......*[tra]......Rudras[e]na-putrasa rajñaḥ Kṣatra.........*
Damaged.

194 — Do. Weight—35 grains.
Obverse—As on No. 1.
Reverse—Pellet border; symbols damaged.
Legend : (II) *[rajño...kṣa]trapasa Rudrasana-[putra]sa rajña[ḥ Kṣatra].........*

XII. *Mahākṣatrapa,* son of Rudrasena II

195 Śaka 200+? — Do. Weight—32½ grains.
Obverse—As on No. 1.
Reverse—As on No. 1; but with

		the symbols blurred and the star damaged. Legend : (II) [*rajño Mahakṣa*]-*trapasa Rudrasena-putrasa rajñaḥ* [*Maha*(?) *kṣatra*]...... Damaged.
196	Śaka [200+10+2]	Do. Weight—30 grains. *Obverse*—As on No. 1. *Reverse*—As on No. 1; but with the star damaged. Legend : (II)...... [*kṣatra*]*pasa Rudrasana-putrasa rajño Ma*[*hakṣa-tra*]......
197	Rubbed off	Do. Weight—32½ grains. *Obverse*—As on No. 1. *Reverse*—Pellet border; symbols damaged. Legend : (II)......[*kṣatrapa*]*sa Rudrasena-putrasa ra*[*jño Mahakṣa*]...

XIII. *Kṣatrapa* or *Mahākṣatrapa*, son of Rudrasena II

198	Śaka [200+10]	Do. *Obverse* and *Reverse*—As on No. 1. Legend : (II) [*ra*]*jño Mahakṣa-trapasa Rudrasana-pu*[*tra*]...........
199	Cut off	Do. *Obverse*—As on No. 1. *Reverse*—As on No. 1; but with the star cut off. Legend : (II) *rajñ*[*o*] *Mahākṣa-tra*[*pasa*] *Rudrasana-putrasa rajñ*[*o*] .... *Pa* in *Mahakṣatrapasa* looks like *na*.
200	Cut off; slight traces	Do. Weight—27 grains. *Obverse*—As on No. 1. *Reverse*—No pellet border; symbols damaged. Legend ; (II) *rajño Mahakṣa-*

		trapasa Rudra[*sena-putra. rajña*]...... Damaged
201	Cut off	Do. Weight—32½ grains. *Obverse*—As on No. 1. *Reverse*—Pellet border; traces of the hill and the wavy line; no crescent, no star. Legend: (II).........[*tra*]*pasa R*[*u*]*drasana-putrasa rajña*...........
202	Damaged; traces of the hundred symbol	Do. *Obverse*—As on No. 1. *Reverse*—As on No. 1; but with symbols blurred and the star cut off. Legend : (II) [*rajño Mahakṣatrapasa Rudrasena*].........
203	Do.	Do. *Obverse*—As on No. 1. *Reverse*—As on No. 1; but with symbols damaged. Legend : (II) [*rajño Mahakṣa*]*trapasa* [*Rudra*].......................... Damaged.
204	Damaged	Do. Weight—30 grains. *Obverse* and *Reverse*—As on No. 203. Legend : (II) ....[*sa Rudrasena-putrasa rajña*]...... Do.

XIV. *Kṣatrapa* Viśvasena (Śaka 216-26)

205.	Śaka [200+x+x]; mostly cut off	Do. Weight—32½ grains. *Obverse*—As on No. 1. *Reverse*—As on No. 1; but with traces of the wavy line. Legend : (II)....................[*tṛma*]*-putrasa rajño Kṣat*[*ra*]*pasa* [*V*]*iś*[*va*]*sa*...... Damaged. Cf. Rapson, *loc.cit.*, p. 166, No. 745.

206	Do.	Do. Weight—30 grains. *Obverse*—As on No. 1. *Reverse*—As on No. 1; but with traces of the crescent and star. Legend : (II)...........[*ṭṛda*]*ma-putrasa rajño Kṣatrapasa Vi*[*ś*]*va*...... Damaged.
207	Damaged; slight traces of 200	Do. Weight—32½ grains. *Obverse*—As on No. 1. *Reverse*—As on No. 1; but with the star damaged. Legend : (II) *rajño Mahakṣatra-pasa Bha*[*rt*]*ṛ*...... [*Kṣatra*.... *Vi*]-*śvasanasa*. *Ha* in *Mahakṣatrapasa* looks like *na*.
208	Śaka [200+x+4 or 6]	Do. Weight— 30 grains *Obverse* and *Reverse*—As on No. 1. Legend : (II) [*rajño*......*kṣatra*] ...*Bhatṛdama-putrasa rajño Kṣatrapasa V*[*iś*]*va*...........
209	Śaka 200+[10+ 4 or 6]	Do. Weight—32½ grains. *Obverse* and *Reverse*—As on No. 1. Legend : (II) *rajño Mahakṣatra-pasa Bha*[*tṛ*.........*ś*]*vasanasa*. *Ha* in *Mahakṣatrapa* resembles *na*. Cf. Rapson, *loc.cit.*, p. 162, Plate XVI, No. 719.
210	Śaka 200+10+ [4 or 6]	Do. Weight—35 grains. *Obverse* and *Reverse*—As on No. 1. Legend : (II) *rajño Mahakṣatra-pasa*...........[*kṣatrapasa*] *V*[*i*]*śva-sanasa*. Do.
211	Śaka [x+x+6]	Do. Weight—27 grains.

		Obverse—As on No. 1. *Reverse*—As on No. 1; but no trace of the crescents. Legend : (II) [*rajño Mahakṣat*]*ra*-[*pasa Bhartṛ*[*dama*]-*putrasa rajño Kṣatrapasa Viś*[*va*].........
212	Śaka 200+10+6	Do. Weight—32½ grains. *Obverse*—As on No. 1. *Reverse*—Pellet border; symbols blurred; star of 4 dots. Legend : (II)......[*kṣatra...sa*] *Bhartṛda*[*ma*]......*sa rajño Kṣatrapasa* [*Viś*]*va*...... Cf. Rapson, *loc. cit.*, as No. 209 above.
213	Śaka [200+10+6]; cut off	Do. Weight—25 grains. *Obverse*—As on No. 1. *Reverse*—As on No. 1; but with no trace of the star. Legend : (II) *rajñ*[*o Mahakṣatra*]-*pasa Bhartṛda*[*ma-pu*]*trasa rajña*[*ḥ Kṣatrapasa ...ś*]*va*[*senasa*]. Damaged. Cf. Rapson, *loc. cit.*
214	Śaka [200+20]	Do. Weight—30 grains. *Obverse* and *Reverse*—As on No. 1. Legend : (II) *rajñ*[*o......kṣatra...... tṛ...p*]*utrasa rajño Kṣatrapasa Viśva-s*[*e*]*nasa.* *A. R. Ep.*, 1956-57, Plate VII, No. 15.
215	Śaka [200+20+x]; cut off	Do. *Obverse*—As on No. 1. *Reverse*—Pellet border; symbols blurred; traces of the star. Legend : (II) *rajñ*[*o Maha*]*kṣatra ......*[*tṛ...p*]*utrasa rajño Kṣatrapasa Vi*[*śva*]*sanasa.* Cf. Rapson, *loc. cit.*, p. 164, Plate XVI, No. 732.

216	Śaka 200+[20+2]	Do. Weight—23 grains. *Obverse*—As on No. 1. *Reverse*—As on No. 1; but with traces of the wavy line and star. Legend : (II) *rajño Mahakṣa*[*tra ....Kṣatrapa*]*sa Viśvasanasa*. *Ha* in *Mahakṣatra*...looks like *na*. Cf. Rapson, *loc. cit.*, p. 165, Plate XVI, No. 737.
217	Damaged	Do. Weight—30 grains. *Obverse*—As on No. 1. *Reverse*—As on No. 1; but with dots of the star mixed up with the outline of the hill. Legend : (II) *rajño Maha*[*kṣatrapasa*] *Bhartṛdama-putrasa rajño Kṣatrapasa V*[*iś*]*vas*[*e*]*nasa*.
218	Cut off	Do. *Obverse* and *Reverse*—As on No. 1. Legend : (II) *rajño Mahakṣatra-*[*pasa Bhar*]*tṛ*[*dama-p*]*u*[*t*]*ra*[*sa*] *rajño Kṣatrapasa Viśvasanasa*. *Ha* in *Mahakṣatrapasa* looks like *na*.
219	Cut off	Do. Weight—35 grains. *Obverse*—As on No. 1. *Reverse*—No pellet border; rest as on No. 218. Legend : (II) *rajñ*[*o*] *Ma*[*ha**]-*kṣa*[*tra...........putrasa*] *rajña Kṣatrapasa Viśvasenasa*. *Kṣa* in *Mahakṣatrapasa* looks like *kcha*. Cf. Rapson, *loc. cit.*, p. 167, Plate XVI, No. 749.
220	Illegible	Do. *Obverse* and *Reverse*—As on No. 1. Legend : (II) [*rajño Maha*]*kṣa-*

		tra[pasa] Bha[r]tṛdama-putrasa rajño Kṣatrapasa V[iś]va.................. Do.
221	Cut off	Do. *Obverse*—As on No. 1. *Reverse*—As on No. 1; but with star of 6 dots. Legend : (II) *rajñ[o] Mahakṣatrapasa Bhatṛdama-putrasa rajñ[o] Kṣatra......śva...sa.* *Ha* and *kṣa* in *Mahakṣatrapasa* look respectively like *na* and *kcha*. Cf. Rapson, *loc. cit.*, as No. 219 above.
222	Damaged and cut off	Do. Weight—27 grains. *Obverse*—As on No. 1. *Reverse*—Pellet border; symbols damaged. Legend : (II) *rajño Mahāk[ṣa]tra[pasa] Bhartṛdama-putrasa rajñaḥ Kṣatra[pasa] V[iśvasanasa].*
223	Rubbed off	Do. Weight—32½ grains. *Obverse*—As on No. 1. *Reverse*—As on No. 1; but with no trace of the crescent on the hill. Legend : (II) *rajño Mahakṣatrapasa Bhartṛdama-putra[sa rajño] Kṣatrapasa V[iś]va[sanasa].* *Ha* and *kṣa* in *Mahakṣatrapasa* resemble respectively *na* and *kcha* and *da* in *Bhatṛdama* looks like *na*.
224	Cut off	Do. Weight—30 grains. *Obverse* and *Reverse*—As on No. 1. Legend : (II) *rajñ[o Maha]kṣatra-*

pasa Bhartṛdama-putrasa rajño Kṣatra-[pasa Viś]va[sanasa].

225 Śaka [200+10+4] Do.

Obverse—As on No. 1.

Reverse—As on No. 1; but with dots of the star mixed up with the outline of the hill.

Legend : (X) [*rajño*] *Mahakṣatra-pasa Bhartṛdama-putrasa* [*Kṣatra*]......

The name *Bhartṛdāman* looks like *Bhartṛipana* and *ha* in *Mahakṣa-trapasa* like *na*. The arrangement of the letters of the legend is different.

226 Do. Weight—32½ grains.

Obverse—As on No. 1.

Reverse—Pellet border; symbols damaged.

Legend : (II) [*rajño*] *Ma*[*hakṣa-tra*]*pasa Bhartṛdama-pu*[*t*]*ra*.........

227 Do. Weight—30 grains.

Obverse—As on No. 1.

Reverse—As on No. 1; but with traces of the hill and the wavy line.

Legend : (II) [*rajño Ma*]...[*pa*]-*sa Bhartṛdama-putrasa rajño* [*Kṣa-tra*]............

XV. *Mahākṣatrapa*

228 Cut off Do. Weight—27 grains.

Obverse—As on No. 1.

Reverse—As on No. 1, but with star cut off.

Legend : (II).........*trasa rajño Maha*[*kṣatrapasa*]......

Damaged.

XVI. *Kṣatrapa* Rudrasiṁha II (Śaka 225?-235)

229 Śaka[x+20+5] Do. Weight—30 grains.

		Obverse—As on No. 1. *Reverse*—As on No. 1; but with both the crescents to the left of the hill. Legend : (II) *svami-Jivadama-put[ra]sa [rajñaḥ] Kṣatrapasa Rudrasahasa.* The date is doubtful. *Va* in *Jivadama* and *ha* in *Rudrasahasa* look like *na.* The arrangement of the letters is irregular. *A.R. Ep.*, 1956-57, Plate VII, No. 16.
230	Cut off	Do. *Obverse*—As on No. 1. *Reverse*—As on No. 1; but with the crescents damaged. Legend : (XI) *[s]vam[i]-J[i]va-dama-putrasa rajña Kṣatrapasa Rudrasaha[sa].* *Va* in *Jivadama* and *ha* in *Rudrasahasa* look like *na.* *Sa* is peculiar in *putrasa, Kṣatrapasa* and *Rudrasahasa.* The arrangement of the letters is irregular.

XVII. *Kṣatrapa* Yaśodāman II (Śaka 238-254)

231	Śaka 200+[40]	Do. *Obverse* and *Reverse*—As on No. 1. Legend : (II) *rajña Kṣatra[pasa Rudrasa]ha-putrasa rajña Kṣatra-pasa Yaśadamna..* *Ha* in *Rudrasaha* resembles *na.* Cf. Rapson, *op. cit.*, p. 175, Plate XVII, No. 759.
232	Śaka [200+40]	Do. Weight—32½ grains. *Obverse* and *Reverse*—As on No. 229. Legend : (II) *rajña Ksatrapasa Rudrasaha-putrasa rajña Kṣatra-[pasa]......* Cf. *loc. cit.*

XVIII. Defective Specimens.

233 Do. Weight—37½ grains.

Obverse—As on No. 1; but with no date.

Reverse—Bust damaged.

A.R. Ep., 1956-57, Plate VII, No. 17

234 Do. Weight—35 grains.

Obverse—As on No. 1.

Reverse—Bust to left; no ornamental Greek letters.

235 Do. Weight—30 grains.

Obverse and *Reverse*—As on No. 234.

CHAPTER X

SOME PROBLEMS OF TRIBAL COINS

I

More than six thousand copper coins of the Mālavas were discovered in 1871-73 by A. C. Carlleyle at Nagar (ancient Mālava-nagara) in the Uniyara Tahsil of the present Tonk District of Rajasthan.[1] According to Carlleyle's report, he 'found the small green old coins in some places lying as thick as shells on the sea-shore'. The Mālava coins were later discussed by A. Cunningham,[2] E. J. Rapson,[3] V. A. Smith,[4] R. O. Douglas,[5] K. P. Jayaswal,[6] J. Allan,[7] S. K. Chakrabortty[8] and others

Carlleyle and Cunningham assigned the Mālava coins to the period between 250 B.C. and 250 A.D. or 350 A.D. at the latest. But Rapson and Smith thought that the initial date is not earlier than 150 B.C. As regards the later limit, Rapson observed, "The coins on which *Mālavānāṁ jayaḥ* has been read were formerly regarded as ancient; but both the characters of their inscriptions and the fact that they are in fabric somewhat similar to the coins of the Nāgas of Padmāvatī point to the date not earlier than the fifth century A.D." But Smith said that 'the cessation of the local coinage is adequately accounted for by Samudragupta's conquest of Northern India about 330 A.D.' and that 'none of the coins in the Indian Museum are as late as the fifth century, and...........330 A.D. may be taken as the limiting date.' Of course, Smith failed to note that 330 A.D. is too early for Samudragupta's conquest of Northern India. It is interesting to note that, in a copy of Smith's *Catalogue of the Coins in the Indian Museum* (from which the two passages have

1. *ASI Rep.*, Vol. VI, pp. 162 ff. (cf. pp. 173-83).
2. *Ibid.*, Vol. XIV, pp. 149 ff.
3. *Indian Coins*, pp. 12-13.
4. *Catalogue*, pp. 160 ff., 170 ff.
5. *JASB*, 1923, Num. Suppl., No. XXXVII, pp. 42 ff.
6. *Hindu Polity*, Vol. I, p. 218.
7. *Catalogue* (Anc. Ind.), pp. civ ff.
8. *Ancient Indian Numismatics*, pp. 189 ff.

been quoted), preserved in the Calcutta University Library, the words 'Samudragupta's conquest of Northern India about 330 A.D.' in the first extract and '330 A.D.' in the second are found corrected in Smith's own handwriting respectively as 'the extension of the power of Candragupta II about 380 A.D.' and '380 A.D.'

In Allan's opinion, the letter *ma* in the legend of the Mālava coins exhibits an 'Early Gupta' form, so that the coins should be assigned to the period between the second century A.D. and the earlier part of the fourth century. He seems to be right.

Numismatists have divided the Mālava coins into three classes, the first of them bearing the legend *Mālavānāṁ jayaḥ* or *Mālavagaṇasya jayaḥ* which reminds us of similar legends on the coins of the Yaudheyas and the Ārjunāyanas.[1] The coins have the vase, lion, bull, king's head, 'fan-tail' peacock and other objects as their reverse design. Their weight and size vary. The bigger coins are in some cases a little above half an inch in diameter and their weight is generally between 10.5 and 40.3 grains. But most of the specimens are small and light, one measuring only .2 inch in diameter and weighing 2.5 grains.

The two other classes of coins are ascribed to the Mālavas primarily because they were found along with the Mālava coins and resemble the latter in fabric. The coins of the second class do not bear any legend, while those of the third category have meaningless legends in which the name of the Mālavas cannot normally be traced. In our opinion, the coins of these second and third categories are mere imitations of Mālava coins and not genuine issues of the Mālava Republic. Among the coins of the first class also, those on which the word *Mālavānāṁ* has been read as *Mālavahṇa* and others on which the legend has to be read from right to left appear to us to be similar imitations.

Smith regarded the Mālava coins as 'the most curious and enigmatical' in the vast range of Indian coinages. This is partly due to the meaningless legends on the third class of the coins referred to above and partly also to the light weight and small size of many of the coins. The size and weight of the coins of the first category, which are the genuine Mālava issues in our

1. Cf. *Ārjunāyanānāṃ jayaḥ*, *Yaudheya-gaṇasya jayaḥ*, etc. (Allan, *op. cit.*, pp. 121, 276).

opinion, have already been discussed. The coins of the second class bearing no legend are generally small and light, one of them measuring .2 inch in diameter and weighing 1.7 grains only. These are amongst the smallest coins of the world.

The meaningless legends on the third class of coins ascribed to the Mālavas have been read as follows : *Bhapaṁyana*, *Gajava*, *Gojara*, *Harāya* (supposed wrongly to stand for the royal title *Mahārāya*), *Jāmaka*, *Jāmaku*, *Jamapaya*, *Magacha*, *Magaja*, *Magajaśa*, *Magojava*, *Majupa*,[1] *Mapaka*, *Mapaya*, *Mapojaya*, *Maraja*, *Māśapa*, *Pacha*, *Paya*, *Yama*, etc. These legends have been regarded as puzzling by the writers on early Indian numismatics.

Smith suggested that they are the names of certain foreign rulers who issued the coins in question, though Douglas and Chakrabortty[2] regarded them as Mālava chiefs. While rejecting Smith's suggestion, Allan rightly pointed out, "They certainly do not look like Indian; but it is difficult to think what invaders could have struck them. They are too late for the Śakas and too early for the Hūṇas ; in addition, out of over twenty names, not one bears any resemblance to any Śaka or Hūṇa name."[3] He further observed that these legends cannot be regarded as names of rulers since 'in not one, there is any trace of a genitive.'[4]

We may add a few more points to Allan's observations. In the first place, while it is difficult to believe that certain [Mālava] chiefs issued coins at the same time for circulation in the same area in addition to the monetary issues of the Mālava Republic, it is even more difficult to accommodate so many rulers using the 'Early Gupta' type of *ma* in the period before or after the age covered by the genuine issues of the Mālavas. Secondly, the well-known story of the gradual Indianisation of the foreign-

1. On Coin No. 70 in Smith's *Catalogue* (p. 175), the legend has been read as (1) *Malavā* (2) *Majupa*, both lines read from right to left. This imitation coin may be regarded as connecting the Mālavas with the coins bearing meaningless legends.

2. Chakrabortty draws our attention to the coins of the Rājanya Republic and those of Rājanya Mahīmitra whom he regards as the executive head of the Rājanyas. But it is doubtful whether the coins of the Rājanyas and of Mahīmitra were issued at the same time. Moreover the existence of Rājanya Mahīmitra seems to depend on misunderstanding. Alternatively Chakrabortty suggests that Bhapaṁyana and others may have been feudatories of the Mālava Republic.

3. *Op. cit.*, p. cvi.

4. *Ibid.*, p. cvii.

ers during the early-centuries of the Christian era, as indicated, among others, by their adoption of Indian names within a few generations, makes it difficult to believe that so many foreign rulers could have successively resisted the Indianisation of their names. Thirdly, since the Mālavas are actually known to have been an indigenous Indian tribe, it is difficult to explain such an intimate relation between their Republic and a group of foreign chiefs, so that both issued coins at the same time for circulation in the same region.

Jayaswal noted that many of the legends begin with the letter *ma* and therefore suggested that it is a contraction of the royal title *Mahārāja*. But Allan rightly rejected the suggestion on the following grounds. Firstly, even if *ma* is taken to stand for *Mahārāja*, the remaining letters of the legends do not offer any intelligible name. Secondly, there is no instance of such a contraction in Indian numismatics.

Allan's own conclusion on the puzzling legends of the Mālava coins runs as follows: "I am inclined to think [that] they are not names, but, in most cases, meaningless attempts to reproduce parts of *Mālavānāṁ jayaḥ*. This accounts for so many of them beginning with *ma* and for the frequency of *ma* as another letter of the inscriptions, and, indeed, for the limited number of consonants which form these inscriptions." Certainly this is the correct approach to the problem. But Allan failed to note that, considering the large number of the coins bearing meaningless legends, it is difficult to regard them as the genuine monetary issues of the Mālavas. On the other hand, the meaninglessness of the legends is no doubt easily explained if the coins are regarded as imitations of the Mālava money. Of course, there is ample evidence to show that, in ancient and medieval India, minting of coins was largely in the hands of the goldsmiths, so that some of the coins with meaningless legend may be supposed to have been issued by inefficient goldsmiths side by side with the regular Mālava coins minted by others. It is, however, difficult to explain in that case how the circulation of the two types of coins at the same time and in the same area should have been allowed by the Mālava Republic over a fairly

1. *Loc. cit.*
2. *Loc. cit.*

long period of time. We are therefore inclined to think that, when the Mālavas were no longer in a position to issue their own coins, local goldsmiths minted the imitation coins in order to meet the requirements of the people of the area in question, who were used to the Mālava coinage.

The rôle of local conservatism in Indian numismatics has often been emphasised and we have actually coins imitated from the Mālava types, which were issued by the Imperial Guptas[1] and local chiefs of the Mālava region such as Rāmagupta.[2] Among other notable imitation coins, mention may be made of the imitations of Kuṣāṇa coins discovered in Orissa, Rajasthan and the Punjab,[3] the imitation Gupta coins of Bengal[4] and local South Indian imitations of the Imperial Roman coinage.[5]

II

The unique silver coin of king Rudravarman in the Punjab Museum has been discussed by Cunningham,[6] Bergny,[7] Rapson,[8] Whitehead,[9] Allan,[10] S. K. Chakrabortty[11] and R. C. Kar.[12]

Formerly Rudravarman was regarded as a scion of the Audumbara clan because the elephant and trident-battleaxe represented on the coin were believed to have suggested its attribution to the Audumbaras. Thus even Allan says, "The Kharoṣṭhī legend also shows that the word before the king's name is *Vemaki* (for *Vaimaki*, like *Oduṁbara* for *Audumbara*). The legend means 'of the victorious king Rudravarman the Vimaki', the latter being an otherwise unknown family of the Audum-

1. Cf. the copper coins of Candragupta II with the vase on the reverse in Allan's *Catalogue* (Gupta), pp. lxxxviii, 60; below, p. 222.

2. *Ep. Ind.*, Vol. XXXIII, pp. 95-96; below, pp. 222-23; 226 ff.

3. Rapson, *op. cit.*, pp. 13, 35; Allan, *Catalogue* (Anc. Ind.), pp. cxxi-cxxii.

4. Allan, *Catalogue* (Gupta), pp. cvi-cvii; *JASB*, 1923, Num. Suppl., No. XXXVII, pp. 58 ff.

5. Cf. *Indian Archaeology*, 1957-58, p. 9.

6. *Coins of Ancient India*, pp. 66-68, Plate IV, No. 6.

7. *JRAS*, 1900, p. 419.

8. *Ibid.*, p. 429, note 2.

9. *Catalogue*, Vol. I, p. 167, No. 137, Plate XVI.

10. *Catalogue* (Anc. Ind.), pp. lxxxv-lxxxvi; cf. p. 125, No. 23, Plate XIV, No. 13.

11. *Op. cit.*, pp. 214-15.

12. *Ind. Hist. Quart.*, Vol. XX, pp. 59 ff. Allan and Kar do not refer to Chakrabortty's work published in 1931.

baras." Of course, there are a few errors in this statement, to which reference will be made below.

While R. D. Banerji was doubtful about the attribution of the coins not bearing the name of the Audumbaras to that people,[1] Chakrabortty suggests, "There seems to be some relationship between the Vimakas and the Ąudumbaras; perhaps they were neighbours." Kar points out that king Rudravarman of the coin belonged to the Vaimaki clan which he identifies with the Vaimakas of a text ascribed to an early astronomer named Parāśara[2] in Utpala's commentary on Varāhamihira's *Bṛhatsaṁhitā* and the Vaiyāmakas of the *Mahābhārata*.[3] He further draws our attention to Rapson's emphasis on the Indian coin-types being predominantly local in character[4] and observes that the close resemblance of Rudravarman's coin-type with the type of the Audumbara coins merely suggests the proximity of the mints and the areas of circulation of both the Vaimaki and Audumbara coins.

The dynastic or clan name of king Rudravarman has sometimes been read as *Vamaki*, although the correct form is now believed to be *Vemaki* which, as we have seen, has been taken to stand for Sanskrit *Vaimaki* derived from the name *Vimaki*. But *vemaka* in the sense of 'a weaver' is a common Sanskrit word, while Vemaka is the name of a sage whose wife, according to a tradition in the *Harivaṁśa* (III. 1. 14-15) and *Brahma Purāṇa* (13. 136-37), brought up the Kaurava king Ajapārśva, the great-great-grandson of Janamejaya Pārikṣita.[5] It seems therefore that the family or clan name *Vaimaki* is derived not from the

1. *JASB*, 1914, Num. Suppl., No. XXIII, p. 248.

2. Cf. *atha prāg-uttarasyāṃ Kaulūta-Brahmapura-Kuṇinda-Divādina-Pārata-Naṣṭarājya-Vanarāṣṭra-Vaimak-Āinabhalla-Siṃhapura-Cāmara-Taṅgaṇa-Sāryaka-Parvataka-Kāśmīra-Darada-Darvābhimu(sā)ra-Jaṭāsura-Paṭola-Sairindhra-Kucintana-Kirāta-Paśupāla-Cīna-Survarṇabhūmi-devasthala-devodyānāni.*

3. II. 52. 13-16 :

Kairātā Daradā Darvāḥ śūrā Vaiyāmakās=tathā ।
Audumbarā Durvibhāgāḥ Pāradā Vāhlikaiḥ saha ॥
Kāśmīrāś=ca Kumārāś=ca Ghorakā Haṃsakāyanāḥ ।
Śibi-Trigarta-Yaudheyā Rājanyā Madra-Kaikayāḥ ॥
Ambaṣṭhāḥ Kaukurās=Tārkṣyā Vastrapāḥ Pahlavaiḥ saha ।
Vaśātayaś=ca Mauleyāḥ saha Kṣudraka-Mālavaiḥ ॥
Pauṇḍrikāḥ Kukkurāś=c=aiva Śakāś=c=aiva viśāmpate ।
Aṅgā Vaṅgāś=ca Puṇḍrāś=ca Śāṇavatyā Gayās=tathā ॥

4. *Catalogue*, p. xi.

5. Some manuscripts of the *Brahma Purāṇa* read *Remaka* for *Vemaka*.

name *Vimaki*, but from *Vemaka* through the intermediate form *Vaimaka* just as the clan name *Audumbari* is derived from *Udumbara* through the intermediate form *Audumbara*.[1]

The identification of Parāśara's *Vaimaka* with *Vaiyāmaka* of the *Mahābhārata*, as suggested by Kar, may not be improbable It should, however, be noticed that *Vaimaka* and *Vaiyāmaka* are derived from two distinctly separate names, viz. *Vemaka* and *Vyāmaka* respectively. Thus, if we have to identify the Vaimakas and Vaiyāmakas, it has to be suggested that the person called Vemaka also bore the name Vyāmaka or that Vemaka and Vyāmaka were two distinguished rulers of the clan in question so that the people were named after both of them.

The full legend on the silver coin of Rudravarman, in Kharoṣṭhī on the obverse and in Brāhmī on the reverse, runs as follows : *rajña Vemakisa Rudravarmasa vijayata*, standing for Sanskrit *rājñaḥ Vaimakeḥ Rudravarmaṇaḥ vijayataḥ*, "[This is the coin] of the victorious king Rudravarman who is a scion of the Vaimaka clan." But Allan has offered some new suggestions.

In the body of Allan's *Catalogue*,[2] he reads the Kharoṣṭhī legend as *raña Vamakisa Rudravarmasa vijayata*, while his eye-copy of the Brāhmī legend would read *rajña Vamakisa Rudravarmasa vajaya[ka ?]*. But, in the Introduction,[3] the following readings have been proposed :

1. Udumbara was the name of a descendant of the sage Viśvāmitra and the founder of a *gotra* of the Kauśika group. For the tradition, see, in the first instance, *Harivaṃśa*, I. 27. 48 ff. (Audumbara); *Vāyu Purāṇa*, 91. 96 ff. (Udumbara); *Brahmāṇḍa Purāṇa*, III.66. 68 ff. (Udumbara). Among the authorities on *gotra* and *pravara*, Baudhāyana assigns the Vaiśvāmitra, Daivarāta and Audala *pravaras* to the Audumbari *gotra* and the Vaiśvāmitra, Kātya and Ātkila *pravaras* to the Audumbarāyaṇa *gotra*. This latter group of *pravaras* is assigned to the Audumbari or Audumbarāyaṇi *gotra* by Āpastamba and to the Udumbari *gotra* by the *Matsya Purāṇa*. It appears that Udumbara, Udumbari, Audumbara, Audumbari, Audumbarāyaṇa and Audumbarāyaṇi are variants of the same *gotra* name, although originally the Audumbari *gotra* may have been regarded as separate from, but allied with, the Audumbarāyaṇa *gotra*, the former falling in the Viśvāmitra-Kuśika group and the latter in the Kata group. See J. Brough, *The Early Brahmanical System of Gotra and Pravara*, pp. 35, 147-48, 153, 157, etc. In any case, the fact that the Audumbaras thus claimed descent from Viśvāmitra explains the representation of the sage, called *Viśpamitra* in Prakrit in the Kharoṣṭhī legend, on the obverse of the silver coin of the Audumbara king Dharaghoṣa (Allan, *op. cit.*, p. 124). According to a Puranic tradition, the Udumbaras (Audumbaras) were one of the six branches of the Sālva tribe (Sircar, *Stud. Geog. Anc. Med. Ind.*, p. 21, note 3)

2. See p. 125.

3. Cf. pp. lxxxv-lxxxvi.

Kharoṣṭhī—*vijayaya-raña Vemakisa Rudravarmasa.*

Brāhmī—*vijayaka-rajñ[o] Vemakisa Rudravarmasa.*

And, in respect of these readings, we have Allan's observations in the following words: "In the text (p. 125), I had adopted the reading *vijayata*, given by Cunningham, Rapson and others, for the word in the exergue in Kharoṣṭhī. There is no doubt, however, that the word is *vijayaya*, a Prakrit equivalent of *vijayaka* (on *ya* for *ka*, cf. Pischel, *Grammatik der Prakrit Sprachen*, 1900, $ 598) which, and not *vijaya* (sic), is the correct reading of the corresponding word in the Brāhmī inscription where it begins the legend. It is an adjective meaning 'victorious'......" We find it difficult to agree with Allan in respect of the reading and interpretation of the word *vijayaya* in Kharoṣṭhī and *vijayaka* in Brāhmī.

In the first place, we have no doubt that the reading is *vijayata* (Sanskrit *vijayataḥ*, 'of the victorious') in both Kharoṣṭhī and Brāhmi. In Sanskrit syntax, it is of course immaterial whether the word stands at the beginning or at the end of the legend, though, in the former position, it may have been changed to *vijayato* in *Sandhi*.

Secondly, it is doubtful whether the author of the legend would have written *vijayaka-rājñaḥ* for *vijaya-rājasya* because, although the suffix *ka* is sometimes added to nouns without changing the meaning of the words, it generally indicates diminution, deterioration, endearment or similarity; *e.g.*, *vṛkṣaka*, 'a small tree'; *putraka*, 'a dear or little son'; *aśvaka*, 'a bad horse'; etc. The expression *vijayaka-rāja* would then have the derogatory sense of 'a king having a small victory to his credit', a probable meaning which a sane officer is expected to have avoided in the description of his master.

III

While writing, some years ago,[1] on the tribal and monarchical states flourishing on the decline of the Kuṣāṇa power in various parts of North India, we pointed out that the fashion of mentioning the name of the ruling authority on the coin-legend was inspired and popularised in India by the foreign

1. *The Age of Imperial Unity*, ed. Majumdar, Bombay, 1951, p. 159.

kings beginning with the Indo-Greeks and that most of the coins bearing legends should preferably be assigned to dates later than the earlier decades of the second century B.C. It was also indicated that the word read as *Bhagavata* on certain tribal coins and often taken to stand for Sanskrit *Bhāgavata*, 'a devout worshipper of the Bhagavat (i.e. the god Viṣṇu)' and regarded as an epithet of the ruler who issued the coins, really stands for *Bhagavataḥ*, 'of the Lord', and refers to the deity in whose name the coins in question were issued and that sometimes the name of the deity was mentioned side by side with that of a king without the said epithet.[1]

In J. Allan's *Catalogue of the Indian Coins in the British Museum* (*Catalogue of the Coins of Ancient India*), published in 1936, the legends on the coins of the Audumbari kings Śivadāsa, Rudradāsa and Dharaghoṣa have been read respectively as *Mahadevasa raña Sivadasasa*, *Mahadevasa raña Rudradasasa* and *Mahadevasa raña Dharaghosasa*, in which *Mahadeva* (*Mahādeva*) has been regarded as a 'regal title.'[2] In our opinion, Mahādeva here is the well-known name of the god Śiva and the coins were issued in the name of the said god as well as of the ruling king of the Audumbaris, apparently because Mahādeva or Śiva was the deity enjoying the special devotion of the clan in question.

On a class of coins attributed to the Audumbaris, the legend has been read and interpreted as *Bhagavata-Mahadevasa rajaraña* (or *rajaraja*[*sa*]), Sanskrit *Bhāgavata-Mahādevasya rājarājasya*, 'of Mahādeva, the worshipper of the Bhagavat [and] the king of kings.'[3] But, in our opinion, the coins were issued in the name of the god Mahādeva conceived as a ruler apparently because the kingdom had been dedicated to the deity. A similar case of the medieval age is the representation of the god Puruṣottama-Jagannātha (Viṣṇu) of Purī as the overlord of the later Eastern Gaṅga kings of Orissa and their political successors, in medieval Orissan records, as a result of the dedication of the Gaṅga kingdom to the said god by king Anaṅgabhīma III (1211-39 A.D.).[4]

1. Cf. *ibid.*, p. 161, notes 1 and 4.
2. *Op. cit.*, pp. lxxxiii-lxxxiv.
3. *Ibid.* p. lxxxv.
4. *Ep. Ind.*, Vol. XXX, pp. 19,47 ff. There are several cases of the type.

On certain coins attributed to the Kuṇindas, the legend has been read as *Bhāgavata-Catreśvara-Mahātmanaḥ.*[1] But the intended reading is no doubt *Bhagavataḥ Catreśvara-mahātmanaḥ* "[This is the coin] of Lord Catreśvara, the Supreme Being." Catreśvara, apparently a form of Śiva whose figure holding the trident appears on the obverse of the coins, was probably the deity to whom the Kuṇindas were specially devoted.

On the coins of the Yaudheyas, the legends have been read and interpreted as follows : (1) *Bhagavata-svāmino Brahmaṇya* [*sya*] *Yaudheya* or *Yaudheya-bhāgavata-svāmino Brahmaṇyasya*, "of Brahmaṇya (a name of Kārttikeya), the divine lord of the Yaudheyas," and (2) *Bhāgavata-svāmino Brahmaṇyadevasya Kumārasya*, "of Kumāra the divine lord Brahmaṇyadeva."[2] But the intended readings of the two legends are apparently (1) *Bhagavataḥ Svāmino Brahmaṇyasa Yaudheyānām* "[This is the coin] of the Divine Lord Brahmaṇya [and] the Yaudheyas"; and (2) *Bhagavataḥ Svāmino Brahmaṇyadevasya Kumārasya*, "[This is the coin] of the Divine Lord Brahmaṇyadeva *alias* Kumāra." Thus the first series of the coins was issued in the name both of the Yaudheya people and the deity to whom they were specially devoted, viz., the god Brahmaṇyadeva Kumāra, while the second series was issued in the name of the god alone.

A number of copper coins were discovered at Agroha (in the Hissar District of the Eastern Punjab) and its neighbourhood.[3] They have two distinct varieties. The legend of the first of the varieties reads *Agodakā Agāca-janapadasa*, which reminds us of the legend, *Majhamikāya Śibi-janapadasa* (Sanskrit *Madhyamikāyāḥ Śibi-janapadasya*), "[This is the coin] of the Śibi-janapada from (*i.e.* struck at) Madhyamikā," and seems to stand for Sanskrit *Agrodakāt Agratya-janapadasya*, "[This is the coin] of the *janapada* or corporation of the Agratyas from (*i.e.* struck at) Agrodaka." Thus the legend refers to the Agratya people whose territory consisted of or had its headquarters at the city of Agrodaka which is no doubt modern Agroha. The real name of the place seems to have been Agra, which or the headquarters or office-area of which may have been called Agrodaka

1. Allan, *op. cit.*, p. ciii.
2. *Ibid.*, pp. cxlix-cl.
3. Allan, *op. cit.*, pp. clvii-clviii, 282-83; Barnett in *BSOS*, Vol. X, p. 279; P. L. Gupta in *JNSI*, Vol. IV, pp. 49 ff.

owing to the existence of a tank.[1] The name *Agratya* probably means 'the inhabitants of Agra' and the form *Agāca* is derived from it through Prakrit *Aggacca*=*Aggāca*, the latter giving *Agāca* in epigraphic Prakrit by avoiding re-duplication in *ggā* and modifying it to *gā*.

The legend on another group of Agroha coins has been read by Barnett as *Agāca-mitrapad-ābhiṣṭhāyinaṁ* in which he finds a reference to a *mitrapada* and interprets it 'as an allied State', *i.e.* a state allied to the Agāca people. It appears, however, that the intended reading and interpretation are *Agratya-mitra-pad-ābhiṣṭhāyinām*, "[This is the coin] of those who dwell at the feet of [the god] Agratyamitra." The name Agratyamitra means 'the friend of the Agratyas' and the god appears to have been the deity specially worshipped by the Agratya people. Thus the Agratyas are mentioned here indirectly as devotees of 'the friend of the Agratyas'. In this case, therefore, the coins are not represented as the issues of the deity to whom a people were particularly devoted. On the other hand, a people (*i.e.* Agratyas of Agrodaka, the same as the Agravālas of today) that issued the coins, is represented as devoted to the god enjoying their special devotion.

1. Cf. *JNSI*, Vol. IV, p. 52.

Chapter XI

COINS OF KUMĀRAGUPTA I, HARIGUPTA AND RĀMAGUPTA

I

A few gold coins of the Gupta emperor Kumāragupta I (413-55 A.D.), belonging to the Rhinoceros-slayer type, have been discovered, and the question whether these coins have any bearing on the extent of Kumāragupta's empire has been discussed by scholars. M. M. Nagar observed, "The portrayal of rhinoceros.........is very important as it suggests that nearly 1500 years ago this animal was frequently met with in Āryāvarta, although it has since become entirely extinct from here. Or alternatively it may suggest that Assam (ancient Kāmarūpa), the marshy jungles of which are even today the abode of rhinoceroses, was included in the vast empire of Kumāragupta I and that sometime during his lifetime the king had visited the place and hunted there these wild and hefty animals. The latter view, however, appears more plausible, as it is supported by similar coin types of other Imperial Gupta emperors, the Tiger-slayer type of Samudragupta marking his conquest of East Bengal and Assam (Samataṭa-Ḍavāka-Kāmarūpa) areas, where alone the tigers are found, and the Lion-slayer type of Candragupta II commemorating his conquest of Kathiawar, the only place where lions are found in India."[1]

Unfortunately Nagar indulged in the above speculations without caring to examine the question whether ancient and medieval Indian literature and the works of foreign travellers speak of the existence of the rhinoceros, tiger and lion in areas other than those where they flourish today. Indeed a study of such sources, which would have sapped the foundation of Nagar's theory, was not undertaken by any one. On the

1. *JNSI* Vol. XI, Part I, 1949, p. 8. There are other observations of this nature in Nagar's article "We know from other sources that Kumāragupta I inherited a vast empire from his father Candragupta II which included both Kathiawar and Assam, and it is very probable that he might have visited both these parts of his empire, hunted lions and rhinoceroses and perpetuated these exploits on his coins."

other hand, P. J. Chinmulgund offered unqualified support to Nagar's views when he declared, "Nagar seems to be right in his conclusion that Kumāragupta's empire included Assam and that the king might have hunted the rhinoceros there. We know that, except towards the end of his reign, Kumāragupta's rule was peaceful and prosperous and the king might have visited different parts of his vast empire and hunted tigers in Bengal, lions in Kathiawar (Saurāṣṭra) and the rhinoceros in Assam; and quite appropriately these exploits were commemorated on his coinage."[1]

S. V. Sohoni, however, rightly drew attention to the views of S. H. Prater on the distribution of the rhinoceros in India, and this latter authority says, "Formerly extensively distributed in the Indian Peninsula. Today it is restricted to parts of Nepal and Assam. In Nepal, it is found only in the country to the east of the Gandak river, known as Chaitwan, in Assam in isolated areas of the plains."[2]

Unfortunately, the word 'formerly' in the passage quoted from Prater does not make it clear whether the rhinoceros was 'extensively distributed in the Indian Peninsula' before or even after the age of the Imperial Guptas (from the 4th to the 6th century A.D.). That is why even Sohoni could not free himself completely from the influence of Nagar's speculation. He said, "It is not necessary to hold that Kumāragupta I had to go to Kāmarūpa to hunt a big one-horned rhinoceros.......... It is more probable that Kumāragupta I's hunt of rhinoceros took place in North Bihar jungles adjoining the Chaitwan region in Nepal, not far away from Vaiśālī, than in distant Assam. A ruler of Pāṭalipatra would have found this more convenient."[3] Sohoni further observed, "It could be safely assumed on account of this variety's extensive distribution in North India centuries ago, that Kumaragupta I could have hunted a big one-horned rhinoceros much nearer home than in Assam."

1. *Ibid.*, Vol. XVII, Part ii, 1955, pp. 105-06. For other recent writings on the coin type, see *ibid.*, Vol. XXIV, pp. 152 ff. ; Vol. XXV, Part i, pp. 29 ff. B.N. Mukherjee appropriates Nagar's views when he tries to prove that the said coins were issued to commemorate Kumāragupta's conquest of Kāmarūpa (*IHQ*, Vol. XXXI, 1955, pp. 175 ff.).

2. *JNSI*, Vol. XVIII, Part ii, 1956, p. 179; Prater, *The Book of Indian Animals*, pp. 101 ff. Instead of 'Rhinoceros-slayer', Sohoni calls the type *Khaḍga-trātā* (Rhinoceros-saviour).

3. *JNSI*, Vol. XVIII, Part ii, p. 179.

But, if the rhinoceros flourished in early times in the valley of the Ganges on which the Gupta capital stood, how can it be possible to determine the exact spot where Kumāragupta I might have encountered a rhinoceros ?

There is evidence to show that the rhinoceros flourished in the Ganges valley at least as late as the 11th century A.D. The celebrated Muslim savant Abu Rihān Al-Bīrūnī, who wrote his *Kitābul Hind* in 1031 A.D., says, "The *gaṇḍa* exists in large numbers in India, more particularly about the Ganges. It is of the build of a buffalo, has a black scaly skin, and develops hanging dewlaps down under the chin. It has three yellow hoofs on each foot, the biggest one forward, the others on both sides. The tail is not long; the eyes lie low, further down the cheek than is the case with all other animals. On the top of the nose there is a single horn which is bent upwards. The Brāhmaṇas have the privilege of eating the flesh of the *gaṇḍa*.[1] I have myself witnessed how an elephant coming across a *gaṇḍa* was attacked by it. The *gaṇḍa* wounded with its horn a forefoot of the elephant, and threw it down on its face."[2]

II

It was early in the year 1949 that A. S. Altekar sent to various scholars photographs of Kumāragupta's 'Apratigha' type of coins in the Bayānā hoard and requested them to give him their opinion especially on the reading of the marginal legend on the obverse.[3] I was amongst those who received the photographs; but I felt diffident to offer any suggestion on the marginal legend because it appeared to me that no satisfactory reading of the said section of the legend was possible on the basis of the photograph. I was eager to examine some plaster-casts ; but none was available to me. People bolder than myself of course published the results of their study of the coins in the pages of the *Journal*

1. The flesh of the rhinoceros is perscribed as the proper Aryan food by Bodhāyana (1.12.5), Manu (V. 18), Gautama (17.27), Āpastamba (1.17.37), Viṣṇu (51.6, 26-27), etc., though Vasiṣṭha (14.39-40,44,47) says that there are conflicting opinions regarding the flesh of the wild boar and rhinoceros. See G.N. Jha, *Manusmṛti Notes*, Part III, pp. 365-66.

2. Sachau, *Alberuni's India*, Part I, pp. 203-04.

3. Cf. A. S. Altekar, *Catalogue of the Gupta Gold Coins in the Bayana Hoard*, p. cxi.

of the Numismatic Society of India,[1] and their views were discussed by Altekar in the introductory part of his *Catalogue.* Several notes on the subject also appeared after the publication of Altekar's *Catalogue,* one of them from the pen of Altekar himself.[2] But none of the suggestions on the 'Apratigha' coins appeared to me to be of any worth. There are two smaller lagends, viz. the king's name on either side of the lower part of the central one of the three standing human figures on the obverse pointing to its identity and one of the king's titles on the reverse. These could be confidently read from the photograph.

Recently, S. V. Sohoni kindly sent me a few plaster-casts of a Bayānā coin of the 'Apratiga' type, now preserved in the Bhārat Kalā Bhavan attached to the Hindu University, Varanasi. This seems to be Coin No. 10 on Plate XXXI in Altekar's *Catalogue.* On this specimen, the syllables between III and VI are somewhat better preserved than elsewhere and I have been tempted to offer my tentative reading of these letters in the following lines. The casts were not quite satisfactory. It is also a matter of regret that casts of all the coins of this type were not available to me.

Much has already been written on the 'Apratigha' type of Kumāragupta's coins, as indicated above, and the points raised by various scholars are expected to be quite familiar to the students of Gupta numismatics. I am therefore submitting my suggestions generally without arguments for or against the views on the subject expressed by previous writers. It is, however, necessary to make one point clear at the outset : I have no doubt that the smaller legend giving the name of the central one of the three human figures on the obverse of the coins and the royal title on the reverse respectively read *Kumāraguptaḥ* and *Apratighaḥ* and that I consider *Mihirakulaḥ* and *Śripratāpaḥ,* as read by some scholars in their place, to be definitely wrong.

Of the three figures on the obverse of the coins, the

1. Vol. XII, pp. 68 ff., 72 ff.

2. *Ibid,* Vol. XVI, pp. 210. ff.; Vol. XVIII, pp. 56 ff.; Vol XXI, pp. 34 ff., 71-72; Vol. XXIII, pp. 345 ff. (cf. *The Indian Numismatic Chronicle,* Vol. II, pp. 99 ff.); Vol. XXIV, pp. 164 ff.; *Ind. Hist. Quart.,* Vol. XXXIV, pp. 270 ff.; Vol. XXXV, pp. 265 ff.

central one, labelled as 'Kumāragupta' is shorter in stature than the male figure on his right and the female figure on his left and seems therefore to be represented as a boy.[1] His hair is tied in a top-knot on the head and his hands folded on the chest. As regards the first of these two characteristics, it has to be pointed out that, though bearded Indian ascetics tied their hair in a top-knot, the practice was by no means confined to them. Indeed, the malefolk in ancient India generally kept long hair and tied it in a top-knot.[2] The folded hands of the central figure, *i. e.* the boy Kumāragupta, indicate his reverential attitude towadrs the male and female figures on either side. He is not represented as looking at either of the side figures. This is apparently due to an attempt to represent him as exhibiting exactly equal reverence to both.

The male figure to the right of the boy Kumāragupta holds a shield in his left hand and the Garuḍa-dhvaja in the right. He is depicted in the attitude of presenting the Garuḍa-dhvaja to the boy. It seems, however, that he is really offering both the shield and the Garuḍa-dhvaja to Kumāragupta. The female figure to the left of Kumāragupta is also depicted as offering to him some unidentifiable object held on the palm of her extended right hand.

As indicated above, the folded hands of the boy Kumāragupta point to the reverence shown by him to the male and female figures on his sides. There is also little doubt that the scene depicted on the obverse of the 'Apratigha' coins relates to an incident in Kumāragupta's life and that it is closely associated with his title *Apratigha*, 'Invincible', found on the reverse of the coins. It is thus not impossible that the presents received by Kumāragupta from the two well-wishers, including the shield and Garuḍa-dhvaja, made it possible for young Kumāragupta to attain the invincibility referred to in the title. The marginal legend is expected to

1. The small size of Kumāragupta may also be due to the fact that he was a man while the other two were divinities.

2. Cf. Motichandra in *Journal of the Indian Society of Oriental Art*, Vol. VIII, 1940, pp. 90, 92, etc.; Hopkins in *Journal of the American Oriental Society*, Vol. XIII, pp. 193 note, 307 note. Cf. *Mṛcchakaṭika* IX. 2: *Kṣaṇena granthiḥ kṣaṇa-jūṭako me kṣaṇena bālā kṣaṇa-kuntalā vā* |, *kṣaṇena muktāḥ kṣaṇa ūrdhva-cūḍā citro vicitrohaṁ rāja-śyālaḥ* ||

contain the expression *Apratigha* though it has not yet been traced therein.

It is indeed difficult to understand the real implication of the scene, especially in view of the fact that the marginal legend has not been satisfactorily read to offer us the expected clue. Under the circumstances, we have merely to conjecture a possible explanation. Suppose, Kumāragupta lost his father at a young age and was defeated in battle by his adversaries who even snatched away the Garuḍa-dhvaja which was the banner of the Imperial Gupta house. Suppose, when he was in that deplorable condition, a male and a female friend, probably believed to have been divine personages in desguise, appeared to him and gave him certain objects which ultimately helped him in overpowering his enemies and making himself invincible. The permissibility of such a conjecture of course depends on the support it gets from the marginal legend when the latter is satisfactorily deciphered.

The syllables between III and VI are ten in number, the first five of which appear to read *a* (or *pra*) *ptapatako* standing for *āpta-patāko* or *prāpta-patāko*, i.e. '[Kumāragupta] who has received his *patākā*, i.e., flag or banner'. The question is whether the word *patākā* in this context means the Garuḍa-dhvaja represented as being offered to Kumāragupta by his male well-wisher in the scene. In an excellent discussion on the meanings of *dhvaja*, *ketu* and *patākā* in the *Mahābhārata*, Hopkins shows that *dhvaja* is often a synonym of *ketu*, though sometimes the former means the whole arrangement including the staff and the image or banner, while the latter indicates only the symbol or banner alone. He further points out that *ketu* is sometimes synonymous with *patākā* or flag and the *dhvaja* is the metallic top-piece of the staff, or that together with the staff which bore flags beneath the emblem.[1] It is interesting, however, to note that the *Amarakoṣa* (Kṣatriya-varga, VIII. 101) regards *patākā*, *vaijayantī*, *ketana* and *dhvaja* as synonymous words. Thus the Garuḍa standard represented on the coins as being presented to Kumāragupta may be the *patākā*, men-

1. See *Journal of the American Oriental Society*, Vol. XIII, pp. 243 ff.; *Ep. Ind.*, Vol. XXXIII, p. 136.

tioned in the passage describing Kumāragupta as *āpta-patāka* or *prāpta-patāka*.

I am less confident about the reading of the next five syllables which may be *nukapadaptaḥ*, i.e. [*a*]*nukampā-dīptaḥ*, meaning '[Kumāragupta] who was stimulated by the sympathy [of friends].' The following three syllables, which are partially preserved, look like *narapa*, though it is difficult to conjecture the intended word without examining some other specimens of the type.

The metrical legends on Imperial Gupta coins mostly contain half or quarter of a stanza. The marginal legend on the 'Apratigha' coins of Kumāragupta, however, appears to exhibit a complete stanza.

III

A copper coin of a king named Harigupta, stated to have been found at Ahicchatrā (modern Rāmanagar in the Bareily District, U. P.), was published by Cunningham in his *Coins of Medieval India*.[1] Its weight is given as 41 grains and size .6 inch. The obverse of the coin contains the representation of a *pūrṇa-kumbha*[2] on a pedestal while the legend in two lines on the reverse was read as [*śrī*]-*mahār*[*āja*]-[*Ha*]*riguptasya*. Allan who entered the coin in his *Catalogue of the Coins of the Gupta Dynasties*,[3] however, observed that the reading of the legend is very uncertain, *guptasya* alone being clear. But, as regards the reading, we are inclined to agree with Cunningham. Elsewhere in the same work,[4] Allan admits his inability to offer any suggestion regarding the identity of the king who issued the coin, but observes[5] that the palaeography of the legend suggests a date in the fifth century A.D.

Assuming the correctness of the reading of the name Harigupta in the legend, we have to see what relations the ruler might have had with the Imperial Gupta dynasty of Magadha. It has to be pointed out that the Ahicchatrā coin of Harigupta is not without resemblance with the copper coinage of the Imperial

1. See p. 19, Plate II, No. 6.
2. This is often described as a flower-vase.
3. Cf. p. 152, No. 616; Plate XXIV, No. 16.
4. See p. lxi.
5. Cf. p. cv.

Guptas in type and style. One type of copper coins issued by the Gupta emperor Candragupta II (*c.* 376-413 A.D.) shows a *pūrṇa-kumbha* (with flowers or leaves hanging down its sides) within a dotted border on the obverse and the legend *Candra* beneath a crescent within a similar border on the reverse.[1] Elsewhere Allan, suggests that this type was probably struck in Malwa in imitation of the Mālava tribal issues just as Candragupta II imitated the coins of the Śaka rulers in his silver coinage meant for circulation in Western India conquered from the Śakas.[2] The vase within a dotted border is a well-known feature of the coins of the Mālavas.[3] It has to be admitted that the weight of the seven coins of this type of Candragupta II in the British Museum cabinet varies between 3.3 and 18 grains, while the weight of the Ahicchatrā coin of Harigupta is 41 grains. But a number of copper issues of the Gupta monarch are known to weigh between 40.5 and 49.5 or more grains.[4] Now we have to determine whether Harigupta imitated the copper coinage of Candragupta II or whether he ruled over a tract near about the Malwa region and imitated the tribal issues of the Mālavas.

In this connection we have also to see whether Harigupta of the Ahicchatrā coin was related to another ruler of the Malwa region who bore a name ending with the word *gupta* and some of whose coins have been discovered in East Malwa. A few years ago, six copper coins of a ruler named Rāmagupta were discovered in a locality near Bhilsa (near the capital of the ancient Ākara or Daśārṇa country comprising East Malwa) and were published in the *Journal of the Numismatic Society of India.*[5] Their obverse exhibits, within a dotted border, a lion sitting, facing left, with its tail raised and curled, while their reverse shows the legend *Rāmaguta* or *Rāmagupta* beneath a crescent within a similar border. The weight of these coins varies between 2.5 and 31.3 grains. It may be pointed out that the lion is a familiar device on the Mālava coins, although generally they

1. *Ibid.*, p. 60 ; Plate XI, Nos. 21-26. Allan describes the *pūrṇa-kumbha* as a flower-vase.

2. *Catalogue of the Coins of Ancient India*, p. cvi.

3. See Smith, *Catalogue of the Coins in the Indian Museum*, Vol. I, pp. 171 f.

4. Cf. Allan, *Catalogue* (Gupta), pp. 52 ff., Nos. 141-45, 147-48, 152-53, 160-61.

5. Vol. XII, pp. 103 ff.

exhibit the animal in a standing posture.[1] The palaeography of the legend on Rāmagupta's coins suggests that they were issued sometime in the fourth or fifth century A.D. Another group of four copper coins, similar to the above six, also found at Bhilsa, have been published in the same journal.[2]

There has been a controversy whether Rāmagupta of the Bhilsa (now named Vidiśā) coins was a local ruler of the said region or should be identified with the Gupta king of the same name who, according to literary traditions, succeeded the Gupta emperor Samudragupta (*c*. 335-76 A.D.), but was ousted by his younger brother Candragupta II.[3] It is difficult to be definite on this point. The Prakritic form of the name *Rāmaguta* found on some of the coins may be a mistake not suggesting a date earlier than the time of Samudragupta who is the first Gupta monarch to have extended his supremacy in the Malwa region.[4] But a point which can scarcely be ignored in this connection is that, if Rāmagupta really belonged to the Imperial Gupta dynasty and ruled as an emperor even for a short period, we would have by now discovered at least a few of his gold coins, since the largest number of Gupta coins so far found are gold issues, the Gupta silver and copper coinage being far less copious. The genuineness of the literary tradition regarding the existence of a Gupta emperor named Rāmagupta has not yet been proved by any other evidence.

The problem to be solved now is : if Rāmagupta is regarded as a local ruler of the Malwa region unconnected with the Gupta, should he be assigned to a date somewhat earlier than the expansion of Gupta supremacy in the said area about the middle of the fourth century A.D. ? Should Harigupta of the Ahicchatrā coin, on which the reading of the name has been doubted by Allan, be regarded as a scion of Rāmagupta's family or of any other local ruling house and as flourishing before

1. Smith, *op. cit.*, p. 172.
2. *JNSI*, Vol. XIII, pp. 128 ff.
3. See *ibid.*, Vol. XII, pp. 103 ff.
4. One of Samudragupta's inscriptions has been found engraved on a pillar at Eraṇ in the Saugor District of Madhya Pradesh (i.e. in East Malwa) and his Allahabad pillar inscription refers to his success against the Āryāvarta king Rudradeva who is apparently the Śaka ruler Rudrasena III of Western India. See *Select Inscriptions*, pp. 257, 260 ff.; *Proc. IHC*, Madras, 1944, pp. 78 ff.

the middle of the fourth century ? The problem of this ruler is, however, rendered more complicated by two factors. In the first place, a newly discovered copper coin of the king not only gives the name quite clearly as Harigupta, but is also a very clear imitation of a type of the copper coinage of Candragupta II. Secondly, we have an inscription testifying to the fact that a king named Harirāja, who claimed to have been a scion of the Gupta dynasty, ruled over the region comprising the present Banda District of U. P. sometime in the fifth century and it is very probable that he is identical with the issuer of the Ahicchatrā coin.

A copper coin, now exhibited in the Allahabad Municipal Museum, was examined by me when I visited Allahabad in December 1957. The Curator of the Museum was kind enough to allow me to take a plaster-cast of the coin. There can be no doubt that the prototype from which this coin was imitated is the second variety of the second type of the copper coinage of Candragupta II described and illustrated by Allan in his *Catalogue of the Coins of the Gupta Dynasties*.[1] The prototype may be described as follows :

Obverse : King standing to left (three-quarter length), apparently casting incense on altar with uplifted right hand (as on similar gold coins of the Chatra type); left hand behind on hip; behind the king a dwarf attendant holding the parasol over him.

Reverse : The bird Garuḍa (the emblem of the Guptas) standing, facing, with outspread wings (without human arms with bracelets as seen on the first variety of these copper coins); legend below the above reading *Mahārāja-śrī-Candraguptaḥ* in one line.

The size of the coins is about three quarters of an inch and weight between 36.5 and 101.5 grains. On the coin of Harigupta, the obverse does not clearly show the parasol in the hands of the attendant and the proper right side of the bird on the reverse is blurred, while the legend beneath the bird reads *Mahārāja-śrī-Hariguptasya* in two lines in character similar to those of the legend on the Ahicchatrā coin. The size of our coin is .85

1. See p. 53, Nos. 144-47; Plate XI, No. 4.

inch and its weight 49 grains, although its exact findspot seems to be unknown. We have no doubt that the same *Mahārāja* Harigupta also issued the Ahicchatrā coin, even though Allan doubted the reading of the name on it.

An inscription on a bronze image found in the ruins of Dhanesar Kherā in the village of Ichchhawar or Nichchhawar in the Banda District, U. P., was published by Smith and Hoey as early as 1895,[1] although they could not decipher the record satisfactorily. The correct reading of this record in two lines is as follows :—

1. *Deya-dharmmō=ya(ṁ*) Gupta-vaṅśo (vaṁś-ō)dita-śrī-Harirājasya ra(rā)jñī-Mahādevyā[ḥ] (।*) yad=attra puṇya(ṁ*) tad=bhavatu*
2. *sa[rvva]-sa[tvā(ttvā)nā](ṁ*) māta(tā)-pitṛ-pū[rvva]-ṅgama(me)na anuttara-pada-jñāna(n-ā)vāptaye(।*)*[2]

It seems that the ruins of Dhanesar Kherā referred to above represent the site of the headquarters of Harirāja mentioned in the inscription. We know that, about the fifth century A.D., the title *Mahārāja* was enjoyed by the subordinates and feudatories of the Gupta *Mahārājñādhirājas*.[3] Our Harirāja, called *Mahārāja* in the legend on his coins, thus appears to have been a subordinate of the contemporary Gupta emperor. The first question now is : if Harirāja belonged to the Imperial Gupta family, why was he called Harirāja and not Harigupta ? We know that from the assumption of imperial status by Candragupta I about 320 A.D., his descendants assumed names ending in the word *gupta*. But we also know that the second name of Candragupta II is sometimes quoted as both *Devagupta* and *Devarāja*.[4] Thus mere mention of the ruler's name as *Harirāja* instead of *Harigupta* does not prove anything. The second question to be answered then is : if Harirāja-Harigupta was a scion of the Imperial Gupta family even from his mother's side, why is his family relationship with the contemporary Gupta emperor not specified in the inscription ? The answer to this seems to be that the relation ship was not a very close one.

Thus, even if the problem of the Ichchhavar inscription

1. *JASB*, Vol. LXIV, 1895, Part i, pp. 159 ff. and Plate.
2. See *JOR*, Vol. XVIII, 1949, pp. 185 ff.
3. Cf. *IHQ*, Vol. XXII, pp. 64-65. The Gupta emperors were rarely called *Mahārāja*.
4. *Select Inscriptions*, pp. 273, 420.

can be solved, the Ahicchatrā and Allahabad Museum coins offer yet another difficulty. The king enjoyed the feudatory title *Mahārāja* and there is no doubt that he imitated a type of the copper coins of Candragupta II. The question now is whether a subordinate ruler was allowed by his Gupta suzerain to issue coins of his own. This seems to be extremely doubtful in the present state of our knowledge. As we have already seen, *Mahārāja* Harigupta of the Ahicchatrā and Allahabad Museum coins cannot be assigned to an age earlier than the expansion of Gupta supremacy in Malwa and Central India since he certainly imitated one of the types of the copper coins issued by Candragupta II, the obverse design of which was itself a copy of the well-known Chatra type of the same monarch's gold coinage. But when did Harirāja-Harigupta issue his copper coin of the same type ? The answer to this question may be that Harigupta issued the coins on the decline of Gupta power about the last quarter of the fifth cetury A.D. He seems to have selected some of the popular types of Imperial Gupta coinage prevalent in the area over which he ruled. Considering the problem of local conservatism in ancient Indian numismatics, it does not appear necessary to think that Harigupta's coins were issued shortly after the issue of their prototypes.

IV

It has been indicated above that some coins bearing the name of Rāmagupta on the obverse and the figure of a lion on the reverse were discovered a few years ago.[1] These coins are of copper and were found in the region of East Malwa. They resemble the monetary issues of the Mālavas of Rajasthan and the Nāgas of Malwa. There was a controversy on the position of the issuer of the coins. Some scholars favoured his identification with an Imperial Gupta ruler who, according to the story of Viśākhadatta's drama entitled *Devīcandragupta*, bore the name Rāmagupta and was the immediate predecessor of

1. Above, pp. 222-23; *JNSI*, Vol. XII, pp. 103-06, Plate IX, Nos. 1-6; Vol. XIII, pp. 128-30, Plate VIII, Nos. 1-8; Vol. XVII, pp. 108-09, Plate VIII, No. 1.

Candragupta II Vikramāditya (376-413 A.D.). But there were others who took Rāmagupta of the copper coins to be a local ruler of the Malwa region since they were doubtful about the historicity of Rāmagupta known from the tradition recorded in the *Devīcandragupta*.

Recently K.D. Bajpai has published some more coins of Rāmagupta, which were collected by him from Vidiśā and Eraṇ in East Malwa.[1] They are also of copper and some of them are of the lion type known from Rāmagupta's coins published previously. But a number of the coins now published by Bajpai bear the symbol of Garuḍa, facing with outspread wings, instead of the lion emblem, on the reverse. Since Garuḍa was the family emblem of the Imperial Guptas of Magadha and is found on many of their monetary issues, Bajpai is confident that 'the coins bearing the name Rāmagupta are not the issues of any local officer of the Imperial Guptas, nor of any feudatory king named Rāmagupta', but that 'they were issued by Rāmagupta, the elder brother of Candragupta II Vikramāditya.' In our opinion, however, the discovery of these Garuḍa type copper coins of Rāmagupta does not prove that the issuer was an Imperial Gupta monarch. On the other hand, they really show that, like many other rulers of his type, he was a chief who issued coins in imitation of Gupta money on the decline of the Gupta family about the close of the fifth century A.D.

Bajpai's other conclusions, based on the discovery of these coins at Vidiśā and Eraṇ, are that Rāmagupta was appointed the governor of East Malwa by his father Samudragupta (c. 335-76 A.D.), that circumstances compelled him to stay there on even after his father's death and that the murder of the Śaka king and later of Rāmagupta himself by Candragupta II, as known from the *Devīcandragupta* story, took place at Vidiśā or Eraṇ. All these are conjectures based on the belief that the discovery of the Garuḍa type coins of Rāmagupta proved the genuineness of the tradition recorded in the *Devīcandragupta*. But this is entirely unwarranted.

We have seen above that a ruler named Harigupta, who

1. *Ibid.*, Vol. XXIII (Golden Jubilee Volume), pp. 340 ff., Plate X, Nos. 1. 12.

enjoyed the title *Mahārāja* known to have been assumed by the non-imperial rulers of Northern India during the Gupta age, issued copper coins, one class of which was imitated from the Chatra type gold coins of Candragupta II and exhibits Garuḍa, facing with outstretched wings, above the legend on the reverse.[1] It is also clear that, even if this Harigupta is identified with Harirāja described in a Bundelkhand inscription of about the fifth century A.D. as *Gupta-vaṃś-odita*, he has no place among the Imperial Gupta monarchs.

The *gupta*-ending name of another imitator of the monetary issues of the Imperial Guptas is revealed by two copper coins recently discovered in the course of excavations at Kumrahar near Patna in Bihar.[2] They have the bust of king, to left, on the obverse and Garuḍa above the legend *Indragupta* on the reverse. It is palpably impossible to regard this Indragupta as one of the Gupta emperors of Magadha.

If therefore the Garuḍa type coins of Harigupta and Indragupta do not prove that they were emperors belonging to the Gupta house, no such thing is proved by the similar Garuḍa type copper coins issued by Rāmagupta. On the other hand, the similarity of their coin types and names would point to the fact that all the three rulers, viz. Rāmagupta, Harigupta and Indragupta, enjoyed similar positions, if not that they belonged to the same region and also to the same family. They appear to have flourished on the decline of the Imperial authority of the Guptas in the outlying provinces of the Gupta empire about the close of the fifth and the beginning of the sixth century A.D., which saw the rise of such ruling families as the Parivrājaka, Uccakalpīya and Śarabhapurīya houses.[3] The palaeography of the legend on the coins in question, do not appear to militate against the above dating.

It will be seen that, while Rāmagupta and Indragupta do not employ any royal title along with their names, Harigupta is called a *Mahārāja*. This may suggest that Harigupta flourished later than the other two rulers.[4]

1. *Ep. Ind.*, Vol. XXXIII, pp. 95 ff.; above, pp. 224-25.
2. Altekar and Mishra, *Report on Kumrahar Excavations*, 1951-55, p. 100, Nos. 1 and 3.
3. Cf. *Select Inscriptions*, pp. 370 ff., 374 ff.; *Ep. Ind.*, Vol. XXXI, pp. 267-68.
4. A recent writer speaks of a coin bearing the *pūrṇa-kumbha* symbol

If the three rulers are believed to have flourished in the regions of Bundelkhand and Malwa, we have to think that the coins of Indragupta and Harigupta travelled respectively to Kumrahar (ancient Pāṭaliputra, capital of Magadha) and Rāmnagar (ancient Ahicchatrā, capital of North Pañcāla) in the course of trade. The general belief among numismatists that copper coins, being made of a cheap metal, did not travel away from the land of their issue does not appear to be strictly correct, because some rulers and ruling families issued only copper money which was thus the principal currency in their States and copper was considerably costlier in early India than in later times. Apart from the very high purchasing power of the ancient Indian money, it has to be noticed that 16 copper Paṇas of 80 Ratis each were regarded as equal to one silver Kārṣāpaṇa of 32 Ratis each thus making 40 Ratis of copper equal to one Rati of silver in value. Even in the early medieval age, 16 copper Paṇas were regarded as equal to one silver Dramma, 16 of which were equal to a gold Niṣka. In the age of the Mughuls, 40 Akbarī Dāms of copper were equal to one Akbarī Rupee of silver while, in Alamgīr's time, 46⅓ Dāms were regarded as equal to a Rupee. Later, a much higher number of copper Dāms were considered as equivalent to a silver Rupee.[1]

on the reverse and the name of *Mahārāja* Devagupta as published by Cunningham (cf. *Ind. Hist. Quart.*, Vol. XXXIII, p. 378). This reverse symbol would associate Devagupta with Harigupta, one type of whose copper coins bears the same emblem on the reverse (Cunningham, *Coins of Medieval India*, p. 19, Plate II, No. 6). It may, however, be that Harigupta has seen wrongly mentioned as Devagupta. It is not improbable that the so-called Later Guptas, first of Mālava (East Malwa) and then of Magadha, were related to the family represented by the issuers of the copper coins discussed above.

1. According to the medieval *Śukranītisāra* (IV. 2. 92-93), gold=16 times silver, and silver=80 times copper.

CHAPETR XII

COIN OF MUHAMMAD BIN SĀM AND PṚTHVĪRĀJA

I

An interesting billon coin bearing the names of both the Ghaznavide Sulṭān Muizuddīn Muḥammad bin Sām (1173-1205 A.D.) and the Cāhamāna king Pṛthvīrāja III (1179-92 A.D.) was described by H. N. Wright in his *Coinage and Metrology of the Sultans of Delhi*, p.12, No. 36-A. One side of the coin has a recumbent bull with the legend *srī(śrī)-Mahamada-Sāma* in Nāgarī characters and the other side a horseman with the Nāgarī legend *srī(śrī)-Pṛthvīrājā(ja)deva.*

Wright believed that the coin was issued by the Muslim ruler 'as a suzerain of Pṛthvīrāja of Ajmer'. He observes, "No. 36-A shows the transition stage, the obverse bearing the name of the conqueror and the reverse that of the conquered Pṛthvīrāja."[1] In the ancient history of the north-western part of India, we have many such cases of coins bearing the name of the overlord or the senior partner in kingship on the obverse and that of the feudatory, viceroy or junior partner on the reverse.[2] But there is reason to believe that such coins were issued by the subordinate party. Under ordinary circumstances, a ruler is not expected to mention the name of a subordinate on his coins as that of a joint issuer. Thus it is not unnatural to think that the coin in question was issued by Pṛthvīrāja as a subordinate of Muḥammad bin Sām or by the latter as a subordinate of the former. Unfortunately the known facts of the relations between the said two rulers do not speak of any period when one of them could have issued coins as a subordinate of the other.

Kunwar Devi Singh recently published an article (in Hindī), entitled *Pṛthvīrāj aur Muhammad Gorīkā Saṁyukt Sikkā* (i. e. Joint Coin of Pṛthvīrāja and Muḥammad Ghūrī), in the *Nāgarī Pracāriṇī Patrikā*, Vol. LVII, pp. 59-60. A summary of this article, prepared by P. L Gupta, also appeared in the *Journal of the Numismatic Society of India*, Vol. XIV, 1952, p.147.

1. *Op. cit.*, p. 67.
2. Cf., e.g., *The Age of Imperial Unity*, pp. 123 ff.

Singh thinks that the type in question was issued by Muizuddīn Muḥammad bin Sām, who considered it wise to retain on it, at least for some time, the name of the Cāhamāna king Pṛthvīrāja overthrown by him. It is suggested that Pṛthvīrāja III was not killed at the battle of Tiraurī, but was captured by the Ghaznavide ruler and was living in captivity. Singh points out that the Muslim conqueror of the western part of Northern India copied the Cāhamāna coins in the western portion of his Indian possessions and the Gāhaḍavāla coinage in the east. According to him, the Muslim ruler retained the name of the Cāhamāna king on the above type of his coins just to make them popular in the newly conquered territory. He further surmises that the Sulṭān ought to have issued similar coins with the name of the Gāhaḍavāla king Jayaccandra; but the absence of such issues is sought to be explained by pointing to the fact that Jayaccandra is said to have drowned himself in the waters of the Ganges after his defeat at the hands of the Musalmans. Singh does not say anything in this connection regarding the Gāhaḍavāla king Hariścandra who succeeded his father Jayaccandra and was ruling as late as 1197 A.D.

Of course local conservatism is a remarkable characteristic of Indian numismatics and we have many instances in which a conqueror is known to have issued coins in imitation of the prevalent coinage of the subdued territory. But it is really difficult to understand why the name of the overthrown king, even if he was continuing a precarious existence in the victor's prison, should have been mentioned as that of a joint issuer of the latter's coins. I do not find any similarity between this coin and those issued by the East India Company in the name of Shāh 'Alam II because the circumstances were not quite similar. Such a position therefore appears to me to be rather unnatural, unless there was a special circumstance to justify it. Let us imagine such a circumstance. We know that, according to Hasan Nizāmī, a son of Pṛthvīrāja was installed to succeed his father as a feudatory of the Muslims.[2] This Cāhamāna viceroy of the Muslims, if his father was living in the Muslim prison,

1. Bhandarkar's List, No. 433.
2. Ray, *DHNI*, Vol. II, p. 1092; *CHI*, Vol. III, p. 41.

could possibly have issued coins of the type under discussion in the name of both his present and former suzerains. The shortness of his rule may be supposed to explain the paucity of such issues. There are however other facts to consider.

In Gupta's summary of Singh's paper, the views expressed in it were characterised as unconvincing, although no arguments were offered to disprove any of them. Some time later, Gupta published his comments on Singh's views in the *Nāgarī Pracāriṇī Patrikā*, Vol. LVII, pp. 270-73. The main points in Gupta's note may be summarised as follows.

The coins of the Hindu Śāhī kings of Kabul have the recumbent bull on one side and the horseman on the other. This coinage was often imitated, e.g., by the Sulṭāns of Ghaznī and several Khalifas as well as, in India, by the Cāhamānas, Tomaras and others. The coin of Muḥammad bin Sām in question represents a similar imitated type. The Ghaznavide coins imitated from the Śāhī issues have, on one side, the name of the Sulṭān in Kufic characters and on the other the bull together with the name of an old Śāhī king called Sāmantadeva. Similarly, *Śrī-Sāmantadeva* occurs on one side of the coins of the Cāhamānas and Tomaras. This shows that the imitators of the bull-and-horseman type coins of the Śāhīs continued to mention the name of the Śāhī king Sāmantadeva on their issues. On Pṛthvīrāja's own coins, the side with the horseman has the legend *Śrī-Pṛthvīrājadeva* while that with the bull has *Aśāvarī-Śrī-Sāmantadeva*. The coin under discussion resembles the issues of the Cāhamāna king in as much as the horseman side is similar in both the cases although the bull side has the name of the Ghaznavide ruler instead of that of the Śāhī king Sāmantadeva. On similar other issues of Muḥammad bin Sām, the name of Pṛthvīrāja is replaced on the horseman side with the legend *Śrī-Hammīra*, *Hammīra* being the Indianised form of the Sulṭān's title *Amīr*. It is clear that Muizuddīn Muḥammad bin Sām continued the old process of imitation in issuing his own coins in India, but that, owing to a mistake of his mint officers, Pṛthvīrāja's name was put on the side that should have properly borne the Sulṭān's name while the latter was used to replace the traditionally handed name of Sāmantadeva on the other side of the coin. As soon, however, as the mistake was noticed, the officers replaced Pṛthvīrāja's name by the Sulṭān's title.

The occurrence of the Cāhamāna king's name on the coin of Muḥammad bin Sām therefore has no bearing on the question whether Pṛthvīrāja was alive or dead at the time of its issue.

It is however difficult to believe that the mint masters of Muḥammad bin Sām could have committed such a strange mistake and taken considerable time in detecting it. But if it is suggested that the type represented by the coin in question was issued by a private agency, its characteristics can possibly be easily explained even if the Cāhamāna king was already dead at the time of its issue. It is well known that in India sometimes the adherents of a king, either dead or overthrown by the enemies, dated their records in the years of his *atīta-*, *gata-* or *vinaṣṭa-rājya.*[1]

The Ghaznavide rulers are actually known to have allowed the currency of privately minted coins in their dominions. This is clear from a passage of the *Jamī'ul Hikāyat* by Muḥammad 'Ufī as given in Elliot and Dowson's *History of India as told by its own Historians*, Vol. II, p. 188.[2] The passage runs as follows : "When Yaminuddaula Mahmūd (997-1030 A.D.) came to the throne and the effects of his greatness spread through all countries, and his rule swept away the idol temples and scattered the worshippers, some sharp men of India formed a plan [for enriching themselves]. They brought out a Dirham of great purity and placed a suitable price upon it. Time passed on and the coin obtained currency. Merchants coming from Muhammadan countries used to purchase these Dirhams and carry them to Khurasan. When the people grew accustomed to the value of the coin, the Indians began by degrees to debase the standard. The merchants were unaware of this depreciation and, finding a profit upon silver, they brought that metal and gold from all parts of the world and sold it for [the debased coins of] copper and brass, so that by this trick the wealth of the Muhammadans was drawn to Hindustan. When 'Alāuddaula (Mas'ud III, 1099-1114 A.D.) ascended the throne, this grievance had become intolerable, and he determined to remedy it, and consulted with the merchants as to the measures to be taken to effect this purpose. They ad-

1. Cf. *Journ. As. Soc.*, Letters, Vol. XVII, pp. 27-31; *Ep. Ind.* Vol. XXXV, pp. 234 ff.

2. Cf. *JRAS*, Old Series, Vol. XVII, p. 181.

vised that the debased coinage should be exchanged for good ones from the royal treasury. Accordingly 'Alāuddaula gave the necessary orders and 100,000,000 Dirhams were issued from the treasury to the mint and thence distributed to the servants of the Almighty as redress and compensation. The fame of this act spread the lustre of 'Alāuddaula's glory throughout the world."

The influence of private agencies on the minting of coins in India has not always been realised. Some years ago we had occasion to discuss this point in discussion note on the Marāṭhā mint under the Peshwās.[1] The Peshwās granted license to goldsmiths for minting coins. But in spite of the fact that they were not inclined to tolerate unlicensed mints and debased coins, in some provinces of their dominions the land-holders often established their own mints from which counterfeit coins were issued. Of course the licensees also had a fairly free hand whenever the state was in difficulties. Thomas[2] is therefore right when he points out that the royal prerogative of coining money was not properly understood and jealously guarded in India. According to Ferishta,[3] in 1357-74 A.D. goldsmiths and dealers in bullion were authorised, by prescriptive right, to fabricate money at will on their own account, without being subjected to any check or control on the part of the ruling power. Malcolm[4] says, "There are mints at almost all the principal towns in Central India...The right of coining is vested in no particular body or individuals; any banker or merchant sufficiently conversant in the business has merely to make application to Government, presenting at the same time a trifling acknowledgement, engaging to produce coin of the regulated standard, and pay the proper fees on its being assayed and permitted to pass current." May this fact not explain the vagaries of the coin that forms the subject under study? At least the mistakes in the orthography of the legend may better be attributed to goldsmiths who could boast of little learning rather than to royal officials. It is interesting to note that this very suggestion has been offered in order to explain the errors in the legends

1. *JNSI*, Vol. VII, pp. 78-82 ; below, pp. 273 ff.
2. *Ancient Indian Weights*, p. 57, note 4.
3. Thomas, *Pathan Kings of Delhi*, p. 344.
4. *Central India*, Vol. II, 1832, p. 10.

on Śivājī's coins.[1] We also know how, in medieval India, any coin could enter into currency and remain in circulation for centuries.[2] The same was apparently the case also in ancient India. The *Arthaśāstra* may be taken to refer to the manufacture of coins by the government;[3] but, in reality, it seems to give us a picture that is not unlike that of the Marāṭhā mint. The evidence of Buddhaghoṣa and his commentators moreover suggests that the silver punch-marked coins called Purāṇa were manufactured, no doubt by private agencies, in the age of the Śātavāhanas and the Guptas.[4]

A word may be said here about the mention of Sāmantadeva on the coins of various rulers of different dynasties. There is a difficulty in regarding this Sāmantadeva as a single individual like an old Śāhī king in all the cases. Under ordinary circumstances, it can hardly be expected that so many kings would issue coins consciously retaining on them the name of an old monarch who had been dead many years ago. This could have been possible only when there were special circumstances justifying this strange behaviour of the rulers. On some such coins, we have clearly *Asāvarī-śrī-Sāmantadeva*, *Mādhava-śrī-Sāmantadeva*, *Kutāmāṇa-śrī-Sāmantadeva*, etc.[5] The expressions *Asāvarī*, *Mādhava*, *Kutāmāṇa*, etc., found in this connection on the issues of different rulers, appear to be the names of the tutelary or family deities of the kings in question. It is thus not impossible to think that at least some of the supposed issuers of such coins were inclined to present themselves as the *sāmanta* or feudatory of the deities in question. There are many instances in Indian history of kings ruling their dominions, in a theoretically subordinate capacity, in the names of deities or saints either living or dead.[6] There are also several instances of the mention of tutelary deities on certain types of early Indian coins.[7] It should however be admitted that the expression *śrī-Sāmantadeva* looks more like a name than an epithet.

1. *JNSI*, Vol. VII, p. 81; below, p. 276.
2. *JNSI*, Vol. VII, pp. 78, 88; below, pp. 273-74, 290-91.
3. *JNSI*, Vol. XIV, p. 182.
4. Cf. *ibid.*, Vol. XIII, pp. 187 ff.; above, p. 104.
5. Smith, *Catalogue*, pp. 260 ff.
6. Cf. *Orissa Hist. Res. Journ.*, Vol. 1, pp. 18 ff.; *Ep. Ind.*, Vol. XXX, pp. 19, 47 ff.
7. See above, pp. 211 ff.

But *Sāmantadeva* may in such cases be compared with the subordinate title *Sāmantarāya* (Sanskrit *Sāmantarāja*, same as the modern Oriya-Bengali family name *Sāntrā*) found in the medieval inscriptions of Orissa.

It will be seen from the foregoing lines that we have offered some comments on the views of several scholars regarding the interpretation of the evidence supplied by a coin bearing the names of the Ghaznavide ruler Muizuddīn Muḥammad bin Sām and Cāhamnāna Pṛthvīrāja and on some associated problems. We admit that the real significance of the coin under study is not easy to explain and is likely to remain doubtful until further evidence on the point is forthcoming. But it seems to us that, if the so-called imitation coins are regarded as issued from private mints and not as royal issues, some of their characteristics can possibly be explained.

II

Since only one coin of this type has so far been discovered, Altekar is inclined to support the view of Gupta that it was due to a mistake of the mint. He points out that, as late as the time of 'Allāuddīn Khaljī, Hindu mint masters like Ṭhakkura Pheru used sometimes to be in charge of the mint. It is likely that, after annexing the Cāhamāna kingdom, officers of the conqueror occupied the royal mint which contained a large number of the dies of Pṛthvīrāja showing the Bull and the legend *Sāmantadeva* on one side and the Horseman and Pṛthvīrāja's name on the other. Muḥammad eventually decided to have for his currency intended for his Indian subjects the type having the Bull and the legend *Sāmantadeva* on one side and the Horseman and the legend *Śrī-Hammīra* on the other. Coins were issued with two such dies for the two sides and it is unlikely that, at the early stage when all the old dies had not been removed from the mint, a mint employee put the obverse die of the earlier reign by mistake along with the reverse die of the new one, giving rise to the coin under discussion. "The mistake must have been seen before half a dozen coins were issued and corrected immediately by putting the proper obverse die of the new reign. Hence the extreme rarity of this coin type......The solitary coin of Samudragupta which gives him the title *Śrī-Vikrama* may be due to a similar mistake of using the reverse die of Candragupta along with the obverse one of Samudragupta of the Standard type."[1]

As regards these views, it may be admitted that, as indicated above, we hesitate to explain such numismatic problems by putting the blame on the mint employee. Samudragupta's Śrī-Vikrama coin appears to us to be a forgery, the coin being carelessly represented as belonging to an old hoard. Moreover, such a mistake on the part of a Hindu officer, so soon after the overthrow of Hindu rule, must have been regarded as high treason by his Turkish Muslim master.

III

D. Sharma draws our attention to Hasan Nizāmī's *Tāj-ul-ma'asir*, according to which the Rāī of Ajmīr (i.e. Pṛthvīrāja) was taken prisoner during the action, though his life was spared. It is said that the Rāī of Ajmīr, who had managed to obtain his release or, at least, immunity from punishment, was possibly detected in some intrigue so that orders were issued for his death and he was killed.[2] Sharma suggests that Cāhamāna Pṛthvīrāja ruled for a short time as a vassal of Muḥammad and that the coin may have been minted during that period.[3]

But, when Hasan Nizāmī's evidence is considered along with what we learn from the *Hammīramahākāvya*, it appears that Pṛthvīrāja had no chance to rule for sometime as a vassal of Muḥammad : "When Udayarāja, a great friend and ally of Pṛthvīrāja, heard of his captivity, he sat down before Delhi and besieged it. During the siege, a courtier of the Ghūrī Sulṭān suggested to his master that it would be becoming on his part to release the Cauhān. Muizuddīn, it is said, was so incensed by the proposal, that he denounced the adviser as a traitor and ordered Pṛthvīrāja to be imprisoned in the citadel where, a few days afterwards, he breathed his last."[4]

1. See *JNSI*, Vol. XV, pp. 134-35.

2. *Ibid.*, Vol. XVI, p. 122; *Ind. Cult.*, Vol. XI, pp. 57 ff.; Elliot and Dowson, *History of India*, etc., Vol. II, p. 215.

3. Some scholars wrongly ascribe this fate, on the same authority, to the son of the Rāī of Ajmīr. Cf. Ray, *DHNI*, Vol. II, p. 1091.

4. Ed. Kirtane, intro., pp. 20-21; Hodivala, *Studies in Indo-Muslim History*, pp. 175-79.

Chapter XIII

COINS OF KĀKATĪYA PRATĀPARUDRA I

I

In a small note appearing in the *Journal of the Numismatic Society of India*, Vol. XXI, Part i, pp. 37-38 (Plate IV, Nos. 6-9), Dinkar Rao published four copper coins which he ascribed to the Rāṣṭrakūṭa king Kakka II (972-73 A.D.). The coins, which are circular and apparently .8 inch in diameter, are stated to have been secured from a locality near Mālkheḍ, old Mānyakheṭa which was the capital of the Rāṣṭrakūṭas, in the Gulbarga District of the former Hyderabad State, now in Mysore. He reads the legend on the obverse and reverse of the coins as follows :

Obverse	Reverse
Śrīmadevara	*idava vi-*
Kākarāya	*jaya karavu*
[*dhī*]*yaru*	....

The legend was translated as follows : "This is the auspicious coin of king Karkarāya, the wise and learned."

Unfortunately, to any student of Indian epigraphy and palaeography, the reading of the legend offered by Dinkar Rao would appear to be quite untenable, while his translation would likewise puzzle the students of Indian languages. Another puzzle has been created by Dinkar Rao by illustrating only the negative of the reverse of Coin No. 7.

It is really surprising that two quite obvious points in regard to these coins have escaped the notice of the author of the note. In the first place, it is quite clear that the characters of the legend are Southern Nāgarī of about the twelfth or thirteenth century A. D. and it is impossible to assign the coins, against the evidence of palaeography, to the third quarter of the tenth century when Rāṣṭrakūṭa Kakka II flourished. Secondly, Kakka II was the last of the Imperial Rāṣṭrakūṭas and ruled only for about a year before he was overthrown by Taila II, the founder of the Later Cālukya dynasty of Kalyāṇa. In view of the facts that the fortune of the Imperial Rāṣṭrakūṭas was at the lowest ebb at the time of Kakka II and that we have no coins issued by the mighty emperors of the house such as Govinda III, Indra III and Kṛṣṇa III,[1] it is difficult to believe that Rāṣṭrakūṭa Kakka issued any coins at all.

Owing to the unsatisfactory nature of the illustrations of the coins, it is not possible to read the entire legend on their obverse and reverse. But the name of the king who issued them and the dynasty to which he belonged can be read with absolute certainty.

What Dinkar Rao has read in the second line on the obverse as *Kākarāya* is undoubtedly *Kākatīya,* the *ī-mātrā* of *tī* resembling the sign for medial *ā* as is often noticed in the Southern Nāgarī inscriptions of the Kākatīya age.

On an examination of the illustrations of the coins, I find that what Dinkar Rao has read as *⁰ru idava* (*ru* at the end of the third or last line on the obverse and *idava* at the beginning of the first on the reverse) is quite clearly *Rudradeva.* Again what has been read as [*dhī*]*ya⁰* in the third line on the obverse is really *pratāpa.* This is clearer on the illustration of coin No. 7 than on that of coin No. 6.

As to the other parts of the legend, it may be observed that the first word on the obverse is no doubt *śrīmat* joined with another word in *Samāsa* while the word following *dradeva* at the beginning of the writing on the reverse is certainly *vijaya.* The other words of the legend cannot be satisfactorily read from the illustrations. The date of the issue, in the Śaka era, seems to have been written in the last line on the reverse, as suggested by the traces of numerical figures in the reproduction of coins Nos. 6 and 8.

There is thus no doubt that the copper coins published by Dinkar Rao were issued by the Kākatīya king Pratāparudra, although, owing to our inability to read the date, it is difficult to say whether the king is Pratāparudra I (1158-96 A. D.), also called Rudradeva, or Pratāparudra II (1291-1323 A.D.).

There are two copper coins of the same type in the pos-

1. The silver coins bearing the name of Kṛṣṇarāja were apparently issued by the Kalacuri ruler of that name. See *JNSI,* Vol. XVI, pp. 107 ff.

session of I. Mahadevan who published a note on them, without illustration, in *The Hindu*, Madras, dated the 28th June 1959. They are thick round pieces, about .8 inch in diameter, exactly as Dinkar Rao's coins, and were likewise secured from the old Hyderabad State. Mahadevan reads the legend as follows:

Obverse	Reverse
śrīmad-vikra-	*dradeva-vi-*
ma-Kākatīya-	*jaya-vatsara*
Pratāparu-	123..

Since the date, which is a year between 1230 and 1239, is no doubt a year of the Śaka era and would correspond to a year between 1308 and 1317 A.D., Mahadevan assigns his coins to Kākatīya Pratāparudra II. But I have doubts about his reading of the date and of some other letters of the legend although his reading cannot unfortunately he checked for the absence of any illustration. There can however be no doubt that he has read quite correctly the name of Kākatīya Pratāparudradeva, which baffled Dinkar Rao.

Another copper coin of the same type, measuring .82 inch in diameter and weighing 125.5 grains, has been recently published by J. Ramayya[1] who reads the legend as follows :

Obverse	Reverse
śrīmad-vikra-	*dradeva-vi-*
ma-Kākatīya-	*jaya-Kaṭaka*
Pratāparu-	[12 ?] *Saka*

The expression *vijaya-kaṭaka* can be read from the illustration (No. 5-A). But *śrīmad-vikrama* at the beginning of the legend is not clear while 12 *Saka* at the end seems to be wrong.

II

Plaster-casts of three coins of the same type in the possession of Dinkar Rao of Hyderabad were recently available to me for examination and were noticed in the *Annual Report on Indian Epigraphy*, 1959-60, Nos. E 100-02. They clearly demonstrate the errors in the published readings of the legends on the obverse and reverse of the coins. The three coins together give us the following legends :

1. *JNSI*, Vol. XXI, pp. 181 ff., Plate XI, Nos. 5, 5-A and 5-B.

Obverse	Reverse
Śrīmad-Veṅka-	*dradeva-vi-*
ṭa-Kākatīya-	*jaya-kaṭaka*
Pratāparu-	*Śa-* 1108 *ka*

The date in the last line on the reverse stands for *Śaka* 1108 corresponding to 1186-87 A.D. On some specimens, the date is given as *Śa-* 1109 *ka*, i.e. Śaka 1109=1187-88 A.D. The numeral 9 is written with a globular mark attached to the right upper end of the figure for 8. This is of palaeographical interest since these types of 8 and 9 resemble their forms in the Kaithī and Gurumukhī alphabets, even though the characters of the legends are South Indian Nāgarī.

The dates on these coins show that they were issued by the Kākatīya king Pratāparudra I (1158-96 A.D.). In the inscriptions of the Kākatīya kings, often the royal name follows the family name, *e.g.*, *Kākatīya-Pratāparudra*, though the family name is spelt variously as *Kākatīya*, *Kākatiyya*, *Kākati*, *Kākita*, *Kākatya*, etc., while, in some cases, expressions like *Kākatiyya-puravar-ādhiśvara*, *Kākatīyamanuma*, *Kākatīya-kumāra*, etc., are found in place of the dynastic name. Kākati was also the name of the tutelary deity of the family. In the expression *Veṅkaṭa-Kākatīya* in the obverse legend on the coins in question, Veṅkaṭa may have been a secondary name of king Pratāparudra I

There is a forged document[1] purported to have been issued by Kāketa-Rudra-Veṁkkaṭarāya śrī-Pratāparudradeva who is endowed with the *viruda* *Vīra-śrī-Gajapati-Gauḍeśvara-nava-koṭi-Karnnāṁ* (*rṇā*) *ṭa-Kalubarigeśvara*. It will be seen that the persons responsible for the fabrication of the document represented the donor of the grant, viz. Rudra Veṅkaṭarāya Pratāparudra, as a Kāketa, i.e. Kākatīya, though they wrongly attributed to him the epithet *Vīraśrī-Gajapati*, etc., suitable to the Sūryavaṁśī Gajapati king Pratāparudra (1497-1540 A.D.) of Orissa. There is thus a confusion between Kākatīya Pratāparudra and Gajapati Pratāparudra. But the epithet *Kāketa-Rudra-Veṅkaṭarāya* suggests that Kākatīya Pratāparudra was also known as Veṅkaṭarāya.

The three coins may be described as follows :

1. Butterworth and Chetty, *Nellore District Inscriptions*. Part I, pp. 184-85, No. 22; *A. R. Ep.*, 1945-46, No. A6.

1. Copper, round. Weight 155 grains. Diameter .8 inch.
   Obverse—Three-line legend in the Sanskrit language and South Indian Nāgarī characters : [*Śrī*] *mad-v* [*eṁ*]*ka-* / *ṭa-Kākatīya* ·/...[*ru*]
   Reverse—Continuation of the legend : .../ *jaya-kaṭa*... / ...1209...
2. Copper, round. Weight 152 grains. Diameter .8 inch.
   Obverse—Three-line legend : *Śrīmad-Veṁka-* / *ṭa-Kākatī*.../...*tāpa*...
   Reverse—Continuation of the legend...*va-v*[*i*].../ *ya-kaṭaka* /...08 *ka.*
3. Copper, round. Weight 140 grains. Diameter .8 inch.
   Obverse—Three-line legend : *Śrīmad-V*[*eṁka*] /... *Kākatīya-* /...*tāparu*
   Reverse—Continuation of the legend : *dradeva- vi-* / *jayakaṭaka* /......[1]

1. For a recent note, see *JNSI*, Vol. XXVIII, pp. 71-72.

CHAPTER XIV

GAJAPATI PAGODA, GAṄGA FANAM AND RĀMA-ṬAṄKĀ

I

Writers on Indian numismatics generally assign two types of gold coins to Orissa. The bigger and heavier of the two is called 'Gajapati Pagoda' because the figure of a caparisoned elephant appears on the coins and the Europeans applied the name Pagoda or Pagode to the South Indian gold issues locally known as the Gadyāṇa, Varāha or Hon, often regarded as weighing 48 Ratis or 87 grains. The name Pagoda or Pagode is derived from *Pagodi* which is a South Indian corruption of Sanskrit *Bhagavatī*, 'the Mother-goddess', no doubt owing to many such coins bearing the figures of deities and their temples.[1] The smaller and lighter of the two types is called 'Gaṅga Fanam' because the coins are regarded as issued by the Eastern Gaṅga kings of Orissa and resemble small South Indian gold coins known to the Europeans as 'Fanam', the name being derived from Tamil *Paṇam* (Sanskrit *Paṇa*).[2]

V. A. Smith, in his *Catalogue of the Coins in the Indian Museum, Calcutta*, Vol. I, speaks of a Gajapati or Elephant Pagoda (size —.45 in diameter, weight—51.3 grains) which he assigns to the thirteenth century A.D.[3] and also of some Fanams of the Eastern Gaṅga monarch Anantavarman Coḍagaṅga (1078-1147 A.D.), which measure between .4 and .53 inch in diameter and weigh about 7.7 grains.[4] While no Orissan find of the Gajapati Pagoda is known, several hoards of 'Gaṅga Fanams' have been reported from Orissa as we shall see below.

What C. J. Brown says about these coins in his *Coins of India*, 1922, p. 60, is based on the views of such earlier writers as G. Bidie in his article published in the *Journal of the Asiatic Society of Bengal*, Vol. LII, Part i, 1883, p. 40, Plate I, No. 7,[5]

1. Cf. Yule and Burnell, *Hobson-Jobson*, s.v. *Pagoda*.
2. See *ibid.*, s.v. *Fanam*.
3. *Op. cit.*, p. 318, Plate XXX, No. 18.
4. *Ibid.*, pp. 314-15, Plate XXX, No. 7.
5. Cf. *Proceedings of the Asiatic Society of Bengal*, 1882, pp. 141-42.

W. Elliot in his *Coins of Southern India*, 1885, p. 116, Plate III, Nos. 118-19, and E. J. Rapson in his *Indian Coins*, 1898, p. 36, Plate V, No. 12.[1] Brown's observations run as follows :"The original home of the Gajapatis or Elephant-lords was Koṅgu-deśa—Western Mysore and the modern Districts of Coimbatore and Salem. About the ninth century, these Cera kings fled before the invading Coḷas to Orissa, and there were coined the famous Elephant Pagodas and Fanams which Harṣadeva of Kashmir (A.D. 1089) copied." That the Fanams were also copied by the Kashmirian king is a fanciful addition to what we learn from such authorities as Rapson who says, "The date of these gold coins, the chief type of which is the elephant (Plate V. 12) is limited to a period before c. 1090 A.D., as they are imitated by Harṣadeva of Kashmir." But all this is unfortunately wrong.

In the first place, the Early Western Gaṅgas of Mysore were neither Ceras nor did they rule in Koṅgudeśa, while the Eastern Gaṅgas began to rule in the Śrīkākulam region of Andhra Pradesh, from the close of the fifth century A.D., and Anantavarman Coḍagaṅga belonging to a branch of this family was the first to annex the Purī-Cuttack region to the Eastern Gaṅga empire about the beginning of the twelfth century. The early members of the Imperial branch of the Eastern Gaṅga family were matrimonially related to the Coḷas and were subordinate allies of the latter.

Secondly, Kalhaṇa's *Rājataraṅgiṇī* (middle of the twelfth century) states that king Harṣa (1089-1101 A.D.) of Kashmir issued coins in imitation of the monetary issues of Karṇāṭa in Dākṣiṇātya,[2] while the location of this Karṇāṭa is quite clear from another section of the same work, according to which the said Kashmirian king wanted to marry queen Candalā after having killed her husband Parmāṇḍi, the king of Karṇāṭa.[3]

1. See also A. Cunningham, *Coins of Medieval India*, 1893, p. 35; R. D. Banerji, *Prācīn Mudrā*, 1322 B. S. (1915 A. D.), p. 181.
2. VII. 926 :
Dākṣiṇāty=ābhavad=bhaṅgiḥ priyā tasya vilāsinaḥ ।
Karṇāṭ-ānuguṇaṣ=ṭaṅkas=tatas=tena pravartitaḥ ॥
3. VII. 1119 and 1121 :
Karṇāṭa-bhartuḥ Parmāṇḍeḥ sundarīṃ Candal-ābhidhām ।
ālekhya-likhitāṃ vīkṣya so='bhūt=Puṣpāyudha-kṣataḥ ॥
Sa-viṭ-odrecito vīta-trapaś=cakre sabh-āntare ।
pratijñāṃ Candal-āvāptyai Parmāṇḍeś=ca viloḍane ॥

A third section of the work also refers to Dākṣiṇātya and to Harṣa's desire to kill the king of Karṇāṭa, to enter Kalyāṇapura and to marry Candalā and Pimmalā.[1] The identity of this king Parmāṇḍi of Karṇāṭa, who has his capital at Kalyāṇapura, with Harṣa's Dākṣiṇātya contemporary, Permāṇḍi Vikramāditya VI (1076-1126 A.D.) of the Cālukya dynasty of Kalyāṇa in the present Bidar District formerly in the Hyderabad State but now in Mysore, one of whose queens was the Śilāhāra princess Can dralekhā or Candaladevī, is so obious that nobody can have any doubt about it. The identification is again quite clearly supported by a fourth section of the *Rājataraṅgiṇī*, accord ing to which the Kashmirian poet Bilhaṇa who had gone away from the country during the reign of king Kalaśa (1063-89 A.D.), father of Harṣa, and had been made the *Vidyāpati* (*i.e.* the chief court poet) by the Karṇāṭa king Parmāḍi (Parmāṇḍi), when he heard of Harṣa's munificence to artists and literary men, thought even his great honour at the Karṇāṭa court a mere deception.[2] It is well known that this Bilhaṇa was the court poet of Cālukya Vikramāditya VI and wrote his celebrated *Vikramāṅkadevacarita* on his patron's career.

If therefore the evidence of the *Rājataraṅgiṇī* is taken into consideration, it may be supposed that at least some of the so-called Gajapati Pagodas were issued by the Western Cālukyas of Kalyāṇa probably including Vikramāditya VI. Cup-shaped gold coins resembling the Padma-ṭaṅka (bearing the lotus symbo) have been found to bear either the lion or the temple symbol in place of the lotus or no symbol at all and also the names of Jayasiṁha, Jagadekamalla and Trailokyamalla who have been

1. VII. 1123-24 :
Bhāṣā-veṣa-viśeṣataḥ parigatas=tvaṃ Dākṣiṇātyo='dhvago
gandhād=apy=avadhāritaṃ yad=uta te karpūra-kolaṃ kare ।
pakvaṃ ced=idam=aṅga Harṣa-nṛpates=tat=kalpay=opāyanaṃ
no cet=tiṣṭhatu nālikera-kuhare sampraty=amuimin=yataḥ ॥
Ā Karṇāṭa-vasundharā-dhava-dhād=ā Candal-āliṅganād=
ā Kalyāṇapura-praveśana-vither=ā Pimmalā-darśanāt ।
ā rāj-āśraya-kānan-ānta-vasudhā-pārardhi-kautūhalād=
Devena pratiṣiddham=iddha-mahasā potāsa-saṃcarvaṇam ॥

2. VII. 935-37 :
Kāśmīrebhyo viniryāntaṃ rājye Kalaśa-bhūpateḥ ।
vidyāpatiṃ yaṃ Karṇāṭaś=cakre Parmāḍi-bhūpatiḥ ॥
prasarpataḥ karaṭibhiḥ Karṇāṭa-kaṭak-āntare ।
rājño='gre dadṛśe tuṅgaṃ yasy=aiv=ātapavāraṇam ॥
Tyāginaṃ Harṣadevaṃ sa śrutvā sukavi-bāndhavam ।
Bilhaṇo vañcanāṃ mene vibhūtiṃ tāvatīm=api ॥

regarded as Western Cālukya kings of Kalyāṇa.[1] It has to be believed in that case that the Western Cālukya kings issued coins in some cases with and in others without legend. It seems, however, that the Gajapati Pagodas without any legend were minted mostly by the temple authorities or the goldsmiths of Karṇāṭa for centuries with the permission of the royal authority. This is probably supported by the fact that the epigraphic records of the Karṇāṭa country often speak of such coins named after particular persons or places, e.g., Bhairava-gadyāṇa named after a person called Bhairava and Lokki-gadyāṇa named after the locality called Lokki, *i.e.* Lokkiguṇḍi (modern Lakkuṇḍi in the Dharwar District).[2]

H. Heras contended that the Gajapati Pagodas were issued by the Vijayanagara king Mallikārjuna who ruled in 1446-65 A.D.[3] But this can only be partially true if it is true at all. R. D. Banerji's suggestion that they are the issues of the Sūryavaṁśī Gajapati king Kapilendra (Kapileśvara, 1435-67 A.D.)[4] does not appear to be supported by any evidence. In any case, it is quite clear that the coins imitated by king Harṣa of Kashmir about the close of the eleventh century could not have been issued by any ruler of the Sūryavaṁśī Gajapati family of Orissa or the Vijayanagara dynasty of Karṇāṭa as these flourished much later. It is again impossible to believe that the author of the *Rājataraṅgiṇī* confused Karṇāṭa with Orissa. Indeed it is doubtful whether any Orissan king including the Eastern Gaṅgas issued such coins at all. It has, however, to be admitted that a gold coin of similar weight is well known from medieval Orissan records. It is the Māḍha or Māḍhā, called Māḍa in Telugu inscriptions and Māḍai in Tamil epigraphs and often regarded as weighing 40 Ratis or 73 grains.

As regards the ascription of the Gajapati Pagodas to Kapilendra, it may be pointed out that no coin assignable to any monarch of the Sūryavaṁśī Gajapati family has as yet been

1. Cf. Elliot, *op. cit.*, p. 67; Rapson, *op.cit.*, p. 37; Smith, *op. cit.*, p. 317; Brown, *op. cit.*, p. 59. See also Hultzsch in *Ind. Ant.*, 1896, p. 322, Plate II, No. 34.

2. Cf. *Ep. Ind.*, Vol. XXXIII, p. 55; *SII*, Vol. XI, Part ii, No. 136.

3. *Journal of the Asiatic Society of Bengal*, Numismatic Supplement, No. XLIV, 1933, pp. 17-22, Plate I, Nos. 4-8.

4. *History of Orissa*, Vol. I, p. 304.

discovered. But a verse in *Kaviḍinḍima* Jīvadev-ācārya's *Bhakti-bhāgavata* states that king Pratāparudra (1497-1540 A.D.), grandson of Kapilendra, issued gold coins bearing the figure of Gopāla (*i.e.* Kṛṣṇa) and the king's name and that the said coins were in circulation in many lands.[1] Since the book was written in 1510 A.D. during the reign of Pratāparudra, the patron and disciple of Jīvadeva, the information seems to be genuine. But, considering the late date, it is strange that no such coin has so far been noticed.

As to the so-called Gaṅga Fanams, which generally bear only certain symbols and the date in the regnal reckoning of some unknown rulers, it is impossible to assign any particular coin of this class to a particular king of any ruling family of Orissa. Like the Gajapati Pagoda of Karṇāṭa, the Gaṅga Fanam of Orissa also appears to have been issued mostly by licensed goldsmiths or temple authorities over many centuries.

II

In recent years no less than three hoards of small gold coins, usually known as Gaṅga Fanam, were discovered in the Angul and Cuttack regions of Orissa and were acquired for the Orissa Museum. The three hoards contained 40, 58 and 130 coins respectively; that is to say, they together consisted of 228 coins. Another Gaṅga Fanam was secured for the Orissa Museum in the year 1934. The size of the coins varies between .37″ and .42″ in diameter and their weight between 6.87 and 8.37 grains. An interesting analysis of the coins was published by S. C. De in the *Journal of the Kalinga Historical Research Society*, Vol. I, 1947, pp. 367ff.[2]

The reverse of all these coins bears a symbol resembling the Oriya *sa*, placed horizontally above, with the left face downwards, below which stands a number expressed in one

1. *Gopāla-mūrti-rucirā nava-hema-mudrā*
yan-nāma-varṇa-likhan-āṅkana-bhāsamānā ı
sarvāsu dikṣu viharanti yadīya-sūkti-
muktāś=ca kaṇṭha-kuhare sudhiyāṃ luṭhanti ıı

See *Navabhārata* (Oriya), Vol. VI, No. 6, p. 295; *Utkal University Souvenir*, 1948, p. 113. Cf. *Ep. Ind.*, Vol. XIX, p. 299, text line 20.

2. There is a reference to the addition of 49 Gaṅga Fanams to the Orissa Museum (*JNSI*, Vol. XIII, pp. 91-92). They were formerly in the collection of the ruler of the old Sonepur State; but they have not yet been published.

numerical figure or two. But in many cases this *sa*-like symbol is flanked by two other symbols looking respectively like the *aṅkuśa* or elephant-goad and the *kuṭhāra* or axe. The *sa*-like symbol was explained by Hoernle as a contraction of the word *Saṁvat* or *Saṁvatsara*, while the number beneath has been regarded by numismatists as the year of issue of particular coins. De agrees with these views. He takes the numbers on the coins as regral years of the issuer or issuers, counted according to the well-known *Aṅka* system, adopted by the medieval Gaṅga rulers of Orissa and their successors. The obverse of these coins usually represents a recumbent bull flanked by various symbols. De has classified the symbols both on the obverse and the reverse of the coins and has published their sketches in several charts accompanying his paper.

Four Plates (which may be referred to as A, B, C and D for the sake of convenience) illustrating 28 of the coins discussed by De have also been appended to the paper. Plates A and D illustrate respectively 4 and 15 coins, which bear consecutive numbers while Plates B and C offer respectively 5 and 4 coins which have not been similarly numbered. The illustrations clearly bear out De's description of the coins. It is however interesting to find that the Plates bear two notes from the pen of the Joint-Editor of the Journal saying that the legend *Patna* (probably intending *Pāṭanā*) or its part *tna* (possibly intending *ṭana*) in some cases is clear on the reverse of the coins. It is apparent that the *sa*-like symbol has been read as *tna* and the same symbol flanked by the *aṅkuśa* and *kuṭhāra* symbols has been supposed to be *Patna*. From a footnote at page 362 of the same issue of the *Journal of the Kalinga Historical Research Society*, it is seen that the Joint-Editor, who offered the above reading of the symbols, is P. C. Rath who was Superintendent of Archaeology of the old Patna (Pāṭanā) State, now merged in Orissa. It is, however, a matter of great regret that Rath considered it wise to offer such an absolutely unwarranted and absurd suggestion. It is quite impossible to make out the name of *Pāṭanā* in any form on the reverse of the so-called Gaṅga Fanams illustrated in De's paper.

De's article contains two interesting charts[1] one illustrating the forms of the numerals as read by him and the other giving the number of coins bearing a particular year of the *Aṅka* reckoning of the issuers of the coins. It may however be noted that no less than three numerical figures have been deciphered wrongly by De. In the first place, what has been read by him as 2 is really 7. Secondly, the first of the two figures read as 3 is undoubtedly 2. Thirdly, the figure doubtfully read by him as 7 is actually a slightly modified form of the regular 3. There should moreover have been no query after the figure for 9. The above readings of the numerical figures are supported by numerous medieval Orissan records, both published and as yet unpublished, including the Kendupatna and other plates of Narasiṁha II, Puri Plates of Bhānu II, Puri plates (B) of Narasiṁha IV, Polsara plates of Arkeśvara, etc., etc. Under the circumstances, De's chart giving the number of coins bearing particular dates, which is full of mistakes, should be thoroughly recast.

With the exception only of three, the numbers on all the other 25 coins illustrated in De's Plates are clear and can be read satisfactorily. The third coin of Plate A gives the date 22. The five coins of Plate B have respectively the dates 5, 21, 10, 10 and 8, while the four on Plate C have respectively 4, 23, 18 and 2. The fifteen coins on Plate D have similarly 4, 4, 5, 7, 10, 7, 10, 13, 4, 9, 21, 25, 34, 2 and 5.

In this connection it is also necessary to refer to another hoard of similar coins discussed by P. C. Rath in an interesting but extremely misleading article in the *Journal of the Numismatic Society of India*, Vol. V, 1943, pp. 61-64. The title of Rath's paper is "Parimalgiri Hoard of the Gold Coins of Cauhān King Rāmadeva" and it is indicated in a foot-note that the article was written with the help of A. S. Altekar, the then editor of the Journal.[2]

It is said that small gold coins numbering 119 were discovered at a place called Parimalgiri in the old Patna State

1. *Op. cit.*, p. 369.

2. The importance of Rath's dubious paper was recognised by Altekar by including a discussion on it in the article entitled "Numismatic Discoveries and Researches during 1941-50" published in *JNSI*, Vol. XIII, pp. 1 ff. (vide p. 15).

sometime in 1942. Out of these, only 80 coins could be secured for the State treasury. Of these again, only 12 were discussed by Rath in his article and were illustrated in the Plate (*JNSI*, Vol. V, Plate IV-B) accompanying it. Although the representation of the coins in the Plate is not quite satisfactory, many of the mistakes in Rath's description can fortunately be seen clearly from it.

It is well known that the obverse of the so-called Gaṅga Fanams bears such representations as the couchant bull, lion with raised paw, two fishes, Śiva-liṅga, etc.[2] The obverse symbols of the Parimalagiri coins, as described by Rath, therefore do not offer any peculiarity at all, although he may not be quite accurate in their description in all the cases. As regards the reverse, Rath says, "On the reverse of these coins there is a legend in three lines. The first reads *Srī-Rāma*, the second *Patanā* (possibly intending *Pāṭanā*) and the third gives the date of issue in numerals. The dates on the 12 coins illustrated on the Plate are 8, 33, 34, 35, 55, 56, 56, 56, 56, 56, 59 and 33 respectively" (*op. cit.*, p. 62). According to Rath, Śrī-Rāma was the king who issued the coins and ruled for 59 years as indicated by the eleventh coin illustrated and, since only king Rāmadeva, founder of the so-called Cauhān dynasty of Patna, is supposed (on no satisfactory grounds) to have ruled for 59 years (*c.* 1212-71 A.D.), he must have issued the coins of the Parimalgiri hoard. Rath also says, "The weight of these coins is slightly higher than the Fanams of Anantavarman, which seem to have been accepted as his model for weight by Śrī-Rāma." The statement about the weight is difficult to understand. The size and weight of the coins are said to vary between .41″ and .44″ and between 7.37 and 7.42 grains respectively.

As regards the numerical figures on the Parimalgiri coins, Rath's readings are unfortunately more inaccurate than De's. Those numbers which are clear on the Plate and are beyond doubt are the following: Coins No. 3—'24'; No. 4—'21'; No. 5—'11'; No. 8—'17'; No. 9—'17'; No. 10—'17'; No. 11—'19'; No. 12—'22'. It will be seen that these numbers, viz., 24, 21, 11, 17, 17, 17, 19 and 22, have been wrongly read by Rath respectively as 34, 35, 55, 56, 56, 56, 59 and 33. He has thus read 5 in place of 1, 3 in place of 2 and 6 in place of 7. The highest number exhibited by the coins is 24, although Rath speaks of 59. The numbers 56 and 59 in Rath's readings, on which the suggestion regarding the length of the reign of the issuer of the Parimalgiri coins as well as his identification with Cauhān Rāmadeva of Patna are based, are really 17 and 19 respectively and would hardly support the theories propounded by Rath.

What has been read by Rath as *Paṭnā* (probably intending *Pāṭanā*) is the same as the symbols described by De as the Oriya *sa* flanked by the *aṅkuśa* and *kuṭhāra*. It is really unfortunate that the central one of the three symbols, which is commonly found on the Gaṅga Fanams either singly or flanked by other symbols, were not recognised as such. Rath's editorial comment on De's article, noticed above, seems to show that, in his opinion, all such coins were issued from Patna by the earliest Cauhān ruler. Needless to say that the theory is absolutely unwarranted. It is not easy to prove that the petty rulers of Patna ever issued any gold coins or even any coins at all. In case the central top symbol is read as an Oriya *sa,* the coins may be palaeographically assigned to a date not much earlier than the rise of the Sūryavaṁśis of Orissa in the fifteenth century.

Under the circumstances I consider it extremely desirable that the so-called Gaṅga Fanams referred to in these lines, especially those on which Rath has written in the *Journal of the Numismatic Society of India,* should be re-examined by more careful students of Indian epigraphy and numismatics.

Before concluding this discussion, I may refer to the forms of the numerals that have been wrongly read by either De or Rath or by both of them. The figure 1, which has been read correctly by De and wrongly by Rath, is of the Telugu-Kannaḍa type and resembles a convex. It is found in many medieval Orissan records including the Kendupatna plates of Narasiṁha II.[1] The figure 2 is of the medieval Bengali type and resembles the

1. Cf. *JASB,* Vol. LXV, 1896, Part i, Plate VIII, left margin.

modern forms of Telugu and English 3.[1] This figure has been read wrongly by both De and Rath. The figure 3 is of the Nāgarī type sometimes showing slight variation in the form.[2] The figure 7 is of the usual type which stands midway between its modern forms in Oriya and Bengali and resembles a staff with its head considerably carved towards the left. It is found in numerous early and medieval records from different parts of India.[3]

III

Some time ago, I received for examination a late medieval silver coin which is said to have been found somewhere in Bihar. Its owner is supposed to have in his possession a few more coins of the same type. Unfortunately, none of these other coins was available to me for examination.

The coin is round in shape, its diameter, thickness and weight being respectively 2.4 cm. (.97 in.), .31 cm. (.12 in.) and 11.79 grams (182 grains). The edge is unmilled; but there is a cut-like mark at the top edge. The specimen may be regarded as belonging to the series of medieval silver coins known as *ṭaṅka*.

The obverse of the coin exhibits a crudely executed pair of human forms, a male to the right and a female to the left. The breasts of the female figure are not marked ; but the lower part of her body, from the waist down to the legs, is covered by the lower end of her *sāḍī*. The male figure wears a piece of *dhotī* in the tight fashion, and the two ends of his *uttarīya* fly behind his back, one below the other. He faces left, with left hand resting on his waist and right hand touching the lower part of the back of the female who partly faces right. The male figure wears a three-pronged crown or headgear on his head, each of the prongs ending in a knob. The female form holds on her head, by her right hand, what looks like a basket containing some roundish objects. A scarf or the upper end of her *sāḍī* hangs down from her right shoulder, her left hand

1. For its occurrence in medieval Orissan records, see *ibid.*, Plate X, left magin, and Mazumdar, *Orissa in the Making*, Plate facing p. 202, line 22.
2. See *JASB*, *op. cit.*, Plate XII, left margin; Mazumdar, *loc. cit.*
3. Vide Ojha, *Palaeography of India* in Hindi, Plates LXXI, LXXV, LXXVI.

hanging with a slant towards the male. The scene seems to refer to a story of Kṛṣṇa, in the guise of a toll-collector, harassing his beloved milkwoman Rādhā on the plea that she had evaded payment of the usual *dāna* or royal dues on marketabl e commodities.

There is a legend in one line all around the scene described above. Some of the letters, e.g., *pajapa* (VII to IX) in late medieval Nāgarī are fairly clear, and *ja* therein is of the modern type not found in records earlier than the fourteenth or fifteenth century. The initial vowel *a* of the late Eastern type seems to occur once each on the obverse and the reverse. Unfortunately, the upper part of the letters is cut off owing to the flan being shorter than the die. It is therefore extremely difficult to read and interpret the legend satisfactorily without some help from other specimens.

The reverse of the coin, which is as crude as the obverse, depicts another scene of a cowherd driving his cattle. There are four heads of cattle with the cowboy, holding a stick in each of his raised hands, behind them. There is a tree in the background. This tree has a number of ball-like fruits or flowers. The cowboy is endowed with the *śikhaṇḍaka* or *mayūra-puccha* looking like three knobs on his head. There is no doubt that the scene represents the cowboy Kṛṣṇa tending cattle. The tree in the background thus appears to be a *kadamba*, so famous in the Kṛṣṇa mythology of Eastern India in the late medieval period.

As in the case of the obverse, the legend on the reverse also runs in one line all around the scene described above and has the top of the letters cut off. It is not possible to read and interpret it without the help of other coins of the same type.

The coin may be assigned to the late medieval period, roughly to the sixteenth or seventeenth century. But, unless the legend on both the obverse and the reverse are satisfactorily deciphered and interpreted, it is difficult to say whether it was minted on behalf of a ruler or belongs to the category of coins called Rāma-ṭaṅkā manufactured by private agencies, like temple authorities, and sold to the pilgrims at the holy places of Northern India.[1]

1. For some gold Rāma-ṭaṅkās of South Indian origin (often cup-

If the cut sign at the top edge is regarded as a shroff mark, the coin would appear to have been in circulation. The Rāma-ṭaṅkās were, however, primarily meant for preservation and not for circulation. But it should be remembered in this connection that, in ancient and medieval India, coins issued by any agency and even lumps of metal were usually circulating in the market.

The diameter and weight of the silver coin described above remind us of the silver Ṭaṅkas of the Muslim sovereigns of Delhi. The weight of the Ṭaṅkas of the Delhi rulers was theoretically 96 or 100 Ratis, i.e. 11.33 or 11.85 grams (175 or 183 grains), 1 Rati weighing .118 grams (1.83 grains).[1] Our coin follows the heavier weight standard and does not appear to be earlier than the age of Sher Shāh (1539-45 A.D.).

The Rāma-ṭaṅkās are generally associated with Rāma and appear to have been originally manufactured in the Ayodhyā (Fyzabad District, U.P.) region. But there are also coins of the same type, which have the representation of other deities with or without Rāma's association. Modern coins of this type are usually made of base silver, German silver or brass.

The popular type of Rāma-ṭaṅkā represents Rāma and Lakṣmaṇa with a legend on the obverse and the scene of Rāma's coronation on the reverse. Often it bears a date which is usually fictitious. Rāma-ṭaṅkās of this type are sold at Ayodhyā and other pilgrim spots of Northern India.

A modification of the above type of Rāma-ṭaṅkā exhibits the same reverse, but has the triad worshipped in the Jagannātha temple at Purī in Orissa on the obverse. Such Rāma-ṭaṅkās may have been issued on behalf of the Purī temple.

Among specimens without any association of Rāma, we have seen one exhibiting the goddess Kālī (as now worshipped in Bengal) on one side and Rādhā and Kṛṣṇa on the other and bearing legend in modern Bengali and Nāgarī characters. It was apparently manufactured in Bengal if not in Calcutta where the Kālī of Kālīghāṭ is the most celebrated deity. The

shaped), see *PASB*, 1882, p. 47 and Plate for one exhibited by Gibbs; his paper on 'The Medals known as Rāma-ṭankis' in *JASB*, Vol. LIII, pp. 207 ff. ; M.M. Chakravarti, 'Rāma-taṅkis' in *JASB*, Vol. LXI, pp. 104 ff. and Plate; cf. Bidie in *JASB*, Vol. LIII, No. 2, 1884, p. 212; Elliot, *Coins of South India*, p. 152E.

2. See above, pp. 3, etc. Cf. V. A. Smith, *Catalogue of Coins in the Indian Museum*, Vol. I, p. 134; H. N. Wright, *ibid.*, Vol. II, pp. 6 and IX.

representation of Kṛṣṇa on the coin seems to be explained by the fact that many of the pilgrims visiting the Kālīghāṭ temple are those who received their initiation into the Viṣṇu *mantra*.

We describe below the silver coin of the Rāma-ṭaṅkā type along with the specimens of certain types of Rāma-ṭaṅkā, some of which have been discussed above.

TYPE I. DĀNA-LĪLĀ (RĀDHĀ-KṚṢṆA) : GOPĀLA (COWHERD)-KṚṢṆA.

No. 1. Silver, round ; size 2.5 cm ; weight 11.79 grams (182 grains).

Obverse : Rādhā and Kṛṣṇa in a scene of the *Dāna-līlā* (already described above) ; partially preserved marginal legend all around.

Reverse : Cowherd Kṛṣṇa driving four heads of cattle by a *kadamba* tree (already described above); partially preserved marginal legend all around.

TYPE II. RĀMA-LAKṢMAṆA: RĀM-ĀBHIṢEKA

Variety A, with a possible date in the legend.

No. 2. Base silver ; round ; size 2.8 cm; weight 11.5 grams ; border obliquely milled.

Obverse : Rāma and Lakṣmaṇa wearing *dhotī*; standing in *tri-bhaṅga* pose ; with crown on head and bow on left arm ; Rāma alone has trident in right hand. Legend in Hindī written in modern Nāgarī characters—above (IX to IV)—*Rāma Lachamana Jānaka java(ya) ta Hanamānaka* (Victorious are Rāma, Lakṣmaṇa, Jānakī and Hanumat) ;
below—17 *śana* 40 (probably meaning Vikrama-saṁvat 1740=1683 A. D.).

Reverse : Rāma and Sītā on throne, under *chatra*, with Lakṣmaṇa at the right side, Bharata and Śatrughna at the left and Hanumat below. No legend.

Variety B, with an imaginary and absurd date in the legend.

No. 3. Base silver ; size 2.8 cm ; weight not recorded.

Obverse : Same as in No. 2 (Type II, Variety A). But both Rāma and Lakṣmaṇa have trident in right hand, and the date in the lower part reads '517—40', probably meaning the year 51740 of some fictitious era (cf. No. 7 below).

Reverse : Same as in No. 2 (Type II, Variety A).

N.B. We have many classes of this variety.

TYPE III. JAGANNĀTHA TRIAD : RĀM-ĀBHIṢEKA

No. 4. Base silver ; round, size 2.9 cm; weight 10.35 grams.

Obverse : Jaganātha, Subhadrā and Balarāma, standing. Legend (IX to III) in Sanskrit written in modern Nāgarī—*śrī-śrī-Jagannāthasva* (*s*=*tra*)*yi* (the Jagannātha triad).

Reverse : Same as in Nos. 2-3 (Type II, Varieties A and B).

TYPE IV. KĀLĪ : RĀDHĀ-KṚṢṆA

No. 5. Brass; round, size 2.8 cm ; weight 11.35 grams.

Obverse : Four-armed Kālī trampling on the chest of the prostrate figure of Śiva ; the goddess holding *kharpara* in the lower right hand under a severed human head, held by its hair in the goddess' upper right hand, for receiving the blood dripping from the head. In the upper left hand, the goddess holds a heavy sword (*khaḍga*) and her lower left hand is in the *varada* pose. She wears a thick necklace and a girdle of skulls. Legend—*Kālī-mātā* once in modern Bengali characters in the border to the left of the goddess and again in modern Nāgarī to her right.

Reverse : Kṛṣṇa standing in the well-known *tri-bhaṅga* pose with *śikhi-puccha* on the head, playing on flute ; Rādhā standing on his left, each standing on a lotus under a separate *kadamba* tree. Legend—*Rādhā-Kṛṣṇa* once in modern Bengali characters in the left margin and again in modern Nāgarī in the right.

TYPE V. HANUMAT : NUMERICAL FIGURES

No. 6. Brass ; round, 2.85 cm in diameter ; weight 9.75 grams ; dotted border ; obeverse and reverse not adjusted.

Obverse : The monkey-god Hanumat flying with the Gandhamādana (indicated by a triangular object) in the right hand and a mace in the left hand; crowned with coronet made of dots; facing left ; with torso covered by tight jacket (indicated by dots); ends of the *uttarīya* hanging on the left and the right ; upper part of the thighs covered by tightly worn *dhotī* with one of the ends hanging between the thighs; long tail passing above the head to the other side ; a star each in the upper right and left fields indicating Hanumat's movement in the sky during night time, the land below being indicated by a number of horizontal strokes.

Reverse : Nine numerical figures (in modern Nāgarī) arranged three in a row in spaces created by a pair of parallel straight lines at right angles so that the total of any of the three figures in a row would be 15 in all cases —

4	3	8
9	5	1
2	7	6

TYPE VI. COW : LAKṢMĪ

No. 7. Silver; round, 2.85 cm in diameter, .23 cm in thickness; weight 12.1 grams ; dotted border beyond circle ; obverse and reverse not adjusted; bearing an imaginary and absurd date.

Reverse : Cow to left with a fodder-tub containing leaves in the left field; modern Nāgarī legend above the cow—152100, and below the cow—*sana* (apparently intended to mean that the coin belongs to hoary antiquity and is dated in the year 152100 of some imaginary *San* or era).

Obverse : Four-armed deity seated cross-legged on a lotus ; lotus buds in the upper hands ; crown on the head with locks of hair conventionally represented as hanging from the head and on the soulders and the upper part of the arms ; conventional representation of a lotus plant with flower on either side. It is a crude modern adaptation of the figure of seated Lakṣmī on the reverse of the Archer type gold coins of Candragupta II and his successors. The coin appears to have been fabricated sometime after the beginning of the study of Gupta numismatics, probably not earlier than the close of the nineteenth century.[1]

1. The coin belongs to Abanimohan Ghosh of Dubrajpur (Birbhum District, West Bengal), who says that such coins are kept in the cash-box by the housewives as a token of the goddess of prosperity (Lakṣmī).

Chapter XV

COINS OF BHAIRAVASIMHA

I

An interesting paper on a late medieval silver coin was recently published by R. K. Choudhary in the *Journal of the Numismatic Society of India*, Vol. XX, Part i, pp. 55 ff., Plate IX, No. 5. There are two supplementary notes added to the article, which are equally interesting. One of these comes from the pen of A. S. Altekar, while the other is contributed by P. L. Gupta. Choudhary and Altekar have read the name of the Oinvār ruler Rāmabhadra in the legend on the coin. But, curiously enough, whereas the former reads it in the central section on the reverse, the latter finds it on the borders around the corresponding section on the obverse. P. L. Gupta seems to be doubtful about the reading of the name in the central section, while he considers the writing in the margin as mere decorative symbols. It may, however, be pointed out that the name of Rāmabhadra does not occur anywhere in the legend, either in the central section or in the margin, and, consequently, the attribution of the coin to a ruler of that name is entirely untenable. There can also be no doubt about the existence of the marginal legend on both sides of the coin.

About the end of November 1957, while I was passing through Patna in the course of a tour, Choudhary kindly met me and showed me the coin in question. I could then read only a few letters of the legend. Choudhary was, however, good enough to allow me to prepare plasticine moulds of the coin, from which plaster-casts of it were made at my office on my return to Ootacamund about the beginning of January 1958. The casts were at first studied by one of the numismatists at the office of the Government Epigraphist for India, who unfortunately submitted them to me after some weeks without being able to read the legend either on the obverse or on the reverse. I then myself took up the casts for examination and realised that the legend was not decipherable without very considerable labour.

As a result of repeated attempts on the first day, I could satisfactorily read only *mahārāja-śrī-...nārāyaṇ-ātmaja*[1]...*siṁhasya* in the central sections on both sides of the coin. Since the legend is written in the medieval characters of Eastern India, I was searching for a ruler of the said area and age, whose name ended in *siṁha* and whose father had a name ending in *nārāyaṇa*. However, I was then rather doubtful whether I should ever be successful in deciphering the whole legend satisfactorily. But repeated attempts of several days enabled me to decipher the passage *Tīrabhukti-rāja* in the upper half of the legend in the central section on the reverse. This encouraged me considerably and I continued my efforts. After some days, I succeeded in completing the decipherment of the writing in the central sections on both the obverse and reverse of the coin. These parts read: *mahārāja-śrī-Darppanārāyaṇ-ātmaja-Tīrabhukti-rāja-śrī-Bhairavasiṁhasya.* It was therefore a coin of king Bhairavasiṁha, the lord of Tīrabhukti and the son of *Mahārāja* Darpanārāyaṇa. It was later learnt by me that the coin belonged to a hoard discovered at Bairmo in the Darbhanga District of Bihar.

But I had yet to solve the problem of decipherment of the marginal writing beyond the four sides of the central section on both the faces of the coin. From the very beginning, they appeared to me to be dates; but I could not reconcile two different dates, one on the obverse and another on the reverse of the same coin. When I was struggling with the decipherment of these parts of the legend, I learnt from Choudhary that his article on the coin was being published in the *Journal of the Numismatic Society of India*, although I felt certain that there was none who could offer a satisfactory reading of the entire legend on the coin in a short time and there were only a few who would be able to read it at all. I therefore continued my struggle with the marginal writing and after many more efforts ultimately succeeded in deciphering the border legend on the obverse as *Śaka-sa* 1411 and that on the reverse as *rājya* 15.

1. Altekar also read these eleven *akṣaras* correctly.

II

The coin is round in shape and has a diameter of one inch. Its weight is stated to be 10.52 grams or 161.79 grains. On both obverse and reverse of the coin there is a square made of raised lines, within a circular line of the same type. In the four semi-circular spaces between the arms of the square and the outer line, there is in each case a letter or one or more nu merical figures between two angular ornamental designs. Inside the square the legend is written in raised letters in five lines diagonally arranged between the upper and lower angles on both the obverse and the reverse. The reverse legend is a continuation of the writing on the obverse. There are thirteen letters on the obverse and an equal number of them on the reverse. Of these thirteen letters arranged in five lines, line 3 at the centre has five *aksharas*, lines 2 and 4 have three each and lines 1 and 5 only one each. The same arrangement has been followed on both the sides.

The characters belong to the Gauḍīya alphabet as prevalent in Bihar in the fourteenth and fifteenth centuries A.D. The letters *ra* and *śa* have been written both in the Nāgarī and Gauḍīya fashions. The two types of *ra* are very similar respectively to *n* and *v* as found in the legend, while *ya* resembles *pa*. Some letters of the legend have suffered from effects of later punching by the shroffs.

The writting on the obverse and reverse reads as follows—

Obverse	Reverse
1 *Ma-*	1 *Tī-*
2 *hārāja-*	2 *rabhukti-*
3 *śrī-Da[rppa]nārā-*	3 *rāja-śrī-Bhaira-*
4 *yaṇ-ātma-*	4 *vasiṁha-*
5 *ja-*	5 *sya* (॥*)

The legend may be translated as : "[This coin is] of the illustrious Bhairavasiṁha, the lord of Tīrabhukti [and] the son of the illustrious *Mahārāja* Darpanārāyaṇa."

In the spaces outside the square on the obverse, we have respectively in the upper left, upper right, lower left and lower right :

[Śa]-	*ka-*
sa	1411

In the corresponding spaces on the reverse, there are similarly :

rā- *jya*
[1] 5

Of the writing on the reverse, the central slanting line of *jya* is not clearly made, while the left part of the figure for 1 is cut off. These writings no doubt quote the date of the issue of the coin under study, the obverse giving *Śaka-sa* (i.e. *Śaka-saṁvatsare*) 1411 and the reverse *rājya* (i.e. *rājya-saṁvatsare*) 15, i.e. the regnal year 15. Thus the coin was issued by king Bhairavasiṁha of Tīrabhukti (i.e. Tirhut or Mithilā in North Bihar), who was the son of king Darpanārāyaṇa, in the 15th year of his reign, which corresponded to Śaka 1411 or 1489-90 A.D. Bhairavasiṁha thus ascended the throne of Tirhut about Śaka 1397 or 1475-76 A.D.

There is no doubt that the king who issued the coin under study is identical with Bhairavasiṁha *alias* Rūpanārāyaṇa *alias* Harinārāyaṇa who was the son of Narasiṁha Darpanārayaṇa of the Oinvār dynasty of Tirhut, which flourished in the period between the middle of the 14th to the first half of the 16th century A.D. The coin was then the only known issue of Bhairavasiṁha and one of the very few of the Oinvārs as yet published. As a matter of fact, very few of the Oinvār rulers issued coins. Our coin throws some light on the rather obscure history of the king as well as of the small ruling family of mediaval India, to which he belonged.

III

There is another coin of the same class in the cabinet of the Archaeological Section of the Indian Museum. It was examined by V.A. Smith and was noticed as No. 3 under the head 'Sundry Coins' at the last page (p. 333) of his *Catalogue of the Coins in the Indian Museum*, Vol. I, 1906. He correctly gives the metal, weight and size of the coin respectively as silver, 164 grains and .9 inch. Unfortunately, Smith, who thought that the provenance of the coin might be Nepal, failed to read any part of the five-line (not four-line as supposed by him) legend on the obverse and the reverse. In the *Annual Report of the Archaeological Survey of India*, 1913-14, p. 259 (Plate LXIX,

No. 31), R. D. Banerji made an unsuccessful attempt to read the legend.

The present coin (No. 2) was struck on a flan slightly smaller than that of Bhairavasiṁha's other coin (No. 1) dealt with above. As a result of this, some of the letters and numerical figures that can be seen on Coin No. 1 are cut off on Coin No. 2. The two coins, although they apparently bear the same date, were struck from two different dies. In some cases, the forms of the letters are different on the two specimens; cf. *ha* in *mahārāja*, *sa* in *siṁha*, etc. As on Coin No. 1, some letters on Coin No. 2 are damaged owing to later punching by the shroffs; cf. *ya* in *nārāyaṇa* and *ra* in *Tīrabhukti*. Similarly, two forms of the letters *ja*, *ra* and *ha* have been used in the legend on No. 2 as in that of No. 1. The *akṣara śrī* before *Bhairava*, which exhibits the sign of later punching on Coin No. 1, seems to be badly shaped on Coin No. 2. In spite, however, of these differences, the arrangement of the letters and numerical figures in the legends on both the coins is the same. But, as indicated above, some of these letters and figures in the spaces outside the central square are cut off on Coin No. 2. The legend in the central squares on both sides of Coin No. 2 reads as follows :

Obverse	Reverse
1 *Ma-*	1 *Tī-*
2 *hārāja-*	2 *rabh*[*u*]*kti-*
3 [*śrī*]-*Darppanārā-*	3 *rāja-*[*śrī*] *-Bhaira-*
4 *yaṇ-ātma-*	4 *vas*[*iṁ*]*ha-*
5 *ja-*	5 *sya* (॥*)

Of the letters and numerical figures in the spaces outside the square on the obverse, *Śa* in the upper left is partly visible while *ka* in the upper right is quite clear. *Saṁ* in the lower left is almost totally cut off, though only the lower parts of the figures 1411 in the lower right are lost. Similarly, in the spaces outside the central square on the reverse of the coin, it is difficult to recognize *rā* in the upper left and *jya* in the upper right, while the numerical figure in the lower left and that in the lower right are both cut off. The *akṣara jya* is fully preserved, but is not properly shaped.

IV

The history of the rulers of the Oinvār house of Tirhut is little known and their chronology full of confusion. The confusion is due to many factors such as the uncertainty about the initial year of the Lakṣmaṇasena-saṁvat or La-saṁ used in the dating of many of the literary records of the period and tract in question, the possibility of contemporaneous or conjoint rule for some years of the predecessor and successor in several cases, and the unreliability of some of the local traditions. Since the late medieval period, the La-saṁ is calculated as starting from 1108 A.D.; but, as regards the earlier dates, the initial year varies between 1108 and 1119 A.D.[1] For the sake of convenience, we have tentatively taken 1119 A.D. as the starting point of the era in our calculations in the following pages. Another great difficulty is that even when the La-saṁ year is mentioned together with the corresponding Śaka year and verifiable astronomical details are provided for a date, it is generally irregular according to Swamikannu Pillai's *Indian Ephemeris*. This is evidently due to the fact that the local almanacs, from which the dates were quoted, were based on defective calculations.[2]

Harisiṁha, the last ruler of the Karnāṭa dynasty of Mithilā, was overthrown by Sulṭān Ghiyāsuddīn Tughlug Shāh (1320-25 A.D.) of Delhi about 1324 A.D.[3] Sometime later, about the middle of the fourteenth century, a Brāhmaṇa named Kāmeśvara Ṭhākura, who may have originally been the *Rājapaṇḍita* at Harisiṁha's court, obtained the Zamindari of a considerable part of the country from Sulṭān Fīrūz Shāh (1351-87 A.D.). The dynasty founded by the Brāhmaṇa is called Oinavāra (Oini-

1. Sircar, *Indian Epigraphy*, pp. 271 ff.
2. *Ibid.*, pp. 227-28. Here we are offering a sketch of Oinvār history and chronology on the basis of the following works : (1) M. M. Chakravarti, 'History of Mithilā during the Pre-Mughal Period' (*JASB*, N. S., Vol. XI, 1915, pp. 406-433; especially pp. 415-33); (2) R. K. Choudhary, 'The Oinvāras of Mithilā' (*JBRS*, Vol. XL, pp. 99-121); (3) J. Eggeling, *Catalogue of Sanskrit Manuscripts in the Library of the India Office*, Part IV, pp. 874-76, No. 2564; (4) G.A. Grierson, (a) 'Vidyāpati and his Contemporaries' (*Ind. Ant.*, Vol. XIV, 1885, pp. 182 ff.); (*b*) 'On Some Medieval Kings of Mithilā' (*ibid.*, Vol. XVIII, 1899, pp. 57-58); (*c*) *An Introduction to Maithilī Language*; (5) S. N. Singh, *History of Tirhut*, 1915; and (6) U. Thakur, *History of Mithilā*, 1956, Chapter VI : The Oinavāras (pp. 290-339).
3. I. Prasad, *Hist. Med. Ind.*, p. 266.

vāra) or Oinvār after the village of Oinī in the Muzaffarpur District, which one of his ancestors received from a Karṇāṭa king. The family is sometimes also named after Sugaunā, Kāmeśvara's residence near modern Madhubani in the Darbhanga District. After a short time, Fīrūz Shāh gave Kāmeśvara's throne to the latter's son Bhogīśvara.[1] According to some doubtful traditions, Bhogīśvara ruled for 33 years and died in 1360 A.D.[2] Bhogīśvara's son and successor was Gaṇeśvara who, according to Vidyāpati's *Kīrtilatā*, was defeated and killed by an enemy named Aslān, apparently a Musalmān, aided probably by certain members of the Oinvār family. The date of this event is given in the work in a corrupt passage which may mean the 5th of the first (i.e. dark) half of Agrahāyana in La-saṁ 252 (1371 A.D.).[3] His eldest son Vīrasiṁha seems to have been ruling over a part of the country in La-saṁ 228 (1347 A.D.) when a manuscript of the *Liṅgavārttika* was copied in his territory.[4] That he was a ruler is also suggested by the title *Mahārājādhirāja* applied to him in the *Kīrtilatā.*[5] Sometime after Gaṇeśvara's death his son Kīrtisiṁha became king with the help of Ibrāhim Shāh Sharqī (1401-40 A.D.) of Jaunpur. The next king was Bhavasiṁha, a younger son of Kāmeśvara, and he was succeeded by his eldest son Devasiṁha Garuḍanārāyaṇa. Since a manuscript of Śrīdatta's *Ekāgnidāna-paddhati*, composed at Devasiṁha's request, was copied on Monday, Pauṣa-śudi 9, La-saṁ 299 (1418 A.D.), he seems to have ascended the throne before that date.[6] According to a poem ascribed to Vidyāpati, Devasiṁha died on Thursday, Caitra-vadi 6, La-saṁ 293 corresponding to Śaka 1324 (1403 A.D.) which is supposed to be a mistake for Śaka 1334 (1413 A.D.).[7] As Śrīdhara's *Kāvyaprakāśaviveka* was composed on

1. *JASB*, N. S., Vol. XI, 1915, p. 416.
2. Thakur, *op. cit.*, p. 297; *JBRS*, Vol. XI, p. 102.
3. *JASB*, *op. cit.*, p. 416 and note 2: *JBORS*, Vol. XIII, p. 297.
4. Thakur, *op. cit.*, p. 302.
5. *JASB*, *loc. cit.* The same title was often enjoyed by the ministers of the Oinvār rulers, e.g. Caṇḍeśvara and Rāmadatta, probably because they were ruling over parts of the country as viceroys or enjoyed extensive *jāgīrs* together with regal title.
6. *Ibid.*, pp. 417-18. Doubtful traditions assign Bhavasiṁha's accession to 1348 A.D. and Devasiṁha's to 1385 A.D. (Eggeling, *op. cit.*, p. 875).
7. *JASB*, *op. cit.*, pp. 418-19; D.C. Sen, *Baṅgabhāṣā-o-Sāhitya*, 5th ed., pp. 216-17. Thakur (*op. cit.*, p. 306) ascribes to M.M. Chakravarti the view that

Kārttika-vadi 10, La-saṁ 291 (1411 A.D.) when Devasiṁha's son Śivaisṁha Rūpanārāyaṇa is stated to have been ruling over Tīrabhukti, the son seems to have been reigning jointly with the father as *Yuvarāja* (or at least over parts of the kingdom) and to have been a patron of Śrīdhara. Devasiṁha ruled from Devakulī about 2 miles to the north of Darbhanga while Śivasiṁha had his headquarters at Gajarathapura or Śivasiṁhapura about 5 miles to the south-east of Darbhanga. Three spurious copper-plate charters of king Śivasiṁha, recording the grant of the village of Bisapī in favour of the poet Vidyāpati, bear respectively the dates Vikrama 1455, Śaka 1321 and La-saṁ 293 equated with Vikrama 1455, Śaka 1321 and San 807, i.e. probably 1399 A.D.[1] Śivasiṁha is described by Vidyāpati as the 'lord of the Five Gauḍas' and as one who subdued the king or kings of Gauḍa. This vague and conventional claim may suggest that, unlike his predecessors who owed allegiance to the Muhammadans, Śivasiṁha ruled for sometime as an independent monarch. The result, however, was fatal and, according to tradition, Śivasiṁha was defeated by the Musalmāns and carried away to Delhi.[2] The same source suggests that, after the tragic end of Śivasiṁha's reign, his queen Lakhimādevī ruled for 12 years and was succeeded by Padmasiṁha who was the younger brother of Śivasiṁha (and ruled for 6 years according to one tradition)[3] and that Padmasiṁha's queen Viśvāsadevī ruled for 12 years after her husband's reign of one year. It is also believed that Lakhimā, accompanied by the poet Vidyāpati, took shelter at Purāditya's court at Rājabanauli where Vidyāpati wrote his *Likhanāvalī* in 1418 A.D. and copied the *Bhāgavata* in La-saṁ 309 (1428 A.D.).[4] The next king was Harasiṁha,

Devasiṁha ascended the throne in Śaka 1263 (1342 A.D.). But there is no such statement in Chakravarti's article refered to above.

1. Cf. Bhandarkar's List, Nos. 736, 1126 and 1470. The date of Śivasiṁha's accession is assigned by tradition to 1446 A.D. ((*An. Rep. A.S.I.*, 1913-14, p. 249; Eggling, *loc. cit.*).

2. *Ind. Ant.*, Vol. XVIII, p. 58.

3. *JBRS*, Vol. XL, p. 120.

4. Cf. *loc. cit.* Traditions, referred to by Eggeling (*loc. cit.*), assign the accession of Lakhimādevī to 1449 A.D. and of Viśvāsadevī to 1458 A.D., but omit Padmasiṁha. According to Vidyāpati's *Likhanāvalī*, the work was composed (in La-saṁ 299=1418 A.D.) at the request of king Purāditya Girinārāyaṇa of the Droṇavāra family, who had killed a king named Arjuna

younger son of Devasiṁha, and his son and successor was Narasiṁha Darpanārāyaṇa whose Kandaha inscription is dated Śaka 1375 (1453 A.D.).[1] Narasiṁha was succeeded by his son Dhīrasimha Hṛdayanārāyaṇa during whose rule a manuscript of Śrīnivāsa's *Setudarpaṇī* (a commentary on the *Setubandha*) and another of the Karṇaparvan of the *Mahābhārata* were copied respectively on Saturday, Kārttika-vadi 15, La-saṁ 321 (1440 A.D.) and in La-saṁ 327 (1446 A.D.).[2] For some years Dhīrasiṁha appears to have been ruling jointly with his father or at least over an area of the country. He was succeeded by his younger brother Bhairavasiṁha Rūpanārāyaṇa-Harinārāyaṇa who ruled from Baruāra in the Bacchaurā Pargana of the Darbhanga District. According to some, he assended the throne in 1496 A.D. when Vardhamāna composed his *Gaṅgākṛtyaviveka* and Vācaspati-miśra wrote his *Mahādānanirṇaya* (earliest copy dated in La-saṁ 392 or 1511 A.D.) during his rule, while it is also suggested that he died about 1515 A.D.[3] Bhairavasiṁha's successor was his son Rāmabhadra Rūpanārāyaṇa whose rule is placed by some before 1490 A.D. but by others in 1520-27 A.D.,[4] although both the theroies appear to be wrong. The *Tantrapradīpa* was composed by Gadādhara (a grandson of Dhīrasiṁha) during his reign, while certain manuscripts are known to have been copied at Gadādhara's instance on Friday, Śrāvaṇa-vadi 1, La-saṁ 372 (1491 A.D.) and on Wednesday, Kārttika-sudi 5, La-saṁ 374 and Śaka 1426 (1504 A.D.).[5] The known dates of Rāmabhadra's son and successor Lakṣmīnātha Kaṁsanārāyaṇa offer some difficulty unless it is believed that he was ruling jointly with his father or at least over a part of the country. A manuscript of the *Devīmāhātmya* was copied during Lakṣmīnātha's rule on Wednesday,

and was ruling at Rājabanauli in Nepal. This Arjuna is identified with the son of Bhavasiṁha's son Tripurasiṁha and is believed to have contributed to the murder of Gaṇeśvara (*JBRS*, Vol. XL, pp. 117-19).

1. *JBORS*, Vol. XX, pp. 15-19. Jayaswal wrongly interpreted the chronogram *śar-āśva-madana* as 1357. Traditions referred to by Eggeling (*loc. cit.*) omit Harasiṁha and assign Narasimha's accession to 1470 A.D.

2. *JASB*, *op. cit.*, pp. 425-26; *JBORS*, Vol. X, p. 47. According to M. M. Chakravarti, La-saṁ 321, Kārttika-vadi 15, Saturday, corresponds to October 18, 1438 A.D. Traditions referred to by Eggeling (*loc. cit.*) assign Dhīrasiṁha's accession to 1471 A.D.

3. Cf. Thakur, *op. cit.*, pp. 333-34. Traditions assign Bhairavasiṁha's accession to 1506 A.D. and his successor's to 1520 A.D. (cf. Eggeling, *loc. cit.*).

4. See *JASB*, *op. cit.*, pp. 329-30.

5. *Loc. cit.*

Pauṣa-vadi 3, La-saṁ 393 (1512 A.D.).[1] Lakṣmīnātha's Bhagīrathpur inscription is dated in La-saṁ 394 (1513 A.D.).[2] About this time, Tirhut became a bone of contention between Sulṭān Sikandar Lodī (1489-1517 A.D.) of Delhi and Husain Shāh (1493-1519 A.D.) of Bengal; ultimately the latter's son Naṣrat Shāh (1519-32 A.D.) invaded Tirhut, put the king (probably Lakṣmīnātha) to death and appointed his brothers-in-law, 'Alāuddin and Makhdum-i-'Alam, governors of the country.[3] This account of the Muslim historians is corroborated by a stanza giving the date of Lakṣmīnātha's death as Tuesday, Bhādra-sudi 1, Śaka 1449 (1527 A.D.), although according to a tradition followed by Eggeling he was ruling in 1532 A.D. and, according to another followed by Grierson, in 1542 A.D.[4]

The Oinvār or Sugaunā Dynasty[5]

(middle of the 14th century to 1527 A.D.)

1. *Ibid.*, p. 430.
2. *JBRS*, Vol. XLI, Part 3, pp. 271 ff. The date is given in the chronogram *veda-randhra-Haranetra*.
3. Badāunī, *Muntakhābut Tawārikh*, trans., Vol. I, pp. 415-17; *Hist. Beng.*, Dacca University, Vol. II, pp. 145 ff.; *Camb. Hist. Ind.*, Vol. III, p. 272; Thakur, *op. cit.*, pp. 338-39.
4. Eggeling, *loc. cit.*; Grierson, *Introduction to Maithili Language*, Part II, p. 96; Thakur, *op. cit.*, p. 339 and note 2.
5. The genealogy quoted by Grierson (*Ind. Ant.*, Vol. XIV., p. 196) represents Kāmeśvara as the son of Lakṣmaṇa, grandson of Govinda, great-grandson of Viśvarūpa and great-great-grandson of Atirūpa. Udayasiṁha is mentioned as another son of Bhavasiṁha, and Sarvasiṁha is represented as the only son of Tripurasiṁha. Ratneśvarasiṁha (Raṭāya), Raghusiṁha Vijayanārāyaṇa and Brahmasimha Harinārāyaṇa are mentioned as brothers of Narasiṁha Darpanārāyaṇa. A brother of Candrasiṁha was Durlabhasiṁha or Raṇasiṁha whose son was Viśvanātha Naranārāyaṇa. Rāmacandra and Pratāparudra are represented as the sons of Viśvanātha, and Ratnasiṁha as the son of Rāmacandra. Puruṣottama seems to be mentioned as Garuḍanārāyaṇa. A brother of Lakṣmīnātha Kaṁsanārāyaṇa was Balabhadra and his two step-brothers were Ratinātha and Bhavanātha Hṛdayanārāyaṇa. Mention is also made of Dhīrasiṁha's son Jagannārāyaṇa whose sons were Madhusūdana, Śrīnātha, Kīrtisiṁha, Rudranārāyaṇa and Vīravara.

I. Kāmeśvara (3rd quarter of the 14th cent.)

II. Bhogīśvara (3rd quarter of the 14th cent.) V. Bhavasiṁha

III. Gaṇeśvara (killed in La-saṁ 252)

Vīrasiṁha (La-saṁ 228)

IV. Kirtisiṁha (early years of the 15th cent.)

VI. Devasiṁha Garuḍanārāyaṇa (died in La-saṁ 293, Śaka 1324 or 1334)

XI. Harasiṁha

Tripurasiṁha

XII. Narasiṁha Darpanārāyaṇa (Śaka 1375)

Arjunasiṁha

Amara

VII. Śivasiṁha Rūpanārāyaṇa (La-saṁ 291) + VIII. Lakhimādevī

IX. Padmasiṁha + X. Viśvāsadevī

XIII. Dhīrasiṁha Hṛdayanārāyaṇa (La-saṁ 321, 327)

XIV. Bhairavasiṁha Harinārāyaṇa Rūpanārāyaṇa (Śaka 1411-15th regnal year)

Candrasiṁha

Rāghavasiṁha

Gadādhara (La-saṁ 372, 374; contemporary of Rāmabhadra)

XV. Rāmabhadra Rūpanārāyaṇa (La-saṁ 372,374) Puruṣottama

XVI. Lakṣmīnātha Kaṁsanārāyaṇa (La-saṁ 393, 394; died Śaka 1449)

V

Besides the few facts about Bhairavasiṁha mentioned in the above sketch, some more are also known. It seems that he was originally ruling the kingdom (or part of it) jointly with his elder brother Dhīrasiṁha with the secondary name Rūpanārāyaṇa and that on his brother's death he succeeded to the throne with the name Harinārāyaṇa, his son Rāmabhadra then assuming the name Rūpanārāyaṇa. The reason why Rāghavasiṁha, son of Dhīrasiṁha, was deprived of his father's throne is unknown.

Many of the Oinvār kings patronised men of letters. Bhairavasiṁha was also a great patron of learning and under his patronage Rucipati wrote his *Anargharāghavaṭīkā*, Vācaspatimiśra his *Vyavahāracintāmaṇi*, *Kṛityamahārṇava* and *Mahādānanirṇaya*, and Vardhamān-opādhyāya his *Daṇḍaviveka*. Vācaspati was his *Pariṣada* or *Pāriṣada* (i.e. councillor) and Vardhamāna his *Dharmādhikaraṇika* or judge. Vācaspati's *Dvaitanirṇaya* was written at the request of Bhairavasiṁha's queen Jayā or Jayātmā, mother of *Rājādhirāja* Puruṣottama who seems to have ruled a part of the kingdom under his father. Miśaru-miśra wrote his *Vivādacandra* and *Padārthacandra* at the instance of the wife of Candrasiṁha who was a brother (probably step-brother) of Bhairavasiṁha. According to the *Mahādānanirṇaya*, Bhairavasiṁha excavated many tanks, gave away some towns and townships and performed a *Tulāpuruṣadāna*.[1]

Vidyāpati's *Durgābhaktitaraṅgiṇī* mentions Bhairavasiṁha as *śaury-āvarjita-pañca-Gauḍa-dharaṇinātha* and Vardhamāna's *Daṇḍaviveka* describes him as *Gauḍ-eśvara-pratiśarīram=atipratāpaḥ Kedārarāyam=avagacchati dāra-tulyam.*[2] The vague claim of victory over the rulers of the Five Gauḍas, which is conventional and seems to point to the independent status claimed by Bhairavasiṁha, reminds us of the fact that the only other Oinvār ruler with similar claims is Śivasiṁha who is called *Pañca-Gauḍ-eśvara*, i.e. lord of the Five Gauḍas, in Vidyāpati's songs and is described in the same poet's *Śaivasarvasvasāra* as

1. For references, see *JASB*, *op. cit.*, pp. 426-28.

2. *Ibid.*, p. 426, note 2; p. 427, note 4. Kedārarāya, whom Bhairavasiṁha treated as his own wife (*i.e.* as a subordinate), may have been a general of the Muslim king of Bengal. The ruler of Tirhut probably defeated and humiliated him. The claim may be compared with the title *Ripu-rāja-gopī-govinda* assumed by a medieval ruler of Sylhet (*Hist. Beng.*, Dacca University, Vol. I, p. 256).

śaury-āvarjita-Gauḍa-mahīpāla (i.e. one who conquered the king or kings of Gauḍa by his prowess) and in his *Puruṣaparīkṣā* as one having earned fame in battles with the kings of Gauḍa and Gajjana.[1] These facts appear to show that amongst the Oinvārs at least Śivasiṁha and Bhairavasiṁha aspired for independent status. Besides the Muslim rulers of Delhi, those of Jaunpur and Bengal were also each eager to spread their influence in Tirhut, and the Oinvārs, who owed allegiance to Delhi, had sometimes to submit to these powers as well.[2] But on occasions a few of them got an opportunity to assume independence temporarily as a result of quarrels amongst the said Muslim powers or of their weakness or preoccupations. It is interesting in this connection to note that, as feudatories of the Muslims, the Oinvārs were not expected to issue coins in their own names. That Bhairavasiṁha ruled for sometime as an independent ruler of Tirhut is indicated by his issue of silver coins, two of which are now known. It is also interesting to note that Śivasiṁha is the only other Oinvār king whose coins have been discovered.

In 1913 three small gold coins, out of a lot discovered at the village of Pipra in the Champaran District, were received in the Indian Museum, Calcutta. They were noticed by R. D. Banerji in the *Annual Report of the Archaeological Survey of India*, 1913-14, pp. 248-49, Plate LXVIII, Nos. 1-3. The coins are round in shape with diameter varying between .3 and .325 inch and weight between 13.6 and 14 grains. As on the coins of Bhairavasiṁha discussed above, the legend on the Pipra gold coins runs on from the obverse to the reverse. The legend on the obverse reads *śrī-* and that on the reverse in two lines runs (1) *Śiva-* (2) *sya.* King Śiva, who issued these coins, has been

1. *JBBRS*, Vol. XL, p. 121, note 4; Thakur, *op. cit.*, pp. 310-11. By Gajjana rulers, the successors of the representative of the early Ghazna rulers at Delhi appear to be meant.

2. We have seen how Kāmeśvara and Bhogīśvara obtained rulership from Firūz Shāh Tughluq of Delhi and Kīrtisiṁha from Ibrāhim Shāh (1402-36 A.D.) of Jaunpur. Khwāja Jahān (1394-99 A.D.) of Jaunpur succeeded in extending his influence over Tirhut (*Camb. Hist. Ind.*, Vol. III, p. 251) and Husain Shāh (1458-79 A.D.) crushed the semi-independent landholders of that country before 1466 A.D. (*ibid.*, p. 255). For a short time Iliyās Shāh (1343-57 A.D.) of Bengal occupied Tirhut (*ibid.*, p. 176). Some of the songs attributed to Vidyāpati speak of Muslim rulers like Gyāsadina Suratāna, Nāsira Sāha, *Pañca-Gauḍeśvara Rāya* Nasarata Sāha and Ālama Sāha (*JBRS*, Vol. XL, p.p. 10--10). There is considerable difference of opinion about the identification of these rulers.

rightly identified by Banerji with king Śivasimha of the Oinvār dynasty of Tirhut. A similar coin was previously published by Cunningham in his *Coins of Medieval India*, p. 54, Plate VI, No. 18. Banerji seems to assign the copper coins[1] bearing the name of Campakāraṇya to the dynasty of Śivasimha; but they were issued by the rulers of the Brāhmaṇa dynásty of Champaran and not by the Oinvārs of Tirhut.

The importance of Bhairavasiṁha's coins is two-fold. In the first place, they show, as already indicated above, that Oinvār Bhairavasiṁha ruled for sometimes as an independent monarch and signalised the achievement with the issue of some silver coins. Secondly, we learn for the first time from them that Bhairavasiṁha ascended the throne about 1475-76 A.D. and ruled at least for about 15 years down to 1489-90 A.D. The view assigning his accession to 1496 A.D. is thus wrong.

1. See V. A. Smith, *JASB*, Vol. LXVI, 1897, Part i, p. 309; and *Catalogue* (Indian Museum, Calcutta), p. 293; C. J. Rodgers, *Catalogue* (Lahore Museum), p. 12, Plate IV.

Chapter XVI

MARĀṬHĀ MINT UNDER THE PESHWĀS

Not much is known about the problems regarding the ancient Indian mint and currency. But we have some idea of the monetary problems relating to the late medieval period of Indian history. It may be suggested that a number of facts known about the mint and money of the seventeenth or eighteenth century India were also true in the case of minting in the pre-Musalman days. Thus the facts which are summarily discussed in the following pages are not without bearing also on the study of early Indian numismatics.[1]

The Hindu view as regards mint and currency is supposed to be reflected in the following observation: "No Government has the right to close its mints or to say that the currency of the country was either deficient or redundant. That is a question solely for the bankers, traders and merchants to consider. If they do not require money, they will not purchase bullion to be coined. The duty of the Government is merely to assay all bullion brought to the mint for coinage and to return the value of the bullion in money."[2] The great Śivājī advocated the above policy. This is apparent from his reply to the prayer of the English merchants of the East India Company that their 'money should go current in his dominions'. The English were informed that the Marāṭhā king 'forbids not the passing of any number of coins, nor on the other side can he force his subjects to take those monies whereby they shall be losers; but if their coin be as fine an alloy and as weighty as the Mughul's and other princes', he will not prohibit it."[3] The inevitable result of such a policy was that no less than 26 different sorts of gold coins were current in Śivājī's realm, some of which were foreign issues.[4] Sabhāsad

1. See above, pp. 233-34; also the Sections on the Cowrie-shell and the Rupee below, pp. 279 ff., 289 ff.

2. Cf. Ranade, *Miscellaneous Writings*, p. 330.

3. Sabhāsad, p. 95; Sen, *Śiva Chatrapati*, pp. 134 f.

4. Sen, *Administrative System of the Marāṭhās*, p. 318.

enumerated 32 different kinds of gold coins and 6 varieties of silver money while giving an account of the treasures of Śivājī.[1] The same condition of things was true for the Marāṭhā country also during the later period. In an official list published for the guidance of the civil courts in the Bombay Presidency, no less than 38 gold coins and more than 120 silver issues are mentioned as current in different parts of the country, so as to give the relative instrinsic values of the local currencies in exchange for Queen Victoria's coins.[2]

The natural corrollary of this system, as we see in the Peshwā period, was private minting which was not free but licensed. The owner of private mints was usually a *Sonār* or goldsmith who had to pay for the license. The fee was paid in the shape of a royalty to the government, which varied in different cases. The holder of the mint license was responsible for preserving the purity of the metal for coining and for keeping up the standard proportion in the alloy. Violation of the contract led to punishment by fine or cancellation of the license. There is an interesting record which illustrates the system of private minting in the dominions of the Peshwā. "Bālājī Bāpujī is permitted to establish a mint at Kasba Nagothane and to coin pice 10 *māṣas* in weight. If pice of the prescribed weight is coined, it will be all right; but, if the pice is made less weighty, he will be fined."[3] It was a license for the period of 3 years, for which Bālājī Bāpujī had to pay Rs. 50 for the first year (in 4 instalments of Rs. 12.8 as. each), Rs. 75 for the second year (in 4 instalments of Rs. 18.12 as. each), and Rs. 100 for the third year (in 4 instalments of Rs. 25 each).[4]

The Peshwās naturally did not tolerate unlicensed mints and debased coins. In some provinces of the Peshwās' dominions, however, the land-holders established their own mints from which counterfeit coins were issued. The province of Dharwar was especially notorious for minting debased coins. The first reference to this fact is probably contained in a record of 1760-61 A.D. of the time of Bālājī Bājī Rāo.[5] "In Subha

1. *Ibid.*, p. 108; cf. below, 290-91.
2. Ranade, *op. cit.*, p. 331.
3. *P. D.*, Vol. II, p. 157.
4. Sen, *Ad. Syst. Mar.*, p. 319.
5. *P. D.*, Vol. II, p. 164.

Dharwar, the mints for coining Hons, Mohars and Rupees issue false coins. In the old mints, good coins were struck. Recently the Zamindārs have established mints almost at every house and are issuing bad coins." In order to remedy this evil, it was proposed to abolish the spurious mints and to establish a central mint. A license for the proposed central mint was granted to Pāṇḍuraṅg Murār. "It causes loss to the Government. You represented that all these mints should be abolished and in their place a central mint should be established at Dharwar. Bad coins should be discontinued and good ones issued. Such a measure will be profitable to the Government. Therefore, agreeing with your views that the continuation of the issue of bad coins is not desirable and should be discontinued, the management has been entrusted to you. You should pull down the mints established in different places and found a central mint at Dharwar. You should also destroy the bad coins and issue good ones. The customary charge from former times is one Mohar for each thousand Mohars and one Rupee per thousand. The work of the mint should be profitable; therefore the Sawkārs have been exempted from this charge for one year from Rabilakhar, San Ihide, to Rabilakhar, San Issanne Sitain. After this, you should take the customary dues of 6 per thousand coins and remit the same to the Government. In addition to this, take one coin more with the free consent of the Sawkārs in your own name and remit that also to the Government. Your dues will be afterwards fixed aocording to your service."[1]

It is interesting to note that the customary mint charges were 7 coins per thousand—6 for the Government and 1 for the manager of the mint. The reform referred to in the document, however, could not be carried out till 1765-66. In that year, Peshwā Mādhava Rāo I had to issue a circular letter to the Kamavisdārs, Zamindārs and Sawkārs informing them that no payment would be accepted in future except in new coins.[2] There are other instances of the Peshwās' attempts to suppress spurious mints and false coins. But the Peshwā Government never assumed the actual control of the currency. It remained satisfied with supervision only.[3]

1. *Ad. Syst. Mar.*, pp. 320-21.
2. *Ibid.*, p. 321.
3. *Loc. cit.* Sāhu and the Rājā of Kolhāpur had their own mints.

As to the working of the mints, the following account of the Çhandor mint, closed in 1830 A.D., is very interesting. "A certain quantity of silver of the required test was handed over to each man who divided it into small pieces, rounded and weighed them, greater care being taken that the weights should be accurate than that size should be uniform. For this purpose, scales and weights were given to each of the 400 workmen, and the Manager examined them every week. When the workmen were satisfied with the weight of the pieces, they were forwarded to the Manager who sent them to be stamped. In stamping the rupee, an instrument like an anvil was used. It had a hole in the middle with letters inscribed on it. Piece after piece was thrown into the hole, the seal was held by a workman called *batekari*, and a third man gave a blow with a six pound hammer. Three men were able to strike 2000 pieces an hour, or 20000 in a working day of ten hours. As the seal was a little larger than the piece, all the letters were seldom inscribed."[1]

It has been suggested that the above description holds good also for the mints of Śivājī's time. The suggestion can no doubt be proved by an examination of the legends on the Śivarāya coins, which are always found incomplete apparently because the little circular pieces had originally been hammered on a seal of much larger size. The goldsmiths in charge of the mints could evidently boast of very little learning. On the copper coins alone, we find no less than eight different spellings of the words *Śrī Rājā Śiva Chatrapati.*[2] As a matter of fact, however, the same conditions were undoubtedly present also in ancient India. Mistakes and incompleteness are by no means rare in the legends on old Indian coins.[3]

The Mārāṭhā currency of the Peshwā period was supplemented by the extensive use of *huṇḍīs* or credit instruments. The revenue officers were always instructed to make use of *huṇḍīs* in transmitting money to the central treasury. The popularity of the credit instrument is illustrated by a letter referring to a person who remitted by *huṇḍī* the small sum of Rs. 13.8 as.

1. *Bombay Gazetteer*, Vol. XVI, p. 429.
2. Sen, *op. cit.*, p. 110.
3. Note, *e.g.*, the defective legends on some silver coins of Kumāragupta I; cf. Nos. 368-84 of Allan's *Catalogue* (Gupta), pp. 105-07.

only.[1] That the Indian currency was supplemented largely by the use of *huṇḍīs* also in the ancient period is suggested by the chronicle of Kashmir.[2]

With what we have learnt about the Marāṭhā mint of the late medieval period may be compared what the *Kauṭilīya Arthaśāstra* says about the ancient Indian mint. "The Superintendent of Mint (*Lakṣaṇādhyakṣa*) shall carry on the manufacture of silver coins (*rūpya-rūpa*) made up of 4 parts of copper and $\frac{1}{16}$ part (*māṣa*) of any one of the metals *tikṣṇa*, *trapu*, *sīsa* and *añjana*. There shall be a Paṇa, half a Paṇa a quarter and one-eighth. Copper coins (*tāmra-rūpa*) made up of 4 parts of an alloy (*pāda-jīva*) shall be a Māṣaka, half a Māṣaka, Kākaṇī, and half a Kākaṇī. The examiner of coins (*Rūpadarśaka*) shall regulate currency both as a medium of exchange (*vyayahārikī*) and as legal tender admissible into the treasury (*kośa-prāveśya*). The premia levied on coins paid [into the treasury] shall be 8 per cent known as *rūpika*, 5 per cent known as *vyājī*, $\frac{1}{8}$ Paṇa per cent known as *pārīkṣika* (testing charge), besides a fine of 25 Paṇas to be imposed on offenders other than the manufacturer, the seller, the purchaser and the examiner."[3] "The state goldsmith shall employ artisans to manufacture silver and gold coins (*rūpya-suvarṇa*) from the bullion of citizens and country people. The artisans employed in the office shall do their work as ordered and in time. [The goldsmith of the mint] shall return [to the owners, coins] of the same weight and of the same quality (*varṇa*) as that of the bullion (*nikṣepa*) which was received [at the mint]. With the exception of those [coins] which have been worn out or which have undergone diminution (*kṣiṇa-pariśirṇa*), the same coins shall be received [back into the mint] even after the lapse of a number of years. The state goldsmith shall gather from the artisans employed in the mint information concerning pure god, metalic mass (*pudgala*), coins (*lakṣaṇa*) and the rate of exchange (*prayoga*). In getting a Suvarṇa coin [of 16 *māṣas*] manufactured from gold or from silver, one *kākaṇī* ($\frac{1}{4}$ *māṣa*) weight of the metal more shall be given to the mint towards the loss in manufacture. When the quality

1. *Ad. Syst. Mar.*, p. 321.
2. Cf. *Rājataraṅgiṇī*, V. 27.
3. Cf. Shama Sastry's trans., pp. 95-96.

(*varṇa*) of a coin less than the standard of a Māṣa is lowered, the artisans [concerned] shall be punished with the first amercement. When its weight is less than the standard weight, they shall be punished with the middlemost amercement. Deception in the exchange of manufactured coins (*kṛta-bhāṇḍ-opadhau*) shall also be punished with the highest amercement. Whoever causes [gold and silver coins] to be manufactured in any place other than the mint or without being noticed by the state goldsmith shall be fined 12 Paṇas, while the artisan who does the work shall, if found out, be punished with twice the above fine. If he is not found out, measures........shall be taken to detect him. When thus detected, he shall be fined 200 Paṇas or shall have his fingers cut off. The weighing balance and counter-weights shall be purchased from the Superintendent in charge of them. Otherwise a fine of 12 Paṇas shall be imposed."[1]

1. Cf. *ibid.*, pp. 94-95.

CHAPTER XVII

COWRIE-SHELL

I

Cowrie-shells are known to have been used as money in India, as in many other parts of the world, from very early times. The celebrated Chinese pilgrim, Fa-hien, who travelled in India about the beginning of the fifth century A.D., says about the people of the Madhyadeśa that, in buying and selling commodities, they use cowries.[1] Apparently the pilgrim had occasion to make only small transactions and hardly came into contact with rich people. That is probably why he does not appear to have met with the copper, silver and gold coins issued by the early emperors of the Gupta dynasty.[2] It is interesting to note that the same story is told also by the foreigners who visited India during the late medieval period. Thomas Bowry, for instance, visited a village in Eastern Orissa in the latter half of the seventeenth century, where he found the cowrie-shell to be the only money known to the village

1. Raychaudhuri, *Pol. Hist. Anc. Ind.*, 1938, pp. 469-70.

2. It should be remembered that coins had very high purchasing power in early times. In Kashmir, one *khārī* of paddy (117 pounds or $2\frac{1}{4}$ maunds) was sold in ordinary years at 200 cowries and at 36 cowries in a year of abundance in the ninth century A.D. About the end of the eleventh century, the famine price of one *pala* ($\frac{1}{20}$ seer) of wool was 6 cowries and that of 2 *palas* of grapes only 1 cowrie. In Akbar's time, 8 seers of grapes were sold at a single Akbarī Dām of copper. Ibn Batūta's account gives the same picture for the fourteenth century Bengal. Husked rice was sold at the rate of 25 Delhi *rothls* (about 9 Bengal maunds) for a silver *Dīnār* (about one Rupee). The quantity of paddy sold for 1 *Dīnār* was 80 Delhi *rothls* (2300 lbs. or 1976 lbs., i. e. $28\frac{3}{4}$ or $24\frac{3}{4}$ maunds). A milch cow was sold for 3 silver *Dīnārs* (3 Rupees) and 8 fat fowls for a *Dirham* ($\frac{1}{2}$ Rupee). Even at the end of the seventeenth century, 580 lbs. ($7\frac{1}{2}$ maunds) of rice were sold at Chittagong for one Rupee, which was also the price of 60 good tame poultry. See Stein, *Kalhaṇa's Rājataraṅgiṇī*, Vol. II, pp. 308-28. Thomas Bowry, in the latter half of the 17th century, found that, in Bengal, a very good cow was sold for 4s. 6d. (2 Rupees), a good hog for $\frac{3}{4}$ Rupee and 40 or 50 fowls for one Rupee. See *A Geographical Account of the Countries round the Bay of Bengal*, 1669 to 1679, ed. R.C. Temple, 1905, pp. 193-94. According to tradition, 8 maunds of husked rice were sold at one Rupee in Bengal during the viceroyalty of Shāistā Khān in the latter half of the seventeenth century.

folk.[1] He further records that the whole population of an Oriya village was unable to change a single Rupee into cowries, and that the villagers were even unable to distinguish between silver and German silver.[2]

The cowrie-shell has ceased to have any monetary value in eastern India for a long time; but it has retained its old position, theoretically at least, in the village *Pāṭhaśālās* of Bengal even today. In Bengali arithmetical works known as the *Dhārāpāta*, we still find a table styled *Kaḍākiyā*, the unit of its calculation being the *kaḍā* or *kaḍi* which are the Bengali words for 'cowrie'. According to this table,

4 Kaḍās=	1 Gaṇḍā			
20 ,,	= 5 ,,	=1 Buḍi		
80 ,,	=20 ,,	=4 ,,	=1 Paṇa	
1280 ,,	=320 ,,	=64 ,,	=16	=1 Kāhaṇa (Sanskrit *Kārṣāpaṇa*)

It is well known that according to several authorities, Paṇa was only another name for the copper Kārṣāpaṇa, *i.e.* a copper coin weighing one Karṣa (=80 Ratis=146.4 grains).[3] The Kāhaṇa=Kārṣāpaṇa is no doubt the silver coin of that denomination, which must have orginally weighed one *Karṣa*, but was later made 32 Ratis (58.56 gr.) in weight, and was otherwise known as Purāṇa or Dharaṇa.[3] According to the Bengali practice, the *Buḍi*, *Paṇa* and *Kāhaṇa* are written respectively as the Pice (=¼ Anna), Anna (=4 Pice) and Rupee (=16 Annas). The words *anna* and *paṇa* are morever used synonymously in the Bengali language. That Buḍi was a smaller copper coin, ¼ of a copper Paṇa in value, is probably suggested by the *Mṛcchakaṭika* and *Līlāvatī*. The former refers to the Voḍika

1. Bowry, *op. cit.*, p. 200.
2. *Ibid.*, p. 199.
3. Manu, VIII. 136; Yājñavalkya, I (Ācār-ādhyāya). 364; *Amarakoṣa*, II. 9. 88. Relying on the commentaries on Manu, some scholars (cf. Rapson, *Catalogue*, p. clxvix; Bhandarkar, *Anc. Ind. Num.*, pp. 81-82) take Manu's Kārṣāpaṇa, not in apposition to Purāṇa or Dharaṇa, but as a copper coin only. This view seems to be rendered untenable if Manu is read together with Yājñavalkya and Amara.

(=*Boḍi*=*Buḍi*) in connection with the Suvarṇa (gold coin) and Kārṣāpaṇa (silver coin).[1] Apparently the same coin or a similar one was known as Kākinī at least in the Marāṭhā country about the end of the thirteenth century when the great astronomer Bhāskar-ācārya composed his *Līlāvatī*. There is practically no difference between the table quoted above and the following one from Bhāskar-ācārya's work.[2]

20 cowries	=1 Kākinī (same as Buḍi)				
80 ,,	=4 ,,	= 1 Paṇa			
1280 ,,	=64 ,,	= 16 ,,	=1 Dramma (same as Kāhaṇa)		
20480 ,,	=1024 ,,	= 256 ,,	=16 ,,	= 1 Niṣka (gold coin)	

It is interesting to note that 1280 cowrie-shells were considered equivalent to the old silver coin not only in medieval Bengal, but also in Maharashtra during the early medieval period. As regards the other equation, 16 silver Drammas = 1 gold Niṣka, it may be pointed out that, according to the Baigram inscription of 448 A. D., 16 silver Rūpakas were equal to 1 gold Dīnāra during the regime of the Imperial Guptas.[3] But such equations must have necessarily depended on the weight of the coins as well as on the value of the metals in the locality in question. Thus we have an inscription[4] of the first quarter of the second century A.D. at Nasik in Maharashtra, according to which 35 Kārṣāpaṇas of silver were equivalent to 1 Suvarṇa of gold. The relation of a cowrie with the standard silver coin of a locality therefore could not have been the same in different parts of India even on a particular date. In Kashmir, for instance, 100 cowrie-shells were regarded as equal

1. *Mṛch.*, Act VIII, v. 40; *attham sadam demi suvaṇṇaaṁ de kahāvaṇaṁ demi sa-voḍiaṁ de* (*arthaṁ śataṁ dadāmi suvarṇakaṁ te kārṣāpaṇaṁ dadāmi sa-voḍikaṁ te*).

2. *Līlāvatī*, 1. 2.

3. Sircar, *Select Inscriptions*, p. 343, note.

4. Sircar, *op. cit.*, p. 159. It is probable that, in this case, the silver coins were lighter. These may have been the same as the coins of Nahapāna, which were about 36 grains in weight while the Suvarṇa may be the gold coin (124 grains) of the Kuṣāṇas (*ibid.*, p. 158, note 5).

to one copper coin which consequently came to be styled *Śata* (literally, 'one hundred'), in modern pronunciation *Hat.*[1] The relation of the copper Śata with the silver money of ancient Kashmir cannot be determined; but Stein has suggested that, in the Mughul period, the Akbarī Dām (a copper coin of 323½ grains), 40 of which were equivalent to the Akbarī Rupee (silver coin), was also known as Hat. Modern Kashmirian Hat is considered to be of the same value as the British Indian Pice. We do not know whether the Akbarī Dām was called Śata=Hat, because the two denominations were almost equal in weight, or because Dām became the standard copper coin in place of the old Śata after the annexation of Kashmir to the Mughul empire in 1586 A.D. It has, however, been suggested that the value of an Akbarī Dām in Kashmir was 100 cowries and that of an Akbarī Rupee 4000 cowrie-shells. But, in Eastern India, the Kāhaṇa was recognised in the late medieval period only as ⅜ of a Mughul Rupee. In Eastern India, therefore, the number of cowrie-shells sold for a Rupee was not the same as in medieval Kashmir.

It is well known to students of the accounts of foreign travellers, who visited India during the late medieval period, that cowrie-shells were imported into India from the Maldive Islands,[2] and that 3200 of them were taken to be equivalent to one Rupee in Eastern India. The Rupee here referred to is no doubt the Mughul silver coin corresponding roughly to 2s. 3d. or 2s. 6d.[3] One Mughul Rupee was thus considered equal to 2½ Kāhaṇas of cowrie-shells.

Although 1 Rupee=3200 cowries was the recognised ratio, the value of the cowrie-shell used to rise and fall according to the plenty or scarcity of them in the market. At Hooghly, the cowrie was sometimes 5, 6 or 10 per cent dearer than at Balasore.[4] According to some observers, the price of the shell seldom rose or fell more than 2 Paṇas (160 shells) in one Rupee;[5] others, however, have noticed that

1. Stein, *loc. cit.*
2. Bowry, *op. cit.*, pp. 179-80, 200.
3. *Ibid.*, p. 218.
4. *Ibid.*, p. 217.
5. *Ibid.*, p. 219.

sometimes 31 Paṇas (2480 shells), 37 Paṇas (2960 shells), 38 Paṇas (3040 shells) or 40 Paṇas (3200 shells) were going for a Rupee.[1] Thus the fall of 6¼ per cent in the value of the cowries may not have been quite unusual, though, in abnormal circumstances, the percentage could have risen to 22½. The *Anglo-Indian Dictionary* by Whitworth of the Bombay Civil Service, which was published in 1885, recognises cowrie as 'a small shell, the *cypraea moneta*, still used as money in Northern India; about 6500 go to the Rupee'. Thus the decrease in the eighteenth century in the price of the cowrie shell is more than cent per cent of what it was a century earlier. This is apparently due to the fact that cowries were no longer regarded as money by the government of British India. It should be remembered that the shells continued to be used as money by the poor people for a long time after it had ceased to be recongnised by the Anglo-Indian Government about a century and a half ago.

Cowries were sold by tale and not by weight. In the Maldive Islands, 40 or 42 Paṇas (3200 or 3360 shells) could be purchased at 6 or 7 Annas.[2] A Dollar was taken to be equal to 32 Annas (2 Rupees), and 240 or 250 Paṇas (19200 or 20000 shells) were sold at a Dollar. At the West Indian port of Surat where cowries were bought, they did not cost above 2 Dollars (4 Rupees) per hundredweight or thereabouts. Thus between 9000 and 10000 cowrie-shells were purchased at a Rupee in the Maldives; but they were sold in Bengal between 2500 and 3200 shells per Rupee. There was apparently a very great profit in the trade of cowrie-shells. But the question is whether the Maldive Islands supplied cowries to India also in the ancient period. No definite answer to this question can be offered in the present state of our knowledge; but possibly they did.

A cowrie-shell became useless only when it was perforated. A worthless shell was known in Bengal as the *kāṇā-kaḍi*, literally, 'a one-eyed cowrie.' It is an interesting convention.

1. *Ibid.*, p. 219n, note.
2. *Loc. cit.*

II

K. P. Jayaswal published the text of a judgment issued in Śaka 1716 (1794 A. D.) by a Maithil Pandit named Sacalamiśra in a dispute between Tulārāmaśarman and others (plaintiffs) and Maṇināthaśarman (defendant).[1] Tulārāma claimed that Maṇinātha should restore to him the possession of a slave girl named Saito, who was a daughter of the plaintiff's slave Matī, together with her children. The defendant, in his answer which was a plea of denial, stated that the girl together with her children was no doubt living with him, but that he did not know what her real status was and from which source she had come to his family. The plaintiff was then asked, on the authority of the ancient law-giver Vyāsa, to prove his case.

After the above introductory details, the judgment, as quoted by Jayaswal, goes on to say : *atha Tulārāmaśarmā pratijñāta-Matīdāsa-putrītvam=eva pramāṇam=upanyastavān ; tataḥ pratyarthī Maṇirāmaśarmā Gaurīvavāṭikā-grahaṇa-yogyāyāṁ dāsa-putryāṁ vyābhicāritvena ceṭītvam=asādhayad=idam=aprayojakam=ity=ūcivān ; na ca dāsaputrītva-rūpa-sāmānyadharmasy=āgamakatve='pi Matīdāsa-putrītvam=eva tath=āstām=iti vācyaṁ Matī-putrī-mātrasya pakṣatven=āsādhāraṇyāt.*

Jayaswal's translation of the passage runs as follows : "Now Tulārāmaśarman proposed to prove the fact of her being the daughter of the slave (father) Matī. Thereupon the Defendant Maṇināthaśarman replied that it would be immaterial on account of the fallacy of not proving the slave status of a slave's daugther......that if it were alleged that, in the absence of evidence of the general factor of the status of a slave's daughter, the fact of her being the daughter of Matī Dāsa should be taken to be that evidence, it would be begging the question, for the point of Matī's daughterhood was the hypothesis."[2]

As regards the passage omitted in the translation, Jayaswal says, "The text of the judgment, *Gaurīva......yogyāyāṁ*, is

1. *Journal of the Bihar and Orissa Research Society*, Vol. VI, 1920, pp. 251-52.
2. *Ibid.*, p. 253.

not clear to me. The text seems to be corrupt. I am not sure that the reasoning which follows has been fully brought out in the above translation."

We are inclined to translate the passsage quoted above as follows : "Now Tulārāmaśarman brought forward the very fact of [Saito] being the daughter of [his] slave Matī, which had been declared by him, as the evidence. Then the defendant Maṇināthaśarman said, 'It is pointless due to the fallacy that it does not prove that one's slave's daughter, who is useful to one for getting Gaurīvavāṭikā (as read by Jayaswal), is also one's slave.' It cannot also be said that, if the general position of being a slave's daughter is proved, the status of being the daughter of the slave Matī is proved as well, because the fact of being particularly the daughter of Matī is a premiss to be proved owing to the special nature of the point."

In another paper on the same subject,[1] Ganganatha Jha offered the following comment on Jayaswal's note on *Gaurīva-vāṭikā-grahaṇa-yogyāyāṁ* occurring in the passage quoted above : "On the outer cover of a palm-leaf manuscript in my possession, I have found a document, more then 300 years old, which is a deed of sale pertaining to a slave. In the document the deed is referred to as *Gaurīva-cāṭikā-patram*. From this it would seem as if *Gaurīva-cā* (or *vā*) *ṭikā* were a technical term referring to 'slavery' or 'service'. So that the expression in the judgment may be taken to mean—'who is fit for being received as a slave (or servant)', or more probably 'who is fit for being emancipated from slavery'." In his translation of the said document, Jha translates the expression *Gaurīvacāṭikā-patra*, as read by him, as a 'deed of sale relating to slavery (or deed of emancipation)'.[2]

While commenting on Jha's views Jayaswal further observed[3] on the subject as follows : "The unexplained passage on which Dr. Jha kindly writes is *Gaurīva-vāṭikā*, as the expression has been found in two short documents discovered recently by Pandit Vishnu Lal Jha in the Raj Library at

1. *Ibid.*, Vol. VIII, 1921, Parts 2-3, p. 121.
2. *Ibid.*, p. 122.
3. *Ibid.*, p. 123.

Darbhanga. They are dated in Lakṣmaṇasena era 528 and 549. In the latter of the two documents, a passage occurs in Maithilī (*deśavyavahāre*) as in Dr. Jha's document. Both documents are deeds of transfer of slave girls. The slave girl in each case was bought evidently to be married to the slave of the purchaser. The doument is called a deed of *Gaurīva-vāṭikā* (*Gaurīva-vāṭikā-patra*) drawn by the old master in favour of the new one, giving up all his right, title and interest in the slave. All these three documents show that the slave girl had been a virgin at the time of the transfer. The expression commencing with *Gaurī*, 'virgin', may have something to do with the unmarried status of the slave."

The latest writer on the subject seems to be Jayakanta Mishra. In his *A History of Maithili Literature*,[1] Mishra accepts the reading *Gaurīva-cāṭikā* quoted by Jha and altogether ignores Jayaswal's reading of the expression as *Gaurīva-vāṭikā*. He says, "On a careful study of the documents where this name occurs it appears that it was a name applied to the act of emancipating the daughter of one's 'Bahiā' servant when she was married to someone else."

It seems to us that the readings *Gaurīva-vāṭikā* and *Gaurīva-cāṭikā* are both wrong. There can be little doubt that the correct reading, or at least the reading intended, is *Gaurī-varāṭikā*. The word *gaurī* means 'a young girl eight years old, a young girl prior to menstruation, a vigin, maid'. The word *varāṭikā* is used in the sense of *varāṭa* or *varāṭaka*, *i.e.* a cowrie, in the *Bhāminīvilāsa*.[2] That cowrie-shells were used as coins in India down to the days of the East India Company's rule is well known to all.[3] It has also to be noticed that words denoting the standard coin (including cowrie, *kauḍ̤ī* in Hindi and *kaḍ̤i* in Bengali) were used in most of the modern Indian languages also in the general sense of 'money'. Thus the expression *Gaurī-varāṭikā* really means 'virgin-money'. It was used in Mithilā technically in the sense of 'money to be paid to the master of a slave girl of marriageable age by the master of her bridegroom'.

1. Vol. I, Allahabad, 1949, p. 382.
2. II. 42; cf. Apte, *The Practical Sanskrit-English Dictionary*, s.v.
3. Cf. *JNSI*, Vol. VII, pp. 82-86; above, pp. 267 ff.

After this transaction called *Gaurī-varāṭikā-grahana* or 'acceptance of virgin-moiney' leading to her marriage, the girl apparently became the slave of her husband's master who really purchased her from her old master. Thus the expression *Gaurīvarāṭikā-grahaṇa-yogyā dāsa-putrī* in the judgment quoted above certainly means 'a slave's daughter who was useful, in the matter of getting virgin-money, to one'. The defendant's argument in the dispute referred to above was apparently that, even if Saito was the daughter of the plaintiff's slave Matī and for that reason originally belonged to the plaintiff, the plaintiff might have sold her by accepting virgin-money and thereby lost his ownership over her. The idea was that, even if Saito was proved to be the daughter of the plaintiff's slave, she could herself not be regarded as a slave of the plaintiff without further evidence.

In conclusion, we quote below, with translation, the copy of a document, which is a *Gaurīvarāṭikāpatra* received by us sometime back from a Maithil friend.

Text

1. Gaurīvarāṭikā-patram ।
2. Gaurīvarāṭikā-patram=idaṁ(dam ।) Māṇḍara-saṁ-śrī-Bhavadevaśarmā Pālī-saṁ-śrī-Sāhebaśarmasu patram=-rpayati ।
3. tad=etat-sakāśād=rājata-mudrā-trayam=ādāya Āmāta-jātīyāṁ Tulaī-putrīṁ śyāma-varṇāṁ ṣaṭ (ṣaḍ)-varṣa-
4. vayaskāṁ Bādari-putrāya pariṇetuṁ dattā (।*) atashpa (taḥpa) raṁ mama svatvaṁ n=āsti (।*) Śāke 1645 Sana
5. 1131 Sāla Mulakī Āṣāḍha-śukla-dvitīyāyāṁ Gurau (।*) śāchi(kṣiṇau) śrī-Vāsudeva-Jhā śrī-Vighneśa-
6. Jhā (।*) likhitam=ubhay-ānumatyā śrī-Ghogheśarmaṇā (।*) likhāpana ānā tīni ।।।

Translation

A deed of [the acceptance of] Virgin-money.
This is a deed of [the acceptance of] Virgin-money.

Śrī Bhavadevaśarman of [a family originally] hailing from Māṇḍara issues the deed in favour of Śrī-Sāhebaśarman of [a family originally] hailing form Pālī: that, having accepted three silver coins (i.e. three Rupees) from this [person, *i.e.* Sāhebaśarman], the six-year-old dark-complexioned daughter of [my female slave] Tulaī, belonging to the Āmāta caste, is given to be married to the son of Sāhebaśarman's [slave] Bādari. Henceforth my right [over her] ceases. On Thursday, the second *tithi* of the bright half of Āṣāḍha in the Śaka year 1645, San 1131 Sāl Mulkī. Witnesses—śrī-Vasudeva-Jhā, śrī Vighneśa-Jhā. Written with the permission of both [parties] by Śrī-Ghogheśarman. The perquisite for getting [the deed] written is three Annas [only].

REMARKS

The names of the bride and bridegroom, a slave girl and a slave boy, are not mentioned is the document. They were both very young. The date of the record is irregular for Śaka 1645 and seems to correspond to Thursday, the 11th June, 1724 A.D., falling in the next expired Śaka year. For *saṁ* in *Māṇḍara-saṁ* standing for a word like *saṁbhūta* and the usual rate of a writer's perquisite in medieval Mithilā at one Anna per Rupee of the amount involved in the transaction, see *Praceedings of the Indian Historical Records Commission*, Vol. XVIII, 1942, p. 88; Sircar, *Studies in the Society and Administration of Ancient and Medival India*, Vol. I, pp. 219 ff.

CHAPTER XVIII

RUPEE AND PICE

I

The Sultāns of Delhi issued silver coins weighing 100 Ratis (variously quoted as 172·8 grains, 175 grains, etc.), often called Tanka, during the 13th and 14th centuries, while Sher Shāh (1539-45 A.D.) re-introduced the same coin (weight variously quoted as 175, 178 or 179 grains), which was adopted by the Mughul emperor Akbar (1556-1605 A.D.) and his successors. This Sūr-Mughul silver coin became famous as Rūpiya or Rupee.[1]

The mint was a source of income to the Muslim governments. A heavy royalty was levied for coining bullion which was debased when occasion demanded. In order to give the mint sufficient work to do, the people were forced by the Mughul government to have their money recoined every year. For each year passed from the date of issue recorded on the coin, a heavy percentage was deducted from its value irrespective of its actual deterioration. A Rupee that had been in circulation for one year lost 3 per cent and after two years' circulation no less than 5 per cent. People had therefore to present the coins to the mints for getting them recoined before the end of the first or second year after their issue. Thus the mint had a flourishing business in Mughul times at the people's expense.

The Mughul government recognised silver as the only circulating medium. Gold coins called Muhar were no doubt struck; but they were treated as bullion. The Muhar were therefore sold at different prices according to the current price

1. Cf. *Encyclopaedia Britannica*, *Hobson-Jobson* and Wilson's *Glossary* under *Rupee*, *Rūpiya*. The weight and metallic purity of the coin varied. According to the *Hobson-Jobson*, the weight did not go very far on either side of 170 grains while the amount of pure silver in the coin was, in some cases, 140 grains and, in exceptional cases, even 100 grains. The theoretical weight of the coin was 179.5511 grains, the fineness being 98 per cent pure silver (W. W. Hunter, *Annals of Rural Bengal*, p. 290, note). *Rūpiya* is the same as Sanskrit *Rūpya*, 'stamped with figures', 'a coin'.

of gold—sometimes for 13, 14 or 15 Sikka Rupees (i.e. fresh issues of the standard silver coin). Copper coins were similarly sold not at their denomination value, but 'at a lower rate, the proportion deducted depending on the locality and the comparative demand for silver and copper coins.'[1]

One of the most coveted insignia of sovereignty in Muslim India was the striking of coins. Even little potentates who acknowledged the suzerainty of the Great Mughul tried to maintain their independent right of coinage. "As it was the last privilege to which fallen dynasties clung, so it was the first to which adventurers rising into power aspired."[2] Silver money thus issued by various authorities in different parts of the country passed from province to province with wandering merchants and in payment of tribute. Different mints produced Rupees of different weight and fineness and very few of them even adhered to their own nominal standard. Moreover, the coins were subjected to various attempts at debasement when they reached the public. In the absence of an ideal standard coin, it became necessary to fix one by which to calculate the value of the different specie. The situation was faced in the following way. "When a sum of Rupees is brought to a *Shroff* (banker or money-changer), he examines them piece by piece, ranges them according to their fineness, then by their weight. Then he allows for the different legal *battas* (deductions) upon Siccas and Sunats;[3] and, this done, he values in gross by the Current Rupee (i.e. the Rupee of the accounts) what the whole quantity is worth. The Rupee Current, therefore, is the only coin fixed, by

1. Hunter, *op. cit.*, p. 298.

2. *Ibid.*, p. 299. As early as 1685, when the English merchants of the East India Comany had only a few houses and gardens in Bengal, they sought for the dignity of having coins of their own. The Company began to issue coins in the name of the contemporary Mughul emperors. Previously, however, 'the Rupee of Bombaim' was struck in 1677 A.D. in the name of king Charles II of England at Bombay, received by the Company on lease from the Stuart king in 1668 A.D. (cf. *Hobson-Jobson*).

3. The name *Sunat* or *Sonat* (*Sanwāt*, plural form of *sonat*, 'a year') was applied to the Rupee in the third year of its currency. The Sikka or fresh Rupee was rated 116 to 100 of the Current Rupee (i.e. the Calānī Rupee of the accounts); but in the second and third years the ratio was respectively 113 to 100, and 111 to 100 (cf. Wilson's *Glossary*). Soon the name Sikka came to mean the silver coins struck at the Murshīdābād mint and bearing the date of the 19th regnal year of Shāh 'Alam II. See below, p. 295 and note 3.

which coin is at present valued; and the reason is, because it is not a coin itself and therefore can never be falsified or worn."[1]

The vitiated Indian currency of the mid-eighteenth century has been described as the refuse of twenty different dynasties and petty potentates, which had been 'clipped, drilled, filed, scooped out, sweated, counterfeited and changed from its original value by every process of debasement' during a period of four centuries.[2] Small coins could not change hands without a calculation regarding the amount that had to be deducted from their face value. When Bengal passed under the British rule, the treasury officers exacted from the land-holders a 3 per cent discount for coins that were in circulation for one year and 5 per cent for coins that were two years old. The discount was allowed, as already noticed, even where no actual deterioration had taken place. The land-holders naturally, demanded a double allowance from the middlemen who, in their turn, exacted a quadruple from the poor peasants. This charge in exchanging old Rupee was called *batta* which was the most undefined and oppressive of the illegal cesses that caused sufferings to the tillers of the soil. The rapacity of the collecting officers was unlimited owing to the absence of any recognised standard of the *batta* as regards the different types of coins in circulation. The great variety of coins in use was another source of difficulty to the poor peasant, because he never knew whether the coins for which he sold his crops would be accepted when he came to pay his rent. There were cowries (shells), copper coins of every denomination, lumps of copper without any denomination whatever, pieces of iron beaten up with brass, 32 different kinds of Rupees from the full Sikka to the Viziery ($\frac{87}{100}$ of the Sikka), Dollars of different standards of purity (worth from 6s. 8d. to 8s. 6d. according to weight and the current rates of exchange), gold Muhars worth from 25s. to 30s. each, and a diversity of Asiatic and European coins.[3]

1. J. Steuart *Principles of Money applied to Bengal*, 1772, p. 17; Hunter, *op. cit.*, p. 300.
2. Hunter, *op. cit.*, p. 293.
3. *Ibid.*, pp. 294-95; cf. above, pp. 273-74.

At some treasuries of the East India Company (like that at Sylhet), payments in cowries were accepted; but at others (like that at Birbhum), they were not. Some of the Company's Collectors accepted payment in gold, while others refused to do it. The people had to receive payment for their crops in coins whose value they did not understand. They had to pay their rent and taxes in those coins according to a calculation which also they could not follow. The old custom of paying rent in the produce of the soil was no doubt free from such difficulties and was certainly a boon to the peasant.

The coins in circulation were insufficient for the commerce of the country. The Ango-Indian government, however, repeatedly attributed the scarcity to the tricks of the bankers in raising the *batta* or exchange, to the extortions of usurers or to the combination of monied harpies. The remedy of the trouble was apparently to call in all the old coins and supercede the old currency by a new coinage of fixed weight and purity. But the East India Company had not the required bullion. The public would hardly bring their debased coins to the mint when recoinage cost them a heavy percentage.[1] They received back only $\frac{3}{5}$ of what they brought to the mint and that also after the lapse of a considerable period of time. As a result, Rupees disappeared and business came to a stand-still.

The fourfold currency of gold, silver, copper and notes, gradually introduced by the Anglo-Indian Government, was faced with great difficulties. Offences against the coin such as counterfeiting, etc., could not be punished more severely than as cases of ordinary cheating. The notes were unpopular and were forced into circulation. The East India Company paid all salaries or fixed disbursements over £1200 per annum half in notes and half in cash. As a matter of fact, often there was nothing but paper in the Company's treasury and its officials had to be paid only with notes. In this way, the people even of remote places were saddled with the 'Company's

1. For reference to a profit to the merchant of gold—3 per cent+a *batta* on the gold Muhar—3 per cent+a charge of coinage and duties—2 per cent=8 per cent, see N.L. Chatterji, 'Bimetallic Scheme of Clive', in *Bhārata-Kaumudī*, Part I. p. 187.

papers' which they could get rid of only at a loss. Unfortunately, however, the Company's Collectors were not instructed to accept payments if they had been tendered in notes.

The Company's attempt to mitigate the scarcity of silver coins by issuing a gold currency was a failure. The Council had not the requisite bullion for the purpose and had to induce the people to bring their gold for coinage by attaching an arbitrary value to the Muhar. The gold coin was to pass 'at a rate which exceeded by 17½ per cent its market value in silver'.[1] The arbitrary fixation of the ratio between gold and silver at 16.45 to 1 in place of the market ratio of 14 to 1[2] was the cause of great distress to the poor. "The Council by fixing the value of the new coins (Muhars) at arbitrary rates had rendered it 17½ per cent more profitable to make payments in gold, but it had only done so by rendering it 17½ per cent less profitable to pay in silver. The gains of the fortunate few who held gold had to be paid by a thousand-fold by the unfortunate many who held silver."[3] According to the regulations of 1766, a Muhar containing 149.72 grains of pure gold passed for Rs. 14, *i.e.* at 10.694 grains to the Rupee; but, according to the regulations of 1769, a Muhar with 190.086 grains of pure gold passed for Rs. 16, *i.e.* at 11.88 grains per Rupee. People found that they could always get the market value of their gold; but it was not possible for them to know what liberty the English merchants might take with their gold coins. As a result, they refused to bring their gold to the mint for coinage.

There were other causes also of the scarcity of coins in India during the second half of the eighteenth century. India always depended on foreign countries for a supply of precious metals.[4] The people of this country moreover absorbed in jewellery and domestic articles a vast quantity of silver coins that poured into the land in exchange for Indian goods.

1. Hunter, *op. cit.*, p. 302.
2. Chatterji, *op. cit.*, p. 191.
3. Hunter, *op. cit.*, pp. 302-03.
4. That silver and gold coins were imported into India also in ancient times is known from the *Periplus of the Erythream Sea*, §49. See also W.H. Schoff's trans., p. 287.

As early as the first century A.D., the celebrated Roman author Pliny complains, "The subject is one well worthy of our notice, seeing that in no year does India drain us less than 550000000 Sesterces (22000000 Dollars=61111111 Rupees) giving back her own wares which are sold among us at fully hundred times their first cost."[1] The Venetians, Portuguese, Dutch and English had all in their turn lamented the exportation of their coins in exchange for Indian products. In the seventeenth century a single West Indian port, viz. Surat, 'received by way of the Persian Gulf alone half a million Stirling per annum in specie'.[2] The quantity of bullion which the trade of the East India Company carried out of England annually was for a long time deplored by the English people. Upto 1765, the Company's business was to send silver from England and to bring back Indian goods in exchange. In the above year, however, the revenues of Bengal passed to the Company's hands and the annual surplus enabled it to discontinue importing specie for the purchase of goods.[3] Moreover, it was observed as early as 1750 that the payment of the Mughul emperor's revenue 'sweeps away almost all the silver, coined or uncoined, which comes into Bengal'. "It goes to Delhi from where it never returns to Bengal; so that after such treasure is gone from Muxadabad, there is hardly currency enough left in Bengal to carry on any trade, or even to go to market for provisions and necessaries of life, till the next shipping arrives to bring a fresh supply of silver."[4] Now that the annual influx of coins from England ceased, the scarcity of coins became very serious, especially as the consumption of metals went on as before. The evil was aggra-

1. *Ibid.*, p. 219. A large number of Roman coins of the Imperial period have been discovered in India. See Sewell, 'Roman Coins found in India' in *JRAS*, 1904, pp. 591-637.

2. Hunter, *op. cit.*, p. 304.

3. Hunter points out (*op. cit.*, p. 304), "If a district yielded, as in the case of Beerbhoom, £90,000 of revenue, the council took care that not more than £5,000 or £6,000 were spent in governing it. From the remainder, ten thousand pounds or so were deducted for general civil expenses, ten thousand more for the maintenance of the army, and the surplus of say £60,000 was invested in silks, muslins, cotton cloths and other articles, to be sold by the authorities in Leadenhall Street."

4. Cf. Mandeville's letter dated 27th November, 1750; Hunter, *op. cit.*, p. 305.

vated by other contributory factors such as (1) the drain of silver from Bengal to the Company's settlements in Bombay, Madras and China; (2) the decline of trade with the neighbouring countries; (3) the suspension of silver importation by other European companies; (4) the expenses incurred on troops stationed outside Bengal;[1] (5) Nawāb Mīr Qāsim's flight with specie worth about 13 millions Stirling; (6) the annual tribute of 26 lacs paid to the Mughul emperor Shāh 'Alam II; and (7) the use of the surplus revenues for the provision of the Company's investments.[2]

To remedy the evils of *batta*, Warren Hastings enacted that no deduction should be made from an old coin unless it was actually deteriorated and that all future issues should bear one date from 1773. It is for this reason that the coins of the Banāras mint, issued between Hijrī 1190 and 1229, all bear the same date of Shāh 'Alam's reign—year 17. Numerous gold and silver coins of the Murshīdābād mint likewise bear the date—the 19th year of the auspicious reign of Shāh 'Alam.[3]

But the scarcity of coins was not mitigated. In 1780, the Calcutta shops remained shut for several days owing to a dispute about the value of the Sikka Rupee. In 1789, Lord Cornwallis issued an order to the effect that, if a Rupee was the genuine product of a recognised mint, no matter to what extent it had been clipped or drilled, the treasury officers were to receive it by weight according to fixed rates hung up in the Collector's office. The indefinite and arbitrary discount exacted by the treasury officers from very early times was thus put a stop to. These officers had so long the privilege of deducting from a coin whatever they liked and then returned it to circulation as payments of merchants' investments at rates fixed at their own will. Thus, although they

1. Cf. "Bengal from the very first seems to have been the milch cow from which the other Presidencies drew their support;" "the Council complains that the Bengal treasuries are completely emptied by sending coin to the other Presidencies." See Hunter, *op. cit.*, p. 303, note 98.

2. Chatterji, *op. cit.*, pp. 183-84.

3. For these and similar Farrukhābad (Bengal Presidency) Rupees of his year 45 and Sūrat (Bombay) Rupees of his year 46 and the Arkāt (Madras) Rupees of year 6 of 'Alamgīr II, see Lane-Poole, *Catalogue* (Moghul), pp. 267 ff.

received a salary of £40 per year, they actually earned an income of £4000 or more. Very soon the treasury officers were made responsible not only for the net sums received, but also for the actual coin in which they were paid. The ruin of the profitable career of a treasury officer was complete.

The coins were now divided into two classes : (a) the statutory coinage to be received at its full value, and (b) the deteriorated coins to be received at published rates and to be sent off to Calcutta at the end of each month. Coins requiring deduction from its nominal value were made unfit to be returned to circulation and the treasury officers were now required to specify the rates at which they received the coin in an invoice to be forwarded together with the coin to the Presidency mint. The officers grumbled and wanted to disobey. But the English Collectors of the Districts now came to be fined for the offences of their subordinates and they took ample vengeance on their Indian treasury officers. The attempt of the Anglo-Indian government at currency reform was at last going to be successful.

But the policy of calling in debased coins, which formed two-thirds of the currency, required an adequate number of fresh coins to be issued by the Government. This the Council was not in a position to do, especially owing to the drainage due to wars with Tīpū Sulṭān of Mysore. As a result of the scarcity and consequent dearth of coins, prices of local produce sank to nominal rates. The poor peasant had to sell his hole crop at the cheap rate for his necessities or to give it to the money-lender in return for a few Rupees advanced to him in the spring season. The distress was terribly increased by the urgent necessity of funds to prosecute the Mysore wars. In spite of all difficulties, however, the old Calcutta mint as well as those newly established at Dacca, Murshīdābād and Pāṭnā were set up to vigorous work. On January 1, 1791, the 'new milled' Rupees were issued at the four mints. On the 18th November of the same year, the Governor-General declared, 'in future the sale of gold and silver coin shall be as free and unrestrained in every respect as the sale of gold and silver bullion, and the exchangeable value or price of each determined by the course of trade, in the same manner as the price of every other commodity that comes into the market.'[1] On the 24th October, 1792, Lord Cornwallis further declared that, after the first day of the Bengali year 1200, i.e. the 10th April, 1794, the new coinage should be the only legal tender and that no person should be permitted to recover any sum of money under a bond or other writing, by which any species of Rupees, excepting the Sikka Rupees of the 19th San, was stipulated to be paid.[2] In the year 1794, however, a grace of another year was granted; but, in the year following, in Hunter's words, the Company's 'new and uniform currency at last completely ousted the multitudinous, battered and debased Rupees which had so long afflicted the people.'

Still, however, different kinds of Rupee were current in the three Presidencies of Bengal, Bombay and Madras, the following Rupees being current in the Bengal Presidency : (1) Sikka which latterly weighed 192 grains and contained 176 grains of pure silver; (2) Farrukhābādī latterly weighing 180 grains and containing 165.215 grains of pure silver; and (3) Banārasī (upto 1819) weighing 174.76 grains including 168 grains of pure silver. There was also the Calānī or Current Rupee, in which the Company's accounts were kept, 116 of them being regarded as equivalent to 100 Sikka Rupees. The Bharī (i.e. the Company's Arcot Rupee minted at Calcutta) was 3½ per cent less than the Sikka. The Bombay Rupee (adopted from the Rupee of Surat) weighed (from 1800 A.D.) 178·32 grains inclusive of 164.94 grains of pure silver. The Madras Rupee, adopted from the Rupee of the Nawabs of Arcot (Arkāt) and usually called Arcot Rupee, weighed from 171 to 177 grains with pure silver from 160 to 170 grains. In 1811, the Madras mint issued Rupee weighing 188 grains with 169.20 grains of pure silver in imitation of the Spanish Dollar.[3]

The first step towards the assimilation of these different Rupees was taken in Regulation VII of 1833. This assimilated the Rupees of other parts of British India, but unfortunately retained the exceptional Sikka of Bengal. According to the

1. Hunter *op. cit.*, p. 320.
2. *Ibid.*, p. 321.
3. See *Hobson-Jobson*, s.v. *Rupee*.

currency reform of 1835, however, Rupee of the uniform weight, size and fineness was made the only currency of the whole of British India. This is the Company's Rupee of 180 grains with 165 grains of pure silver. The Sikka was abolished as a coin by Act XIII of 1836.[1] From this time, the Company's Rupee bore the effigy and name of the king of England, the earliest issue being the one struck in 1835-39 in the name William IV (1830-37) as well as of the East India Company, though they bear the date 1835 only and the king died in 1837 and was succeeded by his niece Victoria (1837-1901). Coins with the portrait and name of Victoria as well as the name of the Company began to appear from 1840. This is due to the delay in transporting fresh dies from England to India.

Queen Victoria's Rupee can be divided into three classes, the first being similar to those bearing the name of William IV. It shows the queen's uncrowned head to left on the obverse and the value of the coin in English and Persian together with the name of the Company and the date (1840) on the reverse. The Rupee of the second variety bearing the initials of W. Wyan of the Royal Mint, London, also bore the date 1840, but continued to be struck till 1861 considerably after the Company's rule had ended on the 1st of November, 1858, and the government of India transferred to the queen of England. The second class of Victoria's Rupee started from 1862 and bore the name and crowned bust of the queen, the Company's name being omitted. The name of India is added and the value of the coin is indicated in English only. The coins of this class bear the dates 1862, 1874, 1875 and 1876.

The third class of Victoria's coins, resembling those of the second class, begin with her assumption of the title Empress on the 1st of January 1877. Due to the fall in the value of silver, no Rupee was minted in 1894-96 and 1899 and the value of the coin was fixed at 1 shilling 4 pence in 1899 (*i.e.* £ 1=Rs. 15). Down to 1873, the Rupee was regarded as equal to 2 shillings, though later, for sometime, its value fell as low as 1 shilling.

1. Cf. *loc. cit.*; *Encyclopaedia Britannica*, s. v. *Rupee*.

Among the successors of Queen Victoria, her son Edward VII (1901-10), grandson George V (1910-36) and great-grandsons Edward VIII (1936) and George VI (1937-52), no Rupee was issued in the name of Edward VIII. The Rupee of quarternary silver (an alloy of 50 per cent silver, 40 per cent copper, 5 per cent nickel and 5 per cent zinc) was introduced during the rule of George VI though it was soon replaced by pure nickel in 1946. A new type of nickel Rupee was minted in 1947, the year that witnessed India gaining her independence and the end of the Indo-British coinage. The silver coins had straight milling while those of alloy and nickel have 'the security edge'. The nickel Rupee has on the reverse the figure of a tiger to right (in place of the old floral design) together with the value written in English, Ūrdū and Hindī as well as the name of India and the date of issue. It is slightly smaller in shape than the silver Rupee, but has the same weight of 180 grains.[1]

The nickel Rupee of the independent Republic of India somewhat resembles the nickel Rupee of George VI.

II

The word *viṁśopaka* is mentioned in a number of inscriptions as the name of a coin as also of a land measure. The derivative meaning of the word is uncertain; but it seems to be wrongly Sanskritised from Prakrit *vīsovaga*=Sanskrit *viṁśopaga*, 'belonging to twenty', and the Viṁśopaka was the twentieth of the standard silver coin in value and of the standard land measure in area.

That twenty Viṁśopakas made one silver Dramma was known to scholars from the celebrated Siyadoni inscription, line 20 of which mentions half of a Vigrahatuṅgīya-Dramma as equal to ten Viṁśopakas.[2] This record comes from the Jhansi District of U.P. The recently published charter (592 A.D.) of Viṣṇuṣeṇa likewise represents five Viṁśopakas as the same as one-fourth of the silver coin called Rūpaka.[3] This inscription

1. See *The Indian Numismatic Chronicle*, Patna, Vol. II, 1961, pp. 125 ff.
2. See D. R. Bhandarkar, *Carmichael Lectures*, 1921, p. 210; *CII*, Vol. IV, p. clxxxix, note 7.
3. *Ep. Ind.*, Vol. XXX, p. 175, note 2; p. 180, text line 23.

comes apparently from the Gujarat region. Some early medieval inscriptions of the same area speak of Viṁśopaka as the name of a land measure.[1]

We have seen that twenty Viṁśopakas are regarded as equal to the silver coin called Dramma in one record and Rūpaka in another. This raises the question whether Dramma and Rūpaka may be different names of the same coin. According to Bhāskar-ācārya's *Līlāvatī* (thirteenth century),

20 cowrie-shells	= 1 Kākinī		
80 ,,	= 4 ,,	= 1 Paṇa	
1280 ,,	=64 ,,	=16 ,,	=1 Dramma;

and the same work further says that the Dharaṇa (i. e. the silver Kārsāpaṇa or Purāṇa), apparently the same as Dramma, was, in weight, equal to twentyfour Ratis and to one-half of a Gadyāṇa.[2] According to a table of equation popular in Eastern India during the late medieval period, as we have seen above,

4 cowrie-shells	= 1 Gaṇḍā		
80 ,,	= 20 ,,	= Paṇa	
1280 ,,	=320 ,,	=16 ,,	=Kāhaṇa (Kārṣāpa ṇa)[3]

The two tables make it clear that the Dramma and Kārsāpaṇa (Purāṇa and Dharaṇa) were regarded as the same, even though the weight of the former is given as twentyfour Ratis while that of the latter, as known from older works like the *Manusmṛti*, was thirtytwo Ratis. This is because the name Kārṣāpaṇa here indicates the silver coin introduced by the Śaka Satraps of Western India and imitated by the Traikūṭakas, Kalacuris, Guptas, etc. In the fifth century A.D. when Buddhaghoṣa flourished, this new Kārsāpaṇa was called Rudradāmaka-Kārṣāpaṇa (after the celebrated Śaka Satrap Rudradāman I 130-50 A. D.) and was regarded as three-fourths of the old Kārṣāpaṇa (weighing thirtytwo Ratis) in weight and value.[4] The theoretical weight of the new Kārṣāpaṇa was thus twentyfour Ratis although it was probably somewhat lighter actually. That the same silver coin was

1. A. K. Majumdar, *The Caulukyas of Gujarat*, p. 244.
2. I. 2-3; *JNSI*, Vol. VII, pp. 82 ff.; above, p. 281.
3. See above, p. 280.
4. *JNSI*, Vol. XIII, pp. 189-90 ; cf. *Select Inscriptions*, pp. 158-59; above, p. 98.

called Rāpaka since the age of the Guptas is clearly indicated by epigraphic evidence. Thus the Gupta silver coins, imitated from the Śaka silver currency, are called Rūpaka in the Baigram copper-plate inscription (448 A. D.),[1] while Kalacuri Kṛṣṇarāja's silver coins of the same type are likewise mentioned as Kṛṣṇarāja-Rūpaka in the Anjaneri plates (710 A.D).[2]

Just as twenty Viṁśopakas were equal to a silver Dramma = Kārṣāpaṇa = Rūpaka (twenty four Ratis theoretically), the Ṣoḍaśikā was one-sixteenth of the same silver coin in value. Since the Ṣoḍaśikā is comparable to the old copper Paṇa sixteen of which made the old Kārṣāpaṇa (Purāṇa or Dharaṇa) weighing thirtytwo Ratis, there is no doubt that the Viṁśopaka and Ṣoḍaśikā were copper coins. The fact that the Viṁśopaka was equal to about one Ratī of silver also suggests that it was a coin of copper and not of silver, such small silver coins being rare.

The coin name *Viṁśopaka* is sometimes found in the Prakrit form *Vīsovā* in West Indian epigraphs like the Patan inscription of the time of Siṅghaṇa.[3] Apparently the same coin is called Vīsa (Sanskrit *Viṁśa*) in Kannaḍa inscriptions as in *Lokkīya-vīsa* or the Vīsa minted at Lokki or Lokkiguṇḍi, i.e. modern Lakkundi in the Dharwar District of Mysore.[4]

As regards the land measure called Viṁśopaka, there is little doubt that the name survives in the modern Biswa (Marāṭhī *Viśva*) which is the twentieth part of a property, especially of the standard land measure called Bīghā, according to Wilson's Glossary.

If twenty Viṁśopaka (Vīsovā, Vīsa) coins of copper were equal to one silver coin equated with 1280 cowrie-shells, one Vimśopaka would be equal to 64 cowrie-shells. But the number of cowrie-shells to be equated with a Dramma is sometimes given differently. Thus, according to a scheme popular in the Rajasthan region during the late medieval period,

1. *Select Inscriptions*, p. 343 and note 5.
2. *Ep. Ind.*, Vol XXV, p. 229. Pratīhāra Bhoja's silver coins (Smith's *Catalogue*, pp. 241-42), probably called Ādivarāha-dramma in the Siyadoni inscription, were usually double Dramma.
3. *Ep. Ind.*, Vol. I, p. 343 ; *CII*, Vol. IV, p. clxxxix, note 7.
4. *A.R. Ep.*, 1933-34, B.K. No. 120.

5 cowrie-shells	= 1 Pāvīsā			
100 ,,	= 20 ,,	= 1 Lohaḍiyā		
2000 ,,	=400 ,,	=20 ,,	=1 Dramma.[1]	

Although it is difficult to say whether this Dramma is the same silver money weighing twenty four Ratis theoretically or the silver Ṭaṅka or Rūpiya issued by the Muslim rulers, the name Pāvisā in the above table is interesting since it is clearly Sanskrit *Pāda-viṁśaka* or quarter-Viṁśopaka. The gap between the old and new rates of exchange, viz. 80 quarter-Viṁśopakas =20 Viṁśopakas=1 Dramma, and 400 Pāvīsās=100 Vīsās or Viṁśopakas=1 Dramma, may of course suggest that the Dramma here is a heavier coin such as the Muslim silver money like the Rūpiya of 80 or 96 Ratis.

The old rate equating 20 Viṁśopakas with the Dramma= Kārṣāpaṇa=Rūpaka would suggest the equation of 80 Pāvīsās=Pāda-viṁśakas=Pāda-viṁśopakas with one silver coin, and this rate seems to suggest further that the word *Pāvīsā* was later modified to *Paisā* through an intermediate form like *Paīsā*=Sanskrit *Pada-viṁśaka*, which is the same as *Pāda-viṁśaka* (*Pāda-viṃśopaka*).

According to Wilson's Glossary, *Paisā* (variously written as *Pysa*, *Pyce*, *Pice*, etc., in English) was a copper coin which, under the native government, varied considerably in weight and value, the East India Company's Pice being fixed at the weight of 100 grains and rated at 64 to the silver Rupee. That it was sometimes rated, like the quarter-Viṁśaka (Viṁśopaka) to the Dramma, at 80 to the Rupee is also known from Fryer (1673 A.D.) as quoted in the *Hobson-Jobson*.

It is interesting to note that the word *Paisā* (*Pada-viṁśaka*, '$\frac{1}{4}$ of $\frac{1}{20}$' i.e. $\frac{1}{80}$) is not only used to indicate the copper coin a number of which are equated with the Rupee, but that, in Marāṭhī, it also means a land measure which is now regarded as equal to $7\frac{1}{2}$ Bīghās. The area of land, of which the Paisā was $\frac{1}{80}$, was originally about 600 Bīghās. The fixation of the rent of a Viṁśopaka of land at the high rate of 24, 20, 16

1. *Ep. Ind.*, Vol. XXXIII, p. 238.

or 10 Drammas in the early medieval records of Gujarat indeed seems to refer to a big area.[1]

1. A. K. Majumdar, *The Caulukyas of Gujarat*, p. 244. The purchasing power of a silver coin was very high and the price of the produce of the fields was very cheap. Under the cirucmstances, 10 Drammas could have been the rent for a Viṁśopaka of fallow land only if it was a very big area. See above, p. 279, note 1. For the Viṁśopaka coin, see also R.C. Agrawala in *JNSI*, Vol. XVII, Part ii, pp. 80-82; S. Bandyopadhyay, *ibid.*, Vol. XXVIII, pp. 21-24, 149-52; L. Gopal, *The Economic Life of Northern India*, pp. 204-05.

Appendix I

DISCOVERY OF COINS REPORTED IN 1955-1956

I

In 1948 a proposal was received from the Indian Embassy at Kabul to send a small body of archaeologists to Afghanistan; but it was dropped owing to financial considerations. The proposal was, however, renewed in 1951, and the Central Advisory Board of Archaeology recommended in 1954 that steps should be taken to organise and send an archaeological mission to Afghanistan for exploration and search of sculptures, inscriptions, coins, etc. The Government of India agreed to the scheme in September 1955 and accordingly an archaeological delegation headed by T. N. Ramachandran of the Department of Archaeology was sent to Afghanistan in May 1956. The delegation stayed in Afghanistan for two months and a half and returned about the end of July 1956. The members of the delegation studied the collections of the Kabul Museum and visited various sites including Jalalabad, Ghazni, Kandahar, Farah, Herat, Mazar-i-sharif, Haibak, Qunduz, Bamiyan and Begram.

The delegation saw thousands of early and medieval coins in the museums at Kabul, Kandahar, Herat and Mazar-i-sharif as well as in certain collections of antiquities at Shindand, Gulbahar, Bala Hisar and Maimana. All these coins have not yet been examined by experts. Some of the Indo-Greek, Scytho-Parthian and Kuṣāṇa coins found in Afghanistan and its neighbourhood have been recently noticed in the *Trésors Monétaires d'Afghanistan* by Raoul Curiel and Daniel Schlumberger, published in 953 from Paris as Volume XIV of the *Mémoires de la Délégation Archéologique Francaise en Afghanistan.* A section of this book deals with the Mir Zakah hoard as well as the coins in the private collections of S. A. R. Shah Mahmoud Khan and Marc le Berre. It also contains brief notices of the coins in the private collections of J. M. Casal, J. Sénécal and K. A. Gai.

The Indian archaeological delegation selected, out of the various collections it had an opportunity to examine, hundreds of coins that would interest the students of early Indian history and got them photographed. These photographs are now being studied in India.

The coins of the Qunduz, Mir Zakah, Chaman Hazuri and Kotla-i-Khairkhaneh hoards are now preserved in the Kabul Museum. The Qunduz hoard, said to be of 628 silver coins, was discovered in 1918 somewhere between Qunduz and Khanabad. It contains coins of the Attic standard issued by seventeen Greek kings of Bactria and India including those of Lysias, Antialcidas, Theophilus, Archebius, Philoxenus, Amyntas and Hermaeus, which were noticed in the *Numismatic Circular* for May 1953 and May 1954, *Journal of the Numismatic Society of India*, Vol. XVII (1955), *Journal of the Asiatic Society*, Letters, Vol. XXI (1955), etc.

Over 20,000 coins were found from the bed of a sacred spring called Karez Gai (Sanskrit *Gomukha*) at Mir Zakah, 20 miles from Gardez and 95 miles to the south of Kabul. According to tradition, the earlier name of the spring, which is now also called Khor-Khotai, was Gaṅgā. The find of such a huge hoard of coins in its bed seems to suggest that they were offerings of pious pilgrims in the holy waters of the spring. 191 copper and 8459 silver coins from Mir Zakah are arranged in three show-cases in the Kabul Museum, the remainder of the coins found there still lying in the store rooms of the Museum. Of the Mir Zakah coins in the show cases, punch-marked (including the long-bar and bent-bar types) and tribal coins alone are about 4500 in number. There are many tribal coins including those of the Taxila and Kauśāmbī types. Amongst the coins of the Indo-Greeks, mention may be made of those of Menander, Lysias, Pantaleon, Philoxenus, Agathokleia (jointly with Strato I) and Strato I. There are also 238 coins of Azes I and Azes II and a large number belonging to Azilises, Gondophernes, Abdagases and Soter Megas. The collection contains about 100 copper coins of different kings of the Kuṣāṇa family.

The coins found at Chaman Hazuri have been noticed by Schlumberger in the section entitled *L'argent Grec dans l'empire Achemenide* in the joint work of Curiel and himself, referred to above. Out of the 118 silver coins found there, 30 are of the Athenian Drachma type and 8 are Persian Siglos, while 20 are miscellaneous Greek coins of the sixth century B.C. They also include 12 bent-bar punch-marked coins. The Kotla-i-Khairkahneh hoard of 308 silver coins belong to the early Sassanian rulers. The Moidan hoard consists of 10 gold coins which are Kuṣaṇo-Sassanian issues.

In the Kandahar Museum, there are 6 gold, 363 silver and 815 copper coins, all of them collected from the neighbouring areas. There are one punch-marked silver coin and a copper coin with the incomplete Brāhmī legend reading *divi*. The collection also includes some coins of Spalapatideva and Sāmantadeva and of Kumārapāla as well as some silver Rāmaṭaṅkās. Many coins of these types have been discovered in India. The coins of Spalapatideva and Sāmantadeva are issues of the Śāhī dynasty of North-Western Bhāratavarṣa. Kumārapāla, issuer of some of these coins, was supposed by Cunningham to have belonged to the Tomara ruling family of Delhi and Ajmer, although we have no definite evidence in favour of the existence of any Tomara king of that name.

The collection of coins in the Herat Museum, which is housed in the Herat Hotel, consists of 29 gold, 370 silver and 600 copper coins. Most of the early coins belong to the Greek rulers of Bactria and India (including Diodotus, Menander and others), Scythians, Parthians, Kuṣāṇas and Sassanians. Some Kuṣāṇo-Sassanian gold coins of the collection bear the name of Vāsudeva. A few of the gold coins belong to the Kalacuri king Gāṅgeyadeva Vikramāditya who flourished in the period c. 1015-41 A.D. There are also a few silver Gaḍhaiyā coins and 75 copper coins bearing the representation of a crouching animal with a long tail on both the obverse and reverse, but without any legend.

The Museum at Mazar-i-sharif, 389 miles north-west of Kabul and about 12 miles form Balkh, has a collection of 4083 coins. Of these, 88 are of gold, 2000 of silver and 1995 of copper. As many as 374 Kuṣāṇa coins of the collection are reported to have been found at Balkh. There are coins of the Greek rulers of Bactria and India as well as of the Scythians, Parthians, Kuṣāṇas and Sassanians. The collection includes some coins bearing the name of Vāsudeva and others that of

Varahran I. A few gold coins of Kalacuri Gāṅgeyadeva and of Gāhaḍavāla Govindacandra, who flourished in the period c. 1114-55 A.D., as well as some issues of Spalapatideva and Sāmantadeva belong to the collection. There are also some silver coins of *Rājā* Gīrvāṇa Yuddhavikrama of Nepal.

A number of coins (including some Sassanian issues) are in the private collection of the Governor of Maimana, while the coin collection housed in the Government Hotel at Shindand on the road between Farah and Herat contains some Parthian issues. Among the antiquities housed in the Nashir Library at Bala Hisar, there is a Rāma-ṭaṅkā and a number of Kuṣāṇa coins. Some antiquities have been collected at Gulbahar from the neighbourhood of the town. These are housed in a local factory and contain a number of coins including one copper issue bearing the representation of a horseman and probably the name of Spalapatideva.

II

A reference may be made to the finds of coins reported in the year 1955 from different parts of India. There is, however, little doubt that the information is incomplete and many discoveries remain unreported. The finds that came to our notice are : (1) 51 silver coins from Gondarmau near Bhopal, (2) gold coins of Mahendrāditya and Prasannamātra from Bhandara in the Chanda District, Maharashıra, (3) 139 Indo-Sassanian copper coins from Sirsa in the Durg District of Madhya Pradesh, (4) 178 copper coins from Khokra Kot in the Rohtak District, East Punjab, (5) 3 silver coins of the Mughul emperor Shāh 'Alam II from Ludhiana in the same State, (6) 10 gold coins of the Kalacuri kings Ratnadeva and Pṛthvīdeva from Ratnapur in the Puri District, Orissa, (7) 25 copper coins of the Cāhamānas from Isarda in the Sawai Madhopur District, Rajasthan, (8) 50 gold coins, including the issues of kings Devarāya, Kṛṣṇarāya and Rāmarāya of Vijayanagara, from Gollapalli in the Krishna District, Andhra Pradesh, (9) 4 silver coins of the Later Mughuls and some issued by the English and French East India Companies, from Malreddipalli in the Anantapur District of the same State, (10) 35 gold Fanams from Puthudy Thavalam in the Devicolam Taluk, Kottayam District, Kerala, (11) 29 Indo-British coins of different metals from Singampunari and Soachani in the Ramanathapuram District, Madras, (12) 8 Mughul silver coins from Puraina in the Basti District, Uttar Pradesh, (13) 23 silver coins of the Sulṭāns Nāṣiruddīn Maḥmūd and ʻAlauddīn Muḥammad Shāh of Delhi from Bankasia in the same District, (14) 7 silver coins, including the issues of the Mughul emperors Shāh Jahān and Aurangzīb, from Muhammadabad in the Azamgarh District of the same State, (15) 22 gold coins of the Kalacuri king Gāṅgeyadeva Vikramāditya from Basarwa in the same District, (16) 40 silver coins of the Later Mughuls from Kaolas in the Nanded District, Maharashtra, (17) 101 silver coins of the Mughul emperors from Bhose in the Aurangabad District of the same State, (18) 19 Mughul silver coins from Golapnagari in the same District, and (19) 20 small South Indian gold coins from a locality near Sangli, now in the possession of the Director of Archives, Bombay.

The above finds numbering a dozen and a half account for 756 coins in different metals and of various periods; but the total number of coins discovered in different localities in the old Hyderabad State alone is reported to be more than 1400, although detailed information about all the Hyderabad finds is not available.

During the last few months of the year, the office of the Government Epigraphist for India, Ootacamund, received the following hoards of coins for examination : (1) 57 South Indian copper coins from Karur, Tiruchirapalli District, Madras. (2) 4 copper coins from Maski, Raichur District, formerly in the Hyderabad state but now in Mysore, (3) 40 coins (39 lead and 1 copper) from Nagarjunikonda, Guntur District, Andhra Pradesh, and (4) 10 copper Gadhaiyā Paisās from Kotda in the Anjar Taluk, Kutch.

A.S. Altekar and H. V. Trivedi were responsible for the rediscovery of nearly fifteen thousand coins including about a dozen of gold, about five thousand of silver and about ten thousand of copper. A large number of these coins belong to the medieval and modern periods, being issues of the Sulṭāns of Delhi, Mandu and Gujarat, the Mughul emperors and the former Native States. They also contain a good number of Gadhaiyā coins of both silver and copper. A majority of these coins were previously preserved in the treasuries of the former States of Ratlam, Dhar, Rajgarh and Barawani. With the merger of the States and the formation of the State of Madhya Bharat (now merged in Madhya Pradesh), they were transferred to the Central Treasury at Gwalior. Altekar and Trivedi succeeded in convincing the Madhya Bharat Government as to the desirability of the transference of the coins from the Treasury to the State Museums. It is interesting to note in this connection that the small States referred to above received certain coins from the treasure-trove finds at places like Yeotmal, Nandurbar, Prakasha, Vikrama, etc., through the Museums of Bombay and Madhya Pradesh apparently for preservation and exhibition in their Museums, although they were sent to the State treasuries as, unfortunately, none of the States had any Museum worth the name. If a vigorous search is made in the treasuries of all the former States throughout the country, many thousands of coins—ancient, medieval and modern, are sure to come to light.

III

During the year 1956, reports of the discovery of numerous hoards of coins were received by us from various sources including the Treasure Trove officers of the different States.

A word may be said here in regard to the working of the Treasure Trove Act. Coins acquired by the State Governments under this Act are distributed amongst various museums and institutions in different parts of India. This no doubt gives an opportunity to a student of numismatics to study the coins prevalent in different ages and different parts of the country in a museum in his own area without undergoing the trouble of visiting the museums in the different States. But the difficulty is that this distribution of hoards is often done without a proper examination of their composition. Thus, if five hundred coins of a hoard are scattered among twentyfive institutions in various parts of India, it becomes extremely difficult for one to form an idea about the nature and contents of the hoard, which are often of very great importance to the student of the subject. It is probably desirable to preserve the hoards of coins descovered in a particular State intact in the principal Museum of that State, though it cannot be done without a revision of the Treasure Trove Act. If, however, the present policy of distributing the coins of a hoard is continued, it will have to be seen that the State Museums do not scatter the hoards without keeping a careful and complete record of them. Such a record should contain all necessary information regarding the weight, size, shape and metal contents of each coin. Indeed it will be proper if a fully equipped Numismatic Section of the National Museum of India undertakes this work of examination and disbursement of the Treasure Trove coins.

Out of the numerous hoards of coins discovered during the year throughout the country, three deserve prominent mention owing to the huge number of coins in each one of them. The first of these in a large hoard of Kuṣāṇa coins discovered at Bhuteswar near Mathura in U. P. It includes the issues of Wema Kadphises, Kaniṣka and Vāsudeva. The coins of this hoard weigh no less than one Maund, two Seers and three Chhatacks. But one of the largest hoards of coins ever discovered in India was found at Chhapra in the Saran District of Bihar.

While digging the lawn of the palace of the Rājā of Hathwa at Chhapra, 9,40,000 silver coins weighing 9,23,179 Tolas (i. e. 257 Maunds, 9 Seers, and 59 Tolas) were discovered. They were found in 59 brass and copper jars. As reported to the press by the District Magistrate of Saran, the coins bear the names of Shāh 'Alam II and of Queen Victoria and came from the mints of the English East India Company at the Fort William (Calcutta), Banaras, Farrukhabad and Murshidabad. The maximum and minimum numbers of coins in a jar were 94,000 and 11,000 respectively. We do not know where these coins are now and whether they have been properly studied. Such a huge number of coins is likely to yield, if closely studied, valuable information regarding the weight-standard and fabric and specially the mint-marks of the East India Company's coinage, regarding which our knowledge is still insufficient. They may also throw light on the Company's mints in Calcutta, Bombay and Madras. The coins appear to have been hidden during the days of the Indian Mutiny about the middle of the nineteenth century.

In that case, those with the names of Queen Victoria are expected to be issues of 1840 and to belong to two classes, viz. one with a larger and the other with a smaller flan.

The third of the large hoards was discovered at Dhotra in the Amraoti District of the Maharashtra State. It contained copper coins of the Bahmanīs of Gulbarga. The weight of the hoard is stated to be about sixteen Seers.

In this connection, the discovery of another hoard of coins may also be mentioned. A news-item appeared in the Madras papers regarding the discovery of about 50 silver coins of the Western Satraps from a locality in the Guntur District of Andhra Pradesh. The coins were said to be in the custody of the District Magistrate of Gunter. It was also reported that they yielded the name of a new king besides a few other known rulers. The find of these coins far away from the dominions of the Śakas of Western India raised considerable interest and their examination was expected to throw some light on the history of the period in question. Unfortunately such reports are often found to be erroneous.[1]

Besides the hoards of coins noticed above, information regarding the discovery of the following hoards were also received during the said year from numerous other localities in diffierent parts of the country :

(1) 8 copper coins belonging to the Tughluqs and Mughuls of Delhi and the Sulṭāns of Gujarat from Jhaloregarh in the Mehsana District of Gujarat ; (2) 1 silver coin of A. H. 1109 belonging to Aurangazīb and 6 silver coins of Sulṭān Mahmūd Shāh of Gujarat from Khadiarpara in the Kaira District of the same State ; (3) 20 gold coins from Walve in the Satara District of the Maharashtra State ; (4) 6 silver coins of the Later Mughuls and 4 copper coins from the city of Ahmedabad in the Gujarat State ; (5) 37 Mughul coins from Paidipalli in the Warangal District of Andhra Pradesh ; (6) 4 copper coins of the Mughuls and 28 coins of the Quṭbshāhīs from Janagama in the Nalgonda District of the same State; (7) 12 gold coins of the Sulṭāns of Delhi and 279 coins of Aurangzīb from a locality in the Guna District of Madhya Pradesh ;

1. See above, pp. 150 ff., for a detailed report on this hoard.

(8) 14 silver coins of the Mughuls from Gummi in the Buldana District of the Maharashtra State ; (9) 15 silver coins of the Mughuls and 685 copper coins of the Bahmanīs from Borakhedi in the same District ; (10) a hoard of silver coins of the Later Mughuls from Chhindwara in Madhya Pradesh; (11) 114 silver coins of the Mughuls from Barela in the Chhindwara District of the same State ; (12) 41 silver coins of the Mughuls from a locality in the Saugor District of the same State ; (13) 109 coins of Kalacuri Gāṅgeyadeva from Barela in the Jabalpur District of the same State ; (14) 118 Indo-British coins of silver, 15 Svāmi-Pagodas of gold issued by to the East India Company and 1 silver Half-Rupee of Balarāmavarman of Travancore from different localities of the Madras State ; (15) 10 gold coins of Kaṇṭhīrava Narasarāja Woḍaiyar of Mysore from Thippur in the Mandya District of Mysore ; (16) 2 coins of the Sulṭāns of Malwa, viz. 1 gold issue of Ghiyāṣuddin Khaljī dated A. H. 880 and 1 copper coin of Sulṭān 'Alāuddīn Mahmūd Shāh bearing legend in Nāgarī, from Chitorgadh in Rajasthan ; (17) 9 Gadhaiyā coins from Badoli in the Chitorgardh District of the same State ; (18) 165 coins including tribal, punch-marked and Kṣatrapa issues from Nagari in the same District ; (19) 61 silver coins of the Mughuls from Jodhpur in the same State ; (20) 3 coins of the Tughluq dynasty from Gagraun in the Jhalawar District of the same State ; (21) 44 copper coins including 1 of Sulṭān 'Alāuddīn Muḥammad Shāh of Delhi and 15, 23 and 1 respectively of three Sulṭāns of Gujarat, viz. Ahmad Shāh II, Mahmūd Shāh and Muzaffar Shāh II, from Talaja in the Gohilwad District of the Gujarat State ; (22) 2 copper coins from Pindara in the same State ; (23) 2 coins of the Kṣatrapas (one of silver and the other of copper) from Naisra in the same State ; (24) 61 gold coins and a large number of silver issues from Porbandar in the same State ; (25) 35 gold Rāśipaṇams from Puttady Thavalam in the Devicolam Taluk of the Kerala State ; (26) 8 and 20 silver coins respectively of Shāh Jahān and Aurangzīb from Bhedauha in the Basti District of U.P. ; and (27) 110 silver coins of the East India Company from Bagadiha in the same District.

APPENDIX II

Date of the Satraps of Mathura

Numismatists usually describe the coins of Hagāna and Hagāmaṣa (both those issued jointly by them and those issued alone by Hagāmaṣa) before those of Rañjuvula. Allan[1] assigns the issues of Hagāmaṣa to *c.* 50-40 B. C. and those of Rañjuvula to *c.* 40-20 B. C. while the joint issues of Hagāna and Hagāmaṣa are placed between the above two classes.[2] Apparently however the joint issues of Hagāna and Hagāmaṣa should have been described earlier than the coins issued by Hagāmaṣa alone. This is no doubt suggested by the mention of Hagāna before Hagāmaṣa in the coin legend : *Khatapāna Hagānasa Hagāmaṣasa*, indicating that Hagāna was the senior partner in the combination.

Another interesting fact, to which we draw the attention of scholars in this connection, is that Rañjuvula was apparently the earliest known Scythian ruler of Mathurā and was certainly earlier than Hagāna and Hagāmaṣa. This is definitely indicated by his coins. Rañjuvula's earlier coins bear legends in Greek and Kharoṣṭhī; but his later issues have legends only in Brāhmī which was the script prevalent in Mathurā. His son Śoṇḍāsa as well as the other Kṣatrapas of Mathurā (including Hagāna and Hagāmaṣa) used Brāhmī only in their coin legends. The facts that Rañjuvula's coins were found in the Punjab and the western parts of Uttar Pradesh and that his commonest type is copied from the coins of Strato I and II, while his rarest issues are imitated from the local rulers of Mathurā show that the Śaka chief, who seems to have been a semi-independent general of Maues (Moga), established himself at Mathurā late in his life.[3]

1. *Catalogue of Indian Coins in the British Museum* (Ancient India), pp. 183-85.
2. Cf. also Rapson, *CHI*, Vol. I, pp. 527, 538; Smith, *Catalogue*, pp. 190, 195.
3. *Select Inscriptions*, p. 112.

As regards the date of Rañjuvula, it may be pointed out that we are inclined to identify the older of the two eras, used by the Scytho-Parthians and Kusāṇas, with the Vikrama-saṁvat of 58 B.C. and to believe that year 72 of that era, in which Śoṇḍāsa's inscription is dated, corresponds to 15 A.D.[1] We have also assigned Rañjuvula to *c.* 1-15 A.D. and his son Śoṇḍāsa to *c.* 10-25 A.D.[2] It has further been suggested that this era started from the accession of Vonones, founder of an independent kingdom in East Iran about the middle of the first century B.C., and was carried to India by Maues (*c.* 25 B.C.-25 A.D.).[3]

1. Cf. *Vikrama Volume*, ed. R.K. Mookerji, 1948, pp. 579ff.; *The Age of Imperial Unity*, ed. Majumdar, 1951, pp. 125 note, 144 note.
2. *Select Inscriptions*, 1942, p. 112.
3. See also Sircar *Indian Epigraphy*, pp. 248 ff., 251 ff.

APPENDIX III

Bangala Couplet on Akbarī Rupee

Bangāla is mentioned in Abū'l Fazl's *'Aīn-i-Akbarī* as one of the mint-towns of the Mughul emperor Akbar (1556-1605 A.D.), and the name has been traced in the Persian *bait* on certain square Akbarī Rupees.[1] Out of the words found on the coins, the following couplet has been reconstructed :

sikkah-i-Bangālah za ān dil-khwāh shud
ke ābrūsh zarb Akbar Shāh shud.

"The coin of Bangāla became pleasing from this
That its honour lay in the striking by Akbar Shāh."[2]

There has been controversy among scholars about the location of the Bangāla mint of Akbar, the problem being related to the identification of the city of Bengala mentioned by medieval European travellers, notably the Portuguese.

In a well-written article on the Bangāla mint of Akbar, S.H. Hodivala came to the conclusion that 'Bangāla was not the real or fixed name of any town or city, but an alternative or honorific designation by which the capital of the province at the time being was known'. He further observed that Bangāla might have been Gaur in Munim Khān's time, that the name was possibly applied to Tānda during the subsequent twenty years, and that Bangāla on Akbar's coins of the 39th and following years would probably be identical with Akbarnagar.[3]

Sometime ago, I myself came to a similar conclusion in respect of the city of Bangāla mentioned by the medieval European writers. I pointed out that Europeans other than

1. Cf. Vost in *Numismatic Supplement*, No. XI, Article No. LXV, in *JASB*, 1909; H.N. Wright, *Catalogue of the Coins in the Indian Museum, Calcutta*, Vol. III, 1908, p. 35, No. 315 (a-b); R.B. Whitehead, *Catalogue of the Coins in the Punjab Museum, Lahore*, Vol. II, 1914, p. 39 and note 1; C.J. Brown, *Catalogue of the Coins in the Provincial Museum, Lucknow: Coins of the Mughal Emperors*, Vol. II, 1920, pp. 32-33, Nos. 362-65.

2. See, e.g., Brown, *op. cit.*, Vol. I, p. 18; also Vost, *loc. cit.*

3. See *Numismatic Supplement*, No. XXXIV, pp. 199-212, in *JPASB*, 1920.

the Portuguese sometimes considered Bengala to be a misnomer and had no memory of it after the collapse of the Portuguese in Bengal, that the Bengal records and traditions do not speak of any city called Vaṅgāla in South-East Bengal during the late medieval period, and that the Bengala of the Portuguese must have been known to the Bengalis by a different name. I therefore concluded that the Portuguese originally applied the name Bengala to the chief city of the Vaṅgāla country, which lay then in the Dacca region, and that after the Portuguese port in the Chittagong area had become a flourishing centre of trade in Bengal, they began to call it the city of Bengala. I further observed that this was possibly done when Sonārgāon near Dacca passed out of the picture due to the transference of the provincial capital first to Rajmahal and then to Dacca.[1]

Recently Whitehead opened up the question in a very small note appearing in the *Journal of the Numismatic Society of India*, Vol. XVIII, 1956, pp. 213-14. He quoted the views both of Tome Pires who wrote in 1515 A.D. that the principal port of Bengal was the city of Bengala, another port being Satgāon on the Orissa side, and also of Hosten who observed that the European travellers applied the name Bengala to a variety of places, usually what was, or what they thought was, the chief port at the time. But Whitehead came to the conclusion that Akbar's mint of Bangāla and the city of Bengala of the medieval Europeans are both identical with Satgāon. He did not discuss the difficult problem of identification, roughly indicated above, apparently because be thought that an Akbarī Rupee in the British Museum 'puts an end to the controversy'. However, I find it difficult to agree with him in the evaluation of the new evidence.

Whitehead quoted the legend on the British Museum Rupee as follows :

khallada Allāhu mulkahu
Akbar Shāh shud.........6
Kābrūsh zarb
Bangālah za ān dil-khwāh
zarb Bandar Satgānū.

1. See Sircar, *Stud. Geog. Anc. Med. Ind.*, pp. 129-30; cf. *Bhār. Vid.*, Vol. V, 1944, pp. 34 ff.

It will be seen that, besides the damaged date of issue, the above legend contains the same *bait* with the omission of the word *sikkah* at the beginning and *shud* at the end, but with the addition of the two passages *khalada Allāhu mulkahu* (may God perpetuate his kingdom) and *zarb Bandar Satgānū* (struck at the port of Satgāon). This coin was no doubt issued from Akbar's mint at Satgāon. But, in my opinion, this hardly proves that Satgāon is identical with the Bangāla of the passage *sikkah-i-Bangālah* (the coin of Bangāla) or that all the Akbarī Rupees bearing the Bangāla couplet were minted at Satgāon. Considering the problems involved, there is little doubt that the *bait* mentions Bangāla in the sense of the Sūba of Bangāla, so that the legend on the British Museum Rupee in question merely means that the coin was minted at the port of Satgāon in the Sūba of Bangāla.

That the passage *sikkah-i-Bangālah* need not be interpreted as 'the coin struck at the Bangāla mint', but would also mean 'the coin struck in the land of Bangāla' is clearly suggested by the following *bait* in the legend on the Kashmīr coins of the Mughul emperor Jahāngīr (1605-27 A.D.), son and successor of Akbar :

jahān-fīrūz gasht ba Kashmīr ke zar
za nūr-i-nām Jahāngīr Shāh Shāh Akbar.
"The coin of Kashmīr became world-conquering
By the light of the name of Jahāngīr Shāh, [son of] Akbar Shāh."[1]

Some of Jahāngīr's Kashmīr coins contain the passage *zarb Kashmīr* (struck in Kashmīr).[2] But, as is well known, Kashmīr was not the name of a city, but was really a Sarkār in the Sūba of Kābul and had its headquarters at the city of Shrīnagar.[3]

Thus Whitehead's contention can only be proved if we get coins bearing the mint-name as *Bangālah Satgāon* (as in the

1. See, e.g., Brown, *op. cit.*, Vol. I, p. 25.
2. Cf., e.g., Wright, *op. cit.*, p. 80, No. 691.
3. See *'Ain-i-Akbarī*, trans. Jarrett and Sarkar, Vol. II, pp. 349 ff., 356.

case of *Akbarpūr Tāndah*)[1] or as *Bangālah 'urf Satgāon* (as in the case of *Kālpī 'urf Muḥammadābād*[2] and *Qanauj 'urf Shāhgarh*).[3]

1. Cf. Wright, *op. cit.*, p. 41, Nos. 365-66; Brown, *op. cit.*, Vol. II, pp. 23-24, No. 271-73.

2. Cf. Wright, *op. cit.*, p. 51, Nos. 455-57; Brown, *op. cit.*, p. 84, Nos. 1020-21.

3. Cf. Wright, *op. cit.*, p. 58, Nos. 514-16; Brown, *op. cit.*, p. 84, Nos. 1012-17.

INDEX

S

U

V

ADDENDA ET CORRIGENDA

Page 11, line 8.—*Add Note*—Coins travelled in the course of trade. Stray Kuṣāṇa coins have been found in Scandinavia and Wales while a hoard of them has been discovered at Dabra Dammo in Abyssinia. See *JRAS*, 1912, p. 672; *Convengo internazionale di studi Etiopici*, Rome, 1959, pp. 249ff.

„ 13, line 15.—*Read*—Vāsiṣṭhīputra

„ 14, line 31.—*Read*—Eucratides I

„ 16, line 21.—*Read*—Lakṣmī

„ „ line 26.—*Add Note*—Coins bearing the name Sāmantadeva were current over a long period and one such specimen was found in distant Poland. See *JRAS*, Vol. IX, 1848, p. 178.

„ 19, lines 5-6.—*Read*—A. H 418 (1027-28 A.D.) and 419 (1028-29 A.D.). Cf. *JNSI*, Vol. XVI, p. 113.

„ „ line 11.—*Add*—Certain gold coins (179 grains) of Mahmūd bear the legend saying, "This Dīnār [is struck] for the cities [subdued] during the holy war against Hind [in] A. H. 397 (1006-07 A.D.)." See *JNSI*, Vol. XVI, p. 123.

„ 21, line 19.—*Read*—Jājnagar

„ 24, line 28.—*Read*—Mughul

„ 28, line 21.—*Add*—A popular type adopted by Haidar 'Alī bears the representation of Śiva and Pārvatī.

„ 31, line 23.—*Read*—Cakram

„ „ line 32.—*Read*—round shape

„ 32, line 4.—*Read*—appeared

„ 47, line 21.—*Read*—youngsters

„ 53, line 9.—Read—*Ā-Mā*

„ 78, line 24.—Read—*tāmra-rūpa*

„ 81, line 23.—*Read*—Muṣṭis or handfuls according to Kullūka

„ 84, line 32.—*Read*—a man

„ 89, line 3.—*Read*—Suvarṇas

„ 97, line 25.—Read—*Porāṇakassa Kahāpaṇassa*

„ 107, note 3.—*Add*—For a silver coin of Vāsiṣṭhīputra Śātakarṇi, see K. Gopalachari's *Early History of the Andhra Country*, 1941, pp. 99 (note 32), 135 (note 45), Plate I (2).

Page 109, line 22.—Read—*Vāsiṣṭha* or *Vāsiṣṭhī*
,, 111, line, note 3, line 3.—*Read*—Tirunelveli
,, 116, line 15.—*Read*—Ptolemy's
,, 117, note 3, line 2.—Read—*Brāhmī*
,, 117, note 3, line 2.—Read—*Brāhmī*
,, 136, line 23.—*Read*—Cuṭuka-Cuṭukula
,, 144, line 3.—*Read*—Cuṭu
,, 151, line 1.—*Read*—Peṭlūripālem
,, 152, line 17.—*Read*—indicate ancient
,, 153, 155, 157, 169, 197, 201, top.—*Read*—Peṭlūripalem
,, 155, line 16.—Read—*Bhartṛpana*
,, 157, line 16.—*Read*—Rapson, *op. cit.*, p.
,, 165, line 25.—Read—*A. R. Ep.*, 1956-57, Plate
,, 171, lines 6-7 and 16.—Read—*Rudras*[*e*]*nasa*
,, 182, line 25.—Read—*Bha*[*rt*]*ṛ*
,, 183, lines 4-5.—Read—*Bha*[*rt*]*ṛ*......
,, 185, lines 30-31.—Read—*Bhart*[*ṛ*]*da*[*mna*]
,, 190, line 1.—Read—*Bhar*] *tṛ*-[*damnaḥ*]
,, 201, line 11.—Read—*Bhartṛpana*
,, 218, line 7.—*Read*—legends
,, 224, line 3.—*Read*—a newly
,, 227, line 27.—*Read*—Vidiśā
,, 230, line 8.—Read—*Sultāns of Dehlī*
,, 232, line 9.—Read—*Pracāriṇī*
,, 234, note 3.—Read—*Dehlī*
,, 236, top.—*Read*—Indian
,, ,, line 9.—*Read*—Cāhamāna
,, ,, line 20—*Read*—'Alāuddīn
,, ,, line 21.—*Read*—Pherū
,, 253, top.—*Read*—Rāma-ṭaṅkā
,, 256, line 11.—*Read*—Jagannātha
,, 266, note 1, line 3.—*Read*—Eggeling
,, 268, line 8.—*Read*—'Alāuddīn
,, 270, line 14.—Read—*Kṛtyamahārṇava*
,, 274, line 8.—*Read*—intrinsic values
,, 277, line 32.—*Read*—pure gold
,, 286, line 25.—*Read*—a virgin
,, 287, line 1.—Read—*Gaurī-varāṭikā-grahaṇa*
,, ,, line 2.—*Read*—virgin-money
,, 288, line 11.—*Read*—Vāsudeva-Jhā
,, ,, line 16.—*Read*—in the document
,, 300, line 8.—Read—*Līlāvatī*
,, 301, line 1.—*Read*—called Rūpaka

KEY TO PLATES

PLATE I

Purchase of the Jetavana Park.

Jetavana at Śrāvasti was purchased by the *Śreṣṭhin* Anāthapiṇḍika in order to dedicate it for the Buddha's use. The owner of the park was Prince Jeta who agreed to sell it on condition that its price should be the gold coins required to cover the entire ground. The scene, as depicted in a Barhut sculpture, exhibits a bullock cart which brought the coins to the park and two persons engaged in spreading them on the ground. The coins are rectangular in shape. Anāthapiṇḍika carries a waterpot for pouring water in the Buddha's hands, indicative of the ceremonial offering of a gift. There are two temples or cottages bearing the labels *Kosabakuṭi* (*Kauśāmbakuṭī*) and *Gadhakuṭi* (*Gandhakuṭī*) respectively. The whole scene bears the label—*Jetavana Anāthapeḍiko deti koṭi-saṁthatena ketā* (*Jetavanam=Anāthapiṇḍiko dadāti koṭi-samstṛtena krītvā*), "Anāthapiṇḍika dedicates the Jetavana, having purchased it with a layer of crores [of coins]." The sculpture belongs to c. 2nd century B. C.

Cf. N. G. Majumdar, *A Guide to the Sculptures in the Indian Museum*, X-b.

PLATE II

II/1-1 A. Bent-bar. Silver (100-Rati standard)—4.43 cm., 177.4 grains= 11.5 grammes.

Obverse and side view : two six-armed symbols each represented by a circular knob-like centre which has a handle and is surrounded by a circle having six tridents standing on it all around, with counter-marks in between.

Reverse : blank (not reproduced).

Cf. C. Valdettaro, *Cat.* (unpublished), No. 2. The symbols on the bent-bar coins were punched on semi-molten pieces of metal.

II/2-2 A. Bent-bar. Silver (100-Rati standard)—4.76 cm., 175 grains= 11.35 grammes.

Obverse and side view : two six-armed symbols, one on left and the other on right, resembling those on No. II/1 (but looking more like lotuses) with counter-marks in between.

Reverse : blank (not reproduced).

Cf. Valdettaro, *Cat.* (unpublished), No. 1.

II/3. Single Type (from North India). Silver (16-Rati ½-Kārṣāpaṇa)— oblong; .5×.2 inch, .25.5 grains.

Obverse : symbol represented by an oblong knob-like centre with a leaf issuing from the upper right and left and lower right and left corners and with taurus on the right and left between two of the leaves.

Reverse : blank (not reproduced).

Cf. J. Allan, *BMC* (AI). I.9. The symbols on the single-type coins were punched on semi-molten pieces of metal.

II/4. Single Type (from North India). Silver (16-Rati ½-Kārṣāpaṇa)— oblong, .35 inch, 25.5 grains.

Obverse : symbol represented by a crossed circle at the centre, which has five leaves and a handle around.

Reverse : blank (not reproduced).

Cf. Allan, *BMC* (AI). I.6. See No. II/7 below.

II/5. Single Type (from North India). Silver (16-Rati ½-Kārṣāpaṇa)—oblong, .35 inch, 25.5 grains.

Obverse : symbol represented by circular knob-like centre with mushroom-like signs (tree or umbrella) standing onits four sides, a circular knob mark standing between any two of them.

Reverse : blank (not reproduced).

Allan, *BMC* (AI).I.8.

II/6. Single Type (from 'North-West India'). Silver (100-Rati standard)—oblong, .95×.6 inch, 173.6 grains.

Obverse : two overlapping six-armed symbols each represented by a circular knob-like centre which has a handle and is surrounded by a circle having six tridents standing on it all around.

Reverse : blank (not reproduced).

Cf. Allan, *BMC* (AI). I.1 (reduced).

II/7. Single Type (from 'North-West India'). Silver (12-Rati standard)—round—.45 inch, 19.6 grains.

Obverse : six-armed symbol represented by a crossed circle at the centre which is surrounded by six circular leaves standing on it.

Reverse : blank (not reproduced).

Cf. Allan, *BCM* (AI). I.5. See No. II/4 above.

II/8. Single Type. Sultanpur (South-West India—near Wai, Satara District, Maharashtra). Silver (64-Rati Double-Kārṣāpaṇa)—round, .85 inch, 98.3 grains.

Obverse :. symbol repesented by a circle with knob-like centre, with two wing-like projections above.

Reverse : blank (not reproduced).

Cf. Allan, *BMC* (AI). I.16.

II/9. Single Type. Silver (thick—24-Rati ¾-Kārṣāpaṇa)—1.32 cm, 45 grains=2.9 grammes.

Obverse : one big symbol similar to those on No. II/10.

Reverse : blank (not reproduced).

Cf. Valdettaro, *Cat.* (unpublished), No. 51. See No. II/13 below.

II/10. Saucer-shaped. Silver (32+16=48-Rati 1½-Kārṣāpaṇa)—oval, 2.96×2.46 cm, 4.95 grammes.

Obverse : two bigger symbols with two smaller lotus-like symbols, with minute counter-marks.

Reverse : blank (not reproduced).

Cf. Valdettaro, *Cat.* (unpublished), No. 38. The symbols on the saucer-shaped coins were punched on semi-molten pieces of metal.

II/11. Saucer-shaped. Silver (8-Rati ¼-Kārṣāpaṇa)—oval, 2.22×1.39 cm, .9 gramme.

Obverse : two bigger symbols like those on No. II/10.

Reverse : blank (not reproduced).

Cf. Valdettaro, *Cat.* (unpublished), No. 42.

II/12. Saucer-shaped. Silver (4-Rati ⅛-Kārṣāpaṇa)—round, 1.5 cm, 7.2 grains=.47 grammes.

Obverse : one big symbol as on No. II/10.

Reverse : blank (not reproduced).

Cf. Valdettaro, *Cat.* (unpublished), No. 48.

II/13. Punch-marked. Silver (32-Rati Kārṣāpaṇa).

Obverse : five different symbols, one of them being a partially preserved sun.

Reverse : not reproduced.

Cf. Whitehead, *The Pre-Mohammedan Coinage of Northwestern India*, X.2. The symbols on the 'punch-marked' coins were punched separately on hard metal strips.

II/14. Punch-marked. Silver (32-Rati Kārṣāpaṇa).

Obverse : Several symbols—three-peaked hill surrounded by crescent, wheel, 'Ujjayinī symbol', etc.

Reverse : symbol looking like three signs for Brāhmī '80' put together one above the other; often described as the caduceus.

Cf. Whitehead, *The Pre-Mohammedan Coinage of Northwestern India*, X.1.

II/15. Punch-marked. Silver (32-Rati Kārṣāpaṇa)—round, about 50 grains.

Obverse : figure of an animal, solar symbol, etc.

Reverse : three symbols.

Cf. Brown, *CI*. I. 1.

II/16. Single type. Silver (thick—32-Rati Kārṣāpaṇa)—oval, 1.32 × 1.12 cm, 48 grains=3.1 grammes.

Obverse : one big symbol slightly different from those on No. II/10.

Reverse : blank (not reproduced).

Cf. Valdettaro, *Cat.* (unpublished), No. 52. It should have properly been put along with Nos. II/3-9.

II/17-17A. Cast. Copper (pair showing join)—1×.5 inch, 71 grains.

Obverse (in both) : three-peaked hill with crescent above.

Reverse (in both) : elephant to left.

Cf. Allan, *BMC* (AI). XII.1.

II/18. Almora. Śivapālita. Silver (base—160-Rati ½ Śatamāna)—round, 1 inch, 281 grains.

Obverse : crude human figure (Śiva) in centre; bull before tree in railing; Brāhmī legend (c. 2nd century A.D.)—*Sivapālita*[*sa*],' [Coin] of Śivapālita.'

Reverse : altar bearing ornate *nandipada*, surmounted by triangle-headed post (banner ?) and flanked by two palm trees on either side.

Cf. Allan, *BMC* (AI). XIV.8.

II/19. Audumbara. Dharaghoṣa. Silver (20-Rati ½-Śāna or Dramma)—round .7 inch, 37.5 grains.

Obverse : Viśvāmitra standing, facing, with right hand raised; traces of deer-skin on left arm; Kharoṣṭhī legend—*Viśpamitra* (in front), *Mahadevasa, raña Dharaghoṣasa* (around) and *Odubarisa* (below), 'Viśvāmitra. [Coin] of Mahādeva. [Coin] of king Dharaghoṣa, the Audumbari.'

Reverse : trident with axe on right; tree in enclosure on left; Brāhmī legend (c. 3rd century A.D.)—*Mahādevasa, rāño Dharaghoṣasa* (around) and *Odubarisa* (below).

Cf. Allan, *BMC* (AI). XIV. 14. The coin was issued by Audumbari Dharaghoṣa, claiming descent from Viśvāmitra, in the name of the god Mahādeva (Śiva).

II/20. Ayodhyā. Cast. Copper (20-Rati ¼-Paṇa)—round, .5 inch, 34 grains.

Obverse : four crescents joined to four sides of a central knob.

Reverse : *svastika*.

Cf. Allan, *BMC* (AI). XVI. 7.

II/21. Ayodhyā. Cast. Copper (20-Rati $\frac{1}{4}$-Paṇa)—round, .5 inch, 26.8 grains.

Obverse : *svastika* above fish to left.

Reverse : taurus above battle-axe.

Cf. Allan, *BMC* (AI). XVI. 10.

II/22. Ayodhyā. Āryamitra. Copper (60-Rati $\frac{3}{4}$-Paṇa)—round, .65 inch, 105 grains.

Obverse : humped bull to left before spear or post; Brāhmī legend (c. 2nd century A.D.) below—*Ayyamitasa*, "[Coin] of Āryamitra."

Reverse : cock to right on left and palmyra tree on right.

Cf. Allan, *BMC* (AI). XVII. 18.

II/23. Ayodhyā. Dhanadeva. Copper (60-Rati $\frac{3}{4}$-Paṇa)—square, .75 inch, 103 grains.

Obverse : bull to left, with fodder-tub in front; Brāhmī legend (c. 1st century A.D.) above—*Dhanadevasa*, "[Coin] of Dhanadeva."

Reverse : six symbols—(1) *svastika*, (2) 'Ujjayinī symbol', (3) *triratna*, (4) post in railing, with fruit-like objects hanging from its bent top, and (5) snake or river.

Cf. Allan, *BMC* (AI). XVII. 1.

PLATE III

III/1. Ayodhyā. Kumudasena. Copper (80-Rati Paṇa)—round, .85 inch, 120 grains.

Obverse : humped bull standing to left between standard in railing in front and uncertain object behind; Brāhmī legend (c. 2nd century A.D.) below—*rājña Kumudasenasa*, "[Coin] of the king Kumudasena."

Reverse : *triratna* in square.

Cf. Allan, *BMC* (AI). XVIII. 10.

III/2. Eran (Saugor District, M.P.). Copper (40-Rati $\frac{1}{2}$-Paṇa)—square, .65 inch, 73 grains.

Obverse : five symbols—(1) six-marks (alternate taurus and umbrella or tree), (2) eight-petalled lotus, (3) tree in railing, (4) triangle-headed post (banner ?) between two small trees in the same railing, and (5) alternate taurus and *svastika* in river.

Reverse : blank (not reproduced).

Cf. Allan, *BMC* (AI). XVIII. 10.

III/3. Eran. Copper (60-Rati $\frac{3}{4}$-Paṇa)—square, .85 inch, 98 grains.

Obverse : four symbols—(1) 'Ujjayinī symbol' with circle inside each of the four orbs, (2) elephant, (3) horse and (4) alternate *svastika* and taurus in bed of river.

Reverse : blank (not reproduced).

Cf. Allan, *BMC* (AI). XVIII. 7.

III/4. Eran. Copper (120-Rati standard)—square, 1.1 inch, 192 grains.

Obverse : five symbols—(1) 'Ujjayinī symbol' as on No. III/3 above, (2) elephant, (3) horse, (4) tree in railing, and (5) triangle-headed post (banner ?) between trees in the same railing.

Reverse : blank (not reproduced).

Cf. Allan, *BMC* (AI). XVIII. 11.

III/5. Eran. Dharmapāla. Copper (100-Rati standard)—square. .95 inch, 179 grains.

Obverse : negative Brāhmī legend (c. 2nd century B.C.) to be read from right to left due to defect in the die—*Dhamapālasa*, '[Coin] of Dharmapāla.'
Reverse : blank (not reproduced).
Cf. Allan, *BMC* (AI). XVIII. 6.

III/6. Cast. Kāḍa. Copper—round, .9 or 9.5 inch.
Obverse : below snake or river, Brāhmī legend (c. 2nd century B.C.) —*Kāḍasa*. "[Coin] of Kāḍa."
Reverse : similar as the obverse (not reproduced).
Cf. Rapson, *IC*. III. 7.

III/7. Kanauj. Viṣṇudeva. Copper (40-Rati ½-Paṇa)—round, .8 inch, 65 grains.
Obverse : three symbols—(1) tree in railing, (2) hare on ornate crescent, and (3) symbol surmounted by umbrella or tree; Brāhmī legend (c. 1st century A.D.) below—*Viṣṇudevasa*, "[Coin] of Viṣṇudeva."
Reverse : horse to left before *yūpa* (?).
Cf. Allan, *BMC* (AI). XIX. 13.

III/8. Kauśāmbī. Cast. Copper (80-Rati Paṇa)—circular, 1 inch, 152.5 grains.
Obverse : leafy tree in three-barred railing ; six-peaked hill below; *triratna* above wheel on left; 'Ujjayinī symbol' above *svastika* on right.
Reverse : humped bull to left, facing triangle-headed post (banner ?); above—four crescents in four directions with a globular knob at the centre.
Cf. Allan, *BMC* (AI). XX. 14.

III/9. Kauśāmbī. Bṛhaspatimitra (II). Copper (60-Rati ¾-Paṇa)—round, .75 inch. 98 grains.
Obverse : tree in railing in centre; *triratna* with triangle-headed post on platform on left and river or snake on right; Brāhmī legend (c. 1st century A.D.) below—*Bahasatimitasa*, "[Coin] of Bṛhaspatimitra."
Reverse : bull to right before three-peaked hill above enclosure, surmounted by *triratna*; 'Ujjayinī symbol' above.
Cf. Allan, *BMC* (AI). XX. 2.

III/10. Kauśāmbī. Dhanadeva. Copper (40-Rati ½-Paṇa)—round, .8 inch, 60 grains.
Obverse : in square—tree in enclosure between unidentified objects; Brāhmī legend (c. 2nd century A.D.) below—*Dhanadevasya*, "[Coin] of Dhanadeva;" below—river-bed (?).
Reverse : humped bull moving to left, with three-peaked hill symbol on left and trident in background.
Cf. Allan, *BMC* (AI). XX. 12.

III/11. Kulūta. Vīrayaśas. Silver (40-Rati Śāna or Double-Dramma)—round, .75 inch, 75.7 grains.
Obverse : wheel surrounded by circle of dots; Brāhmī legend (c. 3rd century A.D.) around—*Rājña Kulūtasya Vīrayaśasya*, "[Coin] of the Kulūta king Vīrayaśas;" two other symbols—(1) triangle-headed post, and (2) *triratna*.
Reverse : four symbols—(1) *svastika*, (2) *triratna*, (3) *śrīvatsa* or Liṅga with serpent on either side; Kharoṣṭhī legend—*raña*, the two letters being written on right and left respectively of ten-peaked hill standing on river and surmounted by tree.
Cf. Allan, *BMC* (AI). XVI. 4.

III/12. Kuṇinda. Amoghabhūti. Silver (20-Rati ½-Śāna or Dramma) —round, .8 inch, 34.6 grains.
Obverse : Deer to right; Lakṣmī standing on lotus, facing, holding flower in uplifted right hand; tree or umbrella in railing above the back of

deer; double-serpent above head of deer; three-peaked hill surmounted by crescent below deer; Brāhmī legend (c. 3rd century A.D.) —*Rājña Kuṇidasa Amoghabhūtisa Mahārājasa* ([Coin] of the Kuṇinda king *Mahārāja* Amoghabhūti), followed by circle of small horizontal strokes around a central dot.

Reverse : five symbols—(1) *svastika*, (2) *triratna*, (3) six-peaked hill surmounted by tree or umbrella, (4) tree in railing, (5) river or snake, and (6) triangle-headed post in railing ; Kharoṣṭhī legend—*Raña Kuṇidasa Amoghabhutisa* (around) and *Maharajasa* (below).

Cf. Allan, *BMC* (AI). XXII. 5.

III/13. Kuṇinda. Amoghabhūti. Copper (32-Rati Kārṣāpaṇa)—round, .85 inch, 58 grains.

Obverse : same as the obverse of No. III/12 above.

Reverse : same as the reverse of No. III/12 above; but border of dots, and Kharoṣṭhī legend omitted.

Cf. Allan, *BMC* (AI). XXIII. 1.

III/14. Mālava. Copper (8-Rati $\frac{1}{10}$-Paṇa)—round, .55 inch, 14 grains.

Obverse : Brāhmī legend (c. 1st century A.D.) in two lines—(1) *jaya* (2) *Mālivānāṃ*, "Victory of the Mālavas."

Reverse : corroded (not reproduced).

Cf. Smith, *IMC*. XX. 13.

III/15. Mālava. Copper (thick—20-Rati $\frac{1}{4}$-Paṇa)—.52 inch, 31.4 grains.

Obverse : Brāhmī legend (c. 1st century A.D.)—*jaya* in bold characters on blank surface.

Reverse : corroded (not reproduced).

Cf. Smith, *IMC*, XX. 14.

III/16. Mālava. Copper (4-Rati $\frac{1}{20}$-Paṇa)—rectangular, .35×3 inch, 7.3 grains.

Obverse : Brāhmī legend (c. 2nd century A.D.) in two lines—(1) *Malava-*(2) *na jaya*, "Victory to the Mālavas.'

Reverse : vase in dotted border.

Cf. Smith, *IMC*. XX. 15.

III/17. Mālava. Copper (4-Rati $\frac{1}{20}$-Paṇa)—rectangular, .32 inch, 6 grains.

Obverse : tree or palm branch; tree in railing; Brāhmī legend (c. 1st century A.D.)—*Malavā-*(on right), *ṇa jaya* (on left).

Reverse : lion to right.

Cf. Smith, *IMC*. XX. 16.

III/18. Mālava (imitation). Copper (5-Rati Māṣa)—rectangular, .37×.3 inch, 8.5 grains.

Obverse : Brāhmī legend (c. 4th century A.D.) in two lines —(1) *Malava-* (2) *hṇa jaya* (Victory to the Mālavas); no device.

Reverse : humped bull walking to left.

Cf. Smith, *IMC*. XX. 17. Imitation coins Nos. III/18 and IV/2 and 4-6 appear to have been issued by private agencies on the subjugation of the Mālavas by Samudragupta (c. 335-76 A.D.).

PLATE IV

IV/1. Mālava. Copper (5-Rati Māṣa)—circular, .43 inch, 9 grains.

Obverse : surface divided into upper and lower by trident; Brāhmī legend (c. 2nd century A.D.)—*Mālava-* (above) and *ṇa jaya* (below), "Victory to the Mālavas."

Reverse : recumbent bull to right.

Cf. Smith, *IMC.* XX. 19.

IV/2. Mālava (imitation). Copper (4-Rati $\frac{1}{20}$ Paṇa)—circular, .4 inch, 7 grains.

Obverse : similar to the obverse of No. IV/1, but Brāhmī legend (c. 4th century A.D.) is reversed and has to be read from right to left.

Reverse : as the reverse of No. IV/1 (not reproduced).

Cf. Smith, *IMC.* XX. 20.

IV/3. Mālava. Copper (5-Rati Māṣa)— circular, .4 inch, 8 grains.

Obverse : uncertain device in centre; marginal Brāhmī legend (c. 3rd century A.D.)—*Mālavagaṇa...*, "...the Mālava Republic."

Reverse : human head crudely represented.

Cf. Smith, *IMC.* XX. 21.

IV/4. Mālava (imitation). Copper (4-Rati $\frac{1}{20}$-Paṇa)—circular, .38 inch, 6.3 grains.

Obverse : crude device; reversed Brāhmī legend (c. 4th century A.D.) to be read from right to left—*[Mā] lava-ga...*

Reverse : peacock with expanded tail (not reproduced).

Cf. Smith, *IMC.* XX. 23.

IV/5. Mālava (imitation). Copper (8-Rati $\frac{1}{10}$-Paṇa)—square, .4 inch, 15 grains.

Obverse : tree in railing; marginal Brāhmī legend (c. 4th century A.D.)—*bhapaṁyana.*

Reverse : lion or tiger to left.

Cf. Smith, *IMC.* XX. 24.

IV/6. Mālava (imitation). Copper (4-Rati $\frac{1}{20}$ Paṇa)—rectangular, 35·×.3 inch, 5.2 grains.

Obverse : in incuse—Brāhmī legend (c. 4th century A.D.)—*magojava.*

Reverse : lion sitting to right.

Cf. Smith, *IMC.* XXI. 3.

IV/7. Mālava (imitation). Copper (5-Rati Māṣa)—squarish, .42 inch, 9.8 grains.

Obverse : tree in railing; on right—vertical Brāhmī legend (c. 1st century B.C.)—*ya ma.*

Reverse : probably circle in centre surrounded by several circles.

Cf. Smith, *IMC.* XX. 25. The fabricators of the coin appear to have used the Brāhmī characters of an earlier period.

IV/8. Mathurā. Gomitra. Copper (60-Rati $\frac{3}{4}$-Paṇa)—round, .8 inch, 110.5 grains.

Obverse : standing Lakṣmī, facing, holding lotus in up-lifted right hand; conventional tree on left, 'Ujjayinī symbol' and a variant of 'Liṅga with a serpent on either side' (as on the Pañcāla coinage) on right, river bed with fishes below; Brāhmī legend (c. 1st century B.C.)—*Gomitasa.* "[Coin] of Gomitra."

Reverse : three elephants with riders holding goads, the central animal facing and the other two respectively to left and right.

Cf. Allan, *BMC* (AI). XXV. 5-6.

IV/9. Mathurā. Sūryamitra. Copper (60-Rati $\frac{3}{4}$-Paṇa)—round, .8 inch, 106 grains.

Obverse : Lakṣmī standing facing between conventional tree on left and 'Ujjayinī symbol' and variant of 'Liṅga with a serpent on either side' on right; Brāhmī legend (c. 1st century B.C.)—[*Sū*]*yamitasa*, "[Coin] of Sūryamitra."

Reverse : three elephants with riders holding goads; the central animal facing and the other two respectively to right and left.

Cf. Allan, *BMC* (AI). XXV. 17.

IV/10. Nāga. Gaṇapati (Gaṇendra). Copper—circular.

Obverse : Brāhmī legend (c. 4th century A.D.) from about X—*śrī-Gaṇapati*[*nāga*].

Reverse : humped bull to left.

Cf. Rapson, *IC*. V. 2.

IV/11. Nāga. Gaṇendra (Gaṇapati). Copper (8-Rati $\frac{1}{10}$-Paṇa)—circular, .35 inch, 12 grains.

Obverse : Brāhmī legend (c. 4th century A.D.) from about XII—*Mahārāja-śrī-Gaṇendra*, "the illustrious *Mahārāja* Gaṇendra."

Reverse : in dotted circle—recumbent bull.

Cf. Smith, *IMC*. XXI. 10.

IV/12. Pāñcāla. Bhūmimitra. Copper (40-Rati $\frac{1}{2}$-Paṇa)—round, .7 inch, 53 grains.

Obverse : above—the three Pāñcāla symbols—(1) tree in railing, (2) variant of Liṅga-flanked-by-snake, and (3) symbol looking like the Brāhmī character *mya*; Brāhmī legend (c. 2nd century A.D.)—*Bhūmimitasa*, "[Coin] of Bhūmimitra."

Reverse : Agni with flaming hair standing, facing, between two pillars in railing.

Cf. Allan, *BMC* (AI). XXVIII. 5. The figure of the goddess Earth (Bhūmi) was expected on the reverse of the coin. The figure of Agni occurs on the reverse of Pāñcāla Agnimitra's coins.

IV/13. Pāñcāla. Phalgunīmitra. Copper (160-Rati Double-Paṇa)—round, 1 inch, 267 grains.

Obverse : the three Pāñcāla symbols as on No. IV/12 above; Brāhmī legend (c. 2nd century A.D.)—*Phagunimitasa*, "[Coin] of Phalgunīmitra."

Reverse : Lakṣmī (or Phalgunī) standing, facing, on lotus, holding uncertain object in raised right hand; another variant of the Liṅga-flanked-by-serpents on left; headdress-like symbol above the head of the deity.

Cf. Allan, *BMC* (AI). XXVII. 11.

IV/14. Taxila. Copper (single-die issue—80-Rati Paṇa)—square, .8 inch, 126 grains.

Obverse : in incuse—pile of balls arranged in the shape of a pyramid on left; three-peaked hill surmounted by crescent on right; below—snake or river with vine branches with grapes at the bottom.

Reverse : blank (not reproduced).

Cf. Allan, *BMC* (AI). XXXII. 9.

IV/15. Taxila. Copper (60-Rati $\frac{3}{4}$-Paṇa)—square, .9 inch, 107 grains.

Obverse : Brāhmī legend (c. 2nd century B.C.)—(1) *I* (2) *Negamā*, "1; the guild of merchants."

Reverse : Kharoṣṭhī legend—*Dojaka*, "[the township of] Dojaka"; below—axe or steelyard.

Cf. Allan, *BMC* (AI). XXXI. 2.

IV/16. Taxila. Copper (double-die—100-Rati standard)—about 180 grains.

Obverse : elephant moving to right, with three-peaked hill above back.

Reverse : in incuse—lion standing to left, with *svastika* above back and three-peaked hill surmounted by crescent in front.

Cf. Whitehead, *The Pre-Mohammedan Coinage of Northwestern India*, X. 2; see also Brown, *CI.* I. 5; Rapson, *IC.* I. 18.

IV/17. Vaimaki. Rudravarman. Copper—round, .7 inch.
Obverse : bull to right, lotus in front; Kharoṣṭhī legend—*Raña Vamakisa Rudravarmasa vijayata*, "[Coin] of the Vaimaki king Rudravarman, the Victorious."
Reverse : elephant to right; trident with axe on left; Brāhmī legend (c. 2nd century A.D.)—*rajña Vamakisa Rudravarmasa vijayato.*
Cf. Allan, *BMC* (AI). XIV. 13.

IV/18. Vaṭāśvaka. Copper (80-Rati Paṇa)—round, .9 inch, 144 grains.
Obverse : three-peaked hill surmounted by crescent above balls arranged in the shape of a pyramid; on right—human figure in *udicyaveśa* to left, with folded hands, standing on Brāhmī symbol for '10'; Brāhmī legend (c. 2nd century B.C.) below—*Vaṭasvaka*, "[the guild of the township of] Vaṭāśvaka" or "[the person or people called] Vaṭāśvaka."
Reverse : blank (not reproduced).
Cf. Allan, *BMC* (AI). XXXIX. 2.

IV/19. Vṛṣṇi. Jñāgaṇa. Silver (20-Rati ½-Śāna or Dramma)—round, .6 inch, 32 grains.
Obverse : post in railing, surmounted by *triratna*; with animal (half-lion and half-elephant) in front; Brāhmī legend (c. 3rd century A.D.) above—*Vṛṣṇirāja-Jñāgaṇasya tratarasya*, "[Coin] of the Vṛṣṇi king Jñāgaṇa, the Saviour."
Reverse : ornate wheel; Kharoṣṭhī legend around—*Vriṣṇirāja-Jñāgaṇasya tratarasya.*
Cf. Allan, *BMC* (AI). XVI. 5.

IV/20. Yaudheya. Copper (100-Rati standard)—.94 inch, 165.8 grains.
Obverse : Kārttikeya standing with spear in right hand; peacock to left at his left foot; Brāhmī legend (c. 3rd century A.D.)—*Yaudheya-gaṇasya jayaḥ dvi*, "Victory to the Yaudheya Republic. Two."
Reverse : wife of Kārttikeya walking to left, with right hand raised and left hand on hip; flower-vase on left and inverted *triratna* on right; border of dots.
Cf. Brown, *CI.* IV. 11; see Smith, *IMC.* XXI. 19. The meaning of the word *dvi* in the obverse legend is doubtful.

PLATE V

V/1. Yaudheya : God Brahmaṇyadeva. Copper (100-Rati standard)—round, 1 inch, 165.7 grains.
Obverse : Six-headed Brahmaṇyadeva (Kārttikeya), standing on lotus, facing, with left hand on hip and right hand raised towards barbed spear; Brāhmī legend (c. 3rd century A.D.)—*Bha[gavato] Brahmaṇyadevasya*, "[Coin] of Lord Brahmaṇyadeva."
Reverse : six-headed goddess (Kārttikeya's wife) standing on lotus, facing tree in railing on right; six-peaked hill surmounted by tree or umbrella, and *nandipada* on left.
Cf. Smith, *IMC.* XXI. 15.

V/2. Yaudheya : God Brahmaṇya. Silver (16-Rati ½-Kārṣāpaṇa)—round, .7 inch, 26 grains.
Obverse : Six-headed Kārttikeya, standing, facing, holding spear in right hand and with left hand on hip; Brāhmī legend (c. 3rd century A.D.)—*Bhagavato Svāmino Brahmaṇyasya, Yaudheyānām*, "[Coin] of the Divine Lord Brahmaṇya. [Coin] of the Yaudheyas."

Reverse : wife of Kārttikeya standing, facing, on lotus; *triratna* and six-peaked hill surmounted by tree or umbrella on left; tree in railing on right; snake or river below.

Cf. Allan, *BMC* (AI). XXXIX. 21.

V/3. Śātavāhana. Gautamīputra Śātakarṇi (c. 106-30 A.D.). Potin—.7 inch, 121.6 grains.

Obverse : elephant standing to right, with trunk upraised; above—conch-shell (?) and a variant of 'the Ujjayinī symbol'; traces of legend—[*raña siri-Sātakaṇisa* (?)].

Reverse : tree (with large leaves) in railing divided into lozenge-shaped sections with a dot in each of them.

Cf. Rapson, *BMC.* IV. 59.

V/4. Śātavāhana. Vāsiṣṭhīputra Puḷumāvi (c. 130-59 A.D.). Gudivada (Krishna District, A. P.). Lead—round, .7 inch, 85 grains.

Obverse : three-peaked hill above snake or river; Brāhmī legend around —*raño Vāsiṭhiputasa siri-Puḷumāvisa,* "[Coin] of the illustrious king Vāsiṣṭhīputra Puḷumāvi."

Reverse : 'Ujjayinī symbol', each of its orbs made of a pellet surrounded by two circles.

Cf. Rapson, *BMC.* V. 89.

V/5. Śātavāhana. Vāsiṣṭhīputra Śātakarṇi (c. 159-66 A.D.). Silver (20-Rati standard)—circular, .6 inch, 28 grains.

Obverse : head of king to right with hair tied with ribbon, and crest-jewel above forehead; Brāhmī legend—*raño Vāsiṭhiputasa* (XII-IV) *siri-Sātakaṇisa* (VIII-XII), "[Coin] of the illustrious king Vāsiṣṭhīputra Śātakarṇi."

Reverse : symbols as on the reverse of No. V/6 below ; legend in Drāviḍī Brāhmī—*arahaṇaṣa Vahaṭṭi-mākanaṣa tiru-Hātakaṇiṣa* which is the translation of the obverse legend in Drāviḍī Prakrit.

Cf. *Ep. Ind.*, XXXV. Plate facing p. 251. The reading of *ṣ* and *h* seems to be supported by the Bhattiprolu and Nanaghat (cf. *Hakusiri*) inscriptions.

V/6. Śātavāhana. Gautamīputra Yajña-Śātakarṇi(c. 174-202 A.D.). Sopara (Thana District, Maharashtra). Silver (20-Rati standard)—round, .6 inch, 34 grains.

Obverse : head of king to right; Brāhmī legend—*raño Gotamaputasa siri-Yaña-Sātakaṇisa,*"[Coin] of the illustrious king Gautamīputra Yajña-Śātakarṇi."

Reverse : 'Ujjayinī symbol' on left and six-peaked hill on right, both surmounted by crescent; legend in Drāviḍī Brāhmī below weavy line (river or snake)—*arahaṇaṣa Gotamaputaṣa hiru-Yaña-Hātakaṇiṣa* which is the translation of the obverse legend in Drāviḍī Prakrit.

Cf. Rapson, *BMC.* VII. E1. Cf. No. V/5 above.

V/7. Rudra. Lead—.6 inch, 53 grains.

Obverse : elephant with upraised trunk, standing to right; legend (IX)—*siri-Ruda...*, 'the illustrious Rudra...."

Reverse : 'Ujjayinī symbol' with orbs made by pellets surrounded by circle (not reproduced).

Cf. Rapson, *BMC.* VII. G. P. 2. This coin, assigned by Rapson to a Śātavāhana king named Rudra-Śātakarṇi, may have been issued by the Ikṣvāku king Rudrapuruṣadatta (4th century A.D.) of Vijayapurī in the Nagarjunikonda Valley. See *A. R. Ep.*, 1957-58, p.11; 1959-60, p. 30.; also Sircar, 'Coins of the Ikṣvākus' in *Buddha Jayanti Souvenir*, Jaggayyapeta, ed. P. Srinivasachary,1956, pp. 94ff.

V/8. Vīra. Chittala (Yernagudem Taluk [?], Godavari District, A. P.). Lead—round, 1.55 inch, 559.5 grains.

Obverse : lion standing to left; Brāhmī legend (c. 3rd century A.D.)

above—*Varasa raño,* "[Coin] of king Vīra."

Reverse : blank (not reproduced).

Cf. Rapson, *BMC.* I. 4E. The coin does not appear to be assignable to the Ikṣvāku king Vīrapuruṣadatta of Vijayapurī in the Nagarjunikonda valley.

V/9. Kura. Vāsiṣṭhīputra Viḷivāyakura. Kolhapur (?). Potin—.8 inch, 59.2 grains.

Obverse : bow with string downwards, fitted with arrow pointing upwards; dot in the left field; Brāhmī legend (c. 2nd century A.D.)—*raño Vāsiṭhīputasa Viḷivāyakurasa,* "[Coin] of king Vāsiṣṭhīputra Viḷivāyakura."

Reverse : six-peaked hill with tree above and ornate railing or river below; *nandipada* on left and triangle-headed post (banner ?) on right.

Cf. Rapson, *BMC.* II. 17.

V/10. Kura. Māṭharīputra Śivalakura (restruck coin of Vāsiṣṭhīputra Viḷivāyakura). Kolhapur (?). Lead—1.25 inches, 254.9 grains.

Obverse : Brāhmī legend (c. 2nd century A.D.) around bow—*raño Maḍharīputasa Sivalakurasa* on the original ...*putasa Viḷi......*

Reverse : six-peaked hill surmounted by crescent, with river-bed below and tree on right—type struck obliquely over the type of hill with a dot on the body of each peak.

Cf. Rapson, *BMC.* II. 29.

V/11. Kura. Gautamīputra Viḷivāyakura. Kolhapur (Maharashtra). Lead—round, 1.2 inches, 180.2 grains.

Obverse : bow with string downwards and arrow pointing upwards; Brāhmī legend (c. 2nd century A.D.)—*raño Gotamīputasa Viḷivāyakurasa.* "[Coin] of king Gautamīputra Viḷivāyakura."

Reverse : ten-peaked hill with river below and crescent above; tree on right.

Cf. Rapson, *BMC.* III. G. P. 4.

V/12. Ānanda. Cuṭukaḍānanda. Karwar (North Kanara District, Mysore). Lead—1.15 inch, 210.4 grains.

Obverse : eight-peaked hill above horizontal line (river ?); Brāhmī legend (c. 3rd century A.D.)—*raño Cuṭukaḍānaṁdasa,* "[Coin] of king Cuṭukaḍānanda."

Reverse : tree in railing; *nandipada* above *svastika* on left; triangle-headed post (banner ?) below a variant of Liṅga-flanked-by-serpents on right.

Cf. Rapson, *BMC.* VIII. G. P. 2.

PLATE VI

VI/1. Ānanda. Muḍānanda. Karwar (North Kanara District, Mysore). Lead—1.05 inches, 250 grains.

Obverse : eight-peaked hill above horizontal line (river ?); Brāhmī legend (c. 3rd century A.D.)—*raño Muḍānaṁdasa,* "[Coin] of king Muḍānanda."

Reverse : tree in railing with a variant of *triratna* on left and a variant of 'Liṅga flanked by serpents' above triangle-headed post (banner?) on right.

Cf. Rapson, *BMC.* VIII. G. P. 4.

VI/2. Sagama. *Mahāsenāpati* Cuṭukula. Kondapur (Medak District, A. P.). Lead—circular, 1.8 inches, 458 grains.

Obverse : around *svastika,* Brāhmī legend (c. 3rd century A.D.)—*Mahasenapatasa [Bharada]japata[sa] Sagamāna Cuṭakulasa,* "[Coin] of *Mahāsenāpati* Bhāradvājīputra Cuṭukula of the Sagama dynasty."

Reverse : in pellet border— thunderbolt, and traces of arrow.

Cf. *Ep. Ind.*, XXXV. No. 6 of Plate facing p. 77.

VI/3. Persian Siglos. Silver—83.5 grains=5.41 grammes.
Obverse : Early Achaemenid king represented as an archer, half-kneeling to right; punch-mark, symbol like triskelis or Brāhmī '10' or *ma*.
Reverse : not reproduced.
Cf. Rapson, *IC.* I. 3.

VI/4. Persian Siglos. Silver—84.5 grains=5.47 grammes.
Obverse : not reproduced.
Reverse : incuse; counter-mark resembling Brāhmī *yo*.
Cf. Rapson, *IC.* I. 4.

VI/5. Persian Double Daric (struck in India). Gold—262.7 grains=17.02 grammes.
Obverse : Achaemenid king (probably Darius III Codomannus, 337-330 B.C.) represented as an archer, half-kneeling to right; Greek legend —=*sta* (behind) and *mna* (below), i. e. "2 Staters=1 Mina"; monogram combining the Greek letters *lambda* below and *phi* above (in front).
Reverse : irregular incuse, with conventional pattern formed by curved line in relief.
Cf. Rapson *IC.* I. 5.

VI/6. Yavana (Greek). Athenian coin (Indian imitation). Silver (Attic Tetradrachm)—257.8 grains=16.7 grammes.
Obverse : Head of Athena to right; behind—monogram combining the Greek letters *eta*, *mu* and *omicron*.
Reverse : owl to right, with the letters *Athe* in front and a bunch of grapes behind.
Cf. Rapson, *IC.* I. 6.

VI/7. Sophytes. Silver (32-Rati Kārṣāpaṇa)—58.3 grains=3.77 grammes.
Obverse : helmeted head of king to right.
Reverse : cock to right with caduceus above back and facing Greek legend—*Sōphutou*, "[Coin] of Sophytes."
Cf. Rapson, *IC.* I. 8. The Indian weight standard probably suggests that Sophytes (Saubhūti) was not an early Central Asian ruler of the Oxus valley (*Num. Chron.*, 1943, pp. 60-72; *JNSI*, VII, pp. 23-26; *Comp. Hist. Ind.*, II, ed. K. A. N. Sastri, p. 122 and note).

VI/8. Athenian coin (Indian imitation). Silver (32-Rati Kārṣāpaṇa)—54 grains=3.49 grammes.
Obverse : head of Athena to right, with a bunch of grapes behind.
Reverse: eagle to left looking back.
Cf. Rapson, *IC.* I. 7.

VI/9. Yavana (Greek). Diodotus (II ?—latter half of the 3rd century B.C.). Silver (Attic Tetradrachm)—about 268 grains.
Obverse : in pellet border—diademed head of Diodotus to right ; border of dots.
Reverse : in pellet border—naked Zeus thundering, standing on line, to left; eagle in his front; wreath above eagle; vertically written Greek legend—*Basileōs* (right), *Diodotou* (left), "[Coin] of the king Diodotus."
Cf. A.N. Lahiri, *CIGC.* XIII. 9.

VI/10. Yavana (Greek). Diodotus (II ?—latter half of the 3rd century B.C.). Copper.
Obverse : head of Zeus to right, lauriate.
Reverse : Artemis clad in short chiton, running to right; with torch in both hands, quiver at shoulder and hound running beside her; vertically written Greek legend—*Basileōs* (right), *Diodotou* (left).
Cf. Lahiri, *CIGC.* XIII. 12.

VI/11. Yavana (Greek). Euthydemus (c. 215-190 B.C.). Silver (Attic Tetradrachm)—about 268 grains.

Obverse : in pellet border—diademed head of elderly king to right.

Reverse : bearded Heracles seated, naked, to left, on rock with lion's skin spread on it, with left hand resting on rock behind and right hand grasping a club resting on his knee; Greek legend—*Basileōs* (right), *Euthydemou* (left), "[Coin] of king Euthydemus,"—written vertically from upside downwards; monogram.

Cf. Lahiri, *CIGC*. XIII. 7.

VI/12. Yavana (Greek). Euthydemus (c. 215-190 B.C.). Copper.

Obverse : in pellet border, head of bearded Heracles to right.

Reverse : in pellet border, horse pranching to right; Greek legend—*Basileōs* (above), *Euthydemou* (below), "[Coin] of king Euthydemus."

Cf. Lahiri, *CIGC*. XIX. 6.

PLATE VII

VII/1. Yavana (Greek). Euthydemus (II ?). Silver (Attic Tetradrachm) —about 268 grains.

Obverse : in pellet border—diademed and draped head of king to right.

Reverse : young Heracles, facing, ivy-crowned; with wreath of ivy in right hand and club and lion's skin in left hand; vertical Greek legend *Basileōs* (right), *Euthydemou* (left), "[Coin] of king Euthydemus;" monogram.

Cf. Whitehead, *The Pre-Mohammedan Coinage of Northwestern India*, II. 2.

VII/2. Yavana (Greek). Euthydemus (II ?). Silver (Attic Obol)—about $11\frac{1}{6}$ grains.

Obverse : in pellet border— diademed and draped head of king to right.

Reverse : tripod-lebes; vertical Greek legend—*Basileōs* (right), *Euthydemou* (left).

Cf. Lahiri, *CIGC*. XIX. 5.

VII/3. Yavana (Greek). Demetrius (c. 190-165 B.C.). Copper.

Obverse : bearded bust of Heracles to right, wearing ivy-wreath; with knot of lion's skin in front of neck and club over left shoulder.

Reverse : Artemis standing to front, with head radiate; wearing chiton and buskins and holding bow in left hand, right hand drawing arrow from quiver at back; vertical Greek legend —*Basileōs* (right), *Demetriou* (left), "[Coin] of king Demetrius;" monogram.

Cf. Lahiri, *CIGC*. XII. 8.

VII/4. Yavana (Greek). Demetrius (c. 190-165 B.C.). Silver (Attic Tetradrachm)—about 268 grains.

Obverse : in pellet border—diademed head of mature king to right, with elephant's sculp on head.

Reverse : naked Heracles standing to front, crowning himself with right hand and carrying club and lion's skin in left hand; Greek legend—*Basileōs* (right), *Demetriou* (left), "[Coin] of king Demetrius,"—written vertically from the upper side downwards.

Cf. Lahiri, *CIGC*. XI. II.

VII/5. Yavana (Greek). Demetrius (c. 190-165 B.C.). Silver (Attic Obol)—about $11\frac{1}{8}$ grains.

Obverse and Reverse : same as on No. VII/4; monogram.

Cf. Lahiri, *CIGC*. XII. 4.

VII/6. Yavana (Greek). Demetrius (II ?). Silver (Attic Tetradrachm) —about 268 grains.

Obverse : in pellet border, diademed head of king to right.

Reverse : Athena standing, half-right, with long spear in right hand and aegis (shield) resting on the field in left hand; vertical Greek legend —*Basileōs* (right), *Demetriou* (left), "Coin of king Demetrius;" monogram.

Cf. Lahiri, *CIGC.* XIII. 1.

VII/7. Yavana (Greek). Demetrius (III ?). Silver (Indian 20-Rati standard)—about 36 grains.

Obverse : Draped and diademed head of king in Kausia; Greek legend—*Basileōs Anikētou* (above), *Demetriou* (below), "[Coin] of king Demetrius the unconquered."

Reverse : Zeus standing, facing; with thunderbolt in right hand and long sceptre in left hand; Kharoṣṭhī legend—*Maharajasa aparajitasa* (above), *Dimetriyasa* (below),. "[Coin] of king Dimetriya the unconquered."

Cf. Lahiri, *CIGC.* XII. 10. We are not much in favour of duplicating and triplicating kings on the basis of dubious numismatic evidence since difference in coin types may be due to varions factors including the difference in mints and areas of circulation. There are already too many Indo-Greek rulers to be accommodated in too short a period, so that we have to suggest that several of the rulers flourished in different regions at the same time throughout the period of Indo-Greek rule. Naturally the position becomes far worse if the number of rulers is increased by suggesting the existence of too many rulers of the same names.

VII/8. Yavana (Greek). Demetrius (III?). Silver (Indian 20-Rati standard) —square, about 36 grains.

Obverse : head of king with elephant's sculp to right; Greek legend —*Basileōs* (left), *Anikētou* (above), *Demetriou* (right), "[Coin] of the unconquered king Demetrius."

Reverse : winged thunderbolt; Kharoṣṭhī legend—*Maharajasa* (right), *aparajitasa* (above), *Dime[triyasa]* (left); monogram.

Cf. Lahiri, *CIGC.* XII. 1. See note on No. VII/7 above.

VII/9. Yavana (Greek). Antimachus I. Silver (Attic Tetradrachm)— about 268 grains.

Obverse : in pellet or astragalus border—diademed head of king to right, wearing Kausia.

Reverse : diademed and bearded Poseidon, standing, facing, wearing himation and holding long trident in right hand with palm bound with fillet under left arm; Greek legend—*Basileōs Theou* (right), *Antimakhou* (left), "[Coin] of the Divine Antimachus,"—written vertically from top downwards; monogram.

Cf. Lahiri, *CIGC.* VI. 3.

PLATE VIII

VIII/1. Yavana (Greek). Pantaleon. Silver (Attic Tetradrachm)—about 268 grains.

Obverse : in pellet border, diademed head of king to right.

Reverse : Zeus seated to left; with sceptre in left hand and three-headed Hecate in outstretched right hand; Greek legend —*Basileōs* (right), *Pantaleontos* (left), "[Coin] of king Pantaleon," —written vertically from the upper side downwards; monogram.

Cf. Lahiri, *CIGC.* XXVII. 7.

VIII/2. Yavana (Greek). Pantaleon. Copper (100-Rati standard)—square, about .8 inch, about 165 grains.

Obverse: in incuse square—panther to right; Greek legend—*Basileōs* (above), *Pantaleontos* (below), "[Coin] of king Pantaleon."

Reverse : dancing girl in Indian dress holding flower in right hand, to left; Brāhmī legend (c. 2nd century B.C.)—*Rajane* (right), *Patalevasa* (left), "[Coin] of king Pantaleva."

Cf. Lahiri, *CIGC*. XXVII. 11; see Whitehead, *BMC* (i). II. 35.

VIII/3. Yavana (Greek). Agathocles. Silver (Attic Tetradrachm)—about 268 grains.

Obverse : in pellet border—diademed head of king to right.

Reverse : Zeus standing, facing; with sceptre in left hand and three-headed Hecate (carrying torches in both hands) in left hand; Greek legend—*Basileōs* (right), *Agathokleous* (left), "[Coin] of king Agathocles,"—written vertically; monogram.

Cf. Lahiri, *CIGC*. II. 3.

VIII/4. Yavana (Greek). Agathocles. Silver (Attic Drachm)—about 67 grains.

Obverse : in pellet border—diademed and draped head of king to right.

Reverse : Zeus standing, facing with sceptre in left hand and three-headed Hecate (carrying torches in both hands) in right hand; Greek legend—*Basileōs* (right), *Agathokleous* (left)—written vertically from upper side downwards ; monogram.

Cf. Lahiri, *CIGC*. II. 4.

VIII/5. Yavana (Greek). Agathocles. Silver (Attic Tetradrachm)—about 268 grains.

Obverse : in pellet border, head of Alexander in lion's sculp to right; Greek legend—*Alexandrou* (right), *tou Philippou* (left), "[in the name] of Alexander, the son of Philip."

Reverse : Zeus seated on throne to left, holding eagle in outstretched right hand and long sceptre in left hand; Greek legend —*Basileuontos* (in exergue), *Dikaiou* (right), *Agathokleous* [left], "[Coin] of the pious ruling king Agathocles;" monogram.

Cf. Lahiri, *CIGC*. I. 9.

VIII/6. Yavana (Greek). Agathocles. Silver (Attic Tetradrachm)—about 268 grains.

Obverse : diademed head of Diodotus I to right; Greek legend—*Diodotou* (right), *Sōteros* (left), "[in the name] of Diodotus, the Saviour."

Reverse : naked Zeus striding to left, hurling thunderbolt with right hand and holding aegis (shield) on outstretched left arm, with eagle; Greek legend—*Basileuontos* (in exergue), *Dikaiou* (right), *Agathokleous* (left), "[Coin] of the pious ruling king Agathocles,"—written vertically from upper side downwards; monogram.

Cf. Lahiri, *CIGC*. I. 11.

VIII/7. Yavana (Greek). Agathocles. Copper—round.

Obverse : in pellet border—head of Dionysus to right, with ivy-wreath on head and thyrsus over left shoulder.

Reverse : panther to right, touching a vine with right paw; Greek legend—*Basileōs* (above), *Agathokleous* (below); monogram.

Cf. Lahiri, *CIGC*. II. 7; Gardner, *BMC*. IV. 8. This king's square copper coins of the Indian 80-Rati Paṇa standard (.95 8 inch, 175.5 grains) are similar to those of Pantaleon. See Smith, *IMC*. II. 2.

VIII/8. Yavana (Greek). Agathocles(Akathukreya). Copper—square, .6 inch.

Obverse : six-peaked hill; legend in Kharoṣṭhī below—*Akathukreyasa* "[Coin] of Akathukreya."

Reverse : symbol described as tree in railing, but may be variant of 'Liṅga flanked by serpents'; Kharoṣṭhī legend below—*Hirañasame*, "Hiraṇyāśrama."

Cf. Rapson, *IC*. I. 16; see Whitehead, *PMC* (i) II. 51.

VIII/9. Yavana (Greek). Eucratides (c. 175-150 B.C.). Silver (Attic Tetradrachm)—about 268 grains.

Obverse : in astragalus border—helmeted bust of king to right.

Reverse : mounted Dioscuroi charging with long level spears; Greek legend—*Basileōs Megalou* (above), *Eukratidou* [below], "[Coin] of the great king Eucratides;" monogram.

Cf. Lahiri, *CIGC*. XVI. 4.

PLATE IX

IX/1. Yavana (Greek). Eucratides (c. 175-150 B.C.). Silver (Attic Drachm)—about 67 grains.

Obverse : In astragalus border—diademed bust of king, to right, wearing smooth helmet; Greek legend—*Basileus Megas* (above), *Eukratides* (below), "the great king Eucratides."

Reverse : in astragalus border—conjugate bust of Heliocles and Laodice to right; Greek legend—*Heliokleous* (above), *kai Laodikes* (below), "[in the name] of Heliscles and Laodice;" monogram.

Cf. Lahiri, *CIGC*. XV. 4.

IX/2. Yavana (Greek). Eucratides (c. 175-150 B.C.). Silver (Indian 20-Rati standard)—about 36 grains.

Obverse : in astragalus border—head of king to right, wearing smooth helmet; Greek legend—*Basileōs Megalou* (above), *Eukratidou* (below) "[Coin] of the great king Eucratides."

Reverse : the Dioscuroi standing side by side, holding spears and swords; Kharoṣṭhī legend—*Rajasa mahatakasa* (above), *Evukratidasa* (below), "[Coin] of the great king Evukratida"; monogram.

Cf. Lahiri, *CIGC*. XVII. 1.

IX/3. Yavana (Greek). Eucratides (c. 175-150 B.C.). Silver (Indian 20-Rati standard)—square, about 36 grains.

Obverse : diademed head of king to right, wearing smooth helmet; Greek legend—*Basileōs* (left), *Megalou* (above), *Eukratidou* (below).

Reverse : mounted Dioscuroi (with palms) charging to right with spears; Kharoṣṭhī legend—*Maharajasa* (above), *Evukratidasa* (below), "[Coin] of the great king Evukratida"; monogram.

Cf. Lahiri, *CIGC*. XVII. 8. *Maharajasa*=*Rajasa mahatakasa* of No. IX/2.

IX/4. Yavana (Greek). Eucratides (c. 175-150 B.C.). Copper.

Obverse : diademed and helmeted bust of king to right, Greek legend *Basileōs* (left), *Magalou* (above), *Eukratidou* (right).

Reverse : female deity wearing mural crown, seated on throne, to front, holding wreath and palm; on right of throne—forepartof elephant to right, and on left—probably a pilos (conical cap worn by the Dioscuroi); Kharoṣṭhī legend—*Kaviśiye* (right), *Nagara-* (top), *devata* (left), "the city divinity of Kāpiśī."

See Whitehead, *PMC* (i). III. 131.

IX/5. Eucratides (II). Silver (Attic Tetradrachm)—1.25 inches, 262 grains.

Obverse : in astragalus border—diademed bust of king to right.

Reverse : Apollo standing to left, wearing chlamys and boots, holding in right hand arrow and in left hand bow resting on ground; monogram in lower left field; Greek legend—*Basileōs* (right), *Eukratidou* (left), "[Coin] of king Eucratides,"—written vertically.

Cf. Gardner, *BMC.* VI. 8.

IX/6. Yavana (Greek). Plato. Silver (Attic Tetradrachm)—about 268 grains.

Obverse : in reel-and-bead border—diademed head of king to right, wearing smooth helmet.

Reverse : in quadriga—Helios or Mithra (Sun-god), radiate, clad in chiton and chlamys, on four horses, to right; Greek legend—*Basileōs Epiphanous Platonos,* "[Coin] of king Plato, the God-Manifest"; monogram.

Cf. Lahiri, *CIGC.* XXIX. 2.

IX/7. Yavana (Greek). Haliocles. Silver (Attic Tetradrachm)—round, 1.3 inches, 246 grains.

Obverse : in astragalus border—diademed head of king to right.

Reverse : Zeus standing, facing, with thunderbolt in right hand and long sceptre on ground in left hand; Greek legend—*Basileōs* (right), *Dikaiou* (below), *Heliokleous* (left), "[Coin] of the pious king Heliocles"; monogram.

Cf. Whitehead, *PMC*(i). III. 133.

IX/8. Yavana (Greek). Apollodotus (middle of the 2nd century B.C.). Silver (Indian 20-Rati standard)—square, about 36 grains.

Obverse : elephant standing, to right; Greek legend—*Basileōs* (left), *Apollodotou* (above), *Sōteros* (right), "[Coin] of king Apollodotus, the Saviour."

Reverse : humped bull to right; Kharoṣṭhī legend—*Maharajasa* (right), *Apaladatasa* (above), *tratarasa* (left), "[Coin] of the great king Apaladata, the Saviour;" monogram.

Cf. Lahiri, *CIGC.* VII. 4.

IX/9. Yavana (Greek). Apollodotus (middle of the 2nd century B.C.) Copper—square.

Obverse : Apollo, naked and lauriate, standing to front; with arrow in right hand and bow (resting on ground) in left hand; Greek legend—*Basileōs* (left), *Apollodotou* (above), *Soterōs* (right).

Reverse : in dotted square—tripod-lebes with pronounced foot; Kharoṣṭhī legend—*Maharajasa* (right), *Apaladatasa* (above), *tratarasa* (left); monogram.

Cf. Lahiri, *CIGC.* VII. 7.

IX/10. Yavana (Greek). Apollodotus (II ?). Silver (Indian 80-Rati standard)—round, about 146 grains.

Obverse : diademed head of king, to right; Greek legend—*Basileōs Megalou Sōteros kai Philopatoros* (above), *Apollodotou* (below), "[Coin] of the great father-loving king Apollodotus, the Saviour."

Reverse : Athena standing, to left, with aegis (shield) over extended left arm, hurling thunderbolt with right hand; Kharoṣṭhī legend—*Maharajasa tratarasa* (above), *Apaladatasa* (below), "[Coin] of the great king Apollodotus, the Saviour;" monogram.

Cf. Lahiri, *CIGC.* VIII. 11.

IX/11. Yavaṇa (Greek). Apollodotus (II ?). Copper (140-Rati— $1\frac{3}{4}$-Paṇa)—255.55 grains.

Obverse : Apollo clad in chlamys and boots, standing to right, holding arrow in both hands, with quiver on his back; Greek legend—*Basileōs Sōteros* (above), *Apollodotou* (below), "[Coin] of king Apollodotus, the Saviour."

Reverse : tripod-lebes; Kharoṣṭhī legend—*Maharajasa tratarasa* (above), *Apaladatasa* (below), "[Coin] of the great king Apaladata, the Saviour;" monogram.

Cf. Brown, *CI.* II. 3.

IX/12. Yavana (Greek), Antialcidas (close of the 2nd century B.C.). Silver (Indian 20-Rati standard)— about 36 grains.

Obverse : diademed head of king to right, wearing Kausia; Greek legend—*Basileōs Nikēphorou* (above), *Antialkidou* (below), "[Coin] of the victorious king Antialcidas."

Reverse : Zeus seated on throne, to left; with long sceptre (resting on left shoulder) in left hand; Nice bearing wreath and palm in outstretched right hand and forepart of elephant in left field; Kharoṣṭhī legend—*Maharajasa Jayadharasa* (above), *Aṁtialikitasa* (below), "[Coin] of the victory-carrying great king Antyalikita;" monogram.

Cf. Lahiri, *CIGC.* V. 9.

PLATE X

X/1. Yavana (Greek). Menander (c. 115-90 B.C.). Silver (Indian 80-Rati standard)—about 146 grains.

Obverse : diademed head of king to right, wearing Medusa helmet; Greek legend—*Basileōs Sōteros* (above), *Menandrou* (below), "[Coin] of king Menander, the Saviour."

Reverse : helmeted Athena standing to left, holding aegis (shield) on outstretched left arm and hurling thunderbolt with right hand; Kharoṣṭhī legend—*Maharajasa tratarasa* (above), *Menadrasa* (below), "[Coin] of king Menandra, the Saviour; " monograms.

Cf. Whitehead, *The Pre-Mohammedan Coinage of Northwestern India*, VII. 2.

X/2. Yavana (Greek). Menander (c. 115-90 B.C.). Silver (Indian 20-Rati standard)—37.7 grains.

Obverse : diademed bust of king to left, thrusting javelin with right hand; Greek legend—*Basileōs Sōteros* (above), *Menandrou* (below).

Reverse : Athena to left with aegis (shield) on outstretched left arm, hurling thunderbolt with right hand; monogram to right; Kharoṣṭhī legend —*Maharajasa tratarasa* (above), *Menadrasa* (below).

Cf. Brown, *CI.* II. 4.

X/3. Yavana (Greek). Menander (c. 115-90 B.C.) Copper (20-Rati ¼-Paṇa)—square, 38 grains.

Obverse : elephant's head with bell hanging from chain round neck, to right; Greek legend—*Basileōs* (left), *Sōteros* (above), *Menandrou* (right).

Reverse : club of Heracles with the thick end up; two symbols; Kharoṣṭhī legend—*Maharajasa* (right), *tratarasa* (above), *Menadrasa* (left).

Cf. Brown, *CI.* II. 6.

X/4. Yavana (Greek). Agathocleia. Silver (Indian 20-Rati standard)—about 36 grains.

Obverse : diademed head of queen to right; Greek legend—*Basilissēs theotropou* (above), *Agathocleias* (below), "[Coin] of the divine queen Agathocleia."

Reverse : figure of warrior (Strato ?) to right, diademed and clad in short sleeveless tunic, with shield and lance on left arm, right arm extended, with dagger on right side; Kharoṣṭhī legend—*Maharajasa tratarasa dhrami-*

kasa (above), *Stratasa* (below), "[Coin] of the pious great king Strata;" monogram in right field.

Cf. Lahiri, *CIGC*. I. 5.

X/5. Yavana (Greek). Strato I and Agathocleia. Silver (Indian 80-Rati standard)—about 146 grains.

Obverse : conjugate diademed heads of Strato I and Agathocleia, to right; Greek legend—*Basileōs Sōteros Stratonos* (above), *kai Agathokleias* (below), "[Coin] of king Strato, the Saviour, and of Agathocleia."

Reverse : Athena standing to left with aegis (shield) on outstretched left arm and hurling thunderbolt with right hand; Kharoṣṭhī legend—*Maharajasa tratarasa dhramikasa* (above), *Stratasa* (below), "[Coin] of the pious great king Strata, the Saviour;" monogram.

Cf. Lahiri, *CIGC*. I. 8.

X/6. Yavana (Greek), Strato I. Silver (Indian 80-Rati standard)—about 146 grains.

Obverse : diademed head of king to right; Greek legend—*Basileōs Sōteros kai Dikaiou* (above), *Stratonos* (below), "[Coin] of the pious king Strato, the Saviour."

Reverse : Athena standing to left, with helmet, shield and spear and carrying Nice on her outstretched right hand; Kharoṣṭhī legend—*Maharajasa tratarasa dhramikasa* (above), *Stratasa* (below), "[Coin] of the pious great king Strata, the Saviour;" monogram.

Cf. Lahiri, *CIGC*. XXXI. 10.

X/7. Yavana (Greek). Strato I and II. Silver (Indian 20-Rati standard)—37 grains.

Obverse : diademed head of aged king; Greek legend—*Basileōs Sōteros Stratonos viou Stratonos*, "[Coin] of king Strato, the Saviour, [and] of [his] grandson Strato."

Reverse : Athena to left, with aegis (shield) and thunderbolt; Kharoṣṭhī legend—*Maharajasa tratarasa Stratasa potrasa casa priyapita-Stratasa*, "[Coin] of the great king Strata (I), the Saviour, and of his grandson, the father-loving Strata (II)."

Cf. Brown, *CI*. II. 10.

X/8. Yavana (Greek). Philoxenus. Silver (Indian 20-Rati standard)—27.3 grains.

Obverse : helmeted bust of king to right; Greek legend—*Basileōs* (left), *Anikētou* (above), *Philoxenou* (right), "[Coin] of the unconquered king Philoxenus."

Reverse : king on horseback, to right; Kharoṣṭhī legend—*Maharajasa* (right), *Apadihatasa* (above), *Philasinasa* (left) "[Coin] of the unconquered great king Philasina;" monograms.

Cf. Brown, *CI*. II. 7.

X/9. Yavana (Greek). Hippostratus. Silver (Indian 80-Rati standard)—about 146 grains.

Obverse : diademed head of king to right; Greek legend with square *omicron—Basileōs Megalou Sōteros* (above), *Hippostratou* (below), "[Coin] of the great king Hippostratus, the Saviour."

Reverse : king in full panoply on horse walking to right; Kharoṣṭhī legend—*Maharajasa tratarasa mahatasa jayaṁtasa* (above), *Hipustratasa* (below), "[Coin] of the great king, the great Saviour Hipustrata, the victorious;" monogram.

Cf. Lahiri, *CIGC*. XXIII. 3.

X/10. Yavana (Greek). Hermaeus and Callicpe. Silver (Indian 20-Rati standard)—about 36 grains.

Obverse : conjugate busts of king and queen, to right; Greek legend —*Basileōs Sōteros Hermaiou kai Kalliopes,* "[Coin] of king Hermaeus, the Saviour, and of Calliope."

Reverse : king (helmeted, diademed and fully acoutred) on prancing horse to right; Kharoṣṭhī legend—*Maharajasa tratarasa Heramayasa Kaliyapaya*, "[Coin] of the great king Heramaya, the Saviour, and of Kaliyapā;" monograms.

Cf. Brown, *CI.* II. 9.

X/11. Pahlava-Śaka. Vonones (c. 58-18 B.C.) and Spalagadāman. Silver (Indian 20-Rati standard)—round, .65 inch, 35 grains.

Obverse : diademed king on horseback, to right, with couched spear; Greek legend—*Basileōs Basileōn Megalou* (above—on left, top and right), *Onōnou* (below), "[Coin] of Vonones, the great king of the kings."

Reverse : Zeus radiate, standing to front, leaning on long sceptre in left hand and with thunderbolt in right hand; Kharoṣṭhī legend—*Spalahora-putrasa dhramiasa* (above—on right, top and left), *Spalagadamasa* (below), "[Coin] of the pious Spalagadāman, the son of Spalahora."

Cf. Smith, *IMC.* VIII. 6.

X/12. Śaka. Spalyris and Spalagadāman. Copper (70-Rati standard)—square .85 inch, 122 grains.

Obverse : In square frame—king on horseback to right; Greek legend (with square *omicron*)—*Spalyrisos Dikaiou Adelphou tou Basileōs*, "[Coin] of Spalyris the just, the brother of the king." .

Reverse : naked Heracles, diademed, sitting on rock, supporting club on knee; Kharoṣṭhī legend—*Spalahora-putrasa dhramiasa Spalagadamasa*, "[Coin] of the pious Spalagadāman, the son of Spalahora;" monogram on left.

Cf. Whitehead, *PMC* (i). XIV. 386. The king whose brotherhood was claimed by Spalyris is believed to be Vonones. According to some, 'Brother of the King' was merely a title of nobility and does not indicate any blood relations with the king; cf. *Rājaputya*, literally, 'the king's son.'

X/13. Śaka (Imperial). Maues. (c. 22 B.C.-22 A.D.). Copper (80-Rati Paṇa)—about 130 grains.

Obverse : caduceus; Greek legend—*Basileōs* (right), *Mauou* (left), "[Coin] of king Maues,"—vertically written.

Reverse : in border of reels and pellets—head of elephant with upraised trunk, to right, with bell suspended from neck; monogram.

Cf. Brown, *CI.* III. 4.

X/14. Śaka (Imperial). Maues (c. 22 B.C.-22 A.D.). Copper (80-Rati Paṇa)—square, .95 inch, 180 grains.

Obverse : Poseidon standing to front with long trident in left hand and right foot resting on a small radiate figure underneath him; right hand on knee; Greek legend—*Basileōs Basileōn megalou Mauou* "[Coin] of Maues, the great king of kings."

Reverse : female figure standing to front between trees (supposed to be a Bacchante among vines); monogram on right (Kharoṣṭhī *sa*) and left (Greek *s*); Kharoṣṭhī legend—*Rajatirajasa mahatasa Moasa*, "[Coin] of Moa, the great king of kings."

Cf. Whitehead, *PMC* (i). X. 20.

PLATE XI

XI/1. Śaka (Imperial). Azes I (c. 5-25 A. D.). Silver (Indian 20-Rati standard)—about .7 inch, about 36 grains.

Obverse : king on horse-back, to right; legend—*Basileōs Basileōn Megalou Azou*, "[Coin] of Azes, the great king of kings."

Reverse : Athena standing, to front, with shield on left arm; crowning herself with right hand; Kharoṣṭhī legend—*Maharajasa Rajarajasa mahatosa Ayasa*, "[Coin] of the great king Aya, the great king of kings;" monograms on right and left.

Cf. Whitehead, *The Pre-Mohammedan Coinage of Northwestern India*, VIII. 1.

XI/2. Śaka (Imperial). Azes I (c. 5-25 A.D.). Silver (Indian 80-Rati standard)—round, 142 grains.

Obverse : king on horse-back, to right, holding couched lance; Greek legend—*Basileōs Basileōn megalou Azou*, "[Coin] of Azes, the great king of kings;" Kharoṣṭhī *sa* below.

Reverse : not reproduced.

Cf. Brown, *CI.* III. 7.

XI/3. Śaka (Imperial). Azilises (c. 25-35 A.D.). Silver (Drachm)—about 67 grains.

Obverse : king on horse back, holding elephant-goad in right hand; monogram on right; Greek legend—*Basileōs Basileōn megalou Azilizou,*"[Coin] of Azilises, the great king of kings."

Reverse : Dioscuroi standing side by side, armed with spears; Kharoṣṭhī legend—*Maharajasa Rajatirajasa mahatasa Ayiliṣasa*, "[Coin] of the great king Ayiliṣa, the great king of kings."

Cf. Brown, *CI.* III. 9.

XI/4. Śaka (Imperial). Azes (II, c. 30-45 A.D.). Copper (120-Rati standard)—round, about 220 grains.

Obverse : humped bull to right; Greek monogram above and Kharoṣṭhī monogram in front; Greek legend—*Basileōs Basileōn megalou Azou*, "[Coin] of Azes, the great king of kings."

Reverse : lion, to right; Kharoṣṭhī legend above back—*Maharajasa Rajatirajasa mahatasa Ayasa*, "[Coin]of the great king Aya, the great king of kings."

Cf. Brown, *CI.* III. 5; Smith, *IMC.* VIII. 14; Whitehead, *PMC* (i). XII. 263.

XI/5. Pahlava (Parthian). Gondophernes (c. 21-50 A.D.). Copper (80-Rati Paṇa)—about 1 inch, about 124 grains.

Obverse : diademed bust of king to right; legend probably—*Basileōs Sōteros Yndopherou*, "[Coin] of king Undopherus, the Saviour."

Reverse : winged Nice standing to right; legend probably—*Maharajasa Gondapharṇasa tratarasa*, "[Coin] of the great king Gondapharṇa, the Saviour."

Cf. Whitehead, *The Pre-Mohammedan Coinage of Northwestern India*, VIII. 3; see *PMC* (i). p. 152.

XI/6. Pahlava (Parthian). Gondophernes (c. 21-50 A.D.). Silver (base —Indian 80-Rati standard)—142 grains.

Obverse : king on horse-back, to right, with right arm extended; king's special symbol on right; Greek legend—*Basileōs Basileōn megalou Undopherou*, "[Coin] of king Undopherus, the great king of kings."

Reverse : Zeus standing, to right, with right arm extended; Greek monogram on right and Kharoṣṭhī monogram on left; Kharoṣṭhī legend—*Maharaja-rajatiraja-tratara-devavrada-Gudupharasa*, "[Coin] of the great king Guduphara who is the saviour devoted to the gods [and] is the king of kings."

Cf. Brown, *CI.* III.8. The metal of the coin may be billon or copper.

XI/7. Śaka (?). Heraus or Miaus. Silver (120-Rati standard)—1.2 inches, 196 grains.

Obverse : in reel and pellet border—diademed bust of king to right.

Reverse : king on horse-back, to right, followed by flying figure of Nice with wreath; Greek legend (with square *omicron*) —*Tyannontos Ēaou*

Koiianou; in exergue—*Saka* (or *Sanab*).

Cf. Whitehead, *PMC*(i). XVI. 115.

XI/8. Śaka (?). Hyrcodes. Silver (Indian 100-Rati standard)—184.4 grains=11.94 grammes.

Obverse : diademed bust of king to right; legend (with *w*-like *omega*) —*Yrkōdou.*

Reverse : armed figure, facing, with flames issuing from shoulders; holding spear in right hand; legend—*Makarou Ardēthrou.*

Cf. Rapson, *IC.* II. 2.

XI/9. Kuṣāṇa. Kujula Kara Kadphises (c. 76-80 A.D.). Copper—round, .9 inch.

Obverse : bull to right, with Greek monogram above and Kharoṣṭhī monogram (*pu*) on right; corrupt and illegible Greek legend.

Reverse: two-humped camel to right; Kharoṣṭhī *pa* above and a few letters (*sasaṁ* ?) on right; Kharoṣṭhī legend—*...ra* (*ta* ?)*sa Kayala-Kara-Kapasa...*, "[Coin] of Kayala (Kujula) Kara Kapa...."

Cf. Whitehead, *PMC* (i). XVII. 18. It should have been put after No. XI/14.

XI/10. Kuṣāṇa. Kujula Kadaphes (Kadphises I, c. 15-65 A.D.). Copper (imitation of Roman type).

Obverse : diademed head to right; corrupt Greek legend—*Khoshanou Zaoou Kozola Kadaphes*, "Kozola Kadaphes, the chief of the Khoshana (Kuṣāṇa)."

Reverse : king seated on a chair, to right; monogram behind his back; Kharoṣṭhī legend—*...Kaphsasa sacadhrama-ṭhitasa Khuṣanasa Yuasa*, "[Coin] of Kaphsa, chief of the Kuṣāṇas, steadfast in the True Faith (probably, Buddhism)."

Cf. Brown, *CI.* IV. 2.

XI/11. Kuṣāṇa. Kujula Kadphises (Kadphises I, c. 15-65 A.D.). Copper—round, .9 inch.

Obverse : diademed bust of Hermaeus, to right; corrupt Greek legend (with square *omicron*)—*Kozolou Kadphizou Korsolou*, "[Coin] of Kozola Kadphises the Kuṣāṇa (?)."

Reverse : Heracles standing to front, with right hand resting on club, and lion's skin over left arm; Kharoṣṭhī legend—*Kujula-Kasasa Kuṣana-Yavugasa dhrama-ṭhidasa*, "[Coin] of the Kuṣāṇa chief Kujula-Kasa who is steadfast in religion (probably, Buddhism);" in the field Kharoṣṭhī *saṁ*.

Cf. Whitehead, *PMC* (i). XVII. 8.

XI/12. Kuṣāṇa. Wema Kadphises (Kadphises II, c. 65-75 A.D.). Gold (136-Rati Double-Dīnāra)—244.2 grains.

Obverse : king seated cross-legged, wearing crested helmet and diadem, with thunderbolt in right hand; symbol to left; Greek legend—*Basileus Ooemo Kadphises*, "king Wema Kadphises."

Reverse : Śiva radiate, standing in front of bull, with long trident in right hand; monogram on left; Kharoṣṭhī legend—*Maharajasa rajadirajasa sarvaloga-iśvarasa Mahiśvarasa Vima-Kaṭhphiśasa tradara*[*sa*], "[Coin] of the great king Vima Kaṭhphisa, the king of kings, lord of all the world, the Māheśvara (devotee of Śiva)."

Cf. Brown, *CI.* IV. 3. For Dīnāra, see note on No. XI/13 below.

XI/13. Kuṣāṇa. Wema Kadphises (Kadphises II, c. 65-75 A.D.). Gold (68-Rati Dīnāra)—round, .8 inch; about 124 grains.

Obverse: half-length figure of king to right, wearing helmet and diadem and holding club on right hand and elephant-goad in left hand; monogram on right; Greek legend (with *c*-like *sigma*)—*Basileus Ooemo Kadphises.*

Reverse : Śiva wearing necklace, with matted locks on his head, standing to front, with head to left; with long trident-battle-axe in right hand and gourd and tiger skin in left hand; monograms on right and left;

Kharoṣṭhī legend—*Maharajasa rajadirajasa sarvaloga-iśvarasa mahiśvarasa Vima-Kaṭhphiśasa tradarasa.*

Cf. Whitehead, *PMC* (i). XVII. 33. The matted locks of Śiva are described by some as flames issuing from his head. The Kuṣāṇas imitated the Roman Denarius of 124 grains (68 or 70 Ratis). The Kuṣāṇa gold coin was later called Dīnāra, though it is mentioned as Suvarṇa (actually 146.4 grains) in a Nasik inscription (*Sel. Ins.*, I, 1965, p. 165).

XI/14. Kuṣāṇa. Soter Megas. Copper.

Obverse : diademed and radiate bust of king to right, holding a lance; king's special symbol on left.

Reverse : king on horseback to right; king's special symbol on right; Greek legend—*Basileus Basileōn Sōter Megas*, "the king of kings, the great Saviour."

Cf. Brown, *CI.* III. 6. See *The Age of Imperial Unity*, ed. Majumdar, pp. 140-41.

XI/15. Kuṣāṇa. Kaniṣka (78-102 A.D.). Gold (17-Rati ¼-Dīnāra)—.5 inch, 30.8 grains.

Obverse : half-length portrait of king, to left; with spear in left hand; legend in Greek characters—*Shaonano Shao Kaneshki Koshano*, "Kaniṣka the Kuṣāṇa, the king of kings."

Reverse : bearded fire-god to left, with fillet in right hand and tongs in left hand; monogram on left and legend in Greek characters on right—*Athsho* (Persian *Ātash*, Greek Hephaistos, the god of metals).

Cf. Brown, *CI.* IV. 5; see Whitehead, *PMC* (i). XVII. 67.

PLATE XII

XII/1. Kuṣāṇa. Kaniṣka (78-102 A.D.). Gold (68-Rati Dīnāra)—122 grains.

Obverse : king, radiate, standing to left sacrificing at a small altar, with spear in left hand; legend in Greek characters—*Shaonano Shao Kaneshki Koshano*, "Kaniṣka, the Kuṣāṇa, the king of kings."

Reverse : the Buddha, facing, nimbate, wallet in left hand; symbol on right and legend in Greek characters on left—*Boddo* (Indian *Buddha*).

Cf. Brown, *CI.* IV. 4.

XII/2. Kuṣāṇa. Kaniṣka (78-102 A.D.). Gold (68-Rati Dīnāra) — about .9 inch, about 122 grains.

Obverse : king standing to left, wearing peaked helmet, long heavy coat, and trousers, and sacrificing at altar; long spear in left hand; legend probably—*Shaonano Shao Kaneshki Koshano.*

Reverse : four-armed Śiva to left, holding in the hands—trident, goat, drum and gourd (with elephant-goad) respectively; vertical legend —*Oesho.*

Cf. Whitehead, *The Pre-Mohammedan Coinage of Northwestern India*, IX.2; *PMC* (i). XVII. 65. See No XII/8 below.

XII/3. Kuṣāṇa. Kaniṣka (78-102 A.D.). Gold (68-Rati Dīnāra)—.95 inch, 125.5 grains.

Obverse : king standing to left, wearing peaked helmet, long heavy cloak, and trousers and sacrificing at a small altar; long spear in left hand; legend—*Shaonano Shao Kaneshki Koshano.*

Reverse : draped goddess standing to right, carrying short sceptre or callipers; vertical legend on left—*Nana* (to be read upwards); symbol on right.

Cf. *Numismatic Chronicle*, 1892, VII. 9. Nana was the great Mother-goddess of Western Asia. She was identified with the Indian Mother-goddess conceived as the consort of Śiva; cf. the Oesho-Nana type of Huviṣka's coins (*PMC* [i]. XVIII. 135) and the Vedic word *nanā* used in the sense of 'the mother' (*Ṛgveda*, IX. 112. 3).

XII/4. Kuṣāṇa. Kaniṣka (78-102 A.D.). Copper.

Obverse : king radiate, standing to left, sacrificing at a small altar, with spear in left hand; legend in Greek characters—*Shao Kaneshki*, "king Kaniṣka."

Reverse : wind-god, undraped and radiate, running to left; symbol on left and legend in Greek characters on right—*Oado* (Perso-Indian *Vāta*).

Cf. Brown, *CI*. IV, 6.

XII/5. Kuṣāṇa. Huviṣka (c.106-45 A.D.). Gold (68-Rati Dīnāra)—about 124 grains.

Obverse : bust of king, to left, wearing peaked helmet and coat of mail with cloak; with spear in left hand; legend probably—*Shaonano Shao Oeshki Koshano*, "Oeshki, the king of kings, the Kuṣāṇa."

Reverse : the goddess of abundance (Ardokhsho) standing to right, holding cornucopiae (horn of plenty); legend—*Ardokhsho*; symbol to right.

Cf. Whitehead, *The Pre-Mohammedan Coinage of Northwestern India*, IX. 3.

XII/6. Kuṣāṇa. Huviṣka (c. 106-45 A.D.). Gold (68-Rati Dīnāra)—123 grains.

Obverse : king seated cross-legged, turning to left, with goad in left hand and sceptre in right hand; legend in Greek characters—*Shaonano Shao Oeshki Koshano*.

Reverse : bearded Heracles, with club and lion's skin, standing and having apple in left hand; symbol on left and Greek legend on right—*Herakilo*.

Cf. Brown, *CI*. IV. 8.

XII/7. Kuṣāṇa. Huviṣka (c. 106-45 A.D.). Gold (68-Rati Dīnāra)—120.9 grains.

Obverse : king riding on elephant, to right, holding sceptre and elephant-goad; legend in Greek characters—*Shaonano Shao Oeshki Koshano*.

Reverse : goddess Ardokhsho to right, holding cornucopiae in both hands; symbol on right and Greek legend on left—*Ardokhsho*.

Cf. Brown, *CI*. IV. 7.

XII/8. Kuṣāṇa. Vāsudeva (c. 140-80 A.D.).Gold (68-Rati Dīnāra)—122.3 grains.

Obverse : king, radiate, standing to left sacrificing at altar, wearing suit of chain-mail and holding spear in left hand; legend in Greek characters – *Shaonano Shao Bazodeo Koshano*, "Vāsudeva, the Kuṣāṇa, the king of kings."

Reverse : Many-headed Śiva standing in front of bull, with trident in left hand; symbol on right and legend in Greek characters on left—*Oesho* (Sanskrit *Vṛṣa* or *Bhaveśa* meaning Śiva).

Cf. Brown, *CI*. IV. 9.

XII/9. Kuṣāṇa. Vāsudeva (c. 140-80 A.D.). Gold (68-Rati Dīnāra)—.85 inch, 121 grains.

Obverse : king, nimbate, to left, with peaked helmet and complete suit of chain-mail, making offering with right hand over altar, with long trident in left hand; legend in Greek characters—*Shaonano Shao Bazodeo*.

Reverse : two-armed Śiva standing to front, with noose in right hand and long trident in left hand, bull standing to left behind the god; vertical legend on right—*Oesho*; monogram in upper left field.

Cf. Whitehead, *PMC* (i). XIX. 211. Cf. No. XII/8 above.

XII/10. Kuṣāṇa. Vāsudeva (c. 140-80 A.D.). Copper (68-Rati standard?) —round, about .85 inch, about 117 grains.

Obverse : king standing to left, with peaked helmet and suit of chain-mail, holding long trident in left hand and making offering with right hand on small altar; trident in left field; traces of corrupt legend in Greek characters.

Reverse : two-armed Śiva standing, to front, with noose in extended right hand and long trident in left hand; bull standing to left behind the god; trident-battleaxe on right.

Cf. Whitehead, *The Pre-Mohammedan Coinage of Northwestern India*, IX. 4; see a somewhat similar type in *PMC* (i). XIX. 216.

XII/11. Kuṣāṇa (imitation). Gold (68-Rati Dīnāra)—121.4 grains=7.86 grammes.

Obverse : figure of king and legend copied from those of Kaniṣka; Brāhmī characters—*ha* (left) and *vi* (right), (indicating Huviṣka II ?).

Reverse : goddess seated on throne, facing, holding noose in right hand and cornucopiae in left hand; on left—symbol (above) and the Brāhmī character *la* (below).

Cf. Rapson, *IC*. II. 14.

XII/12. Śaka (Satrapal). Zeionises. Silver (80-Rati standard)—round, 149.6 grains=9.69 grammes.

Obverse : Satrap on horse-back, to right; various Kharoṣṭhī characters in field; symbol in front of horse; debased Greek legend (with *w*-like *omega*) probably intended for—*Manniglou yiou Zatrapou* (above), *Zeiōnisou* (below), "[Coin] of Satrap Zeionises the son of Manniglus."

Reverse : left—Satrap to right; right—city-goddess to left, holding wreath and cornucopiae; Kharoṣṭhī legend—*Manigulasa Chatrapasa putrasa Chatrapasa Jihoniasa*, "[Coin] of Satrap Jihonia, son of Satrap Manigula."

Cf. Rapson, *IC*. II. 3.

XII/13. Śaka (Satrapal—Mathurā). Rañjuvula. Silver (base—20-Rati standard)—round, .55 inch, 38 grains.

Obverse : diademed bust of king to right; corrupt Greek legend—(with *c*-like *sigma* and *w*-like *omega*)—*Basileōs Basileōn Sōteros Razy*, "[Coin] of Raz, the king of kings, the Saviour."

Reverse : Athena to left, holding aegis (shield) in left hand and hurling thunderbolt with right hand; Kharoṣṭhī legend—*Apratihatacakrasa* (left), *Chatrapasa* (right—to be read from outer side), *Rajuvulasa* (below), "[Coin] of the invincible Satrap Rājuvula"; Kharoṣṭhī characters in field—*ga* on left and *a* on right.

Cf. Allan, *BMC* (AI). XXVI. 7.

XII/14. Śaka (Satrapal—Mathurā). Hagāna and Hagāmaṣa. Copper (40-Rati ½-Paṇa)—round, .75 inch, 67.5 grains.

Obverse : symbol looking like a narrow-necked vase on pedestal; Brāhmī legend (c. 1st century A.D.)—(1) *Khatapāna* (2) *Hagānasa* (3) *Hagāmaṣasa*, "[Coin] of the Kṣatrapas Hagāna and Hagāmaṣa."

Reverse : horse to left.

Cf. Allan, *BMC* (AI). XXVI. 6.

XII/15. Kṣaharāta-Śaka (Satrapal—Western India), Bhūmaka (c. 105-10 A.D.). Copper (40-Rati standard ?) —.75 inch, 80.2 grains.

Obverse : arrow pointing upwards on left and thunderbolt on right with a pellet in between; Kharoṣṭhī legend—*Kṣaharadasa Kṣa...sa*, "[Coin] of the Kṣasharāta Satrap [Bhūmaka]."

Reverse : capital of pillar bearing on left—lion with upraised paw, facing left, and wheel; traces of legend probably in Brāhmī.

Cf. Rapson, *BMC*. IX. 237.

PLATE XIII

XIII/1. Kṣaharāta-Śaka (Satrapal—Western India), Bhūmaka (c. 105-10 A.D.). Copper (40-Rati ½-Kārṣāpaṇa)—.8 inch, 69.8 grains.

Obverse : arrow and thunderbolt traces of long legend probably in Kharoṣṭhī.

Reverse : capital of pillar bearing lion and wheel; Brāhmī legend (2nd century A.D.)—*Kṣaharāta......pasa Bhumakasa*, "[Coin]of the Kṣaharāta Satrap Bhūmaka."

Cf. Rapson, *BMC*. IX. 238.

XIII/2. Śaka (Satrapal—Bhṛgukaccha). Nahapāna (c. 110-24 A.D.)—Silver (20-Rati Kārṣāpaṇa).

Obverse : head of Satrap to right; legend in Greek characters apparently intending—*Rannio Sahratas Zatrapas* (or *Satrapas*) *Nahapanas*, "[Coin] of king Nahapāna, the Kṣaharāta Satrap."

Reverse : thunderbolt and arrow; Brāhmī legend (XII)—*Rājño Kṣaharātasa Nahapānasa*; Kharoṣṭhī legend (XI towards left)—*Raño Kṣaharatasa Nahapanasa*, "[Coin] of king Nahapāna the Kṣaharāta."

Cf. Brown, *CI*. II. 11. Nahapāna's silver coins are called Kārṣāpaṇa in an inscription which equates 35 such coins to a Suvarṇa, i.e., a Kuṣāṇa gold coin of 124 grains (*Sel. Ins.*, I, 1965, pp. 165-66), though the Indian silver Kārṣāpaṇa and gold Suvarṇa weighed respectively 58.56 and 146.4 grains.

XIII/3. Kārdamaka-Śaka (Satrapal—Ujjayinī). Caṣṭana (c. 125-35 A.D.). Silver (20-Rati standard)—.6 inch, 30.5 grains.

Obverse : bust of Satrap to right; legend in Greek characters apparently intending—*Rannio Zatrapasa Siastanasa*, "[Coin] of king Ciastana, the Satrap."

Reverse : three-peaked hill, surmounted by crescent, with river below; crescent on left and star on right; Brāhmī legend——*Rājño Mahākṣatrapasa Ghsāmotika-putrasa Caṣṭanasa*, "[Coin] of the Great Satrap, king Caṣṭana, the son of Ghsāmotika;" Kharoṣṭhī legend—*Caṭhanasa*, "[Coin] of Caṭhana."

Cf. Rapson, *BMC*. X. J. B.

XIII/4. Kārdamaka-Śaka (Satrapal—Ujjayinī). Rudradāman I (c. 130-55 A.D.). Silver (20-Rati Rudradāmaka-Kārṣāpaṇa)—.6 inch, 29.2 grains.

Obverse : bust of Satrap to right; traces of legend in Greek characters.

Reverse : three-peaked hill, surmounted by crescent, waved line (river) below, and crescent on left and star on right; border of dots; Brāhmī legend—parts of *Rājño Kṣatrapasa Jayadāma-putrasa Rājño Mahākṣatrapasa Rudradāmasa*, "[Coin] of king Rudradāman, the Great Satrap, the son of the Satrap Jayadāman."

Cf. Rapson, *BMC*. X. 272.

XIII/5. Kāradamaka-Śaka (Satrapal—Ujjayinī). Jivadāman. Śaka year 100...(178 A.D.?). Silver (20-Rati Rudradāmaka-Kārṣāpaṇa)—.6 inch, 34.5 grains.

Obverse : bust of Satrap to right; behind—the Brāhmī numerical symbol—*100* ...; traces of legend in Greek characters.

Reverse : three-peaked hill surmounted by crescent; crescent (left), star (right) and weavy line (river—below); border of dots; Brāhmī legend—parts of *Rājño Mahākṣatrapasa Dāmajadaśriya putrasa Rājño Mahākṣatrapasa Jivadāmna*, "[Coin] of king Jīvadāman, the Great Satrap, the son of king Dāmajātaśrī, the Great Satrap."

Cf. Rapson, *BMC*. XI. 288.

XIII/6. Kārdamaka-Śaka (Satrapal—Ujjayinī). Rudrasiṁha I. Śaka year 115 (193 A.D.). Silver (20-Rati Rudradāmaka-Kārṣāpaṇa)—.6 inch, 37 grains.

Obverse : bust of Satrap to right; traces of legend in Greek characters; behind—in Brāhmī numerical symbols—*100 10* 5.

Reverse : three-peaked hill surmounted by crescent with crescent, star and waved line (river); Brāhmī legend—*Rājño* [*Mahākṣatrapasa Rudradāma*]*-putrasa Rājño Mahākṣatrapasa Rudrasīhasa*, "[Coin] of king Rudra-

siṁha, the Great Satrap, the son of king Rudradāman, the Great Satrap."
Cf. Rapson, *BMC.* XI. 320.

XIII/7. Śaka (Satrapal—Ujjayinī). Svāmi-Rudrasiṁha III. Śaka 310... (388 A.D. ?). Silver (20-Rati Rudradāmaka-Kārṣāpaṇa)—round, .6 inch, 32.7 grains.

Obverse : bust of Satrap to right; meaningless traces of Greek legend around; date behind bust—*300 10...* (partially preserved).

Reverse : three-peaked hill, surmounted by crescent, with crescent, star and waved line (river); Brāhmī legend—*Rājña* [*Mahā*]*kṣatrapasa Svāma-Satyasaha-putrasa Rājño Mahākṣatrapasa Svāma-Rudrasahasa,* "[Coin] of king Svāmi-Rudrasiṁha, the Great Satrap, the son of Svāmi-Satyasiṁha, the king, the Great Satrap."

Cf. Rapson, *BMC.* XVII. 926.

XIII/8. Īśvaradatta. Regnal year 2. Silver (20-Rati standard)—.6 inch, 34.6 grains.

Obverse : bust of king to right, meaningless traces of Greek legend; date behind head—*2.*

Reverse : three-peaked hill surmounted by crescent with crescent, star and waved line (river); Brāhmī legend—*Rajño Mahakṣatrapasa Īśvaradattasa varṣe dvitiye,* "[Coin struck] in the second [regnal] year of king Īśvaradatta, the Great Satrap."

Cf. Rapson, *BMC.* XIII. 479.

XIII/9. Gujarat—latter half of the 2nd century A.D. Silver (32-Rati Kārṣāpaṇa)—square, .55 inch, 50 grains.

Obverse : humped bull, facing; square border of dots.

Reverse : three-peaked hill, surmounted by crescent, with crescent, star and waved line (river); square of dots.

Cf. Rapson, *BMC.* XII. 326.

XIII/10. Sassanian. Varahran V (422-40 A.D.). Gold (imitated from Kuṣāṇa coins—Dīnāra of 68 Ratis)—121 grains=7.84 grammes.

Obverse : figure of king (copied from that of Kuṣāṇa Vāsudeva), wearing head-dress ornamented with ram's horns; dotted border; corrupt legend in Greek characters containing the name and titles of king Varahran V.

Reverse : Śiva and bull (copied from Vāsudeva's coins); dotted border; corrupt legend in Greek characters.

Cf. Rapson, *IC.* II. 15.

XIII/11. Hūṇa. Toramāṇa (c. 500-15 A.D.). Year 52. Silver (20-Rati standard—imitated from Gupta coins)—31 grains=2 grammes.

Obverse : head of king to left; date in front—*50 2.*

Reverse : fan-tailed peacock; Brāhmī legend—*Vijitāvanir=avanipatiḥ śrī-Toramāṇo divaṁjayati* (Upagīti), "The illustrious king Toramāṇa wins the heaven after having conquered the earth."

Cf. Rapson, *IC.* IV. 16. The date may stand for Vikrama-saṁvat 452 (509 A.D.) with the hundred omitted.

XIII/12. Hūṇa. Toramāṇa (c. 500-15 A.D.). Copper.

Obverse : bust of king to right, with the Brāhmī *akṣaras dha* behind and *tra* in front.

Reverse : wheel above; Brāhmī legend below—*Tora.*

Cf. Rapson, *IC.* IV. 19.

XIII/13. Hūṇa. Ṣāhi-Javūvla. Silver (*repoussé*—32-Rati Kārṣāpaṇa)—56 grains=3.62 grammes.

Obverse : head of king to right; Brāhmī legend—*Ṣāhi-Javūvlaḥ*, 'the Ṣāhi prince."

Reverse : not reproduced.

Cf. Rapson, *IC.* IV. 18. Ṣāhi-Javūvla may have been Toramāṇa called *Jaūvla* in the Kura inscription (*Sel. Ins.*, 1965, p. 422).

XIII/14. Hūṇa. Mihirakula (c. 515-35 A.D.). Silver (32-Rati standard) —54.2 grains=3.51 grammes.

Obverse : bust of king to right, with bull-standard in front and trident behind; Brāhmī legend—*Jayatu Mihirakula*[*ḥ*], "Let there be victory to Mihirakula."

Reverse : fire-altar and attendants (copied from Sassanian coins).

Cf. Rapson, *IC.* IV. 20.

XIII/15. Hūṇa. Mihirakula (c. 515-35 A.D.). Copper—.7 inch, 56.3 grains.

Obverse : crude Sassanian bust to right; border of thick dots; Brāhmī legend before face—*Śrī-Mihirakula*, "the illustrious Mihirakula."

Reverse : humped bull walking to left above horizontal line; border of dots; Brāhmī legend below—*Jayatu Vṛṣa*[*ḥ*], "May the Bull (Śiva) be victorious."

Cf. Smith, *IMC.* XXV. 5.

XIII/16. Hūṇa (?). Silver.

Obverse : diademed king on horseback, to right; sword hanging from his waist; lotus with stalk and conch-shell in the upper right field; traces of legend.

Reverse : crude representation of the Sassanian fire-altar.

Whitehead, *The Pre-Mohammedan Coinage of Northwestern India*, XII. 3.

PLATE XIV

XIV/1. Hūṇa (?). Silver.

Obverse : diademed bust of king, to right; border of dots; traces of legend.

Reverse : crude representation of the Sassanian fire-altar.

Cf. Whitehead, *The Pre-Mohammedan Coinage of Northwestern India*, XII. 1.

XIV/2. Hūṇa (?). Billon.

Obverse : bust of crowned king, to right; border of dots; traces of legend.

Reverse : crude representation of the Sassanian fire-altar with attendants; border of dots.

Cf. Whitehead, *The Pre-Mohammedan Coinage of Northwestern India*, XIII. 2.

XIV/3. Gadhaiya Paisā. Silver (base—32-Rati standard)—60 grains.

Obverse : conventional head of king to right; field covered with dots and marks.

Reverse : conventional representation of the Sassanian fire-altar.

Cf. Brown. *CI.* VI. 8.

XIV/4. Gadhaiya Paisā. Billon.

Obverse : crude representation of the bust of king, to right.

Reverse : crude representation of the Sassanian fire-altar; border of dots.

Cf. Whitehead, *The Pre-Mohammedan Coinage of Northwestern India*, XIII. 3.

XIV/5. Gupta. Samudragupta (c. 335-76 A.D.). Gold (68-Rati Dīnāra—Garuḍadhvaja Type)—.9 inch, 114.4 grains.

Obverse : king to left, casting incense on altar, holding spear with left arm; Garuḍa standard on left; *Samudra* written vertically under left arm; marginal Brāhmī legend—*Samara-śata-vitata-[vijayo jita-ripur=ajito divaṁ jayati]* (Upagiti), "Victorious in the conqueror of enemies, who remains unconquered [and] has obtained victory in hundreds of battles."

Reverse : goddess on throne, with feet on lotus; holding cornucopiae on left arm with a mark above it; Brāhmī legend on right—*Parākrama*, "Valour [personified];" monogram.

Smith, *IMC*. XV. 6. With the title *Parākrama*, cf. *Parākramāṅka* in the Allahabad pillar inscription (*Sel. Ins.*, 1965, p. 264, text line 17) and the title *Vikrama*, *Vikramāṅka* or *Vikramāditya* found on the coins of Candragupta II (Allan, *BMC*-[*G*] pp. 24-37, 49-51). *Parākramāṅka* and *Vikramāṅka* are synonymous, both meaning "one whose special mark is valour."

XIV/6. Gupta. Kāca (Samudragupta, c. 335-76 A.D.). Gold (68-Rati Dīnāra)—.8 inch, 115.8 grains.

Obverse : king standing to left, at altar; holding with left arm standard surmounted by rayed disk; vertical Brāhmī legend under left arm—*Kāca*; marginal Brāhmī legend—*Kāco gām=avajitya divaṁ karmabhir=utta-[mair=jayati]* (after conquering the earth, Kāca wins the heaven by his good deeds)—Upagīti.

Reverse : robed goddess standing to left, holding flower in extended right hand and cornucopiae on left arm; monogram; marginal Brāhmī legend—*Sarva-rāj-occhettā*, "the exterminator of all kings."

Cf. Smith, *IMC*. XV. 2. The epithet *Sarvarājocchettā* is applied to Samudragupta in Gupta inscriptions (*Sel. Ins.*, 1965, p. 321).

XIV/7. Gupta. [Samudragupta, c. 335-76 A.D., in the name of] Candragupta I and Kumāradevī and the Licchavis. Gold (68-Rati Dīnāra)—123.8 grains=8.02 grammes.

Obverse : queen Kumāradevī, standing to right, facing king Candragupta I standing to left; Brāhmī legend— *Candragupta* on right and *Kumāradevī* on left.

Reverse : goddess seated on lion, to right, facing, holding noose in right hand and cornucopiae on left arm; symbol in upper left field.

Cf. Rapson, *IC*. IV. 9.

XIV/8. Gupta. Samudragupta (c. 335-76 A.D.). Gold (68-Rati Dīnāra—Archer Type)—.87 inch, 117.2 grains.

Obverse : king standing to left, supporting bow on left arm and holding arrow in right hand; Garuḍa standard, adorned with penons, behind right arm; crescent above Garuḍa; vertical Brāhmī legend below left arm—*Samudra*; marginal Brāhmī legend—parts of *Apratiratho vijitya kṣitiṁ sucaritair=divaṁ jayati* (the unrivalled one wins the heaven by good deeds after having conquered the earth) or *Apratiratho vijitya kṣitim=avanīśo divaṁ jayati* (the unrivalled lord of the earth wins the heaven after having conquered the earth)—Upagīti.

Reverse : goddess Ardokhsho or Lakṣmī seated on throne with noose or fillet and cornucopiae; legend—*Apratirathaḥ*, "the Invincible"; monogram.

Cf. Smith, *IMC*. XV. 8. The coin was collected from Ayodhyā in the Faizabad District, U. P.

XIV/9. Gupta. Samudragupta (c. 335-76 A.D.). Gold (68-Rati Dīnāra—Battle-axe Type)—.77 inch, 113.6 grains.

Obverse : king, facing, with head to left, leaning with left arm on battle-axe; right hand on hip; a dwarf attendant in left field supporting a crescent-tipped standard; verical Brāhmī legend under arm—*Samudra*; marginal legend—parts of *Kṛtāntaparaśur=jayaty=ajitarāja-jet=Ājitaḥ* (Pṛthvī), "victorious is the unconquered subduer of unconquered kings [and] the holder of the battle-axe of the god of death."

Reverse : not reproduced.

Cf. Smith, *IMC*. XV. 9.

XIV/10. Gupta. Samudragupta (c. 335-76 A.D.). Gold (68-Rati Dīnāra—Vīṇā Type)—.92 inch, 115.8 grains.

Obverse : king wearing waist-cloth, seated, to front, on high-backed couch, his feet dangling over its edge; with head to left; playing the Indian lyre (*vīṇā*) resting on his lap; below—footstool and the Brāhmī *akṣara si*; marginal legend—*Mahārājādhirāja-śrī-Samudraguptaḥ*

Reverse : goddess seated, to left, on wicker stool; holding noose in right hand and cornucopiae on left arm; vertical marginal legend separated by vertical line—*Samudraguptaḥ*.

Cf. Smith, *IMC*. XV. 4.

XIV/11. Gupta. Samudragupta (c. 335-76 A.D.). Gold (68-Rati Dīnāra—Aśvamedha Type)—.88 inch, 116.6 grains.

Obverse : horse standing on a plain line to left, facing altar surmounted by bent pole (*yūpa*) with streamers curving above; below—the *akṣara si*; marginal legend—parts of *Rājādhirājaḥ pṛthivīm=avitvā divaṁ jayaty=aprativāryavīryaḥ* (or *āhṛta-vājimedhaḥ*), "the supreme king of kings of invincible prowess wins the heaven after having won the earth" (or 'who has performed the horse-sacrifice' in place of 'of invincible prowess')—Upajāti.

Reverse : chief queen of Samudragupta standing on lotus to left, carrying fly-whisk over right shoulder, with left hand hanging by her side and holding uncertain object; in front—a staff or standard adorned with penons; marginal legend on right—*Aśvamedhaparākramaḥ*, "one whose valour is exhibited by the horse-sacrifice [celebrated by him]."

Cf. Smith, *IMC*. XV. 3.

XIV/12. Gupta. Candragupta II (c. 376-414 A.D.). Gold (68-Rati Dīnāra—Couch Type)—.81 inch, 118 grains.

Obverse : king, wearing waist-cloth, seated on couch, facing, with head turned to left; left hand resting on couch; holding flower in raised right hand; right leg tucked up; left leg on footstool; marginal legend—*Devaśrī-Mahārājādhirāja-Candragupta-Vikramāditya*, "the illustrious king Candragupta Vikramāditya (the Sun in Valour), the supreme king of great kings;" in exergue below couch—*Rūpākṛtī*, 'beauty and form.'

Reverse : goddess seated on throne holding noose and flower respectively in right and left hands; monogram; marginal legend on left—*Śrī-Vikrama* (not reproduced).

Cf. Smith, *IMC*. XV. 10.

XIV/13. Gupta. Candragupta II (c. 376-414 A.D.). Gold (68-Rati Dīnāra—Archer Type)—.77 inch, 121 grains.

Obverse : king standing to right grasping bow in left hand and holding arrow in right hand; Garuḍa standard behind right arm; vertical legend below left arm—*Candra*; marginal legend—*Deva-śrī-Mahārājādhirāja-Candraguptaḥ*.

Reverse : goddess (Lakṣmī) seated on lotus, facing, holding noose in right hand and flower in left hand; monogram; legend —*Śrī-Vikramaḥ*.

Cf. Smith, *IMC*. XV. 14.

XIV/14. Gupta. Candragupta II (c. 376-414 A.D.). Gold (68-Rati Dīnāra—Chatra Type)—oval, .95 inch, 119 grains.

Obverse : king standing to left, casting incense on fire-altar with right hand (as on the Kuṣāṇa coins); dwarf attendant holding, over the king's head, umbrella adorned with streamers; king's left hand resting on sword-hilt; legend—*Śrī-Candragupta-mahārāja*.

Reverse : goddess standing to left, holding noose in right hand and lotus flower in left hand; monogram; legend—*Vikramāditya*, "the Sun of Valour."

Cf. Smith, *IMC*. XVI. 1.

XIV/15. Gupta. Candragupta II (c. 376-414 A.D.). Gold (68-Rati Dīnāra—Lion-slayer Type)—.77 inch, 206.6 grains.

Obverse : king standing, to right, holding bow in left hand and shooting in lion's mouth; the Brāhmī character *ha* sideways before the king's face; marginal legend—*Narendracandraḥ prathita-[śriyā] divaṁjayaty=ajeyo bhuvi Siṅhavikramaḥ* (Vaṁśasthavila), "Siṁhavikrama (valorous like the lion), the invincible moon among kings on the earth, wins the heaven by means of his celebrated splendour."

Reverse : goddess facing, seated on lion to left; holding noose in right hand and lotus in left hand; monogram; legend—*Siṅhavikramaḥ*, "valorous like a lion" or "showing valour to a lion."

Cf. Smith, *IMC*. XV. 16.

XIV/16. Gupta. Candragupta II (c. 376-414 A.D.). Gold (68-Rati Dīnāra—Lion-slayer Type)—.94 inch, 120.2 grains.

Obverse : king to right, holding bow in left hand, shooting in lion's mouth and trampling on lion with left foot; legend—*Narendracandraḥ prathitaśriyā divaṁ jayaty=ajeyo bhuvi Siṅhavikramaḥ* (Vaṁśasthavila).

Reverse : goddess, facing, seated on lion to right, noose in right hand and lotus in left hand; monogram; legend—*Siṅhavikramaḥ*.

Cf. Smith, *IMC*. XV. 17.

XIV/17. Gupta. Candragupta II (c. 376-414 A.D.). Gold (68-Rati Dīnāra—Horseman Type)—.75 inch, 118.3 grains.

Obverse : king on horseback, to left; legend—*Paramabhāgavata-Mahārājādhirāja-śrī-Candraguptaḥ*.

Reverse : goddess seated, on round stool, to left; holding lotus in right hand as well as in left hand; monogram; legend—*Ajita-Vikramaḥ*, "the invincible Vikrama" or "one of invincible valour."

Cf. Smith, *IMC*. XV. 15.

XIV/18. Gupta. Candragupta II (c. 376-414 A.D.). Gold (68-Rati Dīnāra=Horseman Type)—about .75 inch, about 120 grains.

Obverse : king on back of horse, to right; crescent behind head; legend—[*Paramabhāgavata-Mahārājādhirāja*]-*śrī-Candraguptaḥ*.

Reverse : goddess seated on wicker stool, to left; holding fillet or noose in outstretched right hand and lotus (with leaves and roots behind her) in left hand; symbol; legend—*Ajita-Vikramaḥ*.

Cf. Whitehead, *The Pre-Mohammedan Coinage of Northwestern India*, XI. 1; see Allan, *BMC* (G). X. 3.

PLATE XV

XV/1. Gupta. Candragupta II (c. 376-414 A.D). Copper (Chatra Type).

Obverse : king standing to left; with dwarf attendant on right, holding umbrella over king's head.

Reverse : Garuḍa seated, facing; represented with wings and human arms.

Cf. Rapson, *IC*. IV. II.

XV/2. Gupta. Kumāragupta I (414-55 A.D.). Gold (used as a ring which is still attached, 68-Rati Dīnāra—Swordsman Type)—.76 inch.

Obverse : king standing with head to left, casting incense on altar with right hand; left hand on hilt of sword at waist; Garuḍa standard behind right arm; the character *ku* surmounted by crescent below left elbow; marginal legend—*Gām=avajitya sucaritaiḥ Kumāragupto divaṁ jayati* (Upagīti), "Having conquered the earth, Kumāragupta wins the heaven by his good deeds."

Reverse : goddess, seated on lotus, with noose and flower respectively

in right and left hands; monogram; legend—*Śrī-Kumāraguptaḥ*.
Cf. Smith, *IMC.* XVI. 2.

XV/3. Gupta. Kumāragupta I (c. 414-55 A.D.). Gold (68-Rati Dīnāra—Lion-slayer Type)—.8 inch, 126 grains.

Obverse : king facing, half-turned to right, with bow in left hand shooting in the mouth of lion falling backwards; legend—*Kṣitipatir=ajita-Mahendraḥ Kumāragupto divaṁ jayati* (Upagīti), "king Kumāragupta, the unconquered Mahendra (Great Lord), wins the heaven."

Reverse : goddess facing, with one knee tucked up, seated on couchant lion with its head to right ; her right hand holding flower and left hand resting on hip; border of dots; legend—*Śrī-Mahendrasiṁhaḥ*. "the lion in the person of the illustrious Mahendra."

Cf. Smith, *IMC.* XVI. 6.

XV/4. Gupta. Kumāragupta I (c. 414-55 A.D.). Gold (68-Rati Dīnāra—Tiger-slayer Type)—.78 inch, 126.3 grains.

Obverse : king facing, half-turned to left; with bow in right hand shooting in the mouth of tiger falling backwards; under left arm—*ku* with crescent above; legend—*Śrīmāṁ Vyāghrabalaparākramaḥ*, "the glorious one with the strength and valour of a tiger."

Reverse : goddess seated, to left, with left hand holding lotus on hip; feeding peacock with right hand; monogram; marginal legend—*Kumāragupto='dhirājaḥ*, "the supreme king Kumāragupta."

Cf. Smith, *IMC.* XVI. 4.

XV/5. Gupta. Kumāragupta I (c. 414-55 A.D.). Gold (68-Rati Dīnāra—Elephant-rider Type)—.77 inch, 124.1 grains.

Obverse : king riding elephant to left; carrying goad in right hand, with left hand on hip; attendant riding behind and holding umbrella over king's head; marginal legend—*Kṣitipati*............as on No. XV/3 above.

Reverse : Lakṣmī, nimbate, standing, facing, on lotus; holding in right hand lotus flower hanging down and uncertain object in left hand; border of dots; legend—uncertain.

Cf. Smith, *IMC.* XVI. 7.

XV/6. Gupta. Kumāragupta. I (c. 414-55 A.D.). Gold (68-Rati Dīnāra—Kārttikeya Type)—.78 inch, 127.2 grains.

Obverse : king standing, head half-turned to left; feeding peacock from bunch of fruits held in right hand; legend—*Jayati svabhūmau guṇarāśi*........ (right), *Mahendra-Kumāra* (left).

Reverse : god Kārttikeya, nimbate, three-quarters to left, riding on his peacock Paravāṇi (standing on a kind of platform), holding spear (*śakti*) in left hand over left shoulder; spirinkling incense on altar with right hand; border of dots; legend—*Mahendra-Kumāraḥ*, i.e. Mahendrāditya Kumāragupta.

Cf. Smith, *IMC.* XVI. 3.

XV/7. Gupta. Skandagupta (455-67 A.D.). Gold (80-Rati Suvarṇa—Archer Type) —.81 inch, 141.2 grains.

Obverse : king standing to left, grasping bow in left hand and stretching right hand across Garuḍa standard ; *Skanda* written vertically under left arm, with crescent above.

Reverse: Lakṣmī, seated on lotus seat, with noose in right hand and lotus in left hand; symbol; legend—*Kramāditya*.

Cf. Smith, *IMC.* XVI. 8.

XV/8. Gupta. Skandagupta (455-67 A.D.). Gold (80-Rati Suvarṇa—King and Queen Type)—.8 inch, 131.3 grains.

Obverse : Garuḍa standard; king on left and queen (wrongly called

Lakṣmī by some) on right, looking at each other; king standing to right, with right hand on hip and left hand grasping bow with its string parallel to the Garuḍa standard; queen standing to left, holding lotus in left hand and uncertain object in raised right hand; traces of legend which may be *Jayati mahītalaṁ sudhanvī*.

Reverse : Lakṣmī, nimbate, seated on lotus, holding fillet in outstretched right hand and lotus in left hand resting on knee; symbol on left; legend—*Śrī-Skandaguptaḥ*.

Cf. Smith, *IMC*. XVI. 9.

XV/9. Gupta. Skandagupta (455-67 A.D.). Silver (20-Rati Rūpaka, Central India)—33.5 grains.

Obverse : head of king to right; uncertain date in Brāhmī numerals on right.

Reverse : peacock standing, facing, with outstretched wings; legend around—*Vijit-āvanir=avanipatir=jayati divaṁ Skandagupto='yom* (Upagiti), "This is king Skandagupta who has conquered the earth [and] is winning the heaven;" border of dots.

Cf. Brown, *CI*. VI. 2.

XV/10. Gupta. Skandagupta (455-67 A.D.). Gupta year 145 (464 A.D.). Silver (20-Rati Rupāka—Central India)—34.3 grains=2.22 grammes.

Obverse: king's head to right; date in front—*100 40* 5.

Reverse : fan-tailed peacock; legend around—*Vijij-āvanir=avanipatir=jayati divaṁ Skandagupto='yam*, "This is king Skandagupta who has conquered the earth [and] is conquering the heaven."=Upagīti.

Cf. Rapson, *IC*. IV. 10.

XV/11. Gupta. Prakāśāditya. Gold (80-Rati Suvarṇa)—.8 inch, 145.8 grains.

Obverse : king on horse back, to right, carrying bow slung behind and thrusting weapon into tiger's mouth; the letter *u* below horse; marginal legend—*vijitya vasudhāṁ divaṁ jayati*.

Reverse : Lakṣmī seated on lotus, holding noose in right hand and lotus in left hand; symbol; marginal legend—*śrī-Prakāśāditya*.

Cf. Smith, *IMC*. XVI. 10.

XV/12. Gupta (imitation). East Bengal. Gold (60-Rati standard)—.85 inch, 92.5 grains.

Obverse : king standing, to left, holding bow in left hand and arrow in left field ; border of thick dots.

Reverse : goddess standing to right ; marginal legend on right, the reading of which is doubtful.

Cf. Allan, *BMC* (G). XXIV. 18.

XV/13. Gauḍa. Śaśāṅka (c. 600-25 A.D.). Gold (80-Rati Suvarṇa—debased metal and unsatisfactory execution)—.8 inch, 139.7 grains.

Obverse : Śiva half-turned to right, reclining on couchant bull to left; with right hand resting on bull's hump and left hand raised; orb of the moon above bull's neck (indicating *śaśāṅka*, 'moon'); below in exergue—*jayaḥ* (victory); in right margin—*Śrī-Śa* (*śāṅka**) (vertically written).

Reverse : Lakṣmī, nimbate, seated on lotus, facing, with elephant on either side sprinkling water on her; lotus in her left hand resting on knee and right hand outstretched; legend—*śrī-Śaśāṅkaḥ*.

Cf. Smith, *IMC*. XVI. 12.

XV/14. Gauḍa. Śaśāṅka. Gold (80-Rati Suvarṇa)—145 grains=9.39 grammes.

Obverse : Śiva facing, seated on bull to left; legend—*Śrī-Śa* (*śāṅka**) (right) and *jaya* (below), "Victory of the illustrious Śaśāṅka."

Reverse : goddess seated on lotus; legend—*Śrī-Śaśāṅka*.

Cf. Rapson, *IC*. IV. 15.

XV/15. Gauḍa (?). Narendrāditya. Gold (much alloyed; 80-Rati Suvarṇa) —.9 inch, 148.2 grains.

Obverse : king nimbate, standing to left, holding bow in left hand and arrow in right hand; bull-standard on left; legend—*Kapa* (below left arm) and *ca* (between feet).

Reverse : Lakṣmī, nimbate, seated on lotus, facing, holding lotus in left hand and fillet in outstretched right hand; symbol on left; legend—*Śrī-Narendrādityaḥ*.

Cf. Smith, *IMC*. XVI. 11.

XV/16. Narendrāditya. Gold (80-Rati Suvarṇa)—.86 inch, 149 grains.

Obverse : king, nimbate, facing, with head to left; squatted on throne, with left knee raised ; right hand on knee and left hand raised; a standing female attendant on either side; the letter *dha* in front of throne and *Yama* written in small characters vertically above the king's left arm.

Reverse : Lakṣmī standing to left, holding long-stalked lotus in right hand with left hand resting on hip; lotus springing from ground behind her and peacock to left standing in front; legend in right margin—*Śrī-Narendrāditya*.

Cf. Smith, *IMC*. XVI. 13.

XV/17. Traikūṭaka. Vyāghrasena (latter half of the 5th century A.D.). Silver (20-Rati standard)—.5 inch, 32 grains.

Obverse : head of king to right.

Reverse : three-peaked hill with star on right ; legend around—*Mahārāja-Dahra[sena]-putra-Paramavaiṣṇava-śrī-Mahārāja-Vyāghra[sena]*, "*Mahārāja* Vyāghrasena, the great devotee of Viṣṇu [and] the son of *Mahārāja* Dahrasena."

Cf. Rapson, *BMC*. XVIII. 975.

XV/18. Early Kalacuri. Kṛṣṇarāja. Silver (20-Rati Rūpaka)—31 grains=2 grammes.

Obverse : head of king to right.

Reverse : humped bull couching, to right; legend around—*Paramamaheśvara-Māhadevyoḥ pād-ānudhyāta-śrī-Kṛṣṇarājaḥ*, "the illustrious Kṛṣṇarāja meditating on the feet of the Supreme Maheśvara and Mahādevī (Śiva and Durgā)."

Cf. Rapson, *IC*. IV. 17.

XV/19. Maukhari. Īśānavarman (c. 550-75 A.D.) Year 54. Silver (20-Rati standard)—35 grains=2.26 grammes.

Obverse : head of king to left; date in front—*50 4*.

Reverse : fan-tailed peacock; legend around—*Vijit-āvanir=avanipatiḥ śr-Īśānavarmā divaṁ jayati* (Upagīti), "The illustrious king Īśānavarman wins the heaven after having conquered the earth."

Cf. Rapson, *IC*. IV. 13. The date may be the Gupta year 254 (573 A.D.) with omitted hundred.

XV/20. Puṣyabhūti (Sthāṇvīśvara). Śīlāditya (Harṣavardhana). Silver (20-Rati standard)—about 36 grains.

Obverse : head of king to left; uncertain date on left.

Reverse: peacock standing, facing with outspread wings and tail; border of dots; legend around—*Vijit-āvanir=avanipatiḥ Śīlādityo divaṁ jayati* (Upagīti), "Śīlāditya, the king, wins heaven after having conquered the world."

Cf. Whitehead, *The Pre-Mohammedan Coinage of Northwestern India*, XI.4; see Brown, *CI*. VI. 3. *Śrī* is sometimes wrongly aded before the king's name.

XV/21. Valabhī. Silver (20-Rati standard)—30.6 grains=1.98 grammes.

Obverse : king's head to right.

Reverse : trident; legend—not satisfactorily read.
Cf. Rapson, *IC*. IV. 12.

XV/22. South Kosala. Bhīmasena. Silver (20-Rati standard)—34.2 grains=2.21 grammes.
Obverse : head of king to left; traces of date in front.
Reverse : fan-tailed peacock; legend around—*Vijit-āvanir=avanipatir=Bhīmaseno divaṁ jayati*, "king Bhīmasena, conquerer of the earth, [now] wins the heaven."
Cf. Rapson, *IC*. IV. 14. Read *patiḥ Śrī-Bhīmaseno*. See his Arang plate dated in the Gupta year 282 (601 A.D.) in *Ep. Ind.*, IX, pp. 342 ff.

PLATE XVI

XVI/1. Arakan. Silver—1.07 inch, 114.2 grains.
Obverse : recumbent humped bull to left; Brāhmī legend above—*Yarukīya* (probably a place name related to Arakan).
Reverse : a variant of the Linga-flanked-by-snake symbol.
Cf. Smith, *IMC*. XXXI. 10.

XVI/2. Nepal. Aṁśuvarman (first half of the 7th century A.D.). Copper.
Obverse : winged horse to left; border of thick dots; legend above—*śry-Aṁśuvarmā*.
Reverse : cow to left; border of thick dots; legend above—*Kāmadehī*.
Cf. Rapson, *IC*. V. 1. *Kāmadehī=Kama-dhenu*.

XVI/3. Harṣavat *alias* Devapāla. Gold (80-Rati Suvarṇa)—1 inch, 180.5 grains.
Obverse : king wearing *dhotī*, to front, with face turned to left, holding arrow (with one end resting on ground) in extended right hand and bow in extended left hand; legend in East Indian characters (c. 9th century A.D.)—(1) *śrī-* (2) *mā(ṁ*)* (above right hand), (3) *Harṣa-* (4) *vā-* (beneath right hand) (5) *n=Deva-* (5) *pāla*, "the illustrious Harṣavat Devapāla."
Reverse : Lakṣmī, seated cross-legged on conventional double lotus, holding lotus in both left and right hands; with vase on left and on right; legend—*Śrī* (i.e. the goddess Lakṣmī) in upper left field.
Cf. *Journ. Num. Soc. Ind.*, Vol. XIII, pp. 123 ff. and Plate. It is difficult to say whether the coin may be attributed to king Devapāla (c. 810-50 A.D.) of Bengal and Bihar.

XVI/4. Gurjara-Pratihāra (Kanauj). Ādivarāha (Bhoja I, c. 836-85 A.D.). Billon.
Obverse : figure of a human being with boar's head (the boar incarnation of Viṣṇu).
Reverse : indistinct marks in place of which the silver issues have the legend—(1) *Śrīmad-Ā-* (2) *divarāha*, "the illustrious Primeval Boar."
Cf. Whitehead, *The Pre-Mohammedan Coinage of Northwestern India*, XIV. 4. See silver and copper issues of this type in Smith's *IMC*. pp. 41-42. Bhoja assumed the name Ādivarāha.

XVI/5. Kalacuri (Ḍāhala, Tripurī). Gāṅgeya (c. 1015-41 A.D.). Gold (34-Rati ½-Dīnāra) —about 62 grains=40 grammes.
Obverse : legend—(1) *Śrīmad-Gā-* (2) *ṅgeyade-* (3) *vaḥ*.
Reverse : four-armed Lakṣmī, seated, facing.
Cf. Brown, *CI*. VI. 10.

XVI/6. Kalacuri (Ḍāhala, Tripurī) Gāṅgeya (c. 1015-41 A.D.). Gold (34-Rati ½-Dīnāra)—77 inch, 63 grains.
Obverse : legend in bold characters—(1) *Śrīmad-Gā-* (2) *ṅgeyade-* (3) *va*.

Reverse : nimbate four-armed Lakṣmī, seated, facing, cross-legged; arms spread out at sides.
Cf. Smith, *IMC*. XXVI. 7.

XVI/7. Kalacuri (Ratnapura). Jājalla (II, c. 1160-68 A. D.). Gold (34-Rati ½-Dīnāra)—.8 inch. 58 grains.
Obverse : legend—(1) *Śrīmaj-Jā-* (2) *jalladeva*.
Reverse : crude representation of lion to right.
Cf. Smith, *IMC*. XXVI. 12.

XVI/8. Candella. Hallakṣaṇavarman (c. 1100 A.D.). Gold (34-Rati ½-Dīnāra)—63 grains
Obverse : legend—(1) *Śrīmaddha-* (2) *llakṣaṇa-* (3) *varmmadeva*.
Reverse : four-armed Lakṣmī, seated, facing.
Cf. Brown, *CI*. VI. 9.

XVI/9. Candella. Trailokyavarman (c. 1202-49 A.D.). Gold (base—34-Rati ½-Dīnāra)—.75 inch, 62.2 grains.
Obverse : legend—(1) *Śrīmat-Trai-* (2) *lokyava-* (3) *rmmadeva*.
Reverse : crude representation of seated Lakṣmī.
Cf. Smith, *IMC*. XXVI. 9.

XVI/10. Gāhaḍavāla Govindacandra (c. 1114-55 A.D.). Gold (34-Rati ½-Dīnāra)—.81 inch, 59.7 grains.
Obverse : legend—(1) *Śrīmad-Go-* (2) *vindacandra-* (3) [*deva*].
Reverse : seated Lakṣmī.
Cf. Smith, *IMC*. XXVI. 18.

XVI/11. Cāhamāna. Pṛthvīrāja III (c. 1175-93 A.D.). Silver (32-Rati Kārṣāpaṇa)—.6 inch, 52 grains.
Obverse : crude representation of horseman; legend—*Śrī-Pṛthvīrājadeva* (not reproduced).
Reverse : crude representation of bull; legend—*Asāvarī-śrī-Sāmantadeva*.
Cf. Smith, *IMC*. XXVI. 20 (obverse and reverse).

XVI/12. Kashmir (?). Vigraha (c. 7th century A.D.). Copper—.85 inch, 117 grains.
Obverse : barbarous imitation of the standing king on Kuṣāṇa coins; legend—*Kida* under left arm.
Reverse : unrecognisable representation of seated goddess (without head); vertical legend on right—*śrī-Vigra*[*ha*].
Cf. Smith, *IMC*. XXVII. 8.

XVI/13. Kashmir (?). Yaśovarman (8th century A.D.). Gold (base—68-Rati Dīnāra)—112 grains.
Obverse : unrecognisable copy of the standing king on Kuṣāṇa coins; legend—*Kidā*[*ra*] below left arm.
Reverse : barbarous representation of seated goddess (without head); vertical legend on right—*śrī-Ya*[*śa*].
Cf. Brown, *CI*. VI. 16.

XVI/14. Kashmir. Diddā. Copper (50-Rati standard)—about 85 grains.
Obverse : crude representation of standing king, to right.
Reverse : seated goddess; legend—*śrī-* (left), *Diddā* (right).
Cf. Brown, *CI*. VI. 15. For the legend *Di*(*Diddā*)*- Kṣema* on her hunband's coins, see Smith, *IMC*. XXVII. 10.

XVI/15. Kashmir. Harṣa. Gold (40-Rati standard—imitated from the Karṇāṭa or Dākṣiṇātya coinage)—71.8 grains=4.65 grammes.
Obverse : elephant to right.
Reverse : legend—(1) *śrī-Harṣa-* (2) *deva*.

Cf. Rapson *IC*. IV. 23.

XVI/16. Kashmir. Harṣa. Gold (40-Rati standard)—73 grains.
Obverse : horseman to right; legend—*Harṣadeva*.
Reverse : seated goddess.
Cf. Brown, *CI*. VI. 14.

PLATE XVII

XVII/1. Kashmir (?). Copper.
Obverse : crude representation of king standing; trident on right.
Reverse : crude representation of Lakṣmī seated; *ja* on left and *ya* on right.
Cf. Rapson, *IC*. IV. 24. Cunningham read the legend as *Jaga* and attributed the coin to Jāgadeva (1198-1214 A.D.) of Kashmir.

XVII/2. Ṣāhi. Bhīma and Sāmanta. Gold (40-Rati standard)—.8 inch, 68 grains.
Obverse : in border of minute dots—bearded king, wearing *dhotī*, seated cross-legged on throne, extending right hand to a person, standing to right, on left; symbols including trident; legend above—*Ṣāhi-śrī-Bhīmadeva*; with the *akṣara go* below throne.
Reverse : in border of minute dots—bearded king seated in the *rājalīlā* pose with right hand raised (the palm opening inwards) and left hand resting on thigh; Lakṣmī seated, to right, on left, holding lotus in left hand; legend above—*śrīmad-Guṇanidhi-śrī-Sāmanatadeva*.
Cf. *Num. Chron.*, 1952, pp. 133-35 and Plate.

XVII/3. Ṣāhi. Spalapati. Silver (32-Rati standard)—50.6 grains=3.27 grammes.
Obverse : horseman to right; the letter *gu* behind and traces of legend in front.
Reverse : recumbent humped bull to left; legend—*śrī-Spalapatideva*.
Cf. Rapson, *IC*. V. 6.

XVII/4. Ṣāhi. Spalapati. Silver (32-Rati standard)—50 grains.
Obverse : horseman to right; undeciphered legend around.
Reverse : recumbent bull to left; legend—*Śrī-Spalapatideva*.
Cf. Brown, *CI*. VI. 12.

XVII/5. Amṛtapāla. Silver (32-Rati standard)—.6 inch, 45 grains.
Obverse : crude representation of bull to left; legend above—*Amṛta-p[āla]*.
Reverse : crude representation of horseman to right.
Cf. Smith, *IMC*. XXVI. 6. Amṛtapāla was probably a ruler of Budaun. His name was formerly read wrongly as Aśatapāla who was identified with Aśaṭa of Chamba or Jirishta's Ishtpāl, father of Ṣāhi Jayapāla. See *L.* Gopal, *Coin-types of N. Ind.*, p. 32.

XVII/6. Ṣāhi. Sāmanta. Silver (32-Rati standard)—about .8 inch, about 51 grains.
Obverse : crude representation of king in armour, on caparisoned horse, to right; symbols.
Reverse : recumbent humped bull, to left, with trappings with curved sides on rump; legend above—*śrī-Sāmantadeva*.
Cf. Whitehead, *The Pre-Mohammedan Coinage of Northwestern India*, XIV. 1; see Smith, *IMC*. XXVI. 3.

XVII/7. Ṣāhi. Sāmanta. Copper (20-Rati ¼-Paṇa)—about 77 inch, about 37 grains.

Obverse : elephant standing to left; legend above—*Śrī-Sāmantadeva*.

Reverse : crude representation of lion, to right, with tail curved above back.

Cf. Whitehead, *The Pre-Mohammedan Coinage of Northwestern India*, XIV. 2; see Smith, *IMC*. p. 248.

XVII/8. South India. Silver (20 Mañjāḍi or 64-Rati standard)—103.9 grains.

Obverse : lion to right.

Reverse : vase on stand; circle of rays.

Cf. Brown, *CI*. VII. 8.

XVII/9. Eastern Cālukya (Veṅgī). Viṣamasiddhi (title of Kubja-Viṣṇuvardhana [615-33 A.D.,] and his descendants). Silver (base—10-Mañjāḍi or 32-Rati standard)—.61 inch, 50 grains.

Obverse : within dotted border—crudely represented lion to right; above—legend in Telugu characters—*Viṣamasiddhi*, "successful in tackling difficulties."

Reverse : within border of rays—a double trident, surmounted by crescent and flanked by lamps.

Cf. Smith, *IMC*. XXX. 1.

XVII/10. Cola. Uttamacola (973-85A.D.). Silver (12½-Mañjāḍi or 40-Rati standard)—62.6 grains=4.05 grammes.

Obverse : tiger seated under canopy, to right, facing two fishes.

Reverse : Nāgarī legend—*Uttamacola*.

Cf. Rapson, *IC*. V. 13.

XVII/11. Cola. Rājendra (I, 1016-44 A.D.) Silver (10-Mañjāḍi or 32-Rati standard)—52 grains.

Obverse : tiger seated to right under canopy, between bow on left and a pair of fish on right; Nāgarī legend below—*Śrī-Rājendra*.

Reverse : same as the obverse.

Cf. Brown, *CI*. VII. 6.

XVII/12. Western Cālukya (Kalyāṇa). Jagadekamalla (Jayasiṁha, 1015-42 A.D.). Gold (cup-shaped—12½-Mañjāḍi or 40-Rati standard)—1.1 inch, 68 grains.

Obverse : concave, in shallow cup-shape—temple in centre; Kannaḍa legend on basement—*Jagadakamala* (*lla*), "the sole wrestler of the world;" in margin, characters formed by separate punches—*śrī* (3 times) and *Jagadakamala* (4 times).

Reverse : blank (not reproduced).

Cf. Smith, *IMC*. XXX. 3.

XVII/13. Western Cālukya (Kalyāṇa). Gold (Pagoda, 12½-Mañjāḍi or 40-Rati standard) —57.2 grains=3.7 grammes.

Obverse : boar to right, surmounted by various punch-marked symbols.

Reverse : striated.

Cf. Rapson, *IC*. V. 17.

XVII/14. Gajapati Pagoda. Gold (12½-Mañjāḍi or 40-Rati standard)—60.2 grains.

Obverse : ornate elephant to right, facing symbol.

Reverse : floral scroll design.

Cf. Brown, *CI*. VII. 5.

XVII/15. Eastern Cālukya (Veṅgī). Rājarāja I (1019-61 A.D.). Regnal year 35. Gold (12½ Mañjāḍi or 40-Rati standard)—66.8 grains.

Obverse : in centre—boar, to right; Telugu legend around—*śrī*-

Rājarāja-sa 35, "[struck in] the 35th [regnal] year of the illustrious Rājarāja."
Reverse : not reproduced.
Cf. Brown, *CI*. VII. 4.

XVII/16. Pāṇḍya. Gold (12½-Mañjāḍi or 40-Rati standard)—57 grains.
Obverse : two fishes under canopy, with lamp on right and flywhisk on left.
Reverse : undeciphered legend in 3 lines.
Cf. Brown, *CI*. VII. 3.

XVII/17. Pāṇḍya (between the 7th and 10th centuries A.D.). Gold (Pagoda—12½-Mañjāḍi or 40-Rati standard)—57 grains=3.69 grammes.
Obverse : two fishes under canopy, with lamp on right and flywhisk on left.
Reverse : Nāgarī legend—(1) *śrī-Pā(ṁ*)*- (2) *ḍyavaṭā* (3)......
Cf. Rapson, *IC*. V. 10.

XVII/18. Kerala. Vīrakerala (about the 11th or 12th century A.D.). Silver (20-Rati standard)—36.3 grains
Obverse : unread legend (*Guṇabhogasya* ?); border of dots.
Reverse : legend—*śrī-Vīrakeralasya* ; dotted border.
Cf. Brown, *CI*. VII. 9.

XVII/19. Padma-ṭaṅkā. Gold (base, cup-shaped—10-Mañjāḍi or 32-Rati standard)—.9 inch, 53.5 grains.
Obverse : in centre—Hanumat; the Nāgarī letter *Ha* (for *Hanumat*) in cage, and the lotus symbol, four each, interposed around.
Reverse : blank (not reproduced).
Cf. Smith, *IMC*. XXX. 4.

XVII/20. Padma-ṭaṅkā. Gold (cup-shaped—12½-Mañjāḍi or 40-Rati standard)—.73 inch, 58.7 grains.
Obverse : concave; seven-petalled lotus on bottom of cup; on the sides—symbols around including sword and the Nāgarī legend—*śrī-śrī-Rāma*.
Reverse : blank (not reproduced).
Cf. Smith, *IMC*. XXX. 17. It is either a Rāma-ṭaṅkā issued by a temple or was issued by a king like Yādava Rāmacandra (1271-1311 A.D.).

PLATE XVIII

XVIII/1. Ceylon. Parākramabāhu (1153-86 A.D.). Copper.
Obverse : crude representation of standing king.
Reverse : seated goddess; Nāgarī legend—(1) *śrī*- (2) *Parā*- (3) *krama*- (4) *bāhu*.
Cf. Brown, *CI*. VII. 7.

XVII/2. Ceylon, Queen Līlāvatī (1197-1200 A.D. and 1209 A.D.). Copper—octagonal, .83 inch, 65.1 grains.
Obverse : crude figure of king, standing, facing; folds of waist-cloth hanging down on both sides; holding flower in raised left hand; right hand extended above uncertain object.
Reverse : crude figure of seated goddess, with left arm raised; legend below left arm—(1) *śrī*- (2) *Rāja*- (3) *Līlā*- (4) *vatī*.
Cf. Smith, *IMC*. XXXI. 5.

XVIII/3. Ceylon. Sāhasamalla (1200-02 A.D.). Copper—.82 inch, 65.6 grains.
Obverse : crude figure of standing king as on Parākramabāhu's coins.
Reverse : crude representation of seated goddess as on Parākramabāhu's

coins; legend—(1) *śri-* (2) *mat-Sā-* (3) *hasa-* (4) *malla.*
Cf. Smith, *IMC.* XXXI. 6.

XVIII/4. Ghūr Muizuddīn Muḥammad bin Sām (Muḥammad Ghūrī, 1203-06 A.D.). Gold (40-Rati standard)—.8 inch, 66.5 grains.
Obverse : Nāgarī legend—*Srī-Mahamada bini Sāma* (in 3 lines).
Reverse : crude representation of Lakṣmī.
Cf. Wright, *CMSD.* I. 4.

XVIII/5. Ghūr. Muizuddīn Muḥammad bin Sām (Muḥammad Ghūrī, 1203-06 A.D.). Billon—.65 inch, 54.5 grains.
Obverse : Arabic legend—*as-Sulṯānul a'ẕam Muizud-dunyā waddīn* (the supreme king Muizuddīn).
Reverse : Arabic legend—*Kaiqubād*; Nāgarī legend—(1) *sri-Sulatāṁ* (2) *Muijudī.*
Cf. Wright, *CMSD.* IV. B263.

XVIII/6. Slave Dynasty (Delhi). Shamsuddīn Iltutmish (1211-36 A.D.). Silver (96-Rati standard)—about 165 grains.
Obverse : not reproduced.
Reverse : in square—Arabic legend written in a circle—*as-Sulṯānul a'ẕam Shamsud-dunyā waddīn abul-muẕaffar Iltutmish as-Sulṯān,* "the supreme Sulṯān, the sun of the world and the faith, the father of the victorious, Iltutmish, the Ṣulṯān;" incomplete marginal legend.
Cf. Brown, *CI.* VIII. 2.

XVIII/7. Slave Dynasty (Dehli). Shamsuddīn Iltutmish (1211-36 A.D.). Copper.
Obverse : in square—Arabic legend in a circle—*as-Sulṯān* (the king).
Reverse : in hexagon—Arabic legend—*'Adl* (the Just).
Cf. Brown, *CI.* VIII. 1.

XVIII/8. Slave Dynasty (Delhi). Rāziya (1236-40 A.D.). Billon—about 54 grains.
Obverse : horseman to right; Nāgarī legend around—*śrī-Hamīraḥ,* "the Amīr."
Reverse : Arabic legend—*as-Sulṯānul a'ẕam Raẕiyatud-dunyā waddīn,* "the supreme Sulṯān Raẕiyatuddīn (the pleasure of the world and the faith)."
Cf. Brown, *CI.* VIII. 3.

XVIII/9. Slave Dynasty (Delhi). Ghiyāsuddīn Balban (1266-86 A.D.). Billon—about 55 grains.
Obverse : Arabic legend in circle—*Balban*; Nāgarī legend around—*śrī-Sulatāna-Giyāsudīna.*
Reverse : Arabic legend—*as-Sulṯānul a'ẕam Ghiyāsud-dunyā waddīn,* "the supreme Sulṯān Ghiyāsuddīn (the succour of the world and the faith)."
Cf. Brown, *CI.* VIII. 4.

XVIII/10. Khaljī Dynasty (Delhi). 'Alāuddīn Muḥammad Shāh (1296-1316 A.D.). Delhi—A. H. 698 (1298-99 A.D.). Gold (96-Rati standard)—170 grains.
Obverse : Arabic legend—*as-Sulṯānul a'ẕam 'Alā ud dunyā waddīn abul muẕaffar Muḥammad Shāh as-Sulṯān,* "the supreme king 'Alāuddīn Muḥammad Shāh, the Sulṯān, the father of the victorious."
Reverse : Arabic legend in circle—*Sikandaruṣ-ṣānī Yamīnul khilāfatī Nāṣiru Amīrul Mominīn,* "the second Alexander, the right hand of the Khilāfat, the helper of the commander of the faithful;" in margin—*Ẕuriba hazihis-sikkatu bi haẕrati Dehlī fī sinate ṣamāna wa tis'aina wa sittami 'ata,* "struck this coin at the capital, Dehlī, in the year eight and ninety and six hundred."
Cf. Brown, *CI.* VIII. 5.

XVIII/11. Khaljī Dynasty (Delhi). Quṭbuddīn Mubārak (1316-20 A.D.). A. H. 719 (1319-20 A.D.). Billon—80 grains.

Obverse : Arabic legend in cricle—*Khalifatullāh Mubārak Shāh*, "Mubārak Shāh, the Khalifa of God"; around—*as-Sulṭānul wāṣiqu bi'-llāh Amīrul Mominīn*, "the Sulṭān, the truster in God, the commander of the faithful."

Reverse : Arabic legend—*al Imāmul a'zam Quṭbuddunyā waddīn abul Muzaffar*, "the supreme Imām, Quṭbuddīn, the father of the victorious."

Cf. Brown, *IC.* VIII. 6.

XVIII/12. Tughluq Dynasty (Delhi). Muḥammad bin Tughluq (1325-51 A.D.). Dehlī—A. H. 726 (1325-26 A.D.). Gold (110-Rati standard)—199 grains.

Obverse : Arabic legend in circle—*al wāṣiqu bi ta'īdur raḥmān Muḥammad Shāh as-Sulṭān* (the truster in the help of the Merciful, king Muḥammad Shāh); marginal legend—same as on No. XVIII/ 10, but *hazihiddīnār*, and the date written in Arabic words.

Reverse : Arabic legend—*Ashhadu an lā ilāha illallāho wa ashhadu an Muḥammadan 'abduhu wa Ras ūluhu*, "I testify that there is no god but God, and I testify that Muḥammad is his servant and apostle."

Cf. Brown, *CI.* VIII. 7.

XVIII/13. Tughluq Dynasty (Delhi). Muḥammad bin Tughluq (1325-51 A.D.) in the name of Khalifa Al Hakim. Billon—about 140 grains.

Obverse : Arabic legend within quatrefoil—*Al Ḥākim b'amru'llah.*

Reverse : Arabic legend within quatrefoil—*Abul 'abbās Aḥmad.*

Cf. Brown, *CI.* VIII. 8.

XVIII/14. Tughluq Dynasty (Delhi). Muhammad bin Tughluq (1325-51 A.D.). Tughluqpūr—A.H. 730 (1329-30A.D.). Brass (forced currency)—about 140 grains.

Obverse : Arabic legend in circle—*Man atā' as-Sulṭān faqad atā' ar Raḥmān*, "He, who obeys the Sulṭān, surely obeys the Merciful;" marginal legend in Persian—*Dar iqlim-i-Tughluqpūr 'urf Tirhut sāl bar hafṣad sī*, "[struck] in the territory of Tughluqpūr *alias* Tirhut, in the year seven hundred and thirty."

Reverse : Persian legend—*Muhar shud tankah-i-ra'ij dar rūzgāh-i bandah-i-ummīdwār Muḥammad Tughluq*, "stamped as a Tanka current in the reign of Muḥammad, [the son of] Tughluq, the slave hopeful of mercy."

Cf. Brown, *CI.* VIII. 9.

XVIII/15. Tughluq Dynasty (Delhi). Fīrūz Shāh (1351-88 A.D.). Gold (96-Rati standard) —169 grains.

Obverse : Arabic legend in circle—*Fī zamānil imāmi Amīrul mominīn 'Abu 'Abdu'llāh khuldat khilāfatuhu*, "the time of the Imām, the commander of the faithful, 'Abu 'Abdullāh..."; marginal legend—illegible.

Reverse : Arabic legend—*as-Sulṭānul a'zam Fīrūz Shāh Zaffar Shāh ibn-i-Fīrūz Shāh Sulṭānī*, "the supreme Sulṭān Fīrūz Shāh Zaffar Shāh, son of Fīrūz Shāh Sulṭān."

Cf. Brown, *CI.* VIII. 11.

XVIII/16. Tughlaq Dynasty (Delhi). Fīrūz Shāh (1351-88 A.D.). Dehlī—A. H. 773 (1371-72 A.D.). Billon—140 grains.

Obverse : Arabic legend—*al khalifatu Amīrul Mominīn khuldat khilāfatuhu, 773*, "the Khalifa of the Commander of the Faithful; may the Khilāfat be perpetuated."

Reverse : Arabic legend—*Fīrūz Shāh Sulṭanī Zuriba bi ḥazrati Dehlī*, "struck by Sulṭān Fīrūz Shāh at the capital Dehlī."

Cf. Brown, *CI.* VIII. 10.

XVIII/17. Bengal. Sikandar Shāh (1357-93 A.D.). Fīrūzābād—A.H. 783 (1381-82 A.D.). Silver (96-Rati standard)—166 grains.

Obverse : Arabic legend in circle—*Abul mujāhid Sikandar Shāh ibn-i-Ilyās Shāh Sulṭān* (the father of the warrior, Sikandar Shah, the son of Sulṭān Ilyās Shāh); in the margin—names of the Four Companions in four circles; between these—*al Imāmul a'zamul wāṣiqu bi tā'īdur Rahmān*, "the truster in the help of the Merciful......."

Reverse : Arabic legend in the central region—*Yamīni Khalifat'ullāh naṣīru Amīrul Mominīn ghauṣul islām wa muslimīn khallada mulkahu*, "the right hand of the Khalifa of God, the helper of the Commander of the Faithful, the succourer of Islām and the Muslims; may God perpetuate the kingdom;" in the margin—*Ẓuriba hazihissikkatul mubārikatu fī baldati Fīrūzābād*, "struck this blessed coin in the town of Fīrūzābād........"

Cf. Brown, *CI*. IX. 1.

PLATE XIX

XIX/1. Ma'bar (Madura). 'Ādil Shāh (1356-60 A.D.). Copper.

Obverse : Arabic legend—*as-Sulṭān 'Ādil Shāh.*

Reverse : Arabic legend—*as-Sulṭānul a'ẓam.*

Cf. Brown. *CI*. IX. 8.

XIX/2. Kashmir. Zainul Ābidīn (1420-70 A.D.). A. H. 842 (1438-39 A. D.). Silver(50-Rati standard)—96 grains.

Obverse : Arabic legend—*as-Sulṭānul a'ẓam Ẓainul-'ābidīn, 842.*

Reverse : Arabic legend in lozenge—*Ẓuriba Kashmīr* (struck in Kashmīr) ; in marginal segments—*fī shuhūri sina iṣnai wa arb'aina wa ṣemanami'ata*, "in the months of the year two and forty and eight hundred."

Cf. Brown, *CI*. IX. 9.

XIX/3. Bahmanī. 'Alāuddīn Aḥmad II (1436-58 A.D.). A. H. 850 (1446-47 A.D.). Silver (96-Rati standard)—169 grains.

Obverse : Arabic legend—*as-Sulṭānul ḥalīmul Karīmur ra'ufi 'alai 'abdu'llah al ghanīul muhaimīn*, "the Sulṭān, the element, the beautiful, the king to the servants of God, the rich, the confiding one."

Reverse : Arabic legend—*Abul muẓaffar 'Alāud-dunyā waddīn Aḥmad Shāh bin Aḥmad Shāh al wālīul Bahmanī*, "the guardian, the Bahmanī......."

Cf. Brown, *CI*. IX. 2.

XIX/4. Jaunpur. Maḥmūd Shāh (1436-58 A.D.). A.H. 846 (? 1442-43 A.D.). Gold. (96-Rati standard)—175 grains.

Obverse : in Tughra characters—*as-Sulṭān Saifud-dunyā waddīn abul Mujāhid Maḥmūd bin Ibrāhīm*, "the king Saifuddīn Abul Mujāhid Maḥmūd, the son of Ibrāhīm.

Reverse : legend within circle—*fī zamānil imāmi na'ibi Amīrul Mominīn abul fatḥ khuldat khilāfatuhu*; in the margin around —similar to No. XVIII/10.

Cf. Brown, *CI*. IX. 4.

XIX/5. Jaunpur. Husain Shāh (1458-79 A.D.). A.H. 864 (1459-60 A.D.). Copper (96-Rati standard)—150 grains.

Obverse : Arabic legend in circle—*Ḥusain Shāh*; around—*bin Muḥammad Shāh bin Ibrāhīm Shāh Sulṭānī*

Reverse : continued legend—*Nā'ibi amīrul mominīn, 864*, "Husain Shāh, son of Muḥammad Shāh, son of Sulṭān Ibrāhīm Shāh......864. "

Cf. Brown, *CI*. IX.5.

XIX/6. Malwa. Ghiyāṣ Shāh (1469-1500 A.D.). A.H. 880 (1475-76 A.D.). Gold (96-Rati standard)—square, 170 grains.

Obverse : Arabic legend in double square—*al wāṣiqu b'il mulkī al multaji abul fatḥ Ghiyās Shāh*; star above.

Reverse : Arabic legend continued from the obverse—*bin Muḥammad Shāh Sulṭānul Khaljī khallada mulkahu, 880,* "Ghiyāṣ Shāh, the son of king Muḥammad Shāh Khaljī, the truster in the kingdom and seeking refuge in the father of victory; A.H. 880; may God perpetuate the kingdom."
Cf. Brown, *CI*. IX. 3.

XIX/7. Gujarāt. Maḥmūd Shāh III (1533-61 A.D.). A.H. 946 (1539-40 A.D.). Gold(100-Rati standard)—185 grains.
Obverse : Arabic legend reading upwards—*Nasirud-dunyā waddīn Abul-fatḥ al wāsiqu billāhi-i-mannān—*
Reverse : Arabic legend in double square—*Maḥmūd Shāh bin Laṭīf Shāh Sulṭān*; margin—*946,* "Maḥmūd Shāh, the son of Sulṭān Latīf Shāh—the helper of the world and the faith, the father of victory, the truster in the beneficent God, "the helper of the world and the faith, the father of victory, the truster in the beneficent God; A.H. 946."
Cf. Brown. *CI*. IX. 6.

XIX/8. Gujarāt, Maḥmūd Shāh III (1533-61 A.D.). Silver (64-Rati standard)—112 grains.
Obverse : legend—as on No. XIX/7.
Reverse : legend—as on No. XIX/ 7, but without date.
Cf. Brown, *CI*. IX. 7.

XIX/9. Kangra. Meghacandra (c. 1390-1405 A.D.). Copper (30-Rati standard)—.55 inch, 48 grains.
Obverse : legend—(1) *Mahārāja-* (2) *śrī-Megha-* (3) *candradeva.*
Reverse : crude representation of horseman on left and tree on right.
Cf. Smith, *IMC*. XXVII. 21.

XIX/10. Champaran. Madanasiṁha (c. 1450-60 A.D.). Copper or bronze (40-Rati ½-Paṇa)—65 inch, 68 grains.
Obverse : legend—(1)*Govinda-*[*ca*]-(2) *raṇa-praṇa-*(3)*ta-Madana* (*ḥ**).
Reverse : legend—(1) *śrī-Campa-* (2) *kāraṇye*, "[struck] in Campakāraṇya (Champaran); Madana devoted to the feet of Govinda (Kṛṣṇa)."
Cf. Smith, *IMC*. XXVIII. 16.

XIX/11. Oinīvāra. Bhairavasiṁha (c. 1475-90 A.D.). Śaka 1411 (1489-90 A.D.), Regnal year 15. Silver (96-Rati standard)—.9 inch, 164 grains.
Obverse : legend in lozenge—(1) *Ma-* (2) *hārāja-* (3) *śrī-Darppa-nārā-* (4) *yaṇ-ātma-* (5) *ja* : in the marginal spaces—*Śaka-sa 1411;*
Reverse : in lozenge, legend continued from the w[riti]ng in lozenge on the obverse—(1) *Tī-* (2) *rabhukti-* (3) *rāja-śrī-Bhaira-* (4) *vasiṁha-* (5) *sya*; in the marginal spaces—*rājya 15,* "[Coin] of the illustrious Bhairavasiṁha, the king of Tīrabhukti, the son of the illustrious *Mahārāja* Darpanārāyaṇa;Śaka year 1411, Regnal year 15."
Cf. *Ep. Ind.*, XXXII, Plate facing p. 336.

XIX/12. Vīravijayanārāyaṇa. Śaka 1442(?). Silver(96-Rati standard)—1.03 inch, 167 grains.
Obverse : legend—(1) *śrī-śrī Vī-* (2) *ravijayanā-* (3) *rāyaṇa Caṇḍī-* (4) *caraṇaparā-* (5) *1442.* "Śrī-śrī-Vīravijayanārāyaṇa devoted to the feet of Caṇḍī."
Reverse : legend continued from line 4 on the obverse—(1) *yaṇa Hā-* (2) *ceṅgasā-śa-* (3) *kti-mardanade-* (4) *va*; *1424* (probably a mistake for *1442*). "The subduer of the power of Hāceṅgasā [of Cachar]."
Cf. Smith, *IMC*. XXXI. 13; see *Ind. Mus. Bul.*, January, 1967, pp. 24 ff.

XIX/13. Vijayanagara. Harihara II (c. 1379-1406 A.D.). Gold (5-Mañjāḍi or 16-Rati Half-Pagoda)—.42 inch, 26.7 grains.
Obverse : Nandināgarī legend—(1) *śrī-Pra-* (2) *tāpa-Hari-* (3) *hara.*

Reverse : god and goddess seated, to front.
Cf. Smith, *IMC*. XXX. 25.

XIX/14. Vijayanagara. Kṛṣṇadevarāya. Gold (5-Mañjāḍi or 16-Rati= Half-Pagoda)—about 26 grains.
Obverse : Nandināgarī legend—(1) *śrī-Pra-* (2) *tāpa-Kṛṣṇa-* (3) *rāja*.
Reverse : Viṣṇu seated, to front, with discus and conch.
Cf. Brown, *CI*. VII. 11.

XIX/15. Mughul. Bābur (1526-30 A.D.). Lāhor—A.H. 936 (1529-30 A.D.). Silver—69 grains.
Obverse : legend within flattened Mihrabi area—*Zahirud-dīn Muḥammad Bābur Bādshāh Ghāzī, 936*; above—*as-Sulṯānul a'zamul Khāqānu-mukarram* (the greatest Sulṭān, the illustrious emperor), *khallada Allāhu ta'ālā mulkahu wa salṯanatuhu* (May God, the Highest, perpetuate the kingdom and sovereignty), and *Zuriba Lāhor* (struck at Lāhor).
Reverse : in circle—the Kalima; in marginal segments—portions of *Abubakr as Sādiq* (Abubakr the faithful witness), *'Umarul Farūq* ('Umar, the discriminator between right and wrong), *'Usmān abu Nūrain* (Usmān, the father of two lights), and *'Alīul Murtaza* ('Alī, the pleasing to God).
Cf. Brown, *CI*. X. 1.

XIX/16. Mughul. Humāyūn (1530-40 A.D. and 1555-56 A.D.). Gold—16 grains.
Obverse : Arabic legend—*khallada Allāhu ta'āla mulkahu...Muḥammad Humāyūn Bādshāh Ghāzī*.
Reverse : in circle—the Kalima; in the marginal segments—as on the reverse of No. XIX/15.
Cf. Brown, *CI*. X. 2.

XIX/17. Sūr. Sher Shāh (1539-45 A.D.). Āgra—A.H. 948 (1544-45 A.D.). Silver (Rupee)—175 grains.
Obverse : in square—the Kalima; in the margins—*as-Sulṯānul 'ādil abul muzaffar Farīdud-dīn, zuriba Āgrah* (the just Sulṭan, the father of the victorious....).
Reverse : Arabic legend in the square—*Sher Shāh Sulṯān khallada Allāhu mulkahu, 948*; below in Nāgarī—*Śrī-Sīrasāha*.
Cf. Brown, *CI*. X. 3. See note on No. XX/6.

PLATE XX

XX/1. Sūr. Islām Shāh (1545-52 A.D.). Qanauj—A.H. 95*. Copper—315 grains.
Obverse : Arabic legend—*fī 'ahdil amīrul ḥāmiud dīni wad dayān 95** (in the time of the prince, the defender of the faith of the requiter)—bisected by double bar with knot in centre.
Reverse : Arabic legend—*Abul muzaffar Islām Shāh bin Sher Shāh Sulṯān, Zuriba Shergarh 'urf Qanauj, khallada Allāhu mulkahu* (the father of the victorious, Islām Shāh, the son of Sulṭān Sher Shāh, struck [the coin] at Shergarh *alias* Qanauj; may God perpetuate the kingdom).
Cf. Brown, *CI*. X. 4.

XX/2. Sūr. Sikandar (1554-55 A.D.). A.H. 962 (1554-55 A.D.). Silver (Rupee)—174 grains.
Obverse : not illustrated.
Reverse : in square—*Sulṯān Sikandar Shāh Isma'il Sūr, 962*; in the margins—legend illegible.
Cf. Brown, *CI*. X. 5.

XX/3. Mughul. Akbar (1556-1605 A.D.). Āgra—A.H. 981 (1573-74 A.D.). Gold (Muhar)—167 grains.

Obverse : legend—*khallada mulkahu Jalāluddīn Muḥammad Akbar Bādshāh Ghāẕī, Ẕuriba baldati Āgrah* (struck at Agra town).

Reverse: in dotted border—the Kalima; names of the Four Companions and the date *981*.

Cf. Brown, *CI.* X. 6. Muhar=11 Māshās=88 Ratis (*'Ain-i-Akbarī*).

XX/4. Mughul. Akbar (1556-1605 A.D.). Āgra—Ilāhī year 50. Gold—182 grains.

Obverse : not reproduced.

Reverse : within dotted circle, on ornamental ground—duck to right.

Cf. Brown, *CI.* X. 9. The Ilāhī era, counted from the 11th March, 1556 A. D., was introduced in 1584 A.D.

XX/5. Mughul. Akbar (1556-1605 A.D.). Ilāhī year 50. Gold—.8 inch, 74 grains.

Obverse : legend within dotted circle—*Ilāhī 50 Farwardīn.*

Reverse : within dotted circle, Rāma, wearing crown of three cusps and carrying a sheaf of arrows and a stretched bow, followed by Sītā who draws back her long veil from her face.

Cf. Lane-Poole, *BMC* (M). V. 172; also Whitehead, *PMC* (ii). XXI.ii reading the Nāgarī legend above the figures as *Rāma-Sītā.*

XX/6. Mughul. Akbar (1556-1605 A. D.). Ahmadābād—A.H. 982 (1574-75 A.D.). Silver (Rupee)—175 grains.

Obverse : not illustrated.

Reverse : legend within dotted square border—*Jalāluddīn Muḥammad Akbar Bādshāh Ghāẕī, 982*; in the margin—portions of *as-Sulṯānul a'ẕam khallada Allāhu ta'āla mulkahu wa salṯanatuhu, ẕuriba dārus salṯanati Aḥmadābād* (struck at Aḥmadābād, the seat of sovereignty).

Cf. Brown. *CI.*X. 7. Rūpiya=11½ Māshās=92 Ratis (*'Ain-i-Akbarī*).

XX/7. Mughul. Akbar (1556-1605 A.D.). Ilāhī year 43. Silver (Half-Rupee) —87 grains.

Obverse : legend within square dotted border—as on No. XX/8.

Reverse : legend—*Shahrīwar, Ilāhī 43.*

Cf. Brown, *CI.* X. 11.

XX/8. Mughul. Akbar (1556-1605 A.D.). Āgra—Ilāhī year 50. Silver (Rupee)—175 grains.

Obverse : Arabic legend in octagonal border, on ornamental ground—*Allāhu Akbar jalla jalāluhu* (God is great; eminent is his glory).

Reverse : legend within similar border—*Ẕarb-i-Āgrah Amrdād Ilāhī 50* (struck at Āgra in the month of Amrdād, Ilāhī year 50).

Cf. Brown, *CI.* X. 8.

XX/9. Mughul. Akbar (1556-1605 A.D.). Dehlī—Ilāhī year 43. Copper—640 grains.

Obverse : legend—*Tankah-i-Akbar Shāhī, Ẕarb-i-Dehlī* (Tanka of Akbar Shāh, struck at Dehlī).

Reverse : legend—*Māh Dī Ilāhī 43* (in the month of Dī, Ilāhī year 43).

Cf. Brown, *CI.* X. 10. Akbarī Dām=167 Ratis (*'Ain-i-Akbarī*).

XX/10. Mughul. Jahāngīr (1605-27 A.D.). A.H. 1020 (1611-12 A.D.), Regnal year 6. Gold (Muhar)—.85 inch, 168 grains.

Obverse : bust of king, to left, radiate, wearing turban with egret (*jikka*), and brocaded dress, and holding goblet in right hand in front of eyes and the Book in left hand; legend on left—*Shabīh Jahāngīr Shāh Akbar Shāh*; on right—*sana shash julūs* ((the sixth year from accession).

Reverse : lion to right, surmounted by setting sun; legend below—*sana Hijri 1020.*

Cf. Lane-Poole, *BMC* (M). IX. 315.

XX/11. Mughul. Jahāngīr (1605-27 A.D.). Ajmer—A.H. 1023 (1614-15 A.D.), Regnal year 9. Gold (Muhar)—168 grains.

Obverse : Jahāngīr, nimbate, seated cross-legged on throne, head to left, goblet in right hand; legend around—*Qazā bar sikka-i-zar kard taṣwīr / Shabī-i-hazrat-i-Shāh-i-Jahāngīr* (Destiny on the coin of gold has drawn the portrait of His Majesty Shāh Jahāngīr).

Reverse : sun in square compartment in centre; legend on left—*zarb-i-Ajmer, 1023*; on right—*ya Mu'inu* (O thou fixed one=Khwāja Mu'inud-dīn Chishtī) and *Sana 9*; above and below—*Ḥarūf-i-Jahāngīr u Allāhu Akbar/ zi rūz-i-azal dar 'adad shud barābar* (The letters of *Jahāngīr* and *Allāhu Akbar* are equal in value from the beginning of time =288).

Cf. Brown, *CI.* XI. 3.

XX/12. Mughul. Jahāngīr 1605-27 A.D.). Āgra—A.H. 1028 (1618-19 A.D.), Regnal year 14. Gold (Muhar)—168 grains.

Obverse : legend—*Yāft dar Āgrah rū-i-zar ziwar / az Jahāngīr Shāh-i-Shāh Akbar* (the face of gold received ornament at Āgra from Jahāngīr Shāh, [the son of] Akbar Shāh) and *Sana 1028.*

Reverse ; ram skipping to left, surmounted by sun; legend below—*Sana 14 julūs* (the fourteenth year from accession) and *Sana 1028.*

Cf. Brown, *CI.* XI. 2.

XX/13. Mughul. Jahāngīr (1605-27 A.D.). Āgra—A. H. 1030 (1620-21 A.D.). Regnal year 16. Gold (Muhar)—.8 inch, 162 grains.

Obverse : legend—similar to that on the reverse of No. XX/ 12, but *Akbar* above *Shāh* with *1030* and *16* in the dates.

Reverse : crab, erect, surmounted by sun; five stars in field.

Cf. Lane-Poole, *BMC* (M). X. 333c.

XX/14. Mughul. Jahāngīr (1605-27 A.D.). Āgra—A.H. 1032 (1622-23 A.D.), Regnal year 18. Gold (Muhar)—.85 inch, 169 grains.

Obverse : legend similar to that on the reverse of No. XX/ 12.

Reverse : man seated with pitcher over shoulder whence pours a stream of water.

Cf. Lane-Poole, *BMC* (M). X. 356.

XX/15. Mughul. Jahāngīr (1605-27 A.D.) with Nūr Jahān. Sūrat—A.H. 1036 (1626-27 A.D.). Gold (Muhar)—166 grains.

Obverse and Reverse : legend—*Zi hukm-i Shāh Jahāngīr yāft ṣad zi war / Ba nām-i-Nūr Jahān Bādashāh Begam zar* (By order of Shāh Jahāngīr, gold gained a hundred beauties through the name of Nūr Jahān Bādshāh Begam) with *Zarb-i-Sūrat* (struck at Sūrat) on the obverse and *1036* (i.e. A.H. 1036) on the reverse.

Cf. Brown, *CI*, XI. 5.

XX/16. Mughul. Jahāngīr (1605-27 A.D.). A.H. 1014 (1605-06 A.D.), Regnal year 1. Silver (Khair Qabūl).

Obverse : legend within dotted border—*Jahāngīr Bādshāh Ghāzi, 1.*

Reverse : legend—*Khair Qabūl* (May these alms be accepted); *1014.*

Cf. Brown, *CI.* X. 12.

XX/17. Mughul. Jahāngīr (Salīm Shāh, 1605-27 A.D.). Ahmadābād—Regnal year 2. Silver (Rupee)—176 grains.

Obverse and Reverse : legend—*Mālikul mulk sikka zad bar zar / Shāh Sulṭān Salīm Shāh Akbar* (the lord of the realm placed [his] stamp on money—Shāh Sulṭān Salīm, [the son of] Akbar Shāh) with *zarb-i-Ahmadābād* (struck

at Ahmadābād) on the obverse and *Farwardīn Sana 2* (i.e. the month of Farwardīn in the regnal year 2) on the reverse.
Cf. Brown, *CI*. XI. 6.

PLATE XXI

XXI/1. Mughul. Jahāngīr. Āgra—A.H. 1019 (1610-11 A.D.), Regnal year 5. Silver—220 grains.

Obverse : legend within multifoil area on flowered ground—*Dar Isfandārmūz in sikka-ra dar Āgrah zad bar zar* (in Isfandārmuz placed this stamp at Agra on money) and 5.

Reverse : legend continued within multifoil area—*Shāhān Shāh i-zamān Shāh Jahāngīr ibn-i-Shāh Akbar* (the emperor of the age, Shāh Jahāngīr, son of Akbar Shāh) and *1019* (i.e. A.H. 1019).

Cf. Brown, *CI*. XI. 4.

XXI/2. Mughul. Jahāngīr (1605-27 A.D.) Ahmadābād—A.H. 1027 (1617-18 A.D.). Regnal year 13. Silver(Rupee)—.8 inch, 175 grains.

Obverse : legend—*Bādshāh Jahāngīr Bādshāh Akbar ẓarb Ahmadābād, 1027* (the emperor Jahāngīr, [the son of] the emperor Akbar; struck at Ahmadābād, A.H. 1027).

Reverse : fore-part of bull to right, issuing from clouds, under sun; legend beneath—*sana 18 julūs* (the 18th year from accession).

Cf. Lane-Poole, *BMC*(M). XI. 364.

XXI/3. Mughul. Shāh Jahān I (1627-58 A.D.). Ahmadābād—A.H. 1038 (1628-29 A.D.). Regnal year 2. Silver (Rupee)—168 grains.

Obverse : legend—*Ṣāhib-i-qirān sānī Shihābud-dīn Shāh Jahān Bādshāh Ghāzī, sana 1038*, "Shihābuddīn Shāh Jahān, the illustrious emperor, the second Ṣāḥib-i-qirān; A.H. 1038."

Reverse : the Kalima in three lines; legend below—*ẓarb-i-Ahmadābād sana 2 Ilāhī māh Khurdād* (struck at Ahmadābād in the month of Khurdād in the year 2 Ilāhī).

Cf. Brown, *CI*. XI. 7.

XXI/4. Mughul. Shāh Shūjā' (1658 A.D.). Akbarnagar—A.H. 1068 (1657-58 A.D.), Aḥd (Regnal year 1). Silver (Rupee)—177 grains.

Obverse : legend in square—*Muḥammad Shāh Shujā, Bādshāh Ghāzī*; in right margin—*Akbar*[*nagar*].

Reverse : in square the Kalima and *1068*; in margin—names of the Four Companions with epithets.

Cf. Brown, *CI*. XI. 10.

XXI/5. Mughul. Aurangzeb (1658-1707 A.D.). Tatta—A.H. 1072 (1661-62 A.D.), Regnal year 5. Gold (Muhar)—170 grains.

Obverse : legend—*Sikka zad dar jahān chū mihr-i-munīr / Shāh Aurangzeb 'Ālamgīr, 1072* (struck money through the world like the shining sun, Shāh Aurangzeb 'Ālamgīr—A.H. 1072).

Reverse : legend—*ẓarb-i Tatta sana 5 julūs-i-maimanat-i-mānūs* (struck at Tatta in the 5th year of the accession associated with prosperity).

Cf. Brown, *CI*. XI. 9.

XXI/6. Mughul. Aurangzeb (1658-1707 A.D.). Kaṭak—Regnal year 29. Silver (Quarter-Rupee)—about 44 grains.

Obverse : legend in dotted square border, on ornamental ground—*Dirham shar'ī*.

Reverse : legend—*Ẓarb-i-Kaṭak, 29* (struck at Kaṭak in the regnal year 29).

Cf. Brown, *CI.* XI. 11.

XXI/7. Mughul. Shāh Jahān III (1759-60 A.D.). Ahmadnagar Farrukhābād—A.H. 1173 (1659-60 A.D.), Regnal year 1. Gold (Muhar)—1 inch, 167 grains.

Obverse : legend—*sikka-mubārak Shāh Jahān Bādshāh Ghāzī* (blessed coin of the illustrious emperor Shāh Jahān), *1173.*

Reverse : legend—*zarb-i-Aḥmadnagar Farrukhābād āḥad julūs-i-maimanat-i-mānūs* (struck at Ahmadnagar Farrukhābād in the first year of accession associated with prosperity).

Cf. Lane-Poole, *BMC* (M). XXVI. 1087.

XXI/8. Mughul. Shāh 'Ālam II (1759-1806 A.D.). Shāhjahānābād—A. H. 1219 (1804-05 A.D.), Regnal year 47. Gold (Muhar)—166 grains.

Obverse : legend within circular border of roses, shamrocks and thistles —*Sikka-i-ṣāḥib-i-qirānī zad zi tā'īdullāh / Hāmī-i-dīn-i Muḥammad Shāh 'Ālam Bādshāh* (struck coin like the lord of the conjunction by the help of God, Defender of the Faith, Muḥammad Shāh 'Ālam the king), *1219*; mint-marks, umbrella and cinquefoil.

Reverse : legend within similar border—*zarb-i-Shāhjahānābād sana 47 julūs-i-maimanat-i-mānūs* (struck at Shāhjahānābād in the 47th year of the accession associated with prosperity).

Cf. Brown, *CI.* XII. 1.

XXI/9. Bijāpūr. 'Alī 'Ādil Shāh II (1656-72 A.D.). Silver(Larin)—about 71 grains.

Obverse : legend—*'Ādil Shāh* followed by 3 strokes.

Reverse : blurred.

Cf. Brown, *CI.* IX. 10. The name Larin applied to the 'fish-hook' coins was derived from the port of Lar on the Persian Gulf.

XXI/10. Durrānī. Ahmad Shāh (1747-73 A.D.). Shāhjahānābād—A. H. 1170 (1756-57 A.D.), Regnal year 11. Silver (Rupee).

Obverse : legend—*Ḥukm shud az qādir-i-bīchūn ba Aḥmad Bādshāh / sikka zad bar sīm u zar az auj-i-māhī tā-ba māh* (There came an order from the potent incomparable one to Aḥmad the king to strike coin on gold and silver from the zenith of the Pisces to the Moon), *1170.*

Reverse : as on No. XXI/8; but the date is 11.

Cf. Brown, *CI.* XII. 2.

XXI/11. Mysore. Tīpū (1782-92 A.D.). Kalīkūt (Calicut). A.H. 1199 (1784-85 A.D.). Gold (Fanam)—about 5.2 grains.

Obverse : Persian letter—*He* (for *Haidar*); border of dots.

Reverse : Persian legend—*Kalīkūt 1199.*

Cf. Brown, *CI.* VII. 10.

XXI/12. Mysore. Tīpū (1782-92 A.D.). Pattan (Seringapatam). Copper (20-Cash).

Obverse : legend—*Zarb-i-Pattan.*

Reverse : elephant with lowered trunk, to right.

Cf. Brown, *CI.* XII. 5.

XXI/13. Nizām. Sikandar Jāh (1803-29 A.D.). in the name of Akbar II (1806-37 A.D.). Ḥaidarābād—A.H. 1237, Regnal year 16. Silver (Rupee).

Obverse : legend—*sikka-i-mubārak-i-Bādshāh Ghāzī Muḥammad Akbar Shāh* (blessed coin of the illustrious emperor Muḥammad Akbar Shāh), *1237*, with the initial letter of the name of Sikandar.

Reverse : legend—as on No. XXI/8, but the year is *16* and the mint —*Farkhanda bunyād Ḥaidarābād* (Ḥaidarābād of fortunate foundation).

Cf. Brown, *CI.* XII. 4.

XXI/14. Āwadh (Oudh). Wājid 'Alī Shāh (1847-56 A.D.). Lakhnau (Lucknow) in Āwadh—A.H. 1264, Regnal year 2. Gold (Muhar).

Obverse : legend—*Sikka zad bar sīm u zar az fazl-i-tā'īdullāh / Zill-i-haqq Wājid 'Alī Sultān-i-'ālam Bādshāh* (struck coin in silver and gold through the grace of divine help, the shade of God, Wājid 'Alī, Sultān of the world, the king), *2*.

Reverse : coat of arms of Āwadh; legend around—*Zarb-i-mulk-i-Āwadh bāitus-saltanat Lakhnau* (struck in the country of Āwadh, at the seat of sovereignty, Lakhnau), *sana 2 Julūs-i-maimanat-i-mānūs* (in the 2nd year of accession associated with prosperity).

Cf. Brown, *CI.* XII. 3.

PLATE XXII

XXII/1. Tripurā. Vijayamāṇikya (c. 1528-70 A.D.). Śaka 1458 (1536-37 A.D.). Silver.

Obverse : legend in square—(1) *śrī-śrī-Vija-* (2) *yamāṇikya-* (3) *deva-śrī-Lakṣmī-* (4) *mahādevyau*, "the doubly illustrious Vijayamāṇikyadeva and Lakṣmī-madādevī."

Reverse : lion in ornamental circle--crescent above, *1458* below. *JNSI*, XXIX. III. 1.

XXII/2. Tripurā. Govinda (Govindamāṇikya). Śaka 1601 (1679 A.D.). Silver (Quarter-Rupee)—.68 inch, 37.8 grains.

Obverse : legend in square with marginal ornamentation—(1) *śrīśrīyu-* (2) *ta-Govi-* (3) *ndadevaḥ*.

Reverse : in circle surmounted by thick dots—conventional lion, rampant, to left; sun and moon above; legend—*Śaka* (in front of the lion), *1601* (below the lion).

Cf. Smith, *IMC.* XXX. 6. Smith wrongly assigned the coin to Kadamba Viṣṇucitta of Goa.

XXII/3. Tripurā. Rāmagaṅgāmāṇikya. Śaka 1728 (1806 A.D.). Silver (Rupee)—1.02 inch, 162.3 grains.

Obverse : legend in square within ornamental margin—(1) *Śiva-Durgā-pade* (2) *śrīśrīyuta-Rāma-* (3) *gaṅgāmāṇikya-* (4) *deva-śrīmati (tī)- Tā-* (5) *rā-mahādevyau*, "the doubly illustrious Rāmagaṅgāmāṇikyadeva and queen Tārā right at the feet of Śiva and Durgā."

Reverse : conventional lion standing to left with right forefoot raised; trident on his back; star in front and behind; legend below—*Śaka 1728*.

Cf. Smith, *IMC.* XXIX. 16. Smith wrongly read the king's name as *Rāmasiṁhamāṇikya*.

XXII/4. Ahom (Assam). Svarganārāyaṇa Pratāpasiṁha *alias* Susenphā or Cucenphā (1611-49 A.D.). Śaka 1570 (1648-49 A.D.). Silver (Rupee) —octagonal, .82 inch, 175.2 grains.

Obverse : legend (1) *Śrī-śrī-Ha-* (2) *rihara-cara-* (3) *ṇa-parāya-* (4) *ṇasya*.

Reverse : legend—(1) *śrī-śrī-Sva-* (2) *rganārāyaṇa-* (3) *devasya Śake* (4) *1570*, "[Coin] of the doubly illustrious Svarganārāyaṇadeva intent on the feet of Hari (Viṣṇu) and Hara (Śiva), [struck] in Śaka 1570."

Cf. Smith, *IMC.* XXIX. 2.

XXII/5. Ahom (Assam). Supātphā *alias* Gadādharasiṁha (1681-95 A.D.). 1681 A.D. Silver (Rupee)—octagonal, .95 inch, 166 grains.

Obverse : legend—(1) *Cāo Śu-* (2) *pātphā pi-* (3) *n khun lāk* (4) *ni Rāiśān*, "in the year Rāiśān (33rd year of Cycle=1681 A.D.) in the reign of the great Śupātphā"; winged dragon on right, below, and crown on left.

Reverse : legend—(1) *Kāō bay* (2) *phāleṅ* (3) *ḍau heu* (4) *cu*, "I, the king, offer prayer to Indra."

Cf. Smith, *IMC*. XXIX. 1.

XXII/6. Ahom (Assam). Gaurīnāthasiṁha (1780-95 A.D.). Silver (Half-Rupee)—octagonal, 88.4 grains.

Obverse : within dotted border in Bengali-Assamese script—*śrī-śrī-Haragaurī-pada-parasya*

Reverse : legend in continuation of the writing on the obverse—*śrī-śrī-Gaurīnāthasiṁha-nṛpasya*, "[Coin] of the illustrious king Gaurīnāthasiṁha devoted to the feet of Hara and Gaurī."

Cf. Brown, *CI*. XII. 8.

XXII/7. *Jayantīpura*. [Rāmasiṁha.] Śaka 1630 (1708-09 A.D.). Silver (Rupee)—1.12 inch, 150 grains.

Obverse : legend in circle with broad dotted margin—(1) *śrī-śrī-Śi-* (2) *va-caraṇa-ka-* (3) *mala-madhuka-* (4) *rasya*, crescent in upper margin; star at the end of legend; sword on right.

Reverse : continuation of legend in broad dotted margin—(1) *śrī-śrī-Ja-* (2) *yantīpura-pu-* (3) *randarasya Śa-* (4) *ke 1630*, "[Coin] of the king of Jayantīpura, a bee on the lotus feet of Śiva, Śaka 1630;" with horizontal line above date.

Cf. Smith, *IMC*. XXIX. 13.

XXII/8. Rangpur. Bharathasiṁha (1792-93 A.D.). Śaka 1714 (1792-93 A.D.). Silver (Rupee)—octagonal, .95 inch, 175.5 grains.

Obverse : legend—(1) *śrī-śrī-Kṛṣṇa-caraṇ-āravinda-makaranda-pramatta-madhukarasya*

Reverse: legend continued from obverse—(1) *śrī-śrī-Bharga (ga) datta-* (2) *kulodbhava-śrī-Bha-* (3) *rathasiṁha-nṛpasya* (4) *Śaka 1714*; "[Coin] of king Bharathasiṁha of the excellent lineage of Bhagadatta, intoxicated with the nectar of the lotus of the feet of Kṛṣṇa—Śaka 1714;" dragon to right below.

Cf. Smith, *IMC*. XXIX. 9. Smith wrongly reads *pramada* for *pramatta*.

XXII/9. Kachar. Govindacandra. Śaka 1736 (1814-15 A.D.). Silver (Rupee)—.93 inch, 175.75 grains.

Obverse : versified legend—*Hiḍimbapūr-adhīsa* (*śa*)-*śrī-Raṇacaṇḍī-pad-ājuṣaḥ* ।

Reverse : legend continued from obverse—*śrī-śrī-Govindacandrasya rājño='ṅga-try-adri-kau Sa* (*Śa*)*ke*, "[Coin] of the doubly illustrious king Govindacandra, the lord of Hiḍimbapūr and devoted to the feet of śrī-Raṇacaṇḍī; [struck] in the Śaka [year counted by] *aṅga* (6), *tri* (3), *adri* (7) and *ku* (1) (i. e. in Śaka 1736).

Cf. *Ep. Ind.*, XXXV, Plate facing p. 103.

XXII/10. Sikh. Amritsar—Vikrama Saṁvat 1837 (1780 A.D.). Silver (Rupee).

Obverse : corrupt Persian couplet—*Sar tegh-i-Nānak......az fazl-i-fatḥ-i-Govindsingh saḥā* (*shāh* ?) *shāhān sāḥib sikka zad bar sim u zar*.

Reverse : Persian legend—*Zarb-i-Shrī-Ambratsar julūs-i-takht ākāl sanbat 1835* (struck at the illustrious Amritsar, the accession to the eternal throne, in Saṁvat 1835).

Cf. Brown, *CI*. XII. 10.

XXII/11. Holkar (Indore). Yaśovanta Rāo (1798-1811 A.D.). Śaka 1728 (1806 A.D.). Silver (Rupee).

Obverse : versified legend after the benedictory word—*śr-Indraprastha-sthita-rājā cakravartī bhū-maṇḍale* / *tat-prasādāt kṛtā mudrā loke='smin va* (*vai*) *virājate* // [*Śaka 1728*].

Reverse : continuation of versified legend—*Lakṣmīkānta-pad-ambhoja-bhramarāyita-cetasaḥ / Yaśovantasya vikhyātā mudr=aiṣā pṛthivī-tale //* "The king of Indraprastha (Delhi) is the emperor of the world; this coin, issued through his grace, circulates on the earth. This coin of the renowned Yaśovanta, whose heart is the black bee on the lotus-feet of Lakṣmīkānta (Viṣṇu), is famous on the earth; Śaka 1728."

Cf. Brown, *CI.* XII. 7.

XXII/12. Rāma-ṭaṅkā. Silver (Rupee)—round, 2.5 cm., 182 grains.

Obverse. Rādhā and Kṛṣṇa in a scene of the *Dāna-līlā*; partially preserved marginal legend all around.

Reverse ; cowherd Kṛṣṇa driving four heads of cattle by a Kadamba tree; partially preserved legend all around.

Cf. *JNSI,* XXVIII. VI. 9.

XXII/13. Rāma-ṭaṅkā.

Obverse : Rāma and Lakṣmaṇa standing to left, with trident in right hand and bow on left arm; legend—*Rāma Lachamana Jānaka javata Hanamānaka* (victorious are Rāma, Lakṣmaṇa, Jānakī and Hanumat) with imaginary date below—*550* and *40* on left and right of rectangle (intended to be year 55040 of some era).

Reverse : Rāma and Sītā seated on throne, with umbrella above; Hanumat sitting under the throne; Lakṣmaṇa standing on left and Bharata and Śatrughna on right.

Unpublished. cf. *JNSI.* VI. 11.

XXII/14. Rāma-ṭaṅkā.

Obverse : Rāma and Lakṣmaṇa standing to left with trident in right hand and bow on left arm; legend—*Rāma Lachamana Jānaka javata Hanamānaka.*

Reverse : Rāma and Sītā seated on throne; Lakṣmaṇa standing on left, holding umbrella above the seated figures; Bharata and Śatrughna standing on right with right hands raised, and Hanumat seated under the throne.

Unpublished.

PLATE XXIII

XXIII/1. Rāmaṭaṅkā. Vikrama 1740 (1683 A.D.). Silver (base—Rupee)—round, 2.8 cm., 11.5 grammes; border obliquely milled.

Obverse : Rāma and Lakṣmaṇa wearing *dhotī*, standing in *tribhaṅga* pose; with crown on head and bow on left arm; Nāgarī legend in old Hindī above—*Rāma Lachamana Jānaka javata Hanamānaka,* "victorious are Rāma, Lakṣmaṇa, Jānakī and Hanumat;" below—17 *Sana* 40 (i.e. year 1740).

Reverse : Rāma and Sītā on throne, under umbrella, with Lakṣmaṇa on right, Bharata and Śatrughna on left and Hanumat below.

Cf. *JNSI,* XXVIII. VI. 10.

XXIII/2. Rāma-ṭaṅkā. Silver (base—Rupee)—round, 2.9 cm. 10.35 grammes,

Obverse : Jagannātha, Subhadrā and Balarāma standing to front; legend—*śrī-śrī-Jagannāthadeva-sva* (*tra*)*yī,* "the Jagannātha triad."

Reverse : same as on No. XXIII/1.

Cf. *JNSI.* XXVIII. VI. 12. On some specimens, the legend appears to read *śrī-śrī-Jagannāthadevasvāmī.*

XXIII/3. Rāma-ṭaṅkā.

Obverse : Rāma and Sītā seated on throne, with Lakṣmaṇa standing on left and holding umbrella above the seated figures, and Hanumat standing on right with folded hands; Nāgarī legend below—*Rāma-*[*Sī*]*tā.*

Reverse : Hanumat flying in the air with the Gandhamādana; Nāgarī legend above—*Hanuma.*

Unpublised.

XXIII/4. Rāma-ṭaṅkā. Brass—round, 2.8 cm, 11.35 grammes.

Obverse : four-armed Kālī standing on prostrate Śiva as now worshipped in Bengal; legend *Kālīmātā* (Mother Kālī) on left in Bengali and on right in Nāgarī.

Reverse : Kṛṣṇa and Rādhā standing under Kadamba tree on separate lotuses; legend—*Rādhā-Kṛṣṇa* on left in Bengali and on right in Nāgarī.

Cf. *JNSI*, XXVIII. VI. 13.

XXIII/5. Vijayanagara. Veṅkaṭeśvara (c. 1600 A.D.). Gold (10-Mañjāḍi or 32-Rati standard)—.43 inch, 51.6 grains.

Obverse : legend—(1) *śrī-Veṅka-* (2) *ṭeśvarā-* (3) [*ya namaḥ*], "Salutation to Veṅkaṭeśvara."

Reverse : Viṣṇu standing under arch.

Cf. Smith, *IMC*. XXX. 32.

XXIII/6. Mysore. Kṛṣṇarāja (1799-1868 A.D.). Gold (10-Mañjāḍi or 32-Rati standard)—.42 inch, 53 grains.

Obverse : Nandināgarī legend—(1) *Śrī-* (2) *Kṛṣṇarā-* (3) *ja*.

Reverse : Śiva and Pārvatī with trident and antelope.

Cf. Smith, *IMC*. XXX. 34.

XXIII/7. Travancore. Rāmavarman (latter half of the 19th century). Copper—.65 inch, 80.2 grains.

Obverse : spiny murex shell; Malayāḷam legend in margin—*Āra cakram*, "Half-Cakram."

Reverse : 'Solomon's seal' in ornamented circle (*tuṭṭu*).

Cf. Smith, *IMC*. XXX. 14.

XXIII/8. Nepāl. Pratāpamalla (1639-89 A,.). Nevārī year 776 (1655 A.D.). Silver (½-Rupee imitating coins of Jahāṅgīr)—1.08 inch, 83 grains.

Obverse : Jahāṅgīr's name in Arabic characters; also *Pratāpamalla* in Nāgarī characters in the field; date below—*776*; the writing is on ornamental field.

Reverse : corrupt legend in Arabic characters probably meant for Ilāhī date; legend in Nāgarī characters—*śrī-śrī-Kavīndra-jaya*, "victory of the doubly illustrious Kavīndra (literally, 'the Prince of Poets');" the writing is on ornamental field.

Cf. Smith, *IMC*. XXVIII. 3.

XXIII/9. Nepāl. Gīrvāṇa Yudhavikrama (1799-1816 A.D.). Śaka 1724 (1802 A.D.). Gold (Half-Muhar)—1.02 inch, 84.2 grains.

Obverse : legend in ornamental square with *śrī-śrī-śrī* above, around small central circle having ornamental trident inside—*Gīrvāṇa-Yuddhavikrama-sāhadī(de)va*; below—*1724*.

Reverse : legend written in eight-petalled lotus—*śrī-Bhavānī* around dagger or Śivaliṅga (at four sides on the pericarp), and—*śrī-śrī-śrī Gorakhanātha* (one syllable each on the eight petals).

Cf. Smith, *IMC*. XXVIII. 10.

XIII/10. Nepāl. Pṛthvīnārāyaṇa (1768-74 A.D.). Śaka 1693 (1771 A.D.). Silver (Half-Rupee)—1.15 inch, 84.3 grains.

Obverse : legend in square having the sun, moon, stars and other ornaments outside, and around ornamental trident—*śrī-śrī-Pṛthvīnārāyaṇa-sāhadī(de)va*; date below—*1693*; border of dots.

Reverse : in lotus—*śrī-śrī-Bhavānī* (on the pericarp around dagger or Śivaliṅga), and—*śrī-śrī-śrī-Gorakhanātha* (one syllable each on the petals).

Cf. Smith, *IMC*. XXVIII. 9.

XXIII/11. Sikkim. Copper—.9 inch, 64.3 grains.

Obverse : legend in square—(1) *śrī-śrī-śrī-* (2) *Sikima-pa-* (3) *ti-Pratāpa.*
Reverse : legend in square- (1)*śrī-śrī-śrī-* (2) *Sikima-* (3)*sakā(rkā)ra* (the Government of Sikkim).
Cf. Smith, *IMC*. XXIX. 18. The obverse legend was read as—(1)*śrī-śrī-śrī-* (2) *Sikim......* (3) *tibutā rājā.*

XXIII/12. Compagnie des Indes in the name of Shāh 'Ālam II (1759-1806 A.D.). Arkāt (Arcot, really Pondichery)—Regnal year 5. Silver (Rupee)—.9 inch, 172 grains.
Obverse : legend—*Sikka zad bar haft kashūr saya fazal Allāh / hāmī dīn Muḥammad Shāh 'Ālam Bādshāh*; no A.H. date.
Reverse : legend—*Ẓarb-i-Arkāt sana 5* (struck at Arkāt in the regnal year 5), with crescent mark before the date.
Cf. Lane-Poole, *BMC*(M). XXXII. 128.

XXIII/13. [East India Company ?]. 'Three-Svāmī' type (flat). Gold (10-Mañjāḍi or 32-Rati standard)—.5 inch, 53 grains.
Obverse : standing figure of the god Veṅkaṭeśvara, to front, with his two wives on either side, both standing to front.
Reverse : granulated field.
Cf. Smith, *IMC*. XXX. 22.

PLATE XXIV

XXIV/1. East India Company in the name of 'Ālamgīr II (1754-59 A.D.). Arkāt (Arcot, really Madras)—A. H. 1172, Regnal year 6. Silver (Double-Rupee)—1.5 inch, 373 grains.
Obverse : legend—*sikka Bādshāh 'Ālamgīr* (Coin of Bādshāh 'Ālamgīr), *1172.*
Reverse : legend—*Ẓarb-i-Arkāt sana 6 julūs-i-maimanat-i-mānūs* (struck at Arkāt in the year 6 from accession associated with prosperity); with trident before *6.*
Cf. Lane-Poole, *BMC*(M). XXXII. 111.

XXIV/2. [East India Company.] 'Azimābād or Pāṭnā—1774 A.D. Copper (2 Annas).
Obverse : legend in Persian—*'Azimābād Dāk do āne.*
Reverse : legend in English—*Patna Post Two Annas 1774.*
Cf. R. Friedberg, *Coins of the British World*, p. 140, No. 32.

XXIV/3. East India Company in the name of Shāh 'Ālam II (1754-1806 A.D.). Mumbai (Bombay)—A.H. 1188 (1774-75 A.D.), Regnal year 9. Silver (Rupee)—1.0 inch, 179 grains.
Obverse : legend—*sikka mubārak Bādshāh Ghāzī Shāh 'Ālam* (blessed coin of his Imperial Majesty Shāh 'Ālam), *1188.*
Reverse : legend—*Ẓarb-i-Mumbai sana 9 julūs-i-maimanat-i-mānūs* (struck at Mumbai in the year 9 of accession associated with prosperity).
Cf. Lane-Poole, *BMC*(M). XXXI. 79.

XXIV/4. East India Company in the name of Shāh 'Ālam II (1759-1806 A.D.). Murshidābād—Regnal year 19. Silver (Rupee, machine-struck).
Obverse : legend—*Sikka-i-Ṣāḥib-i-qirānī zad zi tā'īdullah* | *Hāmī-i-dīn-i-Muḥammad Shāh 'Ālam Bādshāh*, "struck coin like the Lord of the conjunction, by the help of God, Defender of the Faith, Muḥammad Shāh 'Alam the king."
Reverse : legend—*Ẓarb-i-Murshidābād sana 47 julūs-i-maimanat-i-mānūs*, "struck at Murshidābād in the 47th year of the accession associated with prosperity;" and the company's cinquefoil mark.

Cf. Brown, *CI.* XII. 9.

XXIV/5. East India Company in the name of Shāh 'Ālam II (1759-1806 A.D.). Kalkattā (Calcutta)—A.H. 1176 (1763 A.D.), Regnal year 4. Silver (Rupee)—1.1 inch, 180 grains.

Obverse : legend—*sikka zad bar haft kashūr saya fazal Allāh / hāmī dīn Muhammad Shāh 'Ālam Bādshāh/ 1176.*

Reverse : legend—*Zarb-i-Kalkattā sana* 4 *julūs-i-maimanat-i-mānūs*; cinquefoil.

Cf. Lane-Poole, *BMC*(M). XXXI. 67.

XXIV/6. East India Company in the name of 'Ālamgīr II (1754-59 A.D.). Machhlīpatam (Masulipatam)—A.H. 1194, Regnal year 21. Silver (Double Rupee)—1.25 inches, 348 grains.

Obverse : legend—*sikka mubārak Bādshāh 'Ālamgīr Ghāzī* (the blessed coin of the illustrious emperor 'Ālamgīr), *1194.*

Reverse : legend—*Zarb-i-Machhlīpatam sana 21 julūs-i-maimanat-i-mānūs* (struck at Machhlīpatam in the year 21 of the accession associated with prosperity), with trident mark before the date.

Cf. Lane-Poole, *BMC*(M). XXXII. 145.

XXIV/7. East India Company in the name of Shāh Ālam II (1759-1806 A.D.). Banāras—A.H. 1226. Silver (Rupee)—.95 inch, 172 grains.

Obverse : legend—*sikka zad haft kashūr saya fazal Allāh / hāmī dīn Muhammad Shāh 'Ālam Bādshāh / 1226.*

Reverse : legend—*Zarab-i-Banāras sana 26 julūs-i-maimanat-i-mānūs...... Muhammadābād.*

Cf. Lane-Poole, *BMC*(M). XXXI. 61.

XXIV/8. East India Company in the name of Shāh 'Ālam II (1759-1806 A.D.). Farrukhābād—Regnal year 45. Silver (Rupee)—1.5 inch, 174 grains.

Obverse : legend—*sikka zad bar haft kashūr saya fazal Allāh / hāmī dīn Muhammad Shāh 'Ālam Bādshāh. /*

Reverse : legend—*Zarb-i-Farrukhābād sana* 45 *julūs-i-maimanat-i-mānūs*; cinquefoil.

Cf. Lane-Poole, *BMC*(M). XXXI. 50.

PLATE XXV

XXV/1. East India Company in the name of Shāh 'Ālam II (1759-1806 A.D.). Regnal year 46. Gold (Muhar)—.75 inch, 179 grains.

Obverse : legend—*sikka mubārak Shāh 'Ālam Bādshāh Ghāzī* (the blessed coin of his Imperial Majesty Shāh Ālam).

Reverse : legend—*sana 46 julūs-i-maimanat-i-mānūs* (struck in the year of accession 46 associated with prosperity); star after *julūs*.

Cf. Lane-Poole, *BMC* (M). XXXIII. 87.

XXV/2. East India Company in the name of Shāh 'Ālam II (1759-1806 A.D.). Sūrat—Regnal year 46, 1825 A.D. Silver (Rupee)—1.05 inch, 180 grains.

Obverse : legend—parts of *Sikka mubārak Shāh 'Ālam Bādshāh Gāzī*; but with the crown mark.

Reverse : legend—parts of *sana 46 julūs-i-maimanat-i-mānūs* with star and with *1825* in English figures in raised incuse.

Cf. Lane-Poole, *BMC* (M). XXXII. 85.

XXV/3. East India Company in the name of William IV (1830-37 A.D.). Silver (Rupee)—1835 A.D.

Obverse : king's head to right; English legend—*William* (left), *IV King* (right).

Reverse : legend inside circular floral design—*One Rupee* (above—English), *Ek Rūpiya* (below—Urdū); along the border outside the floral design—*East India Company 1835*.

Cf. R. Friedberg, *Coins of the British World*, p. 132, No. 1—top of the reverse displaced. The 'Company's Rupee' from 1836=180 grains (165 grains silver).

XXV/4. East India Company in the name of Victoria (1837-1901 A.D.). Silver (Half-Rupee)—1840 A.D.

Obverse : head of queen to left; English legend—*Victoria Queen.*

Reverse : legend within circular floral design—*Half Rupee* (above—in English), *Hasht Āna*, "Eight Annas" (below—in Persian); outside the design along the border—*East India Company 1840.*

Cf. R. Friedberg, *Coins of the British World*, p. 132, 6 or 7 (?).

XXV/5. East India Company in the name of Victoria (1837-1901 A.D.). Copper (Half-Anna)—1862 A.D.

Obverse : crowned bust of queen to left; English legend—*Victoria* (left), *Queen* (right); dotted border

Reverse : English legend within circular floral design between dotted borders—(1) *Half* (2) *Anna* and (1) *India* (2) *1862* separated by small horizontal line; between floral design and outer border —*East India Company.* The Company's Paisā (Quarter Anna)=100 grains.

Cf. R. Friedberg, *Coins of the British World*, pp. 132-33, No. 16.

XXV/6. Victoria (1837-1901 A.D.). Copper (Quarter-Anna)—1877 A. D.

Obverse : crowned bust of queen to left; English legend—*Victoria* (left), *Empress* (right); dotted border.

Reverse : English legend within circular floral design between dotted borders—(1) *One* (2) *Quarter* (3) *Anna* (above short horizontal line and (1) *India* (2) *1877* (below the horizontal line).

Cf. R. Friedberg, *Coins of the British World*, p. 133, No. 25—reduced.

XXV/7. Edward VII (1901-10 A.D.). Silver (Rupee—proof)—1901 A.D.

Obverse : head of king to right; Latin legend along dotted border—*Eduardus VII Rex et Imperator.*

Reverse : within circular ornamental design—tiger walking to left with *Ek Rūpiya* (Urdū) above and *Ek Rūpayā* (Nāgarī) below; between the floral design and dotted outer border—*One Rupee* (left) and *India 1901* (right) separated by crown above and wreaths below.

Cf. R. Friedberg, *Coins of the British World*, p. 133, No. 31-a

XXV/8. Edward VII (1901-10 A.D.). Nickel and Bronze (Anna with scalloped edge)—1908 A.D.

Obverse : crowned bust of king to right; English legend—*Edward VII King Emperor.*

Reverse : in lozenze—*1* between *India* above and *1908* below; with *An-* on left and *na* on right ; Indian legend in the four margins—*Ek Ānā* (Nāgarī), *Ek Āna* (Urdū), *Oka Āna* (Telugu), and *Ek Ānā* (Bengali).

Cf. R. Friedberg, *Coins of the British World*, p. 133, No. 32—reduced.

XXV/9. Edward VII (1901-10 A.D.). Silver (Quarter Rupee)—1910 A.D.

Obverse : not reproduced.

Reverse : legend between floral designs on left and right, below crown and above *1910*—(1) $\frac{1}{4}$ (2) *Rupee* (3) *India* (English) and *Chāhār Āna* (Persian).

Cf. R. Friedberg, *Coins of the British World*, p. 133. No. 30.

XXV/10. Edward VII (1901-10 A.D.). Silver (2 Annas)—1910 A.D.

Obverse : not reproduced.

Reverse : legend between floral designs on left and right, below crown and above 1910 (1) *Two* (2) *Annas* (3) *India* (English) and *Do Āna* (Urdū).

Cf. R. Friedberg, *Coins of the British World*, p. 133, No. 31.

XXV/11. George V (1910-36 A.D.). Nickel (½ Rupee)—1919 A.D.

Obverse : crowned bust of king to left; English legend—*George V King Emperor*.

Reverse : within central space encircled by scalloped edge, in square—*8* between *India 1919* above and *Annas* below; Indian legend in the four marginal spaces—*Āṭh Ānā* (Nāgarī—left), *Āṭh Āna* (Urdū—above), *Āṭ Ānā* (Bengali—right) and *Enimidi Ānāla* (Telugu—below).

Cf. R. Friedberg, *Coins of the British World*, p. 134, No. 40.

XXV/12. George V (1910-36 A.D.). Nickel (¼-Rupee with scalloped edge)—1919 A.D.

Obverse : crowned bust of king to left; legend around, between circle and scalloped edge—*George V King Emperor* separated from *India 1919* below.

Reverse : English legend in central square—(1) *4* (2) *Annas*; Indian legends in the marginal spaces—*Cār Ānā* (Nāgarī—left), *Chār Āna* (Urdū—above), *Cāri Ānā* (Bengali—right) and *Nālagu Ānāla* (Telugu—bottom).

Cf. R. Friedberg, *Coins of the British World*, p. 134, No. 31.

PLATE XXVI

XXVI/1. George V (1910-36 A.D.) Nickel (Half-Rupee)—square, 1926 A.D.

Obverse : within circle—crowned bust of king to left; legend—*George V King Emperor*; outside the circle—flower design above, *19*—on left and *26* on right.

Reverse : in central square—(1) *2 Annas* in English, with *Do Ānā* (Nāgarī on left), *Do Āna* (Urdū on top), *Dui Ānā* (Bengali on right) and *Reṁḍu Ānāla* (Telugu at bottom).

Cf. R. Friedberg, *Coins of the British World*, p. 134, No. 42.

XXVI/2. George VI (1937-52 A.D.). Silver (Rupee, edge with conventional or safety reeding)—1938 A.D.

Obverse : crowned head of king to left; legend—*George VI King Emperor*.

Reverse : legend in central circle within ornamental floral design—(1) *One* (2) *Rupee* (3) *India* (4) *1938*.

Cf. R. Friedberg, *Coins of the British World*, p. 134, No. 47.

XXVI/3. George VI (1937-52 A.D.). Nickel-brass (Half-Anna—square, with rounded corners)—1940 A.D.

Obverse : crowned head of king to left; legend—*George VI King Emperor*.

Reverse : legend in lozenge—(1) *India* (2) *An-* ½ *na* (3) *1940*; in the marginal spaces—*Do Paisā* (Hindī, left), *Do Paisa* (Urdū, top), *Dui Paysā* (Bengali, right) and *Reṁḍu Paisa* (Telugu, bottom).

Cf. R. Friedberg, *Coins of the British World*, p. 135, No. 57.

XXVI/4. George VI (1937-52 A.D.). Copper (Quarter-Anna)—1938 A.D.

Obverse : crowned head of king to left; legend—*George VI King Emperor*.

Reverse : legend in central circle within floral design—(1) *One* (2) *Quarter* (3) *Anna* (4) *India* (5) *1938*.

Cf. R. Friedberg, *Coins of the British World*, p. 135, No. 59.

XXVI/5. George VI (1937-52 A.D.). Copper (Pice)—round, with large central hole, 1945 A.D.

Obverse : above—crown, and below—*1945*; upper left—*1 Pice*; upper right—*India*; lower left—*Ek Paisā* (Hindī), and lower right—*Ek Paisa* (Urdū).

Reverse : floral design around central hole.

Cf. R. Friedberg, *Coins of the British World*, p. 135, No. 62.

XXVI/6. George VI (1937-52 A.D.). Nickel (Rupee)—1947 A.D.

Obverse : crowned head of king to left; legend—*George VI King Emperor.*

Reverse : tiger walking to left on horizontal line; legend—*One Rupee* (above), (1) *India* (2) *1947* (below) *Ek Rūpayā* (Hindī, left) and *Ek Rūpiya* (Urdū, right).

Cf. R. Friedberg, *Coins of the British World*, pp. 134-35, No. 50.

XXVI/7. George VI. 1937-52 A.D. Nickel (Half-Rupee)—1946 A.D.

Obverse : not reproduced.

Reverse : tiger walking to left on horizontal line; legend—*Half Rupee* (above), (1) *India* (2) *1946* (below), *Ādhā Rūpayā* (Hindī, left) and *Ādha Rūpiya* (Urdū, right).

Cf. R. Friedberg, *Coins of the British World*, pp. 134-35, No. 51.

XXVI/8. George VI, 1937-52 A.D. Nickel (Quarter-Rupee)—1947 A.D.

Obverse : not reproduced.

Reverse : tiger walking to left on horizontal line; legend—*Quarter Rupee* (above), (1) *India* (2) 1947 (below), *Pāv Rupayā* (Hindī, left) and *Pāv Rūpiya* (Urdū, right).

Cf. R. Friedberg, *Coins of the British World*, pp. 134-35, No. 52.

XXVI/9. India. Pure Nickel (Rupee)—1950 A.D.

Obverse : Aśoka pillar showing three of the four lions; star below; legend—*Government of India.*

Reverse : in the central area—figure *1* flanked by wheat sheaf with *Ek Rūpayā* (Hindī, above) and (1) *1 Rupee 1* (2) *1950* (below).

Cf. R. Friedberg, *Coins of the British World*, p. 135, No. 63.

XXVI/10. India. Nickel (50 Naye Paise in the Decimal Coinage)—1960 A.D.

Obverse : Aśoka pillar; legend—*Bhārat* (Nāgarī, left) and *India* (right).

Reverse : above floral design—(1) *Rūpaye kā ādhā bhāg* (Half of a Rupee) (2) *50* (3) *Naye Paise* (New Pice) (4) *1960.*

Cf. R. Friedberg, *Coins of the British World* pp. 135-36, No. 71.

XXVI/11. India. Cupronickel (Anna) with scalloped edge—1950 A.D.

Obverse : Aśoka pillar above star; legend—*Government of India.*

Reverse : humped bull to left; legends—*One Anna* (left), *Ek Ānā* (Hindī, right), and *1950* (below).

Cf. R. Friedberg, *Coins of the British World*, pp. 135, No. 67—slightly reduced.

XXVI/12. India. Bronze (Pice)—round, 1950 A.D.

Obverse : Aśoka pillar above star; legend—*Government of India.*

Reverse : horse running to left, legend—*One Pice* (left), *Ek Paisā* (Hindī, right) and 1950 (below).

Cf. R. Friedberg, *Coins of the British World*, p. 135, No. 69.

PLATE I

PLATE II

PLATE III

PLATE IV

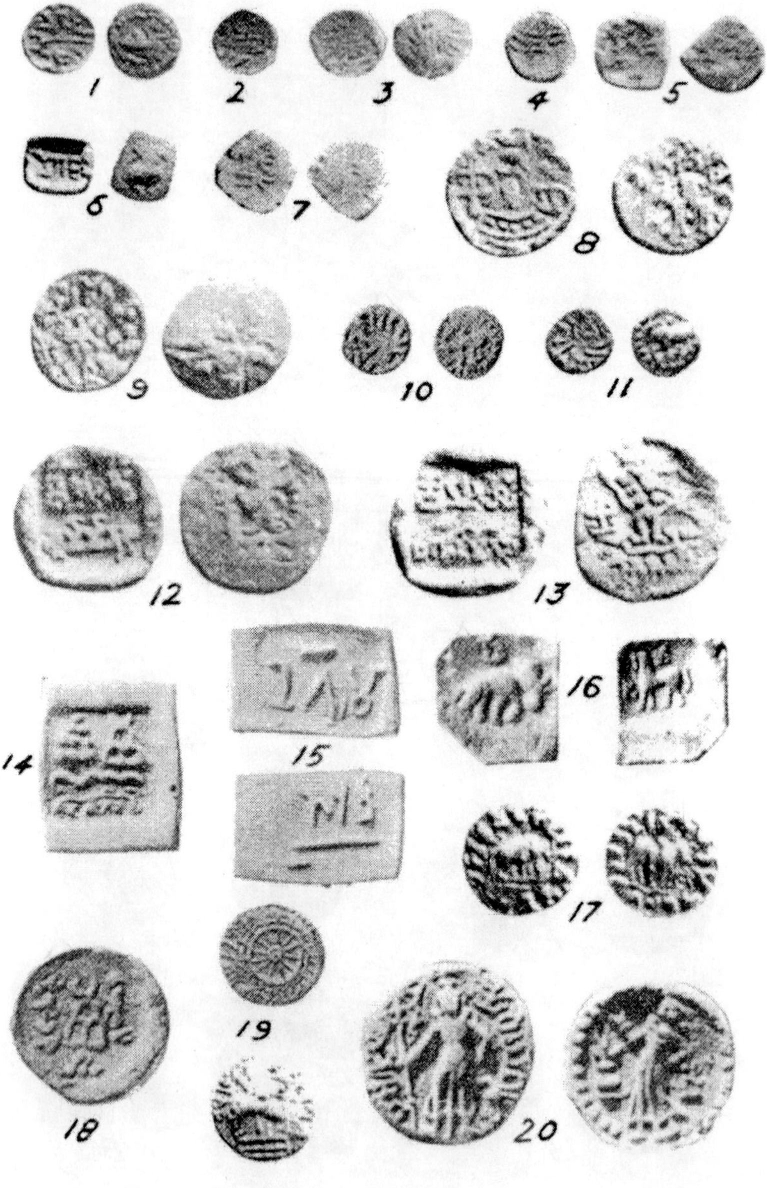

PLATE V

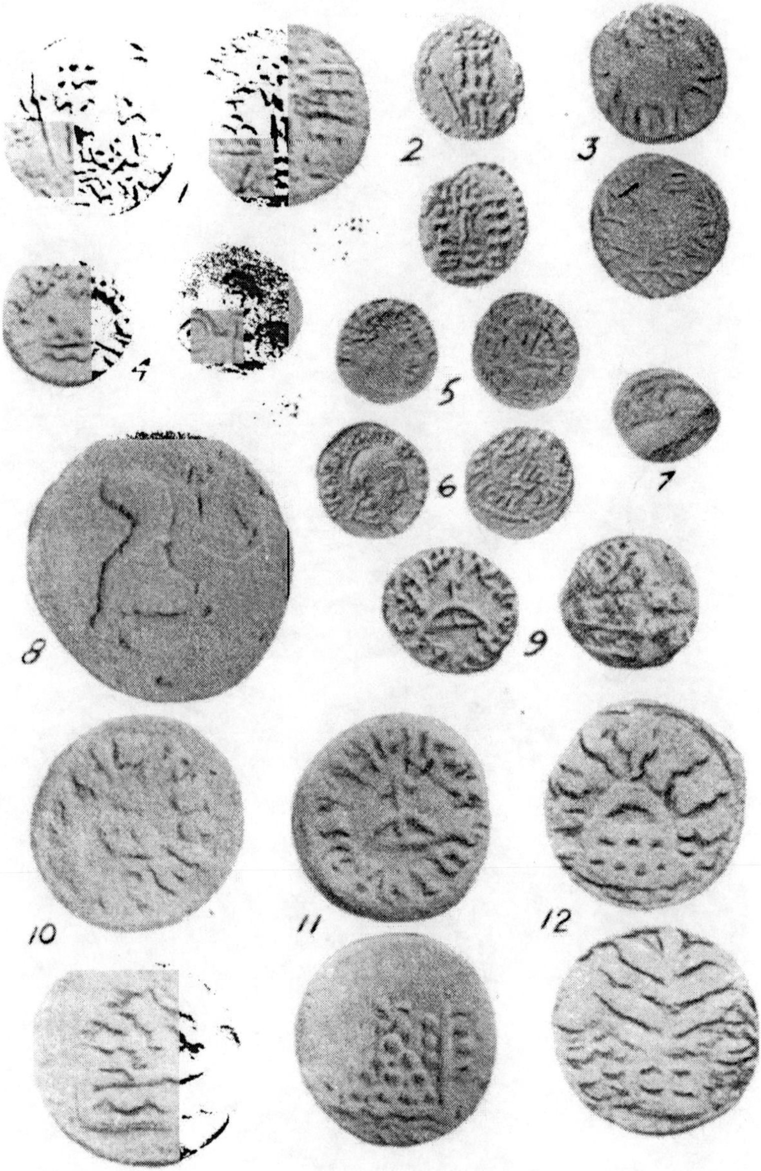

PLATE VI

PLATE VII

PLATE VIII

PLATE IX

PLATE X

PLATE XI

PLATE XII

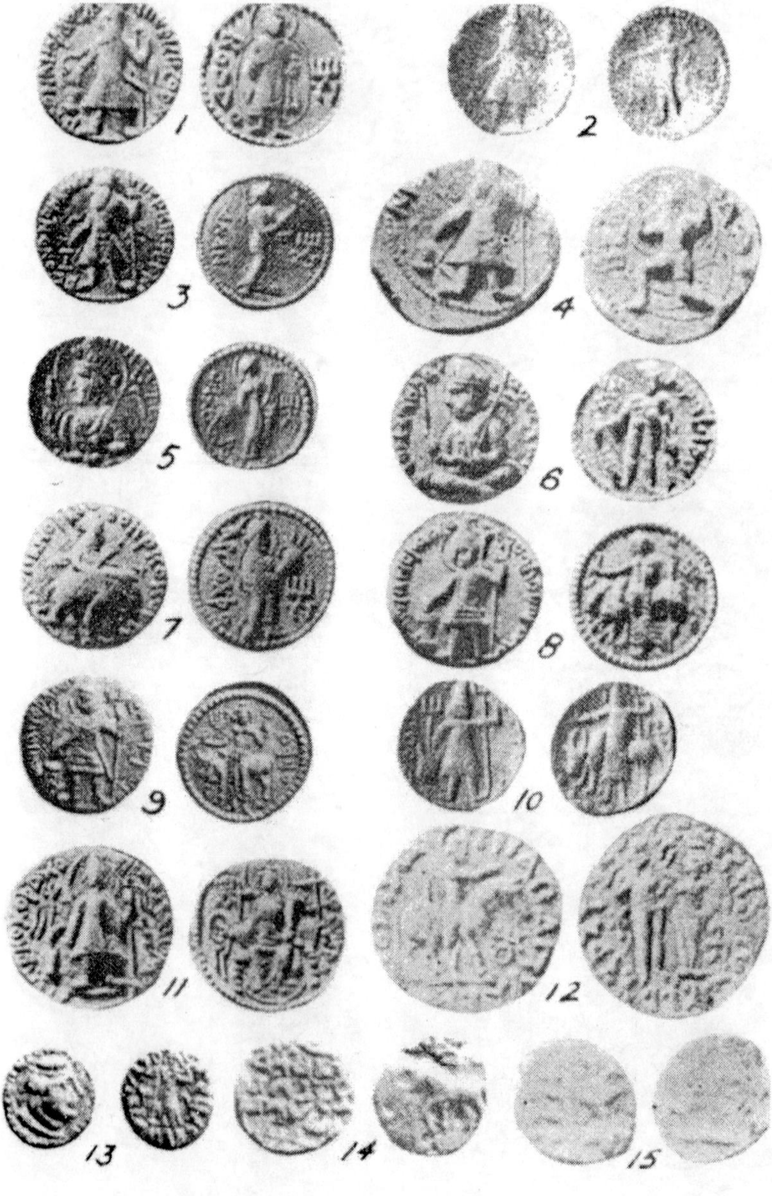

PLATE XIII

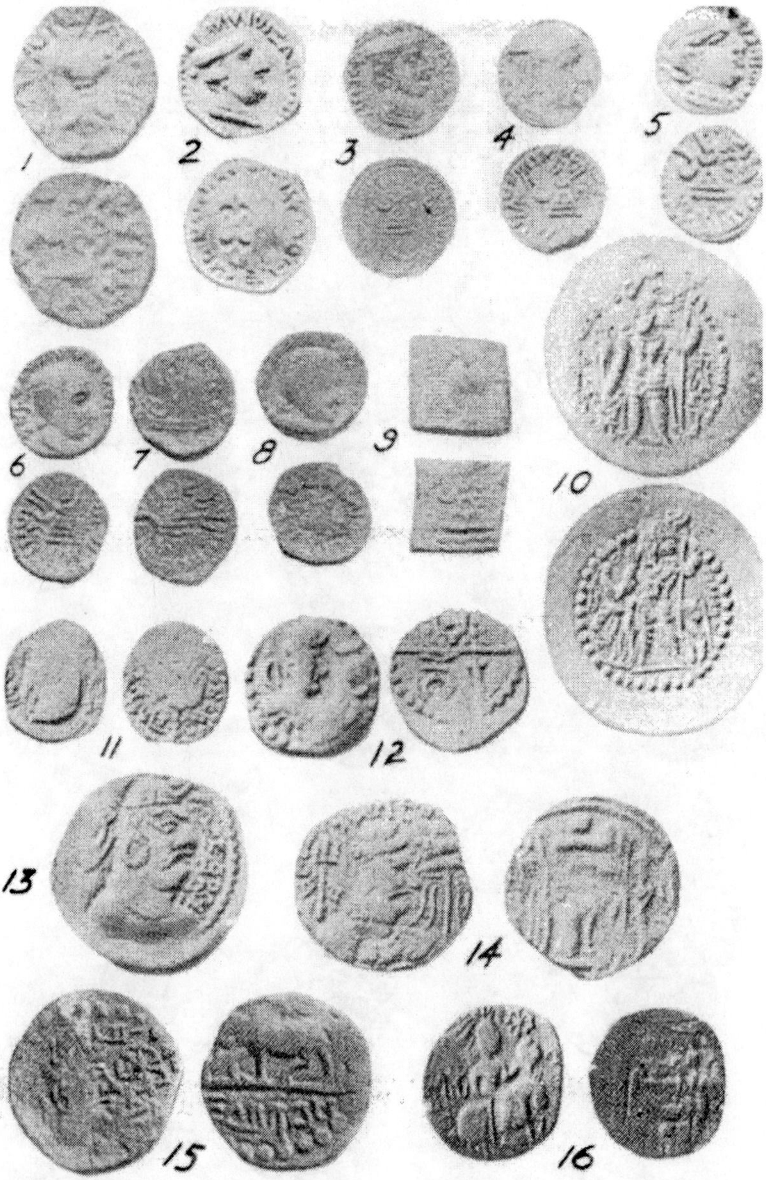

PLATE XIV

PLATE XV

PLATE XVI

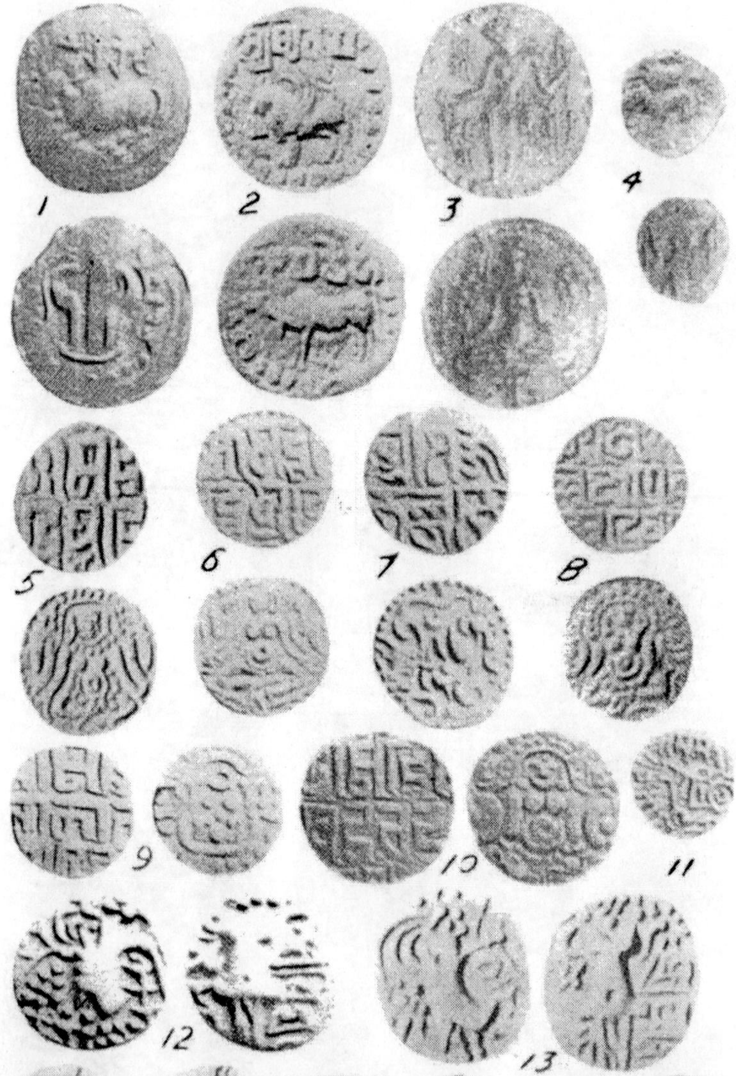

PLATE XVII

PLATE XVIII

PLATE XIX

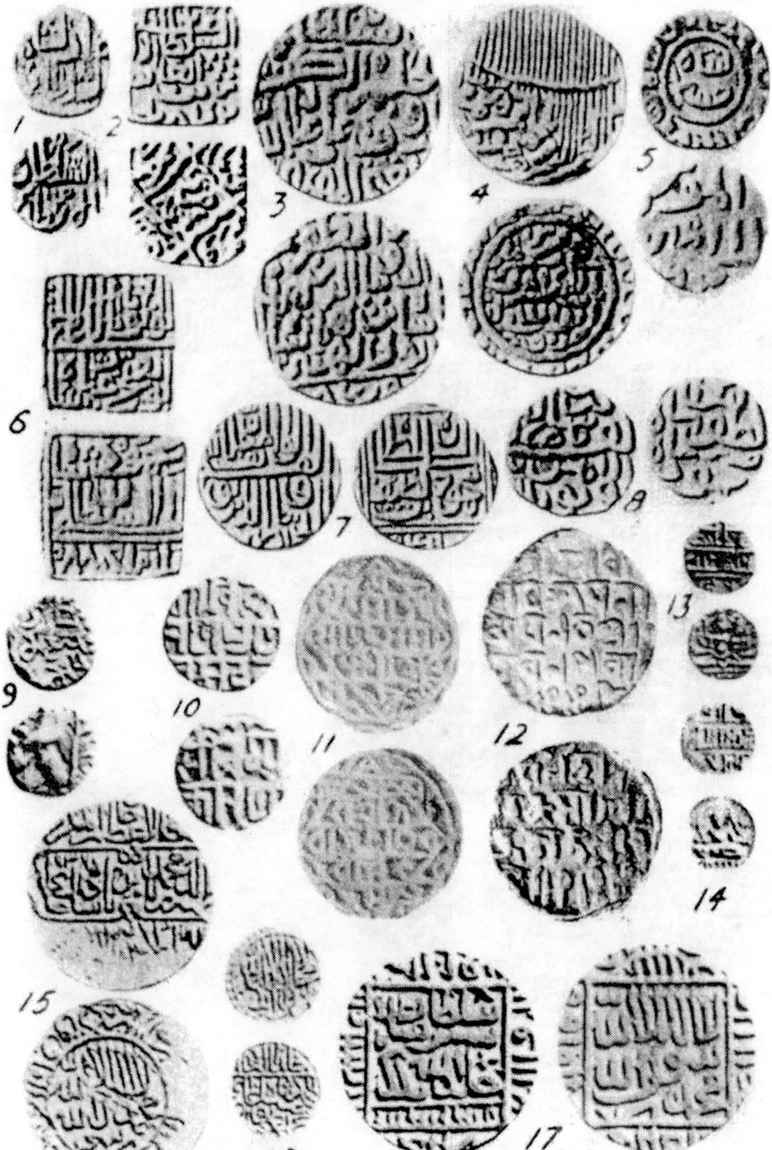

PLATE XX

PLATE XXI

PLATE XXII

PLATE XXIII

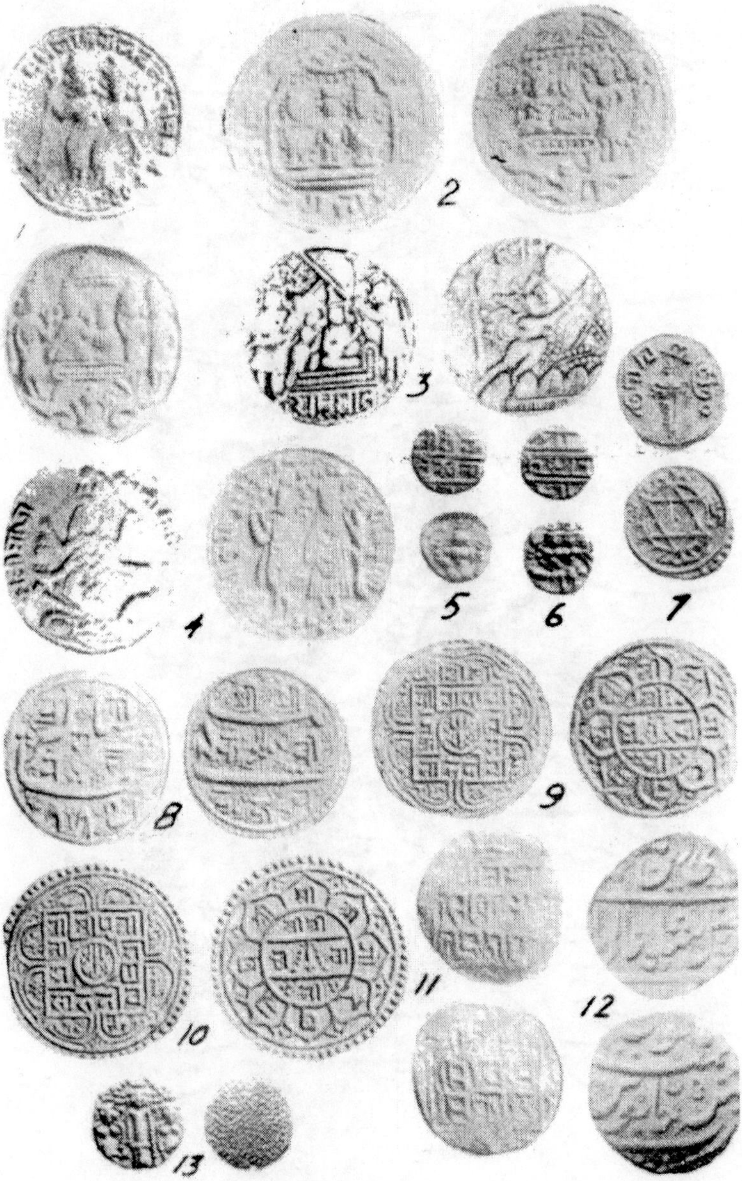

PLATE XXIV

PLATE XXV

PLATE XXIV

ONE QUARTER ANNA INDIA 1938
GEORGE VI KING EMPEROR
ONE RUPEE
INDIA
HALF RUPEE
INDIA
RUPEE
1950
1
2
3
4
5
6
7
8
9
10
11
12